IN

THE WAR

WITH

MEXICO

RANDY W. HACKENBURG

1992
White Mane Publishing Company, Inc.

The abbreviations used under all illustrations not otherwise credited indicate that the illustrations should be credited to:

USAMHI: United States Army Military History Institute
        Carlisle Barracks, Pennsylvania 17013-5008

MOLLUS-Mass: Military Order of the Loyal Legion of the United States--Massachusetts
        Commandery, all of whose records have been deposited at the U.S. Army
        Military History Institute

This White Mane Publishing Company, Inc. publication
was printed by
Beidel Printing House, Inc.
63 West Burd Street
Shippensburg, PA 17257

The acid-free paper used in this book meets the guidelines for permanence and durability of the Committee on Production guidelines for Book Longevity of the Council on Library Resources.

For a complete list of available publications
please write
White Mane Publishing Company, Inc.
P.O. Box 152
Shippensburg, PA 17257

Library of Congress Cataloging-in-Publication Data

Hackenburg, Randy W. (Randy Wayne), 1947-
    Pennsylvania in the war with Mexico : the volunteer regiments /
Randy W. Hackenburg.
      p.   cm.
    Includes bibliographical references and index.
    ISBN 0-942597-39-7 : $44.95
    1. Mexican War, 1846-1848--Regimental histories--Pennsylvania.
2. Mexican War, 1846-1848--Registers.   3. Pennsylvania--History,
Military.   4. Pennsylvania--Genealogy.   5. Soldiers--Pennsylvania-
-Registers.
E409.5.P3H33   1992
972'.05--dc20   92-3733
                                        CIP

Dedicated to the memory of the soldiers of the 1st and 2nd Pennsylvania Volunteer Regiments, 1846 to 1848.

ACKNOWLEDGMENTS ——————————

This book is no different from any other book in that it would not exist without the help of countless people. Each of these people contributed to the completion of this project; some by providing information or leads to it, some by providing services in their line of duty, others simply kept encouraging me on when I felt that the whole thing just wasn't worth it. All I can say to these folks is thank you all very MUCH!

It is impossible for me to remember each person who has aided me along the way, but I do feel constrained to acknowledge those who have been especially helpful. All those listed below have my heartfelt gratitude.

National Archives in Washington, D.C.; The Pennsylvania Historical And Museum Commission, including Mr. John Shelly and the Archives staff, Col. John B. B. Trussell, Mr. Bruce S. Bazelon and Mr. Charles B. Oellig; the State Library of Pennsylvania in Harrisburg, especially the staffs of the Local History Section and the Newspaper Room; the U.S. Army Military History Institute at Carlisle Barracks, Pa. for the use of its magnificent library, and thanks to my friends and co-workers Dr. Richard J. Sommers, Mrs. Norma Umbrell and Mr. Michael J. Winey; Col. James Enos of Carlisle, who did the vast majority of the photography; Mrs. Bonnie Kertland of Carlisle, who drew the maps contained herein; Mr. Roger D. Hunt of Rockville, Md.; Dr. John M. Hyson of Towson, Md.; Mr. Robert T. Lyon of Muncy, Pa.; Mr. Ronn Palm of Kittanning, Pa.; Dr. Richard Sauers of the Pennsylvania State Capitol Flag Preservation Project; the staff of the Historical Society of Berks County; Mrs. Sara Leishman and the staff of the Cambria County Historical Society; the Montour County Historical Society and the Thomas Beaver Free Library in Danville; the Historical Society of Pennsylvania in Philadelphia; President Russell L. Hershberger of the Historical Society of Schuylkill County; Mr. Lee E. Knepp of the Snyder County Historical Society; the staff of the Historical Society of Western Pennsylvania; the staff of the Westmoreland County Historical Society, especially Ms. Gene Berger; the staff of the Wyoming Historical and Geological Society of Wilkes-Barre; Mr. David W. Kraeuter of the Washington and Jefferson College Library; Mr. and Mrs. Elmer Atkinson of the Philadelphia Camp, Sons of Union Veterans and G.A.R. Memorial Hall; Mr. Harry A. Diehl of Wilmington, Del.; Mr. John T. Dyer, Jr. and Mr. Michael Miller at the U.S. Marine

Corps Historical Center; Mr. Richard A. Johnson of Fairfax, Va.; Mr. Michael E. Moss, formerly Curator of Art, now Director, of the U.S. Military Academy Museum at West Point; and Mrs. Joan Popchock of Newport, Pa. who is a direct descendent of Absolom Guiler.

I also owe a deep debt of gratitude to my friends, who kept hearing about this book for years, until they thought it was a fixation with me. Most of all, however, I wish to say that without the support of my family all of this would have collapsed before it got started. My parents have been a real encouragement and have financially supported this book from the beginning. They deserve the lion's share of the credit. My wife, Linda, and my children, Bessie and Scott, have also been an encouragement. Again, without Linda's pushing and forcing me to take time to do this there would be no book.

Ultimately, as a Christian, I believe in the sovereignty of God. He alone provided the interest, led me to the sources and provided the time to complete the work. One of the highlights of this whole project has been to see faith in Jesus revealed through numerous accounts left behind by the soldiers whose story is recounted herein.

Lastly, let me state that I am responsible for all the research. Items which have been omitted were simply not located by me. I also did the writing, typing and organization. What faults are found can surely be laid nowhere else than upon the author.

PREFACE

The period of the Mexican War is such an interesting period of our history, yet it has been overshadowed by the Civil War ever since 1861. It is nonetheless important in its own right. The small Regular Army of the 1840's necessitated a strong and viable militia which could be called up quickly during national emergencies. This system helped our young country through two major wars with Great Britain and had changed but little by 1846.

At that time each state controlled its own militia. The arms and military stores were generally owned by the state, not by the federal government. The Governor served as the Commander-in-Chief of his state's militia forces. One major change that came about shortly after the War of 1812 was the rise in the number of "Volunteer" or "Uniformed Militia" companies. Although many of these "Volunteer" units existed prior to 1812, they reached their height between 1820 and 1860. It is essential to understand that there were great differences between the "Volunteers" and the regular state militia.

The Militia of Pennsylvania in the 1840's was organized geographically. Numbered companies were formed into regiments, brigades and divisions. Enlisted men seldom wore uniforms of any sort, while officers were supposed to wear a uniform conforming to state regulations. The companies normally met for two days of company drill and one battalion drill each year. These drills have often been characterized as more like clowns at a picnic than a military company on parade. Every able-bodied male between the ages of eighteen and forty-five was required by Pennsylvania law to serve in a military company for at least seven years. It is easy to understand, then, that many, if not most, militia members were there only because they had to be.

On the other hand, the "Uniformed Militia" or "Volunteers," (these titles were used interchangeably), developed a tight organization. They adopted uniforms of their own design, or copied from those they had seen. Some were very simple, while others were so ornate they bordered on being ridiculous. They were governed by the same laws as the militia, but they usually performed far beyond the law's requirements. Instead of meeting three times a year the "Volunteers" usually met five or six times, or more, depending of course on the company. For the sake of accountability "Volunteer" companies of a given county were usually battalioned together and attached to their local regiment. The "Uniformed Militia" took their soldiering seriously. Order and discipline were maintained, and violators were dealt with according to the regulations of the corps.

The companies that volunteered to go to Mexico as part of the 1st and 2nd Pennsylvania Regiments were of the latter type. Certainly, many recruits joined the units to enable them to meet the minimum size requirements, but the vast majority of each company were members of the "Volunteer" company they went with. Others had belonged to similar units before joining up for the war.

In 1974 and 1975 I wrote the history of one of these "Volunteer" companies in the form of a masters thesis. I was amazed at how few such histories existed. It would be a great contribution to military history, as well as to local history, if short histories of these companies from each locality could be put together. This would require time and effort by a great many people across the country, but effort well spent. Let me challenge you to look into this subject.

Another observation made at that time was that lists of soldiers from Pennsylvania and brief histories of the units were published for the Revolution and the War of 1812. Samuel P. Bates provided us with his magnificent *History of Pennsylvania Volunteers* for the Civil War. A comparable work exists for our troops in the Spanish-American War, and Governor Martin's five volumes nicely cover the state's 28th Division in World War I. Two good histories cover the World War II service of the 28th Division, although no roster accompanied them. Unfortunately, nothing existed to satisfactorily cover the Mexican War service of the Keystone State. A roster was published in the *Pennsylvania Archives*, Series Six, Volume Ten, but it was ruined by errors and omissions. In fact, the whole of Company F, 2nd Regiment was left out. This book is written to rectify that situation.

This book is about the two volunteer regiments from this state which served in the war. There were other companies of "Volunteers" from Pennsylvania which served; some in the Regular Army, some with other state units, but this book does not cover them. We have left that for someone else to tackle. I do hope one of you will seize upon that opportunity.

Randy W. Hackenburg
Boiling Springs, Pennsylvania
1992

CONTENTS ─────────────────────────────────────

LIST OF MAPS

CHAPTER I

Volunteers Answer the Call

Trouble had been brewing between the United States and Mexico from the time of Texan independence in 1836. Although an independence was won openly in battle, the Mexican government refused to recognize it, and loud threats against Texas continued over the next nine years.

The United States did recognize Texas' independence, and by the early 1840s efforts were being made to bring Texas into the United States. The two countries signed a treaty of annexation in 1844, and U.S. troops were sent to the Texas border to defend the Lone Star State, under command of Brevet Brigadier General Zachary Taylor.

Congress, however, took its time in debating the Texas situation, and it became a key issue of the presidential election of 1844. James K. Polk, the Democratic candidate from Tennessee, came out strongly in favor of annexation, and upon his election the administration of President John Tyler picked up the pace. Polk was inaugurated on 4 March 1845, and on 4 July a convention in Austin, Texas accepted his terms of annexation. The United States Congress voted their final approval on 22 December. Texas became the twenty-eighth state of the Union.[1]

During the same period President Polk stood firm with Great Britain over the Oregon Territory. In this he made a brilliant showing, and considerably advanced American interests.

He evidently thought he could deal with Mexico in the same way, and proceeded accordingly. Ultimately, he hoped to acquire California as well as to resolve the Texas boundary question.[2]

Still not recognizing Texan independence, the Mexican government seemed determined to hold onto at least the land south of the Nueces River, even if they could not keep all of Texas. President Polk, on the other hand, insisted that the Rio Grande formed Texas' southern border. The prevailing opinion

1

in Washington was that Mexico really did not want to fight. Diplomatic efforts, however, fell flat. In Mexico City the relatively cooperative government of José Joaquin de Herrera was forced out of power in January 1846 by the Army, led by conservative generals. This paved the way for the later return of exiled General Antonio López de Santa Anna.[3]

General Taylor received orders to move his command into the disputed area between the Nueces and Rio Grande, which move was begun on 8 March 1846. The Mexican commander demanded that the American forces withdraw to the Nueces. General Taylor simply stated that his orders forbade such a move, and upon receipt of this reply the Mexican general declared that a state of war already existed. Early on the morning of 25 April two squadrons of dragoons, under Captain Seth B. Thornton, were ambushed by Mexican regulars at the Rancho de Carrictitos. Eleven men were killed and six wounded, and most of the survivors of the patrol were captured. Hostilities had begun.[4]

Mexican forces surrounded and besieged Fort Texas across from Matamoros beginning on 3 May. General Taylor, marching from Point Isabel to break the siege, fought and won the battles of Palo Alto and Resaca de la Palma on 8 and 9 May respectively.[5]

The news of Captain Thornton's ambush reached the President in the evening of 9 May, and, after conferring with his cabinet, he decided to ask Congress for a declaration of war. Both House and Senate overwhelmingly passed the war resolution on 13 May and gave authority to the President to call up 50,000 volunteers from the various states. These volunteers were to be recruited to serve either for a year or for the duration of the war.[6]

Governor Francis Rawn Shunk of Pennsylvania received the declaration of war and issued a proclamation in which he stated:

> The Officers and Soldiers of this Commonwealth will, therefore, with that alacrity and zeal which animate Freemen, and for which they are distinguished, hold themselves in readiness promptly to meet and repel the enemies of the Republic, and to preserve the rights and honor, and secure the perpetuity of the Union.
> All Persons who have charge of public arms, and other munitions of war, are reminded by our existing relations, that it is their imperative duty immediately to prepare them for the Public Service.[7]

Colonel Francis M. Wynkoop, commander of the 1st Regiment of Schuylkill County Volunteers, didn't wait for further developments, but went immediately to see Governor Shunk, and, with his encouragement, he went to Washington where he met with President Polk. The President made no commitments to Colonel Wynkoop, but told him to recruit the regiment to full strength and be ready to go. It soon became apparent, however, that both Polk and Secretary of War William L. Marcy were giving Wynkoop and his regiment the runaround. Efforts to have the Schuylkill County Regiment accepted as a body were abandoned after about three months.[8]

It was originally reported that six regiments of the new soldiers were to be from Pennsylvania.[9] This set off a scramble by uniformed militia companies across the commonwealth. Patriotism was not lacking in the Keystone State. It has often been argued that the Mexican War was purely a sectional war at best, or even a war simply to expand the slavery belt of the South. It would appear, however, from the response of the people of Pennsylvania, that such views were not held by the prepondrance of citizens in 1846.

Company after company tendered their services to the government through Governor Shunk, each hoping to have the privilege of representing its own area, as well as the state, on the battlefields of Mexico. By 11 July, the cut-off day for tendering service, ninety fully recruited companies had volunteered, some 7,475 men. In addition there were numerous regiments, battalions and companies that were not accepted because their rosters did not contain 76 privates, the minimum number allowed.[10] The first company to have volunteered was the Washington Guards of McVeytown, Mifflin County, with The Columbia Guards of Danville second.[11]

On 15 July Governor Shunk sent a report to President Polk concerning the availability of volunteers in his state, along with a list of companies that had been approved by Pennsylvania's Adjutant General Purveyance.[12] Recruiting, drilling and general preparation for war continued. Hopes were high that a goodly number of Pennsylvanians would soon be at the front. A central state newspaper made the following observation on 29 May. "Since the War has commenced, the Drum and Fife of Uncle Sam, may be heard daily in all the cities and chief towns of the United States, calling up the volunteer spirit of our citizens."[13]

For weeks after the declaration of war the state's newspapers echoed martial information. The Adjutant General's office in Washington issued the following schedule of pay for volunteer soldiers.

1st Sergeant	$16	per month
2d, 3d, and 4th do.	13	do
Corporal,	9	do
Musician,	8	do
Private,	7	do

The volunteers will be required to clothe themselves, for which they will receive the following allowances from the government.

Seargeant [sic.]	for one year	$38.00
Musician,	do.	38.00
Corporal and Private,		36.00[14]

Gradually the initial excitement tapered off. The six regiments that had been levied upon Pennsylvania were not asked for, and many of the volunteers began to wonder if they would go to Mexico at all. Most of the companies continued their traditional activities. The Wyoming Artillerists helped to play host at the Wilkes-Barre Encampment of 3 July. The Columbia Guards were in attendance, and Governor Shunk was the featured speaker for the occasion.[15]

Numerous other encampments were held around the state, and the militia returned to its pre-war activities and attitudes by mid-July. The rumor was in the air that no troops at all would be accepted from the state. The hopes of those who longed for glory on the field of battle began to fade. The companies which had volunteered in May and June continued to hold themselves in readiness, but no word came to say whether or not they would be needed. That atmosphere blanketed the state's military community until mid-November.

Suddenly, on 16 November the War Department in Washington called for one infantry regiment each from the states of Massachusetts, New York, Pennsylvania, Virginia, North Carolina, South Carolina, Louisiana and Mississippi and one mounted regiment from Texas. The State Adjutant General in Harrisburg issued orders calling for those companies that were ready to go to notify him immediately. Based upon the responses received, and upon what appeared to be political influence, the selection of companies was made. Two of the companies came from Pittsburgh; one was from Wilkes-Barre; one was from Pottsville and six were from Philadelphia. They were all notified between 24 November and 1 December.[16]

The companies of the new Pennsylvania Regiment were ordered to rendezvous in Pittsburgh by 15 December. The Philadelphia soldiers and the Washington Artillery of Pottsville journeyed by rail to Harrisburg and then went either on the Juniata Branch of the Pennsylvania Canal or by the Philadelphia-Pittsburgh Turnpike. The Wyoming Artillerists sailed down the Susquehanna Canal to the Juniata, and west from there. By 15 December all

National Colors of the First Pennsylvania Regiment during the war
Pennsylvania Historical & Museum Commission

ten companies had arrived at the rendezvous. First Lieutenant Horace B. Field of the 3rd U.S. Artillery mustered the companies into federal service: two on the 14th, two on the 15th, four on the 16th and two on the 17th.[17]

The following is the organizational structure of the regiment on 17 December.

Co. A   Jackson Independent Blues — Pittsburgh — Capt. Alexander Hay.

Co. B   Washington Artillery — Pottsville — Capt. James Nagle.

Co. C   Monroe Guards — Philadelphia — Capt. William F. Small.

Co. D   City Guards — Philadelphia — Capt. Joseph Hill.

Co. E   Washington Light Infantry — Philadelphia — Capt. Frederick W. Binder.

Co. F   Philadelphia Light Guards — Philadelphia — Capt. John Bennett.

Co. G   Jefferson Guards — Philadelphia — Capt. Turner G. Morehead.

Co. H   Cadwalader Grays — Philadelphia — Capt. Robert K. Scott.

Co. I   Wyoming Artillerists — Wilkes-Barre — Capt. Edmund L. Dana.

Co. K   Duquesne Greys — Pittsburgh — Capt. John Herron.

Elections for field grade officers were held on the 18th with considerable excitement and political maneuvering. Private J. Jacob Oswandel, of Company C, recorded his observations of the event.

> At 10 o'clock, A.M., the election polls were opened, and generally, like at all other elections, fighting and knocking one another down was the order of the day. Some of our company fought like bull dogs if anyone said aught against Capt. Small. The row was kept up by the different parties concerned nearly the whole day.
>
> In the evening at 6 o'clock the polls were closed.[18]

The results of the day were as follows:

For Colonel

Francis M. Wynkoop	310
William F. Small	306
A. S. Rumford	253
E. Trovillo	16

For Lieutenant Colonel

Samuel W. Black	452
Robert K. Scott	282
Turner G. Morehead	144

For Major

Francis L. Bowman	491
J. C. Brown	334
George McClelland	23
John C. Gilchrist	20
A. W. Foster	1[19]

Some of the Philadelphians, who figured they were out for a lark, decided to arrange a little excitement on the night of the 16th. A party of rowdies and half drunken soldiers of Company D, known as "Killers and Bouncers," pushed past the doorman of a theater in the middle of a performance. They rushed in "whooping and yelling like so many wild Indians." The police were called to the scene to evict the miscreants, but with the cry of "Go in, Killers" they put up a stubborn resistance. A general free-for-all erupted for a while. Tiring of this, the "Killers" moved outside to find more lively sport, allowing the theater crowd to see the remainder of their show in peace. Some of the local toughs then began to shout "hurra for Pittsburgh," at the "Killers." Upon this development the "Killers" armed themselves with brickbats and chased away the "rats and hyenas." At this point the police again tried to intervene, without much success. A few of the rowdies were arrested, but the main body, of about 50 men, moved off to their quarters.[20]

With this one exception the soldiers behaved themselves fairly well and seemed to have the freedom of the city. Upon returning to his quarters on the 19th, one soldier observed:

> Late this evening I noticed several boxes of musketry in our quarters, and it was not long before they were opened and each soldier picked out and helped himself to a musket. They are all old flint muskets, marked Harper's Ferry, U.S.
> Later, every soldier who had helped himself to a musket was ordered to put the musket back into the boxes, as they are not to be opened or used until we arrive at New Orleans.[21]

The field officers of the new regiment were mustered in on the 19th also, and shortly thereafter they announced their staff appointments. Although not a member of the regiment, a sutler, Mr. Samuel D. Karns, was appointed to accompany the troops.[22]

Since their arrival in Pittsburgh, preparations had been underway to transport the men to New Orleans. The government contracted for five steamboats at $4,000 each.[23] The *Messenger* left just after 10:00 A.M. on 21 December, carrying Companies B and C. About two hours later, Companies F and H sailed on the *Cucasian*. The *Aliquippa* carried Companies A and G at about noon on the 22nd, followed by the *St. Anthony* with Companies E and I. Later in the day, the field and staff and Companies D and K sailed on the *New England.* The next day, however, the *New England* was back at the wharf in Pittsburgh, because someone forgot to stow the arms on board.[24]

The War Department in the meantime reconsidered its manpower needs, and on 14 December issued a requisition to Pennsylvania for "an additional Battalion or Regiment of Infantry."[25] Notifications were sent the next day to the ten companies selected, followed by orders on the 16th to rendezvous at Pittsburgh, with all companies expected to be there by 5 January 1847.[26]

The 2nd Regiment drew from a wider geographical base than the 1st, causing its members to have more of a rural background. Each community or city which sent a company to the war took up collections for the men and their families. Many organizations and private individuals made presentations of clothing, equipment or weapons. No soldier who wanted one needed to go off without a Bible. Many, if not most, of the officers were presented with swords. All of the local newspapers were full of articles recounting these events for both regiments.

The newly chosen companies followed roughly the same routes to Pittsburgh as their predecessors. The Philadelphia Rangers had fully expected to be part of the 1st Regiment, but because of confused communications they were not accepted. Being already on their way to Pittsburgh when the 2nd Regiment was called for, they were the obvious choice for first company chosen. They were mustered in on 22 December by Lieutenant Field. The other companies were mustered as they arrived: two on 1 January, one on the 2nd, two on the 3rd, three on the 4th and one on the 5th.[27]

The organizational structure of the 2nd Pennsylvania Regiment on 5 January follows.

Co. A Reading Artillery — Berks County — Capt. Thomas S. Leoser.

Co. B American Highlanders — Summitt, Cambria County — Capt. John W. Geary.

Co. C Columbia Guards — Columbia County — Capt. John S. Wilson.

Co. D Cambria Guards — Ebensburgh, Cambria County — Capt. James Murray.

Pennsylvania in 1846 showing the counties and municipalities which sent companies to Mexico.

Co. E   Westmoreland Guards — Westmoreland County — Capt. John
W. Johnston.

Co. F   Philadelphia Rangers — Philadelphia — Capt. Charles Naylor.

Co. G   Cameron Guards — Dauphin County — Capt. Edward C.
Williams.

Co. H   Fayette County Volunteers — Fayette County — Capt. William
B. Roberts.

Co. I   Independent Irish Greens — Pittsburgh — Capt. Robert Porter.

Co. K   Stockton Artillerists — Carbon County — Capt. James Miller.[28]

A large warehouse belonging to a Mr. R. Christy, fronting on Water Street
and running back to Front Street near a glass factory, was rented to serve as
quarters for the enlisted volunteers in Pittsburgh.[29] One soldier called this the
"Horse Hotel." He noted that the officers found housing at the St. Charles
Hotel.[30]

The fancy militia uniforms and equipment of the pre-war days were either
not worn to Pittsburgh or were sent home from there. It appears that each company was responsible for having its own uniforms made. They were of dark
blue cloth. Company C contracted with a Mr. McCosky at $7.50 a set, coat and
pants.[31] Company E paid a Mr. Digby $7.00 per set of pants and jackets.[32] These
companies were in the 2nd Regiment, but it would appear that all the companies of both regiments were in a similar situation. The Philadelphia companies reportedly procured theirs before leaving home.[33]

The short stay of the 2nd Regiment was not nearly so irksome to the citizens
of the city as was that of the First. It was not without its incidents, however.
On 6 January Private George W. Fenner of Company K accidentally shot a local
teen-ager named Lewis Malisee, "in the right breast near the nipple entering
the lobe of the right lung where it lodged. He was only a few paces off and
the ball glanced along his breast somewhat before entering. After walking a
few steps he fell and immediately expired."[34]

Elections for field officers also took place on the 6th. The returns showed
the following totals.

For Colonel

William B. Roberts   328
J. Hambright   322
Charles Naylor   217
William Larimer, Jr.   10
Samuel H. Montgomery   4

For Lieutenant Colonel

John W. Geary   591
W. Murray   200

Uniform worn by John W. Geary as Captain of the American Highlanders at the time they volunteered to go to Mexico.   *Pennsylvania Historical & Museum Commission*

For Major

William Brindle	511
Robert Klotz	314
W. B. Thompson	12[35]

Preparations having been made for departure, the first two companies, F and K, sailed away from Pittsburgh at about 10:00 A.M. on 8 January aboard the steamer *Brunette*. At about noon Companies A and G sailed on the *Anthony Wayne*. On the same afternoon about 3 o'clock the *North Carolina* headed down river with Companies E and H. At approximately 10 o'clock the next day the *Wisconsin* headed out bearing Companies C and D. Regimental headquarters and Companies I and B followed at about noon on the *Cambria*.[36]

Regimental Order No. 1 indicated the specifics for the departure from Pittsburgh, while Order No. 2 specified the conditions to be maintained on board the steamers.

The Arms will remain boxed, with the exception of those required for guard duty.

Squad drills, without arms, will be had daily, at the discretion of the senior officer of the detachment.

Bars, for the sale or distribution of liquor are strictly prohibited by the commanding officer of the Regiment: and officers commanding detachments will be held responsible for any infringement of this order.

No Soldier will be permitted to leave the boat after leaving Pittsburgh, until he arrives at New Orleans.

The senior officer of each detachment will report his arrival at New Orleans to the Quarter Master.

There shall be, daily, five roll-calls: — the first immediately after Reveille; — the second immediately before Breakfast; — the third immediately before Dinner; — the fourth immediately before Retreat; — the fifth immediately after Tattoo.

The senior officer will detail, daily, a police party, whose duty it shall be to superintend the cleanliness of the transport.

No Revolving Pistols, Bowie Knives, or other arms, will be allowed to remain in possession of the soldiers on board the transports . . . .

The commanding officer expects the officers commanding detachments to secure and preserve strict discipline and decorum among the men . . . .[37]

1. K. Jack Bauer, *The Mexican War 1846-1848* (New York: Macmillan Publishing Co., Inc., 1974), pp. 5-10.
2. *Ibid.*, p. 12.
3. *Ibid.*, p. 26.
4. *Ibid.*, pp. 38, 47-48.
5. *Ibid.*, pp. 50-62.
6. *Ibid.*, pp.68-69.
7. George Edward Reed, ed., *Pennsylvania Archives*, Fourth Series, VII (Harrisburg: The State Of Pennsylvania, 1902), pp. 104-105. See Appendix I for Gov. Shunk's War Proclamation.
8. *The Miner's Journal* (Pottsville), May 23, 1846 and July 4, 1846; *Pittsburgh Daily Gazette And Advertiser*, Dec. 10, 1846.
9. *The Danville Intelligencer*, May 22, 1846.
10. *Pennsylvania Archives*, Fourth Series, VII, pp. 106-111. See Appendix II for Gov. Shunk's Report and list of companies.
11. *The Danville Intelligencer*, June 12, 1846.
12. *Pennsylvania Archives*, Fourth Series, VII, pp. 106-111.
13. *The Danville Intelligencer*, May 29, 1846.
14. *Ibid.*, June 19, 1846.
15. D. C. Kitchen, *Record of the Wyoming Artillerists* (Tunkhannock, Pa.: Alvin Day, Printer, 1874), pp. 9-10.
16. *The Danville Intelligencer*, Nov. 20, 1846 and Dec. 11, 1846; Pennsylvania State Archives, Records of the Department of Military Affairs, Letter from Henry Petrikin to John S. Wilson, Nov. 30, 1846.
17. The National Archives, Record Group 94, Records of the Adjutant General's Office 1780's-1917, Papers of the 1st Pennsylvania Infantry Regiment, 1846-1848.
18. J. Jacob Oswandel, *Notes of the Mexican War 1846-47-48* (Philadelphia: 1885), p. 18.
19. *Pittsburgh Daily Gazette And Advertiser*, Dec. 19, 1846.
20. Oswandel, *Notes*, p. 16; *The Daily Morning Post* (Pittsburgh), Dec. 17, 1846.
21. Oswandel, *Notes*, p. 20.
22. National Archives, RG 94, 1st Pa. Regt. Papers; *Pittsburgh Daily Gazette And Advertiser*, Dec. 23, 1846.
23. *Pittsburgh Daily Gazette And Advertiser*, Dec. 22, 1846.
24. *The Daily Morning Post* (Pittsburgh), Dec. 21, 1846; *Pittsburgh Daily Gazette And Advertiser*. Dec. 23, 1846.
25. *The Danville Intelligencer*, Dec. 18, 1846.
26. *Ibid.*
27. National Archives, RG 94, 2nd Pa. Regt. Papers; J. Thomas Scharf and Thompson Westcott, *History of Philadelphia 1609-1884* (Philadelphia: L. H. Everts & Co., 1884), I, p. 679.
28. Randy W. Hackenburg, "The Columbia Guards, Danville's Volunteer Infantry 1817-1861" (unpublished Masters thesis, Bloomsburg State College, 1975), pp. 37-38.
29. *The Danville Intelligencer*, Dec. 18, 1846.
30. Pennsylvania State Archives, Anonymously written diary, Jan. 3, 1847.
31. *Ibid.*, Jan. 4, 1847.
32. Richard Coulter, "The Westmoreland Guards In The War With Mexico, 1846-1848," *Western Pennsylvania Historical Magazine*, XXIV (June, 1941), p. 103.
33. Scharf & Westcott, *Philadelphia*, p. 680.
34. *Pittsburgh Daily Gazette And Advertiser*, Jan. 7, 1847.
35. *The Danville Intelligencer*, Jan. 15, 1847.
36. *Ibid.*
37. *Ibid.*

CHAPTER II

Off To Mexico

T he long trip down the Ohio and Mississippi Rivers was at times boring, while at others exciting. New sights along the way kept up the interest of the soldiers. Private Oswandel of the 1st Regiment, aboard the *Messenger*, noted on 23 December:

> The soldiers, I am glad to say, are all passing their time first-rate. There seems to be no quarreling or any ill feeling between them, in fact, they act more like so many brothers in place of strangers, for it will be remembered that Co. B, is from Pottsville, and our Co. C, from Philadelphia.
> To-night I notice that most of our soldiers are passing their time in playing cards and singing.[1]

Special preparations had been made for Christmas Dinner aboard the 1st Regiment's steamers. Turkeys, chickens and many other good things were set before the men. All had to wait, however, until the whole meal was ready before any could partake. "The gong rung, then you should [have] seen the rush and tumble for the best seats, and I am sorry to say the soldiers did not eat like men should have done, but like so many starved hogs."[2] The *St. Anthony* with Companies E and I spent Christmas Day passing through the canal at Louisville.[3]

Not all the 1st Regiment enjoyed so peaceful a trip, however. On Saturday afternoon of the 26th, an altercation occurred between two of Captain Hills' soldiers on the *New England*. Private John J. Mayfield claimed someone stole a "Faro Bank" from him, and he ran down the cabin shouting "I am robbed! I am robbed!" Then he jumped on top of a table and split it to pieces. He was immediately arrested and restrained by ropes, under guard. On Sunday before the assembled troops, he was tried by court martial for riotous and disorderly

12

conduct. He was left off with only a severe warning by Colonel Wynkoop, that if he had been tried by a General Court Martial he would have been shot.[4] He must have decided that this military life wasn't for him, because he deserted at New Orleans on 3 January.

The soldiers on the *Messenger* had to go ashore at Louisville and march through the town because of a break in the dam. After a half hour's free time in the town the ship was reboarded and sailed on its way. Privates John F. Perfect and Morris Stemlear were left behind. They followed later on another boat.[5]

The steamers bearing the 1st Regiment arrived at New Orleans between 28 and 31 December. The troops disembarked about seven miles below the city on the famous battlefield of 1815, now appropriately named Camp Jackson.[6] *The New Orleans Delta* recorded a favorable impession of the regiment. "We never saw a finer looking body of citizen soldiers, young, active, and intelligent. They do honor to the old 'Keystone State.' "[7]

They did something else, however, to several businesses located near the camp. A group of men from Company I left camp on the morning of 12 January and headed for a tavern run by a French Creole. They ate and drank till drunk, then proceeded to break the place up. The ring leader was Private Bill Diamond. The proprietor finally turned to his gun to convince the rowdies to leave, but Diamond took it and broke it across the railroad track outside. A neighbor then showed up with a shotgun and fired it at the private, hitting him in the face and neck. He was not seriously injured, but because of his conduct he was dropped from the rolls of his company and left in the hands of New Orleans civil authorities.[8]

Those trouble-makers of Company D, who had terrorized Pittsburgh, wanted to leave their mark on New Orleans as well. On New Years Day they escaped camp and attacked the property of some citizens, for which several were arrested and detained in the city jail for several days. On the 4th they took on a grocery and liquor store near camp and beat up the Spanish proprietor. Some passing officers broke up the scuffle and brought the men back to camp. On the 9th they entered a Frenchman's poultry yard, stealing a dozen or more chickens plus turkeys, geese and a small pet deer. They feasted upon their plunder, while the owner tried to have the whole of Company D arrested. In the early morning of the 16th, just before they were scheduled to sail for Mexico, some of the "Killers" surrounded Captain Hill's tent and attempted to assassinate him. He thereupon submitted his resignation to Colonel Wynkoop, and left for the city. He was warned by men in his command that if he boarded the boat with them he would be killed. Although he was sent for by Major Bowman, he didn't return to the ship but determined to go to Washington, D.C. about the matter. His resignation was never accepted, and he returned to his company in April, 1847.[9]

As the 2nd Regiment was arriving the 1st Regiment was preparing to depart. Companies A, G and K embarked on the sailing ship *Oxnard,* under command of Colonel Wynkoop, on 15 January. The same day E, F, H and I boarded the sailing vessel *Russell Glover*, under Lt. Colonel Black. Companies B, C and D boarded the *Statesman* on 16 January, and were under command of Major Bowman. The vessels sailed into the Gulf of Mexico on the 19th and headed for Brazos Santiago, which was reached on 28 January.[10]

The 2nd Regiment made its way down the Ohio and Mississippi Rivers much as did the 1st. On Sunday, 10 January, Colonel Roberts had Companies B and I line up on the *Cambria's* deck, and he requested that each soldier:

> spend at least 30 minutes in holding communion with his Maker, and I can truly say, that many of our noble fellows did retire to their rooms and invoke the blessing and protection of Him who holds the destinies of all within his hands, while others were engaged in reading their bibles [sic.] and singing hymns.[11]

Despite the ban on all liquors, the bartender of the *Cambria* managed to sneak some whiskey aboard. Colonel Roberts became aware of it, and on the 16th he had about nine gallons of the poison dumped into the river. The bartender feared that his would be the next splash.[12]

The steamers carrying the men of the 2nd Pennsylvania Regiment came into New Orleans between the 14th and 18th of January, carrying them to the old battlefield below the city. Some of the boys from the two regiments who knew each other briefly renewed acquaintances before the 1st Regiment sailed. The volunteers enjoyed seeing the famous and historic places. Some were impressed with New Orleans, while others were disappointed. Camp life too was often found to be depressing. Private William A. Campbell, of Company E, recorded his impressions for a friend on 18 January.

> The majority of the men in all companies, are lower and more vulgar, than I would have possibly believed. Even men who have a character for some decency, are as great outlaws, as there are in the encampment. A soldiers life appears to make every man as low as circumstances can make him . . . .[13]

This impression certainly appeared to have some basis of truth, as Private Fleming Montgomery, a native of Muncy now serving in Company I, was murdered in his tent on the night of 20 January. He had been stabbed three times in the left shoulder, and it happened so quickly that the man sleeping next to him didn't know anything had happened until he tried to awaken him in the morning.[14]

Early on the morning of the 23rd a terrible thunderstorm hit Camp Jackson. Captain John S. Wilson, of Company C, described the scene in a letter to his wife. The "water could not run off, and in the morning the water was between two and three feet deep, so that all our trunks and baggage was floating about and the men walking around and collecting the things[.] our clothes and books

& everything was wet through."[15] The storm simply served to aggravate an already bad situation. The ground was low and unhealthy to begin with, and sickness was beginning to be a problem in the regiment.

Fortunately for them, Companies A, E, H and I, along with Colonel Roberts, had boarded the sailing ship *James N. Cooper* during the 23rd and missed the flood in camp. On the 24th Companies B, D and G, under command of Lieutenant Colonel Geary, boarded the *General Veazie*, bringing with them all their soaked possessions and equipment. Companies C, F and K, under Major Brindle, boarded the *Ocean* on the 24th as well. Bad weather prohibited their immediate departure, but finally the ships were towed down river, and on 31 January they crossed the bar and entered the Gulf of Mexico.[16]

There was considerable dissatisfaction on board the ships during the six days they lay near the city. It seems that the men disliked their rations. In fact, it appeared for a time that the men might cause some real problems over the situation. Promises by the officers to provide better food, and some hard work in finding it, helped to dampen the discontent. Probably the greatest number of desertions during the life of the regiment occurred during those days.[17]

The 1st Regiment had sailed to Brazos Santiago at the mouth of the Rio Grande, where the ships lay at anchor. But none of the troops were debarked. The 2nd Regiment was scheduled to make a short stop at Tampico, but this was made impossible by bad weather. Both regiments were to meet at a small island called Lobos, which served as the rendezvous for General Winfield Scott's army, in preparation for an invasion at Vera Cruz.

The men of the 2nd Regiment had almost a week to become accustomed to their new floating accommodations before leaving the relative safety of the Mississippi Delta. They no longer enjoyed the wide open spaces that they had been used to. One of the Westmoreland Guards wrote home to Greensburgh on the 26th of January about his new lodgings aboard the *James N. Cooper*.

> Sunday I went on board the vessel, and it was a great place, upwards of three hundred men stowed down in the hold, or as they call it the steerage, no light comes in except through a couple of hatchways in my berth (which is made of rough boards as hard as stone) it is so dark at noon that we have to feel for any thing we want; two are put in one berth -.... I laugh for about two hours every night when I get into my berth at the fellows fighting about their beds, of all the kicking and scratching and swearing, all in perfect darkness I never heard.[18]

As if this weren't bad enough, the weather on the Gulf was exceptionally bad. One storm followed another. Late on 1 February a furious gale overtook the small convoy, lasting some forty hours.[19] Private Richard Coulter of Company E penned a colorful description of the scene into his diary on the 3rd.

> Last night was rather a mixture of odd scenes. The excessive tossing of the vessel affected most of the men with seasickness and it was one continual sound of pukeing, spitting, groaning and laughing mixed

with the tumult of the gale. In one place would be a chap laughing at his neighbor's misery telling him to say "New York and go to it," when suddenly he would feel an uneasyness himself at the stomach which a few more lurches would ripen and with a couple of preliminary "Oh G____s" and a few groans, he would "York" it up himself; out it would come in spite of him, and with it a burst of laughter in the surrounding berths from those, who having previously laid out their rations on the deck, were now enjoying a short respite. . . . The gale blew all day and at night was still high. The pukeing continued with little abatement.[20]

By the afternoon of the 3rd the sky had cleared and the Gulf had calmed. The men started to stir, and most were beginning to act alive again by the 4th of February.[21] Private Coulter wrote in his diary on the 7th that the boys were, "unable to remain below on account of stench and very uncomfortable on deck in consequence of the extreme heat."[22] The weather remained favorable for several days, but on the 10th, just when they were to have landed at Tampico, another "Norther" hit, which was even more furious than the first, and lasted

Area of the Gulf of Mexico traversed by the Pennsylvanians

fifty-six hours. No landing could possibly be made in such conditions, so the ships sailed on to Lobos Island.[23]

Both the *Oxnard* and the *Russell Glover*, carrying troops of the 1st Regiment, had arrived at Brazos Santiago by the 24th of January, and on the 27th they sailed for Lobos. Private Oswandel, on the *Statesman*, wrote into his journal on the 28th, "we could plainly see the much talked of and looked for Brazos, Santiago, and a miserable looking place it is; two or three shanties and a few tents along the beach." Surgeon Bunting and a commissary officer went ashore on the morning of the 29th and stayed there until noon on the 1st of February, delaying the *Statesman's* departure.[24]

The first two contingents of the 1st Regiment arrived at Lobos about the 11th or 12th of February, and, after clearing a camp area, debarked with great joy and relief. It was marvelous to breathe clean air and stand on solid ground again. The morning of the 13th saw the arrival of the *Ocean* and *James N. Cooper*, with seven companies of the 2nd Regiment. The men landed the next day and made their camps.[25] On the 16th the *Statesman* dropped anchor, after weathering a severe storm and experiencing a near head-on collision with another ship enroute.[26]

Lieutenant Colonel Geary's contingent of the 2nd Regiment was the last of the Pennsylvanians to arrive, on the *General Veazie*. Some time around the 13th, Private Frederick Shriver of Company B was discovered to have a case of smallpox, so, when the ship dropped anchor on the 18th of February, only Geary and the ship's captain were allowed on land. Every precaution was taken to insure that the dread disease didn't spread. In fact, none of the *Veazie's* troops were permitted on the island until the first week of March, after the rest of the army had embarked for Vera Cruz.[27]

Lobos was located about sixty-five miles south-east of Tampico and some 180 miles north-west of Vera Cruz.[28] John Geary entered a description of it in his diary on 18 February.

> It is situated on a coral rock surrounded with shoal water and a reef distant from the shore from 100 to 300 yards. The island is about 2½ miles in circumference and its surface about 15 or 20 feet above the level of the sea. It is thickly covered with orange, Lemon, Lime, Banian, Gum-Elastic and other trees, bearing fruit. . . .
>
> The greatest abundance of fish are found in the shoal water around the Island — The red fish is the most abundant. they [sic] vary in length from 1 to 4 feet — and are of the most delicious flavor. — The shoal water affords a very fine place for sea bathing and is much enjoyed by the soldiers.
>
> The island is infested with immense numbers of large rats and mice . . . . Vast numbers of striped lizards about 10 or 12 inches in length, run around like so many scared spirits, also square crabs of extraordinary fierceness. — these rats, lizards, & crabs I am assured by men whose veracity I have no reason to doubt made a regular attack upon the first soldiers who landed here and tried every means to prevent encroachments upon their sacred rights. Ants of every description & spiders abound on the island.

Water is obtained by digging 7 or 8 feet, but is so sweet and tasteless as to be faintish and disagreeable to the taste. — The climate is exceedingly mild, being favored with sea breezes from whatever quarter the wind blows.[29]

It seems that Geary's companies weren't the only ones with disease problems. Private Elam B. Bonham of Company C, 2nd Regiment, was thought to have smallpox also, but the company debarked from the *Ocean* anyway, leaving Bonham behind. They were placed in a separate camp area about a quarter of a mile from the rest of the troops, however. Bonham soon recovered and no one else from that ship was affected by it.[30] Jesse G. Clark, of Bonham's company, reported an interesting experience at Lobos to a friend in Danville.

The first night we were encamped here an alarm was given about four o'clock in the morning by the sentinel gun and the long roll of the drum, which roused us out of our slumbers quite unexpectedly, and as we had not yet received our arms, we were placed in rather an awkward situation. We were marched out on our parade ground to get ready for battle, and the company formed, when the captain seeing the situation we were placed in, ordered us to break ranks, go to our tents and arm ourselves with our pistols, knives, axes, hatchets, spades, and whatever a man could in any way defend himself; but in the end it proved to be a false alarm, raised for the express purpose of trying the bravery of Pennsylvania troops, knowing that we were wholly unprepared for the battle field.[31]

In addition to the Pennsylvanians, regiments from North Carolina, South Carolina, New York, Louisiana and Mississippi were on the island for last minute drill and training. The Louisiana and Mississippi regiments soon left for northern Mexico and were not part of the invasion force. General Scott himself arrived on the scene on Sunday, 21 February, aboard the steam ship *Massachusetts.*[32]

General Scott, upon his arrival, named Colonel Wynkoop the senior officer of the volunteers on the island, making him commander of the island. During the early days of the Army's occupancy of the place, several Mexicans landed a boat full of fresh fruit and produce on the island. Fearing that their real business was spying, Captain Binder, of the 1st Regiment's Company E, placed them under arrest. He was exuberant at taking the first enemy prisoners of the campaign. Most of the time on Lobos, however, was spent in drilling, polishing and cleaning. Both Pennsylvania regiments held dress parades to celebrate Washington's Birthday, in fact, parades became almost a daily occurrence.[33]

An election took place in Company D of the 1st Regiment on the 24th to fill the position of captain vacated by Joseph Hill. The candidates were Adjutant Alexander Brown and 1st Lieutenant Julius Kretchmar. Kretchmar won by a nearly unanimous vote.[34]

The time for the invasion was now close at hand. The 1st Regiment boarded their respective vessels on 25 February, and the 2nd Regiment embarked on the 28th and March 1st. The ships weighed anchor two days later, arriving at Anton Lizardo on the 5th of March, within view of the city of Vera Cruz and its castle.[35]

With the departure of the Army, the smallpox-ridden *General Veazie* was allowed to unload. Companies B, D and G disembarked unto the now deserted island on 3 March. By this time there were sixteen men down with the disease, and many others were generally unwell from being on the ship so long. Geary and his men stayed on Lobos until all traces of the smallpox were gone, leaving to catch up with the Army on 8 April.[36]

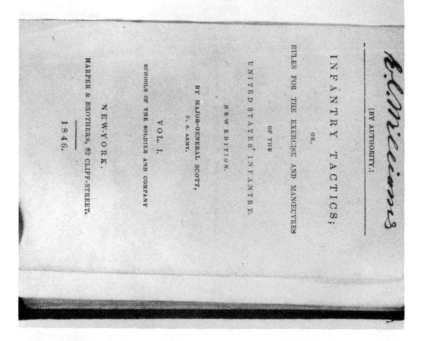

Three volume set of Infantry tactics written by Gen. Winfield Scott, bearing the personal inscriptions of Capt. Edward C. Williams of Company G, 2nd Regiment. He had earlier inscribed the flyleaf as "Capt. E. C. Williams, Cameron Guards, Harrisburg, Penna."

A Private Collection

1. Oswandel, *Notes*, p. 23.
2. *Ibid.*, p. 24.
3. Kitchen, *Wyoming Artillerists*, p. 17.
4. *The Daily Morning Post* (Pittsburgh), Jan. 8, 1847.
5. Oswandel, *Notes*, p. 25.
6. *Ibid.*, p. 27; John H. Niebaum, *History Of The Pittsburgh Washington Infantry* (Pittsburgh: Burgum Printing Company, 1931), p. 36.
7. Niebaum, *Washington Infantry*, p. 36.
8. Oswandel, *Notes*, pp. 39-40; Kitchen, *Wyoming Artillerists*, p. 18; *The Daily Morning Post* (Pittsburgh), Jan. 27, 1847.
9. Oswandel, *Notes*, pp. 30-31, 33, 37-38, 43; *Pittsburgh Daily Gazette And Advertiser*, Jan. 30, 1847; *The Daily Morning Post* (Pittsburgh), Feb. 8, 1847 and Feb. 25, 1847.
10. Oswandel, *Notes*, pp. 42-43.
11. *Pittsburgh Daily Gazette And Advertiser*, Jan. 30, 1847.
12. *Ibid.*, Feb. 1, 1847.
13. *The Daily Morning Post* (Pittsburgh), Feb. 1, 1847.
14. *Pittsburgh Daily Gazette And Advertiser*, Mar. 17, 1847; *The Danville Intelligencer*, Feb. 5, 1847.
15. Letter, J. S. Wilson to Martha Wilson, Feb. 21, 1847, in a private collection.
16. George W. Hartman, *A Private's Own Journal* (Greencastle, Pa.: E. Robinson, 1849), p. 5; Harry M. Tinkcom, *John White Geary, Soldier-Statesman 1819-1873* (Philadelphia: University Of Pennsylvania Press, 1940), p. 8; Pa. Archives, Anonymous Diary, Jan. 24 to Jan. 31, 1847.
17. Pa. Archives, Anonymous Diary, Jan. 25 to 26, 1847; Hartman, *Private's Journal*, pp. 5-6; See rosters for dates of desertions.
18. *The Pennsylvania Argus* (Greensburg), Feb. 12, 1847.
19. John William Larner, Jr., ed., "A Westmoreland Guard In Mexico, 1847-1848: The Journal Of William Joseph McWilliams," *Western Pennsylvania Historical Magazine*, LII (Jul. & Oct., 1969), p. 218.
20. Coulter, "Westmoreland Guards," p. 106.
21. Pa. Archives, Anonymous Diary, Feb. 3-4, 1847.
22. Coulter, "Westmoreland Guards," p. 106.
23. Hartman, *Private's Journal*, p.6.
24. *The Pennsylvania Argus* (Greensburg), Feb. 19, 1847; Oswandel, *Notes*, pp. 48-50.
25. Niebaum, *Washington Infantry*, p. 37; Pa. Archives, Anonymous Diary, Feb. 13-14, 1847.
26. Oswandel, *Notes*, pp. 55-56.
27. Tinkcom, *Geary*, pp. 11-14.
28. Bauer, *The Mexican War*, p. 237.
29. Tinkcom, *Geary*, pp. 11-12.
30. Pa. Archives, Anonymous Diary, Feb. 14-15, 1847.
31. *The Danville Intelligencer*, Mar. 26, 1847.
32. Tinkcom, *Geary*, pp. 12-13; Bert Anson, ed., "Colonel William Barton Roberts In The Mexico City Campaign - 1847," *Western Pennsylvania Historical Magazine*, XXXIX (Winter, 1956), p. 249; Pa. Archives, Anonymous Diary, Feb. 21, 1847.
33. Tinkcom, *Geary*, p. 13; Kitchen, *Wyoming Artillerists*, pp. 22-23; *The Danville Intelligencer*, Mar. 26, 1847; Pa. Archives, Anonymous Diary, Feb. 22-24, 1847.
34. Oswandel, *Notes*, p. 60.
35. Pa. Archives, Anonymous Diary, Feb. 25 to Mar. 3, 1847; Hartman, *Private's Journal*, p. 6.
36. Tinkcom, *Geary*, pp. 14, 16; James K. Greer, ed., "Diary of a Pennsylvania Volunteer in the Mexican War," *Western Pennsylvania Historical Magazine*, XII (No. 3, 1929), p. 151; Anson, "Col. William B. Roberts," p. 256.

Major General Winfield Scott

MOLLUS-Mass. & USAMHI

CHAPTER III

At Vera Cruz

A s the ships sailed quickly from Lobos to Vera Cruz, the men did their last minute preparations for combat. Each spent his time doing the things he felt to be most urgent. Private Oswandel, aboard the *Statesman* with the 1st Regiment's Company C, wrote in his diary on 2 March. "To-night I noticed our Capt. Small and Lieut. Berry making a flag out of blue bunting. The pole is of a ship's boat oar, the spear out of a prong hook, the State of Pennsylvania being too poor to give us a flag."[1]

Other companies had been presented with flags before leaving home. The Pittsburgh companies were supposed to have had them, and the Columbia Guards of Danville were presented with one, made by the ladies of Lewisburg, when they marched through that town on their way to the war. Captain Williams, of the Cameron Guards, claimed to have "borrowed" a Revolutionary War flag from the state library in Harrisburg, which he used during the campaign.[2]

General Scott had his army organized into three divisions: two of regulars commanded by William J. Worth and David E. Twiggs, and one of volunteers under Robert Patterson. Both Pennsylvania regiments and the 1st and 2nd Tennessee Regiments were in Brigadier General Gideon J. Pillow's Brigade of Patterson's Division.[3]

The landing site was south of the city about two miles, near Sacrificios, a small island. The soldiers landed in surf boats which General Scott designed and had built. In preparation, the surf boats transferred the men of the Pennsylvania regiments to the frigate *Potomac*. Worth's Division went in first, and, to everyone's amazement, faced no opposition. Patterson's Division followed Worth's and by dark on 9 March all of the Pennsylvanians were on the beach. Twiggs' Division came on in the third wave. This was the first large scale am-

Flag of the Columbia Volunteer Battalion of Danville. The Columbia Guards were a part of this organization, and a possibility exists
that this is the flag that was made by the ladies of Lewisburg and
raised over Chapultepec by Pvt. Adam Wray.
Pennsylvania Historical & Museum Commission

An imaginative artist pictures U.S. Troops landing at Vera Cruz on
9 March 1847
USAMHI

phibious landing in U.S. history, and it was accomplished without the loss of a single man.[4]

The surf boats could get only to within about twenty yards of the beach, so the men had to jump into waist-deep water and wade ashore. That first night they slept in their wet clothes on the sand. Some time after midnight the whole camp was roused by an alarm. A Mexican force made a loud but not too serious demonstration against the American position. Little real damage was done, but Sgt. John Hantze of Company E, 1st Regiment, sustained a wound in the shoulder. He was the first among many Pennsylvania volunteers to shed his blood for his country in Mexico.[5]

After a breakfast of crackers, salt beef and water, Patterson's Division headed off across the sand hills to extend the line of investment around the city. The Tennesseans took the lead as skirmishers, followed by the 1st and 2nd Pennsylvania. The march was begun at 8 or 9 o'clock on an oppressively hot day. Minor skirmishing occurred all day. A group of mounted Mexicans was chased away from an old powder magazine, and the Tennesseans and 1st Regiment charged upon some 600 enemy on the heights behind Vera Cruz. The Mexicans quickly took off, leaving this key position in American hands. Lieutenant Edward LeClerc of Company C, 2nd Regiment, wrote to his father about a little action he had on that day.

> Our company had a smart skirmish with the enemy, without sustaining any loss upon our side. After receiving their fire, and giving them ours in return, the order to charge was promptly and cheerfully obeyed, and the enemy were completely routed. Our company is the only one of the second Pennsylvania Regiment that has had an opportunity to test its bravery with the enemy.[6]

One of the boys of Company I, 2nd Regiment, wrote home, telling what it was like that day, after; "marching over the plains and hills of hot sand, and buttoned up in tight heavy uniforms and carrying our knapsacks & c. . . Many threw away their knapsacks, blankets and roundabouts. Others fell from the ranks and crawled to the shade completely exhausted."[7] Lieutenant Casper Berry of the 1st Regiment's Company C, was affected by sun stroke on that day, and it was feared that he would die. He returned to duty briefly, but he was later discharged because of its effects.[8]

It soon became obvious to the men that soldiering also meant physical labor. Company E of the 2nd Regiment got their taste of it on 11 March, as they worked all day cutting a road through the chaparral. This road would be used to bring up the big guns after they were landed. The Mexicans in the city kept their eyes open in search of targets for their artillery, and work parties proved convenient ones. Shells and balls of all descriptions flew among the men. Most hit the sand harmlessly, but occasionally they struck someone.[9]

On the night of the 11th, the 2nd Regiment was detailed to guard the railroad. Half watched while the others slept. "Here Gen. Pillow exposed his

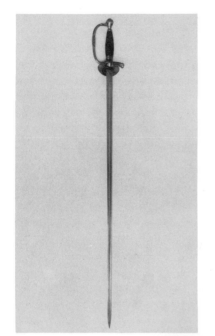
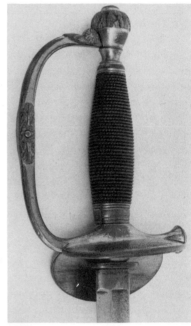

Model 1840 Foot Officers Sword of 2nd Lt. Casper M. Berry, showing it overall, its hilt and
its presentation inscription.

A Private Collection

consumate Generalship by posting the regt. on opposite sides of the road—facing each other about 20 yds apart . . . . Gen. Patterson discovered and rectified the mistake."[10] Private Israel Uncapher of Company E, 2nd Regiment, entered into his journal on the morning of the 13th; "Lay at the Rail Road again last night and stood guard . . . . There are a great many of our boys very easily alarmed, and they fire at any thing that moves; a poor Jackass, not being able to give the countersign, received eleven balls."[11]

Patterson's Division was in the center of the line, with Worth on his right. Twiggs' Division passed on through Patterson's volunteers to extend the line entirely around the city to the left. All communication was then cut off to the defenders. They gave no evidence of capitulating, and to storm the great walls of the city with its well over 100 cannon would be suicide. General Scott used strategy instead of brute force. He had his men prepare fortified works in front of Worth's line for the heavy artillery and mortars. In addition, he had large naval guns removed from the ships and installed into an intrenched position in front of Patterson's line. Most, if not all, the Pennsylvanians got to try their hand with a shovel in preparation for the naval guns. The primary activities of the troops at Vera Cruz were pickett duty, guard duty and fatigue duty.[12]

Foraging was another common occupation of the troops. A party of men from Companies C and G of the 1st Regiment were doing just that on the morning of the 19th when they were overtaken by Mexican lancers. A little fighting and a scramble for shelter ensued. When word of it reached camp, four companies of the 1st Regiment went to aid the foragers. Enroute, the New York Regiment joined the companies, and about four miles out the party was found holed up at a ranch. The rescuers then followed the lancers some distance, but

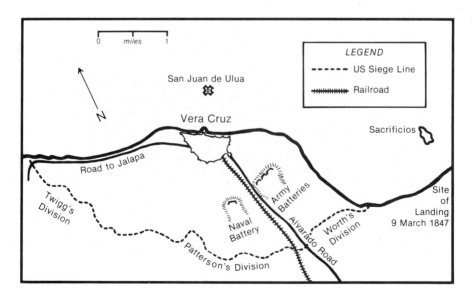

Siege lines at Vera Cruz

were unable to bring them to bay. The mutilated body of Private John F. Miller of Company G was found and brought in for burial.[13]

Hardships and inconveniences are part of warfare. A lieutenant in the 2nd Regiment wrote about some of them in a letter to his parents on 28 March.

> We have not had our clothes off for nearly three weeks, and day after to-morrow will be three weeks since my boots have been off my feet . . . We have not had a tent since we landed. We sleep upon the sand, with a knapsack, a log, or an exploded shell for a pillow.[14]

News of Taylor's victory at Buena Vista on 22 and 23 February reached Scott's army on 17 March and served to boost morale. The arrival of letters from home the next day raised the sagging spirits of the Keystone Boys even higher.[15]

General Scott, on 22 March, offered the commander of Vera Cruz the opportunity to surrender without further endangering his people, but the offer was flatly refused. That same afternoon the now completed batteries in front of Worth's line opened upon the city. The naval squadron also took part in the bombardment. The naval battery was completed, and on the 24th its 32 and 64 pounders joined in raining death and destruction upon the Mexicans.[16]

The Mexican commander sent out a flag of truce on the morning of the 26th, indicating a desire to discuss terms of surrender. A cease fire immediately

James Walker painted "A Siege Battery in Action," at Vera Cruz. Many of the Pennsylvania troops labored to build these batteries.

West Point Museum

Shells were received as well as being dispensed from the heavy batteries at Vera Cruz
USAMHI

went into effect. Arrangements were agreed to, and the formal ceremony of capitulation took place on the 29th.[17]

> The place was a beautiful plain, on the south of the city, three fourths of a mile in width, and about a mile and a half in length, the road passing through this plain—the flag of truce was planted about a mile and a half from the town. On each side of the road, at the distance of about 120 paces, the American Army was stationed. The Mexican soldiers marched out of the town with their National Flag at the head of the column, and their bands playing. When they had reached the flag of truce, they halted, and their bands of music ceased to play. Their flag was then delivered to one of our officers, the musical instruments were laid on heaps, and the soldiers stacked their arms; after which they filed to the right and rested on the ground for some time, while they were furnished with water to drink. While this was going forward, a body of troops, selected for that purpose, were seen marching towards the town and our Steam ships moving towards the Castle . . . . Our troops soon reached the town, and the stars and stripes were seen floating on one of the forts; the Steamships had moved up to the Castle, and soon the stars and stripes of America were also seen floating upon the flag staff of the famed Castle of San Juan de Ulloa.[18]

The Pennsylvania casualties incurred during the siege were twelve in the 1st Regiment and three in the 2nd. Three of these men were killed in action, and one died later from his wound. Their names and companies are as follows:

1st Regiment casualties

Co. A	Pvt. David Harkins
	Pvt. Mansfield B. Mason
Co. D	Pvt. William Beesley (died of wounds)
Co. E	Sgt. John Hantze
	Pvt. Andrew John Kramer
	Pvt. Gottlob Reeb (killed in action)
Co. F	Pvt. Theodore Theiss
Co. G	Sgt. Robert E. Williamson
	Pvt. John F. Miller (killed in action)
Co. I	Pvt. Obed C. Burdin
	Pvt. James H. Stevens
	Pvt. William Vandenburg

2nd Regiment casualties

Co. A	Pvt. John Kutz
Co. F	Pvt. George W. Miller (killed in action)
Co. H	Pvt. Benjamin F. Frey[19]

The soldiers at last saw the famous city up close. Private Richard Coulter noted in his journal that once inside the city it, "does not present the inspiring appearance it did from the sand hills." He wrote that the buildings were old and dilapidated and that "the streets are filthy." Much destruction had occurred because of the shelling. It even appeared to him that the city had been economically hurting for some time.[20] For a week and a half following the surrender the soldiers spent much time looking over the sights. They also did plenty of duty, patrolling streets and standing guard. Orders came down for all to prepare to march, and on the morning of 9 April the army set out for the interior.

Hostile action was not the sole cause of deaths and medical discharges among the volunteers. When the regiments left Vera Cruz, exactly a month after landing there, many were left behind in the hospital or had already been discharged by the surgeons. The diseases stepped in to take their toll. Captain Hay of the 1st Regiment went home to Pittsburgh to recuperate. Captain John S. Wilson of Danville received a leave of absence on the 7th of April and was put on board a ship on the 9th. Just before the ship was to set sail on the 13th, however, Captain Wilson died. His body was brought to the city where it was buried, the military ceremony being performed by the recently arrived Cameron Guards. Major Robert H. Hammond, Paymaster for Scott's Army, read the funeral service of the Episcopal Church. Before the war, Hammond, from

Milton, Pennsylvania, had been a militia brigadier general, and Wilson had served on his staff. Hammond too, would soon fall to disease in this foreign land.[21]

Meanwhile, back on Lobos Island, all the smallpox sufferers having gotten
better, Geary's three companies embarked on the *General Veazie* on 8 April.
Clear weather and a good breeze brought them to Vera Cruz on the 11th, just
two days too late to accompany their regiment into the interior.[22]

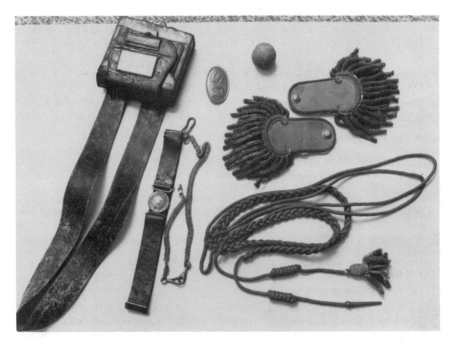

**Epaulettes, Sword Belt, Cartridge Box, Box Plate and Aiguilette worn by John S. Wilson of
Danville as Captain of the Columbia Guards and Brigade Quartermaster on the staff of Brigadier
General Robert H. Hammond.**

A Private Collection

ENDNOTES - CHAPTER III

1. Oswandel, *Notes,* p. 63.

2. Erasmus Wilson, ed., *Standard History of Pittsburgh, Pennsylvania* (Chicago: H. R. Cornell & Co., 1898), p. 414; *The Danville Intelligencer* , Jan. 1, 1847; Dewey S. Herrold, "Brigadier-General Edward Charles Williams," *The Snyder County Historical Society Bulletin,* II (Bulletin No. 4), pp. 502-503; See Appendix IX for Maj. Brindle's Report of the Battle of Chapultepec.

3. Bauer, *The Mexican War,* pp. 241 & 257.

4. *Ibid.,* p. 244; Cadmus M. Wilcox, *History of the Mexican War* (Washington, D.C.: The Church News Publishing Co., 1892), pp. 244-245; Hartman, *Private's Journal,* p. 6; Oswandel, *Notes,* pp. 67-68.

5. Coulter, "The Westmoreland Guards," p. 108; Larner, "A Westmoreland Guard," p. 219; National Archives, RG 94, 1st Pa. Regt. Papers.

6. *The Danville Intelligencer,* May 7, 1847; Larner, "A Westmoreland Guard," p. 220.

7. *The Pittsburgh Daily Gazette,* Apr. 17, 1847.

8. Oswandel, *Notes,* p. 71; See rosters.

9. Hartman, *Private's Journal,* p. 7; Anson, "William B. Roberts," p. 250.

10. Larner, "A Westmoreland Guard," pp. 220-221.

11. Coulter, "The Westmoreland Guards," p. 109.

12. Wilcox, *Mexican War,* pp. 246-f; Bauer, *The Mexican War,* pp. 246-f; *The Pittsburgh Daily Gazette,* Apr. 17, 1847.

13. Historical Society of Pennsylvania, John Kreitzer Journal, 1846-1848, Mar. 19, 1847; Oswandel, *Notes,* pp. 81-82; *The Pittsburgh Daily Gazette,* Apr. 17, 1847.

14. *The Danville Intelligencer,* May 7, 1847.

15. Larner, "A Westmoreland Guard," p. 221.

16. Edward D. Mansfield, *The Mexican War: History Of Its Origin And A Detailed Account Of The Victories Which Terminated In The Surrender Of The Capital; With The Official Despatches Of The Generals* (New York: A. S. Barnes & Co., 1848), pp. 169-171; Bauer, *The Mexican War,* pp. 249-250.

17. Mansfield, *The Mexican War,* p. 171; Bauer, *The Mexican War,* pp. 251-252.

18. *The Danville Intelligencer,* Apr. 30, 1847.

19. National Archives, RG 94, 1st & 2nd Pa. Regt. Papers.

20. Coulter, "Westmoreland Guards," p. 111.

21. National Archives, RG 94, 1st & 2nd Pa. Regt. Papers; *The Danville Intelligencer,* May 7, 1847; See rosters for men discharged and left behind due to illness.

22. Greer, "Diary of a Pennsylvania Volunteer," pp. 151-152; Tinkcom, *Geary,* p. 16; Mary de Forest Geary, *A Story About The Life Of John White Geary* (Brunswick, Ga.: Coastal Books, 1980), p. 19.

CHAPTER IV

Heading For The Interior

Twiggs' Division led the way as the Army moved inland, followed by Patterson's and Worth's Divisions. The march was hard. George Hartman of Company E, 2nd Regiment described it in his diary.

> The road for twelve miles is very bad, nothing but sand half knee deep and very hilly. The weather is extremely warm and water scarce, and what little there is, is very bad. The men lagged very much, many did not get to camp at all that night. The road is strewn with men for miles. We marched to-day twenty miles through a country barren and uncultivated.[1]

The second day's march was not as long or as rapid as the first. They reached the camp site at Puenta de Las Vegas by 2 o'clock. Another hard march followed on the 11th, which brought the Pennsylvanians to Puenta Nacional by evening. The route of the 12th brought them to the Plan del Rio, where Twiggs' Division was preparing to make an assault. The National Road, which they were following, here ran through a long pass, that by nature was a strong defensive position. Santa Anna, now commanding the Mexican Army, selected it as the place he would stop the Americans. The pass was called Cerro Gordo.[2]

General Twiggs intended to have his forces assault a virtually impregnable position. Fortunately, General Patterson came onto the field, and, seeing the situation, cancelled the attack order until a better reconnaissance could be made. A more thorough investigation was undertaken by Scott's engineers, and a path around the enemy position was discovered. However, much hard work would be needed before the artillery could be moved along it. The project immediately commenced, and by the morning of the 17th, Twiggs' men were moving along

Major General Robert Patterson

USAMHI

it to turn and cut off Santa Anna's left flank. The Mexicans discovered the movement and opened fire on the men, but fast movements and courageous actions
captured a key elevation called Atalaya. Three guns from Steptoe's Battery
of the 3rd U.S. Artillery were hauled to the summit during the night. A number
of men from the Pennsylvania regiments were detailed to serve with this battery between 16 April and 8 June.[3]

Scott's plan for the 18th instructed Twiggs to renew his flanking move and
attack early in the morning. Worth's Division was to be on Twiggs' tail. Pillow's
orders were as follows:

> As already arranged, Brigadier-general Pillow's brigade will march
> at six o'clock to-morrow morning along the route he has carefully recon-
> noitred, and stand ready as soon as he hears the report of arms on our
> right, or sooner if circumstances should favor him, to pierce the enemy's

line of batteries at such point—the nearer the river the better—as he may select. Once in the rear of that line, he will turn to the right or left, or both, and attack the batteries in reverse; or if abandoned, he will pursue the enemy with vigor until further orders.[4]

The troops were up at dawn on Sunday and were moving up the highway from their camp by seven o'clock. They marched three or four miles, then halted for some time. During this interlude General Patterson rode along the line and made a short address to each regiment in the brigade. The march then resumed by filing to the left off the National Road into the chaparral. It was obvious that Pillow was not as familiar with the ground as he should have been. Lieutenant Zealous B. Tower, the engineer officer who performed the reconnaissance, knew where to go and how to get there. However, General Pillow forcefully insisted that he knew best and ordered the advance on the right-most of two paths leading into the chaparral. This path led into an open and exposed position in front of the Mexican batteries, whereas the other path was more sheltered and provided greater secrecy. In addition, Pillow decided to modify his orders after the march was in progress. The order of march was 1st Pennsylvania, 2nd Tennessee, 1st Tennessee and 2nd Pennsylvania. The primary position to be attacked was the defile between the two Mexican batteries lying closest to the river. Wynkoop was to form on the left, supported by Colonel William B. Campbell's 1st Tennessee. Colonel William Haskell's 2nd Tennessee was to form on Wynkoop's right, to be supported by Roberts' regiment.

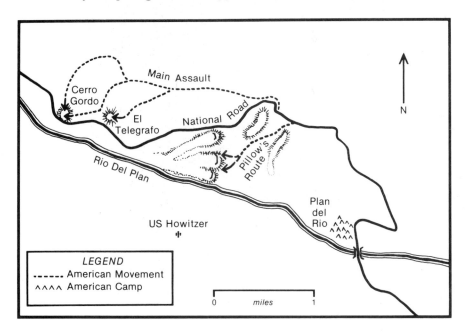

The Battle of Cerro Gordo

Unfortunately, the path followed was very narrow, most of its length re-quiring single file passage. It was almost 9 o'clock before Pillow's troops ap-proached their positions. In the meantime, Twiggs' attack on the right had already begun, and the firing could easily be heard by Pillow's men. Pillow then gave orders for Wynkoop to go along the chaparral behind his assigned position, then file to the right, then file to the right again, thus countermar-ching the regiment into position. Somehow most of this activity was accomplish-ed near the Mexicans without getting their attention. The men were now so close they clearly heard the Mexican officers talking in their batteries. At this point Pillow, in his excitement, shouted out at the top of his voice, "Why the H____l dont Colonel Wynkoop file to the right?"⁵ Almost at once a bugle blared in the Mexican works, and within minutes the enemy cannon opened upon the exposed volunteers.

Haskell's Tennesseans, with a company of Kentucky troops and Charles Naylor's Company F of the 2nd Pennsylvania, were nearly in position. Naylor's,

Gideon J. Pillow, shown in this sketch as a major general
Oswandel's Notes

company was assigned to form part of the attacking force with the 2nd Tennessee. Now under the fire of grape and cannister, some of Haskell's troops took it upon themselves to charge. Pillow then ordered Haskell's force to attack. None of the other regiments, however, were as yet in place. The Mexicans had cleared a fire zone in their front, about 300 yards, by cutting the chaparral and letting it lay on the ground. Once Haskell's men reached the clearing they had difficulty advancing in formation, and the enemy fire intensified. Musketry joined with the artillery from all three batteries. The Tennesseans made for the rear. All of this transpired in probably not over ten minutes.

Although under fire of the artillery, the 2nd Pennsylvania took its place in line behind Haskell and awaited orders to charge to his support. Wynkoop and Campbell also came into position in respectable order on the left. Pillow had ordered both of them not to move from their assigned positions, either forward or backward, until he told them to do so. At that time, the general was squatting behind some bushes about 450 yards to the rear, when a stray ball hit his upper arm. At this he and his aide took off, at a run, for the rear, leaving no orders or instructions.

Colonel Roberts noted that, in an effort to get away, some of the Tennesseans ran right through his regiment knocking a number down. During the charge Naylor's company became disoriented, and when they withdrew they fell back to their left. For the remainder of the engagement they were formed up on the right of the 1st Pennsylvania. After a while Colonel Campbell assumed command of the brigade and was preparing the regiments for a general assault when word passed along that the Mexicans had surrendered. The surrender was not at first believed by the officers or men. They were well aware that their efforts had not seriously intimidated the more than 2,000 defenders in their well placed fortified batteries, with over fifteen pieces of artillery. As the guns fell silent, however, the truth of the capitulation became apparent. Pillow then returned from the rear and ordered a general withdrawal of the brigade.[6]

Numerous interesting incidents occurred during the battle which were recorded by the participants. Lieutenant William J. Ankrimm of Company K, 1st Regiment, wrote to a friend:

> Lieut. Col. Black, who was always in front of the regiment, lost a piece of his coat by a grape shot, but instead of cooling his ardor or courage, this only appeared to increase it. Capt. Herron, when the regiment was advancing, found a man lying down to avoid the iron hail which was flying at the time. Capt. H. gave him a kick, when his foot slipping, he fell forward, and by that accident, no doubt saved his life—for a grape shot at that instant passed over him, and cut down a small tree immediately behind him.[7]

When Private John Shelden of Company C, 1st Regiment, was wounded in the ankle by a grape shot, he was carried back to the National Road on an improvised stretcher by his fellows J. Oswandel and Alburtus Welsh and others. The whole way back he complained pitifully about his injury and expressed fears that he would lose his foot or leg. He died from his wound at Jalapa on 6 May.[8]

A Philadelphian, in a letter home, said that the 1st Regiment's Surgeon Thomas Bunting and his Hospital Steward, Dr. Charles Hardegan, were the only medical officers on the field with Pillow's Brigade during the battle. As such, they were trying to treat the wounded of the whole brigade. During the fight, "Dr. Hardegan's jackass, which carried the medicines, received three balls, and died on the spot." Also, during an operation on the field, "a soldier, who was assisting Dr. Bunting in the act of dressing a wounded man, was himself mortally wounded."[9]

In Company A of the 2nd Regiment, Private John Sheets was struck in the left calf by a grape shot in one of the early discharges. Instead of heading for the rear, he continued to follow the advance of his company for nearly half a mile, until he fell on the path from loss of blood. He was carried from the field and died at Jalapa on the 29th, from lockjaw.[10]

As the troops of the 2nd Regiment filed down the path to get into their line of battle, Corporal John Smith of Company C was behind Lieutenant Frick' and Major Brindle. Frick's sword scabbard fell to the ground, and Smith picked it up and handed it to him. Shortly afterwards, as the men were trying to rapidly move into line, Brindle tripped and fell, dropping one of his pistols.

A bronze cannon captured by the Pennsylvania Regiments at Cerro Gordo was displayed outside the old State Armory in Harrisburg. This gun, being one of two presented to the State by General Patterson in 1847, is now on display at the Pennsylvania Military Museum in Boalsburg.

Pennsylvania Historical & Museum Commission

When he got up, Smith bent over to pick it up and was immediately struck in the face by a grape shot, the ball entering his right eye and exiting the left side of the back of his neck and carrying away the roof of his mouth. The bearers who carried him from the field found him fully conscious and still grasping Brindle's pistol. He lived until 1 May.[11]

A member of Captain Porter's Company I, 2nd Regiment, wrote a short note home about a skulker.

> I am sorry to say, that one of our men, (I will not mention his name,) when under orders to charge, [double quick into line] lay down behind a rock, but was observed by Lieutenant Skelly, who ordered him to get up and go with his company; but he would not obey; and so Skelly struck his sword about three inches into him—that's all![12]

Private James Shaw of Company H, 2nd Regiment, was one of the more fortunate of the casualties. Colonel Roberts said of him, he "had his finger shot off and in less than two hours had the stump cut off and dressed and took his place in ranks."[13]

Considering the fire they faced, the number of casualties incurred by the two regiments was remarkably low. The brigade as a whole reported 106 killed and wounded, the vast majority of these being from Colonel Haskell's 2nd Tennessee Regiment.[14] The list of wounded from the Pennsylvania regiments included ten from the 1st and thirteen from the 2nd. Three in each regiment later died from their wounds. In addition, one man of Company F, 1st Regiment, Private Adolph Bennett, had been wounded at Plan del Rio on the 16th.

1st Regiment casualties

Co. A	Pvt. David Lindsey
	Pvt. John Linhart (died of wounds)
Co. C	Pvt. John Shelden (died of wounds)
	Pvt. George Sutton
Co. D	Pvt. Albert Cudney
	Pvt. Joseph K. Davis
Co. G	Pvt. Benjamin F. Keyser
Co. I	Cpl. Dewitt C. Kitchen
	Pvt. David R. Morrison (died of wounds)
Co. K	Pvt. Aaron Lovett

2nd Regiment casualties

Co. A	Pvt. Abraham Roland (died of wounds)
	Pvt. John Sheets (died of wounds)
Co. C	Cpl. John Smith (died of wounds)
Co. E	Pvt. Jacob P. Miller

Co. F	Pvt. John Chambers
	Pvt. Edward Cruse
	Pvt. Thomas Hann
	Pvt. Jacob B. Simons
Co. H	Pvt. James Shaw
Co. I	Pvt. David M. Davidson
Co. K	Pvt. Josiah Horn
	Pvt. Frederick Sommers
	Pvt. William Wilhelm[15]

The fighting on the Army's right had been overwhelmingly successful. The Mexican Army was defeated, and its line of retreat had been cut off. By 10 o'clock the battle was over. The utter defeat on their left made further defense of the Mexican batteries facing Pillow's Brigade useless. For this reason they surrendered. Some 3,000 prisoners were taken, as well as tons of military paraphernalia.[16]

The day following the battle, the 2nd Regiment was detailed to guard the prisoners, until they were paroled in the afternoon. Ten men from each company of the 1st Regiment were used to bring Steptoe's guns down from Atalaya. General Worth's advancing soldiers occupied Jalapa on the 19th, and, continuing on, they trooped unopposed into Perote on the 22nd.[17]

Bright and early on the 20th Pillow's Brigade, except for the 2nd Tennessee, which was assigned to remain with the sick and wounded, took up the line of march for Jalapa. Leaving their camp at Plan del Rio, they marched up the National Road past the battlefield. Bodies of Mexican soldiers lay scattered about and on piles awaiting burial. Evidence of the pursuit of the 18th was left by the dragoons. "The smell, all along the road on account of the decomposing bodies of men and horses is sickening. There were upwards of forty horses killed in pursuing the enemy. The traveling would be pleasant, were it not for the stench, the road is excellent."[18]

That evening the Pennsylvanians camped near Encero. Close by lay Santa Anna's own hacienda and farm. Colonel Roberts described it as, "one of the most beautiful I have ever seen." He also noted to his wife that the house was well decorated with American made furniture.[19] By noon of the 21st the regiments had reached Jalapa. They marched through the city and encamped on a lovely meadow about three miles west, along the National Road. The site became known as Camp Patterson.[20]

Corporal Dewitt Clinton Kitchen of Wilkes-Barre lay suffering from his wound at Plan del Rio. Years later he wrote of an incident which occurred there, digressing a bit in the progress.

The little dog, Logan, who had followed the fortunes of the company [I, 1st Regt.] through all its engagements and vicissitudes, had been a great source of amusement. His antics were numerous as his affections were inexhaustible. He knew every man in the company and never, by any possibility, mistook his place in the regimental ranks. He would not consort with another dog which belonged to the Pottsville company, but was the veriest martinet as to companionship and company exclusiveness. He was the constant companion of the foragers; went with the men into battle and when a spent cannon ball came skipping along, within his notice, he would bark at it and give it chase, as though he recognized it as an enemy. The wounded were quartered in bambo huts at Plan del Rio. Two days after the battle Pillow's brigade followed the advance of the army to Jalapa, and Logan, of course, went with the company. During the forenoon he returned to the bunk of the writer, whining and seeming in great distress. The person to whom he made his plaints was scarcely in fitting mood to properly answer the earnest appeal for sympathy. Feverish and sore himself, the little dogs pleading was unheeded, and during the day he was found, near the hut, dead. How many times I have reproached myself for that one little act of unkindness. Poor Logan.[21]

The wounded moved up with General John Quitman's column of volunteers on the 21st, arriving in Jalapa on the 23rd. The National College provided fine quarters for the hospital.[22] Along with the sick and wounded came the long lost battalion of the 2nd Regiment. Companies B, D and G received three hearty cheers from their comrades when they reached Camp Patterson. For the first time since leaving New Orleans the 2nd Pennsylvania camped together on the same field.[23]

The soldiers were glad to be at Jalapa. It was a pleasant, progressive city, and its surrounding countryside fairly overflowed with fresh fruits and vegetables. Even the water was good, and healthful to drink. The residents impressed the troops as being intelligent, enterprising and respectful. They seemed to even favor having the Yankees nearby. The senoritas too, attracted much attention. The scene at Jalapa was much in contrast to what the men had encountered previously in Mexico.[24]

Despite what appeared to be a pleasant and advantageous situation, the conditions at Jalapa proved to be disastrous for scores of Pennsylvanians. The rainy season descended just about the time Scott's Army reached the city. A cold rain began to fall on 22 April and continued for days. No tents had, as yet, been brought up for the men because of the lack of horses and wagons. The troops found themselves soaked to the skin and unable to dry out. After a few days they started foraging for scraps with which to erect shelters or huts. The soakings continued at least through the end of the month, and to such an extent that the bivouac became known as Camp Misery.[25]

Bands of Mexican soldiers, guerillas, rancheros and bandits lurked just outside the perimeter of the camp. Numerous unsuspecting soldiers were killed by them. Orders were issued to keep the men inside the camp, but some of Quitman's volunteers insisted on learning the hard way. Several were brought in and buried with full military honors.[26]

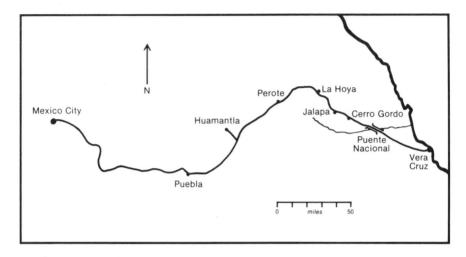

The National Road from Vera Cruz to Mexico City

Artist's View of Jalapa

Oswandel's Notes

The American Army did its share of snooping around the city, and a great quantity of Mexican uniforms was discovered in a warehouse. Lieutenant Colonel Geary noted in his diary on 2 May, that a large number of these were turned over to the men. This provided much amusement, but the need for clothing was a real one, and one not being met by the Army's quartermasters.[27]

Excitement developed in camp on Monday, the 3rd, when the Cameron Guards, or a good sized body of them, registered a complaint with Colonel Roberts about their rations. The Colonel was obviously unable to grant what was not within his power and said so. Unfortunately, some Mexican women had set up food stands nearby, hoping to make money from the soldiers. The Guards made a rush on these ladies and quickly cleaned them out, without paying of course. A few appetites were temporarily quenched, but at the company officers' expense, as they were ordered to pay the women.[28]

The next day one of the "Killers" from Philadelphia was at it again. Private John O'Brien decided to liberate a nice gold watch and cross on a heavy gold chain from a local Roman Catholic priest. O'Brien was tried for the theft by military court, but he established a good alibi through the testimony of his friends, and was acquitted.[29]

At the outbreak of the war several state regiments of volunteers were enrolled for a twelve month period. That enlistment was rapidly running out. General Scott decided that now would be the best time to send these boys home, as they refused to reenlist or extend for the duration of the war. On the morning of 6 May the 1st and 2nd Tennessee, the Tennessee Mounted Volunteer Regiment, the 3rd and 4th Illinois, the 4th Kentucky, the Alabama and Georgia regiments and several independent companies left Camp Misery and headed for Vera Cruz and home. Along with them went Major General Patterson and Brigadier General Pillow. The Army's new organization placed the remaining volunteers, including both Pennsylvania regiments and one each from New York and South Carolina, under command of Brigadier General John A. Quitman of Mississippi.[30]

That same afternoon the 2nd Regiment left camp and moved into the National Guard Barracks in Jalapa, thus becoming the city's new garrison.[31] The 1st Regiment marched on the 7th to Las Vegas, arriving in Perote the following afternoon. It was quartered in the famous castle and garrisoned that city.[32] The men settled in quickly, enjoying the comfortable and spacious quarters. At about noon on 14 May, Companies A, G and I of the 1st Regiment, under Major Bowman, began the return march to Jalapa. Arriving the next day, they added their strength to that of the 2nd Regiment as the city's garrison.[33]

The next weeks passed with little excitement. The troops stood guard duty every few days and held daily dress parades and guard mounts, but they enjoyed much freedom as well. Most familiarized themselves with the cities, their buildings and markets. Some became familiar with the local residents, too. A general court martial pronounced its judgment on four thieves in Jalapa on 19 May. Three were soldiers in the regular army, but one was Private Donald

Revalon, Company B, 2nd Regiment. They were all convicted of horse stealing. The offenders had their heads shaved, and each received thirty-nine lashes
on the bare back. In addition, they were placed in a cart and hauled through
the principal streets with the word "robber" on their backs. The band followed, playing the Rogue's March. Lieutenant Colonel Geary commented in his
diary on the scene: "Although these men doubtlessly deserved punishment, yet
the mode in which it was inflicted is a relic of barbarism, and ought not to
be continued in an enlightened age." Private Revalon was also sentenced to
forfeit four months pay and to spend the remainder of the war incarcerated
in Perote Castle.[34]

One day, First Sergeant Arnold C. Lewis of Company I, 1st Regiment, and
two comrades were exploring the old cemetery at Jalapa. It was located on a
rough hillside and surrounded by an old stone wall. They looked around for
a while, then exited on the far side of the hill.

> Here the ground was broken and uneven and huge masses of lava
> rock so blocked the way that progress was difficult. Proceeding cautious-
> ly, they suddenly found themselves in the presence of five as villainous-
> looking greasers as ever cut a throat. These gentlemen were reclining
> in a little grassy opening in picturesque attitudes, eating, drinking, smok-
> ing and all talking at once. The jabber they made prevented them from
> hearing the approach of our adventurers, who knew the character of the
> men before them and determined upon making a capture. When they
> appeared upon the scene the greasers made an attempt to seize their
> arms, but our boys were too quick and getting between them and the
> rock against which the guns were leaning, with cocked revolvers, com-
> pelled them to take the road to the city, where they were handed over
> to the authorities.[35]

The effects of almost two months of exposure to the elements became very
apparent by the end of May. The weeks of wetness at Camp Patterson especially
took their toll. Private William H. Dietrick of the 2nd Regiment's Company
C wrote home that, "there is at this time some twenty-five or eight, sick; one
half this number are in the Hospital at Jalapa; the others are in the barracks
unfit for duty. It is hoped that they will soon recover. It is not only our company that has the sick, but all, the whole regiment."[36] By the time Dietrick wrote
his letter, three from his unit had already died from disease, and many of the
sick ones he referred to would not recover. Acute diarrhea was by far the most
common complaint. It caused great suffering among hundreds in the Pennsylvania regiments, and it led to many a horrible and pitiful death.[37]

The three companies of the 1st Regiment left Jalapa, accompanying the
sick and hospital stores, on 8 June. General Scott, realizing that his force was
too small, decided to vacate Jalapa and cut his line of communication to the
coast. Only the cities of Vera Cruz, Perote and Puebla would now be occupied
by garrisons. Accordingly, the 2nd Regiment moved from the barracks to Camp
Patterson on the 18th, and the next day moved with Brigadier General George
Cadwalader's train for Perote.[38]

Meanwhile at Perote, General Scott had appointed Colonel Wynkoop Governor of the Castle, with Lieutenant Colonel Black as the troop commander. Wynkoop apparently enjoyed this independence and took the initiative as he saw fit. When the city's mayor cut off the water to the castle, Wynkoop simply told him if he didn't soon restore the water flow, a few shells would be fired into the city. The water quickly returned to its normal flow. On the morning of 22 May, Colonel Wynkoop took Companies F and H to the village of Cruz Blanco in pursuit of a band of guerillas. After spending the day scouting, they returned empty handed. On the 25th, Captain Samuel H. Walker and two companies of mounted riflemen joined the Perote garrison to see to it that the roads to Jalapa and Puebla remained open. Captain Walker escorted a train out for Jalapa on the 27th, and with it went the 1st Regiment's sutler, Samuel D. Karns. He indicated that he had seen enough of Mexico and was going home. He sold his stock to a Mr. Daniel M. Dull of McVeytown, Pennsylvania.[39]

The small adobe town of Tepegahualco lay about ten miles from Perote on the road to Puebla. It had for some time been a sort of headquarters for bands of guerillas in the area, so, on the afternoon of 6 June, Colonel Wynkoop took part of the 1st Regiment and a company of dragoons on an expedition there. No guerillas were seen, but the foray netted a lot of military clothing, arms and ammunition.[40]

The Perote garrison moved on 11 June from the eighty year old stone castle surrounded by a moat, into the city itself. On the same afternoon Companies A, G and I returned from Jalapa and took up residence in the town. Five companies moved back to the castle on the 18th, because of increasing rumors that the Mexicans planned to attack.[41]

Colonel Wynkoop knew Cadwalader's train was on its way from Jalapa, and on the 16th he learned from a courier that the Mexicans planned to challenge his movement at La Hoya Pass. This was a long pass through the mountains, situated between the villages of La Hoya on the east and Las Vegas on the west. A series of excellently prepared fortifications protected it well, and made it a superb defensive position. Late on the 19th, Wynkoop led out a force composed of Companies B, C, F, H and K of the 1st Regiment and Samuel Walker's Company C of the Mounted Rifles, in all about 250 men. They reached Las Vegas early in the morning, and before daylight Walker's company charged the enemy, sending them scurrying. Wynkoop continued the advance upon the enemy position at La Hoya, and Walker stayed out in front of the infantry. Cadwalader's command spent the night at La Hoya and at sun-up proceeded into the pass. For the first two and a half miles the enemy works were empty. Not a Mexican could be seen. Finally, some were spotted on a peak to the left of the road. Captain Winder of the 1st U.S. Artillery led the advance with four companies, one of them apparently being G of the 2nd Pennsylvania Volunteers, which served as skirmishers on the face of the hill. Between the hill and road, on a level wooded area, Company A took its position. Lieutenant Colonel Geary commanded Companies B and D and one from the 1st U.S. Artillery on the road itself. A twelve pounder was brought up and fired four rounds before the enemy began leaving the hill and crossing the road ahead of the column. A chase ensued, and soon Wynkoop's and Cadwalader's troops were mixing with each other. Considerable firing took place, but, before long, the chase became a total route. Mexican casualties were estimated at between 30 and 50 killed, while three U.S. soldiers were injured. None of these were Pennsylvanians.[42]

The pursuit continued for over two miles. Geary's Companies B and D followed the Mexicans through a barley field, over a lava bed, through a thick chaparral, and, at the top of a hill, they sent a volley after them. He wrote:

> I ordered the charge to be continued down the hill, at the foot of which I discovered a cave, into which I directed the men, which was found to be well stored with every luxury to eat, together with live turkeys & chickens, also blankets, trinkets, and jewelry all which was quickly plundered and the charge continued.[43]

In the melee the village of Las Vegas was virtually burned to the ground. Once the troops were reassembled, the combined forces moved up to Rio Frio for the night. At about noon on the 21st, they arrived at Perote.[44]

The time spent at Perote by the 2nd Regiment was only long enough for them to get used to the place. On the 28th, they moved with Colonel Childs' train to Tepegahualco. There they stayed until 3 July, drilling, guarding and being mustered. On the 8th, they finally arrived at Puebla, where the bulk of Scott's Army was encamped.[45] Companies A, C, D, G, I and K of the 1st Regiment left Perote on the 3rd also. They accompanied a train commanded by their old "friend," Gideon Pillow, who, now a major general, was bringing up fresh troops for the Army. They too arrived at Puebla on 8 July. Colonel Wynkoop remained as Governor of Perote, with Major Bowman being the military commander. Companies B, E, F and H of the 1st Regiment, Walker's Mounted Rifles and an artillery battery were the garrison. Wynkoop's responsibility also included the hospital, filled with sick and dying soldiers.[46]

Puebla became a huge camp, with troops quartered in many of the large buildings of the city. It was a metropolis with about 70,000 people. The new soldiers promised by the government finally came up in the trains led by Generals Cadwalader, Pillow and Franklin Pierce. Scott all the while was formalizing his plans and adjusting his forces for the final push on Mexico City.[47]

1. Hartman, *Private's Journal*, p. 10; Kitchen, *Wyoming Artillerists*, p. 33.

2. Oswandel, *Notes*, pp. 109-112.

3. Bauer, *The Mexican War*, pp. 263-265; Mansfield, *The Mexican War*, p. 185; Daniel H. Hill, "Battle of Cerro Gordo," *The Southern Quarterly Review*, XXI (Jan., 1852), pp. 139-140.

4. Mansfield, *The Mexican War*, pp. 186-187.

5. William Starr Myers, ed., *The Mexican War Diary Of George B. McClellan* (Princeton: Princeton University Press, 1917), p. 83.

6. *Ibid.*, pp. 81-87; Anson, "Col. William B. Roberts," pp. 255-257; Oswandel, *Notes*, pp. 122-136; St. George L. Sioussat (ed.), "Mexican War Letters of Col. William B. Campbell of Tennessee," *Tennessee Historical Magazine*, I, 1915, pp. 163-164; Hill, "Battle of Cerro Gordo," pp. 144-145; Wilcox, *Mexican War*, pp. 290-294; Mansfield, *The Mexican War*, pp. 190-192; Bauer, *The Mexican War*, pp. 265-267; Justin H. Smith, *The War With Mexico* (2 vols.; New York: The Mac-Millan Company, 1919), II, pp. 56-58; R. S. Ripley, *The War With Mexico* (2 vols.; New York: Reprint by Burt Franklin, 1970), II, pp. 67-73; John S. Jenkins, *History Of The War between the United States And Mexico from the Commencement Of Hostilities to the Ratification Of The Treaty of Peace* (Philadelphia: John E. Potter And Company, 1851), pp. 282-283; John Bonner, "Scott's Battles In Mexico," *Harpers New Monthly Magazine*, XI (Aug., 1855), pp. 313-314; *Democratic Union* (Harrisburg), May 26, 1847. See Apendices III & IV for Pillow's Report & Wynkoop's account of the battle.

7. *The Daily Morning Post* (Pittsburgh), May 19, 1847.

8. Oswandel, *Notes*, p. 128; National Archives, RG 94, Papers of the 1st Pa. Regt.

9. *The Pennsylvanian* (Philadelphia), May 20, 1847.

10. *Democratic Press* (Reading), May 25, June 1 & June 8, 1847.

11. *The Danville Intelligencer*, June 4, 1847.

12. *The Pittsburgh Daily Gazette*, June 3, 1847.

13. Anson, "Col. William B. Roberts," p. 255.

14. Mansfield, *The Mexican War*, p. 197.

15. National Archives, RG 94, 1st & 2nd Regt. Papers.

16. Smith, *War With Mexico*, II, p. 58; Mansfield, *The Mexican War*, p. 196.

17. Coulter, "Westmoreland Guards," p. 113; Oswandel, *Notes*, pp. 136-137; Bauer, *The Mexican War*, p. 268.

18. Hartman, *Private's Journal*, p. 12; Oswandel, *Notes*, p. 139.

19. Anson, "Col. William B. Roberts," p. 258.

20. Larner, "A Westmoreland Guard," p. 227.

21. Kitchen, *Wyoming Artillerists*, p. 35.

22. *Ibid.*, p. 36; Oswandel, *Notes*, p. 143.

23. Tinkcom, *Geary*, p. 19.

24. Oswandel, *Notes*, pp. 140-146.

25. *Ibid.*, pp. 142-148.

26. *Ibid.*, pp. 147-153.

27. Tinkcom, *Geary*, p. 20.

28. Oswandel, *Notes*, pp. 154-155.

29. *Ibid.*, pp. 155, 158.

30. *Ibid.*, pp. 157-158.

31. Larner, "A Westmoreland Guard," p. 227.

32. Oswandel, *Notes*, pp. 159-160.

33. *Ibid.*, p. 164; Kitchen, *Wyoming Artillerists*, p. 37.

34. Tinkcom, *Geary*, p. 22; John R. Evans, "The Reading Artillerists in the Mexican War," *The Historical Review of Berks County*, XV (Oct., 1949), pp. 135-136; National Archives, RG 94, 2nd Pa. Regt. Papers.

35. Kitchen, *Wyoming Artillerists*, p. 43.

36. *The Danville Intelligencer*, June 25, 1847.

37. National Archives, RG 94, 1st & 2nd Pa. Regt. Papers.

38. Hartman, *Private's Journal*, p. 13; Tinkcom, *Geary*, p. 23.

39. Oswandel, *Notes*, pp. 164-166, 171-172.

40. *Ibid.*, p. 177.

41. *Ibid.*, pp. 184, 187.

42. *Ibid.*, pp. 188-193; Tinkcom, *Geary*, pp. 24-25; Herrold, "Edward C. Williams," pp. 500-501; Executive Documents (After Action Reports of Commanders), 30th Cong., 1st Session, I, (1847), pp. 20-25; *The Philadelphia Grays' Collection of Official Reports of Brigadier-General George Cadwalader's Service during the Campaign of 1847, In Mexico* (Philadelphia: T. K. And P. G. Collins, 1848), pp. 11-12; *The Pennsylvanian* (Philadelphia), Sept. 8, 1847. See Appendices V & VI for Childs' & Wynkoop's Reports of the battle.

43. Tinkcom, *Geary*, p. 25.

44. *Ibid.*

45. Evans, "Reading Artillerists," p. 136.

46. Smith, *War With Mexico*, II, p. 425.

47. Larner, "A Westmoreland Guard," p. 231; Oswandel, *Notes*, pp. 207-243.

CHAPTER V

The Valley of Mexico

The Polk Administration recognized the Army's need for additional soldiers and called for more volunteers. Secretary of War William L. Marcy issued the call on 19 April, asking Pennsylvania for two additional companies. The State's Adjutant General selected the Independent Grays of Bedford, commanded by Captain Samuel M. Taylor, and the Wayne Guards from the southwestern end of Mifflin County, under Captain James Caldwell.[1]

The companies completed their preparations and reported to Pittsburgh, where Lieutenant Horace B. Field of the 3rd U.S. Artillery mustered them into Federal service; the Guards on the 18th of May, and the Grays on the 26th. Second Lieutenant Charles Bower was named Acting Surgeon of the contingent, while First Lieutenant Alexander McKamey became Adjutant, and First Sergeant John M. Gilmore became Sergeant Major. They boarded the steamer, *Colonel Yell* and took to the Ohio River on the 29th. After an interesting trip, the ship docked at New Orleans on 10 June. The next day they rode the train to Camp Carlton, a few miles above the city. The Pennsylvanians were not affected by a serious epidemic of measles infesting the camp. On 22 June the troops embarked for Vera Cruz on the steam ship *Alabama*. A bad Gulf storm caused some exciting moments for the six companies aboard, as water rushed into the ship through cracks in her hull, putting out the fires in her boilers. The crew did some rapid repairs and much bailing, as the soldiers enjoyed the suspense and tried to survive their seasickness. On the 27th they were put ashore just below Vera Cruz.[2]

Brigadier General Franklin Pierce commanded the new troops gathering at Vera Cruz, and he tried to prepare them for the campaign ahead. He staged false alarms, which revealed the lack of discipline. There were also plenty of

Major General John A. Quitman

details, drills, parades, the breaking of wild mules and the inevitable guard duty. The line of march for the interior was taken up on 16 July. The two Pennsylvania companies and a company of Regulars had the opportunity to charge the enemy on the 21st at the National Bridge, thus opening the road for the passage of Pierce's column. No casualties were reported. On the 24th they reached the site of old Camp Patterson just west of Jalapa, and they arrived at Perote on the 31st. The column marched into Puebla on 6 August, and on the following day the two companies became part of the 2nd Regiment; the Grays as Company L and the Guards as Company M.[3]

General Scott reorganized his army then moving on Mexico City. He activated four divisions under Major Generals John A. Quitman and Gideon J. Pillow, and Brigadier Generals David E. Twiggs and William J. Worth. Quitman's 4th Division was composed of two brigades. Brigadier General James Shields commanded the First Brigade, consisting of the Marine Corps detachment and the New York and South Carolina Volunteer Regiments. The Second Brigade was simply the enlarged 2nd Pennsylvania Regiment, under Colonel Roberts.[4]

The four companies of Marines were brought up to be the permanent garrison for Puebla, or so the 1st Pennsylvania thought. When told that they would do that job instead, the regiment became very upset. Lieutenant Colonel Black even went so far as to submit his resignation to General Scott. Scott, of course, refused to accept it and stated that he had great confidence in the regiment and in Black as well. The infantry troops assigned to the garrison of Puebla included Companies A, C, D, G, I and K of the 1st Pennsylvania with Black as their commander. The overall command at Puebla went to Colonel Thomas Childs of the 1st U.S. Artillery. As it turned out, a better choice of troops and commander could probably not have been made.[5]

The day after the new companies joined the 2nd Regiment, 8 August, Quitman's Division left Puebla. The first night they camped at Rio Frieto, and on the 9th they reached San Martin. The next day they began crossing the mountains and got as far as Rio Frio. Heavy rains poured down all that afternoon. The regiment served as the rear guard on the following day. During the 11th's twenty-three mile march, they entered the valley of Mexico to breathtakingly beautiful views. They could see Mexico City in the distance. That night the soldiers camped at an old hacienda near Buena Vista.[6]

The Regiment stayed three days at this location while General Scott's engineers investigated the approaches to the capital. During this time the men explored the countryside and did considerable foraging. Private Jacob C. Higgins of Company M recorded one of his foraging experiences in his journal. For some reason he could not accompany a group when it left camp, but he intended to join them shortly and sent his musket on ahead with them. They went one direction, however, and he went another. He soon entered a village where he expected them to be.

> Naturally when I arrived I did not find the party there. In fact I saw no person at all. The town appeared entirely deserted. I saw the large

double doors of a store standing wide open and I walked in, but saw no one. It was as still as death and close to the front door was a stairway leading up.

Opposite to the front door and in the rear of the room was another door leading to the backyard and the counter was lengthwise across the rear of the room. I walked behind the counter and took a bottle or jar down from a shelf. I opened it and found that it contained honey. I thought I would take that with me to camp.

Just at that time I heard a noise and on looking behind me saw three large brawny Mexicans standing at the front door with large knives or cutlasses in their hands and two others standing in the back door. There I was without any arms whatever to defend myself.

I just leaned back against the counter shelf with a sigh of despair and as my eyes dropped down, as it were, I saw a large Mexican sabre lying under the counter unsheathed almost at my feet. I stooped down, picked it up and walked out from behind the counter in a careless manner, but not a word had been spoken yet either by the Mexicans or myself.

But at this time I raised my sabre, pointing up towards the stairs and called out to my comrades, which I knew were not there, to come down. That threw the Mexicans off their guard and I kept advancing toward the door, swinging the sabre above my head and glancing toward the stairs until I got close enough to strike which I did with all the strength I was able to command. I struck one on the left side of the neck and another on the right side. One fell to the right and the other to the left and the third one jumped out of the way.

I jumped out the door and if ever I did any fast running it was at that time.[7]

Higgins made good his escape, and he acknowledged that his Maker was the one who preserved his life. Unfortunately, Private Thomas McBride of Company H did not fare as well. He went out with a party of foragers near Buena Vista on the 13th, and somehow got separated from the group. The Mexicans quickly took advantage of the situation by killing him and mutilating his body.[8]

Quitman's troops took to the road again early on Sunday the 15th, advancing on the fortified Mexican position at El Penon as a feint. They then counter-marched back through Buena Vista, taking a seldom used, little known road to the south, around the lakes, camping for the night at Chalco. That route avoided the nearly impregnable defenses Santa Anna had placed on all the main approaches to the city. On Monday they moved only about three miles to Capa at Satalco, and another five miles were covered on Tuesday, bringing them to San Gregorio, near Lake Xochimilco. They moved to within a mile of San Augustin on Wednesday the 18th, and the next day they entered San Augustin.[9]

General Scott established his headquarters, trains, and supply depot at that location. Quitman's Division had the task of guarding it. The maneuvering and fighting in front of Mexico City began on the 19th. The stunning victories of San Antonio, Contreras and Churubusco occurred the following day. Shields' Brigade was detached and sent forward for the fighting but Quitman's Second Brigade was not. The Second Brigade could hear the firing not far away, but could not share in the glory. Quitman submitted his resignation to Scott, which

James Walker's painting showing the Army on the march in the Valley of Mexico
West Point Museum

was, of course, not accepted. The Pennsylvanians chafed about it as well. They were ordered to move out toward Churubusco on the 20th, but before they had gone far they had to return as a force of Mexican cavalry was seen coming down from Chalco. General Scott explained in his official report:

> I regret having been obliged, on the 20th, to leave Major General Quitman, an able commander, with a part of his division—the 2d Pennsylvania Volunteers and the veteran detachment of United States Marines—at our important depot San Augustin. It was there that I had placed our sick and wounded; the siege, supply, and baggage trains. If these had been lost, the army would have been driven almost to despair; and considering the enemy's very great excess of numbers, and the many approaches to the depot, it might well have become emphatically the post of honor.[10]

Santa Anna had not yet run out of tricks. His army had again been decisively defeated. But, he knew the United States wanted a satisfactory settlement of the geographical disputes, not the decimation of his country. Mr. Nicholas P. Trist of the State Department was with the Army to, hopefully, achieve a diplomatic settlement, ending the fighting. Santa Anna, therefore, made overtures for a cease fire and the opening of peace negotiations on the morning of the 21st. Scott moved his headquarters and Worth's Division up to Tacubaya, and the next day he agreed to discuss a truce. The terms were signed on the 23rd, and Trist began a series of meetings with the Mexican commissioners, which lasted until 6 September. Although prohibited by the terms, Santa Anna actively moved to improve his defenses and prepare for the final contest. He hoped to take the momentum away from the Americans and even yet to pull a victory out of his hat.[11]

The 2nd Regiment sat at San Augustin from 19 August until 8 September. During this time the men helped with the wounded and sick, as well as guarding the depot and the numerous prisoners taken in the recent battles. Some took time to reflect on their situation and the events occurring around them. John Geary wrote in his diary on Sunday, 29 August,

> I can scarcely realize it—I have not heard a sermon or a prayer since I left old Pennsylvania. God protect and shield me from such a dangerous and sinful situation, and may I be speedily restored to the land where peace reigns and gospel truths abound. I will however say "Welcome sweet day of rest. That saw the Lord arise." and that is the sweetest of the seven. —May the many prayers which are offered up this day in my behalf and for my continued safety be heard at the throne of Grace and be availing as they have been throughout my life from my youth up. —I have always put my trust in God at all times and especially in the hour of danger. He has never deceived nor deserted me, nor will he if I continue to rely upon his Almighty Arms.[12]

Hopes for peace collapsed, forcing Scott to end the armistice. The sick and wounded were moved to Tacubaya on the 7th and 8th of September, Colonel Roberts being one of them as he had a high fever and was spitting up blood. The 2nd Pennsylvania moved from San Augustin to San Angel on the 8th. As they moved they could hear the guns and musketry at the Molino del Rey. Again, they took no part in the bloody action. They spent their time guarding some 2,000 prisoners instead. But Lieutenant Richard Johnston of the 11th U.S. Infantry, formerly a member of Company E, gallantly fell inside the gate of the Molino, at the head of his men.[13]

At sundown of the 11th the troops took to the road again. They marched all night, arriving at Tacubaya about dawn of the 12th. During a rest stop along the way the men dropped beside the road. No sooner had they hit the ground than a cannon carriage ran over and smashed both feet of Private Edward Hansberry of Company E.[14]

Early on the morning of the 12th Major Brindle, with Companies E, I, L and M, was sent to the west of Tacubaya in support of Battery Number 2. They spent the day and night in ditches near the guns. The remainder of the regiment stayed in front of Tacubaya in support of Battery Number 1. The batteries and consequently both battalions came under considerable artillery fire from Chapultepec. Geary stated that nine of his men were wounded from this fire.[15]

The day before, special storming parties were formed, composed of volunteers from the different regiments and including the Marine detachment. Company K of the 2nd Regiment was also detailed to this duty, thus separating it from the regiment during the action at Chapultepec. In addition, fifteen volunteers from throughout the 2nd Pennsylvania, under Second Lieutenant Isaac P. Hare, became part of a storming party.[16]

The objective of the storming parties, as of the whole army, was the castle and fortifications on Chapultepec hill. Its history dated back to the Aztecs, when it served as a palace and stronghold for their princes. Most recently, it was used as the Mexican Military Academy, and her students were now serving in her defense. The hill dominated the surrounding area, and her big guns covered all entrances to the city on the west and south. The guns could be used on the city as well. Clearly, if Scott were to take Mexico City, he had to take Chapultepec.[17]

Sunlight on the 13th brought a renewal of the artillery bombardment, but at about 9 o'clock the American guns went silent. This was the signal to attack. Pillow's Division charged from the west, and Quitman's men went up the Tacubaya Road into the batteries at the bottom of the hill. The now reunited 2nd Pennsylvania Regiment went forward with the New York and South Carolina regiments, following the storming parties. The troops approached to within two hundred yards of the Mexican batteries at the end of the road. But the fire was so heavy and well directed that continuing on would be suicide. General Quitman then ordered the men off the road to the left, across a cornfield and a marsh intersected by deep drainage ditches. During this charge, a spent canister ball hit Lieutenant Colonel Geary, taking him out of action until the castle had fallen. They then came to a wall at the bottom of the hill, the Pennsylvanians going through over an abandoned Mexican battery. Once inside the outer works, the men fought their way up the south side of the hill. There they joined Pillow's troops. The Americans used pick-axes, crowbars, and storming ladders in the assault on the castle at the top of the hill. There was so much confusion and death everywhere that it is now impossible to know all the details of the fall of Chapultepec. Almost every unit involved claimed to have arrived there first, and there are numerous claims to the planting of the first flag. One claimant was Captain Edward C. Williams of Company G. Major Brindle stated in his official report that Williams, "raised the first American Flag over the Fortress."[18]

Samuel H. Montgomery, a captain in the Quartermaster Department, raised a Pennsylvania Flag on the castle, one of the first seen. Montgomery started in the army as a private in Company E.[19]

Enemy resistance was giving out inside the castle. The Americans took several hundred prisoners, including General Bravo, the commander. A high state of excitement existed among the victorious troops, and it took some time

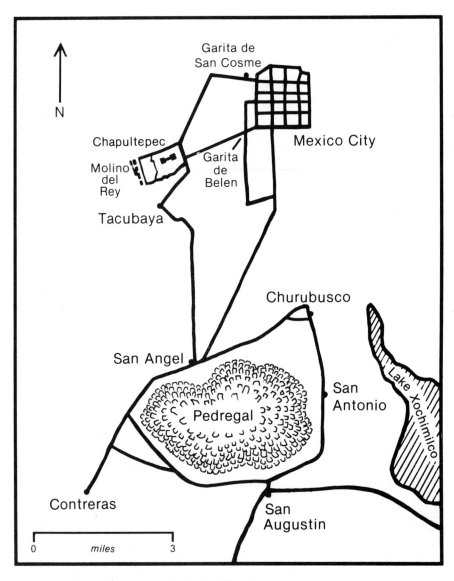

Mexico City Area

The Battle of Chapultepec by James Walker, 1857
U.S. Senate Collection

Another artist's rendition of the fighting at Chapultepec
USAMHI

Captain James Miller who assumed command of the storming party
upon the death of Major Twiggs

MOLLUS-Mass & USAMHI

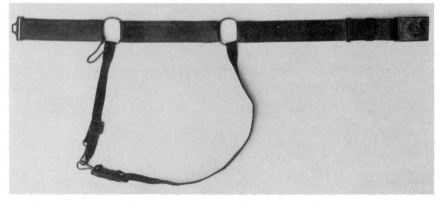

Sword belt worn by Captain Edward C. Williams of the Cameron Guards
during the Mexican War

A Private Collection

to quiet them down. Regiments and companies reformed and prepared for what still lay ahead. General Quitman soon entered the castle and rallying his men to the task, he led them toward the Garita de Belen.

The only approach to the garita, or gate, was down a long causeway, with deep canals and marshes on both sides. A heavy masonry aqueduct ran down the center of the causeway, with fifteen foot high arches that afforded some protection to the attackers. About half way between Chapultepec and the garita, the Mexicans had set up a two gun battery. A larger battery stood closer to the gate, about a mile from Chapultepec. Led by the Rifle Regiment and the South Carolinians, Quitman's men slowly approached the batteries. Captain Simon H. Drum and his men of the 4th U.S. Artillery performed almost super human work, with their own and captured pieces during the fight. Drum, a native of Greensburgh, Pennsylvania, poured shot into the Mexican positions until he was mortally wounded. The price paid by the infantry on the causeway would surely have been much higher without his efforts. The front battery was silenced, then the second position. Quitman's force by this time included his own two brigades, the Rifles, Seymour's regiment of Pierce's Brigade, part of the 6th U.S. Infantry and the residue of Persifor F. Smith's Brigade.[20]

Arch by arch, the troops moved closer to the battery in the garita. All the while musket fire was coming from the walls on both sides. Finally, at twenty minutes past one the army charged with General Quitman in the lead. The force carried the gate and entered Mexico City. The Pennsylvanians were there with the rest. Once inside the gate, they faced a galling fire from the Paseo, or promenade, and from the citadel on their left. The fire was so intense that they were forced back to the minimal shelter offered by the garita. The citadel was an old barracks building with fort-like construction. Quitman's force was in no position to storm it, especially since their artillery ammunition was exhausted. The men kept up a fire with their rifles and muskets, while slowly erecting a breastwork of sandbags and whatever else they could find. A member of Company E wrote home later about a narrow escape enjoyed by First Lieutenant James Armstrong.

> The embrassures of the breastwork were being filled with sand bags by a number of our men, and Armstrong was superintending the work, standing on top of the breastwork in full view of the enemy, a cannon ball struck the work just under his feet; finding he was a mark for them, he fell on his face just as another ball was coming, it passed close over his head and killed and wounded a number of men up the road.[21]

Three times the Mexicans counterattacked Quitman and his troops, each time to be turned back with heavy losses. To prevent the musket fire from the Paseo from enfilading the right flank, Companies A and F moved about a hundred yards in that direction and set up a low sand bag protection. They held up under a sustained heavy fire until nightfall. They constructed more substantial fortifications during the night for three heavy guns and a breastwork on the right for the infantry. They expected dawn to bring a renewal of the carnage, and Quitman hoped his men would be up to it.[22]

General Worth, in the meantime, worked his division around to the northeast side of Chapultepec. By the time of the Mexican retreat there, he was in a position to harass them considerably. He then advanced toward the Garita de San Cosme, and, after heavy fighting, he entered the city about six o'clock.[23]

After dark Santa Anna made the decision to evacuate the city, he and his army retiring to Guadalupe Hidalgo. At first light on the 14th, the Mexicans sent a flag of surrender to General Quitman. Cautiously, the American general proceeded through the streets to the grand plaza. General Scott soon arrived and the American Flag went up over the National Palace. Scott named Quitman Military Governor of the city, and the Army established its headquarters in the Palace. The 2nd Pennsylvania Regiment, however, did not participate in the triumphal entry into the Halls of the Montezumas. It was responsible for garrisoning the citadel, with its stores of military equipment.[24]

The battles for the conquest of Mexico City were a series of brilliant victories for American arms. However, they were costly. The 2nd Regiment was engaged in fighting only on the 12th and 13th of September, but in those two days eight of its men were killed and eighty-nine were wounded. Eleven more of these wounded would soon die from their injuries.[25]

For the first few days after the entering of the city, snipers took to the rooftops and upper floor windows in an effort to hit the U.S. soldiers. That died down as the majority of the populace adjusted to the occupation. The danger of robbery and murder was ever present, however, until the troops left Mexico.[26] For example, the 2nd Pennsylvania remained quartered at the citadel for two days. Private Daniel Kuhns of Company E left its safety to see the sights and was assaulted in the streets. His stab wound eventually caused his death.

On Thursday the 16th the regiment moved to the Grand Plaza and spent the night. George Hartman described the plaza as "a beautiful square, of about three hundred yards. The Nacional Palace is suitated [sic.] on the east side of it, the Cathedral on the north, and large rows of commercial buildings on the south and west."[27] The next day they took up residence in the National University, where most of the men visited the fine museum located there. On the 20th they moved into a large tobacco warehouse on the southern edge of the city, near the San Antonio Garita.[28]

Some of the companies used this time to purchase swords for their favorite officers and have them appropriately engraved. Captain Leoser received one on 3 October. Their men also gave swords to Lieutenants Frick of Company C, Coulter of Company E and Hare of Company F.[29]

On 2 October an earthquake shook the city. Although it caused moderate damage, the quake was not severely destructive. It did attract the attention of the Pennsylvania boys, however, as few, if any, had ever experienced anything like it before. The next night Colonel William B. Roberts went to meet his Maker. He had been sick since mid-August, and had not exercised command

Small Mexican Flag captured by the men of the 2nd Regiment
Pennsylvania Historical & Museum Commission

of the regiment since reaching the Valley of Mexico. He, like many of his men, lingered long and suffered much, but now he was at peace.[30]

On 2 November the announcement was made at dress parade of the elections to fill the vacancy Colonel Roberts' death created.

They were held the next day with the following results:

For Colonel

Lt. Col. John W. Geary	256
Capt. Thomas A. Leoser	152
Sgt. Maj. George W. Todd	87

For Lieutenant Colonel

Maj. William Brindle	379
1st Lt. James Armstrong	87

An election for major followed on the 5th with a larger slate of candidates involved.

For Major

2nd Lt. Richard McMichael	173
Capt. Edward C. Williams	151
1st Lt. Alexander McKamey	73
2nd Lt. Charles McDermitt	62
Pvt. David Duff	40
? Vanster	2
Lt. ? Horne	1
F. Bradly	1[31]

**John White Geary from a daguerreotype taken
about the time of the Mexican War**
Ronn Palm Collection

Major General Scott reviewed the election results, and on 7 November he confirmed the elections of Geary and Brindle but invalidated the election of McMichael because the regiment was too small to have three field grade officers. Some in the regiment believed that intrigue on Geary's part had formed Scott's opinion. A rift developed within the organization which would continue until well after the men returned home. In years to come, many a discussion or letter would raise the blood pressures of the 2nd Pennsylvania veterans, either in favor of or in opposition to the command policies and practices of Geary and Brindle.[32]

General Scott named Captain Naylor, of Philadelphia, in November to be Superintendent of the National Palace. He continued in that capacity throughout the occupation, and Company F was stationed with him, to provide the support necessary to accomplish the task.[33]

1. Bauer, *The Mexican War*, p. 276; E. Howard Blackburn and William H. Welfley, *History of Bedford And Somerset Counties, Pennsylvania* (New York: The Lewis Publishing Company, 1906), pp. 130-131; *History of that part of the Susquehanna And Juniata Valleys, Embraced in the Counties of Mifflin, Juniata, Perry, Union And Snyder, in the Commonwealth Of Pennsylvania* (Philadelphia: Everts, Peck & Richards, 1886), I, p. 149.

2. National Archives, RG 94, 2nd Pa. Regt. Papers; Blackburn, *Bedford & Somerset*, I, p. 131; *Susquehanna & Juniata Valleys*, I, p. 149; Milton V. Burgess, *Minute Men Of Pennsylvania* (Martinsburg, Pa.: Morrisons Cove Herald, 1962), pp. 66-72.

3. Burgess, *Minute Men*, pp. 72, 76-81.

4. Mansfield, *The Mexican War*, pp. 226-227; Anson, "Col. William B. Roberts," p. 263.

5. Oswandel, *Notes*, pp. 244-246; Niebaum, *Pittsburgh Washington Infantry*, p. 41.

6. Hartman, *Private's Journal*, p. 16; Larner, "A Westmoreland Guard," pp. 232-233; Evans, "Reading Artillerists," p. 137; Anson, "Col. William B. Roberts," pp. 262-263.

7. Burgess, *Minute Men*, pp. 84-85.

8. *Ibid.*, p. 86.

9. Evans, "Reading Artillerists," p. 137; Hartman, *Private's Journal*, p. 16; Larner, "A Westmoreland Guard," p. 233.

10. John F. H. Claiborne, *Life And Correspondence Of John A. Quitman, Major-General, U.S.A., And Governor Of The State Of Mississippi* (New York: Harper & Brothers, 1860), I, p. 347.

11. Bauer, *The Mexican War*, pp. 306-307; Mansfield, *The Mexican War*, pp. 274-278.

12. Tinkcom, *Geary*, p. 29.

13. *Ibid.*, pp. 32-33; Larner, "A Westmoreland Guard," p. 236.

14. Larner, "A Westmoreland Guard," pp. 236-237.

15. *The Pennsylvanian* (Philadelphia), Dec. 17, 1847.

16. *Ibid.*

17. Mansfield, *The Mexican War*, pp. 281-284.

18. Quitman's Official Report, Executive Document No. 1, U.S. Senate, 30th Congress, 1st Session, I, (1847), pp. 409-414; Herrold, "Edward C. Williams," pp. 504-505; *The Pennsylvanian* (Philadelphia), Dec. 17, 1847; See Appendices VII through IX for official reports.

19. Larner, "A Westmoreland Guard," p. 239.

20. Claiborne, *John A. Quitman*, pp. 363-364; Smith, *War With Mexico*, II, p. 159.

21. *The Pennsylvania Argus* (Greensburg), Jan. 14, 1848; Claiborne, *John A. Quitman*, pp. 364-365; Smith, *War With Mexico*, II, pp. 158-160.

22. Quitman's Official Report, Executive Document No. 1, U.S. Senate, 30th Congress, 1st Session, I, (1847), pp. 414-416; *The Danville Intelligencer*, Dec. 24, 1847; Smith, *War With Mexico*, II, p. 162.

23. Smith, *War With Mexico*, II, pp. 161-162.

24. *Ibid.*, pp. 163-164; Claiborne, *John A. Quitman*, p. 365.

25. National Archives, RG 94, 2nd Pa. Regt. Papers. See Appendices VII through X for Quitman's, Geary's and Brindle's Reports and the list of casualties as compiled from the rosters.

26. Larner, "A Westmoreland Guard," p. 387.

27. Hartman, *Private's Journal*, p. 20.

28. Greer, "Diary of a Pennsylvania Volunteer," p. 153.

29. Larner, "A Westmoreland Guard," p. 388; *Berks County Press*, Dec. 7, 1847; *The Danville Intelligencer*, Dec. 24, 1847.

30. Evans, "Reading Artillerists," p. 139.

31. Cambria County Historical Society, John A. Blair Diary, Nov. 2-5, 1847.

32. Larner, "A Westmoreland Guard," pp. 390-391; *The Danville Intelligencer*, Sept. 1, 15, 29 and Nov. 10, 1848.

33. National Archives, RG 94, 2nd Pa. Regt. Papers; Oswandel, *Notes*, p. 558.

Flag presented by the Ladies of Pottsville to the Washington Artillery
Pennsylvania Historical & Museum Commission

Guard Mount at Perote Castle

Oswandel's Notes

CHAPTER VI

Puebla Under Siege

The 2nd Regiment marched off with Scott's Army to the Halls of the Montezumas on the 8th of August, leaving the 1st Regiment as garrison at Perote and Puebla. Although they would miss out on the glories to be gained at Chapultepec and Garita de Belen, the 1st Regiment soon found out that not all the action took place at the capital.

Once the Army was beyond supporting distance, Colonel Wynkoop kept his garrison safely quartered in the castle of Perote. This was done for obvious reasons. The "Castle of Perote—built on a large plain, almost impregnable—contained a moat supplied by water from the mountains and armament for 96 guns. The town of Perote, about a mile from the Castle, was a dirty, miserable, and dilapidated old place."[1] "It has already been remarked that Perote was an uninviting place. It is more than that. It is uncomfortable and particularly disagreeable."[2]

Obviously, the soldiers didn't care for Perote, and a little diversion was welcome. Some years earlier a Pottsville Volunteer Militia company visited Philadelphia. A dog attached itself to the unit in that city and returned with it to Pottsville. He stayed there, learning to do tricks and becoming a familiar sight in town, and was referred to as "common property." The dog always took his place in the military activities. When the artillerists left for Pittsburgh and the war with Mexico he went along. He traveled with them to New Orleans, Lobos and Vera Cruz, even taking his place in the line of battle at Cerro Gordo. At Perote he was a real encouragement and served as a tangible link with home for Company B, maybe for the other companies as well.[3]

Colonel Wynkoop continued his policy of making raids on suspected guerilla centers, usually with Walker's Mounted Riflemen. Surgeon John C. Reynolds handled the garrison's medical needs, and watched over the welfare of the hospital and its patients. Many of the sick and wounded recovered their health and supplemented the garrison by forming a provisional company.

The force under Colonel Childs at Puebla was split into three segments. On a high ridge in the northern suburbs was a stone fort, named Fort Loreto. Major Thomas P. Gwynn of the 6th U.S. Infantry commanded there with Captain Hill's Company of the 1st Pennsylvania, Captain H. L. Kendrick's Company of U.S. Regular Artillery, with two 12 pounders and a ten inch mortar, and a company made up of recuperating soldiers from the hospital.

On a somewhat higher location half a mile further east on the same ridge stood the Church of Guadalupe, protected by a ditch and an earthen wall. Its defenders consisted of two mountain howitzers and their crews of the 2nd U.S. Artillery under Lieutenant Edwards, a company of convalescents and Company G, 1st Pennsylvania with Turner Morehead as the commanding officer.

Colonel Childs maintained his headquarters at what was known as the Cuartel de San Jose. It was a large walled-in area in the northeast part of the city and faced upon the Plaza of San Jose. The supplies and ordnance stores, as well as the horses and some of the cattle and sheep were housed here. The sick had originally been scattered in buildings throughout the city, but, with the departure of the Army, they were gathered into buildings in the immediate vicinity of San Jose. Lieutenant Colonel Black commanded San Jose's defenses consisting of Companies A, C, I and K of his own regiment, Captain Lemuel Ford's Company of the 3rd U.S. Dragoons, Captain John H. Miller's Company of the 4th U.S. Artillery serving as infantry and a battery of mountain howitzers under Lieutenant Theodore T. S. Laidley, a regular ordnance officer. Captain Theodore F. Rowe of the 9th U.S. Infantry commanded at the hospital, and Assistant Surgeon Bunting materially assisted with the medical responsibilities. The men under his care, including the convalescent, numbered about 1,800.[4]

Scott's Army was barely out of sight when the atmosphere at Puebla began to change. The majority of the populace wanted no trouble with the American garrison, but Brigadier General Joaquin Rea sent his guerillas into the city to stir the people up. Scott's last division marched out of Puebla on 10 August, and on the 12th some teamsters were attacked while having their wagons loaded with meat near the plaza. The next day Colonel Childs issued an order forbidding all troops from leaving their respective posts without a pass. On Saturday, the 14th, work was undertaken to better fortify the locations. Windows were filled with sandbags, leaving only room for firing of muskets, and holes were cut in walls for that purpose as well. From that time until the end of the siege the men lived in constant expectation of an attack.[5]

The Mexicans used rumors to undermine morale and weaken the little garrison. They claimed that General Scott's Army was badly defeated and that American trains were destroyed on the road between Vera Cruz and Puebla. The Mexican spy company did good work for the United States throughout the conflict, maintaining a flow of accurate information to Colonel Childs. In fact, on the 24th he received the news, and passed it on to the men, of the victories of Contreras, San Antonio and Churubusco.[6]

A large body of guerillas or cavalry succeeded, on the 26th, in raiding the mule-yard where the wagon teams were housed. The men at Guadalupe saw that activity and promptly notified Colonel Childs. A party of mounted volunteers quickly took up the pursuit from San Jose. These were mostly teamsters and wagon masters, but some soldiers did go along. Second Lieutenant Sperry of Company F, 2nd Regiment led the party of about thirty men. The guerillas kept retreating before them, drawing them further from the city. All of a sudden some three hundred lancers charged out of a concealed position onto their flank. The men fought well but were completely overwhelmed. It quickly became a case of every man having to fend for himself. Private Alburtus Welsh of Company C outran two guerillas and hid in a cornfield until dark. He was one of ten who escaped. Morris Stemlear, also of Company C, and John Longstaff of Company K were both taken prisoner. John Preece of Company I was killed as was Lieutenant Sperry. Sperry earlier had become ill and was forced to resign because of his health, being discharged on the 5th of August. Unfortunately for him, his health improved and he wanted to help get the livestock back from the Mexicans. In this case his good health cost him his life. Over the next few days, Mexican farmers brought over a dozen mutilated bodies to San Jose where they were viewed by the troops and buried. The butchery practiced by the guerillas and lancers brought forth many a vow of vengeance against the enemy.[7]

Constant reports of impending attacks seemed to perpetuate themselves. Rumor had it that Fort Loreto was to be stormed on the night of 29 August or the next day. Every night thereafter for about a week one or two companies of the 1st Regiment went up there from San Jose so as to be prepared to hold the key heights. Nothing ever came of it, however, except that the soldiers became more and more tired, weary and hungry.[8]

On the night of 13 September General Rea moved his few thousand troops into Puebla and ordered them to begin a sporadic fire on San Jose and the hospital. This action cut the garrison off from all food supplies in the city, as well as causing them to face the annoying fire. The firing died down during the following day but intensified on the night of the 14th. This action continued with few interruptions for the next twenty-eight days, with most of the firing occurring at night. When the siege began in earnest the garrison had only about thirty head of cattle and 400 sheep. There was little in the way of vegetables or fruit and very little flour.[9]

General Rea invited Colonel Childs to surrender on the 16th, and upon receiving a very negative response he ordered a large body of lancers to charge the San Jose position. The result of this charge caused much work for the Mexican doctors and burial parties, as the horsemen rode straight down a street into the American artillery fire. On the morning of the 22nd the exhilarating news of the capture of Mexico City reached Colonel Childs and soon cheer after cheer after cheer went up from the men. In the afternoon, the Mexicans took their turn at cheering and the ringing of bells in welcome for their gallant but often defeated leader, General Santa Anna. He brought with him such troops as he could scrape together from the Mexico City defenses. Without stopping the firing on the Cuartel of San Jose, a force of about 500 Mexicans moved against Guadalupe on the 23rd. They tried to storm the church, but Captain Morehead and his men sent them packing with heavy casualties. Another try on the following day ended with similar results. Santa Anna on the 25th again demanded that the garrison surrender or leave, and again he was told, absolutely not.[10]

Colonel Childs and his men prepared for the all-out assault promised by Santa Anna, but the Mexicans didn't seem to be in any hurry. The United States forces remained alert, and the firing continued. Private Oswandel wrote his experiences of the 28th into his diary.

> At noon the firing commenced very briskly, and kept up all day. Each sentinel shooting his forty rounds. I myself, from the time I was put on picket-guard, until this morning, shot away sixty rounds, and during this I shot and wounded two umbras and one priest, who were constantly annoying me, and you ought to have seen the old priest jump, and his long stovepipe hat flying off the back of his shaved head. I must have hit him on the left leg (or he played opossum), for he immediately limped, and placed his left hand thereon. The Mexicans seemed to fire at me more than any other sentinel, and I made some very narrow hairbreadth escapes. One bullet cut a lock of my hair off, and grazed the skin a little; it burned like fire.[11]

The previous day Santa Anna had installed several artillery batteries in the city and opened a fire upon San Jose and the hospital. The American guns there and in Fort Loreto replied in kind. The Mexicans began building successively closer breastworks at nights, but the gunfire from Loreto prevented their completion. Occasional forays of company size or smaller groups became necessary to dislodge particular parties of the enemy. Lieutenant Waelder of Company I, who was then serving as Acting Assistant Adjutant General, led one of these missions on the 28th. His men weathered the fire of over 200 enemy muskets and captured a well placed breastwork. In this action Private William Eurick of Company C died from a musket wound in the chest.[12]

Lieutenant Edward C. Lewis led a party out of Guadalupe on the morning of the 29th and attacked a body of Mexicans who were pouring a fire into San Jose. A sharp conflict commenced in which eight of the enemy were killed and numbers more were wounded. Lewis withdrew his men to the church after a hard rain storm caused his men's muskets to misfire. The fight lasted about three hours, and one of the soldiers was seriously wounded, with two others slightly wounded. Another party sallied out of Guadalupe later that same afternoon under Lieutenant William Bryan. This group also inflicted casualties upon the enemy and successfully retired without loss.[13]

Under the cover of darkness the Mexicans placed two six pounders in position and opened with them on the morning of the 30th. Colonel Childs was ready for them because he had one of the 12 pounders, with its crew, moved from Loreto to San Jose late on the 29th. A strong emplacement was prepared for it, where it did good word for the remainder of the siege.[14]

On October 1st, Santa Anna turned command of the siege back over to Rea, and took the majority of the forces for another expedition. He hoped to bottle up and destroy a train coming from Vera Cruz under Brigadier General Joseph Lane.[15]

Rea's men erected a barricade across one of the streets about 500 yards from San Jose, and from its cover rained a constant fire down on the Americans. Fronting on the street was a row of stone buildings, all built side by side with a common wall between them, those buildings ran the entire length of the block. Captain William F. Small was given command of a party of 50 men whose job it was to enter the row of buildings on the San Jose end, and cut through the walls to come out behind the enemy barricade. After about twenty-four hours of hard labor, they breeched the walls. Small's men streamed out of the last house and overwhelmed the Mexicans, killing seventeen of them and wounding others. They then burned the barricade and remained in the buildings they had used until Lieutenant Laidly placed charges and blew them to pieces. Thereafter they returned to their quarters at San Jose for a much deserved rest.[16]

The Mexicans had occupied a brickyard in the same area of the city. A substantial stone wall surrounded a brick house and the yard, creating a natural fort. The firing from it reached unacceptable levels by the 5th of October. On that day Captain John Herron and his Company K were ordered to take and destroy the position. They approached it slowly until they got close, then charged with a shout and rousted the enemy. The company returned to San Jose with several wagons of apples as well as turkeys, chickens and pigs. Morale rose several points at least, due to the fresh goods on the menu.[17]

Two columns of reinforcements joined the Mexicans on the 8th, and firing increased perceptibly. They made motions and noises as if to finally storm the works at San Jose, but the well served guns at Guadalupe and Loreto put an end to that. Heavy firing continued through the night. The following morning, two priests under a white flag, made a request of Colonel Childs. The Bishop of Puebla had died and the people and church desired a three day cease fire on both sides, so as to celebrate his burial in the proper style. Colonel Childs accepted, and the truce began. The troops received instructions not to fire unless fired upon. The Mexicans were either a little slow in getting the word or they chose to ignore it, as numerous instances of firing on the Americans occurred throughout the day.[18]

Private J. Jacob Oswandel experienced a close encounter that night while on picket guard at post nine.

> There is scarcely any firing going on now, so I think the Mexicans
> will obey the armistice during the time named.

**Colonel Thomas Childs of the First
U.S. Artillery**
Oswandel's Notes

Captain William F. Small
Oswandel's Notes

Puebla at the height of the siege. Left to right: San Jose Church, Fort Loreto, Guadalupe Heights, San Jose Quartel and Colonel Childs' Headquarters
Oswandel's Notes

> To-night, about 12 o'clock, while my attention was drawn to our quarters, I was suddenly attacked by three Mexicans from behind; one of these villains tried to stab me in the back, but the point of his dagger, hitting my cartridge-box belt, it glanced off, while the other greaser rushed in front of me, trying to take my rifle from me. At this instant I pushed the Mexican in front of me backwards and he fell into the street; at this time I wheeled around and shot the one who was trying to stab me in the back; he fell, but soon got up again, and the other two carried him off in their arms before I had a chance to reload again. This whole transaction of attempting to assassinate me was all done in about ten seconds. I must have shot the Mexican in the groin, because he was putting his hand there and groaning. The sentinel at Post 5 heard the scrambling and shot fired. I sent for the Sergeant of the guard, who soon reported himself, after which I related to him the circumstances: He remarked that I was the luckiest man in the whole garrison for narrow escapes. Oh! I was wishing I only had a double-barreled gun at the time![19]

Colonel Childs, intent upon keeping the agreement, refused to allow his soldiers to break the cease fire, even when provoked. The Mexicans, on the other hand, openly violated the truce throughout the three days. The firing, however, was only sporadic, relieving the besieged garrison from the constant pressure of the past month, although the soldiers knew that the fighting was not over.

While the beleaguered troops lived from day to day praying for relief, help was at that very moment slowly moving in their direction. Brigadier General Joseph Lane moved his train out of Vera Cruz on 19 September. He experienced problems and delays along the way, but suffering no major setbacks, he overtook an earlier train under Major Folliot T. Lally. Colonel Wynkoop and his four companies of the 1st Pennsylvania Regiment joined the force when they marched out of Perote on 5 October. Lane now commanded some 3,300 men.[20]

Santa Anna's plan was to ambush the American train as it passed through the narrow mountain pass at El Pinal, and he placed about 1,000 of his cavalry there to execute it. The bulk of his forces he concentrated about eight miles away in the town of Huamantla. General Lane could see through this old trick, and his intelligence officers reported Santa Anna's actual whereabouts. The general on 9 October left a substantial force with the wagons east of El Pinal and marched the remainder across country toward Huamantla. Captain Samuel Walker with four mounted companies led the way, and Wynkoop's Pennsylvanians were not far behind. Walker encountered several mounted enemy on the outskirts of the town and elected to charge, without waiting for the infantry to come up. His initial success was overwhelming, but Santa Anna's main body then rode into town and stopped Walker's progress. Lane, meanwhile, rushed the infantry forward. Wynkoop's battalion was to approach from the east, with the artillery. The 4th Indiana, coming from the west, fired several effective volleys, but before the 1st Pennsylvania came within range the Mexicans fled. Although they did little to influence the day's outcome they nonetheless took part in the movement, and suffered the loss of one man, Private Engleheart Leicht of Company F, reported missing in action. Surgeon Reynolds rode that day with Captain Walker and took part in the charge. Readily available for the work he soon was called upon to do. Of course, the most noted casualty of the day was Captain Samuel H. Walker, beloved by his men, and a legend in his own time.[21]

After the soldiers chased the Mexicans away from Huamantla their ambush at El Pinal fell apart as well. Lane's forces returned to the National Road, and on the 10th they continued toward Puebla. The Mexicans in Puebla knew of Lane's approaching column, and began evacuating on the 11th. At about ten o'clock on the morning of the 12th, Lane's forward elements came into view of the troops at Guadalupe, who set the bells pealing the news to the rest of the garrison. A little while later Lieutenant Colonel Black took Companies D and K and headed down the main street to silence a particularly troublesome fire coming from the area of the plaza. As they neared the plaza they saw a body of lancers go down a side street. Captain Herron was then instructed to try to head off their retreat by working his way around them with Company K. In the course of this movement several hundred lancers charged upon them, coming out of several of the cross streets. Herron's men were at once surrounded and the fight turned into a free-for-all. Colonel Black heard the firing and rushed to assist with Company D. In so doing he clearly saved the remainder of Company K, as the lancers would certainly have otherwise annihilated them. This little fight lasted only a minute or two, but in it Company K took more casualties than any other Pennsylvania Company in the war. Of the thirty-one men going into action thirteen were killed outright with four others receiving wounds, Captain Herron being one of the latter.[22]

At about one o'clock General Lane's men entered the city, using several of the main corridors, eventually rendezvousing at the plaza. Stubborn resistance was encountered from a brick building about a block away from San Jose's outer pickett post, and Wynkoop's battalion supported the 4th Illinois Regiment in a charge upon it. The Mexicans quickly fled, but Private John Doyle of Company B was killed in the charge. By 3:30 P.M. the city was fairly well cleared of enemy soldiers and guerillas. At long last, the Siege of Puebla was over. General Scott proved to be correct after all, the 1st Regiment had indeed seen its share of the fighting. Total losses of the Pennsylvania Volunteers at Puebla added up to 55, including five from the 2nd Regiment. Twenty-one of this number were either killed in action or died of their wounds. Colonel Childs reported his total casualties to General Scott as being 72.[23]

At about nine o'clock on the morning of 15 October a service was held for the burial of the thirteen men of Company K killed three days earlier. They laid side by side, and Colonel Black made appropriate comments over the graves. The bodies were later taken home to Pittsburgh for reburial. That same afternoon Captain Small was sent to seize a printing operation run by a hostile Mexican named Rivera. The proprietor was nowhere to be found, but the press was in good shape. It was turned over to Private John Kritser of Company C, and he ran it effectively for several months, printing a newspaper.[24]

Within a very short time the atmosphere of Puebla returned to what it had been before the siege. Commerce resumed, and the populace again fraternized with the troops. The soldiers also reverted to their old ways. In one case a group of them were clustered together watching a fight, and a brand new lieutenant happened upon the scene. Thinking to prove his authority, he drew his sword and charged into the middle of the crowd. Unfortunately for him, they didn't recognize him,

> and, having a most profound contempt for "greenhorns," one of their number quietly disarmed him, while others hustled him out of the crowd in anything but a respectful manner. In fact several hearty and well ad-ministered kicks were delivered upon that part of his person supposed to be most vulnerable.

The lieutenant found Colonel Black and complained bitterly about his treat-ment. The colonel calmly turned and said, "they served you exactly right. What business have you to interfere with my men?"[25]

After nearly two weeks in camp at Puebla the 1st Regiment set out in mid-morning on the 25th of October, heading eastward. They arrived at Perote on Friday the 29th and left there two days later. The men slept Monday night in Jalapa, and on Wednesday camped at Plan del Rio, just below the old battlefield of Cerro Gordo. The primary reason for the trip was to escort a large company of discharged soldiers to the coast so they could be carried by ship back to the United States. The veterans left their escort early in the morning of 4 November and headed for Vera Cruz. The 1st Regiment remained encamped along the river until the 6th, when they retraced their steps to Jalapa. Colonel Wynkoop was named Governor of that city on the 9th, and he immediately ordered a dress parade every evening.[26]

Corporal J. Jacob Oswandel observed in his journal on 10 November:

> This morning, we received clothing from the Quartermaster and all old soldiers got a full suit from head to foot. This being the first regular clothing we drew since we have been in the United States service, and I assure you we all stood much in need thereof. It now being nearly a year since we were in service, and if it was not for the clothing we cap-tured from the Mexicans one-half of our army would have to go naked. Oh how good care our Government is taking of her noble sons, now fighting the bloody Mexicans.[27]

On the 18th Colonel George W. Hughes of the Maryland and District of Columbia Regiment replaced Colonel Wynkoop as Governor of Jalapa. The next night the men of Company E held a dancing party, during which they must have imbibed heartily of strong spirits because the finale of the evening was a knock-down, drag-out fight. Later the 1st Regiment performed the distasteful duty of standing guard for four executions by hanging on the 23rd and 24th. Following the latter, Company C bade farewell to their Captain, William F. Small. He had been elected to a seat in the State Senate of Pennsylvania, and he was returning home to assume his new duties.[28]

Later that same morning the regiment left for Perote, spending Wednes-day night in camp at La Hoya. The men stayed Thursday night at Cruz Blanco, and early on Friday afternoon reached Perote. The march was cold and wet, the men having to contend with snow, ice, hail, rain and mud. They lazed around the city for a couple of days, then, on Monday the 29th, headed for Puebla. That night they camped at Tepegahualco. By mid-afternoon on Wednesday they reached El Pinol, where they made camp. The train occupied Amozoquco on Thursday, the 2nd of December, and about noon of the next day they arrived at Puebla.[29]

The troops prepared to march to Mexico City during the morning of 4 December. The train was composed of the 1st Pennsylvania Volunteers, one regiment from Ohio, one from Massachusetts, Colonel Jack Hays with five companies of mounted Texas Rangers and Major Folliot Lally with some 1,500 recruits. They left around noon, and four days later entered the gates of the capital. Once there, they marched to their quarters near the Grand Plaza, in the heart of the city.[30]

ENDNOTES - CHAPTER VI

1. *Daily Chronicle* (Pittsburgh), July 3, 1847.

2. Kitchen, *Wyoming Artillerists*, p. 56.

3. *The Miner's Journal* (Pottsville), July 24, 1847.

4. Jenkins, *The War between the United States And Mexico*, pp. 455-458; Wilcox, *Mexican War*, pp. 492-493; Smith, *War With Mexico*, p. 174.

5. Bauer, *The Mexican War*, p. 329; Oswandel, *Notes*, pp. 248-252.

6. Oswandel, *Notes*, pp. 254-260.

7. *Ibid.*, pp. 261-265; Kitchen, *Wyoming Artillerists*, pp. 65-66; Jenkins, *War between the United States And Mexico*, p. 456; National Archives, RG 94, 1st & 2nd Pa. Regt. Papers.

8. Oswandel, *Notes*, pp. 267 & f.

9. Smith, *War With Mexico*, p. 174; Wilcox, *Mexican War*, p. 494.

10. Oswandel, *Notes*, pp. 288-299; Bauer, *The Mexican War*, p. 329; Jenkins, *War between the United States And Mexico*, p. 459.

11. Oswandel, *Notes*, p. 309.

12. Oswandel, *Notes*, p. 309; Jenkins, *War between the United States And Mexico*, p. 460; Kitchen, *Wyoming Artillerists*, pp. 67-68; Smith, *War With Mexico*, p. 175; Brooks, *Mexican War*, p. 495.

13. Jenkins, *War between the United States And Mexico*, p. 460.

14. Brooks, *Mexican War*, p. 495.

15. Bauer, *The Mexican War*, p. 329.

16. Wilcox, *Mexican War*, p. 495; Oswandel, *Notes*, pp. 319-323.

17. Oswandel, *Notes*, pp. 327-328.

18. *Ibid.*, pp. 332-336.

19. *Ibid.*, p. 336.

20. Smith, *War With Mexico*, p. 176; Bauer, *The Mexican War*, pp. 329-330.

21. J. M. Wynkoop, *Anecdotes And Incidents: Comprising Daring Exploits, Personal And Amusing Adventures of the Officers and Privates of the Army, and Thrilling Incidents Of The Mexican War* (Pittsburgh: 1848). pp. 61-66; Smith, *War With Mexico*, pp. 176-177; Wilcox, *Mexican War*, pp. 497-499; Jenkins, *War between the United States And Mexico*, pp. 464-465; Bauer, *The Mexican War*, p. 331; Kitchen, *Wyoming Artillerists*, pp. 61-62; National Archives, RG 94, 1st Pa. Regt. Papers.

22. Wilcox, *Mexican War*, pp. 499-500; Jenkins, *War between the United States And Mexico*, pp. 465-467; Smith, *War With Mexico*, p. 178; Oswandel, *Notes*, pp. 341-344; Niebaum, *Pittsburgh Washington Infantry*, pp. 43-45.

23. Oswandel, *Notes*, pp. 344-345; National Archives, RG 94, 1st & 2nd Pa. Regt. Papers; See Appendices XI through XV for Childs', Black's, Gwynn's and Morehead's Reports and list of casualties as compiled from the rosters.

24. Oswandel, *Notes*, pp. 356-357; *The Daily Morning Post* (Pittsburgh), July 21, 1848.

25. Kitchen, *Wyoming Artillerists*, p. 70.

26. Oswandel, *Notes*, pp. 374-384; Kitchen, *Wyoming Artillerists*, pp. 71-75.

27. Oswandel, *Notes*, p. 384.

28. *Ibid.*, pp. 384-394.

29. Oswandel, *Notes*, pp. 394-398; Niebaum, *Pittsburgh Washington Infantry*, p. 46.

30. Oswandel, *Notes*, p. 401; Niebaum, *Pittsburgh Washington Infantry*, p. 46.

CHAPTER VII

Occupation Duty

The arrival of the 1st Regiment at Mexico City on the 8th of December gave great reason for rejoicing. Not only had the victorious Keystone Staters finally entered the capital of their enemy, they were now again united with the 2nd Regiment. For five long eventful months the exigencies of war had kept the two units apart. Now they were together, and it seemed likely that they would stay that way.

Fresh troops were also coming into the country to maintain the hard won peace, causing a reorganization within the Army. A new brigade was organized under command of Brigadier General Caleb Cushing. It consisted of the 1st and 2nd Pennsylvania Volunteers along with the Massachusetts, New York and South Carolina Regiments. All were to garrison San Angel, a few miles south of the city. A dress parade for the whole brigade took place on the 19th, after which the 2nd Pennsylvania marched out to San Angel and occupied their new quarters. They moved into a fine set of buildings known as the Convent of Cormal tes Mauks, which had been built in 1734. The 1st Regiment joined the 2nd in San Angel on the 22nd, and took up quarters in a large building formerly a manufacturing establishment. The village itself presented a pleasant appearance, surrounded by orchards, orange groves and gardens. The men immediately made themselves comfortable, availing themselves of the produce which grew in abundance.[1]

The army celebrated Christmas and New Years without much ado, each soldier doing as he deemed best, or pulling duty as assigned. On the 21st of December another train had arrived from Vera Cruz, bringing with it recruits for both Pennsylvania regiments. The men were processed in the city and assigned to their companies, which they joined on the 29th. Thus, they were on hand

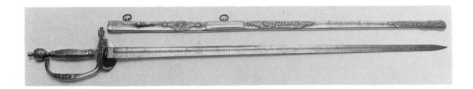

Presentation grade Model 1840 Foot Officers Sword given to 2nd Lieutenant James A. Deany of the Cadwalader Grays

Richard A. Johnson Collection

View of San Angel, showing the 1st Regiment parading in front of their quarters

Oswandel's Notes

to begin 1848 with their comrades, complete with all the excitement and suspense of guard duty and fatigue details. The boredom for many became oppressive. They could not understand why they needed to stay on in Mexico after having beaten the Mexican Army. One of the Westmoreland Guards wrote a letter home on 28 November which typified the sentiments of many of the Keystone soldiers.[2]

> We are all anxious to get home now, for we have accomplished all we came for. We have conquered the Mexicans and subdued the country, and more than that we have sustained the honor of our country and placed our glorious "stars and stripes" on the Palace of the "Montezumas," at least we, the Volunteers, contributed our share to that glorious work. We have conquered Mexico, and if we did not conquer a peace, is it our fault? We did not come here to occupy the country, we came to subdue it; having done all calculated for troops, and nothing is so irksome to us as lying in garrison—it is impossible for us to comply with the army regulations; we can do the fighting well enough, and we can do guard duty, but we can't treat the regular officers with that strict deference and obeissance which they require; . . . .[3]

It is clear from this letter that, in addition to a desire to go home, there was friction between the regular army officers and the volunteers now serving with the army. The majority of existing accounts of the war by regular officers reveal that they genuinely believed the volunteers to be inferior troops, led by inferior officers. Obviously, the volunteers lacked the training, experience and discipline of the West Pointers and pre-war regulars. Also, the government paid little attention to the training of the volunteers before sending them to the front. The Volunteers of Scott's Army, however, when led by competent generals, performed service comparable to the regulars. Also those units raised under the "Ten Regiment Bill," were often made up of militia companies sworn into the regular army as they were. No more training was given them than was tendered to the volunteers. In the case of the 11th U.S. Infantry, the ranks were filled with the friends, neighbors and brothers of the men in the two Pennsylvania volunteer regiments. Also, many of the officers for this organization were drawn straight out of the ranks of the volunteer regiments. The volunteers certainly left room for improvement, but it would appear that much of the criticism directed at them arose out of a bias against them rather than from the facts.[4]

On the 6th of January word reached San Angel that a group of guerillas had occupied the Mexico City road and was harassing soldiers who tried to travel on it. A party of men armed themselves and headed after the guerillas. In the fight that followed, Private John Douty, one of the newly arrived recruits in Company B, 1st Regiment, was killed and two others were wounded. Lieutenant E. M. Daggett and a company of Texas Rangers came charging up the road after the infantry and sent a dozen or more Mexicans into eternity. After this incident, General Cushing put an end to the freedom previously enjoyed by the soldiers to go to Mexico City as they pleased. This restraint probably had its effect on the men for at least a day or two.[5]

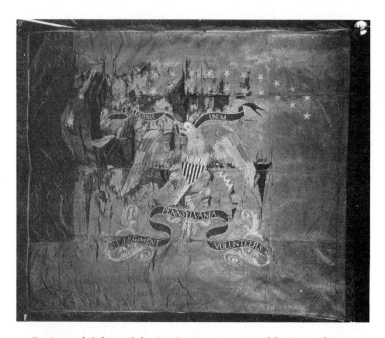

Regimental Colors of the 1st Regiment presented by General Scott
Historical Society of Pennsylvania

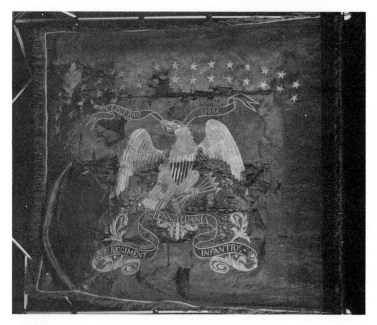

Regimental flag presented by General Scott to the 2nd Regiment
Historical Society of Pennsylvania

Winfield Scott, an outstanding general in many aspects, wanted to show honor to his Army. He contracted with expert seamstresses in Mexico City to have regimental colors made for some thirty regiments which served under his command during the recent campaign. On the 19th of January he presented the 1st and 2nd Pennsylvania Volunteer Regiments with their flags. Neither regiment previously had such a banner. They were richly made, and the men took great pride in them. Following the war the veterans held them dear, and in 1893 they were presented to the Historical Society of Pennsylvania.[6]

A few of the enterprising soldiers of the 2nd Regiment managed to locate musical instruments in the city and set about forming a brass band. Composed of at least sixteen musicians, it gave its first performance on the 7th of February. Thereafter, its presence was much sought after, and its music was thoroughly enjoyed.[7]

Visiting the sights around the city was another key diversion of the troops. Some visited theatrical productions, and once in a while some of the soldiers put on performances to kill the boredom. Others involved themselves in the age old pursuits of soldiers in a foreign land, despite their illegality. Newspapers, too, became very important in the lives of the men. The Pennsylvania regiments contributed heartily to the publications, as many of them had been printers in civilian life. For example, Private John Kritser of Company C, 1st Regiment, took over a printing press in Puebla, which Captain Small had captured. With it he published the bi-weekly *Flag of Freedom*. The first issue was distributed on 20 October, and it cost a half dime. When the 1st Regiment moved out, Kritser remained behind on detached duty so he could continue to publish the *Flag*. It was evidently the only newspaper in Mexico printed by a U.S. soldier. After its Christmas Day, 1847 issue it went from a bi-weekly to a weekly publication and continued as such until its last paper was printed on 26 February 1848. Kritser then rejoined his company in Mexico City, where he was almost immediately detached to work on the *American Star*. Other Pennsylvania volunteers worked on the *Star* also, as well as being detached for duty on other army printing projects. The papers, especially the *American Star*, kept Scott's Army posted on the progress of the treaty and other current events. They also provided a forum for letters, interesting anecdotes, and for advertisements of the enterprising businessmen who followed the Army. Misters A. S. Halsey and C. S. Butler ran daguerreotype galleries in Mexico City, where they took likenesses of the soldiers. They advertised in the *American Star* as early as October, 1847. Almost certainly some of the Pennsylvanians visited one or the other of those establishments.[8]

On 12 February the guard was relieved as usual, but instead of dismissing them, Captain Preston S. Brooks, of the South Carolina Regiment, drilled them intensely for about two hours. This upset the men, and as Brooks started for his quarters they hissed and threw eggs at him, one of the eggs hitting its mark. He shortly returned with an armed guard, one of whom struck a Pennsylvanian on the head with his musket. Brooks then placed two officers under arrest for being with the men and not restraining them. He started to leave but evidently had a second thought, as he grabbed a musket from one of his guards and said he dared anyone to holler now for he would "blow his Brains out." Then he left. Just as he reached the gate, the Pennsylvanians hollered again, but he showed no reaction. The next morning, as the unit stood in the plaza with their muskets stacked awaiting the call to "fall-in," Brooks passed by. The men couldn't resist, and hollered again. This time he drew his revolver and snapped it three or four times at the crowd and strutted away. After the 2nd Regiment was formed and prepared to pass in review for General Cushing, Brooks came along the line and ordered Lieutenants Hiram Wolf of Company K and Biven Davis of Company L placed under arrest. The regiment then passed in review and drilled extensively afterwards. Colonel Geary halted the regiment on the return trip to its quarters and lectured it. He also stated that he would have Lieutenants Wolf and Davis prosecuted for their behavior. Captain Brooks gained greater notoriety in 1856 when he beat Charles Sumner with a cane in the United States Senate chamber.[9]

The soldiers received word in mid-February that the administration in Washington had removed General Scott from command of the Army. The men perceived this not only as an insult to their general but as a slap in the face of each of them as well. Needless to say, Scott was held in the highest esteem by the rank and file. A rumor reached the 1st Regiment at about the same time, that they would be replacing their old flintlock muskets with new percussion cap muskets. It appears that it was indeed only rumor, as no evidence has surfaced to indicate that such an exchange ever took place. Despite the political atmosphere and the excess of all kinds of rumors, military life continued. As a soldier wrote into his journal on the 28th of February:

> This morning all hands were busy in cleaning up their muskets and belts, brightening the brass plates and blackening the cartridge-boxes and shoes, so as to come out tip-top on inspection; for there is a great deal of rivalry between the companies.[10]

Bright and early on the 6th of March, Companies A, D, E, F, H, I and K of the 1st Regiment left San Angel to escort a train heading for Vera Cruz under the command of Lieutenant Colonel Black. Companies B, C and G were ordered to stay behind and care for the quarters as well as the sick of the regiment. Colonel Wynkoop, who usually enjoyed such adventures, stayed back because he had become acting brigade commander on the 16th of February, owing to General Cushing's absence in Puebla. Lieutenant Colonel Black pushed his men, and, without incident, reached Vera Cruz in record time. During their short stay in that city the colonel impressed his men with the casualness of his dress. "He usually wore a sailor's blue shirt, outside of his pantaloons, according to the custom of the country, and looked more like a wagon master than commander of a regiment."[11]

Life continued as usual for the troops left in the capital. A full share of dress parades, formations and drills were "enjoyed." Some, however, insisted on making their own excitement. On the night of 4 April several officers were apparently visiting a gambling establishment. It seems that some ill feeling developed, and before it was over the proprietor was dead and his money disappeared. Lieutenant Isaac P. Hare of Company F, 2nd Regiment, received an arm wound in the course of the evening and was arrested for murder and robbery. The 2nd Regiment's adjutant, Lieutenant Benjamin F. Dutton, was also implicated and arrested. Both were tried by court martial and sentenced to be hung on the 25th of May. But they were reprieved before the sentence could be carried out. The recent signing of the peace treaty with Mexico was given as the reason for the reprieve.[12]

Second Lieutenant A. H. Goff of Wilkes-Barre had been assigned, with his company, to Perote while Colonel Wynkoop was Governor there. He was eventually detached to the Commissary Department, and, when his company left, he stayed on in the city. During his assignment there, Lieutenant Goff spent considerable time at the principal hotel, which was kept by Senora Martinez. As nature would have it, he became quite attached to Fanchette, the beautiful daughter of Mrs. Martinez. She apparently returned his affections, and romance began to bud. Because of her position, however, as the proprietor's oldest daughter, Fanchette was compelled to maintain amicable relations with all the patrons, a job she did well. When Colonel Wynkoop's companies left Perote, the Georgia Volunteer Battalion became the new garrison. A Captain Foster of this command also took quite a liking to Fanchette, and he began to view Lieutenant Goff as an obstacle between himself and his heart's desire. The two argued on the evening of April 9th, until mutual friends helped settle their quarrel. The next morning, however, Foster met Goff at the door of the hotel and, without warning, jumped him with a Bowie knife, stabbing him repeatedly. Fanchette and her mother cared for him, doing all within their power, but on the 13th of April he died. His body was returned to Wilkes-Barre and laid to rest in the familiar soil of the Wyoming Valley.[13]

Lieutenant Colonel Black and his seven companies returned to San Angel from their arduous march on 16 April. They, "gave themselves a good scrubbing, as they nearly all looked like so many wild Indians. Some had caps on, some straw hats, some Mexican military hats, and some had nothing on their heads."[14]

More fresh recruits joined the Keystone State regiments on 19 April. They were evidence of the successful recruiting done by members of the regiments themselves in Pennsylvania. A few officers and non-commissioned officers had left Jalapa for that purpose in early June, 1847. They established recruiting depots in store fronts, public buildings, armories or wherever they could find space. Pittsburgh and Philadelphia proved to be the most fruitful areas. Lieutenant Dutton set up his depot in the State Fencibles' armory as early as July, 1847. Second Lieutenant James A. Deany, of the 1st Regiment, established a depot in Hope's engine house on Sixth Street, Philadelphia in mid-January, 1848. Another was set up in Kensington, at Second and Phoenix Streets, by Private James R. Hughes around the beginning of March. Each regiment recruited strictly for itself, and some men even enlisted for a specific company. In addition to the cities, Pottsville provided some recruits for the 1st Regiment. Recruiting for the 2nd Regiment was also done in Johnstown, Hollidaysburg, Reading, York and Harrisburg. The recruiters themselves came and went. Some were home to recuperate, then involved themselves in recruiting until they could rejoin their companies. The rosters clearly show that not all the recruits made it to Mexico. They also show that the quality of many recruits left a lot to be desired. Fort Mifflin, near Philadelphia, served as the rendezvous for the new enlistees, and from there, they were sent to Mexico in contingents, aboard ships leased by the government. This system was far from efficient, but it did procure much needed manpower to bolster the depleted ranks at the front.[15]

At a dress parade on the evening of 23 April, the sentence of a court martial was read to the troops. Captain Thomas S. Leoser was to forfeit two months pay for not restraining his troops from throwing rotten eggs at a Massachusetts officer. The officer attempted to have a guard bucked and gagged for a trifling offense, and the men took action to prevent a perceived injustice. In fact, it was reported that Leoser rather encouraged them on.[16]

Corporal Oswandel noted in his diary on the 29th; "To-day we drew clothing for the whole regiment, and every company received their letters to put on their caps. So this evening the whole regiment appeared on dress parade with the letter of their respective companies." The next morning they were mustered, and on 1 May the brigade was reviewed by Generals Patterson and Worth.[17]

On the morning of 20 May some twenty-five pounds of powder exploded in the quarters of Company A, 1st Regiment. Private Mansfield Mason was badly burned, but not fatally. Sergeant Charles E. Bruton, on the other hand, wasn't that fortunate. He was "burned almost to a crisp," but lingered until the second of June before he died. The explosion made a mess out of Company A's lodgements.[18]

As the troops faced the boredom of garrison duty, the peace commissioners of both sides labored long and hard on an acceptable peace. With agreements in most areas having been reached, the Treaty of Guadalupe-Hidalgo then had to be passed by both national legislatures. That was finally accomplished, and copies of the ratified treaty were exchanged at Queretaro on the 30th of May, thus officially ending the state of war between the two countries.[19]

The *American Star* kept the soldiers informed of the progress of negotiations, and excitement ran high in San Angel. Rumors and discussions about peace had been prominent for months, but by the end of May the men started singing "We Are Coming Home." Early on the morning of the 30th the volunteer brigade, under Colonel Wynkoop's command, marched away from San Angel for the last time. The day was warm and dry and the road dusty, but the men

Captain Thomas S. Leoser
Historical Society of Berks County

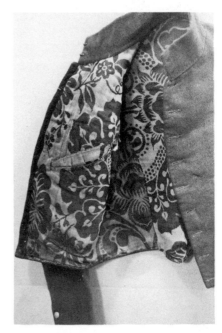

Views of the uniform coat worn home by Private Richard Coulter of the Westmoreland Guards, 2nd Regiment.   *Westmoreland County Historical Society*

marched with bounce in their step, as they thought of home. They passed through Puebla on the morning of 3 June. The bodies of comrades who died there were collected and carried with the regiments for burial in their home soil. The column arrived at Perote before noon on the 7th and spent the night encamped around the castle. On Friday the 9th they passed through Jalapa and spent the night about three miles east of town. From here they clearly saw the Gulf of Mexico off in the distance. A short march the following day brought them to El Encero, where a more formal camp was set up. That camp became a holding area until enough ships arrived at Vera Cruz. Daily drills, parades and reviews reminded the men that they were still in the Army and not civilians yet. On the 15th, the 1st Regiment marched a few miles from Encero, going on to Puente Nacional on the 16th. The 2nd Regiment likewise moved on the 16th, through Cerro Gordo to Plan del Rio. The temperatures were so high in those lower elevations that short marches were necessary. Movements in the early morning and late evening of the 17th carried the regiments to Sante Fe and San Juan respectively. Both regiments reached the outskirts of Vera Cruz on Sunday the 18th.[20]

The 1st Regiment formed on Monday morning and marched through the city to the wharfs. There, six companies boarded the seagoing steamer *Eudora*, which sailed that afternoon. The other four companies embarked on another vessel. The 2nd Regiment set sail on the 20th; Companies A, C, G and M on the barque *Florida*, and B, D, E, F, H, I, K and L on the steamer *Mary Kingsland*. After relatively smooth and uneventful voyages the ships landed at the campground just north of New Orleans. The first four companies of the 1st Regiment arrived on the 25th, followed the next day by the *Eudora's* six companies. The *Mary Kingsland* also cast anchor off New Orleans on the 26th. Seven companies from the *Mary* transferred to the steamboat *Tagliona* on the 27th and headed for Pittsburgh. Company E, 2nd Regiment, sought to make its own arrangements, however, and contracted for cabin accommodations on the riverboat *Charles Hammond*, at a cost of $675.00. The four companies of the 1st Regiment, which had arrived at New Orleans first, boarded and sailed on the *Western World* under command of Lieutenant Colonel Black on the morning of the 27th. That evening the *Charles Hammond* put in at Camp Carlton to pick up Colonel Wynkoop and the remaining six companies of the 1st Regiment. Wynkoop objected as soon as he saw the Westmoreland Guards in cabins, because his men were assigned to the steerage. After a bit of delicate negotiating, the Guards moved to the upper deck of the boat, allowing Wynkoop's contingent to occupy the remainder. It finally left about nine o'clock at night.[21]

The sailing ship *Florida*, with the last four companies of the 2nd Regiment didn't arrive at New Orleans until 29 June. The men shortly transferred to a river steamer and headed for Pittsburgh. Up the Mississippi churned the boats full of excited soldiers. They passed Baton Rouge, Natches, Vicksburg, Memphis and Cairo. At Louisville, the Westmoreland Guards changed to the *Germantown*. The 1st Regiment troops left the *Charles Hammond* at Cincinnati and boarded the smaller boats *Schuylkill* and *Brooklyn*. The vessels began arriving at Pittsburgh on 11 July and continued to do so until the 18th.[22]

Christy's warehouse again housed the returning volunteers. Those from Pittsburgh of course stayed at their own homes, and numerous others paid for rooms in hotels and boarding houses. The crowds on hand for the welcome were overwhelming. Unfortunately, however, the extended time over which the boats came in prevented one huge celebration. By the time the last troops arrived, the desire to extend greetings and hospitality was worn out. Almost every community having a company in service sent a small delegation to Pittsburgh to greet their men. Often these delegations also took charge of the bodies of their fallen heroes.[23]

As the companies arrived they turned over all their muskets, bayonets, accoutrements and other federal property to U.S. Army officers. All of the 2nd Regiment and Companies A, I and K of the 1st Regiment were mustered out at Pittsburgh between 12 and 25 July. The field and staff officers of the 2nd Regiment were mustered out on the 21st. The Philadelphia and Pottsville companies of the 1st Regiment decided that they preferred to end their Federal service at home. So they journeyed to Philadelphia, where they were mustered out between 27 July and 5 August.[24]

As each town received her returning volunteers, parades, speeches, banquets, toasts, presentations and general celebrations were the order of the day. In fact, the rounds of banquets lasted for weeks in most locations. Hundreds sat spellbound as the veterans told of their noble deeds in far-off Mexico. Many more did not get to welcome home those whom they had sent away a year and a half earlier. More than twenty bodies were brought home for burial, but the vast majority of the dead lay under the sod of a foreign land.

A total of 2,415 men served in the two Pennsylvania regiments during the war. Desertion lured away 191. Discharges accounted for 406 more. Death claimed 477, of these 52 were battle related. This brings the loss for the two units to 1,074 men. No matter how the war may be viewed politically, Pennsylvania contributed materially to the support of the central government, and she bore her share of the cost of the victory.[25]

The Pennsylvanians of 1848 had every right to be proud of their volunteers, and of the service they had rendered. A hundred and forty years later, there is still reason to be proud of those men. They volunteered to give their lives for what they believed was a just cause. Their patriotism, courage, stamina, and their faith in the God of heaven who saw them through their ordeal, set an example for years to come.

1. Niebaum, *Pittsburgh Washington Infantry*, p. 46; Oswandel, *Notes*, p. 423; Larner, "A Westmoreland Guard," p. 392; Cambria County Historical Society, John A. Blair Diary; Hartman, *Private's Journal*, p. 21; Evans, "Reading Artillerists," p. 139.

2. Cambria County Historical Society, John A. Blair Diary; Larner, "A Westmoreland Guard," p. 392; National Archives, RG 94, 1st & 2nd Pa. Regt. Papers.

3. *The Pennsylvania Argus* (Greensburg), Jan. 14, 1848.

4. Bauer, *The Mexican War*, p. 276; National Archives, RG 94, 1st & 2nd Pa. Regt. Papers; *The Pennsylvania Argus* (Greensburg), Feb. 26, 1847.

5. Oswandel, *Notes*, pp. 441-442; Larner, "A Westmoreland Guard," p. 393; Cambria County Historical Society, John A. Blair Diary.

6. Oswandel, *Notes*, p. 466; Anonymous, "Mexican War Battle-Flags Presented To The Historical Society of Pennsylvania," *Pennsylvania Magazine of History and Biography*, XVII (1893), pp. 185-189; Niebaum, *Pittsburgh Washington Infantry*, p. 47.

7. Cambria County Historical Society, John A. Blair Diary; Oswandel, *Notes*, pp. 509, 513.

8. Robert L. Bodson, "A Description Of The United States Occupation Of Mexico As Reported By American Newspapers Published In Vera Cruz, Puebla, And Mexico City September 14, 1847 to July 31, 1848" (Doctoral Disertation, Ball State University, 1970), pp. 12-14, 111-112; Oswandel, *Notes*, pp. 431, 484, 511; *The Daily Morning Post* (Pittsburgh), Nov. 29, 1847.

9. Cambria County Historical Society, John A. Blair Diary; Larner, "A Westmoreland Guard," pp. 399-400; National Archives, RG 94, 2nd Pa. Regt. Papers.

10. Larner, "A Westmoreland Guard," p. 401; Oswandel, *Notes*, pp. 488, 507-508.

11. Larner, "A Westmoreland Guard," p. 400, 403; Oswandel, *Notes*, p. 509; Kitchen, *Wyoming Artillerists*, pp. 75-76.

12. Hartman, *Private's Journal*, pp. 23, 25; Oswandel, *Notes*, pp. 525-526, 547, 550, 559, 578, 583-584.

13. Kitchen, *Wyoming Artillerists*, pp. 60, 62-63; National Archives, RG 94, 1st Pa. Regt. Papers; Lieutenant Goff's first name is unknown.

14. Oswandel, *Notes*, p. 530.

15. National Archives, RG 94, 1st & 2nd Pa. Regt. Papers; *The Pennsylvanian* (Philadelphia), July 27, 1847, Jan. 12, 1848 & Mar. 10, 1848.

16. National Archives, RG 94, 2nd Pa. Regt. Papers; Oswandel, *Notes*, pp. 536-537.

17. Oswandel, *Notes*, pp. 538-539.

18. Oswandel, *Notes*, pp. 550, 579; National Archives, RG 94, 1st Pa. Regt. Papers.

19. Bauer, *The Mexican War*, pp. 384, 387.

20. Oswandel, *Notes*, pp. 560-561, 572-583; Hartman, *Private's Journal*, pp. 23-25; Larner, "A Westmoreland Guard," pp. 406-409; Niebaum, *Pittsburgh Washington Infantry*, pp. 47-48.

21. Oswandel, *Notes*, pp. 584-590; Niebaum, *Pittsburgh Washington Infantry*, p. 48; Hartman, *Private's Journal*, pp. 25-26; Larner, "A Westmoreland Guard," pp. 409-410; Coulter, "Westmoreland Guards," p. 119.

22. *The Danville Intelligencer*, July 14, 1848 & July 21, 1848; Evans, "Reading Artillerists," p. 139; Coulter, "Westmoreland Guards," p. 120; Hartman, *Private's Journal*, pp. 27-28; Larner, "A Westmoreland Guard," pp. 410-413.

23. *The Daily Morning Post* (Pittsburgh), July 11, 1848; *The Danville Intelligencer*, July 14, 1848; Oswandel, *Notes*, p. 600.

24. National Archives, RG 94, 1st & 2nd Pa. Regt. Papers.

25. *Ibid.*

ROSTERS

A brief introduction to and explanation of the rosters is in order. They could have been organized in several ways. The companies of both regiments, in almost all cases, had existed before the war as distinct units; hence, their organization here follows that history. The master index will help in locating soldiers for which no company is known.

The information presented here has been extracted from the compiled service record of each soldier. The War Department compilations are extracts from the original muster rolls now in the National Archives. Additional information is in the histories of the counties which provided those units and in the various accounts cited in this book. In the numerous situations where facts were in conflict, the Compiled Service Records and the related original muster rolls were followed. Sometimes a particular fact, such as an age, had so many variations, that a "best guess" was necessary on the part of the author. The spelling of names also follows that used by the War Department, except where the author knew the correct spelling to be different. Variations of spelling are in parentheses with each entry. The rosters are so complex and lengthy that footnoting was impossible. However, the sources of almost all entries are listed in the bibliography, except for the very few cases when one or more of the people listed in the Acknowledgments provided the information.

There is much more information that could have been included in many cases, but it was literally impossible to include all available knowledge. The author hopes that as new information comes to light it will be sent to him so that he can maintain continually updated master rosters.

A list of most of the abbreviations used in the rosters is given below with their explanations.

AWOL	Absent without leave
Bvt.	Brevet
Co.	Company or County
Cpl.	Corporal
disc.	Discharged

enl. . . . . Enlisted
KIA . . . . Killed in action
Lt. . . . . Lieutenant
mi. . . . . Mustered in
mo. . . . . Mustered out
MR. . . . . Muster roll
occ. . . . . Occupation
POW . . . . Prisoner of War
Pvt. . . . . Private
SCD. . . . . Surgeon's certificate of disability
Sgt. . . . . Sergeant
WIA. . . . . Wounded in action

Field and Staff, 1st Regiment

The full membership of the 1st Regiment on 18 December 1846 elected their three field grade officers. The following day First Lieutenant Horace B. Field of the 3rd U.S. Artillery mustered them into federal service. A total of twenty-seven people served in field and staff positions of the regiment during the war. A large turnover was experienced, particularly in the enlisted staff, and other difficulties cropped up because of the division of the Regiment between Perote and Puebla. All three field officers proved to be capable, competent, and popular with their men.

Colonel Wynkoop had been a newspaper proprietor before the war and had also worked his way up to Colonel in the Schuylkill County Militia. After returning home, President Franklin Pierce appointed him U.S. Marshal of the Eastern District of Pennsylvania. He died in a hunting accident in 1857.

Lieutenant Colonel Black and Major Bowman both rendered subsequent military service after the war and were highly thought of by subordinates and superiors alike.

The field and staff officers and men of the 1st Regiment returned to Philadelphia where they were mustered out on 8 August 1848.

John Egbert Farnum pictured as
Lieutenant Colonel of the 70th New York
in the Civil War
*Monmouth County Historical
Association, Freehold, New Jersey*

Lieutenant Colonel Samuel W. Black
pictured as Colonel of the 62nd Pennsylvania
during the Civil War
Civil War Library & Museum - MOLLUS

BALLIER, JOHN FREDERICK: b. 28 Aug 15, enl. 30 Nov 46 at Phila., age 31, mi. 14 Dec 46 at Pittsburgh as 1st Lt., Co. E, placed under arrest 27 Dec 47, appointed Acting Assistant Quartermaster 6 Mar 48, mo. with Co. E, 5 Aug 48. Col. 21st P.V.I. (3 mos.), 29 Apr 61 to 8 Aug 61. Col. 98th P.V.I., 30 Sep 61 to 26 Nov 62 and 12 Mar 63 to 29 Jun 65. WIA at Salem Heights and Fort Stevens. Bvt. Brig. Gen. of Vols. 29 Jun 65. Died at Phila. 3 Feb 93.

BIRCH, JAMES: enl. 20 Nov 46 at Phila., age 32, mi. 17 Dec 46 at Pittsburgh as Pvt., Co. G, appointed Quartermaster Sgt. 22 Apr 47, disc. at Perote 19 Jul 47 on SCD for diarrhea and brain disease.

BLACK, SAMUEL W.: elected Lt. Col. by the Regt. 18 Dec 46, enrolled by virtue of election, commanded Cos. A, C, D, G, I, and K at Puebla from 3 Jul 47 to 12 Oct 47, assumed command of Regt. 15 Feb 48 thru at least 30 Apr 48, mo. with F & S, 8 Aug 48. Col. 62nd P.V.I., 4 Jul 61 until KIA at Gaines Mill, 27 Jun 62.

BOWMAN, FRANCIS L.: enl. 1 Dec 46 at Wilkes-Barre, age 33, mi. 16 Dec 46 at Pittsburgh as 1st Lt., Co. I, elected Maj. 18 Dec 46, Jan-Feb 48 MR lists him as sick at San Angel, mo. with F & S, 8 Aug 48. Appointed Capt., 9th U.S. Infantry, 3 Mar 55, died near Ft. Willamette, Oregon, 10 Sep 56, from fever and exposure. Buried in Wilkes-Barre.

BREECE, SULLIVAN D.: enl. 2 Dec 46 at Phila., age 31, occ. machinist, mi. 16 Dec 46 at Pittsburgh as 1st Lt. of Co. H, appointed Assistant Quartermaster 22 Mar 47, appointed Q.M. 7 Apr 47, was Acting Brigade Q.M. in Apr & May 47, resigned as Q.M. 4 Jun 47, returned to command Co. H from 6 Jun 47, mo. with Co. H, 29 Jul 48.

BROWN, ALEXANDER: enl. 24 Nov 46 at Phila., age 30, mi. 14 Dec 46 at Pittsburgh as 2nd Lt., Co. D, appointed Adjutant 19 Dec 46, promoted to 1st Lt. 30 Mar 47, MRs of Jan-Feb & Mar-Apr 48 list him as sick on duty at San Angel, left sick at New Orleans 29 Jun 48 on the way home, disc. by General Order 20 Jul 48, died in Jul 48.

BUNTING, THOMAS C.: appointed Asst. Surg. of Vols. 17 Sep 46, assigned to the 1st Pa. Regt. 17 Dec 46, joined Regt. 8 Jan 47, served in Puebla during the siege, transferred to 2nd Pa. Regt. 18 Apr 48, died 23 Dec 95.

CASSIDY, ALEXANDER M.: born in & appointed from Ohio, appointed Asst. Surg. of Vols. 9 Aug 47, joined Regt. 19 Apr 48, mo. with F & S, 8 Aug 48.

CLINTON, WILLIAM: enl. 2 Dec 46 at Phila., age 30, occ. carpenter, mi. 16 Dec 46 at Pittsburgh as 2nd Lt. of Co. H, Acting Adjutant from 1 Jan 48, appointed Adjutant 20 Jul 48, mo. with F & S, 8 Aug 48.

DILKS, JACOB: enl. 2 Dec 46 at Phila., age 40 mi. 16 Dec 46 at Pittsburgh as Fifer of Co. H, appointed Principal Musician 20 Dec 46, reduced to Pvt. 1 Jul 47, mo. with Co. H, 29 Jul 48.

DOLORES: enrolled in Mexico City as Matron, attached to Regimental Hospital, listed only on 1st Regt. Hosp. MR of 29· Feb-30 Apr 48.

FARNUM, JOHN EGBERT: b. 1 Apr 24, enl. 1 Dec 46 at Pottsville, age 22, occ. clerk, mi. 15 Dec 46 at Pittsburgh as 2nd Cpl. of Co. B, appointed Sgt. Major 19 Dec 46, detached for recruiting duty from Jun 47, arrived in Pottsville 14 Jul 47, returned to Regt. probably 21 Dec 47, mo. with F & S, 8 Aug 48. Maj., Lt. Col. & Col. of 70th N.Y. Vol. Inf., 29 Jun 61 to 1 Jul 64. Col. of Veteran Reserve Corps, 26 Jul 64 to 30 Jun 66. Bvt. Brig. Gen. of Vols., 3 Jan 66. Died in New York City, 16 May 70.

GILFRY, MATTHEW: enl. 20 Nov. 46 at Phila., age 38, occ. butcher, mi. 17 Dec 46 at Pittsburgh as Pvt. of Co. G, appointed Color Sgt. 9 Mar 47, appears on Co. MRs as Pvt. throughout his service, mo. with Co. G, 29 Jul 48.

GOFF, A. H.: enl. 1 Dec 46 at Wilkes-Barre, age 22, mi. 16 Dec 46 at Pittsburgh as 2nd Lt. of Co. I, appointed Acting Asst. Q.M. 3 Jul 47, detached as Commissary to Dept. of Perote 27 Nov 47, stabbed 10 Apr 48 by Capt. Foster, Georgia Battalion of Vols., in a quarrel over a Mexican Senorita, died 13 Apr 48, his body returned for burial to Wilkes-Barre.

GRAY, WILLIAM H.: b. 12 Mar 24, enl. probably 1 Dec 46 at Phila., age 22, mi. 15 Dec 46 at Pittsburgh as 2nd Lt. of Co. F, Promoted to 1st Lt. 4 Jun 47, appointed Acting Asst. Commissary of Subsistence 1 Dec 47, mo. with Co. F, 28 Jul 48. Col. 20th P.V.I. (3 mos.), 30 Apr 61 to 27 Jul 61. Capt., Co. F, 192nd P.V.I. 12 Jul 64 to 11 Nov 64. Died 12 Nov 12.

HANS, HENRY: (Hains): enl. 2 Dec 46 at Phila., age 21, mi. 14 Dec 46 at Pittsburgh as Pvt. of Co. E, Sick on MR of 14 Dec 46 - 28 Feb 47, detailed for daily duty in hospital on Mar-Apr 47 MR, attendant at hospital 1 to 6 Jun 47, appointed Hospital Steward 7 Jun 47, on duty at Perote Hospital 7 Jun to 22 Jul 47, returned to Co. E, 22 Jul 47, under arrest from 23 Jul 47, reduced to Pvt. 28 Jul 47, fined $30.00 by General Court Martial 2 Sep 47, mo. with Co. E, 5 Aug 48.

HARDEGAN, CHARLES: (Herdegan, Herdegen): enl. 2 Dec 46 at Phila., age 34, occ. physician, mi. 14 Dec 46 at Pittsburgh as Pvt. of Co. E, acted as Hospital Steward from 12 Jan 47 to 28 Feb 47, to more than four Cos. at New Orleans and on ships "Russel Glover" and "Oxnard" and at Lobos Island, served as Steward during the Battle of Cerro Gordo, detached for recruiting duty in Phila. 7 Jun 47, deserted from Ft. Mifflin 20 May 48, rejoined Co. E, 5 Aug 48, dishonorably discharged 5 Aug 48.

HAVILLAND, EDWARD: (Haviland): enl. 2 Dec 46 at Phila., age 22, mi. 16 Dec 46 at Pittsburgh as Pvt. of Co. H, appointed Quartermaster Sgt. 20 Dec 46, disc. 22 Apr 47 at Vera Cruz on SCD.

KERLIN, WILLIAM: (Carlin): enl. 2 Dec 46 at Phila., age 24, occ. bricklayer, mi. 16 Dec 46 at Pittsburgh as Pvt. of Co. H, appointed Hospital Steward for three Cos. 3 Apr 48, mo. with Co. H, 29 Jul 48.

McCULLY, ROBERT: (McCulley, McCullough): enl. 1 Dec 46 at Phila., age 42, mi. 15 Dec 46 as Drummer of Co. F, appointed Principal Musician 19 Dec 46, mo. with F & S, 8 Aug 48.

McDOUGAL, LEON: enl. 1 Dec 46 at Phila., age 22, mi. 15 Dec 46 as Pvt. of Co. F, appointed Quartermaster Sgt. 19 Jul 47, mo. with F & S, 8 Aug 48.

REYNOLDS, JOHN C.: appointed Surgeon 17 Dec 46, joined the Regt. 8 Jan 47, served with Perote garrison Jun-Oct 47, absent on leave from 4 Nov 47 to 17 Apr 48, mo. with F & S, 8 Aug 48.

STAMM, REUBEN (Stamum, Staumm): enl. 1 Dec 46 at Pottsville, age 23, occ. cabinet maker, mi. 15 Dec 46 at Pittsburgh as Fifer of Co. B, appointed Fife Major 30 Jun 47, mo. with F & S, 8 Aug 48.

WHARTON, OLIVIA H.: enrolled as Matron, attached to Regimental Hospital, on MRs from 31 Oct 47 through 30 Apr 48.

WOODS, ROBERT: enl. 26 Nov 46 at Pittsburgh, age 26, mi. 16 Dec 46 at Pittsburgh as Pvt. of Co. A, elected 2nd Lt. 17 Jun 47, Acting Quartermaster from 28 Nov 47, appointed Quartermaster 3 Dec 47, listed as sick at San Angel on Jan-Feb & Mar-Apr 48 MRs, mo. with F & S, 8 Aug 48.

WYNKOOP, FRANCIS MURRAY: enl. 1 Dec 46 at Pottsville, age 28, mi. 15 Dec 46 at Pittsburgh as Pvt. of Co. B, elected Colonel 18 Dec 46, commanding Volunteer Brigade from 15 Feb 48 through at least 30 Apr 48, mo. with F & S, 8 Aug 48. Died 13 Dec 57 at Pottsville, buried in Charles Baber Cemetery in Pottsville.

Company A, 1st Regiment
Jackson Independent Blues

The Jackson Independent Blues was one of Pittsburgh's prominent uniformed militia companies, existing by that name at least from 1822. The unit was reorganized a year or so earlier from the old Pittsburgh Blues, which had served in the War of 1812.

The Blues tendered their services to Governor Shunk sometime before 15 July 1846, and when the 1st Regiment was called for from Pennsylvania they again volunteered. They were notified of their acceptance into the Regiment on 24 November 1846 and immediately began recruiting to fill their ranks. Under command of Captain Alexander Hay, the company was mustered into federal service about 2:00 P.M. on 16 December 1846 by First Lieutenant Horace B. Field of the 3rd U.S. Artillery.

They participated in the siege of Vera Cruz, the battle of Cerro Gordo and the siege of Puebla, eventually doing occupation duty in the Mexico City area. They returned to Pittsburgh on 15 July 1848 and were mustered out of federal service on the 24th of that month by Major George Wright of the 4th U.S. Infantry.

The Jackson Independent Blues continued to exist after the war, eventually becoming Company A, 12th Pennsylvania Volunteer Infantry Regiment in the three months service of 1861.

A total of 107 men served in the company during the war. Of these, nine were recruits who joined it in Mexico. Three men deserted. One man transferred to another unit. One man was missing in action, and thirteen others received wounds. Two of these men died of their wounds, and twenty-one others died from disease or accidents. A total of thirty-one received discharges before the company was mustered out.

ALEXANDER, THOMAS Pvt., enl. 26 Nov 46 at Pittsburgh, age 23, mo. with Co. 24 Jul 48.

ALLEN, WILLIAM G. (Geo. W.): Pvt., enl. 26 Nov 46 at Pittsburgh, age 26, left sick at Perote 3 Jul 47, disc. 8 Nov 47 at Perote on SCD.

ARMSTRONG, JAMES: Pvt., enl. 26 Nov 46 at Pittsburgh, age 23, left sick at Jalapa 7 May 47, died at Jalapa 4 Jun 47.

ARMSTRONG, JEREMIAH: Pvt., enl. 26 Nov 46 at Pittsburgh, age 21, disc. 16 Apr 47 at Vera Cruz on SCD, died 4 Jun 47 at New Orleans on his way home.

BARKER, ELIPHANT: Pvt., enl. 26 Nov 46 at Pittsburgh, age 32, died at Puebla 22 Jul 47.

BARKER, WILLIAM H.: Pvt., enl. 26 Nov 46 at Pittsburgh, age 25, disc. 23 Nov 47 at Jalapa upon his own request by order of Col. Wynkoop.

BARTON, JOHN: Pvt., enl. 26 Nov 46 at Pittsburgh, age 27, died 26 Nov 47 at Puebla from an accidental wound.

BATEMAN, HUGH: Sgt., enl. 26 Nov 46 at Pittsburgh, age 37, died at Perote 6 Jul 47.

BEEBE, ALBERT G.: Pvt., enl. 26 Nov 46 at Pittsburgh, age 22, disc. at Puebla 4 Nov 47 on SCD.

BLACK, SAMUEL: Pvt., enl. 26 Nov 46 at Pittsburgh, age 26, Mar-Apr 47 MR reads, "Clerk at HQ of Gen. Patterson," died at Puebla 12 Aug 47.

BLAKELY, WILLIAM: Pvt., enl. 26 Nov 46 at Pittsburgh, age 22, promoted to 3rd Sgt. 3 Aug 47, sick on Jan-Feb 48 MR, promoted to 2nd Lt. 26 May 48., mo. with Co. 24 Jul 48.

BOWDEN, JAMES: Pvt., enl. 26 Nov 46 at Pittsburgh, age 22, WIA at Puebla 18 Oct 47, disc. at Puebla 15 Dec 47 for wound.

BOWERS, GEORGE L.: Pvt., enl. 26 Aug 47 at Pittsburgh, mi. at Pittsburgh 26 Aug 47, joined Co. in Mexico City 21 Dec 47, mo. with Co. 24 Jul 48.

BOWMAN, FREDERICK: Pvt., enl. 26 Nov 46 at Pittsburgh, age 22, died at Perote 12 Jan 48.

BROWN, MILES: Pvt., enl. 26 Nov 46 at Pittsburgh, age 28, deserted 9 Aug 47 from Puebla but must have returned almost immediately as no action was taken against him, mo. with Co. 24 Jul 48.

BROWN, SAMUEL D.: Pvt., enl. 26 Nov 46 at Pittsburgh, age 25, detailed by Gen. Lane to printing office in Puebla 3 Dec 47, mo. with Co. 24 Jul 48.

BRUTON, CHARLES E. (F.): (Brewton): 4th Cpl., enl. 26 Nov 46 at Pittsburgh, age 21, promoted to 4th Sgt. 18 Jun 47, wounded in a powder explosion at San Angel 20 May 48, died 2 Jun 48.

BRYSON, CHARLES: Pvt., enl. 26 Nov 46 at Pittsburgh, age 19, fined $3.00 by Court Martial according to Jan-Feb 48 MR, mo. with Co. 24 Jul 48. 1st Lt. & Capt. Co. F, 61st P.V.I., 1 Aug 61 to 27 Nov 62. 1st Lt. New Co. G, 87th P.V.I., 9 Mar 65 to 29 Jun 65.

BYERLY, WILLIAM: (Byerley): Fifer, enl. 26 Nov 46 at Pittsburgh, age 26, mo. with Co. 24 Jul 48.

CAIN, THOMAS: Pvt., enl. 26 Nov 46 at Pittsburgh, age 24, died at Puebla 30 Oct 47.

CHALFANT, JAMES: 2nd Sgt., enl. 26 Nov 46 at Pittsburgh, age 32, ruptured on Lobos Island, disc. 28 Feb 47 on the ship "Russel Glover."

CHARLTON, WILLIAM A.: (Charleton): 2nd Lt., enl. 20 Nov 46 at Pittsburgh, age 42, became Acting 1st Lt. 9 Apr 47, was sick at Jalapa at the end of Apr 47, elected Capt. 25 May 48 to rank from 31 Mar 48, mo. with Co. 24 Jul 48.

CONDO, JOHN: Pvt., enl. 26 Nov 46 at Pittsburgh, age 28, disc. at San Angel 29 Feb 48 due to hernia.

COOLLEY, FRANCIS (Fennan) H.: (Cooley): Pvt., enl. 26 Nov 46 at Pittsburgh, age 27, on detached duty in Vera Cruz according to Mar-Apr 47 MR, detached to printing office in Mexico City 19 Dec 47, presumably returned to Co. in Mar 48, mo. with Co. 24 Jul 48.

DENNEY, JAMES O. H. (O'Hara): 1st Lt., enl. 26 Nov 46 at Pittsburgh, age 25, elected Capt. 17 Jun 47, resigned at San Angel 21 Mar 48.

DOLAN, JOHN: (Dolen): Pvt., enl. 26 Nov 46 at Pittsburgh, age 30, wounded at Puebla, on detached duty by order of Lt. Col. Black from 31 Jan 48, mo. with Co. 24 Jul 48.

EDWARDS, EMANUEL: Pvt., enl. 26 Nov 46 at Pittsburgh, age 19, on detached duty with Capt. Steptoe's Battery according to Jul-Aug 47 MR, WIA in the left hand at Puebla, mo. with Co. 24 Jul 48.

FANEMILLER, FREDERICK: (Fammimillar, Fanimiller, Fannimillar, Fannimiller): Pvt., enl. 26 Nov 46 at Pittsburgh, age 24, left sick in Jalapa 23 Nov 47, employed as a nurse in Jalapa Hospital from 1 Jan 48, returned to Co. by 30 Apr 48, mo. with Co. 24 Jul 48.

FENGLE, GEORGE: (Fangle): Pvt., enl. 26 Nov 46 at Pittsburgh, age 42, left sick at Puebla 3 Dec 47, disc. at Puebla 10 Jan 48, died at Pittsburgh.

FERGUSON, ABIJAH: (Furguson): 1st Sgt., enl. 26 Nov 46 at Pittsburgh, age 39, Acting 2nd Lt. from 10 Apr 47, elected 1st Lt. 17 Jun 47, sick in quarters according to Jan-Feb 48 MR, mo. with Co. 24 Jul 48.

FOUST, ELIAS: Pvt., enl. 26 Nov 46 at Pittsburgh, age 20, promoted to Cpl. 1 Jun 48, mo. with Co. 24 Jul 48.

GARMAN, JOHN B.: (Gorman): Pvt., enl. 26 Nov 46 at Pittsburgh, age 21, WIA at Puebla, died of wound at Puebla 14 Oct 47, his body brought home for burial.

GIBNER, JOHN: Pvt., enl. 26 Nov 46 at Pittsburgh, age 26, promoted to Cpl. 18 Jun 47, mo. with Co. 24 Jul 48.

GRAHAM, WILLIAM: Pvt., enl. 26 Nov 46 at Pittsburgh, age 31, disc. at Vera Cruz 16 Apr 47 on SCD due to sickness.

GRIFFITH, JOHN: Pvt., enl. 26 Nov 46 at Pittsburgh, age 26, left Co. without leave and went on Yucatan Expedition, deserted 3 Mar 48, afterwards joining Louisiana Dragoons.

GYRE, DANIEL: (Guyer, Guyre): Pvt., enl. 26 Nov 46 at Pittsburgh, age 20, left sick at New Orleans 17 Jan 47, disc. at New Orleans 28 Feb 47 on SCD due to sickness.

HAGER, DAVID: (Hagar): Pvt., enl. 26 Nov 46 at Pittsburgh, age 20, disc. at Vera Cruz 22 Apr 47.

HAMILTON, STEPHEN: Pvt., enl. 26 Nov 46 at Pittsburgh, age 22, sick in camp according to Mar-Apr 47 MR, detailed to Capt. Steptoe's Battery on Jul-Aug 47 MR, missing since 12 Sep 47 at Battle of the City of Mexico, presumed dead.

HARKINS, DAVID: (Hawkins): Pvt., enl. 26 Nov 46 at Pittsburgh, age 19, wounded in right hand causing loss of fingers while on pickett duty at Vera Cruz, disc. at Vera Cruz 8 Apr 47 on SCD.

HARMAN, JAMES C. (S.): (Harmon): Pvt., enl. & mi. 10 Jan 47 at New Orleans by Col. Wynkoop in place of J. M. Needs who deserted, detached to Capt. Steptoe's Battery according to Jul-Aug 47 MR, mo. with Co. 24 Jul 48.

HAY, ALEXANDER: Capt., disc. at Vera Cruz 2 Apr 47 due to illness. Capt. Co. E, 61st P.V.I. 1 Aug 61 to 20 May 62.

HEINTEEN, FREDERICK: (Hentine): Pvt., Enl. 26 Nov 46 at Pittsburgh, age 20, disc. at Jalapa 19 Dec 47 on SCD for sickness.

HINDS, JOHN: (Heines, Hines): Pvt., enl. 26 Nov 46 at Pittsburgh, age 26, claimed as a deserter by 3rd U.S. Artillery at Vera Cruz 2 Apr 47.

HOLLIDAY, JESSE M.: (Holiday): Pvt., enl. 26 Nov 46 at Pittsburgh, age 35, left sick at Perote 3 Jul 47, rejoined Co., left sick at Perote again 28 Nov 47, died at Vera Cruz in Jun 48 on the way home.

HOOVER, JOHN H.: Pvt., enl. 26 Nov 46 at Pittsburgh, age 28, wounded at Puebla, mo. with Co. 24 Jul 48.

HOSE, BERNARD (Barnard): (Hos): Pvt., enl. 26 Nov 46 at Pittsburgh, age 25, sick in hospital at Jalapa according to Mar-Apr 47 MR, died at Perote 6 Jul 47.

HULL, JAMES C.: (Hall): Pvt., enl. 26 Nov 46 at Pittsburgh, age 19, promoted to Cpl. 1 Dec 47, promoted to Sgt. 1 Jun 48, mo. with Co. 24 Jul 48. Capt. Co. A & Lt. Col. 62nd P.V.I. 4 Jul 61 until death from wounds received at Laurel Hill 22 May 64.

INMETT, SAMUEL: (Immer): Pvt., enl. 26 Nov 46 at Pittsburgh, age 19, sick in camp according to Mar-Apr 47 MR, mo. with Co. 24 Jul 48.

KENNEDY, HIRAM J.: (Kennedey): 3rd Cpl., enl. 26 Nov 46 at Pittsburgh, age 21, promoted to 2nd Sgt. 18 Jun 47, died at San Angel 21 Jan 48.

KENNEDY, WILLIAM: (Kennedey): Pvt., enl. 26 Nov 46 at Pittsburgh, age 19, promoted to 4th Cpl. 18 Jun 47, promoted to Sgt. 24 Jan 48, mo. with Co. 24 Jul 48.

KRINE, JOHN: Pvt., enl. 26 Nov 46 at Pittsburgh, age 25, mo. with Co. 24 Jul 48.

LANDAN, JOSEPH: (Landraw): Pvt., enl. 9 Aug 47 at Pottsville, age 21, mi. at Pottsville by Lt. Kaercher, joined Co. 21 Dec 47, mo. with Co. 24 Jul 48.

LAYBURN, WILLIAM S.: (Leyborne): Pvt., enl. 26 Nov 46 at Pittsburgh, age 22, mo. with Co. 24 Jul 48.

LINDSEY, DAVID: (Lindsay, Lindsy): Pvt., enl. 26 Nov 46 at Pittsburgh, age 31, wounded severely in the right breast at Cerro Gordo with the ball remaining in the wound, wounded in the siege of Puebla, disc. at Puebla 25 Jan 48 on SCD.

LINHART, JOHN: (Lyndhart): Pvt., enl. 26 Nov 46 at Pittsburgh, age 19, WIA at Cerro Gordo 18 Apr 47, died of wound 29 Apr 47.

LYNCH, HENRY: Pvt., enl. 26 Nov 46 at Pittsburgh, age 20, WIA at Puebla, mo. with Co. 24 Jul 48.

MASON, MANSFIELD B.: Pvt., enl. 26 Nov 46 at Pittsburgh, age 19, reportedly wounded at Vera Cruz, fined $3.00 by Court Martial according to Jan-Feb 48 MR, accidently wounded at Puebla 10 Mar 48 but remained on duty, injured when powder exploded in the barracks at San Angel 20 May 48, mo. with Co. 24 Jul 48.

McCAFFREY, JAMES: (McCaffery, McCaffrie): Pvt., enl. 26 Nov 46 at Pittsburgh, age 21, died at Puebla 13 Sep 47.

McCULLY, JOHN W.: (McCulley): Pvt., enl. 26 Nov 46 at Pittsburgh, age 29, left sick at Puebla 24 Oct 47, disc. at New Orleans 28 Nov 47.

McDERMOTT, CHARLES C.: (McDermitt): Pvt., enl. & mi. 15 Jan 47 at New Orleans by Col. Wynkoop in place of George Miller who deserted, deserted from Puebla 19 Aug 47, returned to Co. before 31 Aug 47, mo. with Co. 24 Jul 48. Brother of William McDermott. Age 25.

McDERMOTT, WILLIAM: (McDermitt): Pvt., enl. 26 Nov 46 at Pittsburgh, age 23, deserted from Puebla 9 Aug 47, returned to Co. before 31 Dec 47, mo. with Co. 24 Jul 48. Brother of Charles C. McDermott.

McDONALD, ALFRED: (McDonnald): Pvt., enl. 26 Nov 46 at Pittsburgh, age 19, promoted to Cpl. 24 Jan 48, mo. with Co. 24 Jul 48. 2nd & 1st Lt. Co. A, 62nd P.V.I. 4 Jul 61 to 12 Oct 62.

McINTYRE, THOMAS: (McEntyre, McIntire): Pvt., enl. 26 Nov 46 at Pittsburgh, age 23, fined $3.00 by Court Martial according to Jan-Feb 48 MR, mo. with Co. 24 Jul 48.

McKEE, ROBERT: 2nd Cpl., enl. 26 Nov 46 at Pittsburgh, age 22, died at Puebla 31 Oct 47.

McKUTCHEON, JAMES: (McCutchen, McCutcheon): Pvt., enl. 26 Nov 46 at Pittsburgh, age 40, wounded at Puebla, disc. at Puebla 4 Nov 47 for wound.

McMUTRIE, DAVID: (McMoutrie): Pvt., enl. 26 Nov 46 at Pittsburgh, age 18, left sick at Perote according to Jul-Aug 47 MR, detached by Col. Wynkoop 29 Nov 47, sick in Perote 14 Mar 48 through Apr 48, mo. with Co. 24 Jul 48.

McNALLY, BERNARD: (McNalley, McNulty): Pvt., enl. 26 Nov 46 at Pittsburgh, age 33, mo. with Co. 24 Jul 48.

MILLER, GEORGE: Drummer, enl. 26 Nov 46 at Pittsburgh, age 19, sent home from New Orleans in Jan 47 and his enlistment cancelled because he was under age and enlisted without his parents' consent.

MORTON, JAMES F. (H., T.): Pvt., enl. 26 Nov 46 at Pittsburgh, age 25, promoted to Sgt. 11 Apr 47, Acting 2nd Lt. from 10 Apr 47, promoted to 1st Sgt. 18 Jun 47, sick in quarters according to Jan-Feb 48 & Mar-Apr 48 MRs, mo. with Co. 24 Jul 48.

MOWERY, CHARLES B.: (Mourey, Mowry): Pvt., enl. 26 Nov 46 at Pittsburgh, age 19, disc. at Puebla 4 Nov 47.

NEEDS, JOHN M.: Pvt., enl. 26 Nov 46 at Pittsburgh, age 21, deserted at Pittsburgh 18 Dec 46.

OGDEN, THOMAS E. (James E.) (C.): Pvt., enl. 26 Nov 46 at Pittsburgh, age 21, sick according to 16 Dec 46 - 28 Feb 47 MR, disc. at Lobos Island on SCD 28 Feb 47 for loss of muscular power in his extremities.

PARKER, JOHN: Pvt., enl. 26 Nov 46 at Pittsburgh, age 26, mo. with Co. 24 Jul 48.

PATTERSON, JOHN W.: Pvt., enl. & mi. 11 Jan 47 at New Orleans, age 20, disc. at Vera Cruz 22 Apr 47. Capt. Co. B, 13th P.V.I. (3 mos), 25 Apr 61 to 6 Aug 61. Capt. Co. E, Maj., Lt. Col. & Col. 102nd P.V.I. 16 Aug 61 to 5 May 64, WIA at Fair Oaks, KIA at the Wilderness 5 May 64.

POLEX, JULIUS: (Polax): Pvt., enl. 24 Nov 46 at Pittsburgh, age 28, exchanged from 3rd U.S. Dragoons at Jalapa 9 Jul 47, on duty as Regimental Baker 21 Dec 47 until returning to Co. by 29 Feb 48, mo. with Co. 24 Jul 48.

RASPHILLAR, CHARLES: (Raspeller, Rasspleer): Pvt., enl. 28 Oct 47 at Phila., age 29, mi. 28 Oct 47 at Phila. by Capt. Scott, joined Co. 21 Dec 47, mo. with Co. 24 Jul 48.

REGAN, JOHN: (Ragen, Reagan, Reagon, etc.): Pvt., enl. 26 Nov 46 at Pittsburgh, age 30, mo. with Co. 24 Jul 48.

RICHERBERGER, GEORGE: (Richebuger, Richeburger, Rushelburger): Pvt., enl. 26 Nov 46 at Pittsburgh, age 19, wounded at Puebla, disc. at Perote 29 Nov 47 for wound.

ROWLEY, THOMAS A.: 2nd Lt., enl. 20 Nov 46 at Pittsburgh, age 20, received 30 day furlough 9 Apr 47, disc. effective 15 Apr 47. Capt. Co. H, D.C. & Md. Vols. 4 Oct 47. Col. 13th P.V.I. (3 mos.), 25 Apr 61 to 6 Aug 61. Col. 102nd P.V.I. 6 Aug 61 to 29 Nov 62. Brig. Gen. U.S. Vols. 29 Nov 62 to 29 Dec 64. WIA at Fair Oaks 31 May 62. Died 14 May 92, buried in Allegheny Cemetery.

RUBALD, BALSER (Bolser): (Ribold, Ribolt): Pvt., enl. 26 Nov 46 at Pittsburgh, age 24, died at Vera Cruz 3 Apr 47.

SAVAGE, JOHN: Pvt., enl. 26 Nov 46 at Pittsburgh, age 31, left sick at Mexico City Hospital 19 Dec 47, returned to Co. by 30 Apr 48, mo. with Co. 24 Jul 48.

SCEISEL, ALWAYS (Allawis): (Scisel, Seisel): Pvt., enl. & mi. 18 Sep 47 at Pittsburgh by Lt. Ankrim, age 27, joined Co. 21 Dec 47, mo. with Co. 24 Jul 48.

SCHEISS, FREDERICK: (Scheiz): Pvt., enl. & mi. 1 Sep 47 at Pittsburgh by Lt. Ankrim, age 22, joined Co. 21 Dec 47, mo. with Co. 24 Jul 48.

SCHNIDER, ANTHONY: (Schneider): Pvt., enl. & mi. 24 Jul 47 at Pottsville by Lt. Kaercher, joined Co. 21 Dec 47, mo. with Co. 24 Jul 48.

Thomas A. Rowley pictured as Colonel of the 13th Pennsylvania (3 Months) during the Civil War
MOLLUS-Mass & USAMHI

SHAFFER, JOHN: Pvt., enl. 26 Nov 46 at Pittsburgh, age 19, transferred to Co. B, 2nd U.S. Dragoons 5 Jun 47, disc. at East Pascagoula 13 Aug 48.

SHANNON, JAMES T. (S.), (Thomas J.): (Shanon): Pvt., enl. 26 Nov 46 at Pittsburgh, age 19, left sick in Mexico City Hospital 19 Dec 47, returned to Co. by 30 Apr 48, promoted to Cpl. 1 Jun 48, mo. with Co. 24 Jul 48. Capt. Co. C, 9th Pa. Res. 1 May 61 until his death 12 Sep 62 from wounds received at Second Bull Run.

SHAW, HUGH McC.: Pvt., enl. 26 Nov 46 at Pittsburgh, age 35, died at Jalapa 3 Jun 47.

SKILES, HUGH H. (M.): (Shiles): Pvt., enl. 26 Nov 46 at Pittsburgh, age 24, disc. at Vera Cruz 6 Apr 47 for consumption.

SPITZLEY, JOHN: (Spitsley): Pvt., enl. 26 Nov 46 at Pittsburgh, age 35, died at Jalapa 4 Jun 47.

SPROAT, JAMES: Pvt., enl. 26 Nov 46 at Pittsburgh, age 31, disc. at Vera Cruz 22 Apr 47.

STEWART, ALEXANDER P.: 1st Cpl., enl. 26 Nov 46 at Pittsburgh, age 25, was Acting 1st Sgt. from 11 Apr 47 through at least 30 Apr 47, promoted to 3rd Sgt. 1 Jun 48, mo. with Co. 24 Jul 48.

SULLIVAN, WILLIAM: Pvt., enl. 26 Nov 46 at Pittsburgh, age 21, died at Perote 11 Aug 47.

WALKER, JOHN: Pvt., enl. 26 Nov 46 at Pittsburgh, age 32, listed as deserted on 12 Apr 48 according to Mar-Apr 48 MR, mo. with Co. 24 Jul 48.

WARDROUS, GEORGE: (Wandrass, Waundrass, Wondress): Pvt., enl. & mi. 17 Aug 47 at Pottsville by Lt. Kaercher, age 29, joined Co. 21 Dec 47, mo. with Co. 24 Jul 48.

WILHELM, GEORGE: Pvt., enl. 26 Nov 46 at Pittsburgh, age 26, left sick at Perote according to Jul-Aug 47 MR, died at Perote 12 Jul 47.

WILSON, ROBERT: Pvt., enl. 26 Nov 46 at Pittsburgh, age 23, wounded at Puebla 5 Aug 47, mo. with Co. 24 Jul 48.

WOODS, ROBERT: Pvt., enl. 26 Nov 46 at Pittsburgh, age 26, elected 2nd Lt. 17 Jun 47, Acting Q.M. from 28 Nov 47, appointed Q.M. 3 Dec 47, mo. with F & S 8 Aug 48.

WORTHINGTON, WILLIAM H.: (Worghington): Pvt., enl. 26 Nov 46 at Pittsburgh, age 23, mo. with Co. 24 Jul 48.

WRIGHT, ISAAC: Pvt., enl. 26 Nov 46 at Pittsburgh, age 28, disc. at Vera Cruz 22 Apr 47. Capt. Co. F, 61st P.V.I. 1 Aug 61 to 30 Jan 62. Lt. Col. 136th P.V.I. 23 Aug 62 to 29 May 63. Capt. Co. K, 193rd P.V.I. 19 Jul 64 to 9 Nov 64. Died at New Castle, Pa. 15 Apr 83.

WRIGHT, JAMES B.: Pvt., enl. 26 Nov 46 at Pittsburgh, age 19, sick at Jalapa according to Mar-Apr 47 MR, died at Puebla 5 Aug 47.

YEAGER, FERDINAND: Pvt., enl. & mi. 1 Sep 47 at Phila. by Capt. Scott, age 27, joined Co. 21 Dec 47, mo. with Co. 24 Jul 48.

YEANE, JOHN: (Yance): Pvt., enl. & mi. 10 Aug 47 at Pittsburgh by Lt. Ankrim, age 23, at Carlisle Barracks 31 Aug 47, joined Co. 21 Dec 47, mo. with Co. 24 Jul 48.

YOST, CHRISTIAN (Christopher) F.: (Yoast, Youst): Pvt., enl. 26 Nov 46 at Pittsburgh, age 27, detached to Commissary Dept. in Mexico City 19 Dec 47, mo. with Co. 24 Jul 48.

YOUNG, ELI: Pvt., enl. 26 Nov 46 at Pittsburgh, age 23, disc. at Vera Cruz 22 Apr 47.

YOUNG, OTIS: Pvt., enl. 26 Nov 46 at Pittsburgh, age 25, disc. at Vera Cruz 6 Apr 47 for disease of Scrofula.

YOUNG, ROBERT BRUCE: 4th Sgt., enl. 26 Nov 46 at Pittsburgh, age 25, disc. at Vera Cruz 6 Apr 47 for consumption.

YOUNG, STEPHEN B.: Pvt., enl. 26 Nov 46 at Pittsburgh, age 33, on detached duty at Vera Cruz according to Mar-Apr 47 MR, disc. at Vera Cruz 24 Apr 47.

Company B, 1st Regiment
Washington Artillery

A new uniformed militia company, the Independent Blues, was formed in 1840 and not long afterward renamed the Pottsville Blues. In 1842 the name changed again to the Washington Artillery.

Captain James Nagle and the company offered their services to President Polk as part of the 1st Schuylkill County Volunteer Regiment, under Colonel Francis M. Wynkoop, immediately after the 13 May declaration of war became known. They were accepted instead, on 30 November 1846, to be a part of the 1st Regiment from Pennsylvania.

Departing from Pottsville on a snowy 5 December, the Artillerists rendezvoused in Pittsburgh and were mustered into federal service on 15 December by First Lieutenant Horace B. Field of the 3rd U.S. Artillery.

The artillerists participated in the siege of Vera Cruz, the battles of Cerro Gordo, La Hoya and Huamantla, and performed garrison duty at Perote and finally near Mexico City.

Returning home, the company arrived in Philadelphia on 24 July 1848 and was mustered out there on 27 July by Captain George Taylor of the 3rd U.S. Artillery. The men returned to Pottsville on 5 August for a round of celebrations they would never forget.

A total of 99 men served in the company during the war. Of these, three were recruits who joined the company in Mexico. Thirteen men deserted. One battle casualty was suffered, the soldier being killed. This was one of the seventeen deaths endured by the Artillery. A total of seventeen men also received discharges before their term of service was ended.

Daniel Nagle shown here as Colonel of
the 173rd Pennsylvania in the Civil War
Roger D. Hunt Collection

James Nagle pictured as a Civil War
Brigadier General
USAMHI

BARR, BERNARD: Pvt., enl. 1 Dec 46 at Pottsville, age 33, occ. tailor, promoted to 3rd Cpl. 10 Jan 47, sick on duty according to May-Jun 47 MR, disc. at Perote 30 Oct 47 on SCD.

BERGER, NELSON: Pvt., enl. 1 Dec 46 at Pottsville, age 24, occ. carpenter, left sick at New Orleans 16 Jan 47, rejoined Co. shortly, listed as sick on Jul-Aug 47 MR, mo. with Co. 27 Jul 48.

BOLAND, WILLIAM C.: Pvt., enl. 10 Dec 46 at Lewistown, age 22, occ. boatman, deserted at Louisville, Ky. 24 Dec 46.

BOYER, AUGUSTUS H.: Pvt., enl. 1 Dec 46 at Pottsville, age 21, occ. tailor, promoted to Cpl. 19 May 47, promoted to Sgt. 24 Dec 47, mo. with Co. 27 Jul 48.

BRIGHT, LEVI: Pvt., enl. 1 Dec 46 at Pottsville, age 30, left back near La Hoya 24 Aug 47 while on a march from Perote to Jalapa, supposed to have been killed according to Jan-Feb 48 MR.

BRUMM, CHARLES: (Brunn): Pvt., enl. 1 Dec 46 at Pottsville, age 23, occ. stage driver, deserted at New Orleans 4 Jan 47. 1st Lt. Co. K & Q.M., 76th P.V.I. 18 Nov 61 to 17 Oct 64. Died at Minersville, Pa. 11 Jan 17.

COCHRAN, JAMES: (Cochrane): Pvt., enl. 1 Dec 46 at Pottsville, age 22, occ. teamster, fined $3.00 by Court Martial according to Jul-Aug 47 MR, fined $7.00 by Court Martial 2 Sep 47, listed as sick on Sep-Dec 47 MR, mo. with Co. 27 Jul 48.

DOUTY, JOHN: Pvt., enl. & mi. 9 Aug 47 at Pottsville by Lt. Kaercher, age 20, joined Co. 21 Dec 47, killed by Mexicans near San Angel 6 Jan 48.

DOUTY, PETER: Pvt., enl. 1 Dec 46 at Pottsville, age 22, occ. blacksmith, promoted to Cpl. 19 May 47, promoted to Sgt. 3 Jul 47, sick in hospital at San Angel according to Mar-Apr 48 MR, mo. with Co. 27 Jul 48.

DOYLE, JOHN: Pvt., enl. 1 Dec 46 at Pottsville, age 29, occ. clerk, sick in hospital at Jalapa from 30 Apr 47, rejoined Co. by 30 Jun 47, KIA at Puebla 12 Oct 47.

DUNEGAN, PHILIP: Fifer, enl. & mi. 30 Apr 48 at San Angel, Mexico by Capt. Nagle, age 15, mo. with Co. 27 Jul 48.

EPLER, LEVI: Pvt., enl. 1 Dec 46 at Pottsville, age 28, occ. chair maker, mo. with Co. 27 Jul 48. 1st Lt. & Capt. Co. B, 6th Pa. Res. 6 May 61 to 11 Jun 64, WIA at the Wilderness, Bvt. Major.

FARNUM, J. EGBERT (Egbert J.): 2nd Cpl., enl. 1 Dec 46 at Pottsville, age 22, occ. clerk, appointed Sgt. Major 19 Dec 46, detached for recruiting duty from Jun 47, arrived in Pottsville 14 Jul 47, returned to Regt. probably 21 Dec 47, mo. with F & S, 8 Aug 48. Maj., Lt. Col. & Col. of 70th N.Y. Vol. Inf., 29 Jun 61 to 1 Jul 64. Col. of Veteran Reserve Corps 26 Jul 64 to 30 Jun 66. Bvt. Brig. Gen. of Vols. 3 Jan 66. Died in New York City 16 May 70.

FELLNAGLE, JACOB: (Feltnagle): 2nd Lt., enl. 1 Dec 46 at Pottsville, age 21, listed as sick at Jalapa on Mar-Apr 47 MR, disc. at Jalapa 31 May 47 by Gen. Scott, arrived in Pottsville 25 Jun 47.

FISHER, HENRY: Pvt., enl. 1 Dec 46 at Pottsville, age 21, occ. blacksmith, mo. with Co. 27 Jul 48.

FRAZER, MALCOLM A.: Pvt., enl. 10 Jan 47 at New Orleans, age 25, mi. on ship "Oxnard" 28 Feb 47, deserted at Vera Cruz 8 Apr 47.

GARRETT, GEORGE W.: (Garett): Pvt., enl. 1 Dec 46 at Pottsville, age 24, occ. clerk, promoted to 3rd Cpl. 15 Apr 48, mo. with Co. 27 Jul 48. 1st Sgt. & 2nd Lt. Co. H, 16th Pa. Cav. 27 Sep 62 to 12 Jan 64.

GILLMAN, JOHN C.: (Gilman): Pvt., enl. 1 Dec 46 at Pottsville, age 34, occ. mason, listed as sick on 31 Aug 47 to 31 Dec 47 MR, listed as sick in hospitals at Mexico City and San Angel on Jan-Feb & Mar-Apr 48 MRs, mo. with Co. 27 Jul 48.

GILPIN, THOMAS W.: Pvt., enl. 12 Dec 46 at Pittsburgh, age 21, occ. boatman, fined $3.00 by Court Martial according to Jul-Aug 47 MR, mo. with Co. 27 Jul 48.

GRAEFF, HENRY: Pvt., enl. 1 Dec 46 at Pottsville, age 25, occ. tinsmith, sick in hospital at Jalapa from 30 Apr 47, died at Jalapa 3 May 47 of disease.

GUTHREY, THOMAS W.: (Guthrie, Guthry): Pvt., enl. 1 Dec 46 at Pottsville, age 21, occ. stage driver, left sick in hospital at Vera Cruz 9 Apr 47, disc. at Vera Cruz 22 Apr 47 on SCD.

HAAS, PETER: Pvt., enl. 10 Dec 46 at Lewistown, age 26, occ. saddler, died of disease 11 Jul 48 near Cincinnati, Ohio on the way home.

HAND, JOHN: Pvt., enl. 1 Dec 46 at Pottsville, age 18, occ. shipwright, fined $6.00 by Court Martial according to Jul-Aug 47 MR, deserted from San Angel 15 Apr 48.

HATCHLEY, WILLIAM H.: Pvt., enl. 1 Dec 46 at Pottsville age 25, occ. tobacconist, fined $3.00 by Court Martial according to Jul-Aug 47 MR, in confinement according to 31 Aug-31 Dec 47 MR, fined $7.00 by Court Martial according to Jan-Feb 48 MR, deserted at San Angel 17 Apr 48.

HAYS, JOHN: Pvt., enl. 1 Dec 46 at Pottsville, age 22, occ. teamster, fined $3.00 by Court Martial according to Jul-Aug 47 MR, mo. with Co. 27 Jul 48.

HESSER, GEORGE W.: Pvt., enl. 10 Dec 46 at Waynesburgh, age 27, occ. boatman, mo. with Co. 27 Jul 48.

HINES, WILLIAM: Pvt., enl. 10 Dec 46 at Pittsburgh, age 20, this name appears only on the muster-in roll.

HINEY, ELIAS F.: Pvt., enl. 1 Dec 46 at Pottsville, age 26, occ. printer, promoted to Cpl. 7 Feb 48, mo. with Co. 27 Jul 48.

JENKINS, JOSHUA: Pvt., enl. 15 Dec. 46 at Pittsburgh, age 24, fined $3.00 by Court Martial according to Jul-Aug 47 MR, listed as sick on Jan-Feb 48 MR, listed as sick in hospital at San Angel on Mar-Apr 48 MR, mo. with Co. 27 Jul 48.

JENNING(S), JOSHUA (JOHN): Pvt., enl. 1 Dec 46 at Pottsville, age 24, occ. blacksmith, deserted at New Orleans 12 Jan 47.

JONES, DAVID: Pvt., enl. 1 Dec 46 at Pottsville, age 22, left sick at Vera Cruz 9 Apr 47, disc. at Vera Cruz 22 Apr 47 on SCD.

KAERCHER, EDWARD: (Kaerker): 2nd Sgt., enl. 1 Dec 46 at Pottsville, age 21, occ. machinist, listed sick on Mar-Apr 47 MR, disc. at Jalapa 15 May 47 on SCD.

KAERCHER, FRANKLIN B.: (Carrigers, Kaerker): 2nd Lt., enl. at Pottsville in Dec (probably 1st) 46, age 25, Acting Asst. Commissary of Subsistence of detachment on ship "Oxnard" from 15 Jan 47 to 16 Mar 47, left for recruiting duty 6 Jun 47, arrived in Pottsville 15 Jul 47, rejoined Co. 15 Apr 48, mo. with Co. 27 Jul 48.

KELLY, ELIAS: Pvt., enl. 1 Dec 46 at Pottsville, age 26, occ. watchman, left sick at Vera Cruz 9 Apr 47, disc. at Vera Cruz 22 Apr 47 on SCD.

KEPPLY, JOHN: (Kepley, Keppley): Pvt., enl. 1 Dec 46 at Pottsville, age 28, occ. blacksmith, on extra duty as blacksmith according to Jul-Aug 47 MR, on extra duty at Perote from 29 Nov 47, he became ill there and was sick through Apr 48, mo. with Co. 27 Jul 48.

KIMMEL, SINGLETON: Pvt., enl. 1 Dec 46 at Pottsville, age 22, occ. boatman, mo. with Co. 27 Jul 48.

KNOCKENHOUSE, WILLIAM: Pvt., enl. 1 Dec 46 at Pottsville, age 22, occ. laborer, listed as sick in the hospital at San Angel on Mar-Apr 48 MR, mo. with Co. 27 Jul 48.

LLEWELLEN, DAVID: (Lewellen): Cpl., enl. 1 Dec 46 at Pottsville, age 22, occ. miner, deserted at New Orleans 5 Jan 47.

LUSHT, MICHAEL: Pvt., enl. 1 Dec 46 at Pottsville, age 37, died at Vera Cruz 17 Mar 47 of disease.

LYONS, WILLIAM: Pvt., enl. 1 Dec 46 at Pottsville, age 24, listed as sick on Jul-Aug 47 MR, disc. at Perote 31 Oct 47 on SCD.

MACY, ABLE B.: Pvt., enl. 1 Dec 46 at Pottsville, age 28, fined $2.00 by Court Martial according to Jul-Aug 47 MR, listed as sick on Jan-Feb 48 MR, mo. with Co. 27 Jul 48.

MAMERENK, FREDERICK (Ferdinand): (Mamarenk, Mammarank): Pvt., enl. 1 Dec 46 at Pottsville, age 20, fined $1.00 by Court Martial and reported sick according to Jul-Aug 47 MR, in guardhouse at San Angel from 27 Apr 48, mo. with Co. 27 Jul 48.

MARKLE, WILLIAM: (Merkle): Pvt., enl. 1 Dec 46 at Pottsville, age 25, fined $1.00 by Court Martial 28 Sep 47, missing from San Angel from 3 Jan 48, found murdered by Mexicans near San Angel 13 Feb 48.

MASSON, EDWARD W.: Pvt., enl. 1 Dec 46 at Pottsville, age 23, occ. watchmaker, promoted to Cpl. 18 Dec 46, reduced to Pvt. 18 May 47, on extra duty as Col. Wynkoop's orderly from 21 Nov 47, mo. with Co. 27 Jul 48.

McCORMICK, JOHN: Pvt., enl. 15 Dec 46 at Pittsburgh, age 19, deserted at New Orleans 1 Jan 47.

McDONALD, ALEXANDER: Pvt., enl. 1 Dec 46 at Pottsville, age 22, listed as sick on May-Jun 47 MR, promoted to Cpl. 3 Jul 47, promoted to Sgt. 7 Feb 48, mo. with Co. 27 Jul 48.

McELROY, PATRICK H.: Pvt., enl. 15 Dec 46 at Pittsburgh, age 23, deserted at New Orleans 5 Jan 47.

McGEEN, FRANCIS C.: Pvt., enl. 1 Dec 46 at Pottsville, age 29, promoted to Cpl. 25 Dec 47, in guardhouse at San Angel according to Jan-Feb 48 MR, reduced to Pvt. 8 Mar 48 by Court Martial & to forfeit one month's Cpl's pay.

McLAUGHLIN, SAMUEL: (McGlauchlin): Pvt., enl. 1 Dec 46 at Pottsville, age 35, disc. at Verra Cruz 2 Apr 47 on SCD.

McMICKEN, ISAAC SMITH: Sgt., enl. 1 Dec 46 at Pottsville, age 24, occ. lawyer, remained at Vera Cruz from 8 Apr 47 on three months furlough, appointed Postmaster in Mexico City 1 Nov 47, reduced to Pvt. 25 Dec 47, mo. with Co. 27 Jul 48.

METZ, JOEL: Pvt., enl. & mi. 20 Sep 47 at Pottsville by Lt. Kaercher, age 30, joined Co. 21 Dec 47, mo. with Co. 27 Jul 48. Sgt., Co. E, 6th Pa. Res. 27 May 61 to 11 Jun 64, WIA at Gettysburg.

MILLS, VALENTINE K.: (Miles): Pvt., enl. 1 Dec 46 at Pottsville, age 30, listed as sick on May-Jun 47 MR, died at Perote 4 Aug 47 from disease.

MONTGOMERY, SAMUEL: (Montgeomery): Pvt., enl. 10 Dec 46 at Waynesburgh, age 22, listed as sick on May-Jun 47 MR, died at Perote 26 Aug 47 from disease.

MOONEY, JOHN: Pvt., enl. 1 Dec 46 at Pottsville, age 21, left sick at Pittsburgh 21 Dec 46, later deserted from Pittsburgh.

MYERS, JOHN: Pvt., enl. 1 Dec 46 at Pottsville, age 28, on extra duty as Col. Wynkoop's orderly from 21 Nov 47, listed as sick on Jan-Feb 48 MR, mo. with Co. 27 Jul 48.

NAGLE, BENJAMIN: Pvt., enl. 1 Dec 46 at Pottsville, age 26, fined $2.00 by Court Martial 2 Sep 47, hospitalized from Dec 47, died at San Angel 15 Feb 48 from disease.

NAGLE, DANIEL: Drummer, enl. 1 Dec 46 at Pottsville, age 18, occ. painter, disc. at Perote 31 Oct 47 for disability upon his own request, arrived in Pottsville 30 Nov 47. Capt. Co. D, 6th P.V.I. (3 mos.), 22 Apr 61 to 27 Jul 61. Capt. Co. D & Maj., 48th P.V.I. 23 Sep 61 to 26 Jul 62. Lt. Col. 19th Pa. Emergency Militia 15 Sep 62 to 27 Sep 62. Col. 173rd Pa. Drafted Militia 18 Nov 62 to 17 Aug 63. Died 11 Jan 18.

NAGLE, JAMES: Capt., enl. in Pottsville in Dec (probably 1st) 46, age 24, mo. with Co. 27 Jul 48. Col. 6th P.V.I. (3 mos.) 22 Apr 61 to 27 Jul 61. Col. 48th P.V.I. 1 Oct 61 to 10 Sep 62. Brig. Gen. 10 Sep 62 to 9 May 63. Col. 39th Pa. Emergency Militia 1 Jul 63 to 2 Aug 63. Col. 194th P.V.I. 24 Jul 64 to 6 Nov 64. Died 22 Aug 66.

NAGLE, SIMON S.: 1st Lt., enl. in Pottsville in Dec (probably 1st) 46, age 25, mo. with Co. 27 Jul 48.

NAGLE, WILLIAM S. (F.): Sgt., enl. 1 Dec 46 at Pottsville, age 21, occ. tinsmith, appointed Drummer 7 Feb 48, mo. with Co. 27 Jul 48.

NOLAN, JOHN M.: Pvt., enl. 1 Dec 46 at Pottsville, age 24, listed as sick on Mar-Apr 47 & May-Jun 47 MRs, on extra duty superintending police garrison according to Jul-Aug 47 MR, disc. at Perote 30 Oct 47 on SCD.

PRICE, SETH: Pvt., enl. 1 Dec 46 at Pottsville, age 26, fined $3.00 by Court Martial according to Jul-Aug 47 MR, fined $5.00 by Court Martial 2 Sep 47, listed as sick on 31 Aug-31 Dec 47 MR, listed as sick in hospital at San Angel on Mar-Apr 48 MR, mo. with Co. 27 Jul 48.

PRICHARD, ANDREW: Pvt., enl. 16 Dec 46 at Connellsville, age 22, mi. 4 Jan 47, died at Perote in 1847.

QUITDINGTON, THOMAS: (Quiddington, Quittington): Pvt., enl. 15 Dec 46 at Pittsburgh, age 41, mo. with Co. 27 Jul 48.

REHR, EDWARD: 1st Sgt., enl. 1 Dec 46 at Pottsville, age 32, occ. currier, listed as sick on 15 Dec 46 - 28 Feb 47 MR, elected 2nd Lt. 29 May 47, listed as sick on 31 Aug - 31 Dec 47 MR, mo. with Co. 27 Jul 48.

RICHARDS, HENRY: Pvt., enl. 1 Dec 46 at Pottsville, age 22, fined $17.00 by Court Martial ($12.00 of which went to Pvt. Henry Fisher of Co. B as restitution) according to Jul-Aug 47 MR, on extra duty as hospital attendant according to Jan-Feb 48 MR, died of disease near Wheeling, Ohio 4 Jul 48 on his way home.

ROBBINS, EDWARD: Pvt., enl. 1 Dec 46 at Pottsville, age 21, listed as sick in hospital at San Angel on Mar-Apr 48 MR, mo. with Co. 27 Jul 48.

ROSS, JAMES H. (W.): Pvt., enl. 10 Dec 46 at Waynesburgh, age 20, listed as sick on 31 Aug - 31 Dec 47 MR, listed as sick in San Angel Hospital on Mar-Apr 48 MR, mo. with Co. 27 Jul 48.

RUCKLE, JAMES: Pvt., enl. 1 Dec. 46 at Pottsville, age 23, deserted at New Orleans 29 Dec 46.

SANDS, JAMES: (Sand): Pvt., enl. 1 Dec 46 at Pottsville, age 25, deserted at New Orleans 14 Jan 47, arrested 24 Jul 47, held at Ft. Mifflin, shipped with recruits, rejoined Co. 21 Dec 47, listed on Jan-Feb 48 MR as being in confinement, mo. with Co. 27 Jul 48.

SANDS, MICHAEL: (Sand): Pvt., enl. 1 Dec 46 at Pottsville, age 22, deserted at New Orleans 15 Jan 47, arrested 24 Jul 47 & held at Ft. Mifflin, shipped with recruits, rejoined Co. 21 Dec 47, listed as in confinement on Jan-Feb 48 MR, mo. with Co. 27 Jul 48.

SAVAGE, ROBERT H.: Pvt., enl. 1 Dec 46 at Pottsville, age 28, deserted at New Orleans 12 Jan 47.

SCRIMSHAW, CHARLES: (Schrimshaw): Pvt., enl. 1 Dec 46 at Pottsville, age 23, listed as sick on Jan-Feb 48 MR, mo. with Co. 27 Jul 48.

SEAGRAVES, CHARLES: (Seagreaves): Pvt., enl. 5 Dec 46 at Reading, age 22, disc. at Vera Cruz 2 Apr 47 on SCD, admitted to a hospital in Cincinnati, Ohio 2 May 47, died there 3 May 47 of diarrhea.

SEITZINGER, FRANKLIN: Pvt., enl. 1 Dec 46 at Pottsville, age 20, listed as sick on Jan-Feb 48 MR, sick at San Angel Hospital according to Mar-Apr 48 MR, mo. with Co. 27 Jul 48.

SEITZINGER, GEORGE R. (K.): Pvt., enl. 1 Dec 46 at Pottsville, age 27, listed as sick on May-Jun & Jul-Aug 47 MRs, disc. at Perote 30 Oct 47 on SCD, died at Pittsburgh 27 Dec 47.

SEITZINGER, WILLIAM: Pvt., enl. 1 Dec 46 at Pottsville, age 40, listed as sick on Mar-Apr 47 MR, fined $3.00 & $1.00 by Courts Martial according to Jul-Aug 47 MR, on extra duty at Perote from 29 Nov 47, listed as sick at Perote on Mar-Apr 48 MR, disc. at Perote 15 Apr 48 on SCD.

SHADMAN, SAMUEL: Pvt., enl. 1 Dec 46 at Pottsville, age 22, promoted to 1st Cpl. 19 May 47, left for recruiting duty 6 Jun 47, arrived in Pottsville 12 Jul 47, reported at Ft. McHenry, Md. 20 Jan 48, returned to Co. 15 Apr 48, mo. with Co. 27 Jul 48. Pvt. Co. E, 131st P.V.I. 16 Aug 62 to 23 May 63.

SHAPPELL, DANIEL: Pvt., enl. 1 Dec 46 at Pottsville, age 36, left sick at Perote 29 Nov 47, rejoined Co. after 30 Apr 48, mo. with Co. 27 Jul 48.

SHELL, BENJAMIN: Pvt., enl. 1 Dec 46 at Pottsville, age 20, fined $7.00 by Court Martial 2 Sep 47, mo. with Co. 27 Jul 48.

SHELLY, ELI: Pvt., enl. 1 Dec 46 at Pottsville, age 26, listed as sick on May-Jun 47 MR, died at Perote 29 Jun 47 from disease.

SHELLY, EMANUEL: (Shelley): Pvt., enl. 1 Dec 46 at Pottsville, age 26, fined $3.00 & $7.00 by Courts Martial according to Jul-Aug 47 MR, listed as AWOL on 31 Aug - 31 Dec 47 MR, confined to guardhouse in San Angel from 28 Mar 48, mo. with Co. 27 Jul 48. Drowned in Schuylkill River near Landingville, buried at Pottsville 7 Aug 48, leaving a wife & children.

SHOESTER, JOHN (Shuster): Pvt., enl. 1 Dec 46 at Pottsville, age 22, disc. at Perote 6 Jun 47 on SCD, died in a hospital at Cincinnati, Ohio on his way home, from consumption.

SHOUP, JACOB W.: Pvt., enl. 1 Dec 46 at Pottsville, age 22, fined $1.00 by Court Martial according to Jul-Aug 47 MR, listed as sick on Jan-Feb 48 MR, listed as sick at San Angel Hospital on Mar-Apr 48 MR, mo. with Co. 27 Jul 48.

SIMPSON, THOMAS: Pvt., enl. 1 Dec 46 at Pottsville, age 18, on extra duty as orderly for commanding officer according to Jul-Aug 47 MR, deserted at San Angel 25 Apr 48.

SMINK, HENRY: Pvt., enl. 1 Dec 46 at Pottsville, age 27, mo. with Co. 27 Jul 48.

SMITH, BENJAMIN: Pvt., enl. 1 Dec 46 at Pottsville, age 20, died at Perote 29 Jun 47 from disease.

STACKPOLE, WILLIAM H.: Pvt., enl. 10 Dec 46 at Waynesburgh, age 21, promoted to Cpl. 10 Jan 47, promoted to Sgt. 19 May 47, promoted to 1st Sgt. 1 Jun 47, mo. with Co. 27 Jul 48.

STAMM, ANDREW N. (M.): Pvt., enl. 1 Dec 46 at Pottsville, age 20, listed as sick on Jul-Aug 47 MR, disc. at Perote 30 Oct 47 on SCD.

STAMM, REUBEN: (Stamum, Staumm): Fifer, en. 1 Dec 46 at Pottsville, age 23, occ. cabinet maker, appointed Fife Major by Col. Wynkoop 30 Jun 47, mo. with F & S, 8 Aug 48.

STEGNER, JOHN (Steigner): Pvt., enl. 1 Dec 46 at Pottsville, age 29, disc. at Perote 31 Oct 47 on SCD.

THOMAS, OWEN D.: Pvt., enl. 1 Dec 46 at Pottsville, age 29, disc. at Perote 5 Jun 47 on SCD, died at Perote 11 Jun 47.

WALTER, ROBERT F.: Pvt., enl. 1 Dec 46 at Pottsville, age 26, listed as sick on Jul-Aug 47 MR, promoted to Cpl. 1 Dec 47, died on the way home near Cincinnati, Ohio of disease 10 Jul 48.

WEISHUE, GOTLEIB (Gotlieb): (Weisshue, Wisshue): Pvt., enl. 1 Dec 46 at Pottsville, age 22, left sick at Perote 29 Nov 47, rejoined Co. by 30 Apr 48, mo. with Co. 27 Jul 48.

WELSH, ROBERT: Pvt., enl. 1 Dec 46 at Pottsville, age 22, listed as sick on May-Jun 47 MR, died at Perote 7 Jul 47 of disease.

WHITCOMB, WILLIAM: Pvt., enl. 1 Dec 46 at Pottsville, age 25, on extra duty at Perote from 29 Nov 47, returned to Co. by 30 Apr 48, died of disease on the way home near Cincinnati, Ohio 10 Jul 48.

WOLFINGER, WILLIAM: Pvt., enl. 1 Dec 46 at Pottsville, age 22, mo. with Co. 27 Jul 48.

WYNKOOP, FRANCIS M.: Pvt., enl. 1 Dec 46 at Pottsville, age 28, elected Col. 18 Dec 46, commanding Volunteer Brigade from 15 Feb 48 through at least 30 Apr 48, mo. with F & S, 8 Aug 48. Died 13 Dec 57 at Pottsville, buried in Charles Baber Cemetery in Pottsville.

ZENTMEYER, ENOS: (Zantmeyer): 1st Cpl., enl. 1 Dec 46 at Pottsville, age 25, occ. plasterer, left sick at Vera Cruz 9 Apr 47, disc. at Vera Cruz 22 Apr 47 on SCD.

Company C, 1st Regiment
Monroe Guards

The Monroe Guards, of Philadelphia, was an old uniformed militia company, having served under Captain William F. Small during the riots of 1844.

The men responded quickly to the government's call for volunteers in May 1846, and in November they were notified of acceptance into the state's 1st Regiment. They departed Philadelphia on 9 December and were mustered into federal service at Pittsburgh on 17 December by First Lieutenant Horace B. Field of the 3rd U.S. Artillery.

During the active campaigning which followed, the Monroe Guards participated in the siege of Vera Cruz, the battles of Cerro Gordo and La Hoya and the defense of Puebla. They arrived in Mexico City on 8 December 1847 to assist in occupying the captured capitol.

The Guards returned at about 7:00 A.M. on 24 July 1848 with the other Philadelphia companies of the 1st Regiment. They were mustered out on 29 July by Captain George Taylor of the 3rd U.S. Artillery.

A total of 97 men served in the company during the war. Of these, three were recruits who joined it in Mexico. Eight men deserted, and two were transferred to other units. Five men became battle casualties, with three of them dying, thus bringing to fifteen the number of deaths. An additional twenty-one received discharges before muster out.

115

ACKERMAN, DAVID: Sgt., enl. 18 Nov 46 at Phila., age 33, transferred as Pvt. to Co. F, 1st Pa. Regt. at Perote 11 or 12 Jun 47.

AHL, PETER, JR.: Pvt., enl. 18 Nov 46 at Phila., age 23, granted 30 days furlough from 7 Jan 47 for "urgent private duty," promoted to Cpl. 1 Jun 47, promoted to Sgt. 25 Oct 47, mo. with Co. 29 Jul 48.

AMEY, OTIS: Pvt., enl. 18 Nov 46 at Phila., age 33, deserted at New Orleans 6 Jan 47, apprehended in Phila. 8 May 48, disc. by order of the Adjutant General 24 Jun 48.

BARNES, WILLIAM: Pvt., enl. 18 Nov 46 at Phila., age 19, deserted at Pittsburgh either 19 or 21 Dec 46.

BARR, JOHN: Pvt., enl. 18 Nov 46 at Phila., age 35, disc. at Vera Cruz 5 Apr 47 on SCD for dropsy.

BARTLING, EDWARD: Pvt., enl. & mi. 24 Jul 47 at Phila. by Capt. Scott, mo. with Co. 29 Jul 48.

BEGLEY, JOHN: Pvt., enl. 18 Nov 46 at Phila., age 32, listed a sick on Mar-Apr 47 MR, listed as sick at Perote on May-Jun 47 MR, died at Perote 28 Aug 47 of diarrhea.

BENTLY, MOSES: Pvt., enl. 18 Nov 46 at Phila., age 25, disc. at Vera Cruz 5 Apr 47 on SCD.

BERRY, CASPER M.: 2nd Lt., enl. 18 Nov 46 at Phila., age 24, suffered sunstroke during siege of Vera Cruz, resigned at Vera Cruz 8 Apr 47, disc. at Vera Cruz 9 Apr 47. Major 26th P.V.I. 1 Jun 61 to 7 Jul 62. Lt. Col. 60th Pa. Emergency Militia 19 Jun 63 to 8 Sep 63. Born 8 Apr 22, died 16 Jun 66 at Phila.

BETSON, OSCAR F.: 1st Sgt., enl. 18 Nov 46 at Phila., age 35, disc. at Perote 16 Jun 47 on SCD for diarrhea. Capt. Co. K, 68th P.V.I. 3 Sep 62 to 2 Dec 62.

BONER, JOHN: Pvt., enl. 18 Nov 46 at Phila., age 22, listed as sick in hospital at Jalapa on Mar-Apr 47 MR, listed as sick in hospital at Perote on May-Jun 47 MR, mo. with Co. 29 Jul 48.

BRIGGS, WILLIAM H.: Pvt., enl. 18 Nov 46 at Phila., age 22, died at Puebla 30 Aug 47 of diarrhea, his body was removed to Phila. where it was buried 26 Jul 48.

BROWN, ROBERT C.: Pvt., enl. 18 Nov 46 at Phila., age 23, disc. at Perote 7 Jun 47 on SCD for diarrhea.

BRUSTER, THOMAS: (Brustar): Pvt., enl. 18 Nov 46 at Phila., age 35, promoted to Sgt. 1 Jun 47, died suddenly in quarters at Perote 2 Jun 47 from fever.

BUDDY, EDWARD: Pvt., enl. 18 Nov 46 at Phila., age 22, listed as sick on Mar-Apr 47 MR, died at Puebla 7 Aug 47.

BURNS, WILLIAM: (Burnes): Pvt., enl. 10 Dec 46 at Clarks Ferry, age 26, deserted at Vera Cruz 9 Apr 47.

BYMASTER, LEWIS: Pvt., enl. 10 Dec 46 at Clarks Ferry, age 21, mo. with Co. 29 Jul 48.

CAMPBELL, JOSEPH: Pvt., enl. 18 Nov 46 at Phila., age 21, promoted to Cpl. 12 Jun 47, mo. with Co. 29 Jul 48.

CANNON, FRANCIS: Pvt., enl. 18 Nov 46 at Phila., age 20, mo. with Co. 29 Jul 48.

CAREY, GEORGE: Pvt., enl. 18 Nov 46 at Phila., age 19, promoted to Drummer 1 Jan 47, listed on all subsequent MRs as Pvt., mo. with Co. 29 Jul 48.

COLLISON, CHARLES: Pvt., enl. 18 Nov 46 at Phila., age 24, wounded at Puebla 27 Sep 47, and again on 28 Sep 47 in the foot while on picket duty, mo. with Co. 29 Jul 48.

CORNISH, HENRY: (Cornnish): Pvt., enl. 18 Nov 46 at Phila., age 39, promoted to Cpl. 1 Jun 47, promoted to Sgt. 12 Jun 47, acting 1st Sgt. from 12 Jun 47, promoted to 1st Sgt. 1 Jul 47, reduced to Pvt. 13 Oct 47, mo. with Co. 29 Jul 48.

CORSON, JEREMIAH: Pvt., enl. 18 Nov 46 at Phila., age 32, mo. with Co. 29 Jul 48, died after disc. in Jul 48.

CRAIG, JOHN C.: Pvt., enl. 3 Dec 46 at Phila., age 22, mo. with Co. 29 Jul 48.

CRAVER, DANIEL: (Craven): Pvt., enl. 25 Nov 46 at Phila., age 28, listed as sick on Mar-Apr 47 MR, disc. at Perote 7 Jun 47 on SCD for diarrhea.

CRUTHERS, DANIEL: Pvt., enl. 12 Dec 46 at Clarks Ferry, age 26, listed as sick in hospital at Jalapa on Mar-Apr 47 MR, mo. with Co. 29 Jul 48.

CUSKADEN, JAMES: (Cascaden): Pvt., enl. 27 Dec 47 at Pottsville, age 21, mi. 10 Jan 48 at Ft. Mifflin by Capt. Taylor, joined Co. 19 Apr 48, mo. with Co. 29 Jul 48.

DANNER, JACOB: Pvt., enl. 25 Nov 46 at Phila., age 26, listed as sick in hospital at Jalapa on Mar-Apr 47 MR, hospitalized at Puebla 15 Jul 47, died at Puebla 10 Sep 47 from diarrhea, his body was returned to Little York for burial when the Regt. came home.

DEVLIN, ALEXANDER: Pvt., enl. 25 Nov 46 at Phila., age 24, listed as AWOL on May-Jun 47 MR, confined in guardhouse according to Jan-Feb 48 MR, mo. with Co. 29 Jul 48.

DONAGAN, WILLIAM: (Donegan): Pvt., enl. 25 Nov 46 at Phila., age 26, listed as under arrest and sick on 17 Dec 46 - 28 Feb 47 MR, confined in Perote Castle and forfeited one months pay by Regimental Court Martial 2 May 47, mo. with Co. 29 Jul 48.

DROPSIE, GABRIEL A.: Pvt., enl. 25 Nov 46 at Phila., age 21. mo. with Co. 29 Jul 48.

EURICH, WILLIAM: (Eurick): Pvt., enl. 25 Nov 46 at Phila., age 35, promoted to Cpl. 23 Mar 47, KIA at Puebla 28 Sep 47, his body was returned to Little York for burial when the Regt. came home.

FENEMORE, WILLIAM A.: (Fennemore): Pvt., enl. 25 Nov 46 at Phila., age 35, listed as under arrest on 17 Dec 46 - 28 Feb 47 MR, mo. with Co. 29 Jul 48.

FORD, WILLIAM G.: Pvt., enl. 7 Dec 46 at Phila., age 22, deserted at New Orleans 6 Jan 47.

FOUST, JOSEPH: Cpl., enl. 18 Nov 46 at Phila., age 21, promoted to Sgt. 1 Jun 47, had his nose nearly bitten off by another soldier in Co. C, 1st Pa. Regt. in Feb 48, mo. with Co. 29 Jul 48.

FUNSTON, JOSEPH W.: Pvt., enl. 7 Dec 46 at Phila., age 19, listed as sick in hospital at Perote on May-Jun 47 MR, left sick at Perote 3 Jul 47, wounded in the head with a sword by Capt. Small 27 Oct 47, disc. at Perote 9 Apr 48 on SCD for wound.

GAMBLE, ROBERT: Pvt., enl. 24 Dec 47 at Pottsville, age 26, mi. at Ft. Mifflin 10 Jan 48 by Capt. Taylor, reported at Ft. McHenry, Md. 20 Jan 48, joined Co. 19 Apr 48, mo. with Co. 29 Jul 48.

GILL, JOHN J.: Pvt., enl. 25 Nov 46 at Phila., age 26, deserted at New Orleans 16 Jan 47.

GOLCHER, WILLIAM: Pvt., enl. 25 Nov 46 at Phila., age 19, appointed Fifer 1 Jan 47, listed on all subsequent MRs as Pvt., deserted at Perote 7 Jun 47.

GOSSETT, STEPHEN: Pvt., enl. 25 Nov 46 at Phila., age 22, left sick in hospital at Vera Cruz 9 Apr 47, disc. at Vera Cruz 11 May 47 on SCD for fever.

HAIG, GEORGE H.: Pvt., enl. 25 Nov 46 at Phila., age 19, listed as under arrest on 17 Dec 46 - 28 Feb 47 MR, mo. with Co. 29 Jul 48.

HAINES, AQUILLA: 1st Lt., enl. at Phila., age 28, mo. with Co. 29 Jul 48. Capt. of Capt. Haines' Independent Infantry Co., Pa. Emergency Militia 11 Sep 62 to 22 Sep 62.

HALL, JOSEPH M.: Sgt., enl. 18 Nov 46 at Phila., age 30, elected 2nd Lt. 31 May 47, it is presumed he was mustered out with the Co. on 29 Jul 48 although that is not stated in his service record.

HAMILTON, DANIEL: Pvt., enl. 25 Nov 46 at Phila., age 21, listed as sick on 17 Dec 46 - 28 Feb 47 MR, left sick at Puebla 3 Dec 47, rejoined Co. by 30 Apr 48, mo. with Co. 29 Jul 48.

HANLEY, HENRY: Pvt., enl. 25 Nov 46 at Phila., age 22, listed as under arrest on 17 Dec 46-28 Feb 47 MR, listed as sick on Mar-Apr & May-Jun 47 MRs, disc. at Perote 7 Jun 47 on SCD for diarrhea.

HERRON, JOHN B.: (Hennon): Pvt., enl. 25 Nov 46 at Phila., age 38, listed as sick in hospital at Jalapa on Mar-Apr 47 MR, WIA in the siege of Puebla 30 Sep 47, died from his wound at Puebla 9 Nov 47.

HILL, CHRISTIAN (Christopher) S. (T.): Pvt., enl. 25 Nov 46 at Phila., age 22, promoted to Cpl. 12 Jun 47, promoted to Sgt. 25 Oct 47, AWOL 22 Dec 47 through at least 31 Dec 47, mo. with Co. 29 Jul 48.

HUNTERSON, HENRY: 2nd Lt., enl. at Phila., age 41, on furlough from 4 Nov 47, ordered to recruiting duty according to Mar-Apr 48 MR, working out of Ft. Mifflin 30 Jun 48, mo. with Co. 29 Jul 48.

HUSTED, WILLIAM DAYTON: (Huston): Pvt., enl. 25 Nov 46 at Phila., age 18, listed as under arrest on 17 Dec 46 - 28 Feb 47 MR, listed as sick on May-Jun 47 MR, died at Puebla 30 Jul 47 from diarrhea.

JOHNSON, JOHN H. (J.): (Johnston): Pvt., enl. 7 Dec 46 at Phila., age 30, transferred to Co. H, 1st Pa. Regt. at Perote 7 Jun 47.

JONES, CHARLES A.: Pvt., enl. 7 Dec 46 at Phila., age 30, ruptured doing heavy work at the siege of Vera Cruz, disc. at Perote 7 Jun 47 on SCD. Q.M. 20th P.V.I. (3 mos.) 30 Apr 61 to 27 Jul 61. Q.M. 68th P.V.I. 1 Sep 62 to 11 Nov 62.

JORDAN, AUGUSTUS: Pvt., enl. 7 Dec 46 at Phila., age 19, mo. with Co. 29 Jul 48.

KELLY, GEORGE B.: (Kelley): Pvt., enl. 25 Nov 46 at Phila., age 28, listed as sick on 17 Dec 46 - 28 Feb 47 MR, disc. at Vera Cruz 5 Apr 47 on SCD for consumption.

KIEM, GEORGE W.: (Keim): Pvt., enl. 25 Nov 46 at Phila., age 24, mo. with Co. 29 Jul 48.

KRITSER, JOHN: (Krisker, Kritzer): Pvt., enl. 25 Nov 46 at Phila., age 26, on detached service in Puebla as printer from 24 Oct 47, on detached service in Mexico City as printer on *The American Star* from 20 Apr 48 by order of Lt. Col. Black, mo. with Co. 29 Jul 48.

LEWIS, GEORGE W.: Pvt., enl. 25 Nov 46 at Phila., age 37, promoted to Cpl. 1 Jul 47, mo. with Co. 29 Jul 48.

LINTON, SAMUEL: Pvt., enl. 25 Nov 46 at Phila., age 22, mo. with Co. 29 Jul 48.

MALONE, ROWLAND (Roland) C.: Pvt., enl. 16 Dec 46 at Milesburgh, age 22, promoted to Cpl. 25 Oct 47, ruptured building breast-works, disc. at San Angel 2 Mar 48 on SCD.

MASON, CHARLES: Pvt., enl. 25 Nov 46 at Phila., age 19, died at Puebla 28 Jul 47 from diarrhea.

McDONALD, WILLIAM: Pvt., enl. 7 Dec 46 at Phila., age 22, listed as sick on 17 Dec 46 - 28 Feb 47 MR, disc. at Vera Cruz 5 Apr 47 on SCD for consumption.

MERWIN, ALEXANDER D.: (Merwine): Drummer,. enl. 18 Nov 46 at Phila., age 18, reduced to Pvt. 31 Dec 46, on detached duty as hospital attendant in Jalapa according to Mar-Apr 47 MR, detached from 17 Jul 48 & absent from mo. having remained in Pittsburgh.

MULLIN, WILLIAM: (Mullen): Pvt., enl. 7 Dec 46 at Phila., age 19, disc. at Perote 11 Dec 47 on SCD for diarrhea.

NEWMAN, JOHN: Pvt., enl. 7 Dec 46 at Phila., age 19, promoted to Cpl. 1 May 48, mo. with Co. 29 Jul 48.

NIGHTLINGER, GEORGE: Fifer, enl. 18 Nov 46 at Phila., age 19, reduced to Pvt. 31 Dec 46, confined to guardhouse according to Jan-Feb 48 MR, mo. with Co. 29 Jul 48.

O'NEIL, THOMAS: Pvt., enl. 18 Nov 46 at Phila., age 21, on detached duty as orderly to Brig. Gen. Pillow according to Mar-Apr 47 MR, mo. with Co. 29 Jul 48.

OSWANDEL, J. JACOB (Jacob J.): (Osawandle): Pvt., enl. 12 Dec 46 at Huntington, age 21, occ. boatman, promoted to 3rd Cpl. 25 Oct 47, left sick at Puebla 4 Dec 47, rejoined Co. 20 Dec 47, mo. with Co. 29 Jul 48.

PATTERSON, ROBERT F.: Pvt., enl. 18 Nov 46 at Phila., age 21, disc. at Perote 7 Jun 47 on SCD for diarrhea.

PATTERSON, WILLIAM: Pvt., enl. 18 Nov 46 at Phila., age 19, mo. with Co. 29 Jul 48.

PATTON, JOHN C.: (Patten): Pvt., enl. 18 Nov 46 at Phila., age 26, listed as sick on 17 Dec 46 - 28 Feb 47 MR, disc. at Perote 7 Jun 47 on SCD for consumption, died shortly thereafter at Jalapa.

PERFECT, JOHN F.: Pvt., enl. 18 Nov 46 at Phila., age 27, AWOL from 22 Dec 47 through at least 30 Apr 48, listed as deserted 30 Apr 48 from San Angel, the charge of desertion removed by the Secretary of War 9 Mar 52 & to be listed as mo. with Co. 29 Jul 48.

ROLETT, WILLIAM H.: Pvt., enl. 17 Dec 46 at Pittsburgh, age 38, deserted at New Orleans 16 Jan 47.

ROSCOE, HENRY: Pvt., enl. 7 Dec 46 at Phila., age 21, mo. with Co. 29 Jul 48.

ROYER, GEORGE P.: Cpl., enl. 18 Nov 46 at Phila., age 26, reduced to Pvt. 23 Mar 47, left sick at Vera Cruz 9 Apr 47, disc. at Vera Cruz 11 May 47 on SCD for fever.

SCHAFFER, SIMON: (Schaeffer, Scheaffer): Pvt., enl. 9 Dec 46 at Elizabethton, age 20, listed as sick in hospital at Jalapa on Mar-Apr 47 MR, died at Jalapa 13 May 47 from diarrhea.

J. Jacob Oswandel as a senior citizen
Oswandel's Notes

William F. Small pictured as Colonel of
the 26th Pennsylvania in the Civil War
USAMHI

SCHOPPE, JOHN: Pvt., enl. 8 Dec 46 at Phila., age 35, left sick at Vera Cruz 9 Apr 47, disc. at Vera Cruz 11 May 47 on SCD for diarrhea.

SHELDEN, JOHN: (Sheldon): Pvt., enl. 18 Nov 46 at Phila., age 27, severely wounded in the foot at Cerro Gordo 18 Apr 47, died at Jalapa 6 May 47 from the wound.

SHULTZ, JOHN R.: (Schultz): Pvt., enl. 18 Nov 46 at Phila., age 22, listed as sick in hospital at Perote on May-Jun 47 MR, mo. with Co. 29 Jul 48.

SMALL, GEORGE F.: Sgt., enl. 18 Nov 46 at Phila., age 25, reduced to Pvt. in May or Jun 47, disc. at Perote 7 Jun 47 by order of Col. Wynkoop at his own request because of disability, died not long thereafter.

SMALL, WILLIAM F.: Capt., enl. at Phila., age 28, absent on 90 day furlough from 23 Nov 47, arrived in Phila. 29 Dec 47, rejoined Co. for mo. 29 Jul 48. Col. 26th P.V.I. 1 Jun 61 to 30 Jun 62, WIA at Williamsburg 5 May 62. Col. 60th Pa. Emergency Militia 19 Jun 63 to 8 Sep 63. Died at Phila. 13 Jun 77.

SMITH, CHARLES: Pvt., enl. 25 Nov 46 at Phila., age 37, died at Perote 30 Jul 47 from diarrhea.

SNETHEN, HOSEA: Pvt., enl. 18 Nov 46 at Phila., age 25, listed as sick in Perote Hospital on May-Jun 47 MR, mo. with Co. 29 Jul 48.

STAIR, SAMUEL: Pvt., enl. 18 Nov 46 at Phila., age 21, listed as sick on 17 Dec 46 - 28 Feb 47 MR, listed as sick in Perote Hospital on May-Jun 47 MR, mo. with Co. 29 Jul 48.

STEMLEAR, MORRIS: Pvt., enl. 18 Nov 46 at Phila., age 19, listed as in confinement under charges on Mar-Apr 47 MR, captured in action at Puebla 26 Aug 47, freed by U.S. troops at Chululu in mid-Oct 47, rejoined Co. 18 Oct 47, mo. with Co. 29 Jul 48.

SUTTON, GEORGE H.: Pvt., enl. 8 Dec 46 at Phila., age 19, listed as sick on 17 Dec 46 - 28 Feb 47 MR, WIA slightly at Cerro Gordo 18 Apr 47 causing hospitalization at Jalapa, confined in guardhouse according to Jan-Feb 48 MR, mo. with Co. 29 Jul 48.

SWARTZ, ALLEN: Pvt., enl. 1 Dec 46 at Phila., age 34, listed as sick in hospital at Perote on May-Jun 47 MR, AWOL from 20 Dec 47, returned to Co. before 30 Apr 48, mo. with Co. 29 Jul 48.

TAYLOR, JOSEPH C.: Pvt., enl. 18 Nov 46 at Phila., age 22, mo. with Co. 29 Jul 48.

WALKER, WILLIAM: Pvt., enl. 18 Nov 46 at Phila., age 24, disc. at Perote 7 Jun 47 on SCD for diarrhea.

WATSON, THEODORE: Pvt., enl. 18 Nov 46 at Phila., age 21, mo. with Co. 29 Jul 48.

WELLS, JOHN: Pvt., enl. 18 Nov 46 at Phila., age 26, left sick at Puebla 3 Dec 47, rejoined Co. by 30 Apr 48, mo. with Co. 29 Jul 48.

WELSH, ALBURTUS (Albertus) H.: Pvt., enl. 25 Nov 46 at Phila., age 22, mo. with Co. 29 Jul 48.

WHITTEN, RICHARD F.: Pvt., enl. 18 Nov 46 at Phila., age 22, left sick at Vera Cruz 9 Apr 47, disc. at Vera Cruz 11 May 47 on SCD for diarrhea.

WILHELM, GEORGE: Pvt., enl. 18 Nov 46 at Phila., age 21, mo. with Co. 29 Jul 48.

WILLIAMS, THOMAS: Pvt., enl. 18 Nov 46 at Phila., age 24, died at Perote 25 Jun 47 from diarrhea.

WILSON, EDWARD: Pvt., enl. 18 Nov 46 at Phila., age 25, listed as sick on 17 Dec 46 - 28 Feb 47 MR, confined in guardhouse according to Jan-Feb 48 MR, fined four months pay by Court Martial, mo. with Co. 29 Jul 48.

WILSON, JAMES B.: Cpl., enl. 18 Nov 46 at Phila., age 23, promoted to Sgt. 1 Jun 47, reduced to Pvt. 23 Oct 47, Court Martialed in Nov 47 for stealing a pair of socks while drunk, mo. with Co. 29 Jul 48.

WRAY, ANDREW, JR.: Cpl., enl. 18 Nov 46 at Phila., age 28, disc. at Perote 7 Jun 47 on SCD for diarrhea.

ZEIGLE, THOMAS A.: Pvt., enl. 25 Nov 46 at Phila., age 22, promoted to 1st Sgt. 14 Oct 47, mo. with Co. 29 Jul 48. Col. 16th P.V.I. (3 mos.) 3 May 61 to 30 Jul 61. Col. 107th P.V.I. 23 Dec 61 until his death at Warrenton, Va. 16 Jul 62, buried in York, Pa.

Company D, 1st Regiment
City Guards

The City Guards of Philadelphia were a rough, tough group of men. They existed as a uniformed militia company prior to 1846 and were eager to go when war was declared.

Notified of acceptance into the 1st Regiment in November, they left Philadelphia on 7 December 1846. The unit arrived in Pittsburgh and was mustered into U.S. service on 14 December by First Lieutenant Horace B. Field, 3rd U.S. Artillery. A number of the men showed their troublesome nature in Pittsburgh by starting riots and numerous fights. Captain Joseph Hill had his share of headaches.

During the war, the City Guards took part in the siege of Vera Cruz, the battle of Cerro Gordo and the siege of Puebla. They arrived in Mexico City on 8 December for garrison duty at the enemy capitol.

The Guards returned to Philadelphia at about 7:00 A.M. on 24 July 1848 and were treated to an overwhelming reception. Captain George Taylor of the 3rd U.S. Artillery mustered the company out of the Federal service on 31 July.

A total of 109 men served in the Guards during the war. Of these, sixteen were recruits who joined the company in Mexico. Fourteen men deserted, and one was transferred to another unit. Four men became battle casualties, and two of them died of their wounds. In all, seventeen died in service. An additional twenty-eight received discharges before muster out.

ALTMAN, CHARLES H.: Pvt., enl. & mi. 29 Sep 47 at Pittsburgh by Lt. Ankrimm, age 25, joined Co. 21 Dec 47, mo. with Co. 31 Jul 48.

ANDREWS, CHARLES: 2nd Cpl., enl. 24 Nov 46 at Phila., age 36, promoted to 1st Cpl. in May or Jun 47, wounded at Puebla in Aug 47, died at Puebla 14 Aug 47 from consumption.

ATKINS, EDWARD: Pvt., enl. 24 Nov 46 at Phila., age 19, left sick in hospital at Perote 3 Jun 47, disc. at Perote 29 Oct 47 on SCD. Pvt. Co. H, 95th P.V.I. 21 Sep 61 to 24 Dec 61.

ATKINS, HENRY: Pvt., enl. 24 Nov 46 at Phila., age 23, disc. at Vera Cruz 22 (or 27) Apr 47 on SCD.

BAKER, SAMUEL H.: Pvt., enl. 24 Nov 46 at Phila., age 20, left sick at Vera Cruz 9 Apr 47, disc. at Vera Cruz 13 May 47 on SCD for bronchitis.

BARTON, THOMAS: Pvt., enl. 24 Nov 46 at Phila., age 19, disc. at Jalapa 27 Apr 47 on SCD.

BEAN, IRWIN (Urwin): Pvt., enl. 24 Nov 46 at Phila., age 22, promoted to Cpl. 30 Oct 47, promoted to 3rd Sgt. 1 Jun 48, mo. with Co. 31 Jul 48.

BEESLEY, SYLVESTER: (Beasly): Pvt., enl. 24 Nov 46 at Phila., age 19, promoted to Cpl. in Sep 47, wounded at Puebla 28 Sep 47, disc. at Puebla 12 Nov 47 for wound.

BEESLEY, WILLIAM: (Beasly): Pvt., enl. 24 Nov 46 at Phila., age 20, accidently wounded while on guard duty at Vera Cruz, disc at Vera Cruz 5 Apr 47 for wound, died 6 Apr 47.

BIRKENWALD, MICHAEL: (Berkenward): Pvt., enl. 31 Aug 47 at Phila., age 23, mi. 31 Aug 47 at Ft. Mifflin, joined Co. 21 Dec 47 in Mexico City, mo. with Co. 31 Jul 48.

BLACKELLS, ALEXANDER: Pvt., enl. 24 Nov 46 at Phila., age 28, disc. at Jalapa 15 Apr 47 on SCD for diarrhea.

BRITTON, ELIJAH W.: Pvt., enl. 24 Nov 46 at Phila., age 20, listed as sick in hospital at Perote on May-Jun 47 MR, died at Perote 14 Aug 47 from diarrhea.

BROWN, ALEXANDER: 2nd Lt., enl. 24 Nov 46 at Phila., age 30, appointed Adjutant 19 Dec 46, promoted to 1st Lt. 30 Mar 47, reported sick on duty on Jan-Feb & Mar-Apr 48 MRs, left sick at New Orleans 29 Jun 48 on the way home, disc. by General Order 20 Jul 48, died in Jul 48.

BUCKWATER, ELIAS: Pvt., enl. 24 Nov 46 at Phila., age 20, left sick at Puebla 14 Dec 47, rejoined Co. 10 Apr 48, in confinement according to Mar-Apr 48 MR, mo. with Co. 31 Jul 48.

CAFFIN, EBENEZER: (Caffyn, Coffin): Pvt., enl. 24 Nov 46 at Phila., age 26, it is likely that he was wounded at Vera Cruz, disc. at Vera Cruz 27 Apr 47 on SCD.

CARROLL, EDWARD: Cpl., enl. 24 Nov 46 at Phila., age 21, promoted to 4th Sgt. 14 Apr 47, promoted to 2nd Lt. 10 Jun 47, was sick in Mexico City and San Angel from Dec 47 to Apr 48, mo. with Co. 31 Jul 48. Capt. Co. F, & Lt. Col. 95th P.V.I. 27 Sep 61 until KIA at the Wilderness 5 May 64, also WIA at Gaines' Mill.

CARSON, SAMUEL: (Carston): Pvt., enl. 24 Nov 46 at Phila., age 22, promoted to Cpl. 1 Jun 48, mo. with Co. 31 Jul 48.

CHAPMAN, EDWARD: Pvt., enl. 24 Nov 46 at Phila., age 19, appears to have been wounded at Vera Cruz, disc. at Vera Cruz 5 Apr 47 on SCD.

CLARK, WILLIAM H.: Pvt., enl. 24 Nov 46 at Phila., age 21, deserted at New Orleans 3 Jan 47.

CLINTON, WILLIAM: Pvt., enl. 24 Nov 46 at Phila., age 28, disc. at Puebla 5 Nov 47 on SCD, later died in a hospital in New Orleans of diarrhea.

CLOAK, SAMUEL: Pvt., enl. 24 Nov 46 at Phila., age 19, fined $3.00 by Court Martial according to Jan-Feb 48 MR, mo. with Co. 31 Jul 48. Pvt. Co. H, 72nd P.V.I. 10 Aug 61 to 15 Jul 63.

COLE, EDWARD I.: Pvt., enl. 24 Nov 46 at Phila., age 21, deserted at New Orleans 3 Jan 47.

CONNOR, EDWARD A. (O): Pvt., enl. & mi. 7 Aug 47 at Pottsville by Lt. Kaercher, age 26, joined Co. 21 Dec 47, mo. with Co. 31 Jul 48.

COOPER, DAVID: Pvt., enl. 24 Nov 46 at Phila., age 34, promoted to Cpl. 30 Apr 47, mo. with Co. 31 Jul 48.

CROOKS, JOHN: Pvt., enl. 24 Nov 46 at Phila., age 20, disc. at Vera Cruz 6 Apr 47 on SCD.

CROOKS, THOMAS: Pvt., enl. 24 Nov 46 at Phila., age 23, sick at New Orleans Barracks from 12 Jan 47, disc. at New Orleans 14 Mar 47 on SCD.

CRYSTAL, FRANCIS: (Christal, Chrystal, Cristal): Pvt., enl. 24 Nov 46 at Phila., age 19, found guilty of theft by Court Martial 8 Apr 47 and sentenced to one month's imprisonment in San Juan de Ulloa and loss of one month's pay, fined $3.00 by Regimental Court Martial according to Jan-Feb 48 MR, mo. with Co. 31 Jul 48.

CUDNEY, ALBERT (John A.): Pvt., enl. 24 Nov 46 at Phila., age 22, slightly WIA at Cerro Gordo 18 Apr 47, listed as sick in camp on Mar-Apr 47 MR, listed as sick in hospital at Perote on May-Jun 47 MR, left sick at Perote 3 Jul 47, rejoined Co. before 31 Dec 47, mo. with Co. 31 Jul 48.

DAVIS, JOSEPH K.: Pvt., enl. 24 Nov 46 at Phila., age 21, slightly WIA at Cerro Gordo 18 Apr 47, disc. at Perote 12 Nov 47 on SCD for diarrhea.

DICKSON, DAVID: (Dixon, Dixson): Pvt., enl. 24 Nov 46 at Phila., age 21, promoted to Cpl. 14 Apr 47, died at Puebla 24 Aug 47 from diarrhea.

DIXON, SAMUEL: (Dickson, Dixson): Pvt., enl. 4 Dec 46 at Wilkes-Barre, age 19, mo. with Co. 31 Jul 48.

DOLLHOWER, LEVI: (Delhower, Dolhauer, Dollenhower): Pvt., enl. & mi. 3 Aug 47 at Pittsburgh by Lt. Ankrimm, age 20, reported at Carlisle Barracks 31 Aug 47, joined Co. 21 Dec 47, mo. with Co. 31 Jul 48.

DOYLE, JAMES: Pvt., enl. 24 Nov 46 at Phila., age 20, listed as sick in hospital at Jalapa on Mar-Apr 47 MR, promoted to Cpl. 30 Oct 47, mo. with Co. 31 Jul 48.

DUPER, CHRISTIAN: Pvt., enl. 24 Nov 46 at Phila., age 19, mo. with Co. 31 Jul 48.

EHLERT, JOHN: Pvt., enl. 24 Nov 46 at Phila., age 22, listed as sick on 14 Dec 46 - 28 Feb 47 MR, fined $3.00 by Regimental Court Martial according to Jan-Feb 48 MR, mo. with Co. 31 Jul 48.

EKINS, BERNARD: (Eakins): Pvt., enl. 24 Nov 46 at Phila., age 26, died at Pittsburgh 22 Dec 46 of "mania a potu."

ELLEMAN, WILLIAM L.: Pvt., enl. & mi. 15 Sep 47 at Phila. by Capt. Scott, age 21, joined Co. 21 Dec 47, mo. with Co. 31 Jul 48.

FARR, PETER: Pvt., enl. 24 Nov 46 at Phila., age 28, deserted at New Orleans 16 Jan 47.

FORCE, SAMUEL S.: Pvt., enl. 24 Nov 46 at Phila., age 21, deserted at Puebla 7 Aug 47.

FREESTON, ROBERT: Sgt., enl. 24 Nov 46 at Phila., age 24, died at Cincinnati, Ohio from diarrhea on his way home 9 Jul 48, was buried in Phila. 28 Jul 48.

GLENN, JOHN FRANCIS: Pvt., enl. & mi. 20 Jul 47 at Phila. by Capt. Scott, age 21, joined Co. 21 Dec 47, mo. with Co. 31 Jul 48. Capt. Co. B, 23rd P.V.I. (3 mos.) 21 Apr 61 to 31 Jul 61. Capt. Co. A, Maj., Lt. Col. & Col. 23rd P.V.I. 4 Aug 61 to 8 Sep 64. Died 8 Jan 05.

GODSHALL, FREDERICK: Pvt., enl. & mi. 5 Jan 48 at Phila. by Capt. Scott, age 25, reported at Ft. McHenry, Md. 20 Jan 48, joined Co. 22 Apr 48, left sick at Cincinnati, Ohio 12 Jul 48, disc. at Cincinnati 14 Aug 48.

GRANT, THOMAS: Fifer, enl. 24 Nov 46 at Phila., age 20, listed as sick on 14 Dec 46 - 28 Feb 47 MR, listed as Pvt. on all MRs after Mar 47, disc. at Perote 26 May 47 on SCD.

GRASSENMEYERS, JOSEPH F.: (Grusenmeyers, Grusenmyer, Grussenmyers): Pvt., enl. 24 Nov 46 at Phila., age 19, found guilty of theft by Court Martial 8 Apr 47 & sentenced to one month's imprisonment at San Juan de Ulloa and loss of one month's pay, left sick at Vera Cruz 9 Apr 47, disc. at Vera Cruz 13 May 47 on SCD for intermittent fever.

GREEN, JOHN D.: (Greene): Pvt., enl. & mi. 20 Jul 47 at Phila. by Capt. Scott, age 21, joined Co. 21 Dec 47, mo. with Co. 31 Jul 48.

John F. Glenn shown as Colonel of the
23rd Pennsylvania in the Civil War
Civil War Library and Museum - MOLLUS

Robert E. Winslow shown here as
Lieutenant Colonel of the 68th
Pennsylvania in the Civil War
MOLLUS-Mass & USAMHI

GUNN, DWIGHT B.: Pvt., enl. 24 Nov 46 at Phila., age 21, disc. at Vera Cruz 5 Apr 47 on SCD, died 6 Apr 47 of brain fever.

HANNEY, MOSES M.: (Haney): Pvt., enl. 24 Nov 46 at Phila., age 21, in guardhouse in Mexico City according to 31 Aug - 31 Dec 47 MR, mo. with Co. 31 Jul 48.

HAVILAND, WILLIAM: Pvt., enl. 24 Nov 46 at Phila., age 27, disc. at Puebla 5 Nov 47 on SCD for diarrhea.

HIGGINS, SAMUEL: Pvt., enl. 4 Dec 46 at Wilkes-Barre, age 22, deserted at Pittsburgh 15 Dec 46.

HILL, JOSEPH: Capt., age 32, left the Co. 16 Jan 47 & ordered dropped from the rolls, ordered by Gen. Scott to resume command of Co. 1 Apr 47, AWOL from 6 Nov 47 through 30 Apr 48, mo. with Co. 31 Jul 48.

HILTNER, GEORGE: Pvt., enl. 24 Nov 46 at Phila., age 23, listed as sick in hospital at Jalapa on Mar-Apr 47 MR, fined $3.00 by Court Martial and listed as sick in hospital at San Angel according to Jan-Feb 48 MR, mo. with Co. 31 Jul 48.

HULING, THOMAS: (Hewlings): Pvt., enl. 24 Nov 46 at Phila., age 20, listed as sick on 14 Dec 46 - 28 Feb 47 MR, disc. at Vera Cruz 6 Apr 47 on SCD.

JOHNSON, JOHN: (Johnston): Pvt., enl. 4 Dec 46 at Wilkes-Barre, age 35, died at Vera Cruz 12 Apr 47 from diarrhea.

JONES, HENRY A. P.: Pvt., enl. 24 Nov 46 at Phila., age 19, disc. at New Orleans 10 Jan 47 on SCD, reached Harrisburg in Apr 47 with illness preventing further travel, died in Harrisburg 22 Aug 47 under his mother's care, buried in Harrisburg.

JONES, THOMAS: Pvt., enl. & mi. 13 Jan 47 at New Orleans by Col. Wynkoop, mo. with Co. 31 Jul 48. Age 23.

KANE, LEWIS H.: 1st Sgt., enl. 24 Nov 46 at Phila., age 27, promoted to 2nd Lt. 24 Feb 47, disc. at Jalapa 21 May 47 on SCD.

KEILL, EDWARD: Pvt., enl. 24 Nov 46 at Phila., age 26, deserted at New Orleans 16 Jan 47.

KELLY, MICHAEL: Cpl., enl. 24 Nov 46 at Phila., age 37, reduced to Pvt. 6 Apr 47, disc. at Vera Cruz 6 Apr 47 on SCD for diarrhea.

KENNY, FRANCIS: (Kenney): Pvt., enl. 24 Nov 46 at Phila., age 24, promoted to Fifer 1 Mar 47, mo. with Co. 31 Jul 48.

KERBAUGH, PETER A. B.: Pvt., enl. 6 Aug 47 at Phila., age 21, mi. 6 Aug 47 at Ft. Mifflin, joined Co. 21 Dec 47, mo. with Co. 31 Jul 48.

KERWIN, MICHAEL: (Kervin, Kirwin): Pvt., enl. 26 Jul 47 at Phila., age 32, mi. 29 Jul 47 at Ft. Mifflin, joined Co. 21 Dec 47, mo. with Co. 31 Jul 48. Capt. Co. B, Maj. & Col. 13th Pa. Cavalry 16 Apr 62 to 14 Jul 65.

KNAPP, DEXTER (Baxter) W.: Pvt., enl. 24 Nov 46 at Phila., age 35, deserted at New Orleans 11 Jan 47.

KRETCHMAR, JULIUS C.: 1st Lt., age 32, elected Capt. 24 Feb 47, he sold U.S. Gov't. property of the Co., deserted at Vera Cruz 30 Mar 47, his resignation later accepted by order of the Secretary of War, disc. effective 12 May 47.

LAMBERT, JAMES W.: Pvt., enl. 24 Nov 46 at Phila., age 26, WIA in the hand during the siege of Puebla 28 Sep 47, died from the wound 29 Oct 47.

LINDSEY, JAMES: Pvt., enl. 24 Nov 46 at Phila., age 26, deserted at New Orleans 11 Jan 47.

LOGAN, HUGH: Pvt., enl. 24 Nov 46 at Phila., age 21, mo. with Co. 31 Jul 48.

MacKAY, WILLIAM J.: (MacKey): Pvt., enl. 24 Nov 46 at Phila., age 22, disc. at Vera Cruz 5 Apr 47 on SCD for brain fever.

MacLEER, JOHN: (McAleer, McLear, McLeer): Pvt., enl. 24 Nov 46 at Phila., age 19, left sick at Puebla 14 Dec 47, rejoined Co. 24 Feb 48, listed as in confinement at Mexico City on Mar-Apr 48 MR, mo. with Co. 31 Jul 48.

MAYFIELD, JOHN J.: Pvt., enl. 24 Nov 46 at Phila., age 24, deserted at New Orleans 3 Jan 47.

MAYNES, PATRICK: (Mayens): Pvt., enl. 24 Nov 46 at Phila., age 34, deserted at Pittsburgh 18 Dec 46.

McCLELLAN, WILLIAM: (McClelland): Pvt., enl. 24 Nov 46 at Phila., age 22, disc. at Perote 5 Nov 47 on SCD for diarrhea.

McDERMOTT, STEPHEN: (McDermont) (Dermot, McStephen): Pvt., enl. 24 Nov 46 at Phila., age 27, deserted at New Orleans 16 Jan 47, rejoined Co. 1 Apr 48, mo. with Co. 31 Jul 48.

McKEEVER, PETER: Pvt., enl. 24 Nov 46 at Phila., age 20, fined $3.00 by Regimental Court Martial according to Jan-Feb 48 MR, died at San Angel 7 Jan 48 of stomach cramps after a hard march, his body was returned to Phila. by the Co. where it was buried 30 Jul 48.

McMICHAEL, DANIEL (McMichal): Pvt., enl. 24 Nov 46 at Phila., age 32, left sick at Perote 3 Jul 47, disc. at Perote 29 Oct 47 on SCD for diarrhea.

McMULLIN, WILLIAM: (McMullen): Pvt., enl. 24 Nov 46 at Phila., age 20, promoted to Cpl. 6 Jun 47, promoted to 1st Sgt. 1 Jul 47, mo. with Co. 31 Jul 48.

MEYERS, CHARLES (Myers): Pvt., enl. 24 Nov 46 at Phila., age 19, fined $3.00 by Regimental Court Martial according to Jan-Feb 48 MR, mo. with Co. 31 Jul 48.

MOORE, GEORGE: 2nd Lt., age 34, left the Co. 16 Jan 47 & ordered to be dropped from the roll, ordered to resume command by Gen. Scott 1 Apr 47, commanded the Co. from 6 Nov 47 to mo., mo. with Co. 31 Jul 48.

NEEDHAM, SAMUEL: Pvt., enl. 24 Nov 46 at Phila., age 27, disc. at Vera Cruz 22 Apr 47 on SCD.

NEFF, ALEXANDER: Pvt., enl. 24 Nov 46 at Phila., age 19, left sick in hospital at Jalapa 24 Nov 47, died at Jalapa 21 Dec 47 from brain fever.

NEILL, JEREMIAH F.: Pvt., enl. 24 Nov 46 at Phila., age 20, mo. with Co. 31 Jul 48.

O'BRIEN, JOHN: (O'Brian): Pvt., enl. 24 Nov 46 at Phila., age 20, left sick at Puebla 4 Dec 47, rejoined Co. 1 Apr 48, mo. with Co. 31 Jul 48.

PAULIN, JOHN: Pvt., enl. 24 Nov 46 at Phila., age 27, mo. with Co. 31 Jul 48.

RANKINS, GEORGE: Drummer, enl. 24 Nov 46 at Phila., age 31, died at Perote 16 Jul 47.

REELER, FREDERICK W. (W. F.): (Reeller): Pvt., enl. 24 Nov 46 at Phila., age 25, mo. with Co. 31 Jul 48.

REID, ROBERT (Reed): Pvt., enl. 24 Nov 46 at Phila., age 23, was Cpl. from 1 Sep 47 to 1 Oct 47, transferred to Co. K, 1st Pa. Regt. 1 Oct 47.

REYNOLDS, JOHN: 4th Sgt., enl. 24 Nov 46 at Phila., age 22, promoted to 2nd Sgt. 8 Apr 47, promoted to 1st Sgt. 30 Apr 47, reduced to Pvt. for bad conduct 1 Jul 47, left sick at Puebla 14 Dec 47, rejoined Co. 10 Mar 48, in confinement in Mexico City according to Mar-Apr 48 MR, mo. with Co. 31 Jul 48.

ROAT, HENRY: Pvt., enl. 24 Nov 46 at Phila., age 42, promoted to Sgt. 9 Mar 47, disc. at Vera Cruz 22 Apr 47 on SCD for chronic rheumatism.

RUSK, EDWARD D.: Pvt., enl. 24 Nov 46 at Phila., age 22, deserted at New Orleans 11 Jan 47.

RYLEY, JOSEPH: Cpl., enl. 24 Nov 46 at Phila., age 38, reduced to Pvt. 1 Mar 47, promoted to Sgt. 1 Jun 47, reduced to Pvt. 30 Oct 47, AWOL from 6 Nov 47 through 30 Apr 48 as he went home in company with Capt. Hill, mo. with Co. 31 Jul 48.

SCHEERER, JOHN: (Scherer, Schuerer, Sheerer): Pvt., enl. & mi. 25 Jul 47 at Phila. by Capt. Scott, age 32, joined Co. 21 Dec 47, mo. with Co. 31 Jul 48.

SEPOLD, ADAM (Abraham): (Seapold, Seapole, Seopold): Pvt., enl. 4 Dec 46 at Wilkes-Barre, age 27, mo. with Co. 31 Jul 48.

SHERIDAN, ARTHUR M.: (Scheridan): Pvt., enl. & mi. 6 Aug 47 in Phila. by Capt. Scott, age 19, joined Co. 21 Dec 47, mo. with Co. 31 Jul 48.

SMITH, ISAAC W.: Pvt., enl. 24 Nov 46 at Phila., age 27, promoted to Cpl. 1 Mar 47, disc. at Vera Cruz 27 Apr 47 on SCD.

SMITH, ISAIAH: Pvt., enl. 24 Nov 46 at Phila., age 20, disc. at Vera Cruz 27 Apr 47 on SCD.

SMITH, JAMES E.: 2nd Sgt., enl. 24 Nov 46 at Phila., age 30, Acting 1st Sgt. 1 to 9 Mar & 22 Apr 47, reduced to Pvt. for bad conduct 30 Apr 47 by Court Martial which also fined him $20.00, left sick at Perote 3 Jul 47, fined $3.00 by Regimental Court Martial according to Jan-Feb 48 MR, mo. with Co. 31 Jul 48.

SMITH, SAMUEL S.: Pvt., enl. 24 Nov 46 at Phila., age 19, listed as sick in Perote Hospital on May-Jun 47 MR, left sick at Perote 3 Jul 47, disc. at Perote 29 Oct 47 on SCD for chronic diarrhea.

STEWART, WILLIAM HENRY (W.): Pvt., enl. & mi. 20 Jul 47 at Phila., age 21, joined Co. 21 Dec 47, mo. with Co. 31 Jul 48.

STRANAHAN, ISAAC E.: (Stranaham, Strenaham): Pvt., enl. 24 Nov 46 at Phila., age 21, left sick at Perote 30 Nov 47, rejoined Co. 15 Mar 48, mo. with Co. 31 Jul 48.

STRICKMAN, WILLIAM: Pvt., enl. 24 Nov 46 at Phila., age 23, disc. at Perote 6 Jun 47 on SCD for injury incurred while drawing a cannon at the Battle of Cerro Gordo on 18 Apr 47.

TAGGART, JOSHUA: (Taggert): Pvt., enl. 24 Nov 46 at Phila., age 21, promoted to Cpl. 14 Apr 47, promoted to 3rd Sgt. 30 Apr 47, mo. with Co. 31 Jul 48.

THOMAS, WILLIAM: Pvt., enl. & mi. 4 Jan 48 at Phila. by Capt. Scott, age 26, reported at Ft. McHenry, Md. 20 Jan 48, joined Co. 22 Apr 48, died at Beaver, Ohio 12 Jul 48 from diarrhea while on the way home.

THOMPSON, JOHN L.: Pvt., enl. 24 Nov 46 at Phila., age 22, deserted at New Orleans 16 Jan 47.

TILLMAN, AUGUSTUS: Pvt., enl. & mi. 15 Nov 47 at Jalapa, Mexico by Lt. Carroll, age 19, fined $3.00 by Regimental Court Martial according to Jan-Feb 48 MR, mo. with Co. 31 Jul 48.

VANHORN, JOHN: Pvt., enl. 24 Nov 46 at Phila., age 21, disc. at Puebla 5 Nov 47 on SCD for diarrhea.

VANSANT, WILLIAM C.: (Vansandt, Vanzant, Wanzant): Pvt., enl. & mi. 13 Jan 47 at New Orleans by Col. Wynkoop, age 24, mo. with Co. 31 Jul 48.

WALTZ, FREDERICK: Pvt., enl. 24 Nov 46 at Phila., age 19, disc. at Perote 5 Jun 47 on SCD for diarrhea.

WARD, JOHN: Pvt., enl. 24 Nov 46 at Phila., age 22, fined $3.00 by Regimental Court Martial according to Jan-Feb 48 MR, mo. with Co. 31 Jul 48.

WHITNEY, ALEXANDER B.: Pvt., enl. 24 Nov 46 at Phila., age 19, disc. at Vera Cruz 22 Apr 47 on SCD for diarrhea, died 23 Apr 47.

WINSLOW, ROBERT E.: Pvt., enl. 22 Jul 47 at Phila., age 21, mi. at Phila. by Capt. Scott, joined Co. 21 Dec 47, mo. with Co. 31 Jul 48. 1st Lt. Co. H, 20th P.V.I. (3 mos.) 30 Apr 61 to 7 Jul 61. Capt. Co. C, Maj. & Lt. Col. 68th P.V.I. 4 Aug 62 to 9 Jun 65, WIA at Gettysburg 2 Jul 63. Bvt. Col. & Brig. Gen. 13 Mar 65. Born 1 Jan 29. Died 8 Jan 93. Buried in Phila.

Company E, 1st Regiment
Washington Light Infantry

The Washington Light Infantry of Captain Frederick W. Binder is believed to have existed prior to the war with Mexico. The company was quick to volunteer its services, and in November 1846 Captain Binder was notified that his company was to form part of the 1st Pennsylvania Regiment.

The company left Philadelphia, with two others from the city, on 7 December. They rendezvoused at Pittsburgh where First Lieutenant Horace B. Field of the 3rd U.S. Artillery mustered the unit into Federal service on 14 December.

The Washington Light Infantry played a role in the siege of Vera Cruz, the battle of Cerro Gordo, the garrisonning of Perote and the battle of Huamantla. They also did their share of escort duty between Vera Cruz and Mexico City.

This company, with the others from Philadelphia, arrived in the city at about 7 o'clock on the morning of 24 July 1848. Captain George Taylor of the 3rd U.S. Artillery mustered the men out on 5 August.

A total of 97 men served in the company during the war. Of these, three recruits joined it in Mexico. A total of five men deserted. Three battle casualties were suffered, with one being killed in action. In all twenty-two men died in service. An additional fifteen received discharges before muster out.

ACKERLIN, FREDERICK W.: Pvt., enl. 2 Dec 46 at Phila., age 33, promoted to 4th Cpl. 28 May 47, promoted to 2nd Cpl. 8 Jul 47, reduced to Pvt. 30 Nov 47, promoted to 4th Sgt., died at Jalapa 9 Jun 48 on the way home.

ANGEROTH, CHARLES: 1st Sgt., enl. 2 Dec 46 at Phila., age 36, reduced to Pvt. for cowardice 12 Apr 47, disc. at Vera Cruz 28 Apr 47 on SCD. Lt. Col. 27th P.V.I. 31 May 61 to 7 Sep 61. Col. 2nd Pa. Heavy Art. 8 Feb 62 to 21 Jun 62. Died 23 Jan 82.

AUGRAMM, JOHN S.: (Ingram): 4th Cpl., enl. 2 Dec 46 at Phila., age 38, reduced to Pvt. 9 Mar 47, listed as sick in hospital at Jalapa

John F. Ballier pictured as Colonel 98th Pennsylvania in the Civil War
USAMHI

on Mar-Apr 47 MR, rejoined Co. at Perote 11 Jun 47, left sick at Perote 29 Nov 47, died at Perote 22 Apr 48 from consumption, leaving a wife & 3 children.

BADER, HIERONYMUS: Pvt., enl. 2 Dec 46 at Phila., age 26, Court Martialed 17 Sep 47 for disobedience of an order & fined $5.00, the money was refunded and the sentence was remitted by Col. Wynkoop upon disc., mo. with Co. 5 Aug 48.

BALLIER, JOHN FREDERICK: b. 28 Aug 15. 1st Lt., enl. at Phila., age 31, placed under arrest 27 Dec 47, appointed Acting Asst. Q.M. 6 Mar 48, mo. with Co. 5 Aug 48. Col. 21st P.V.I. (3 mos.) 29 Apr 61 to 8 Aug 61. Col. 98th P.V.I. 30 Sep 61 to 26 Nov 62 and 12 Mar 63 to 29 Jun 65. WIA at Salem Heights and Ft. Stevens. Bvt. Brig. Gen. of Vols. 29 Jun 65. Died at Phila. 3 Feb 93.

BENZINGER, FREDERICK: Pvt., enl. 2 Dec 46 at Phila., age 21, left sick at Jalapa 29 Apr 47, rejoined Co. 11 Jun 47, Court Martialed 17 Sep 47 for disobedience of an order & fined $5.00, the money was refunded and the sentence was remitted by Col. Wynkoop upon disc., mo. with Co. 5 Aug 48.

BERGER, BERNHARDT: Pvt., enl. 2 Dec 46 at Phila., age 29, listed as sick on Dec 46 - Feb 47 MR, left sick at Jalapa 6 May 47, rejoined Co. 11 Jun 47, died at Perote 21 Aug 47 from diarrhea.

BINDER, FREDERICK WILLIAM: Capt., enl. at Phila., age 37, listed as sick from 10 Aug to 31 Aug 47, mo. with Co. 5 Aug 48.

BLUCHER, ADAM: 2nd Lt., enl. at Phila., age 30, listed as sick on Dec 46-Feb 47 MR, took 60 day furlough from 7 May 47 (was AWOL), returned to Co. 22 Dec 47, listed as sick on Mar-Apr 48 MR, mo. with Co. 5 Aug 48.

BOCK, GEORGE: Pvt., enl. 2 Dec 46 at Phila., age 27, died at Jalapa 27 May 47 from consumption.

BOLMAN, JOHN: (Paulman): Pvt., enl. 2 Dec 46 at Phila., age 21, detailed for hospital duty according to Dec 46 - Feb 47 & Mar-Apr 47 MRs, rejoined Co. 7 May 47, listed as sick on May-Jun & Jul-Aug 47 MRs, disc. at Perote 21 Oct 47 on SCD.

BOWMAN, PETER: Pvt., enl. 2 Dec 46 at Phila., age 33, Court Martialed 17 Sep 47 for disobedience of an order & fined $5.00, the money was refunded and the sentence was remitted by Col. Wynkoop upon disc., mo. with Co. 5 Aug 48.

BRAKENWAGER, OTTO: (Brackewagen): Pvt., enl. 2 Dec 46 at Phila., age 22, Court Martialed 16 May 47 for misbehavior and conduct unbecoming a soldier & sentenced to 10 days hard labor, sentence remitted by Col. Wynkoop, Court Martialed 17 Sep 47 for disobedience of an order & fined $8.00, listed as under arrest on Jan-Feb 48 MR, fined $5.00 by Court Martial 11 Feb 48, mo. with Co. 5 Aug 48.

BUSH, GEORGE: (Busch): Fifer, enl. 2 Dec 46 at Phila., age 21, listed as Pvt. on all MRs, Court Martialed 17 Sep 47 for disobedience of an order & fined $5.00, the money was refunded and the sentence was remitted by Col. Wynkoop upon disc., listed as sick in quarters on Mar-Apr 48 MR, mo. with Co. 5 Aug 48.

CONRADT, THEODORE: (Conrad): Pvt., enl. 2 Dec 46 at Phila., age 25, listed as sick on May-Jun & Jul-Aug 47 MRs, died at Perote 19 Oct 47 from consumption.

DUTT, MICHAEL: Pvt., enl. 2 Dec 46 at Phila., age 30, promoted to 3rd Cpl. 9 Mar 47, on extra duty as Baker according to May-Jun 47 MR, promoted to 2nd Cpl. 28 May 47, promoted to 1st Cpl. 8 Jul 47, promoted to 4th Sgt. 8 Sep 47, promoted to 2nd Sgt. 30 Nov 47, promoted to 1st Sgt 31 Jan 48, mo. with Co. 5 Aug 48.

EISENBERGER, JOHN: (Eisenbrecker): Drummer, enl. 2 Dec 46 at Phila, age 27, fined $7.00 by Court Martial 18 May 47, fined $3.00 by Court Martial 12 Jul 47, listed as under arrest on 31 Aug - 31 Dec 47 MR, listed as Pvt. on Jan-Feb 48 MR & all subsequent MRs, mo. with Co. 5 Aug. 48.

FEIX, JOHN F. (J., S.): Pvt., enl. 2 Dec 46 at Phila., age 21, left sick at Jalapa 6 May 47, rejoined Co. 11 Jun 47, Court Martialed 17 Sep 47 for disobedience of an order & fined $5.00, the money was refunded and the sentence was remitted by Col. Wynkoop upon disc., mo. with Co. 5 Aug 48.

FREY, FRANCIS: Pvt., enl. 2 Dec 46 at Phila., age 24, Court Martialed 17 Sep 47 for disobedience of an order & fined $5.00, the money was refunded and the sentence was remitted by Col. Wynkoop upon disc., promoted to Cpl. 1 Dec 47, mo. with Co. 5 Aug 48.

FURSTENBERG, LEWIS (Levis): Pvt., enl. 2 Dec 46 at Phila., age 24, Court Martialed 17 Sep 47 for disobedience of an order & fined $5.00, the money was refunded and the sentence was remitted by Col. Wynkoop upon disc., mo. with Co. 5 Aug 48.

GOERGEN, S. J. B. (Bernhard S.): (Georgn): Pvt., enl. 2 Dec 46 at Phila., age 21, deserted at New Orleans 14 Jan 47.

GRASSELL, JOHN: Pvt., enl. 2 Dec 46 at Phila., age 21, Court Martialed 17 Sep 47 for disobedience of an order & fined $5.00, the money was refunded and the sentence was remitted by Col. Wynkoop upon disc., promoted to 3rd Cpl. 1 May 48, mo. with Co. 5 Aug 48.

GROLL, ANTHONY: (Groell): Pvt., enl. 2 Dec 46 at Phila., age 28, on extra duty as Baker according to May-Jun 47 MR, mo. with Co. 5 Aug 48.

HALTER, CASPER: Pvt., enl. 2 Dec 46 at Phila., age 38, listed as sick on Mar-Apr & May-Jun 47 MRs, rejoined Co. 11 Jun 47, disc. at Perote 30 Oct 47 on SCD.

HANS, HENRY: (Hains): Pvt., enl. 2 Dec 46 at Phila., age 21, listed as sick on 14 Dec 46 - 28 Feb 47 MR, detailed for daily duty at hospital according to Mar-Apr 47 MR, served as hospital attendant from 1 to 6 Jun 47, promoted to Hospital Steward & served at Perote Hospital from 7 Jun 47 to 22 Jul 47, under arrest from 23 Jul 47, reduced to Pvt. 28 Jul 47, fined $30.00 by General Court Martial 2 Sep 47, mo. with Co. 5 Aug 48.

HANTZE, JOHN: (Hanze, Heintze): Sgt., enl. 2 Dec 46 at Phila., age 37, wounded in the shoulder 9 Mar 47 on the beach near Vera Cruz, promoted from 3rd Sgt. to 2nd Sgt. 12 Apr 47, promoted to 1st Sgt. 8 Jul 47, reduced to Pvt. 14 Oct 47, promoted to Cpl. 1 Dec 47, reduced to Pvt. 5 Feb 48, listed as sick in quarters on Mar-Apr 48 MR, mo. with Co. 5 Aug 48.

HARDEGAN, CHARLES (Herdegan, Herdegen): Pvt., enl. 2 Dec 46 at Phila., age 34, detached as Hospital Steward from 12 Jan 47, left for recruiting duty 7 Jun 47, deserted at Ft. Mifflin 20 May 48, returned to Co. 5 Aug 48, dishonorably disc. 5 Aug 48.

HARTMAN, GODFREY: Pvt., enl. 2 Dec 46 at Phila., age 26, on extra duty as Baker according to May-Jun & Jul-Aug 47 MRs, Court Martialed 17 Sep 47 for disobedience of an order & fined $7.00, listed as sick on Jan-Feb 48 MR, left sick at Jalapa 6 Apr 48, mo. with Co. 5 Aug 48.

HASSLACHER, ANDREW: Pvt., enl. 2 Dec 46 at Phila., age 22, on extra duty as Baker according to Jul-Aug 47 MR, Court Martialed 17 Sep 47 for disobedience of an order & fined $5.00, the money was refunded and the sentence was remitted by Col. Wynkoop upon disc., mo. with Co. 5 Aug 48.

HASSLER, GEORGE: Pvt., enl. 2 Dec 46 at Phila., age 36, listed as sick on 14 Dec 46 - 28 Feb 47 MR, left sick at Vera Cruz 9 Apr 47, disc. at Vera Cruz 27 Apr 47 on SCD.

HEMPEL, FERDINAND (Frederick): Pvt., enl. 2 Dec 46 at Phila., age 25, promoted to Cpl. 26 Jan 47, promoted to Sgt. 8 Jul 47, reduced to Pvt. 1 Dec 47, reinstated as Sgt. 10 Jun 48, mo. with Co. 5 Aug 48.

HETTENBACK, MATTHIAS (Mathiew): Pvt., enl. 2 Dec 46 at Phila., age 23, left sick at Jalapa 29 Apr 47, rejoined Co. 7 Jun 47, on extra duty as Baker according to 31 Aug - 31 Dec 47 & Jan-Feb 48 MRs, promoted to Cpl. 8 Sep 47, promoted to 3rd Sgt. 1 Dec 47, mo. with Co. 5 Aug 48.

HOENCK, THOMAS: (Heonck, Hoenk): Pvt., enl. 2 Dec 46 at Phila., age 26, listed as sick on 14 Dec 46 - 28 Feb 47 MR, Court Martialed 17 Sep 47 for disobedience of an order & fined $5.00, the money was refunded and the sentence was remitted by Col. Wynkoop upon disc., listed as sick on Jan-Feb & Mar-Apr 48 MRs, mo. with Co. 5 Aug 48.

HOFFMAN, ADAM: Pvt., enl. 2 Dec 46 at Phila., age 20, Court Martialed 17 Sep 47 for disobedience of an order & fined $5.00, the money was refunded and the sentence was remitted by Col. Wynkoop upon disc., mo. with Co. 5 Aug 48.

HOHNSTEIN, HENRY: (Hohenstein): Pvt., enl. 2 Dec 46 at Phila., age 21, left sick at Jalapa 6 May 47, rejoined Co. 11 Jun 47, Court Martialed 17 Sep 47 for disobedience of an order & fined $5.00, the money was refunded and the sentence was remitted by Col. Wynkoop upon disc., promoted to 4th Cpl. 31 May 48, mo. with Co. 5 Aug 48. 1st Lt. Co. I, 98th P.V.I. 17 Aug 61 until his death 23 Dec 61.

HUBER, JOHN (Joseph): Sgt., enl. 2 Dec 46 at Phila., age 34, promoted from 4th Sgt. to 3rd Sgt. 12 Apr 47, left sick at Jalapa 22 May 47, disc. at Jalapa 22 May 47 on SCD for diarrhea.

HUBER, JOHN: Pvt., enl. 2 Dec 46 at Phila., age 29, listed as sick on 14 Dec 46 - 28 Feb 47 MR, left sick at Vera Cruz 9 Apr 47, died at Vera Cruz 14 May 47.

HULLER, CHARLES ULRICH (Ulrich Charles): Pvt., enl. 2 Dec 46 at Phila., age 29, deserted at Pittsburgh 20 Dec 46.

HUTTNER, GEORGE: Cpl., enl. 2 Dec 46 at Phila., age 33, promoted to 4th Sgt. 12 Apr 47, promoted to 3rd Sgt. 28 May 47, promoted to 2nd Sgt. 8 Jul 47, promoted to 1st Sgt. 14 Oct 47, missing at San Angel from 25 Dec 47 & supposed to have been murdered.

JAGERN, ALBERT: Pvt., enl. & mi. 3 Aug 47 at Perote, Mexico by Col. Wynkoop, age 29, listed as under arrest on Jan-Feb 48 MR, fined $7.00 by Court Martial 11 Feb 48 for disobedience of an order, mo. with Co. 5 Aug 48.

JUNGLANS, HENRY: Pvt., enl. 2 Dec 46 at Phila., age 21, Court Martialed 17 Sep 47 for disobedience of an order & fined $5.00, the money was refunded and the sentence was remitted by Col. Wynkoop upon disc., mo. with Co. 5 Aug 48.

KERN, JACOB: Pvt., enl. 2 Dec 46 at Phila., age 28, listed as sick on May-Jun 47 MR, died at Perote 25 Aug 47 from diarrhea.

KIRCHNER, ADAM (Hubert): Cpl., enl. 2 Dec 46 at Phila., age 32, deserted at New Orleans 14 Jan 47.

KNETSCH, LEWIS: (Knetsh): Pvt., enl. 2 Dec 46 at Phila., age 23, listed as sick on 31 Aug - 31 Dec 47 MR, sick in hospital in Mexico City according to Jan-Feb 48 MR, was moved to Jalapa & left there sick 14 Apr 48, died at Jalapa in Apr 48 from consumption.

KOHLER, WILLIAM Pvt., enl. 2 Dec 46 at Phila., age 35, promoted to 4th Cpl. 12 Apr 47, promoted to 3rd Cpl. 28 May 47, reduced to Pvt. 1 Dec 47, rejoined Co. from Perote 26 Dec 47, mo. with Co. 5 Aug 48. Pvt. Co. C, 98th P.V.I. 6 Sep 61 to 1 Oct 61. Sgt. Co. D, 98th P.V.I. 1 Oct 61 to 23 Feb 63.

KOLB, AUGUSTUS: Pvt., enl. 2 Dec 46 at Phila., age 24, died at Perote 31 Jul 47 from consumption.

KOLTES, JOHN: Pvt., enl. 2 Dec 46 at Phila., age 21, promoted to Cpl. 8 Jul 47, promoted to 3rd Sgt. 1 Dec 47, promoted to 2nd Sgt. 31 Jan 48, mo. with Co. 5 Aug 48. Col. 73rd P.V.I. 17 Sep 61 until KIA at 2nd Bull Run 30 Aug 62.

KORN, VALERIUS (Frederick): (Kern): Pvt., enl. 2 Dec 46 at Phila., age 29, left sick at Vera Cruz 9 Apr 47, disc. at Vera Cruz 28 Apr 47 on SCD.

KRAMER, ADAM: Pvt., enl. 2 Dec 46 at Phila., age 38, Court Martialed 17 Sep 47 for disobedience of an order & fined $5.00, the money was refunded and the sentence was remitted by Col. Wynkoop upon disc., promoted to 1st Cpl. 1 Dec 47, mo. with Co. 5 Aug 48. Pvt. Co. F, 2nd U.S. Dragoons 16 May 57 to 16 May 62. Pvt. & Sgt. Co. I; 1st Lt. Co. B; and Capt. Co. M, 15th Pa. Cavalry 6 Sep 62 to 21 Jun 65. 2nd Lt. 2nd U.S. Cavalry 7 Dec 65 to 12 Feb 66. 2nd Lt., 1st Lt., Capt. & Maj. 6th U.S. Cavalry 27 Apr 66 until retirement 13 Jan 97. Died 10 Nov 01.

KRAMER, ANDREW JOHN (John Andrew): Pvt., enl. 2 Dec 46 at Phila., age 24, wounded in the knee 11 Mar 47 on a sand hill southwest of Vera Cruz, left sick at Vera Cruz 9 Apr 47, disc. at Vera Cruz 28 Apr 47 on SCD.

KRAUSS, CHRISTIAN: (Krausz, Krauz): Pvt., enl. 2 Dec 46 at Phila., age 22, left sick at Jalapa 29 Apr 47, rejoined Co. 11 Jun 47, mo. with Co. 5 Aug 48.

Adam Kramer shown as a captain in the 15th Pennsylvania Cavalry in the Civil War
J. Craig Nannos Collection

KRAUSS, FREDERICK: Pvt., enl. 2 Dec 46 at Phila., age 23, Court Martial-ed 17 Sep 47 for disobedience of an order & fined $5.00, the money was refunded and the sentence was remitted by Col. Wynkoop upon disc., listed as sick on Jan-Feb 48 MR, listed as sick in hospital in San Angel on Mar-Apr 48 MR, mo. with Co. 5 Aug 48.

KRETSCH, CASPAR: (Kretsh): Pvt., enl. 2 Dec 46 at Phila., age 25, Court Martialed 17 Sep 47 for disobedience of an order & fined $5.00, the money was refunded and the sentence was remitted by Col. Wynkoop upon disc., listed as sick in hospital at San Angel on Mar-Apr 48 MR, mo. with Co. 5 Aug 48.

LAGER, HENRY: Pvt., enl. 2 Dec 46 at Phila., age 23, listed as sick on Mar-Apr 47 MR, left sick at Jalapa 6 May 47, rejoined Co. 7 Jun 47, listed as sick on 31 Aug - 31 Dec 47 MR, listed as sick in hospital at Mexico City on Jan-Feb 48 MR, mo. with Co. 5 Aug 48.

LEHN, HENRY: Pvt., enl. 2 Dec 46 at Phila., age 21, left sick at Vera Cruz 9 Apr 47, evidently evacuated to New Orleans, disc. at New Orleans 31 Dec 47 on SCD.

MAGEARY, CHARLES (John): (Maguary, Meaguery): Pvt., enl. 2 Dec 46 at Phila., age 21, on extra duty as Blacksmith according to Jul-Aug 47 MR, mo. with Co. 5 Aug 48.

MAYER, JOHN: (Meyer): Pvt., enl. 2 Dec 46 at Phila., age 26, left sick at Vera Cruz 9 Apr 47, disc. at Vera Cruz 27 Apr 47 on SCD.

MEHLHORN, JOHN: Pvt., enl. 2 Dec 46 at Phila., age 40, listed as sick on May-Jun 47 MR, died at Perote 25 Jul 47 from diarrhea.

MEILEY, BENJAMIN GEORGE: Pvt., enl. 2 Dec 46 at Phila., age 22, Court Martialed 17 Sep 47 for disobedience of an order & fined $5.00, the money was refunded and the sentence was remitted by Col. Wynkoop upon disc., mo. with Co. 5 Aug 48.

MERKEL, MATTHEW: Pvt., enl. 2 Dec 46 at Phila., age 26, Court Martialed 17 Sep 47 for disobedience of an order & fined $5.00, the money was refund-ed and the sentence was remitted by Col. Wynkoop upon disc., mo. with Co. 5 Aug 48.

MEYER, CHARLES: (Mayer): Pvt., enl. 2 Dec 46 at Phila., age 22, listed as sick on Jul-Aug 47 MR, left sick at Perote 29 Nov 47, rejoined Co. at Perote 9 Apr 48, mo. with Co. 5 Aug 48.

MEYER, JOHN: (Mayer): Pvt., enl. 2 Dec 46 at Phila., age 29, left sick at Vera Cruz 9 Apr 47, disc. at New Orleans 31 Dec 47 on SCD.

MOORE, ANDREW: Pvt., enl. 2 Dec 46 at Phila., age 41, left sick at Vera Cruz 9 Apr 47, died at Vera Cruz 27 May 47 from consumption.

MORITZ, JOHN: Pvt., enl. 2 Dec 46 at Phila., age 26, Court Martialed 17 Sep 47 for disobedience of an order & fined $5.00, the money was refunded and the sentence was remitted by Col. Wynkoop upon disc., listed as sick on Jan-Feb 48 MR, fined $5.00 by Court Martial 11 Feb 48 for disobedience of an order, mo. with Co. 5 Aug 48.

MULLER, JOHN: Pvt., enl. 14 Dec 46 at Pittsburgh, age 27, left sick at Vera Cruz 9 Apr 47, disc. at Vera Cruz 27 Apr 47 on SCD.

NEWMANN, NICHOLAS: Pvt., enl. 2 Dec 46 at Phila., age 28, listed as Fifer in Co. descriptive book, disc. at Vera Cruz 7 Apr 47 on SCD.

PFIEFLEY, ANDREW: (Peiffley, Pfeiffley): Pvt., enl. 2 Dec 46 at Phila., age 25, left sick at Jalapa 6 May 47, rejoined Co. 11 Jun 47, Court Martialed 17 Sep 47 for disobedience of an order & fined $5.00, the money was refunded and the sentence was remitted by Col. Wynkoop upon disc., mo. with Co. 5 Aug 48.

PRATT, ANDREW: Pvt., enl. 2 Dec 46 at Phila., age 19, deserted at New Orleans 14 Jan 47.

RAAB, CHRISTIAN: Pvt., enl. 2 Dec 46 at Phila., age 38, mo. with Co. 5 Aug 48.

REEB, GOTTLOB (Gottlieb): (Rueb): Pvt., enl. 2 Dec 46 at Phila., age 35, listed as sick on 14 Dec 46 - 28 Feb 47 MR, KIA on the Navy Battery near Vera Cruz 26 Mar 47.

REISSMAN, MARTIN: (Reissmann): Pvt., enl. 2 Dec 46 at Phila., age 23, left sick at Jalapa 6 May 47, died at Jalapa 29 May 47 from consumption.

RIMON, ABRAHAM: Pvt., enl. 2 Dec 46 at Phila., age 26, listed as sick on Jul-Aug 47 MR, died at Perote 6 Nov 47 from consumption.

SAWER, CHARLES: (Sauer): Pvt., enl. 2 Dec 46 at Phila., age 26, died at Perote 18 Aug 47 from diarrhea.

SCHAFFER, HENRY: (Schaeffer): Pvt., enl. 2 Dec 46 at Phila., age 41, died at Perote 10 Aug 47 from consumption.

SCHEICK, JOSEPH: (Scheik, Shick): Pvt., enl. 2 Dec 46 at Phila., age 21, promoted to Cpl. 1 May 48, died at San Angel 4 May 48 when he accidently drowned while bathing in a small mill pond.

SCHERZER, JOHN: (Scheizer): Pvt., enl. & mi. 3 Aug 47 at Phila. by Lt. Ankrimm, age 21, reported at Carlisle Barracks on 31 Aug 47, hospitalized at Perote in Dec 47, joined Co. at San Angel 27 Apr 48, no further record given.

SCHLINKERT, LEWIS (Frederick): Pvt., enl. 1 Dec 46 at Wilkes-Barre, age 36, left sick at Jalapa 6 May 47, died at Jalapa 12 May 47 from dropsy.

SCHMIDT, FREDERICK: Pvt., enl. 1 Dec 46 at Wilkes-Barre, age 40, disc. at Perote 6 Jun 47 on SCD.

SCHONLE, MICHAEL: (Schoenle): Pvt., enl. 2 Dec 46 at Phila., age 25, on extra duty as Baker according to May-Jun 47 MR, Court Martialed 17 Sep 47 for disobedience of an order & fined $5.00, the money was refunded and the sentence was remitted by Col. Wynkoop upon disc., mo. with Co. 5 Aug 48.

SCHUHE, CHARLES (Schuh): Pvt., enl. 2 Dec 46 at Phila., age 23, Court Martialed 17 Sep 47 for disobedience of an order & fined $5.00, the money was refunded and the sentence was remitted by Col. Wynkoop upon disc., mo. with Co. 5 Aug 48.

SCHUHE, GEORGE: (Schuh): Pvt., enl. 2 Dec 46 at Phila., age 33, Court Martialed 17 Sep 47 for disobedience of an order & fined $5.00, the money was refunded and the sentence was remitted by Col. Wynkoop upon disc., mo. with Co. 5 Aug 48.

SCHULTZ, LEONHARDT: (Schultze, Schulze): Pvt., enl. 2 Dec 46 at Phila., age 26, Court Martialed 17 Sep 47 for disobedience of an order & fined $5.00, the money was refunded and the sentence was remitted by Col. Wynkoop upon disc., mo. with Co. 5 Aug 48.

SCHWEBEL, FRANCIS: Pvt., enl. 2 Dec 46 at Phila., age 25, left sick at Jalapa 6 May 47, rejoined Co. at Perote 7 Jun 47, mo. with Co. 5 Aug 48.

SEIDENSTRICKER, FREDERICK: (Saidenstricker): 2nd Lt., enl. at Phila., age 32, listed as sick on Mar-Apr 47 MR, received one month's furlough from 7 May 47 at the end of which time he resigned, Gen. Scott accepted his resignation 7 Jun 47.

SIMON, HENRY: Pvt., enl. 2 Dec 46 at Phila., age 23, Court Martialed 17 Sep 47 for disobedience of an order & fined $5.00, the money was refunded and the sentence was remitted by Col. Wynkoop upon disc., mo. with Co. 5 Aug 48. Reportedly served in Battery F, 2nd U.S. Artillery in the Civil War, unconfirmed.

SIMON, JACOB: Pvt., enl. 2 Dec 46 at Phila., age 20, Court Martialed 17 Sep 47 for disobedience of an order & fined $5.00, mo. with Co. 5 Aug 48.

SPERLIN, STEPHEN: (Sperlein, Spoerlein): Pvt., enl. 2 Dec 46 at Phila., age 30, left sick at Jalapa 6 Apr 48, rejoined the Co. on the march home, mo. with Co. 5 Aug 48.

SPOERER, HENRY: (Sperer): Pvt., enl. 2 Dec 46 at Phila., age 24, Court Martialed 17 Sep 47 for disobedience of an order & fined $5.00, the money was refunded and the sentence was remitted by Col. Wynkoop upon disc., mo. with Co. 5 Aug 48.

STEEL, JOSEPH: Pvt., enl. 2 Dec 46 at Phila., age 30, left sick at Jalapa 29 Apr 47, rejoined Co. 11 Jun 47, left sick at Puebla 4 Dec 47, rejoined Co. 1 Feb 48, mo. with Co. 5 Aug 48.

STICKEL, JACOB: Pvt., enl. 2 Dec 46 at Phila., age 21, on extra duty as Butcher according to May-Jun & Jul-Aug 47 MRs, on detached service at Perote as Butcher according to Mar-Apr 48 MR, mo. with Co. 5 Aug 48.

STOCK, GEORGE: Cpl., enl. 2 Dec 46 at Phila., age 26, left sick at Jalapa 29 Apr 47, rejoined Co. at Perote 11 Jun 47, promoted to Sgt. 28 May 47, listed as sick on Jul-Aug 47 MR, died at Perote 7 Sep 47 from consumption.

VOLTAIRE, LEWIS (Louis): Sgt., enl. 2 Dec 46 at Phila., age 29, promoted to 1st Sgt. 12 Apr 47, elected 2nd Lt. 8 Jul 47, Court Martialed in Jan 48, mo. with Co. 5 Aug 48. Capt. Co. I, 98th P.V.I. 17 Aug 61 to 30 Jan 64.

VOLTZ, MARTIN: Pvt., enl. 2 Dec 46 at Phila., age 21, disc. at New Orleans 12 Jan 47 on SCD.

WALSCH, FREDERICK: (Waltsch): Pvt., enl. & mi. 4 Aug 47 at Perote, Mexico by Col. Wynkoop, Court Martialed 17 Sep 47 for disobedience of an order & fined $5.00, promoted to Cpl. 1 Dec 47, deserted at San Angel 11 Feb 48.

WANDEL, JOHN: Pvt., enl. 2 Dec 46 at Phila., age 26, on extra duty as Baker according to Jul-Aug 47 MR, Court Martialed 17 Sep 47 for disobedience of an order & fined $5.00, the money was refunded and the sentence was remitted by Col. Wynkoop upon disc., mo. with Co. 5 Aug 48.

WEISS, CHRISTIAN (Carl, Charles): Pvt., enl. 2 Dec 46 at Phila., age 21, Court Martialed 17 Sep 47 for disobedience of an order & fined $5.00, the money was refunded and the sentence was remitted by Col. Wynkoop upon disc., mo. with Co. 5 Aug 48.

WEVELL, WILLIAM: (Wewell): Pvt., enl. 2 Dec 46 at Phila., age 41, listed as sick on May-Jun 47 MR, died at Perote 30 Jun 47 from diarrhea.

Company F, 1st Regiment
Philadelphia Light Guards

It was likely that the Philadelphia Light Guards of Captain John Bennett existed before the beginning of hostilities with Mexico. Having volunteered early for service, the company was notified in November 1846 that it would be included in Pennsylvania's 1st Regiment. The Guards left Philadelphia by train on 7 December for the rendezvous at Pittsburgh. First Lieutenant Horace B. Field, 3rd U.S. Artillery, mustered the Light Guards into Federal service on 15 December.

The Light Guards performed faithful service during the investment of Vera Cruz, the battles of Cerro Gordo and La Hoya, the defense of Perote and the battle of Huamantla. On 8 December 1847 they arrived at Mexico City for occupation duty.

The Philadelphia companies of the 1st Regiment, including the Philadelphia Light Guards, returned to their home city at about 7:00 A.M. on 24 July 1848. The welcome was tremendous. On 28 July, Captain George Taylor, 3rd U.S. Artillery, mustered the veterans out of the U.S. Army.

A total of 98 men served in the company during the war. Only one desertion was recorded. One man transferred to another unit, while two others transferred into the Guards. The company suffered three battle casualties, with one man reported as missing in action. In all, eight men died in service. An additional twenty-four were discharged before their terms had expired.

ACKERMAN, DAVID: Sgt., enl. 18 Nov 46 at Phila., age 33, transferred as Pvt. from Co. C, 1st Pa. Regt. 12 Jun 47 by order of Col. Wynkoop, listed as sick in quarters on Mar-Apr 48 MR, mo. with Co. 28 Jul 48.

ACUFF, WILLIAM: Pvt., enl. 1 Dec 46 at Phila., age 21, listed as sick on Jul-Aug 47 MR, disc. at Perote 29 Oct 47 on SCD for diarrhea.

ALBAUGH, MAURICE (Morris, Morriss): Pvt., enl. 1 Dec 46 at Phila., age 23, fined $3.00 by Regimental Court Martial at Perote, on detached duty at Jalapa from 7 Apr 48, mo. with Co. 28 Jul 48.

ALLEN, JOHN M.: Pvt., enl. 1 Dec 46 at Phila., age 36, disc. at Perote 6 Jun 47 on SCD for diarrhea.

BARD, WILLIAM H.: Pvt., enl. 1 Dec 46 at Phila., age 24, disc. at Perote 6 Jun 47 on SCD for diarrhea.

BASSITT, ISAAC: (Bassett): Pvt., enl. 1 Dec 46 at Phila., age 19, disc. at New Orleans 13 Jan 47 on Habeas Corpus because he was a minor.

BASTION, JOSEPH A.: Pvt., enl. 1 Dec 46 at Phila., age 24, left sick at Perote 29 Nov 47, rejoined Co., listed as sick in quarters on Mar-Apr 48 MR, mo. with Co. 28 Jul 48.

BENNETT, ADOLPH: Pvt., enl. 1 Dec 46 at Phila., age 30, wounded 16 Apr 47 on march from Vera Cruz to Plan Del Rio, hospitalized at Jalapa, rejoined Co. shortly thereafter, mo. with Co. 28 Jul 48.

BENNETT, JOHN: Capt., enl. 1 Dec 46 at Phila., age 25, listed as sick on Jan-Feb 48 MR, mo. with Co. 28 Jul 48.

BISHOP, WILLIAM H.: Pvt., enl. 1 Dec 46 at Phila., age 23, died at Perote 26 Jul 47 from diarrhea.

BLACK, GEORGE: Cpl., enl. 1 Dec 46 at Phila., age 24, promoted to Sgt. 1 Jun 47, mo. with Co. 28 Jul 48.

BROWN, ISAAC CHAUNCEY: 2nd Lt., enl. 1 Dec 46 at Phila., age 31, detailed to duty with Battery A, 3rd U.S. Artillery from May or Jun 47 until rejoining Co. 16 Apr 48, was Acting Ordnance Officer at Perote from 25 Jun 47 to 29 Feb 48, mo. with Co. 28 Jul 48.

BUNDY, AARON: (Bundey): Pvt., enl. 1 Dec 46 at Phila., age 24, listed as in hospital at Jalapa on Mar-Apr 47 MR, disc. at Perote 6 or 15 Jun 47 on SCD for diarrhea.

CALLOWAY, THOMAS J.: (Callaway): Pvt., enl. 1 Dec 46 at Phila., age 22, detailed as Acting Division Commissary Sgt. in Mexico City Dec 47 through Apr 48, mo. with Co. 28 Jul 48.

CAMERON, ALEXANDER: Pvt., enl. 1 Dec 46 at Phila., age 27, left sick in hospital at Mexico City 19 Dec 47, rejoined Co. by Mar 48, mo. with Co. 28 Jul 48.

CARTY, RANDOLPH: Pvt., enl. 1 Dec 46 at Phila., age 32, listed as in hospital at Vera Cruz on Mar-Apr 47 MR, disc. at Vera Cruz 27 Apr 47 on SCD for diarrhea.

COLE, HOWARD M.: 4th Cpl., enl. 20 Nov 46 at Phila., age 25, transferred as Pvt. 23 Jun 47 from Co. G, 1st Pa. Regt. by order of Col. Wynkoop, left sick at Perote 29 Nov 47, rejoined Co. probably in Mar 48, mo. with Co. 28 Jul 48.

COX, JAMES: Pvt., enl. 1 Dec 46 at Phila., age 26, mo. with Co. 28 Jul 48.

CROUT, WILLIAM D.: Pvt., enl. 1 Dec 46 at Phila., age 22, fined $3.00 by Regimental Court Martial according to 31 Aug - 31 Dec 47 MR, mo. with Co. 28 Jul 48.

DAY, WILLIAM: Pvt., enl. 1 Dec 46 at Phila., age 22, died at Perote 4 Jun 47 from diarrhea.

DIVINE, PETER JAMES: (Devine): Pvt., enl. 1 Dec 46 at Phila., age 22, left sick at Perote 9 Apr 48, rejoined Co. on the march home, mo. with Co. 28 Jul 48.

DOWNER, CHARLES A.: Pvt., enl. 1 Dec 46 at Phila., age 23, fined $3.00 by Regimental Court Martial according to 31 Aug - 31 Dec 47 MR, left sick at Perote 29 Nov 47, mo. with Co. 28 Jul 48.

DUNNETT, JESSE: Pvt., enl. 1 Dec 46 at Phila., age 24, deserted at New Orleans 12 Jan 47.

DUNPHY, THOMAS JAMES (James F.): Pvt., enl. 1 Dec 46 at Phila., age 22, mo. with Co. 28 Jul 48.

EALER, LEWIS W.: Pvt., enl. 1 Dec 46 at Phila., age 18, mo. with Co. 28 Jul 48. Sgt. Major, 2nd Lt. & 1st Lt. Co. F, 68th P.V.I. 23 Aug 62 until WIA at Gettysburg 2 Jul 63, died of wounds 6 Oct 63.

ENGLISH, MIZEAL: Pvt., enl. 1 Dec 46 at Phila., age 22, promoted to Cpl. 1 Nov 47, mo. with Co. 28 Jul 48.

FERER, JOHN: Pvt., enl. 1 Dec 46 at Phila., age 23, mo. with Co. 28 Jul 48.

FLEMING, ELIAS: (Flemming): Pvt., enl. 1 Dec 46 at Phila., age 23, listed as sick in quarters on Mar-Apr 48 MR, mo. with Co. 28 Jul 48.

FORBES, WILLIAM: (Forbs): Pvt., enl. 1 Dec 46 at Phila., age 23, listed as sick in hospital at Jalapa on Mar-Apr 47 MR, listed as sick in quarters on Mar-Apr 48 MR, mo. with Co. 28 Jul 48.

FRENCH, WILLIAM: Pvt., enl. 1 Dec 46 at Phila., age 20, mo. with Co. 28 Jul 48.

FUNSTON, THOMAS G.: Pvt., enl. 1 Dec 46 at Phila., age 21, mo. with Co. 28 Jul 48. Capt. Co. B, 68th P.V.I. 19 Aug 62 to 6 Oct 63.

GODSHALL, FREDERICK S. (T.): Pvt., enl. 1 Dec 46 at Phila., age 24, listed as sick in hospital at Vera Cruz on Mar-Apr & May-Jun 47 MRs, disc. at Vera Cruz 27 Apr 47 on SCD for diarrhea.

GRAY, WILLIAM H.: 2nd Lt., enl. at Phila., age 32, promoted to 1st Lt. 4 Jun 47, appointed Acting Asst. Commissary of Subsistence 1 Dec 47, mo. with Co. 28 Jul 48. Col. 20th P.V.I. (3 mos.) 30 Apr 61 to 27 Jul 61. Capt. Co. F, 192nd P.V.I. 12 Jul 64 to 11 Nov 64. Born 12 Mar 24 & died 12 Nov 12.

GROFF, JOHN R.: Pvt., enl. 1 Dec 46 at Phila., age 23, listed as sick on Jul-Aug 47 MR, disc. at Perote 29 Oct 47 on SCD for diarrhea.

HEILMAN, ABRAHAM: (Hileman, Hilman): Pvt., enl. 1 Dec 46 at Phila., age 23, detached to Capt. Wall's Battery of U.S. Art. according to Mar-Apr 47 MR, fined $3.00 by Court Martial according to 31 Aug - 31 Dec 47 MR, listed as sick in quarters on Mar-Apr 48 MR, mo. with Co. 28 Jul 48.

HILDEBRAND, URIAH: (Hildebrant, Hilderbrant): Pvt., enl. 1 Dec 46 at Phila., age 21, mo. with Co. 28 Jul 48.

HITCHCOCK, WILLIAM: Pvt., enl. 1 Dec 46 at Phila., age 22, fined $3.00 by Regimental Court Martial according to 31 Aug - 31 Dec 47 MR, listed as sick in quarters on Mar-Apr 48 MR, mo. with Co. 28 Jul 48.

HOFFMAN, JOHN G.: Pvt., enl. 1 Dec 46 at Phila., age 18, left sick at Vera Cruz 9 Apr 47, disc. at Vera Cruz 25 Apr 47 on SCD for diarrhea.

HUNTLEY, JOSEPH: (Huntly): Pvt., enl. 1 Dec 46 at Phila., age 24, fined $3.00 by Regimental Court Martial according to 31 Aug - 31 Dec 47 MR, mo. with Co. 28 Jul 48.

HUTTON, WILLIAM: Pvt., enl. 1 Dec 46 at Phila., age 28, listed as attendant at Jalapa Hospital on Mar-Apr 47 MR, left sick at Perote 29 Nov 47, rejoined Co. by 30 Apr 48, mo. with Co. 28 Jul 48.

JENKINS, OSCAR D.: Pvt., enl. 1 Dec 46 at Phila., age 22, left sick at Perote 29 Nov 47, disc. at Perote 17 Dec 47 on SCD. 1st Sgt. & 2nd Lt. Co. C, 13th Pa. Reserves 1 Jun 61 to 20 Apr 63, WIA at Fredericksburg. Capt. Co. C & Maj. 194th P.V.I. 18 Jul 64 to 6 Nov 64.

JONES, JOHN: Pvt., enl. 1 Dec 46 at Phila., age 24, had his musket broken by enemy shot at Cerro Gordo 18 Apr 47, listed as sick on Jul-Aug 47 MR, died at Perote 15 Nov 47 from diarrhea.

KEAN, CHARLES: Pvt., enl. 1 Dec 46 at Phila., age 27, listed as sick on Jul-Aug 47 MR, disc. at Perote 29 Oct 47 on SCD for diarrhea.

KEITH, JACOB: Pvt., enl. 1 Dec 46 at Phila., age 21, detached for duty with Capt. Wall's Battery of U.S. Art. according to Mar-Apr 47 MR, mo. with Co. 28 Jul 48.

LARRANTREE, AUGUSTUS A.: (Larrentree): 1st Lt., enl. at Phila., age 45, appointed Acting Asst. Q.M. 14 Jan 47, listed as sick on 15 Dec 46 - 28 Feb 47 MR, died at Anton Lizardo on board the ship "Oxnard" 7 Mar 47 from brain fever.

LARUE, KINSEY: Pvt., enl. 15 Dec 46 at Pittsburgh, age 23, died at Perote 18 Jul 47 from diarrhea.

LEICHT, ENGLEHEART: Pvt., enl. 1 Dec 46 at Phila., age 31, missing after the Battle of Huamantla 9 Oct 47.

LEWIS, DANIEL: Pvt., enl. 1 Dec 46 at Phila., age 20, disc. at Perote 6 Jun 47 on SCD for diarrhea.

LINDSEY, JOSEPH: (Linsey): Pvt., enl. 1 Dec 46 at Phila., age 23, disc. at Perote 29 Oct 47 on SCD for diarrhea.

LINDSEY, THOMAS: (Linsey): Pvt., enl. 1 Dec 46 at Phila., age 25, promoted to Cpl. 1 Jun 47, mo. with Co. 28 Jul 48.

LITTLE, CHARLES: Pvt., enl. 1 Dec 46 at Phila., age 23, listed as sick in quarters on Mar-Apr 48 MR, mo. with Co. 28 Jul 48.

MANCER, STEPHEN: (Manser): Pvt., enl. 1 Dec 46 at Phila., age 25, died at Mexico City 25 Apr 48 of wounds received from the guard 24 Apr 48 while endeavoring to escape arrest.

MANN, WILLIAM: Pvt., enl. 1 Dec 46 at Phila., age 35, mo. with Co. 28 Jul 48.

MARTIN, WILLIAM: Pvt., enl. 1 Dec 46 at Phila., age 27, fined $3.00 by Court Martial according to 31 Aug - 31 Dec 47 MR, listed as sick in quarters on Mar-Apr 48 MR, mo. with Co. 28 Jul 48.

MARTINO, CASPER: Pvt., enl. 1 Dec 46 at Phila., age 21, fined $3.00 by Regimental Court Martial according to 31 Aug - 31 Dec 47 MR, mo. with Co. 28 Jul 48. Capt. Co. K, 7th Pa. Reserves 4 Jun 61 to 27 Jan 62.

McCULLOUGH, GEORGE W.: Cpl., enl. 1 Dec 46 at Phila., age 21, mo. with Co. 28 Jul 48.

McCULLY, ROBERT: (McCulley, McCullough): Drummer, enl. 1 Dec 46 at Phila., age 42, appointed Principal Musician by Col. Wynkoop 19 Dec 46, mo. with F & S 8 Aug 48.

McDOUGAL, LEON: Pvt., enl. 1 Dec 46 at Phila., age 22, appointed Q.M. Sgt. by Col. Wynkoop 19 Jul 47, mo. with F & S 8 Aug 48.

McDOWELL, PAXON: Pvt., enl. 1 Dec 46 at Phila., age 22, disc. at New Orleans 12 Jan 47 on SCD for rupture.

McGLUCKEN, SAMUEL: (McCluken): Pvt., enl. 1 Dec 46 at Phila., age 21, fined $1.50 by Regimental Court Martial according to 31 Aug - 31 Dec 47 MR, mo. with Co. 28 Jul 48.

McLAUGHLIN, JOHN J. (S.): (McLoughlin): Pvt., enl. 8 Dec 46 at Hollidaysburg, age 25, occ. blacksmith, absent with leave at mi., joined Co. at New Orleans 10 Jan 47, mi. at Ship Island 28 Feb 47, transferred to Co. B, 2nd Pa. Regt. 27 Jun 47 by order of Col. Wynkoop.

McMANUS, RICHARD: Pvt., enl. 1 Dec 46 at Phila., age 21, listed as sick in hospital at Jalapa on Mar-Apr 47 MR, listed as sick on Jul-Aug 47 MR, disc. at Perote 29 Oct 47 on SCD for diarrhea.

McQUILLEN, PATRICK: Pvt., enl. 1 Dec 46 at Phila., age 21, disc. at Vera Cruz 7 Apr 47 on SCD for diarrhea & consumption.

MOAN, DENNIS: Fifer, enl. 1 Dec 46 at Phila., age 19, reduced to Pvt. 1 Jun 47, left sick at Perote 29 Nov 47, disc. at Perote 17 Dec 47 on SCD for diarrhea.

MONROE, JOHN E.: (Munroe): Pvt., enl. 1 Dec 46 at Phila., age 25, was sick at Perote 9 Apr 48, mo. with Co. 28 Jul 48.

MULLEN, WILLIAM E.: (Mullin): Pvt., enl. 1 Dec 46 at Phila., age 27, listed as serving with Commissary Dept. on May-Jun & Jul-Aug 47 MRs, disc. at Perote upon his own request 29 Oct 47.

NELSON, FRANCISCO L.: Sgt., enl. 1 Dec 46 at Phila., age 33, listed as sick on Jul-Aug 47 MR, disc. at Perote 29 Oct 47 on SCD for diarrhea.

PELOUZE, CHARLES W. (N.): (Pelouge, Pelouse, Pelowze): Cpl., enl. 1 Dec 46 at Phila., age 22, promoted to 4th Sgt. 1 Nov 47, mo. with Co. 28 Jul 48.

POLK, SAMUEL B.: Pvt., enl. 1 Dec 46 at Phila., age 33, detached for duty in Perote from 9 Apr 48 through at least 30 Apr 48, mo. with Co. 28 Jul 48.

PRICE, SAMUEL: Pvt., enl. 1 Dec 46 at Phila., age 28, listed as on extra duty on May-Jun 47 MR, fined $3.00 by Regimental Court Martial according to 31 Aug - 31 Dec 47 MR, mo. with Co. 28 Jul 48.

READ, GEORGE P.: (Reed): Pvt., enl. 1 Dec 46 at Phila., age 21, mo. with Co. 28 Jul 48.

REED, SAMUEL: Cpl., enl. 1 Dec 46 at Phila., age 24, left sick at Vera Cruz 9 Apr 47, disc. at Vera Cruz 27 Apr 47 on SCD for diarrhea.

REMLEY, LEVI (Levy) H.: (Remely, Remly): Pvt., enl. 1 Dec 46 at Phila., age 22, fined $1.50 by Regimental Court Martial at Perote according to 31 Aug-31 Dec 47 MR, listed as sick in quarters on Mar-Apr 48 MR, mo. with Co. 28 Jul 48.

RIBAUT, JOHN: (Ribant, Ribault, Ribout): Sgt., enl. 1 Dec 46 at Phila., age 32, promoted to 2nd Lt. 11 Jun 47, mo. with Co. 28 Jul 48.

ROBERTSON, FRANCIS: Pvt., enl. 1 Dec 46 at Phila., age 21, mo. with Co. 28 Jul 48.

RUPLEY, JACOB: Pvt., enl. 15 Dec 46 at Hollidaysburg, age 20, left sick at Perote 29 Nov 47, rejoined Co. by 30 Apr 48, mo. with Co. 28 Jul 48.

SANDERS, GEORGE P.: (Saunders): Pvt., enl. 1 Dec 46 at Phila., age 26, detached to serve with Capt. Woll's Battery of U.S. Artillery 15 Apr 47, rejoined Co. by 30 Jun 47, fined $3.00 by Court Martial at Perote according to 31 Aug - 31 Dec 47 MR, mo. with Co. 28 Jul 48. 1st Sgt. & 1st Lt. Co. B, 68th P.V.I. 19 Aug 62 to 9 Jun 65.

SCHAFFER, WILLIAM H.: (Schafer): Pvt., enl. 1 Dec 46 at Phila., age 24, mo. with Co. 28 Jul 48.

SHEIFLEY, GEORGE: (Scheifley, Schiefley, Sheifly): Pvt., enl. 1 Dec 46 at Phila., age 24, mo. with Co. 28 Jul 48.

SHINGLE, CHRISTOPHER: (Schingle): Pvt., enl. 1 Dec 46 at Phila., age 22, mo. with Co. 28 Jul 48.

SHINGLE, HENRY: (Schingle): Pvt., enl. 1 Dec 46 at Phila., age 20, mo. with Co. 28 Jul 48.

SMITH, SAMUEL P.: Pvt., enl. 1 Dec 46 at Phila., age 32, mo. with Co. 28 Jul 48.

STARKS, CHARLES S.: Pvt., enl. 8 Dec 46 at Lewistown, age 23, died at Perote 3 Aug 47 from diarrhea.

STAUNTON, JOHN F.: (Stanton): Pvt., enl. 1 Dec 46 at Phila., age 25, acting as orderly to Col. Wynkoop according to May-Jun 47 MR, disc. at Perote 29 Oct 47 upon his own request on SCD. Col. 67th P.V.I. 24 Jul 61 to 1 Sep 64. Died at Phila. 8 Feb 75.

THEISS, THEODORE: Pvt., enl. 1 Dec 46 at Phila., age 24, wounded on the sand hills south-west of Vera Cruz 11 Mar 47, disc. at Vera Cruz 6 Apr 47 for wound.

THOMAS, ENOCH: Pvt., enl. 1 Dec 46 at Phila., age 28, left sick at Jalapa 7 Apr 48, mo. with Co. 28 Jul 48. 1st Lt. & Capt. Co. A, 68th P.V.I. 18 Aug 62 to 18 Apr 63.

THOMAS, LAFAYETTE: Pvt., enl. 1 Dec 46 at Phila., age 21, listed as in hospital at Jalapa on Mar-Apr 47 MR, mo. with Co. 28 Jul 48.

THOMAS, RICHARD S. (Sermon): Pvt., enl. 1 Dec 46 at Phila., age 21, listed as sick on Jul-Aug 47 MR, listed as on extra duty as Acting Commissary Sgt. on 31 Aug - 31 Dec 47, Jan-Feb 48 & Mar-Apr 48 MRs, mo. with Co. 28 Jul 48.

WALBRIDGE, THOMAS: Pvt., enl. 8 Dec 46 at Lewistown, age 29, listed as sick in quarters on Mar-Apr 48 MR, mo. with Co. 28 Jul 48.

WALLACE, EDWARD E.: Sgt., enl. 1 Dec 46 at Phila., age 20, promoted to 1st Sgt. 11 Jun 47, left sick in hospital at Perote 29 Nov 47, rejoined Co. before 29 Feb 48, mo. with Co. 28 Jul 48. Lt. Col. 91st P.V.I. 4 Dec 61 to 10 Jan 63. Born 1 Mar 25 & died at Phila. 2 Jan 08.

WARNE, ELISHA: (Warren): 1st Sgt., enl. 1 Dec 46 at Phila., age 23, left sick at Vera Cruz 8 Apr 47, reduced to Pvt. 1 Jun 47, disc. at New Orleans date unknown on SCD for diarrhea.

WEBB, JOHN: Pvt., enl. 1 Dec 46 at Phila., age 25, detached to Q.M. Dept. at Perote from 29 Nov 47 through at least 30 Apr 48, mo. with Co. 28 Jul 48.

WEST, JAMES T.: Pvt., enl. 1 Dec 46 at Phila., age 24, detached to Capt. Woll's Battery of U.S. Artillery according to Mar-Apr 47 MR, rejoined Co. by 30 Jun 47, listed as sick in quarters on Mar-Apr 48 MR, mo. with Co. 28 Jul 48.

WHISNER, JACOB I. (S.): Pvt., enl. 1 Dec 46 at Phila., age 21, listed as sick in quarters on Mar-Apr 48 MR, mo. with Co. 28 Jul 48.

WHISNER, SAMUEL D.: Pvt., enl. 1 Dec 46 at Phila., age 25, promoted to 2nd Sgt. 1 Jun 47, listed as sick in quarters on Mar-Apr 48 MR, mo. with Co. 28 Jul 48.

WILKIE, JOSHUA (John) L.: (Wilkey): Pvt., enl. 1 Dec 46 at Phila., age 22, disc. at Perote 29 Oct 47 on SCD for diarrhea.

WILLIAMS, ISAAC: Pvt., enl. 1 Dec 46 at Phila., age 21, promoted to Cpl. 1 Jun 47, mo. with Co. 28 Jul 48.

Company G, 1st Regiment
Jefferson Guards

The Jefferson Guards was probably part of the Philadelphia Volunteer establishment before the crisis with Mexico erupted. The Guards, under Captain Turner G. Morehead, showed themselves up to the situation by volunteering early to do battle for their state and country. They were notified of their selection as part of Pennsylvania's first regiment in November, 1846 and left for Pittsburgh and the regimental rendezvous on 9 December. There First Lieutenant Horace B. Field, 3rd U.S. Artillery, on 17 December, mustered the new soldiers into Federal service.

While in the service of their country they took part in the siege of Vera Cruz, the battle of Cerro Gordo, and the defense of Puebla. Arriving in Mexico City on 8 December 1847, they assisted in garrisoning the vanquished capitol.

The Jefferson Guards, and other companies of the 1st Regiment from Philadelphia, arrived in the "City of Brotherly Love" at about 7 o'clock on the morning of 24 July 1848. Parades, speeches and banquets were the order of the day. On 29 July, Capt. George Taylor, 3rd U.S. Artillery, mustered the Guards out of U.S. service.

A total of 103 men served in the Guards during the war. Of these, nine recruits joined them in Mexico. Nine men deserted, and two were transferred to other companies. Seven men became battle casualties, with one killed in action. A total of fourteen died in service. Twenty-seven received discharges prior to muster out.

151

ADAIR, JAMES: Pvt., enl. 20 Nov. 46 at Phila., age 23, occ. carpenter, mo. with Co. 29 Jul 48.

AECHTERMACHT, WILLIAM: Pvt., enl. 20 Nov 46 at Phila., age 20, listed as sick in hospital at Jalapa on Mar-Apr 47 MR, disc. at Jalapa 24 May 47 on SCD for diarrhea.

ARTHUR, WILLIAM M.: Pvt., enl. 20 Nov 46 at Phila., age 26, occ. clerk, on furlough from 10 Nov 47, disc. at Phila. 4 Jan 48 upon his own request & by order of the Adjutant General.

ATKINSON, C.: Pvt., enl. 20 Nov 46 at Phila., age 30, deserted at Pittsburgh 20 Dec 46.

BARBER, FRANCIS W.: (Barbier, Barbrin): Pvt., enl. 20 Nov 46 at Phila., age 24, promoted to Cpl. 7 Mar 47, disc. at Jalapa 24 May 47 on SCD for liver disease.

BARNARD, BONAFON (Boniface, Bonnifon): (Bernard, Bernhard): Pvt., enl. 20 Jul 47 at Phila., age 21, occ. clerk, mi. 29 Jul 47 at Phila. by Capt. Scott, joined Co. 21 Dec 47, mo. with Co. 29 Jul 48.

BARTLING, EDWARD: Pvt., enl. 24 Jul 47 at Phila., age 32, occ. bricklayer, mi. 29 Jul 47 at Phila. by Capt. Scott, joined Co. 21 Dec 47 in Mexico City, mo. with Co. 29 Jul 48.

BEBEE, OLIVER: (Beebe): Pvt., enl. 20 Nov 46 at Phila., age 25, mo. with Co. 29 Jul 48.

BIRCH, JAMES: Pvt., enl. 20 Nov 46 at Phila., age 32, promoted to Q.M. Sgt. 22 Apr 47, disc. at Perote 19 Jul 47 on SCD for diarrhea and brain disease.

BOMHOWER, WILLIAM: (Bowenhower, Bumhower): Pvt., enl. & mi. 23 Aug 47 at Pittsburgh by Lt. Ankrimm, age 31, occ. gardner, reported at Carlisle Barracks on 31 Aug 47, joined Co. 21 Dec 47 in Mexico City, mo. with Co. 29 Jul 48.

BOWERHILL, ROBERT F.: (Bouerhill): Pvt., enl. 20 Nov 46 at Phila., age 38, died at Puebla 22 Sep 47 from diarrhea.

BRAZELL, JAMES: Pvt., enl. 20 Nov 46 at Phila., age 33, deserted at Pittsburgh 20 Dec 46.

BRIGGS, WILLIAM A. M.: Sgt., enl. 20 Nov 46 at Phila., age 24, promoted to 1st Sgt. 9 Apr 47, promoted to 1st Lt. 9 Nov 47, mo. with Co. 29 Jul 48.

BRYAN, WILLIAM: (Brian): 2nd Lt., enl. 20 Nov 46 at Phila., age 38, was Acting Asst. Surgeon on the ship *Statesman* 12 Jan 47 to 17 Feb 47 and 26 to 28 Feb 47, received 30 days leave of absence 4 Nov 47 due to illness, listed on the detachment roll at Ft. Mifflin 30 Jun 48, never rejoined Co. until it arrived in Phila., mo. with Co. 29 Jul 48.

CAMPBELL, JAMES: Pvt., enl. 20 Nov 46 at Phila., age 21, occ. carpenter, was sick in hospital at San Angel from 1 Feb 48 through Apr 48, mo. with Co. 29 Jul 48.

CARSON, THOMAS: Pvt., enl. 20 Nov 46 at Phila., age 28, occ. bricklayer, mo. with Co. 29 Jul 48.

CAVENAUGH, PHILIP C.: Pvt., enl. 20 Nov 46 at Phila., age 28, disc. at Jalapa 28 Apr 47 on SCD for diarrhea.

CLARE, JOHN: Pvt., enl. 20 Nov 46 at Phila., age 28, died at Perote 15 Jun 47.

CLOW, JOHN D. (B.): Pvt., enl. 20 Nov 46 at Phila., age 39, occ. baker, was on extra duty at Jalapa as baker from 23 Nov 47 through Apr 48, mo. with Co. 29 Jul 48.

COLE, HOWARD M.: 4th Cpl., enl. 20 Nov 46 at Phila., age 25, reduced to Pvt. 19 Apr 47, transferred to Co. F, 1st Pa. Regt. 23 Jun 47.

COOK, JOHN: Pvt., enl. 20 Nov 46 at Phila., age 25, occ. stone cutter, listed as in confinement on 17 Dec 46 - 28 Feb 47 MR, was sick in hospital from 28 Dec 47, sick in hospital at San Angel from 11 Feb 48, mo. with Co. 29 Jul 48.

CRESWELL, JOSIAH: (Cresswell): Pvt., enl. 20 Nov 46 at Phila., age 22, disc. at Pittsburgh 20 Dec 46 for palpitation of the heart.

CROSS, SAMUEL: Pvt., enl. 20 Nov 46 at Phila., age 22, listed as sick in hospital at Perote on May-Jun 47 MR, disc. at Perote 30 Oct 47.

DAY, LEHMAN H.: Pvt., enl. 20 Nov 46 at Phila., age 26, occ. clerk, on extra duty as Steward in hospital at Jalapa from 23 Nov 47 through Apr 48, mo. with Co. 29 Jul 48.

DEAL, GEORGE W.: Pvt., enl. 20 Nov 46 at Phila., age 22, disc. at Perote 29 Nov 47 on SCD for diarrhea.

DICE, CHARLES C.: Pvt., enl. 20 Nov 46 at Phila., age 24, occ. carpenter, mo. with Co. 29 Jul 48.

DIMOND, JOHN H.: (Diamon, Dimon): Pvt., enl. 20 Nov 46 at Phila., age 22, occ. carpenter, promoted to Cpl. 5 Sep 47, sick in hospital at San Angel from 20 Feb 48, mo. with Co. 29 Jul 48.

DOMINUS, JACOB: (Dominos): Pvt., enl. & mi. 31 Aug 47 at Phila. by Capt. Scott, age 22, occ. baker, joined Co. at Mexico City 21 Dec 47, mo. with Co. 29 Jul 48.

EBENER, JOHN: (Ebenner): Pvt., enl. & mi. 25 Sep 47 at Pittsburgh by Lt. Ankrimm, age 22, occ. cabinet maker, joined Co. 21 Dec 47, in guardhouse under arrest according to Jan-Feb 48 MR, mo. with Co. 29 Jul 48.

EINWECHTER, WILLIAM: (Einwechton): Pvt., enl. 20 Nov 46 at Phila., age 29, disc. 28 Apr 47 at Jalapa on SCD for diarrhea.

EVANS, WALTER F.: Pvt., enl. 20 Nov 46 at Phila., age 22, occ. clerk, promoted to Cpl. 2 Sep 47, mo. with Co. 29 Jul 48.

FITZGERALD, ADAM: Pvt., enl. 20 Nov 46 at Phila., age 37, occ. gardener, mo. with Co. 29 Jul 48.

FOSS, AUGUSTUS H. (M.) (N.): Pvt., enl. 20 Nov 46 at Phila., age 23, occ. clerk, promoted to Cpl. 27 May 47, listed as sick in hospital at Perote on May-Jun 47 MR, mo. with Co. 29 Jul 48.

GILFRY, MATTHEW: Pvt., enl. 20 Nov 46 at Phila., age 38, occ. butcher, appointed Regimental Color Sgt. 9 Mar 47, appears on Co. MRs as Pvt. throughout his service, mo. with Co. 29 Jul 48.

HAHN, HENRY: (Hohn): Pvt., enl. 20 Nov 46 at Phila., age 27, occ. farmer, sick in hospital at Perote from 29 Nov 47, rejoined Co. before 30 Apr 48, mo. with Co. 29 Jul 48.

HAINES, JOHN: (Hains): Pvt., enl. 20 Nov 46 at Phila., age 39, on extra duty as Hospital Steward aboard the ship "Statesman" 17 Jan to 17 Feb 47 & 26 to 28 Feb 47, listed as sick in hospital at Jalapa on Mar-Apr 47 MR, on extra duty as Hospital Steward from 15 Jun 47, disc. at Puebla 2 Dec 47 on SCD for diarrhea.

HANDLEN, WILLIAM (Handlin, Hanlan): Pvt., enl. 20 Nov 46 at Phila., age 22, occ. carpenter, mo. with Co. 29 Jul 48.

HARDING, JOHN: Pvt., enl. 20 Nov 46 at Phila., age 35, died in camp near Jalapa 11 Jun 47 from chronic diarrhea.

HARPER, ALFRID M.: Pvt., enl. 20 Nov 46 at Phila., age 21, died at Perote 23 Jun 47 from chronic diarrhea.

HENRY, WILLIAM: Pvt., enl. 20 Nov 46 at Phila., age 25, deserted at New Orleans 14 Jan 47.

HOPE, WILLIAM, JR.: Pvt., enl. 20 Nov 46 at Phila., age 25, died at Puebla 1 Nov 47 from chronic diarrhea.

HOUPT, SAMUEL: Pvt., enl. 20 Nov 46 at Phila., age 33, occ. farmer, slightly wounded during the siege of Puebla, mo. with Co. 29 Jul 48.

HOUSTON, JESSE E.: (Housten): Pvt., enl. 20 Nov 46 at Phila., age 22, listed as sick in hospital at Jalapa on Mar-Apr 47 MR, disc. at Perote 30 Oct 47 on SCD for diarrhea.

JOHNS, WILLIAM A.: Sgt., enl. 20 Nov 46 at Phila., age 28, promoted to 3rd Sgt. 9 Apr 47, listed as sick on May-Jun 47 MR, died at Puebla 1 Sep 47 from diarrhea.

KANE, DANIEL: Pvt., enl. 20 Nov 46 at Phila., age 24, on detached service at Vera Cruz according to Mar-Apr 47 MR, deserted at Vera Cruz 28 Apr 47.

KEINSEL, HENRY: (Kenzel, Kenzell, Kernsell): Pvt., enl. & mi. 25 Sep 47 at Pittsburgh by Lt. Ankrimm, age 39, joined Co. 21 Dec 47, sick in hospital at San Angel from 1 Feb 48, listed as sick at Hollidaysburg, Pa. from 21 Feb 48, mo. with Co. 29 Jul 48.

KEMBLE, WILLIAM P.: Pvt., enl. 20 Nov 46 at Phila., age 22, occ. clerk, mo. with Co. 29 Jul 48.

KERR, THOMAS: Pvt., enl. 20 Nov 46 at Phila., age 35, occ. brick maker, sentenced to confinement in Chapultepec and to forfeit all pay & allowances during the war with Mexico by a General Court Martial in Jan or Feb 48 for striking an officer, mo. with Co. 29 Jul 48.

KEYSER, BENJAMIN F.: Pvt., enl. 20 Nov 46 at Phila., age 26, WIA at Cerro Gordo 18 Apr 47 & relieved of duty for 30 days, died at Puebla 13 Sep 47 from Typhoid Fever.

KOHLHUND, CHRISTIAN: Cpl., enl. 20 Nov 46 at Phila., age 23, occ. painter, promoted to 2nd Sgt. 2 Sep 47, mo. with Co. 29 Jul 48.

LEECH, WILLIAM: Pvt., enl. 20 Nov 46 at Phila., age 24, occ. calico printer, in main guardhouse under charges according to Jan-Feb & Mar-Apr 48 MRs, fined 2 months pay & allowances by General Court Martial 30 Apr 48, mo. with Co. 29 Jul 48.

LENTZ, JACOB H.: Pvt., enl. 20 Nov 46 at Phila., age 22, disc. at Vera Cruz 6 Apr 47 on SCD for sun-stroke.

LEWIS, EDWARD C.: 2nd Lt., enl. at Phila., age 35, on furlough from 10 Nov 47 through at least Apr 48, mo. with Co. 29 Jul 48.

LIST, JOHN: Pvt., enl. 20 Nov 46 at Phila., age 21, occ. carpenter, mo. with Co. 29 Jul 48.

LOGAN, PETER: Pvt., enl. 20 Nov 46 at Phila., age 29, deserted at New Orleans 14 Jan 47.

LYBRAND, THOMAS N.: Pvt., enl. 20 Nov 46 at Phila., age 21, died at Perote 26 Jun 47 from diarrhea.

MARGERUM, EDWIN: Pvt., enl. 20 Nov 46 at Phila., age 21, listed as sick in hospital at Jalapa on Mar-Apr 47 MR, disc. at Jalapa 24 May 47 on SCD for diarrhea.

MARSHALL, SAMUEL: Pvt., enl. 20 Nov 46 at Phila., age 20, occ. boatman, sick in hospital from 28 Dec 47, mo. with Co. 29 Jul 48.

MEYER, HENRY C.: (Meezer, Meiser, Muzer): Pvt., enl. 20 Nov 46 at Phila., age 27, disc. at Jalapa 24 May 47 on SCD for bladder infection.

MILLER, JOHN F. (Q.): Pvt., enl. 20 Nov 46 at Phila., age 21, KIA by lancers during siege of Vera Cruz 19 Mar 47 in a skirmish about 6 miles from the city.

Turner G. Morehead
pictured as Colonel of the
106th Pennsylvania in the
Civil War
MOLLUS-Mass &
USAMHI

MOREHEAD, TURNER G.: Capt., enl. at Phila., age 30, was sick on duty at Jalapa in Apr 47, mo. with Co. 29 Jul 48. Col. 22nd P.V.I. (3 mos.) 23 Apr 61 to 7 Aug 61. Col. 106th P.V.I. 28 Aug 61 to 5 Apr 64. Bvt. Brig. Gen. 15 Mar 65. Born 18 Mar 14 & died 28 May 92 at Asbury Park, N.J.

MORRIS, GEORGE B.: Pvt., enl. 20 Nov 46 at Phila., age 25, listed as sick in hospital at Jalapa on Mar-Apr 47 MR, listed as sick in hospital at Perote on May-Jun 47 MR, disc. at Perote 30 Oct 47 on SCD for diarrhea.

NAFLEY, JOSEPH: (Nafly): Pvt., enl. 20 Nov 46 at Phila., age 21, occ. weaver, fined $3.00 by Court Martial according to Jan-Feb 48 MR, AWOL from 14 Mar 48 through at least 30 Apr 48, mo. with Co. 29 Jul 48.

NICHOLSON, THOMAS: Pvt., enl. 20 Nov 46 at Phila., age 24, listed as sick on 17 Dec 46 - 28 Feb 47 MR, disc. at Vera Cruz 6 Apr 47 on SCD for diarrhea.

O'KANE, DANIEL: Pvt., enl. 20 Nov 46 at Phila., age 21, occ. plasterer, sick in hospital at Perote from 29 Nov 47, rejoined Co. before 30 Apr 48, mo. with Co. 29 Jul 48.

Henry Stainrook shown as
Col. of the 109th Penn-
sylvania in the Civil War
*Civil War Library &
Museum - MOLLUS*

OPP, PETER V. (N.): Pvt., enl. 20 Nov 46 at Phila., age 20, occ. clerk, promoted to Cpl. 27 May 47, promoted to 4th Sgt. 10 Nov 47, mo. with Co.
29 Jul 48.

PARKER, JOSEPH L.: Pvt., enl. 20 Nov 46 at Phila., age 27, occ. clerk, promoted to Cpl. 19 Apr 47, promoted to 3rd Sgt. 27 May 47, absent with leave
at Vera Cruz from 10 Nov 47 to at least 31 Dec 47, mo. with Co. 29 Jul 48.

POLLARD, ROBERT F.: Pvt., enl. 20 Nov 46 at Phila., age 35, listed as sick
in hospital at Jalapa on Mar-Apr 47 MR, listed as sick in hospital at Perote
on May-Jun 47 MR, disc. at Perote 30 Oct 47 on SCD for diarrhea.

RAWDON, CALVIN L.: Pvt., enl. 20 Nov 46 at Phila., age 23, occ. carpenter,
promoted to Drummer 3 Dec 47, mo. with Co. 29 Jul 48. Pvt. Co. B, 105th
Ohio Vol. Inf. 4 Jun 64 to 1 Jun 65. Pvt. Co. K, 38th Ohio Vol. Inf. 1 Jun
65 to 12 Jul 65.

REESE, ANDREW: Pvt., enl. 10 Dec 46 at Lancaster, age 23, sick in hospital
at San Angel from 3 Jan 48, disc. at San Angel 2 Mar 48 on SCD for deafness.

RHINO, GEORGE: (Ryno): Pvt., enl. 20 Nov 46 at Phila., age 37, deserted at
New Orleans 14 Jan 47.

RITMAN, GEORGE L.: Pvt., enl. 20 Nov 46 at Phila., age 21, occ. cabinet maker, listed as sick at Jalapa on Mar-Apr 47 MR, sick in hospital at Perote from 29 Nov 47, rejoined Co. by 30 Apr 48, mo. with Co. 29 Jul 48. Capt. Co. D & Maj. 71st P.V.I. 28 May 61 to 16 Jan 63. Died 19 Feb 04 at Ogden, Utah.

ROBINSON, WILLIAM: Pvt., enl. 20 Nov 46 at Phila., age 21, occ. calico painter, sick in hospital at San Angel from 10 Feb 48, rejoined Co. by 30 Apr 48, drowned in Mississippi River below Vicksburg on the way home 29 Jun 48.

RODGERS, GEORGE E.: (Rogers): Pvt., enl. 20 Nov 46 at Phila., age 21, occ. sash maker, mo. with Co. 29 Jul 48.

ROESCH, LEWIS: (Resch): Pvt., enl. & mi. 9 Oct 47 at Phila. by Capt. Scott, age 26, occ. tailor, joined Co. 21 Dec 47, mo. with Co. 29 Jul 48.

ROWAND, THOMAS (Nicholas) W. (West, Wish): Pvt., enl. 17 Dec 46 at Pittsburgh, age 21, disc. at Vera Cruz 28 Apr 47 on SCD for diarrhea.

RYAN, DANIEL: Fifer, enl. 20 Nov 46 at Phila., age 15, WIA in the arm during the siege of Puebla 25 Sep 47, disc. at Puebla 3 Dec 47.

SEDDINGER, JACOB: (Seddington, Sedinger): Pvt., enl. 20 Nov 46 at Phila., age 26, occ. boatman, AWOL from San Angel from 10 Mar 48 & presumed murdered.

SHRUM, GEORGE: Pvt., enl. 20 Nov 46 at Phila., age 23, died at Puebla 1 Nov 47 from diarrhea.

SHULTZ, WILLIAM N. (A.): Pvt., enl. 20 Nov 46 at Phila., age 33, occ. book binder, was sick in Jalapa Hospital in Apr 47, listed as AWOL on May-Jun 47 MR, wounded at Puebla, confined in guardhouse under charges according to Mar-Apr 48 MR, mo. with Co. 29 Jul 48. Pvt. Co. A, 114th P.V.I. 12 Jan 62 to Jan 65.

SMITH, CHARLES P.: Pvt., enl. 20 Nov 46 at Phila., age 25, died at Jalapa 17 Jun 47 from diarrhea.

SMITH, EDWARD B.: Pvt., enl. 20 Nov 46 at Phila., age 22, occ. printer, listed as sick on 17 Dec 46 - 28 Feb 47 MR, mo. with Co. 29 Jul 48.

STAINROOK, HENRY: (Skinrook, Stairnook, Steinrook): Pvt., enl. 20 Nov 46 at Phila., age 28, occ. plumber, on extra duty as Hospital Steward from 31 Oct 47 through at least 30 Apr 48, mo. with Co. 29 Jul 48. Col. 109th P.V.I. 5 May 62 until KIA at Chancellorsville 3 May 63.

STEEL, JAMES C.: (Steele): Pvt., enl. 20 Nov 46 at Phila., age 24, occ. clerk, promoted to Cpl. 10 Nov 47, mo. with Co. 29 Jul 48.

ST. JOHN, JAMES: Drummer, enl. 20 Nov 46 at Phila., age 16, occ. musician, mo. with Co. 29 Jul 48. 1st Sgt., 2nd Lt., 1st Lt. & Capt. Co. D, 4th Pa. Reserves 25 May 61 to 17 Jun 64.

STOCKTON, THOMAS: Pvt., enl. 20 Nov 46 at Phila., age 21, occ. farmer, listed as sick at Jalapa Hospital on Mar-Apr 47 MR, mo. with Co. 29 Jul 48.

STROUGH, GEORGE: Pvt., enl. 20 Nov 46 at Phila., age 24, occ. tailor, mo. with Co. 29 Jul 48.

VAN OSTEN, JAMES W.: Cpl., enl. 20 Nov 46 at Phila., age 21, occ. clerk, promoted to Sgt. 9 Apr 47, promoted to 1st Sgt. 1 Nov 47, mo. with Co. 29 Jul 48.

VANRONK, DANIEL: (Vanroonk): Pvt., enl. 20 Nov 46 at Phila., age 23, occ. plasterer, left sick at Pittsburgh 22 Dec 46, subsequently enl. in Co. D, 2nd Pa. Regt. 4 Jan 47, was demanded at Jalapa by Capt. Morehead but was not delivered. For Civil War service see Co. D, 2nd Pa. Regt.

VERNERS, ANTHONY: Pvt., enl. & mi. 17 Aug 47 at Pottsville by Lt. Kaercher, age 35, occ. farmer, joined Co. 21 Dec 47, mo. with Co. 29 Jul 48.

WAGER, ADAM: Pvt., enl. 20 Nov 46 at Phila., age 28, deserted near New Orleans 7 Jan 47.

WALTERS, CHARLES B.: Pvt., enl. 20 Nov 46 at Phila., age 22, deserted at Wood Wharf near Memphis, Tenn. 27 Dec 46, arrested 28 Apr 48, held at Ft. Mifflin, disc. 18 Jun 48 by order of the Adjutant General.

WALTERSMIDTZ, PHILIP: (Walderscmidz, etc.): Pvt., enl. 20 Nov 46 at Phila., age 35, disc. at Vera Cruz 28 Apr 47 on SCD for diarrhea.

WARAM, THOMAS H.: (Warham): Cpl., enl. 20 Nov 46 at Phila., age 31, listed as sick on 17 Dec 46 - 28 Feb 47 MR, disc. at Vera Cruz 6 Apr 47 on SCD for an injury of the back received on board ship at sea in Feb 47 when going down a hatch to quarters.

WARNER, SAMUEL G.: Pvt., enl. 20 Nov 46 at Phila., age 24, disc. at Vera Cruz 28 Apr 47 on SCD for diarrhea.

WEIR, THOMAS: (Wier): Pvt., enl. 20 Nov 46 at Phila., age 22, occ. carpenter, promoted to Cpl. 19 Apr 47, reduced to Pvt. 1 Oct 47, mo. with Co. 29 Jul 48.

WHITE, CHARLES I.: Pvt., enl. 20 Nov 46 at Phila., age 22, deserted at Wood Wharf near Memphis, Tenn. 27 Dec 46.

WILKNER, JAMES: Pvt., enl. 20 Nov 46 at Phila., age 37, wounded in the leg during the siege of Puebla 31 Oct 47, hospitalized from then until disc. at Mexico City 17 Feb 48 on SCD.

WILLIAMSON, ROBERT E.: Sgt., enl. 20 Nov 46 at Phila., age 25, wounded in the sand hills southwest of Vera Cruz 11 Mar 47, promoted to 2nd Sgt. 9 Apr 47, disc. at Jalapa 24 May 47 on SCD for disease of the hip.

WILLIS, JOSEPH P.: Pvt., enl. 20 Nov 46 at Phila., age 29, occ. hatter, wounded at Puebla, mo. with Co. 29 Jul 48.

WILSON, JONATHAN P.:   Pvt., enl. 20 Nov 46 at Phila., age 33, disc. at Vera Cruz 28 Apr 47 on SCD for diarrhea.

YOUNG, MONTGOMERY P.:   1st Lt., enl. at Phila., age 35, occ. lawyer, was sick on duty at Jalapa in Apr 47, died at Puebla 5 Oct 47 from fever contracted during the siege.

YOUNG, WARREN L.:   1st Sgt., enl. 20 Nov 46 at Phila., age 30, disc. at Vera Cruz 7 Apr 47 on SCD for fever. Capt. Co. G, 68th P.V.I. 26th Aug 62 to 15 Apr 64.

Company H, 1st Regiment
Cadwalader Grays

The Cadwalader Grays was a uniformed militia company active in Philadelphia before 1846. Under their energetic captain, Robert K. Scott, they were quick to volunteer for service when war was declared against Mexico. Captain Scott received word in November that his company was chosen to be part of Pennsylvania's first regiment. The Grays left Philadelphia on 9 December along with the Monroe Guards and Jefferson Guards. They marched to Pittsburgh where First Lieutenant Horace B. Field, 3rd U.S. Artillery, on 16 December mustered the men into Federal service.

The Grays did service equal to their namesake, participating in the investment of Vera Cruz, the battle of Cerro Gordo, the garrison and defense of Perote, and the battle of Huamantla. In addition they did garrison duty in the Mexico City area, reaching there on 8 December 1847, and they performed escort service between the capitol and Vera Cruz.

The 1st Pennsylvania Regiment's Philadelphia companies, including the Cadwalader Grays, returned to the city at about 7:00 A.M. on 24 July 1848. Parades, speeches and rounds of banquets followed the homecoming. Captain George Taylor, 3rd U.S. Artillery, mustered the Grays out on 29 July.

A total of 97 men served in the Grays during the war. Of these, only one recruit joined the company in Mexico, and another man transferred into it from a different unit. Desertions, at four, were relatively few. Only one man sustained injury from hostile action, however, eleven died in service. Twenty-six received discharges before their enlistments had expired.

ALLEN, JOSEPH: Pvt., enl. 2 Dec 46 at Phila., age 25, occ. confectioner, listed as sick on Jan-Feb 48 MR, mo. with Co. 29 Jul 48.

ANDERSON, JAMES H.: Pvt., enl. 2 Dec 46 at Phila., age 24, deserted at New Orleans 7 Jan 47, arrested in Phila. 29 Oct 47, placed on ship 30 Oct 47, returned to Co. 21 Dec 47, listed as sick on Mar-Apr 48 MR, mo. with Co. 29 Jul 48.

ARRENTRUE, JOHN: Pvt., enl. 2 Dec 46 at Phila., age 31, occ. gentleman, promoted to Cpl. 15 Apr 47, reported as being promoted to Q.M. Sgt. 13 Jun 47 but never appears on F & S MRs, mo. with Co. 29 Jul 48.

ARTHUR, ALBERT: Pvt., enl. 2 Dec 46 at Phila., age 22, occ. blacksmith, promoted to Cpl. 1 Feb 48, mo. with Co. 29 Jul 48.

BLITZ, BAREND B. (John B.): Pvt., enl. 2 Dec 46 at Phila., age 21, detached 15 Apr 47 to Capt. Woll's Battery of U.S. Artillery, rejoined Co. 6 Jun 47, detailed to recruiting duty by Col. Wynkoop 6 Jun 47, doing duty in Phila., was Lance Orderly Sgt. of recruits in transit, rejoined Co. 21 Dec 47, detailed as Gen. Cushing's Orderly 20 Jan 48, listed as Orderly to Col. Wynkoop on Mar-Apr 48 MR, mo. with Co. 29 Jul 48.

BRATTON, GEORGE: Pvt., enl. 2 Dec 46 at Phila., age 29, occ. bricklayer, listed as sick on Mar-Apr 48 MR, mo. with Co. 29 Jul 48.

BREECE, SULLIVAN D.: (Breese): 1st Lt., enl. 2 Dec 46 at Phila., age 31, occ. machinist, appointed Asst. Q.M. 22 Mar 47, appointed Q.M. 7 Apr 47, was Acting Brigade Q.M. in Apr & May 47, resigned as Q.M. 4 Jun 47, commanded Co. from 6 Jun 47, mo. with Co. 29 Jul 48.

BRICKMAN, GEORGE: Pvt., enl. 2 Dec 46 at Phila., age 24, listed as sick on Dec 46 - Feb 47 MR, listed as sick in camp near Jalapa on Mar-Apr 47 MR, disc. at Jalapa 2 May 47 on SCD.

BRINCKLER, JOHN B.: (Brinkloe): Pvt., enl. 2 Dec 46 at Phila., age 20, left sick at Vera Cruz 9 Apr 47, disc. at Vera Cruz 18 May 47 on SCD.

BROWN, HARPULESS: Pvt., enl. 2 Dec 46 at Phila., age 19, occ. bar tender, listed as sick on Mar-Apr 48 MR, mo. with Co. 29 Jul 48.

CARNAN, THOMAS J.: Pvt., enl. 2 Dec 46 at Phila., age 38, left sick at Jalapa 7 May 47, disc. at Perote 29 Oct 47 on SCD. 1st Lt. Co. F, 26th P.V.I. 28 May 61 to 11 Dec 63, WIA at Gettysburg.

CASEY, MICHAEL: Pvt., enl. 2 Dec 46 at Phila., age 24, left sick at Vera Cruz 9 Apr 47, disc. at Vera Cruz 18 May 47 on SCD.

CLENDENNING, JOHN: (Clendening, Clendining, Clindening): Pvt., enl. 2 Dec 46 at Phila., age 20, occ. cabinet maker, mo. with Co. 29 Jul 48.

CLINTON, WILLIAM: 2nd Lt., enl. 2 Dec 46 at Phila., age 30, occ. carpenter, Acting Adjutant from 1 Jan 48, appointed Adjutant 20 Jul 48, mo. with F & S 8 Aug 48.

CLYMER, JAMES M.: Pvt., enl. 2 Dec 46 at Phila., age 21, occ. whip maker, listed as sick on May-Jun 47 MR, mo. with Co. 29 Jul 48.

COCHRAN, HENRY (Kennedy, Kenny): Pvt., enl. 2 Dec 46 at Phila., age 21, detached 15 Apr 47 to Capt. Woll's Battery of U.S. Artillery, accidently shot through the head by the discharge of a musket in the hands of Pvt. Phillip H. Reitzel who was standing sentinel duty at Perote 3 Aug 47, died at Perote 3 Aug 47.

COCHRANE, WILLIAM: (Cochran): Pvt., enl. 2 Dec 46 at Phila., age 22, disc. at Vera Cruz 6 Apr 47 on SCD.

CONE, JOSEPH H.: Pvt., enl. 2 Dec 46 at Phila., age 21, left sick at Vera Cruz 9 Apr 47, disc. at Vera Cruz 18 May 47 on SCD.

COOK, MUNSON: Pvt., enl. 2 Dec 46 at Phila., age 21, listed as sick on 16 Dec 46 - 28 Feb 47 MR, left sick at Jalapa 7 May 47, listed as sick on Jan-Feb 48 MR, mo. with Co. 29 Jul 48.

COOPER, SAMUEL B.: Pvt., enl. 2 Dec 46 at Phila., age 36, disc. at Perote 27 May 47 on SCD, died at Jalapa 14 Jun 47.

CRESS, ALBANUS: Pvt., enl. 2 Dec 46 at Phila., age 21, occ. weaver, mo. with Co. 29 Jul 48.

CRESS, EDWARD: Pvt., enl. 2 Dec 46 at Phila., age 21, occ. weaver, listed as sick on Jul-Aug 47 MR, disc. at Perote 29 Oct 47 on SCD.

CROSSON, JAMES (Crossin): 1st Sgt., enl. 2 Dec 46 at Phila., age 25, occ. cordwainer, detached for recruiting duty at Phila. and Ft. Mifflin from 6 Jun 47, disc. at Ft. Mifflin 13 Jul 47. 2nd Lt. Co. K & Adjutant 101st P.V.I. 14 Dec 61 to 20 Jul 63.

CULLEN, GARRETT B.: (Culin): Pvt., enl. 2 Dec 46 at Phila., age 23, occ. whip maker, mo. with Co. 29 Jul 48.

DARRAH, JOHN: (Darragh): Pvt., enl. 2 Dec 46 at Phila., age 30, occ. tailor, listed as sick on May-Jun 47 MR, died 27 Sep 47 from diarrhea.

DAVIS, MILTON (Miller) D. (L., S.): Pvt., enl. 2 Dec 46 at Phila., age 22, occ. carpenter, detached 15 Apr 47 to Capt. Woll's Battery of U.S. Artillery, rejoined Co. before 30 Jun 47, mo. with Co. 29 Jul 48.

DEANY, JAMES A.: (Deaney): 2nd Lt., enl. at Phila., age 22, occ. tailor, arrested by Col. Wynkoop at 3:00 A.M. 18 Aug 47, absent on sick leave from Nov 47, ordered to recruiting duty in Phila. 11 Jan 48, appointed 2nd Lt. 8th U.S. Infantry 29 Mar 48, accepted 7 Apr 48, died at La Vaca, Texas 24 Dec 48.

DEAVES, EDWIN (Edward): Cpl., enl. 2 Dec 46 at Phila., age 29, occ. painter, listed as sick on 16 Dec 46 - 28 Feb 47 MR, listed as sick in camp near Jalapa on Mar-Apr 47 MR, reported sick but present on May-Jun & Jul-Aug 47 MRs, disc. at Perote 29 Oct 47 on SCD.

DICKENS, JAMES: (Dykins): Pvt., enl. 2 Dec 46 at Phila., age 22, disc. at Vera Cruz 5 Apr 47 on SCD for consumption.

DILKS, JACOB: Fifer, enl. 2 Dec 46 at Phila., age 40, promoted to Principal Musician 20 Dec 46, reduced to Pvt. 1 Jul 47, mo. with Co. 29 Jul 48.

DODSON, JOHN: Pvt., enl. 2 Dec 46 at Phila., age 22, occ. printer, mo. with Co. 29 Jul 48.

DONNELLY, THOMAS L.: (Donnely): Pvt., enl. 2 Dec 46 at Phila., age 24, occ. blacksmith, promoted to Cpl. 1 Apr 48, left sick at Jalapa 7 Apr 48, mo. with Co. 29 Jul 48.

DOYLE, JOHN T.: Sgt., enl. 2 Dec 46 at Phila., age 22, occ. printer, disc. at New Orleans 7 Jan 47.

FISS, JOSEPH L. (S.): Pvt., enl. 2 Dec 46 at Phila., age 23, detached 15 Apr 47 to Capt. Woll's Battery of U.S. Artillery, rejoined Co. by 30 Jun 47, promoted to Cpl. 1 Jun 48, mo. with Co. 29 Jul 48.

FRANKLIN, WILLIAM: Pvt., enl. 2 Dec 46 at Phila., age 26, occ. carpenter, mo. with Co. 29 Jul 48.

GIVENS, WILLIAM: Pvt., enl. & mi. 26 Feb 47 at Lobos Island, age 26, listed on Mar-Apr 47 MR as "absent on leave to assist in the printing office, to join when orders to march are given," confined to guardhouse at Perote according to May-Jun 47 MR, died at Perote 4 Aug 47 from diarrhea.

GRAFF, JOHN A.: Pvt., enl. 2 Dec 46 at Phila., age 23, occ. farmer, wounded at Jalapa 27 Aug 47, left sick at Perote 29 Nov 47, disc. at Perote 7 Jan 48 on SCD for wound.

HANSELL, WILLIAM W.: Pvt., enl. 2 Dec 46 at Phila., age 27, disc. at Vera Cruz 5 Apr 47 on SCD.

HAVILLAND, EDWARD: (Haviland): Pvt., enl. 2 Dec 46 at Phila., age 22, appointed Q.M. Sgt. 20 Dec 46, disc. at Vera Cruz 22 Apr 47 on SCD.

HAYS, WILLIAM: (Hayes): Pvt., enl. 2 Dec 46 at Phila., age 26, listed as under arrest on 31 Aug - 31 Dec 47 MR, fined $3.00 by Court Martial according to Jan-Feb 48 MR, listed as sick on Mar-Apr 48 MR, mo. with Co. 29 Jul 48.

HUGHES, PETER (Patrick): Pvt., enl. 2 Dec 46 at Phila., age 23, mo. with Co. 29 Jul 48.

JOHNSON, JOHN H. (J.): (Johnston): Pvt., enl. 7 Dec 46 at Phila., age 30, transferred from Co. C 1st Pa. Regt. 7 Jun 47, deserted at Vera Cruz 2 Apr 48, returned to Co. after 30 Apr 48, mo. with Co. 29 Jul 48.

JONES, LEWIS A.: Pvt., enl. 2 Dec 46 at Phila., age 29, occ. printer, listed as sick on Jan-Feb 48 MR, mo. with Co. 29 Jul 48.

KERLIN, WILLIAM: (Carlin): Pvt., enl. 2 Dec 46 at Phila., age 24, occ. bricklayer, appointed Hospital Steward to three Cos. 3 Apr 48, mo. with Co. 29 Jul 48.

KIRBY, CHARLES T.: Pvt., enl. 2 Dec 46 at Phila., age 25, occ. printer, detached for duty in printing office & fined $10.00 by Court Martial according to 31 Aug - 31 Dec 47 MR, on furlough from 21 Dec 47, listed as sick on Mar-Apr 48 MR, mo. with Co. 29 Jul 48.

LANG, CHARLES H.: Pvt., enl. 2 Dec 46 at Phila., age 22, occ. machinist, listed as sick on May-Jun 47 MR, fined $10.00 by Court Martial according to 31 Aug - 31 Dec 47 MR, under arrest & fined $7.00 by Court Martial according to Jan-Feb 48 MR, mo. with Co. 29 Jul 48.

LEIDY, SAMUEL R.: (Leichy): Pvt., enl. 2 Dec 46 at Phila., age 25, occ. tailor, disc. at Vera Cruz 5 Apr 47 on SCD.

LOURILLARD, ALEXANDER: (Lourilliard): Pvt., enl. 2 Dec 46 at Phila., age 21, occ. tailor, listed as sick in camp near Jalapa on Mar-Apr 47 MR, promoted to Cpl. 6 Jun 47, promoted to Sgt. 1 Jun 48, mo. with Co. 29 Jul 48. 1st Lt. Co. K, 82nd P.V.I. 4 Sep 61 to 14 May 62.

LOWER, GEORGE: Pvt., enl. 2 Dec 46 at Phila., age 25, occ. farmer, listed as sick on 16 Dec 46 - 28 Feb 47 MR, promoted to Sgt. 7 Jan 47, promoted to 1st Sgt. 30 Apr 48.

LOWER, HENRY: Pvt., enl. 2 Dec 46 at Phila., age 24, died at Plan Del Rio 17 Apr 47 from diarrhea, buried at Whitemarsh, Montgomery County.

LUFF, JOHN S. (D): Pvt., enl. 2 Dec 46 at Phila., age 25, occ. clerk, left for recruiting duty in Phila. 6 Jun 47, disc. at Ft. Mifflin 3 Feb 48 on SCD for fistula.

MALLON, JAMES: (Mallen): Pvt., enl. 2 Dec 46 at Phila., age 22, occ. coppersmith, disc. at Perote 3 Oct 47 on SCD.

McCALLION, JAMES: (Macallion, McCalleon, McCallin): Pvt., enl. 2 Dec 46 at Phila., age 24, occ. cordwainer, detached 15 Apr 47 to Capt. Woll's Battery of U.S. Artillery, rejoined Co. by 30 Jun 47, listed as sick on Mar-Apr 48 MR, mo. with Co. 29 Jul 48. 1st Lt. & Capt. Co. D, 68th P.V.I. 23 Aug 62 to 9 Jun 65.

McCAULLY, JOHN G. (James T.): (Maccauley, etc.): Pvt., enl. 2 Dec 46 at Phila., age 32, occ. oil cloth manufacturer, mo. with Co. 29 Jul 48.

McDONALD, PATRICK (McDonnell): Pvt., enl. 2 Dec 46 at Phila., age 26, occ. gentleman, arm broken at Ojo de Aqua 13 Mar 48, left sick at Perote 16 Mar 48, mo. with Co. 29 Jul 48.

McLEARN, GEORGE: (McLean): Pvt., enl. 2 Dec 46 at Phila., age 22, occ. chair maker, mo. with Co. 29 Jul 48. Capt. Co. D, 68th P.V.I. 23 Aug 62 until KIA at Gettysburg 2 Jul 63.

MONTOYA, GEORGE: (Montonia, Montonill, Montonya, Montoyne): Pvt., enl. 2 Dec 46 at Phila., age 30, listed as sick on 16 Dec 46-28 Feb 47 MR, detached to Capt. Woll's Battery of U.S. Artillery 15 Apr 47, rejoined Co. by 30 Jun 47, promoted to Cpl. 29 Oct 47, mo. with Co. 29 Jul 48.

MOUILLE, JOHN: (Moulle): Pvt., enl. 2 Dec 46 at Phila., age 32, occ. cooper, mo. with Co. 29 Jul 48.

MOUILLE, STEPHEN: Sgt., enl. 2 Dec 46 at Phila., age 23, occ. lamp maker, detached 15 Apr 47 to Capt. Woll's Battery of U.S. Artillery, disc. at Perote 6 Jun 47 on SCD.

MOYLAN, ALFRED: (Meylain, Moylain): Pvt., enl. 2 Dec 46 at Phila., age 21, occ. tinsmith, detached 15 Apr 47 to Capt. Woll's Battery of U.S. Artillery, rejoined Co. by 30 Jun 47, listed as sick on 31 Aug - 31 Dec 47 MR, mo. with Co. 29 Jul 48. 1st Lt. Co. I, 61st P.V.I. 29 Oct 61 until dying from wounds 8 Jul 62.

MURRAY, WILLIAM: (Murry): Pvt., enl. 2 Dec 46 at Phila., age 22, disc. at Vera Cruz 26 Mar 47 on SCD.

O'BRIEN, JAMES: (O'Brian): Pvt., enl. 2 Dec 46 at Phila., age 32, occ. tailor, mo. with Co. 29 Jul 48.

PACKER, CHARLES B.: Pvt., enl. 2 Dec 46 at Phila., age 29, occ. fancy workbox maker, listed as sick on May-Jun 47 MR, died at Perote 3 Aug 47 from diarrhea.

PALMER, LAFAYETTE: Sgt., enl. 2 Dec 46 at Phila., age 22, occ. machinist, elected 2nd Lt. after 30 Apr 48, mo. with Co. 29 Jul 48. 1st Lt. Co. A, 12th Pa. Reserves 30 May 61 to 8 Oct 61.

PAYNTER, THEODORE: Pvt., enl. 2 Dec 46 at Phila., age 29, left sick at Vera Cruz 9 Apr 47, deserted from hospital at Vera Cruz 10 Apr 47.

PERNIER, FRANCIS: (Pernice, Pounier): Cpl., enl. 2 Dec 46 at Phila., age 24, occ. bricklayer, left sick at Vera Cruz 9 Apr 47, disc. at Vera Cruz 18 May 47 on SCD.

RACKSTRAW, THOMAS P.: (Rakestraw): Pvt., enl. 2 Dec 46 at Phila., age 26, detached 15 Apr 47 to Capt. Woll's Battery of U.S. Artillery, left sick in hospital at Jalapa 7 May 47, died at Jalapa 22 May 47 from diarrhea.

REISS, WILLIAM S.: (Reese, Reess, Reesse): Pvt., enl. 2 Dec 46 at Phila., age 23, mo. with Co. 29 Jul 48.

REITZELL, PHILIP H.: Pvt., enl. 2 Dec 46 at Phila., age 24, occ. printer, promoted to Fifer 5 Jan 47, reduced to Pvt. before 30 Apr 47, while a sentinel at Castle Perote 3 Aug 47 his musket accidently discharged killing Pvt. Henry Cochran, disc. at San Angel 25 Feb 48 on SCD.

ROBERTS, JAMES: Pvt., enl. 2 Dec 46 at Phila., age 24, occ. printer, died at Plan Del Rio 18 Apr 47 from diarrhea & fever.

ROSE, CHARLES F.: Pvt., enl. 2 Dec 46 at Phila., age 36, occ. cabinet maker, Acting Cpl. from 20 May 47 to 6 Jun 47, left for recruiting duty in Phila. 6 Jun 47, mo. with recruits at Ft. Mifflin 13 Jul 48.

Robert K. Scott as a Civil
War Brigadier General
MOLLUS-Mass &
USAMHI

SAWYER, JAMES A.: Pvt., enl. 2 Dec 46 at Phila., age 22, listed as sick on 16 Dec 46 - 28 Feb 47 MR, on leave of absence to printing office in Jalapa from 25 Apr 47, furloughed by Col. Wynkoop to printing office in Puebla from 1 Jun 47, worked on the *American Star* in Mexico City, listed as sick on Mar-Apr 48 MR, mo. with Co. 29 Jul 48.

SCOTT, ROBERT KINGSTON: Capt., enl. at Phila., age 31, occ. attorney, relinquished command & went on recruiting duty to Phila., departed from Perote 7 Jun 47, arrived in Phila. by 7 Jul 47, disc. at Ft. Mifflin 31 Jul 48. Lt. Col. & Col. 68th Ohio Vol. Inf. 30 Nov 61 to 12 Jan 65. Brig. Gen. of Vols. 12 Jan 65 to 6 Jul 68. Bvt. Brig. Gen. & Maj. Gen. of Vols. Died in Henry County, Ohio 12 Aug 00 & buried in Napoleon, Ohio.

SEAVEY, AMOS W.: Pvt., enl. 2 Dec 46 at Phila., age 26, disc. at Vera Cruz 5 Apr 47 on SCD.

SMITH, EDWARD L.: Pvt., enl. 2 Dec 46 at Phila., age 29, occ. blacksmith, on extra duty with Q.M. Dept. according to Jul-Aug 47 MR, mo. with Co. 29 Jul 48.

SOUDERS, JESSE F.: (Sinders, Sowder): Pvt., enl. 2 Dec 46 at Phila., age 21, occ. umbrella maker, listed as sick on May-Jun 47 MR, mo. with Co. 29 Jul 48.

SPARKS, WILLIAM H.: Pvt., enl. 2 Dec 46 at Phila., age 21, occ. chair maker, listed as sick on 16 Dec 46 - 28 Feb 47 MR, mo. with Co. 29 Jul 48.

SPRINGER, FRANCIS G. (J.): Pvt., enl. 2 Dec 46 at Phila., age 29, listed as sick in hospital at Jalapa on Mar-Apr 47 MR, left sick at Jalapa 7 May 47, disc. at Perote 29 Oct 47 on SCD.

ST. JOHN, JAMES: Drummer, enl. 2 Dec 46 at Phila., age 40, reduced to Pvt. 5 Jan 47 at his own request, mo. with Co. 29 Jul 48.

STUBBINS, THOMAS G. (S.): (Steblins): Pvt., enl. 2 Dec 46 at Phila., age 23, listed as sick in camp near Jalapa on Mar-Apr 47 MR, was under arrest at Chapultepec, fined $14.00 by Court Martial according to Jan-Feb 48 MR, listed as sick on Mar-Apr 48 MR, mo. with Co. 29 Jul 48.

STULTZ, JOHN W.: Pvt., enl. 2 Dec 46 at Phila., age 23, occ. baker, on extra duty as Baker according to May-Jun 47 MR, detached to bakery in Mexico City from 21 Dec 47, rejoined Co. before 29 Feb 48, mo. with Co. 29 Jul 48.

THOMAS, JACOB H. (S.): Pvt., enl. 2 Dec 46 at Phila., age 27, deserted at New Orleans 11 Jan 47, arrested at Phila. 27 Jan 48, mo. at Ft. Mifflin 13 Jul 48 without pay.

TORBERT, HENRY: (Tolbert): Pvt., enl. 2 Dec 46 at Phila., age 32, listed as sick on 16 Dec 46 - 28 Feb 47 MR, disc. at Vera Cruz 27 Mar 47 for varicose veins in the right arm & loss of muscular power therein, a non-service related disability.

TOWNLEY, SMITH: Pvt., enl. 2 Dec 46 at Phila., age 22, detached 15 Apr 47 to Capt. Woll's Battery of U.S. Artillery, listed as sick on May-Jun 47 MR, died at San Angel 12 Jan 48 from diarrhea.

TREVASCUS, JOHN: (Trevassus): Pvt., enl. 2 Dec 46 at Phila., age 30, detached 15 Apr 47 to Capt. Woll's Battery of U.S. Artillery, mo. with Co. 29 Jul 48.

WANDS, ALEXANDER H.: (Wards): Pvt., enl. 2 Dec 46 at Phila., age 21, occ. printer, promoted to Cpl. 20 May 47, listed as sick on Jan-Feb 48 MR, disc. at Vera Cruz 29 Mar 48 on SCD for consumption.

WARR, GEORGE: Pvt., enl. 2 Dec 46 at Phila., age 21, died at Perote 13 May 47 from diarrhea.

WARRINGTON, SMILEY (Samuel, Smilet): Pvt., enl. 2 Dec 46 at Phila., age 25, promoted to Drummer 5 Jan 47, listed as sick on 16 Dec 46 - 28 Feb 47 MR, on detached duty at Puebla from 13 Jun 47, rejoined Co. before 31 Dec 47, reduced to Pvt. according to 31 Aug - 31 Dec 47 MR, listed as sick on Mar-Apr 48 MR, mo. with Co. 29 Jul 48.

WELDEN, JAMES: (Weldin): Pvt., enl. 2 Dec 46 at Phila., age 26, deserted at New Orleans 11 Jan 47.

WHITAKER, EBEN (Elon): Cpl., enl. 2 Dec 46 at Phila., age 20, occ. cord-wainer, left sick at Perote 19 Nov 47, disc. at Perote 29 Dec 47 on SCD for diarrhea.

WHITMAN, ANDREW: (Whiteman): Pvt., enl. 2 Dec 46 at Phila., age 26, occ. weaver, listed as sick on Mar-Apr 48 MR, mo. with Co. 29 Jul 48.

WIGMORE, CHARLES A.: Pvt., enl. 2 Dec 46 at Phila., age 24, occ. victualler, listed as sick in camp near Jalapa on Mar-Apr 47 MR, disc. at Jalapa 2 May 47 on SCD.

WILLIAMS, THOMAS M.: Pvt., enl. 2 Dec 46 at Phila., age 23, occ. painter, died at Puebla 1 Nov 47 from diarrhea.

WOOD, JOHN F.: (Woods): Pvt., enl. 2 Dec 46 at Phila., age 33, occ. laborer, on detached duty at Jalapa from 27 Aug 47, returned to Co. by 31 Dec 47, mo. with Co. 29 Jul 48. 2nd Lt. & Capt. Co. K, 58th P.V.I. 31 Aug 61 until dying at Richmond, Va. 25 Nov 65.

WRAY, LINDSAY H.: Pvt., enl. 2 Dec 46 at Phila., age 26, left sick at Vera Cruz 9 Apr 47, disc. at Vera Cruz 18 May 47 on SCD.

YOKILL, GEORGE: Cpl., enl. 2 Dec 46 at Phila., age 28, occ. bricklayer, promoted to Sgt. 6 Jun 47, mo. with Co. 29 Jul 48.

Company I, 1st Regiment
Wyoming Artillerists

The Wyoming Artillerists were recruited and organized in 1842 by Francis L. Bowman, who became their first commander. The first lieutenant was Edmund L. Dana. In a very short period this company became one of the leading uniformed militia units in northeastern Pennsylvania.

Quick to volunteer for service in the war with Mexico, the Artillerists departed from Wilkes-Barre on 6 December 1846. They reached Pittsburgh, and First Lieutenant Horace B. Field, 3rd U.S. Artillery, mustered the men into Federal service on 16 December.

During their year and a half away from home the Wyoming cannoneers helped besiege Vera Cruz, storm Cerro Gordo and defend Puebla, later garrisoning Mexico City.

The Artillerists were mustered out at Pittsburgh on 20 July 1848 by Major George Wright, 4th U.S. Infantry, and they arrived home in Wilkes-Barre on 30 July.

The Wyoming Artillerists continued to exist as an active military organization after the war. In 1861 they became part of the 8th Regiment of Pennsylvania Volunteers, and in 1862 were redesignated Company C of the 143rd Pennsylvania Volunteer Infantry Regiment. They became part of the state's National Guard establishment in the early 1870's.

A total of 111 men served in the company during the war, and there were only two desertions. Fifteen new recruits joined the Artillerists in Mexico. Ten men sustained battle injuries, from which two died. In all, twenty-three deaths were recorded during the war. Twenty-eight got discharged before muster out.

Edmund L. Dana as Colonel, 143rd
Pennsylvania in the Civil War
MOLLUS-Mass & USAMHI

William T. Wilson as Colonel, 123rd
Ohio in the Civil War
MOLLUS-Mass & USAMHI

ABEL, GRANDISON: Pvt., enl. 1 Dec 46 at Wilkes-Barre, age 20, on detached duty as teamster for three months from 1 Feb 48, mo. with Co. 20 Jul 48. Sgt. Co. E, 9th Iowa Cavalry 25 Aug 63 to 3 Feb 66.

ALWARD, JOSEPH: Pvt., enl. 1 Dec 46 at Wilkes-Barre, age 39, occ. shoemaker, residence Danville, mo. with Co. 20 Jul 48.

BACHMAN, WILLIAM C.: Pvt., enl. 1 Dec 46 at Wilkes-Barre, age 20, promoted to Cpl. 1 May 48, mo. with Co. 20 Jul 48.

BARNES, JOHN: Drummer, enl. 1 Dec 46 at Wilkes-Barre, age 22, left sick at Cincinnati 24 Dec 46, never heard from afterwards.

BEAUMONT, WILLIAM H.: Cpl., enl. 1 Dec 46 at Wilkes-Barre, age 21, listed as AWOL on 31 Aug - 31 Dec 47 MR, promoted to 2nd Sgt. 1 Nov 47, left sick at Jalapa 6 Apr 48, promoted to 1st Sgt. 1 May 48, mo. with Co. 20 Jul 48. Died at Wilkes-Barre from apoplexy in Jun 74.

BELDING, WALLACE I.: Pvt., enl. 1 Dec 46 at Wilkes-Barre, age 19, promoted to Fifer 27 Dec 46. disc. at Jalapa 18 May 47 on SCD for chronic rheumatism.

BENTLEY, ALFRED: Pvt., enl. 1 Dec 46 at Wilkes-Barre, age 40, died at Jalapa 27 May 47.

BOWMAN, FRANCIS L.: (Bouman): 1st Lt., enl. 1 Dec 46 at Wilkes-Barre, age 33, elected Major 18 Dec 46, listed as sick at San Angel on Jan-Feb 48 MR, mo. with F & S, 8 Aug 48. Appointed Capt., 9th U.S. Infantry 3 Mar 55, died near Ft. Willamette, Oregon 10 Sep 56 from fever & exposure, buried in Wilkes-Barre.

BURDIN, OBED (Ovid) C.: (Burden, Burdon): Pvt., enl. 1 Dec 46 at Wilkes-Barre, age 20, slightly wounded on the sand hills south-west of Vera Cruz 11 Mar 47, left sick at Perote 9 Apr 48, evidently rejoined Co. at Perote on the march home, mo. with Co. 20 Jul 48.

BURKE, LUKE: Pvt., enl. 1 Dec 46 at Wilkes-Barre, age 21, left sick at Puebla 12 Oct 47, disc. at Puebla 5 Nov 47 on SCD.

CARKHUFF, WILLIAM H.: (Carkhiff): Pvt., enl. 1 Dec 46 at Wilkes-Barre, age 21, listed as sick on 16 Dec 46 - 28 Feb 47 MR, left sick at Perote 3 Jul 47, died at Perote 20 Jul 47.

CLINGER, ELIAS: (Clirger, Klinger): Pvt., enl. 1 Dec 46 at Wilkes-Barre, age 26, died at sea 31 Jan 47 off Lobos Island from effects of the voyage from New Orleans.

COLDER, LLOYD M.: Pvt., enl. 9 Dec 46 at Lewistown, age 23, died at Perote 1 Jul 47.

COLLINGS, E. B.: 2nd Lt., age 26, elected 1st Lt. 19 Dec 46, disc. at Vera Cruz 8 Apr 47. Died at Wilkes-Barre in 1872.

COLLINGS, GEORGE: Pvt., enl. 1 Dec 46 at Wilkes-Barre, age 18, promoted to Cpl. 1 Jun 48, mo. with Co. 20 Jul 48. 2nd Lt., 1st Lt. & Capt. Co. G, 143rd P.V.I. 10 Oct 62 to 8 Aug 64. Died at Wilkes-Barre in 1873 or 1874.

CONNER, WILSON B.: (Connor): Pvt., enl. 1 Dec 46 at Wilkes-Barre, age 20, promoted to Drummer 27 Dec 46, disc. at Jalapa 18 May 47 on SCD for a "chronic affection of the nerves and muscles of the lumbar region." Living in Wilkes-Barre in 1874.

COOPER, JACOB L. (D.): Pvt., enl. 1 Dec 46 at Wilkes-Barre, age 26, left sick at Perote 3 Jul 47, rejoined Co. by Dec 47, left sick at Jalapa 6 Apr 48, mo. with Co. 20 Jul 48. Died of diabetes in a barber shop in Berwick, Pa. while waiting for a shave, date unknown.

DANA, EDMUND LOVELL: (Danna): Capt., enl. at Wilkes-Barre, age 29, listed as sick in Mexico City on 31 Aug - 31 Dec 47 MR, mo. with Co. 20 Jul 48. Col. 143rd P.V.I. 18 Nov 62 to 18 Aug 65, WIA & captured at Wilderness 5 May 64, Bvt. Brig. Gen. from 26 Jul 65. Born 29 Jan 17 & died at Wilkes-Barre 25 Apr 89.

DEBERGER, M. M.: (DeBurger): Pvt., enl. 1 Dec 46 at Wilkes-Barre, age 22, left sick at Vera Cruz 9 Apr 47, disc. at Vera Cruz 11 May 47 on SCD.

DEVANNY, DOMINICK: Sgt., enl. 1 Dec 46 at Carbondale, age 26, listed as sick at Jalapa on Mar-Apr 47 MR, reduced to Pvt. 16 Mar 47, promoted to 4th Sgt. 1 Jul 47, wounded at Puebla, sick at Perote from 29 Nov 47, rejoined Co. in Mar on Apr 48, mo. with Co. 20 Jul 48. Sgt. & 1st Sgt. Co. I, 24th Wisconsin Vol. Inf. 14 Aug 62 to 26 Apr 63.

DIAMOND, WILLIAM: Pvt., enl. 1 Dec 46 at Wilkes-Barre, age 25, disc. at New Orleans 14 Jan 47; delivered over to civil authorities on account of assault & riot and left at New Orleans 16 Jan 47; he broke up a bar, being slightly wounded by a shotgun blast in the process.

DILL, JAMES F.: Pvt., enl. 1 Dec 46 at Wilkes-Barre, age 31, left sick at Perote 3 Jul 47, died at Perote 14 Aug 47.

DRINKHOUSE, JOHN C.: Pvt., enl. 1 Dec 46 at Wilkes-Barre, age 18, disc. at Vera Cruz 26 Mar 47 on SCD for consumption.

DRIPS, THOMAS G.: (Dripps): Pvt., enl. 11 Dec 46 at Lewistown, age 26, promoted to Cpl. 1 Jul 47, promoted to 3rd Sgt. 1 May 48, mo. with Co. 20 Jul 48. Living in Clayton County, Iowa in 1874.

EHLERS, AUGUSTUS: (Ehler): Pvt., enl. & mi. 9 Aug 47 at Pottsville by Lt. Kaercher, mo. with Co. 20 Jul 48.

ELLIS, JAMES: Pvt., enl. 10 Dec 46 at Huntingdon, age 36, wounded at Puebla, promoted to Cpl. 1 Nov 47, left sick at Vera Cruz 1 Apr 48, disc. at New Orleans 28 Jun 48 on SCD. Served in the Civil War, unit(s) unknown.

EMERY, LEVI: Pvt., enl. 7 Dec 46 at Wilkes-Barre, age 23, left sick at Puebla 4 Dec 47, rejoined Co. by 29 Feb 48, mo. with Co. 20 Jul 48.

FELL, GEORGE W.: Pvt., enl. 7 Dec 46 at Wilkes-Barre, age 18, listed as on extra duty taking care of Maj. Bowman's horse on Jan-Feb 48 MR, mo. with Co. 20 Jul 48.

FIST, LANDLIN: Pvt., enl. & mi. 6 Oct 47 at Pottsville by Lt. Kaercher, age 28, joined Co. 21 Dec 47, mo. with Co. 20 Jul 48.

FLOYD, LUKE: Pvt., enl. 7 Dec 46 at Wilkes-Barre, age 34, had two fingers of his right hand shot off at Puebla 22 Sep 47, was sick in hospital at Mexico City from 19 Dec 47 having been beaten by cut-throats, rejoined Co. by 30 Apr 48 but never fully recovered either physically or mentally, mo. with Co. 20 Jul 48. Died in the early 1850's.

FOX, SAMUEL: Pvt., enl. 7 Dec 46 at Wilkes-Barre, age 24, listed as sick in hospital at Jalapa on Mar-Apr 47 MR, disc. at Jalapa 18 May 47 on SCD for phthisis pulmonalis.

FUNK, FREDERICK: Pvt., enl. 7 Dec 46 at Wilkes-Barre, age 25, mo. with Co. 20 Jul 48.

GANGEWERE, AARON: (Gangawer, Gangawere): Pvt., enl. 7 Dec 46 at Wilkes-Barre, age 38, mo. with Co. 20 Jul 48.

GARDON, ERNEST: (Gorden): Pvt., enl. & mi. 19 Aug 47 at Pittsburgh by Lt. Ankrimm, age 19, reported at Carlisle Barracks 31 Aug 47, mo. with Co. 20 Jul 48.

GAREY, JOSEPH C.: Pvt., enl. 7 Dec 46 at Wilkes-Barre, age 24, listed as sick on 16 Dec 46 - 28 Feb 47 MR, disc. at Vera Cruz 16 Mar 47 on SCD for spinal disease.

GAUL, JOHN: Pvt., enl. & mi. 6 Aug 47 at Pittsburgh by Lt. Ankrimm, age 26, reported at Carlisle Barracks 31 Aug 47, mo. with Co. 20 Jul 48.

GERDEN, CHARLES: (Gerdon, Gergen, Yergen): Pvt., enl. 26 Oct 47 at Pittsburgh, age 25, mi. 10 Jan 48 at Ft. Mifflin by Capt. Taylor, reported at Ft. McHenry, Md. 20 Jan 48, joined Co. 19 Apr 48, mo. with Co. 20 Jul 48.

GILROY, PATRICK: Pvt., enl. 7 Dec 46 at Wilkes-Barre, age 22, listed as sick at Vera Cruz on Mar-Apr 47 MR, disc. at Vera Cruz 16 Apr 47 on SCD.

GOFF, A. H.: 2nd Lt., enl. 1 Dec 46 at Wilkes-Barre, age 22, Acting Asst. Q.M. from 3 Jul 47, transferred as Commissary to Dept. of Perote 27 Nov 47, stabbed by Capt. Foster of the Georgia Volunteer Battalion 10 Apr 48 in Perote over a Mexican Senorita, died of wound 13 Apr 48, his body was taken home to Wilkes-Barre for burial.

GOODERMOOTH, JOHN: (Goodermuth, Gudermuth): Pvt., enl. 10 Dec 46 at Lewistown, age 25, died at Puebla 16 Oct 47.

GOUNERMAN, MAGNUS: (Gonnerman): Pvt., enl. 10 Dec 46 at Lewistown, age 22, left sick at Perote 3 Jul 47, died at Perote 29 Jul 47.

HARBERHOLD, ANTHONY: (Haberhold): Pvt., enl. 1 Dec 46 at Wilkes-Barre, age 21, mo. with Co. 20 Jul 48.

HARVEY, NATHANIEL G.: Pvt., enl. 1 Dec 46 at Wilkes-Barre, age 28, left sick at Perote 3 Jul 47, died at Perote 20 Aug 47.

HILLSMAN, WILLIAM: Pvt., enl. 4 Jan 48 at Phila., age 20, mi. 10 Jan 48 at Ft. Mifflin by Capt. Taylor, reported at Ft. McHenry, Md. 20 Jan 48, mo. with Co. 20 Jul 48.

HINE, PETER: Pvt., enl. 1 Dec 46 at Wilkes-Barre, age 23, left sick at Perote 3 Jul 47, disc. at Perote 29 Oct 47 on SCD for consumption.

HORNBRADT, HENRY: (Hernbroad, Hernbrok): Pvt., enl. 1 Dec 46 at Wilkes-Barre, age 28, promoted to Cpl. 1 May 48, mo. with Co. 20 Jul 48.

HOWARD, DAVID H. (W.): Pvt., enl. 1 Dec 46 at Wilkes-Barre, age 20, mo. with Co. 20 Jul 48.

HOWARD, JOHN: Pvt., enl. 1 Dec 46 at Wilkes-Barre, age 25, left sick at Vera Cruz 9 Apr 47, rejoined Co. by 30 Apr 48, mo. with Co. 20 Jul 48.

HUNT, JOHN: Pvt., enl. 1 Dec 46 at Wilkes-Barre, age 20, listed as sick on Mar-Apr 47 MR, disc. at Vera Cruz 16 Apr 47 on SCD.

HUNTINGTON, ALEXANDER F.: Pvt., enl. 8 Dec 46 at Danville, age 22, occ. miner, residence Danville, mo. with Co. 20 Jul 48. Pvt. & Cpl. Co. A, 132nd P.V.I. 6 Aug 62 to 24 May 63. Pvt. Co. D, 53rd Pa. Emergency Militia 28 Jun 63 to 19 Aug 63. Died at Danville 10 Apr 96.

JOHNSON, CHARLES: Pvt., enl. 1 Dec 46 at Wilkes-Barre, age 19, mo. with Co. 20 Jul 48. Sgt. Co. B, 12th Pa. Reserves & 190th P.V.I. 15 May 61 until KIA at Petersburg.

KELLY, WILLIAM: Pvt., enl. 1 Dec 46 at Wilkes-Barre, age 22, deserted at New Orleans 9 Jan 47.

KIDDER, LYMAN C.: Pvt., enl. 1 Dec 46 at Wilkes-Barre, age 40, disc. at Jalapa 18 May 47 on SCD for chronic rheumatism.

KING, PATRICK: Pvt., enl. 1 Dec 46 at Wilkes-Barre, age 33, mo. with Co. 20 Jul 48.

KITCHEN, DEWITT C.: Cpl., enl. 1 Dec 46 at Wilkes-Barre, age 21, listed as sick on 16 Dec 46 - 28 Feb 47 MR, severely WIA at Cerro Gordo 18 Apr 47, left sick at Perote 3 Jul 47, disc. at Perote 29 Oct 47 on SCD for wound. Reportedly served in the Civil War in the 12th Pa. Reserves & Harnes' Independent Battery (both unconfirmed). Pvt., 1st Sgt. & 2nd Lt. Co. B, 132nd P.V.I. 11 Aug 62 to 24 May 63. Living in Tunkhannock, Pa. in 1874.

KNORR, SAMUEL: Pvt., enl. 6 Jan 48 at Phila., age 40, mi. 10 Jan 48 at Ft. Mifflin by Capt. Taylor, reported at Ft. McHenry, Md. 20 Jan 48, joined Co. 19 Apr 48, lost near National Bridge, Mexico & it was supposed that he had died in Jun 48.

LeBARD, JOSEPH: (Lebard, Lebhard, Leopard, Leopert): Pvt., enl. 1 Dec 46 at Wilkes-Barre, age 23, occ. carpenter, residence near Danville, left sick at Puebla 13 Apr 48, mo. with Co. 20 Jul 48. Pvt. Co. H, 5th Pa. Reserves 21 Jun 61 to 10 Mar 63. His last years were spent at the Soldier's Home in Erie, Pa., where he died 17 Jan 93. Buried at Lewisburg, Pa.

LEHMAN, FREDERICK: Pvt., enl. 1 Dec 46 at Wilkes-Barre, age 22, disc. at Vera Cruz 30 Mar 48 on SCD for disease of sensorium.

LEWIS, ARNOLD C.: 1st Sgt., enl. 1 Dec 46 at Wilkes-Barre, age 20, on furlough to Vera Cruz according to Jan-Feb 48 MR, promoted to 2nd Lt. 29 May 48 to date from 13 Apr 48. Major 46th P.V.I. 17 Aug 61 until 22 Sep 61 when he was killed by one of his own men who objected to being disciplined.

LEWIS, SAMUEL A.: Pvt., enl. 1 Dec 46 at Wilkes-Barre, age 29, detached to duty in printing office in Puebla from 24 Oct 47, left sick at Jalapa 6 Apr 48, mo. with Co. 20 Jul 48. Living & farming in Nebraska in 1874.

LUTES, CHARLES W.: (Lutz): Pvt., enl. 1 Dec 46 at Wilkes-Barre, age 25, listed as sick at Vera Cruz on Mar-Apr 47 MR, disc. at Vera Cruz 11 May 47 on SCD.

MARKS, SAMUEL: Pvt., enl. 10 Dec 46 at Lewistown, age 18, mo. with Co. 20 Jul 48. Served in unknown unit(s) during the Civil War.

McKOWEN, JOHN: (McKeown):   Pvt., enl. 8 Dec 47 at Phila., age 28, mi. 10 Jan 48 at Ft. Mifflin by Capt. Taylor, reported at Ft. McHenry, Md. 20 Jan 48, joined Co. 19 Apr 48, mo. with Co. 20 Jul 48.

MEISSLER, FREDERICK: (Meisler):   Pvt., enl. & mi. 12 Oct 47 at Pottsville by Lt. Kaercher, age 30, joined Co. 21 Dec 47, mo. with Co. 20 Jul 48.

MILLER, WALKER B.:   Pvt., enl. 11 Dec 46 at McVeytown, age 18, left sick at Vera Cruz 9 Apr 47, disc. at Vera Cruz 11 May 47 on SCD.

MINER, JOSEPH W.:   4th Sgt., enl. 1 Dec 46 at Wilkes-Barre, age 21, occ. lawyer, promoted to 3rd Sgt. 16 Mar 47, elected 1st Lt. 15 Jun 47, on special duty attending the trial of Capt. Foster at Jalapa from 25 Apr 48, mo. with Co. 20 Jul 48.

MOREHOUSE, JOHN: (Moorehouse):   Pvt., enl. 1 Dec 46 at Wilkes-Barre, age 23, mo. with Co. 20 Jul 48.

MORRISON, DAVID R. (K.):   Pvt., enl. 10 Dec 46 at Lewistown, age 21, WIA at Cerro Gordo 18 Apr 47, died at Jalapa 12 May 47 from wounds.

MYERS, JOHN W.:   Pvt., enl. 1 Dec 46 at Wilkes-Barre, age 22, left sick at Perote 3 Jul 47, disc. at Perote 29 Oct 47 on SCD.

O'CRAFT, GEORGE (G. O.): (Craft):   Pvt., enl. 22 Dec 47 at Phila., age 18, mi. 10 Jan 48 at Ft. Mifflin by Capt. Taylor, reported at Ft. McHenry, Md. 20 Jan 48, joined Co. 19 Apr 48, supposed to have fallen off the steam boat and drowned on the way home 3 Jul 48.

O'DONNELL, PATRICK: Pvt., enl. 1 Dec 46 at Carbondale, age 33, died at New Orleans 2 Jan 47.

PHILIPS, JULES (Philip, Phillips):   Pvt., enl. 1 Dec 46 at Wilkes-Barre, age 24, on extra duty as servant to Lt. Col. Black according to Jan-Feb 48 MR, mo. with Co. 20 Jul 48.

PHILLIPS, CHARLES: Pvt., enl. 1 Dec 46 at Wilkes-Barre, age 21, deserted at New Orleans 5 Jan 47.

POTTER, JOSEPH W.:   2nd Sgt., enl. 1 Dec 46 at Wilkes-Barre, age 23, left sick at Perote 3 Jul 47, disc. at Perote 29 Oct 47 on SCD for chronic disease of the cerebrum.

PREECE, JOHN: Pvt., enl. 1 Dec 46 at Wilkes-Barre, age 25, KIA at Puebla 26 Aug 47 in an effort to drive cattle into the besieged garrison.

PRICE, JOHN B. (D.):   Pvt., enl. 8 Dec 46 at Danville, age 20, occ. printer, residence Danville, died at Jalapa 12 Jun 47.

PRICE, THOMPSON: Fifer, enl. 1 Dec 46 at Wilkes-Barre, age 26, reduced to Pvt. 27 Dec 46, left sick at Perote 3 Jul 47, disc. at Perote 29 Oct 47 on SCD for chronic diarrhea and general anasarca.

RIGG, JAMES W.: Pvt., enl. 10 Dec 46 at Lewistown, age 20, fined one month's pay by Court Martial according to 31 Aug - 31 Dec 47 MR, mo. with Co. 20 Jul 48. Pvt. Co. H, 110th P.V.I. 28 Aug 62 until KIA at Chancellorsville 3 May 63.

ROBINHOLT, ADAM: (Robenholt): Pvt., enl. & mi. 21 Sep 47 at Pottsville by Lt. Kaercher, joined Co. 21 Dec 47, died on a steam boat on the Ohio River 13 Jul 48 on the way home.

ROTHERMELL, ISAAC: (Rothshimer): Pvt., enl. 8 Dec 46 at Danville, age 28, occ. laborer, died on board ship at Vera Cruz 13 Mar 47.

SHADELL, JOHN (Jon): (Shaddell, Shadle): Pvt., enl. 11 Dec 46 at Danville, age 18, mo. with Co. 20 Jul 48.

SISTY, WILSON E.: Pvt., enl. 1 Dec 46 at Wilkes-Barre, age 19, disc. at Perote 29 Oct 47 on SCD for chronic rheumatism and diarrhea. Living at "Home Farm," Idaho Springs, Colorado in 1874.

SLIKER, JAMES: Pvt., enl. 1 Dec 46 at Wilkes-Barre, age 22, listed as on detached duty on Jul-Aug 47 MR, absent serving as a teamster from 1 Feb 48 through at least 30 Apr 48, mo. with Co. 20 Jul 48.

SLIKER, JOHN: Pvt., enl. 1 Dec 46 at Wilkes-Barre, age 28, left sick at Perote 3 Jul 47, died at Perote 7 Jul 47.

SMITH, JOHN: Pvt., enl. 4 Jan 47 at New Orleans, age 19, mi. at New Orleans 11 Jan 47 by Col. Wynkoop, left sick at Perote 3 Jul 47, died at Perote 28 Aug 47.

SPENCER, HIRAM: Pvt., enl. 1 Dec 46 at Wilkes-Barre, age 31, promoted to Cpl. 16 Mar 47, left sick at Perote 3 Jul 47, disc. at Perote 29 Oct 47 on SCD for chronic diarrhea.

STEVENS, JAMES H. (W.): (Stephens): Pvt., enl. 1 Dec 46 at Wilkes-Barre, age 20, severely wounded by a bayonet 11 Mar 47 in the left thigh while chasing a burro through a thicket near Vera Cruz, disc. at Vera Cruz 5 Apr 47 on SCD for lameness resulting from his wound. Living and farming in Iowa in 1874.

STEVENS, LEVI H.: (Stephens): Pvt., enl. 1 Dec 46 at Wilkes-Barre, age 22, promoted to Cpl. 1 Nov 47, on special duty attending the trial of Capt. Foster in Jalapa from 25 Apr 48, promoted to 4th Sgt. 1 May 48, mo. with Co. 20 Jul 48. Living and farming in Iowa in 1874.

STOUT, CHARLES MINER: Cpl., enl. 1 Dec 46 at Wilkes-Barre, age 20, promoted to Sgt. 16 Mar 47, appointed 2nd Lt. in 11th U.S. Infantry 29 Mar 48, accepted his commission 6 May 48, mo. 16 Aug 48. Mi. to Co. E, 7th Pa. Reserves 27 Jul 61, was also 2nd Lt. & Adjutant, dismissed 12 Nov 64. Died in Washington, D.C. just after the Civil War.

SWAN, JOHN: Pvt., enl. 11 Dec 46 at Lewistown, age 22, detached to care for David Morrison at Jalapa until he died 12 May 47, mo. with Co. 20 Jul 48. 1st Lt. Co. F. 205th P.V.I. 2 Sep 64 to 2 Jun 65.

TANNER, GEORGE: Pvt., enl. 1 Dec 46 at Wilkes-Barre, age 36, died at Perote 29 Jun 47.

TOBY, WILLIAM C.: (Tobey): Pvt., enl. & mi. 4 Jan 47 at New Orleans by Col. Wynkoop, age 29, disc. at Jalapa 22 May 47 on SCD. He was originally ordered by his employer, the Phila. "North American," to accompany the 1st Pa. Regt., but permission to do so was denied, so he enlisted. After disc. he remained in Mexico until the war was over.

TRIPP, CHARLES: Pvt., enl. 1 Dec 46 at Wilkes-Barre, age 38, died at Puebla 12 Sep 47.

VANDENBURG, WILLIAM (M.): (Vandenbeck, Vanderbark, Vanderberg, Vanderberk, Vandermark): Pvt., enl. 7 Dec 46 at Wilkes-Barre, age 21, slightly wounded 11 Mar 47 on the sand hills south-west of Vera Cruz, mo. with Co. 20 Jul 48. Living in West Zanesville, Ohio in 1874.

VANGORDEN, GERSHAM B. (J. B.): (Vangordon): Pvt., enl. 1 Dec 46 at Wilkes-Barre, age 25, died at Perote 23 May 47.

VANWINKLE, NORMAN: Pvt., enl. 1 Dec 46 at Wilkes-Barre, age 28, left sick at Perote 3 Jul 47, disc. at Perote 29 Oct 47 on SCD for chronic rheumatism.

VAUGHAN, HOLDEN T.: (Vaughn): Pvt., enl. 1 Dec 46 at Wilkes-Barre, age 22, disc. at Jalapa 19 May 47 on SCD for chronic diarrhea and debilitation. Pvt. Co. H, 52nd P.V.I. 29 Oct 63 to 12 Jul 65. Living in Providence, Pa. in 1874.

VAUGHAN, JOHN B.: (Vaughn): Cpl., enl. 1 Dec 46 at Wilkes-Barre, age 23, listed as sick on Mar-Apr 47 MR, disc. at Jalapa 17 May 47 on SCD for phthisis pulmonalis.

VERNERT, ANTHONY: (Varnet, Vernest, Vernete): Pvt., enl. & mi. 17 Aug 47 at Pottsville by Lt. Kaercher, age 35, joined Co. 21 Dec 47, mo. with Co. 20 Jul 48.

WAELDER, JACOB: enl. 1 Dec 46 at Wilkes-Barre, age 25, elected 2nd Lt. 19 Dec 46, was Acting Asst. Adjutant Gen. to Col. Childs at Puebla from 20 May 47 at least through Apr 48, mo. with Co. 20 Jul 48. Living in San Antonio, Texas in 1874.

WANDEL, EDMUND (Edward) W.: (Wandall): Pvt., enl. 1 Dec 46 at Wilkes-Barre, age 19, mo. with Co. 20 Jul 48. Capt. Co. G, 143rd P.V.I. 15 Nov 62 to 19 Nov 63. Died in Wilkes-Barre in 1871 or 1872.

WARD, WALSINGHAM (Walshingham) G.: Pvt., enl. 1 Dec 46 at Wilkes-Barre, age 25, listed as sick on 16 Dec 46 - 28 Feb 47 MR, disc. at Vera Cruz 5 Apr 47 on SCD for debility incurred from two attacks of typhoid fever. He later became a judge in Scranton, Pa. where he was living in 1874.

WEHLE, HENRY: Pvt., enl. & mi. 9 Aug 47 at Pottsville by Lt. Kaercher, age 33, reported at Carlisle Barracks, Pa. 31 Aug 47, joined Co. 21 Dec 47, mo. with Co. 20 Jul 48.

WESTHOVEN, ARMON D.: Pvt., enl. 8 Dec 46 at Wilkes-Barre, age 30, promoted to Cpl. 1 May 48, mo. with Co. 20 Jul 48. Pvt. Co. F, 46th Ohio Vol. Inf. 20 Nov 61 to 3 Sep 62.

WHITAKER, WILLIAM H.: Pvt., enl. 8 Dec 46 at Wilkes-Barre, age 22, residence Danville, mo. with Co. 20 Jul 48.

WILSON, THOMAS I.: Pvt., enl. 1 Dec 46 at Wilkes-Barre, age 21, left sick at Plan Del Rio 19 Apr 47, removed to Jalapa, died at Jalapa 27 May 47.

WILSON, WILLIAM TECUMSEH: (Willson): Pvt., enl. 12 Dec 46 at Huntington, age 22, detached to printing offices at Puebla & Mexico City from 24 Oct 47, promoted to Cpl. 1 Nov 47, rejoined Co. by 30 Apr 48, reduced to Pvt. 1 Jun 48, mo. with Co. 20 Jul 48. Capt. Co. C, 15th Ohio Vol. Inf. (3 mos.) 23 Apr 61 to 27 Aug 61. Lt. Col. 15th Ohio Vol. Inf. 12 Sep 61 to 10 Aug 62. Lt. Col. & Col. 123rd Ohio Vol. Inf. 9 Sep 62 to 12 Jun 65. Bvt. Brig. Gen. 13 Mar 65. Born 6 Oct 23 & died 5 Jun 05 at Columbus, Ohio.

WITZELL, DANIEL W.: (Weitzele, Weitzell, Whitesell): Pvt., enl. 8 Dec 46 at Wilkes-Barre, age 27, on extra duty helping Q.M. Woods according to Jan-Feb 48 MR, on detached duty at Perote from 9 Apr 48 through at least 30 Apr 48, mo. with Co. 20 Jul 48. He admitted to being a coward. He ran from a skirmish at Vera Cruz and shirked at Cerro Gordo. Killed in a gambling affray in Virginia, date unknown.

WOLFSTEIN, MICHAEL: (Wolfstien): Pvt., enl. & mi. 31 Aug 47 at Phila. by Capt. Scott, age 30, joined Co. 21 Dec 47, mo. with Co. 20 Jul 48.

WRIGHT, THOMAS I.: Pvt., enl. 8 Dec 46 at Wilkes-Barre, age 19, mo. with Co. 20 Jul 48.

YARLOTT, DAVID W.: (Yarlett): Pvt., enl. 1 Dec 46 at Wilkes-Barre, age 22, wounded at Puebla, acting as Co. Commissary according to Jan-Feb 48 MR, mo. with Co. 20 Jul 48.

Company K, 1st Regiment
Duquesne Greys

The Duquesne Greys of Pittsburgh were organized in 1831 and quickly assumed a prominent role in the military life of the city. Upon the breaking out of war with Mexico the Greys offered their services to the government. Their acceptance as part of the 1st Regiment was received on 23 November. Preparations immediately began for departure to the seat of war. First Lieutenant Horace B. Field, 3rd U.S. Artillery, mustered the company, under Captain John Herron, into federal service on the afternoon of 16 December.

During their active service the Greys were involved in the siege of Vera Cruz, the battles of Cerro Gordo and La Hoya and the siege of Puebla, taking heavy casualties in the last encounter. They entered Mexico City at the end of 1847 and did occupation duty there. The company arrived home in Pittsburgh on 16 July 1848 and was mustered out of federal service on the 24th by Major George Wright of the 4th U.S. Infantry.

The Duquesne Greys returned to their pre-war routine and continued to prosper as a uniformed militia unit. They became Company B of the 12th Pennsylvania Volunteer Infantry Regiment in 1861.

A total of 121 men served in the Greys during the war. Of these, twenty were recruits who joined them in Mexico. Eight men became deserters, while one other transferred out and two transferred in. Twenty-four battle casualties were inflicted, with thirteen deaths resulting therefrom. In all, twenty-eight Greys died in service, and twenty-seven more received discharges before muster out.

ALWARD, HENRY W.: Pvt., enl. 8 Dec 46 at Pittsburgh, age 23, mo. with Co. 25 Jul 48, died shortly after returning home.

ALWARD, HUGH BELLAS: Pvt., enl. 8 Dec 46 at Pittsburgh, age 24, listed as on extra duty with sutler being disabled with poisoned feet on Mar-Apr 47 MR, died in hospital at Puebla 24 or 26 Oct 47.

ANDERSON, ROBERT: 2nd Sgt., enl. 8 Dec 46 at Pittsburgh, age 28, on detached duty in Puebla as Acting Postmaster from 13 Oct 47 to 23 Jan 48, promoted to 1st Sgt. 1 Apr 48, promoted to 2nd Lt. 26 May 48, mo. with Co. 25 Jul 48.

ANKRIMM, WILLIAM J.: 2nd Lt., enl. 8 Dec 46 at Pittsburgh, age 27, promoted to 1st Lt., apparently disabled in Apr or May 47, left for recruiting duty 6 Jun 47, commanded Pittsburgh recruiting station from 1 Jul 47 to Jun 48, disc. in Phila. in the summer of 1848.

BAKER, JOHN: Pvt., enl. 8 Dec 46 at Pittsburgh, age 32, disc. at Vera Cruz 27 Apr 47 on SCD, re-enl. 28 Oct 47 at Pittsburgh, mi. at Ft. Mifflin 10 Jan 48, reported at Ft. McHenry, Md. in Jan 48, rejoined Co. 19 Apr 48, mo. with Co. 25 Jul 48.

BARNDOLLAR, WILLIAM S.: Pvt., enl. & mi. 27 Aug 47 at Phila., age 21, joined Co. in Mexico City 21 Dec 47, mo. with Co. 25 Jul 48.

BATES, HENRY: Pvt., enl. 8 Dec 46 at Pittsburgh, age 19, died at Perote 21 Jul 47.

BECK, THEODORE: Pvt., enl. & mi. 18 Aug 47 at Pottsville, age 38, joined Co. in Mexico City 21 Dec 47, mo. with Co. 25 Jul 48.

BENNETT, HAMILTON: Pvt., enl. 8 Dec 46 at Pittsburgh, age 30, promoted to Cpl. 1 May 48, mo. with Co. 25 Jul 48.

BLAKEMAN, CHARLES W.: Pvt., enl. 8 Dec 46 at Pittsburgh, age 21, WIA at Puebla 12 Oct 47, disc. at Puebla 1 Nov 47 on SCD for wounds.

BLEEN, PHILIP: Pvt., enl. 8 Dec 46 at Pittsburgh, age 20, deserted at Pittsburgh 16 Dec 46.

BLOCKER, JOHN: Pvt., enl. & mi. 6 Aug 47 at Pittsburgh, age 25, reported at Carlisle Barracks, Pa. 31 Aug 47, joined Co. in Mexico City 21 Dec 47, mo. with Co. 25 Jul 48.

BOSLER, JOHN: Pvt., enl. & mi. 26 Nov 47 at Pittsburgh, age 33, joined Co. 19 Apr 48, mo. with Co. 25 Jul 48.

BRADEN, JAMES M.: Pvt., enl. 8 Dec 46 at Pittsburgh, age 23, deserted at Pittsburgh 16 Dec 46.

BROWN, WILLIAM A.: Pvt., enl. & mi. 10 Sep 47 at Phila., age 20, joined Co. in Mexico City 21 Dec 47, hospitalized for illness at Mexico City 12 Jan 48, was sick through Apr 48, mo. with Co. 25 Jul 48. Supposed to have served with Co. I, 11th Pa. Cavalry in the Civil War (unconfirmed).

BURNS, WILLIAM: Pvt., enl. 8 Dec 46 at Pittsburgh, age 22, promoted to Cpl. 1 May 48, mo. with Co. 25 Jul 48.

CALHOUN, JAMES: Pvt., enl. 8 Dec 46 at Pittsburgh, age 21, mo. with Co. 25 Jul 48.

CAREY, HENRY W.: Pvt., enl. & mi. 7 Sep 47 at Pittsburgh, age 18, joined Co. in Mexico City 21 Dec 47, mo. with Co. 25 Jul 48.

CEYMORE, ISAAC: (Ceymour): Pvt., enl. 8 Dec 46 at Pittsburgh, age 18, disc. at Vera Cruz 27 Apr 47 on SCD, missing ever since.

CHRISTY, URIAH W.: Pvt., enl. & mi. 27 Jul 47 at Pittsburgh, age 21, reported at Carlisle Barracks, Pa. 31 Aug 47, listed as sick in hospital at Phila. 31 Oct 47, reported at Ft. McHenry, Md. 20 Jan 48, joined Co. in Mexico City 19 Apr 48, mo. with Co. 25 Jul 48.

CLAMMER, DAVID: Pvt., enl. 8 Dec 46 at Pittsburgh, age 19, mo. with Co. 25 Jul 48.

COLLINS, ROBERT D.: Pvt., enl. 8 Dec 46 at Pittsburgh, age 24, disc. at Vera Cruz 7 Apr 47 on SCD for loss of fingers by the accidental discharge of a musket.

CUMMINGS, JOHN (James) A.: Pvt., enl. 8 Dec 46 at Pittsburgh, age 23, transferred at Vera Cruz to Co. H, 2nd Pa. Regt. 30 Mar 47.

CUNNINGHAM, RICHARD: Fifer, enl. 8 Dec 46 at Pittsburgh, age 18, reduced to Pvt. 1 Jan 47, disc. at Vera Cruz 27 Apr 47.

DALZELL, JOHN: Pvt., enl. 8 Dec 46 at Pittsburgh, age 21, disc. at Vera Cruz 27 Apr 47.

DAVIS, THOMAS M.: Pvt., enl. 8 Dec 46 at Pittsburgh, age 24, in hospital at Vera Cruz according to 16 Dec 46 - 30 Apr 47 MR, disc. at Vera Cruz 27 Apr 47. Moved to Oregon.

DIETRICH, JOSEPH: (Detrich, Detrick): Pvt., enl. 27 Aug 47 at Pottsville, age 29, mi. 31 Aug 47 at Ft. Mifflin, joined Co. in Mexico City 21 Dec 47, mo. with Co. 25 Jul 48.

DONAGER, GOTLIEB (Gottlieb): (Doneger, Doniger, Donniecker): Pvt., enl. & mi. 4 Aug 47 at Pittsburgh, reported at Carlisle Barracks, Pa. 31 Aug 47, joined Co. in Mexico City 21 Dec 47, taken prisoner 3 Jan 48, returned to Co. 16 Feb 48, mo. with Co. 25 Jul 48.

DOWNS, JONATHAN: (Downes): Pvt., enl. 8 Dec 46 at Pittsburgh, age 38, died at Puebla 3 Oct 47.

DRUM, RICHARD COULTER: Pvt., enl. 8 Dec 46 at Pittsburgh, age 21, appointed 2nd Lt. of Infantry in the Regular Army 18 Feb 47, disc. at Vera Cruz 17 Mar 47 to accept this commission, assigned to 9th U.S. Inf. 9 Apr 47, Bvt. 1st Lt. 13 Sep 47, transferred to 4th U.S. Art. 8 Mar 48, promoted to 1st Lt. 16 Sep 50, Bvt. Capt. Asst. Adjt. Gen. 16 Mar 61, Maj. A.A.G. 3 Aug 61, Lt. Col. A.A.G. 17 Jul 62, Bvt. Col. 24 Sep 64, Bvt. Brig. Gen. 13 Mar 65, Col. A.A.G. 22 Feb 69, Brig. Gen. & Adjt. Gen. 15 Jun 80, retired 28 May 89. Born 28 May 25 and died 15 Oct 09 at Bethesda, Md.

**Richard C. Drum as a Brigadier
General after the Civil War**
MOLLUS-Mass & USAMHI

**John Poland as Major of the 102nd
Pennsylvania in the Civil War**
Ronn Palm Collection

**Oliver H. Rippey as Colonel of the 61st
Pennsylvania in the Civil War**
Roger D. Hunt Collection

James S. Negley shown as a militia officer in the 1850s

USAMHI

EBBERT, THEODORE S.: (Ebert): Pvt., enl. 8 Dec 46 at Pittsburgh, age 19, sick at San Angel from 23 Feb 48, left sick at Puebla 12 Apr 48, absent sick at mo., died shortly thereafter.

ELLIOTT, JOHNSON: Pvt., enl. 8 Dec 46 at Pittsburgh, age 25, promoted to Cpl. 8 Feb 47, wounded, disc. at Puebla 1 Nov 47 on SCD for wounds.

EVANS, EDWARD (Evan) E. (R.): Pvt., enl. 10 Jan 47 at New Orleans, age 19, mi. on ship *Oxnard* 26 Feb 47, listed as missing on 16 Dec 46 - 30 Apr 47 MR.

FEOCK, CHARLES: Pvt., enl. 8 Dec 46 at Pittsburgh, age 19, deserted at Pittsburgh 16 Dec 46.

FROST, RALPH: Pvt., enl. 8 Dec 46 at Pittsburgh, age 32, left sick at Puebla 12 Apr 48, rejoined Co. for march home, mo. with Co. 25 Jul 48.

FURMAN, THOMAS B.: (Furnam): Pvt., enl. 8 Dec 46 at Pittsburgh, age 20, wounded at Puebla, mo. with Co. 25 Jul 48.

GARDNER, JOHN H.: Drummer, enl. 8 Dec 46 at Pittsburgh, age 23, left sick at Puebla 3 Dec 47, rejoined Co. during Mar or Apr 48, mo. with Co. 25 Jul 48.

GILCHRIST, JOHN C.: Pvt., enl. 8 Dec 46 at Pittsburgh, age 26, KIA at Puebla 12 Oct 47.

GLENN, CHARLES, JR.: 1st Sgt., enl. 10 Jan 47 at New Orleans, appointed 1st Sgt. the day he enrolled, mi. 28 Feb 47 on ship *Oxnard,* detached for recruiting duty at Pittsburgh 6 Jun 47, disc. at Pittsburgh in Mar 48 on SCD.

GLENN, GEORGE S. (L.): Pvt., enl. 8 Dec 46 at Pittsburgh, age 26, mo. with Co. 25 Jul 48.

GLENN, SAMUEL A.: Pvt., enl. 8 Dec 46 at Pittsburgh, age 22, deserted at New Orleans 10 Jan 47.

GRAY, JAMES: Pvt., enl. 16 Dec 46 at Pittsburgh, disc. at Vera Cruz 6 Apr 47.

GUTHRIE, ROBERT B.: 1st Sgt., enl. 8 Dec 46 at Pittsburgh, age 25, his name was not taken up on the Co. MRs.

HAGUE, JOHN W., JR.: 2nd Lt., enl. at Pittsburgh, age 24, was Court Martial-ed, under arrest and in confinement from 19 Dec 47 through Jan 48, sick in San Angel from 20 Feb 48, on three months leave of absence from 29 Feb 48, disc. at Mexico City 25 May 48, returned home with Co. Capt. Co. I, 134th P.V.I. 1 Sep 62 to 26 May 63, WIA at Fredericksburg.

HAMBRIGHT, CHARLES W.: Cpl., enl. 8 Dec 46 at Pittsburgh, age 23, on ex-tra duty as Commissary Sgt. according to 16 Dec 46 - 30 Apr 47 MR, pro-moted to Sgt. 8 Feb 47, detailed to recruiting duty 6 Jun 47, at Carlisle Barracks from 25 Aug 47, at Pittsburgh from Sep 47 to Jun 48, then at Ft. Mifflin, mo. at Ft. Mifflin 13 Jul 48.

HAMILTON, JOHN S.: Pvt., enl. 8 Dec 46 at Pittsburgh, age 23, sick in hospital at Mexico City 19 Dec 47, on detached duty at Post Office in Mexico City from 20 Dec 47, listed as sick on Mar-Apr 48 MR, mo. with Co. 25 Jul 48.

HEROD, JOHN H.: (Herrod): Pvt., enl. 8 Jan 47 at New Orleans, mi. 28 Feb 47 on ship *Oxnard*, KIA at Puebla 12 Oct 47.

HERRON, JOHN B.: Capt., enl. at Pittsburgh, age 31, WIA at Puebla 12 Oct 47, left sick at Puebla 3 Dec 47, rejoined Co. at Puebla 12 Apr 48, mo. with Co. 25 Jul 48. Born 6 Apr 23 & died 19 Apr 94. Buried in Allegheny Cemetery, Pittsburgh.

HESS, KELEAN (Kelly): Pvt., enl. & mi. 30 Aug 47 at Pottsville by Lt. Kaercher, age 25, joined Co. in Mexico City 21 Dec 47, mo. with Co. 25 Jul 48.

HICKMAN, JOHN POWELL: Pvt., enl. & mi. 14 Sep 47 at Pittsburgh, age 30, joined Co. in Mexico City 21 Dec 47, mo. with Co. 25 Jul 48.

HOFFMAN, CHARLES: (Huffman): Pvt., enl. 8 Dec 46 at Pittsburgh, age 24, promoted to Cpl. 29 Feb 48, promoted to Sgt. 1 Apr 48, mo. with Co. 25 Jul 48.

JACKSON, B. C.: Pvt., listed only on 30 Apr 47 - 31 Dec 47 & Jan-Feb 48 MRs, informally mustered as a substitute and was not a regular member of Co.

JOHNS, FRANCIS B.: Pvt., enl. 8 Dec 46 at Pittsburgh, age 23, KIA at Puebla 12 Oct 47.

JONES, EDWARD H.: Pvt., enl. 8 Dec 46 at Pittsburgh, age 23, KIA at Puebla 12 Oct 47.

KEELEY, THOMAS C. M.: (Keely): Pvt., enl. 8 Dec 46 at Pittsburgh, age 23, left sick at Jalapa 7 Apr 48, died at Jalapa 8 Jun 48.

KEENAN, JAMES, JR.: Pvt., enl. 8 Dec 46 at Pittsburgh, age 23, disc. at Vera Cruz 27 Apr 47. 2nd Lt. 11th U.S. Inf. 6 Sep 47, mo. 16 Aug 48.

KELLY, PLINY: Pvt., enl. 8 Dec 46 at Pittsburgh, age 23, promoted to Cpl. 1 May 48, mo. with Co. 25 Jul 48. Supposed to have served with Co. E, 2nd Mass. Vols. in the Civil war (unconfirmed).

KERR, FRANCIS J.: Pvt., enl. 8 Dec 46 at Pittsburgh, age 33, mo. with Co. 25 Jul 48.

KINKEAD, JOSEPH M. (W.): (Kinkaid): Cpl., enl. 8 Dec 46 at Pittsburgh, age 23, disc. at Vera Cruz 27 Apr 47. Adjt. 13th P.V.I. (3 mos.) 25 Apr 61 to 6 Aug 61. Lt. Col. & Col. 102nd P.V.I. 6 Aug 61 to 27 May 63. Died at Pittsburgh 13 Apr 92.

KNAPP, VALENTINE: Pvt., enl. 8 Dec 46 at Pittsburgh, age 22, listed as in hospital at Vera Cruz on 16 Dec 46 - 30 Apr 47 MR, disc. at Vera Cruz 27 Apr 47.

KRUTZLEMAN, HENRY: (Krulzelman): Pvt., enl. 8 Dec 46 at Pittsburgh, age 23, KIA at Puebla 12 Oct 47.

LEIPER, BENHAM (Bartram, Bernhard) G.: (Leper): Pvt., enl. 8 Dec 46 at Pittsburgh, age 20, listed as in hospital at Jalapa on 16 Dec 46 - 30 Apr 47 MR, left sick at Puebla according to 30 Apr - 31 Dec 47 MR, rejoined Co. 16 Feb 48, on detached duty at Puebla from 12 Apr 48, mo. with Co. 25 Jul 48.

LONGSTAFF, JOHN: Pvt., enl. 8 Dec 46 at Pittsburgh, age 19, listed as in hospital at Jalapa on 16 Dec 46 - 30 Apr 47 MR, captured in action at Puebla 26 Aug 47, released by our troops at Chululu in mid-Oct 47, left sick at Puebla 3 Dec 47, rejoined Co. 14 Feb 48, on daily duty with Lt. Col. Black from 14 Feb 48, mo. with Co. 25 Jul 48.

LOOMIS, SETH: Pvt., enl. 8 Dec 46 at Pittsburgh, age 28, left sick at Vera Cruz 9 Apr 47, disc. at Vera Cruz 17 Apr 47 on SCD, died in hospital at New Orleans 27 Sep 47 from diarrhea.

LOVETT, AARON: Pvt., enl. 8 Dec 46 at Pittsburgh, age 22, slightly WIA at Cerro Gordo 18 Apr 47, left sick at Puebla 3 Dec 47, mo. with Co. 25 Jul 48.

LOWRY, THOMAS: Pvt., enl. 2 Nov 47 at Pittsburgh, age 25, mi. 10 Jan 48 at Ft. Mifflin, reported at Ft. McHenry, Md. 20 Jan 48, joined Co. 19 Apr 48, mo. with Co. 25 Jul 48.

LYONS, JOHN: Pvt., enl. 8 Dec 46 at Pittsburgh, age 21, listed only on Co. muster-in roll.

MANN, BENJAMIN F.: Pvt., enl. 8 Dec 46 at Pittsburgh, age 30, disc. at Vera Cruz 27 Apr 47. Died shortly thereafter.

MANN, WILLIAM F.: Pvt., enl. 8 Dec 46 at Pittsburgh, age 26, elected 2nd Lt. 31 Dec 47, mo. with Co. 25 Jul 48.

MARSHALL, ANDREW E.: Pvt., enl. 8 Dec 46 at Pittsburgh, age 19, wounded at Puebla, on duty with Lt. Col. Black from 20 Sep 47, sick in hospital at San Angel from 14 Feb 48, listed as in hospital at Mexico City on Mar-Apr 48 MR, mo. with Co. 25 Jul 48.

McCLELLAND, GEORGE C.: Graduated from the U.S. Military Academy at West Point with the Class of 1843, Bvt. 2nd Lt. 3rd U.S. Inf. 1 Jul 43, resigned 30 Apr 46. Cpl., enl. 8 Dec 46 at Pittsburgh, age 28, appointed 2nd Lt. of Inf. in the Regular Army 17 Feb 47, disc. at Vera Cruz 17 Mar 47 to accept this commission, assigned to 11th U.S. Inf. 9 Apr 47, cashiered 13 Oct 47. Died 26 Oct 88.

McCLINTOCK, DRYDEN S.: Cpl., enl. 8 Dec 46 at Pittsburgh, age 23, promoted to 4th Sgt. 15 Nov 47, promoted to 1st Sgt. 26 May 48, mo. with Co. 25 Jul 48.

McDOWELL, JAMES: (McDowells): Pvt., enl. 8 Dec 46 at Pittsburgh, age 27, died in quarters at Puebla 12 Sep 47.

McGIFFIN, NORTON: Pvt., enl. 8 Dec 46 at Pittsburgh, age 22, mo. with Co. 25 Jul 48. Lt. Col. 12th P.V.I. (3 mos.) 25 Apr 61 to 5 Aug 61. Lt. Col. 85th P.V.I. 7 Nov 61 to 12 May 62. Capt. Co. A, 6th Pa. Emergency Militia 15 Sep 62 to 28 Sep 62. Born in 1824 & died 30 Jul 05 at Washington, Pa.

McILROY, JOHN D.: (McElroy): 2nd Sgt., enl. 8 Dec 46 at Pittsburgh, age 29, disc. at Puebla 1 Nov 47.

McMINN, JEREMIAH: Pvt., enl. 8 Dec 46 at Pittsburgh, age 34, died at Perote 8 Aug 47.

MEREDITH, WILLIAM: Pvt., enl. 16 Dec 46 at Pittsburgh, age 27, died at Perote 25 May 47. Had no relations in the U.S.

MILLER, JOHN: Pvt., enl. 8 Dec 46 at Pittsburgh, age 19, left sick at Puebla 3 Dec 47, rejoined Co. 8 Feb 48, mo. with Co. 25 Jul 48.

MILLER, ROBERT F.:   Pvt., enl. 8 Dec 46 at Pittsburgh, age 19, sick in hospital at San Angel from 10 Jan 48, disc. at San Angel 28 Feb 48 on SCD for induratis and diseased testicle.

MITCHELL, DAVID A.:   Pvt., enl. 8 Dec 46 at Pittsburgh, age 28, disc. at Perote 6 Jun 47 on SCD, died on the way home.

MOSGROVE, ANDREW: Pvt., enl. 8 Dec 46 at Pittsburgh, age 25, disc. at Perote 6 Jun 47 on SCD, died on the way home.

MUNDAY, HENRY D. (G., I.): (Mundy):   Pvt., enl. 8 Dec 46 at Pittsburgh, age 22, listed as in hospital at Vera Cruz on Mar-Apr 47 MR, disc. at Vera Cruz 27 Apr 47 on SCD. Died shortly thereafter.

NEGLEY, JAMES SCOTT: (Neagly, Negely):   Pvt., enl. 8 Dec 46 at Pittsburgh, age 20, wounded at Puebla, promoted to 2nd Cpl. 2 Dec 47, promoted to 4th Sgt. 1 Jun 48, mo. with Co. 25 Jul 48. Brig. Gen. of Pa. Vols. 19 Apr 61 to 20 Jul 61. Brig. Gen. of U.S. Vols. 1 Oct 61 to 29 Nov 62. Maj. Gen. of U.S. Vols. 29 Nov 62 to 19 Jan 65.

NELLIS, JEREMIAH M.:   Pvt., enl. & mi. 17 Nov 47 at Pittsburgh, age 25, reported at Ft. McHenry, Md. 20 Jan 48, joined Co. in Mexico City 19 Apr 48, mo. with Co. 25 Jul 48.

NOBLE, JAMES: Pvt., enl. 8 Dec 46 at Pittsburgh, age 22, died at Perote 23 May 47.

OLIVER, JOSEPH: Pvt., enl. 8 Dec 46 at Pittsburgh, age 26, listed only on Co. muster-in roll.

OWENS, THOMAS R.:   Pvt., enl. 8 Dec 46 at Pittsburgh, age 20, died at Perote 8 Aug 47.

PARK, JOSEPH W.: (Parke):   Pvt., enl. 8 Dec 46 at Pittsburgh, age 28, disc. at Puebla 1 Nov 47 on SCD, died shortly thereafter.

PATRICK, HOLMES C.:   Pvt., enl. 8 Dec 46 at Pittsburgh, age 20, on detached duty in printing office in Mexico City from 19 Dec 47 through Apr 48, mo. with Co. 25 Jul 48.

PHILLIPS, JAMES: (Philips):   Pvt., enl. 16 Dec 46 at Pittsburgh, age 26, KIA at Puebla 12 Oct 47.

PHILLIPS, WILLIAM: Pvt., enl. 8 Dec 46 at Pittsburgh, age 25, disc. at Vera Cruz 27 Apr 47 on SCD.

PHILLIPS, WILLIAM A.: (Philips): Pvt., enl. 8 Dec 46 at Pittsburgh, age 41, in hospital at Jalapa in Apr 47, KIA at Puebla 12 Oct 47.

POLAND, JOHN: Pvt., enl. 8 Dec 46 at Pittsburgh, age 20, mo. with Co. 25 Jul 48. Capt. Co. K, 13th P.V.I. (3 mos.) 26 Apr 61 to 6 Aug 61. Maj. 102nd P.V.I. 6 Aug 61 until KIA 1 Jul 62 at Malvern Hill.

POTTER, WILLIAM H.: Pvt., enl. 8 Dec 46 at Pittsburgh, age 25, appointed Fifer 1 Jan 47, absent on leave from Aug 47, rejoined Co. as Pvt. 1 May 48, mo. with Co. 25 Jul 48.

REAMS, GEORGE: Pvt., enl. 8 Dec 46 at Pittsburgh, age 23, disc. at Perote 6 Jun 47, died shortly thereafter.

REES, RICHARD J.: Pvt., enl. & mi. 20 Nov 47 at Pittsburgh, age 28, reported at Ft. McHenry, Md. 20 Jan 48, joined Co. in Mexico City 19 Apr 48, mo. with Co. 25 Jul 48.

REID, ROBERT: (Reed): Pvt., enl. 24 Nov 46 at Phila., age 23, transferred as Pvt. from Co. D, 1st Pa. Regt. 1 Oct 47, wounded at Puebla, mo. with Co. 25 Jul 48.

RIPPEY, OLIVER H.: Pvt., enl. 8 Dec 46 at Pittsburgh, age 21, on extra duty in Commissary Dept. from 22 Jun 47 through at least 30 Apr 48, mo. with Co. 25 Jul 48. Lt. Col. 7th P.V.I. (3 mos.) 23 Apr 61 to 30 Jul 61. Col. 61st P.V.I. 24 Jul 61 until KIA 31 May 62 at Fair Oaks.

ROBBINS, JAMES: Pvt., enl. 8 Dec 46 at Pittsburgh, age 20, disc. at Perote 6 Jun 47, died on the way home.

ROBINSON, LEWIS G.: Sgt., enl. 8 Dec 46 at Pittsburgh, age 33, disc. at Lobos Island 7 Feb 47 on SCD, died shortly thereafter.

SCHMITDZ, WILLIAM: (Schmidt, Schmitz, Smid): Pvt., enl. 8 Dec 46 at Pittsburgh, age 23, KIA at Puebla 12 Oct 47.

SCOTT, ROBERT LIGHTNER: Pvt., enl. 8 Dec 46 at Pittsburgh, age 19, drowned in Mississippi River 5 Jul 48 on the way home.

SEWELL, SAMUEL D.: Pvt., enl. 8 Dec 46 at Pittsburgh, age 23, KIA at Puebla 12 Oct 47.

SLOOP, SAMUEL: Pvt., enl. 9 Mar 47 on the ship *Oxnard,* mi. 1 May 47 at camp near Jalapa, WIA at Puebla 12 Oct 47, disc. 1 Nov 47 on SCD for wounds. Moved to England.

SMITH, ANDREW JACKSON: (Schmidt): Pvt., enl. & mi. 20 Sep 47 at Pottsville, age 23, joined Co. in Mexico City 21 Dec 47, mo. with Co. 25 Jul 48.

SMITH, CHARLES: Pvt., enl. 8 Dec 46 at Pittsburgh, age 25, deserted at New Orleans 7 Jan 47.

SMITH, SAMUEL C. (A.) Pvt., enl. 8 Dec 46 at Pittsburgh, age 38, deserted at New Orleans 14 Jan 47.

SPENCER, JOSEPH M. (C., W.): Pvt., enl. 8 Dec 46 at Pittsburgh, age 19, listed as sick on 16 Dec 46 - 28 Feb 47 MR, in hospital at Jalapa according to Mar-Apr 47 MR, died at Jalapa 4 Jun 47.

STEIN, ADAM: Pvt., enl. 8 Dec 46 at Pittsburgh, age 28, deserted at Pittsburgh 16 Dec 46.

THOMAS, FRANCIS I. (Frederick J.): Pvt., enl. 8 Dec 46 at Pittsburgh, age 25, was with the New York Regt. from 8 Aug 47 to 9 Dec 47 & had $28.00 of his pay withheld because of this absence, mo. with Co. 25 Jul 48.

THORNBURGH, THOMAS: (Thornburg): Pvt., enl. 8 Dec 46 at Pittsburgh, age 24, listed as sick on 16 Dec 46 - 28 Feb 47 MR, wounded at Puebla 9 Oct 47 while on post as sentinel, disc. at Puebla 1 Nov 47 on SCD for wounds.

TROVILLO, WILLIAM: 1st Lt., enl. at Pittsburgh, age 26, hospitalized at Vera Cruz 9 Apr 47, placed on leave of absence until 9 May 47 at which date his resignation became effective and he was to be considered honorably discharged.

TROYER, SAMUEL: Pvt., enl. 8 Dec 46 at Pittsburgh, age 20, KIA at Puebla 12 Oct 47.

VAN DYKE, FRANCIS: Pvt., enl. 8 Dec 46 at Pittsburgh, age 23, KIA at Puebla 12 Oct 47.

VERNOVY, DAVID S.: (Vernoy): Pvt., enl. 8 Dec 46 at Pittsburgh, age 25, KIA at Puebla 12 Oct 47.

WALKER, JOHN: Pvt., enl. & mi. 4 Sep 47 at Pittsburgh, age 22, joined Co. in Mexico City 21 Dec 47, mo. with Co. 25 Jul 48.

WARR, ISAAC: Pvt., enl. & mi. 11 Oct 47 at Phila., age 19, joined Co. in Mexico City 21 Dec 47, mo. with Co. 25 Jul 48.

WHELAND, JOB B.: (Wheeland): Pvt., transferred from the New York Regt. 8 Aug 47, disc. at Puebla 4 Nov 47 on SCD, died shortly thereafter.

WILSON, JOSEPH: Pvt., enl. 8 Dec 46 at Pittsburgh, age 21, KIA at Puebla 12 Oct 47.

WINIBIDDLE, WILLIAM C.: (Winebiddle): Pvt., enl. & mi. 10 Jan 47 at New Orleans, age 26, wounded at Puebla, sick at San Angel from 7 Feb 48, rejoined Co. by 30 Apr 48, mo. with Co. 25 Jul 48.

WIRE, THEODORE B.: Pvt., enl. & mi. 4 Dec 47 at Pittsburgh, age 22, reported at Ft. McHenry, Md. 20 Jan 48, joined Co. in Mexico City 19 Apr 48, mo. with Co. 25 Jul 48.

WOODS, BENJAMIN F.: Pvt., enl. 8 Dec 46 at Pittsburgh, age 22, on extra duty as butcher according to Mar-Apr 47 MR, deserted at Jalapa 4 May 47.

Unassigned Recruits, 1st Regiment

ALLISON, THOMAS: Pvt., enl. 8 Feb 48 at Phila., age 21, mi. 29 Feb 48 at Ft. Mifflin, mo. 13 Jul 48 at Ft. Mifflin.

ASH, EDWARD T.: Pvt., enl. 13 Mar 48 at Pittsburgh, age 27, mi. 30 Apr 48 at Ft. Mifflin, AWOL from 30 Jun 48, listed as absent on muster-out roll of 13 Jul 48.

BAPTIST, JOHN: (Babtist): Pvt., enl. 12 Feb 48 at Pittsburgh, age 32, mi. 28 Feb 48 at Ft. Mifflin, mo. 13 Jul 48 at Ft. Mifflin.

BARNHAM, CHARLES: Pvt., enl. 1 Mar 48 at Pittsburgh, age 22, mi. 30 Apr 48 at Ft. Mifflin, mo. 13 Jul 48 at Ft. Mifflin.

BARR, HENRY: Pvt., enl. 2 Dec 47 at Phila., age 22, mi. at Phila. in Dec 47, deserted 24 Dec 47.

BAUER, RUDOLPH: Pvt., enl. 5 Jun 48 at Pittsburgh, age 23, mi. 30 Jun 48 at Ft. Mifflin, mo. 13 Jul 48 at Ft. Mifflin.

BENDER, JEROME: Pvt., enl. 1 Mar 48 at Phila., age 20, mi. 30 Apr 48 at Ft. Mifflin, deserted 12 Mar 48, returned 23 May 48, disc. on Habeus Corpus 28 May 48 being a minor.

BLANCHARD, CHARLES: Pvt., enl. 24 Feb 48 at Phila., age 18, mi. 28 Feb 48 at Ft. Mifflin, disc. 31 May 48 on Habeus Corpus.

BOYD, WILLIAM C.: Pvt., enl. 6 Aug 47 at Phila., age 21, mi. at Ft. Mifflin on the same day, deserted 3 Sep 47.

BOYLE, JOHN T.: Pvt., enl. 18 Jan 48 at Phila., age 37, mi. at Ft. Mifflin 31 Jan 48, deserted 18 Feb 48, arrested 17 Apr 48, disc. 24 Jun 48 by order of the Adjt. Gen.

BRADY, BARNEY: Pvt., enl. 24 Aug 47 at Pittsburgh, age 31, mi. at Pittsburgh, reported at Carlisle Barracks 31 Aug 47, deserted 15 Sep 47.

BROWN, SAMUEL: Pvt., enl. 15 Feb 48 at Phila., age 21, mi. at Ft. Mifflin 28 Feb 48, mo. 13 Jul 48 at Ft. Mifflin.

BRUMMER, JOHN: (Brunner): Pvt., enl. 25 Mar 48 at Pittsburgh, age 32, mi. 30 Apr 48 at Ft. Mifflin, mo. at Ft. Mifflin 13 Jul 48.

BURTON, ISAAC: Pvt., enl. & mi. 10 Aug 47 at Phila., rejected by Dr. King because of size, disc. 10 Aug 47.

BUTLER, CORNELIUS S.: Pvt., enl. 3 Jan 48 at Phila., age 20, rejected due to injury to right eye.

BYERLY, JOHN: (Byerley): Pvt., enl. 25 Mar 48 at Pittsburgh, age 32, mi. at Ft. Mifflin 30 Apr 48, mo. at Ft. Mifflin 13 Jul 48.

CLARK, WILLIAM: Pvt., enl. 1 Oct 47 at Pittsburgh, age 38, deserted at Ft. McHenry, Md. 20 Jan 48.

COMMEFORD, DENNIS L.: (Commefford, Cummeford): Pvt., enl. 29 Jan 48 at Phila., age 31, mi. at Ft. Mifflin 29 Feb 48, employed in Phila. by Lt. Hunterson as Recruiting Sgt. according to 29 Feb 48 MR, deserted 29 May 48.

CONNOR, BENJAMIN F.: (Conner): Pvt., enl. 7 Feb 48 at Phila., age 28, mi. at Ft. Mifflin 30 Apr 48, employed in Phila. by Lt. Hunterson as Recruiting Sgt. according to 29 Feb 48 & 30 Apr 48 MRs, deserted from this post.

CONNOR, SAMUEL: Pvt., enl. 5 Aug 47 at Phila., age 30, mi. at Ft. Mifflin 6 Aug 47, deserted from Ft. Mifflin 7 Aug 47.

COX, GEORGE W.: Pvt., enl. & mi. 9 Sep 47 at Pittsburgh disc. at Phila. by Dr. King 30 Sep 47.

CRAMMER, ISAAC R.: (Cranner): Pvt., enl. 10 Apr 48 at Phila., age 25, mi at Ft. Mifflin 30 Apr 48, mo. 13 Jul 48 at Ft. Mifflin.

CRAWFORD, GEORGE: Pvt., enl. 4 Sep 47 at Pittsburgh, age 26, deserted near Phila. 26 Oct 47.

CROWLEY, DANIEL: Pvt., enl. 12 May 48 at Phila., age 29, mi. at Ft. Mifflin 31 May 48, mo. 13 Jul 48 at Ft. Mifflin.

DAVIS, THOMAS M.: Pvt., enl. 2 Nov 47 at Pittsburgh, age 27, stationed at Ft. Mifflin by 10 Jan 48, listed as permanent party on 30 Apr 48 MR, mo. at Ft. Mifflin 13 Jul 48.

DENNISON, JAMES: Pvt., enl. 6 Apr 48 at Pittsburgh, age 36, mi. at Ft. Mifflin 30 Apr 48, mo. at Ft. Mifflin 13 Jul 48.

EGE, JACOB: Pvt., enl. 28 Feb 48 at Phila., age 24, mi. at Ft. Mifflin 29 Feb 48, mo. at Ft. Mifflin 13 Jul 48.

FATZINGER, THOMAS: Pvt., enl. 2 Feb 48 at Phila., age 23, mi. at Ft. Mifflin 29 Feb 48, mo. at Ft. Mifflin 13 Jul 48.

FAULKNER, THOMAS: Pvt., enl. in Dec 47 at Phila., rejected because of hemorrhoids according to 10 Jan 48 MR.

GAMBLE, WASHINGTON F.: Pvt., enl. 23 Jul 47 at Phila., rejected because his guardian refused consent, disc. 26 Jul 47.

GAW, THOMAS: Pvt., enl. 12 Apr 48 at Phila., age 34, mi. at Ft. Mifflin 30 Apr 48, mo. at Ft. Mifflin 13 Jul 48.

GLENN, DAVID: Pvt., enl. 8 Mar 48 at Phila., age 27, mi. at Ft. Mifflin 30 Apr 48, serving as Recruiting Sgt. at Lt. Bryan's rendezvous in Phila. according to 30 Apr 48 MR, mo. at Ft. Mifflin 13 Jul 48.

GOODES, THOMAS: Pvt., enl. 26 Nov 47 at Phila., age 21, rejected for varicose veins about 10 Jan 48.

GORMLEY, HENRY: Pvt., enl. 8 Mar 48 at Phila., age 21, mi. at Ft. Mifflin 30 Apr 48, mo. at Ft. Mifflin 13 Jul 48.

GREENE, WILLIAM K.: Pvt., enl. 27 Jul 47 at Phila., age 19, disc. on Habeus Corpus by Judge Campbell 28 Aug 47.

GUISON, JEAN T.: Pvt., enl. 19 Aug 47 at Pittsburgh, age 29, reported at Carlisle Barracks 31 Aug 47.

HACKETT, PETER: Pvt., enl. 23 Feb 48 at Phila., age 21, delivered up to Capt. George Taylor of 3rd U.S. Artillery who claimed him as a deserter before 29 Feb 48.

HARPER, ALEXANDER: Pvt., enl. 20 Mar 48 at Phila., age 25, mi. at Ft. Mifflin 30 Apr 48, mo. at Ft. Mifflin 13 Jul 48.

HARRAR, JOSEPH W.: Pvt., mi. at Ft. Mifflin 11 Feb 48, deserted 15 Feb 48, apprehended 18 May 48, disc. by order of the Adjt. Gen. 8 Jun 48.

HENRICK, ADAM: Pvt., enl. 4 Mar 48 at Pittsburgh, age 43, mi. at Ft. Mifflin 30 Apr 48, mo. at Ft. Mifflin 13 Jul 48.

HENRY, WILLIAM A.: Pvt., enl. 29 Jan 48 at Phila., age 24, mi. at Ft. Mifflin 2 Feb 48, mo. at Ft. Mifflin 13 Jul 48.

HINKLE, JOHN HENRY: (Hinckel, Hinckle): Pvt., enl. 5 Nov 47 at Phila., age 32, mi. at Ft. Mifflin 10 Jan 48, fined one month's pay by Court Martial according to muster-out roll, mo. at Ft. Mifflin 13 Jul 48.

HOLMES, THOMAS: Pvt., enl. 18 Jan 48 at Phila., age 32, deserted from Ft. Mifflin 21 Feb 48.

HUGHES, JAMES R.: Pvt., enl. 25 Feb 48 at Phila., age 21, mi. at Ft. Mifflin 30 Apr 48, serving as Recruiting Sgt. at Lt. Bryan's rendezvous in Phila. according to 30 Apr 48 MR, mo. at Ft. Mifflin 13 Jul 48.

ICKES, JOSEPH D. B.: Pvt., enl. 12 Mar 48 at Phila., age 2?, mi. at Ft. Mifflin 30 Apr 48, mo. at Ft. Mifflin 13 Jul 48.

JACOBY, HENRY: Pvt., enl. 4 Aug 47 at Phila., age 23, rejected for varicose veins, disc. 5 Aug 47.

JOHNSON, JAMES W.: Pvt., enl. 13 May 48 at Phila., age 23, mi. at Ft. Mifflin 31 May 48, mo. at Ft. Mifflin 13 Jul 48.

JONES, JOHN: Pvt., enl. 10 Feb 48 at Phila., age 32, mi. at Ft. Mifflin 29 Feb 48, deserted from Ft. Mifflin 10 Apr 48, arrested 15 Apr 48, dishonorably disc. 30 Jun 48.

KELCH, THOMAS M.: Pvt., enl. 14 Oct 47 at Phila., "absent when Rolls were signed. Went out in the ship." Listed only on the detachment Roll of 31 Oct 47 at Ft. Mifflin.

KELLY, MICHAEL: Pvt., enl. 23 Jul 47 at Phila., disc. at Phila. 26 Jul 47 "being intemperate."

KELLY, WILLIAM: Pvt., enl. 28 Feb 48 at Phila., age 28, mi. at Ft. Mifflin 29 Feb 48, mo. at Ft. Mifflin 13 Jul 48.

KENNIN, CHARLES F.: (Kinnin): Pvt., enl. 18 Jan 48 at Phila., age 2?, mi. at Ft. Mifflin 29 Feb 48, mo. at Ft. Mifflin 13 Jul 48.

KERNS, MORGAN: Pvt., enl. 27 Jan 48 at Phila., age 31, mi. at Ft. Mifflin 29 Feb 48, mo. at Ft. Mifflin 13 Jul 48.

KIRKPATRICK, MOORE: (Moore, Kirkpatrick): Pvt., enl. 22 Jan 48 at Phila., age 2?, mi. at Ft. Mifflin 29 Feb 48, employed as Recruiting Sgt. in Phila. by Lt. Deaney from 29 Feb 48, mo. at Ft. Mifflin 13 Jul 48.

LEVIS, SAMUEL J.: Pvt., enl. 8 May 48 at Phila., age 2?, deserted 16 May 48.

LONG, EDWARD H.: Pvt., enl. 2 Feb 48 at Phila., age 21, mi. same day at Ft. Mifflin, employed as Recruiting Sgt. in Phila. by Lt. Hunterson according to 29 Feb 48 MR, deserted from Phila. 23 Apr 48, arrested 23 Apr 48, disc. 6 May 48.

LOWER, JOSEPH, JR.: Pvt., enl. 4 Aug 47 at Phila., age 35, mi. at Ft. Mifflin 6 Aug 47, deserted 8 Aug 47.

LUKENS, JOSEPH: (Lukins): Pvt., enl. 8 Feb 48 at Phila., age 2?, mi. at Ft. Mifflin 29 Feb 48, mo. at Ft. Mifflin 13 Jul 48.

McCANDLESS, WILLIAM J.: Pvt., enl. 14 Jan 48 at Pittsburgh, age 20, mi. at Ft. Mifflin 29 Feb 48, mo. at Ft. Mifflin 13 Jul 48.

McCOY, ALEXANDER: Pvt., enl. 1 Mar 48 at Phila., age 20, disc. on Habeus Corpus 15 Mar 48 being a minor.

McKELVEY, JOHN F.: Pvt., enl. 1 Mar 48 at Phila., age 19, disc. at Ft. Mifflin on Habeus Corpus 29 Apr 48 being a minor.

MEHAFFY, JAMES: Pvt., enl. 9 Dec 47 at Phila., deserted 24 Dec 47, arrested 25 Jan 48, escaped 13 Feb 48.

MILLER, SAMUEL D.: Pvt., enl. 31 Jan 48 at Phila., age 21, deserted from Ft. Mifflin 18 Feb 48.

MILLINGER, SAMUEL: Pvt., enl. 16 Feb 48 at Phila., age 34, rejected by Dr. King, disc. 22 Feb 48 for disability.

MILLS, GEORGE: Pvt., enl. 29 Feb 48 at Phila., age 21, mi. at Ft. Mifflin 29 Feb 48, absent on leave on 30 Apr 48 MR, mo. at Ft. Mifflin 13 Jul 48.

MORRIS, ANDREW: Pvt., enl. 6 May 48 at Phila., age 2?, mi. at Ft. Mifflin 31 May 48, mo. at Ft. Mifflin 13 Jul 48.

MULHOLLAND, PATRICK: Pvt., enl. 24 Apr 48 at Pittsburgh, age 34, mi. at Ft. Mifflin 7 Jun 48, mo. at Ft. Mifflin 13 Jul 48.

MULLEN, JAMES: Pvt., enl. 31 Jan 48 at Phila., age 21, mi. at Ft. Mifflin 29 Feb 48, mo. at Ft. Mifflin 13 Jul 48.

NEAMULLER, ANTOINE: Pvt., enl. 5 Jun 48 at Pittsburgh, age 23, mi. at Ft. Mifflin 30 Jun 48, mo. at Ft. Mifflin 13 Jul 48.

PIPER, DANIEL: Pvt., enl. 7 Jan 48 at Pittsburgh, age 24, mi. at Ft. Mifflin 29 Feb 48, mo. at Ft. Mifflin 13 Jul 48.

PRESTON, WILLIAM: Pvt., enl. 20 Mar 48 at Phila., age 21, mi. at Ft. Mifflin 31 Mar 48, mo. at Ft. Mifflin 13 Jul 48.

QUINN, JAMES P.: Pvt., enl. 22 Mar 48 at Phila., age 22, mi. at Ft. Mifflin 31 Mar 48, deserted from Ft. Mifflin 29 May 48.

RAMAGE, WILLIAM (David): Pvt., enl. 8 Mar 48 at Phila., age 25, mi. at Ft. Mifflin 31 Mar 48, mo. at Ft. Mifflin 13 Jul 48.

RANG, FREDERICK: Pvt., enl. 1 Mar 48 at Pittsburgh, age 22, mi. at Ft. Mifflin 30 Apr 48, mo. at Ft. Mifflin 13 Jul 48.

RIELLY, WILLIAM W.: (Reily): Pvt., enl. 3 Apr 48 at Pittsburgh, age 22, AWOL on 30 Apr 48 MR, rejected, disc. at Ft. Mifflin 18 May 48.

ROSE, ELIAS: Pvt., enl. 22 Jul 47 at Phila., age 41, rejected because of piles, disc. at Ft. Mifflin 29 Jul 47.

ROSELL, JOHN P.: Pvt., enl. 6 Aug 47 at Phila., age 24, mi. at Ft. Mifflin 6 Aug 47, AWOL on 31 Aug 47 MR, deserted 5 Sep 47.

RUGGLES, THOMAS: Pvt., enl. 2 Aug 47 at Pottsville, age 27, mi. at Ft. Mifflin 31 Aug 47, deserted 5 Sep 47.

SHIELDS, PETER: Pvt., enl. 11 Jan 48 at Pittsburgh, age 30, mi. at Ft. Mifflin 29 Feb 48, mo. at Ft. Mifflin 13 Jul 48.

SITLER, ISAAC W. D.: Pvt., enl. 14 Feb 48 at Phila., age 22, mi. at Ft. Mifflin 29 Feb 48, AWOL from 24 Feb 48, returned before 29 Feb 48, mo. at Ft. Mifflin 13 Jul 48.

SMALL, PATRICK: Pvt., enl. 13 Apr 48 at Phila., age 39, mi. at Ft. Mifflin 30 Apr 48, disc. 5 May 48 by order of the Adjt. Gen.

SMITH, PATRICK D.: Pvt., enl. 21 Oct 47 at Phila., age 25, deserted from recruiting rendezvous, brought to Ft. Mifflin 27 Apr 48 as a deserter, rejected for disability, disc. 16 May 48.

SMITH, WILLIAM: Pvt., enl. 24 Feb 48 at Phila., age 19, mi. at Ft. Mifflin 29 Feb 48, disc. at Ft. Mifflin 31 May 48 on Habeus Corpus being a minor.

STANLEY, WILLIAM H.: Pvt., enl. 18 May 48 at Pittsburgh, age 33, mi. at Ft. Mifflin 7 Jun 48, mo. at Ft. Mifflin 13 Jul 48.

STULL, JAMES: Pvt., enl. 2 Feb 48 at Phila., age 20, mi. at Ft. Mifflin 29 Feb 48, disc. on Habeas Corpus 29 May 48 being a minor.

SWORDS, WILLIAM ADAM: Pvt., enl. 24 Jan 48 at Phila., age 24, mi. at Ft. Mifflin 29 Feb 48, mo. at Ft. Mifflin 13 Jul 48.

TAYLOR, WILLIAM: Pvt., enl. 6 Jan 48 at Phila., age 33, rejected for disability before 10 Jan 48.

WAGONER, CHRISTOPHER: (Waggoner): Pvt., enl. 24 Dec 47 at Pittsburgh, age 27, mi. at Ft. Mifflin 29 Feb 48, mo. at Ft. Mifflin 13 Jul 48.

WARNER, FREDERICK: Pvt., enl. 11 Oct 47 at Pottsville, age 25, listed on only one detachment Roll at Phila. 31 Oct 47.

WELLS, CHARLES: Pvt., enl. 7 Jan 48 at Pittsburgh, age 31, mi. at Ft. Mifflin 29 Feb 48, mo. at Ft. Mifflin 13 Jul 48.

WHITE, CHARLES: Pvt., enl. 4 Apr 48 at Pittsburgh, age 30, mi. at Ft. Mifflin 30 Apr 48, mo. at Ft. Mifflin 13 Jul 48.

WHITE, SAMUEL SMITH: Pvt., enl. 21 Aug 47 at Phila., age 35, rejected because of his teeth, disc. 23 Aug 47.

WHITEMAN, WILLIAM H. H.: (Whitman): Pvt., enl. 25 Jan 48 at Phila., age 26, rejected for disability, disc. 19 Apr 48.

WILLIAMS, HIRAM: Pvt., enl. 6 Jan 48 at Phila., age 39, rejected because of hemorrhoids.

WILLIAMS, JACKSON: Pvt., enl. 18 Jan 48 at Phila., age 22, mi. at Ft. Mifflin 29 Feb 48, deserted 10 May 48.

WILLIS, ROBERT W.: Pvt., enl. 28 Aug 47 at Pittsburgh, age 21, deserted 26 Oct 47.

WILSON, JAMES: Pvt., enl. 17 Feb 48 at Phila., age 25, mi. at Ft. Mifflin 29 Feb 48, deserted 26 May 48.

WINTERS, JOHN HUNNA: Pvt., enl. 14 Feb 48 at Phila., age 29, mi. at Ft. Mifflin 29 Feb 48, mo. at Ft. Mifflin 13 Jul 48.

ZEIGLER, GEORGE W.: Pvt., enl. 20 Sep 47 at Pittsburgh, age 44, deserted from Pittsburgh 23 Sep 47, present at Ft. Mifflin from at least 29 Feb 48, disc. after 30 Jun 48 because of previous desertion.

Field and Staff, 2nd Regiment

The field officers of the 2nd Regiment were elected on 6 January 1847, and First Lieutenant Horace B. Field mustered them in the next day. A total of thirty-three people served in the field and staff of the regiment during the war. As with the 1st Regiment, there was considerable turnover in the staff positions.

Colonel Geary graduated from Jefferson College and worked as an engineer for the Allegheny Portage Railroad Company. He was also active in local military activities. Following the war he served as Postmaster and as Mayor of San Francisco, California. He was appointed Governor of Kansas Territory in 1856, serving until March 1857. He distinguished himself as a soldier for the Union during the Civil War and won promotions to Major General. The people of Pennsylvania elected him Governor in 1866, and he served in that capacity until 1873.

The field and staff of the Second Regiment returned to Pittsburgh and were mustered out by Major George Wright on 21 July 1848.

BARBARA: Matron, listed only on 2nd Regt. Hospital MR of Sep-Oct 47.

BOMANA, HOLORUS C.: Matron, listed only on 2nd Regt. Hospital MR of Sep-Oct 47.

BOWER, CHARLES: (Brown): enl. 5 May 47 at Newton Hamilton, age 30, occ. physician, mi. 18 May 47 at Pittsburgh as 2nd Lt. Co. M, appointed Acting Asst. Surg. 26 May 47 upon departure from Pittsburgh, acted in that capacity through 31 Oct 47, on 3 months furlough from 1 Nov 47 because of diarrhea, tendered his resignation 29 May 48, it was accepted 5 Jun 48. Surgeon 6th Pa. Reserves 22 Jun 61 to 11 Jun 64. Surgeon 193rd P.V.I. 19 Jul 64 to 9 Nov 64. Bvt. Lt. Col. & Col. 13 Mar 65. Died in 1867.

BOWER, FRANCIS: enl. 26 Dec 46 at Danville, age 25, occ. stone cutter, mi. 3 Jan 47 at Pittsburgh as Pvt., Co. C, hospitalized at Jalapa according to Mar-Apr 47 MR, serving as Asst. Hospital Steward & Ward Master in regimental hospital from 2 Sep 47 through at least 30 Apr 48, mo. with Co. C, 20 Jul 48.

BRINDLE, WILLIAM: enl. 26 Dec 46 at Danville, age 28, residence Muncy, mi. 3 Jan 47 at Pittsburgh as 2nd Lt., Co. C, elected Maj. 5 Jan 47, promoted to Lt. Col. 4 Nov 47, mo. with F & S 21 Jul 48. Died in Dec 1902, buried in Pottsville.

BUNTING, THOMAS C.: appointed Asst. Surg. of Vols. 17 Sep 46, assigned to 1st Pa. Regt. 17 Dec 46, transferred by Special Order #40 to 2nd Pa. Regt. 18 Apr 48, mo. with F & S, 21 Jul 48. Died 23 Dec 95.

CHRISTENA: Matron, attached to regimental hospital 1 Mar 48, listed only on 2nd Regt. Hospital MR of Mar-Apr 48.

CLARK, JESSE G.: enl. 26 Dec 46 at Danville, age 22, occ. printer, residence Danville, mi. 3 Jan 47 at Pittsburgh as Fifer of Co. C, appointed Fife Maj. 5 Jan 47, reduced to Fifer of Co. C, 1 May 47, mo. with Co. C, 20 Jul 48.

CONFER, JACOB M.: (Carfer, Cenfer, Cowfer): enl. 21 Dec 46 at Hollidaysburg, age 21, occ. medical student, mi. 3 Jan 47 at Pittsburgh as Pvt. in Co. B, promoted to 4th Sgt. 8 Jan 47, detached to regimental hospital as Ward Master 5 Aug 47, reduced to Pvt. & appointed Hospital Steward 16 Nov 47, mo. with Co. B 14 Jul 48. Surgeon 29th Indiana Vol. Inf. 10 Feb 63 to 8 Dec 63.

DOLORUS: Matron, attached to regimental hospital 1 Oct 47, listed only on 2nd Regt. Hospital MR of Sep-Oct 47.

DUFF, DAVID: enl. 26 Dec 46 at Huntingdon, age 25, occ. lawyer, mi. 3 Jan 47 at Pittsburgh as Pvt. in Co. B, on duty as clerk for Col. Geary from Nov 47 through May 48, promoted to Sgt. Major 10 Jun 48 to rank from 12 Feb 48, mo. with F & S 21 Jul 48.

DUTTON, BENJAMIN F.: enl. 1 Dec 46 at Phila., age 30, mi. 22 Dec 46 at Pitts. as 1st Lt. in Co. F, appointed Adjutant 7 Jan 47, left Jalapa for recruiting duty 8 Jun 47, was recruiting in the State Fencibles' armory in Phila. by 27 Jul 47, rejoined Regt. 28 Dec 47, he was involved in a bank robbery and murder in Mexico City 4 Apr 48, removed from the post of Adjutant by Col. Geary 6 Apr 48, was in confinement according to Mar-Apr 48 MR, his sentence (hanging) was read to the troops 19 May 48, was reprieved, mo. with F & S 21 Jul 48.

ELIGERDO: Matron, attached to regimental hospital 1 Mar 48, listed only on 2nd Regt. Hospital MR of Mar-Apr 48.

John White Geary as a Brigadier General in the Civil War
MOLLUS-Mass & USAMHI

GEARY, JOHN WHITE: enl. 21 Dec 46 at Summitt, age 28, mi. 3 Jan 47 at Pittsburgh as Capt. of Co. B, elected Lt. Col. 6 Jan 47, assumed command of Regt. 1 Sep 47, slightly WIA in charge on Chapultepec 13 Sep 47, promoted to Col. 3 Nov 47, mo. with F & S 21 Jul 48. Col. 28th P.V.I. 28 Jun 61, Brig. Gen. of Vols. 25 Apr 62, Maj. Gen. of Vols. 12 Jan 65 to Jul 65. Died 8 Feb 73.

GIVEN, JOHN G. (J.): enl. 16 Dec 46 at Ebensburgh, age 26, occ. printer, mi. 4 Jan 47 at Pittsburgh as 2nd Lt. of Co. D, appointed Acting Asst. Commissary of Subsistence 25 May 47, mo. with Co. D 14 Jul 48. Reported as living in Mexico, Indiana in 1907.

GUILLOT, FRANCIS: Steward, attached to regimental hospital as Steward 16 Sep 47, listed only on 2nd Regt. Hospital MR of Sep-Oct 47.

HOOVER, JOHN B.: enl. 11 Dec 46 at Ebensburgh, age 22, occ. printer, mi. 4 Jan 47 at Pittsburgh as Pvt. in Co. D, appointed Fife Maj. 1 May 47, listed as sick in quarters on Sep-Oct 47 MR, hospitalized in Mexico City according to Nov-Dec 47 & Jan-Feb 48 MRs, mo. with F & S 21 Jul 48.

HORN, SAMUEL: (Horne, Horner): enl. 20 Dec 46 at Mauch Chunk, age 44, occ. hatter, mi. 1 Jan 47 at Pittsburgh as Drummer of Co. K, appointed Drum Maj. 10 Jul 47, listed as absent on Sep-Oct 47 MR, reduced to Drummer of Co. K in Nov or Dec 47, listed as sick in quarters on Nov-Dec 47 MR, mo. with Co. K 12 Jul 48.

JOHNSTON, JAMES: (Johnson, Johnstone): enl. 24 Dec 46 at Greensburgh, age 27, occ. law student, mi. 1 Jan 47 at Pittsburgh as Pvt. in Co. E, appointed Q.M. Sgt. 7 Jan 47, disc. at Jalapa 22 May 47 on SCD.

KLOTZ, ROBERT: enl. 20 Dec 46 at Mauch Chunk, age 27, occ. merchant, mi. 1 Jan 47 at Pittsburgh as 2nd Lt. of Co. K, on furlough from 4 May 47, while marching from Vera Cruz to rejoin his Co. he was detailed to Co. K, 11th U.S. Inf. & participated in the skirmish of Puente Nationale, rejoined Co. 7 Dec 47, on furlough in Mar 48, appointed Adjutant 7 Apr 48, absent on leave at mo. Col. 19th Pa. Emergency Militia 15 Sep 62 to 27 Sep 62. Died 1 May 95.

LeCLERC, EDWARD E.: enl. 26 Dec 46 at Danville, age 27, occ. lawyer, residence Wilkes-Barre, mi. 3 Jan 47 at Pittsburgh as 2nd Lt. of Co. C, listed as sick on Sep-Oct 47 Mr, appointed Q.M. 8 Nov 47, promoted to 1st Lt. 12 Nov 47, mo. with Co. C 20 Jul 48. Died at Phila. 12 Aug 49.

McMICHAEL, RICHARD: (McMichaels): enl. 16 Dec 46 at Reading, age 30, occ. pattern maker, mi. 5 Jan 47 at Pittsburgh as Pvt. of Co. A, appointed Sgt. Maj. 7 Jan 47, promoted to 2nd Lt. of Co. A 9 Sep 47, mo. with Co. 21 Jul 48. Lt. Col. 14th P.V.I. (3 mos.) 30 Apr 61 to 1 Aug 61. Lt. Col. 53rd P.V.I. 7 Nov 61 to 19 May 64. Lt. Col. 194th P.V.I. 24 Jul 64 to 6 Nov 64.

McMILLAN, ROBERT: (McMillen): had been Surgeon's Mate in the 5th U.S. Inf. 4 Dec 19, hon. disc. 1 Jun 21. Asst. Surg. 1 Jul 22. Major, Surgeon 3 Sep 32, resigned 1 Dec 33. enl. 27 May 47 at Jalapa, appointed Surg. of Vols. 8 Jun 47, not accounted for after Dec 47, hon. disc. 20 Jul 48.

MILLER, FREDERICK W.: commissioned Asst. Surg. 18 Jan 47, joined Regt. at camp near Vera Cruz 29 Mar 47, AWOL from 8 Jun 47, appointed Surg. 10 Mar 48, rejoined Regt. 3 Jun 48, mo. with F & S 21 Jul 48.

MUHLENBERG, BENJAMIN SCHAUM: commissioned Surg. 4 Jan 47, verified as present with the Regt. only in Mar 47, resigned 30 Apr 47.

NEWELL, GEORGE M. (W.): (Neuell, Newal): enl. 1 Dec 46 at Phila., age 26, mi. 22 Dec 46 at Pittsburgh as Sgt. of Co. F, appointed Drummer of Co. F 8 Jan 47, appointed Drum Maj. 1 Mar 47, reduced to Drummer of Co. F 10 Jul 47, transferred to 1st Massachusetts Regt. 1 Mar 48 in trade for Drummer Henry S. Moore.

ROBERTS, WILLIAM B.: enl. 16 Dec 46 at Uniontown, age 38, occ. furniture maker, mi. 4 Jan 47 at Pittsburgh as Capt. of Co. H, elected Col. 6 Jan 47, sick from Sep 47. Died in Mexico City 3 Oct 47, his remains were returned to Uniontown for burial.

RUTLEDGE, HUGH ROSE: appointed Asst. Surg. of Vols. 10 Sep 47, assigned to 2nd Regt. in Mexico City 3 Jan 48 by the Army's Medical Director, on duty with Regt. through Apr 48, disc. 12 Jul 48.

SHELCROSS, JAMES P.: (Schellcross, Shallcross, Shalleroys): enl. 3 Jan 47 at Pittsburgh, age 39, mi. 3 Jan 47 at Pittsburgh as Pvt. of Co. B, appointed Q.M. Sgt. 8 May 47, mo. with F & S 21 Jul 48.

SIMONS, SAMUEL: enl. 6 Dec 46 at Harrisburg, age 28, occ. blacksmith, mi. 2 Jan 47 at Pittsburgh as Drummer of Co. G, appointed Drum Maj. 8 Nov 47, mo. with F & S 21 Jul 48. Musician Co. K, 2nd P.V.I. (3 mos.) 20 Apr 61 to 26 Jul 61.

TINKCOM, JOHN L.: (Tinckcum, Tincom, Tinkem, Tinkom, Tinkum, Truckain): enl. 21 Dec 46 at Armagh, age 23, occ. carpenter, mi. 3 Jan 47 at Pittsburgh as Drummer of Co. B, appointed Drum Maj. 7 Jan 47, reduced to Pvt. in Co. B 1 Mar 47, left sick at Perote 28 Jun 47, disc. at Perote 29 Oct 47 on SCD.

TODD, GEORGE W.: enl. 4 Dec 46 at Ebensburgh, age 22, occ. clerk, mi. 4 Jan 47 at Pittsburgh as Pvt. of Co. D, promoted to 1st Sgt. 26 Jan 47, appointed Sgt. Maj. 10 Sep 47, promoted to 2nd Lt. of Co. D 10 Jun 48 to rank from 11 Feb 48, mo. with Co. D 14 Jul 48. Major 91st P.V.I. 4 Dec 61 until 19 Dec 62 when he died of wounds received at Fredericksburg 13 Dec 62, Bvt. Lt. Col. 13 Dec 62.

WATERBURY, ISAAC S.: enl. 6 Dec 46 at Harrisburg, age 27, occ. tailor, mi. 2 Jan 47 at Pittsburgh as 2nd Lt. of Co. G, appointed Acting Adjt. 8 Jun 47, returned to Co. G 28 Dec 47, listed as sick in quarters on Nov-Dec 47 MR, mo. with Co. G 20 Jul 48. Adjt. 2nd P.V.I. (3 mos.) 20 Apr 61 to 26 Jul 61. Capt. Co. G, 55th P.V.I. 28 Aug 61 until dying at Bermuda Hundred 8 May 64.

Company A, 2nd Regiment
Reading Artillerists

The Reading Artillerists organized under that name in 1820 and became widely known and highly respected as a uniformed militia company. In 1844 they were called to duty in Philadelphia to help quell a series of violent riots.

Upon the declaration of war against Mexico the Artillerists unhesitatingly volunteered their services. Captain Thomas Leoser was notified on 16 December 1846 that his company was given a position in Pennsylvania's 2nd Regiment. The Artillerists departed from Reading on 26 December, heading for Pittsburgh by way of Philadelphia and Harrisburg. First Lieutenant Horace B. Field, 3rd U.S. Artillery, mustered the unit into U.S. service on 5 January 1847.

Captain Leoser's men upheld their reputation throughout their Federal service. They participated in the siege of Vera Cruz and the battles of Cerro Gordo, La Hoya, Chapultepec and Garita de Belen. Arriving back in Pittsburgh on 18 July 1848, they were mustered out there on 21 July by Major George Wright, 4th U.S. Infantry. Most of the company arrived in Reading at different times during the day of 29 July. The organization and traditions of the Reading Artillerists continued on after the war.

A total of 102 men served in the company during the war, six of them recruits who joined it in Mexico. Thirteen deserted the colors. Seventeen men suffered battle related injuries, five of whom died. In all, twenty-eight Artillerists died in service, and an additional twelve received discharges prior to muster out.

AKER, ELLIS L.: (Acher, Acker): 3rd Sgt., enl. 16 Dec 46 at Reading, age 23, occ. carpenter, promoted to 2nd Lt. 1 Jun 48, mo. with Co. 21 Jul 48.

ALBERT, PAUL: Pvt., enl. 16 Dec 46 at Reading, age 26, deserted from Camp Jackson near New Orleans 25 Jan 47.

ALEXANDER, JOSEPH W.: Pvt., enl. 16 Dec 46 at Reading, age 24, occ. laborer, left sick at Puebla 7 Aug 47, disc. at Vera Cruz 3 Dec 47 on SCD, died at New Orleans on his way home.

ALOCHER, JEFFERSON: (Arlocher): 2nd Cpl., enl. 16 Dec 46 at Reading, age 27, occ. laborer, promoted to 1st Cpl. 1 Nov 47, promoted to 2nd Sgt. date unknown, promoted to 1st Sgt. 13 Apr 48, mo. with Co. 21 Jul 48.

ANDERSON, JOHN L.: Pvt., enl. 16 Dec 46 at Reading, age 28, occ. laborer, in hospital at Vera Cruz from 8 Apr 47, disc. at Vera Cruz 17 May 47 on SCD, arrived in Reading 17 Jun 47.

ARMBRIESTER, JACOB: (Aowpriester, Armpriester): Pvt., enl. 16 Dec 46 at Reading, age 21, slightly WIA in charge at Chapultepec 13 Sep 47, mo. with Co. 21 Jul 48.

ARTHUR, JOHN (Jon) ELLIOTT: (Arther): Pvt., enl. 16 Dec 46 at Reading, age 22, occ. laborer, severely WIA in charge at Chapultepec 13 Sep 47, hospitalized in Mexico City 15 Sep 47, returned to Co. in Mar or Apr 48, promoted to 3rd Cpl. 13 Apr 48, mo. with Co. 21 Jul 48. Capt. Co. B & Lt. Col. 93rd P.V.I. 12 Oct 61 to 14 Nov 62. Lt. Col. 42nd Pa. Emergency Militia 6 Jul 63 to 12 Aug 63. Died in Reading 15 Mar 00.

BACHMAN, GEORGE: (Baukman, Bokman): Pvt., enl. 16 Dec 46 at Reading, age 26, occ. engineer, listed as on detached duty as teamster to Q.M. Dept. on Sep-Oct 47, Nov-Dec 47, Jan-Feb 48 & Mar-Apr 48 MRs, mo. with Co. 21 Jul 48.

BAUGHTER, HIRAM: (Bauehter, Bochter): Pvt., enl. 16 Dec 46 at Reading, age 20, occ. carpenter, left sick at Perote 22 Jun 47, rejoined Co. by 31 Dec 47, mo. with Co. 21 Jul 48.

BEAN, NEHEMIAH (NEIHM): Pvt., enl. 16 Dec 46 at Reading, age 22, occ. shoemaker, promoted to 4th Cpl. 13 Apr 48, mo. with Co. 21 Jul 48.

BEIDINGER, HENRY: (Beidinjer, Beitinger, Bitinger, Reidinger): 2nd Sgt., enl. 16 Dec 46 at Reading, age 21, occ. carpenter, left sick at Puebla 7 Aug 47, died at Puebla 1 Sep 47 from diarrhea.

BITTING, FRANKLIN: Pvt., enl. 16 Dec 46 at Reading, age 21, occ. printer, hospitalized at Jalapa 28 Apr 47, rejoined Co. by 31 Aug 47, listed as on extra duty on Sep-Oct 47 MR, detached to printing office in Mexico City according to Nov-Dec 47 MR, hospitalized in Mexico City 31 Dec 47, rejoined Co. by 30 Apr 48, mo. with Co. 21 Jul 48.

BOYER, HENRY: Pvt., enl. 16 Dec 46 at Reading, age 21, occ. printer, slightly WIA at Chapultepec 13 Sep 47, detached to "Star" printing office in Mexico City according to Jan-Feb 48 & Mar-Apr 48 MRs, mo. with Co. 21 Jul 48.

BRIESTLEY, JOHN: (Breistley, Briestly, Bristley): Pvt., enl. 16 Dec 46 at Reading, age 20, occ. shoemaker, listed as sick on Sep-Oct 47 MR, mo. with Co. 21 Jul 48.

BROWN, LEWIS: Pvt., enl. 16 Dec 46 at Reading, age 23, left sick at Perote 22 Jun 47, rejoined Co. after 30 Apr 48, mo. with Co. 21 Jul 48.

BUMBARGER, ADAM: (Bamberger): Pvt., enl. 8 Sep 47 at Phila., age 24, occ. baker, mi. at San Angel & joined Co. 31 Dec 47, mo. with Co. 21 Jul 48.

BURNS, SAMUEL: (Burms, Burnes): Pvt., enl. 26 Dec 46 at Danville, age 34, occ. laborer, transferred from Co. C, 2nd Pa. Regt. and promoted to Musician 1 May 47, mo. with Co. 21 Jul 48.

CARRAGAN, THOMAS: Pvt., enl. 16 Dec 46 at Reading, age 20, occ. carpenter, mo. with Co. 21 Jul 48.

CLINGER, CHARLES: Pvt., enl. 16 Dec 46 at Reading, age 18, deserted from Camp Jackson near New Orleans 25 Jan 47.

COBB, CYPRIAN: Pvt., enl. 16 Dec 46 at Reading, age 22, deserted from Camp Jackson near New Orleans 25 Jan 47.

COLDRICK, PATRICK (Parish): (Colerick, Colrick): Pvt., enl. 25 Aug 47 at Pittsburgh, age 27, occ. laborer, mi. at San Angel & joined Co. 31 Dec 47, mo. with Co. 21 Jul 48.

COLEMAN, JACOB: Drummer, enl. 16 Dec 46 at Reading, age 21, occ. mason, listed as on extra duty on Sep-Oct 47 MR, detached to regimental hospital as cook from 23 Feb 48 through at least 30 Apr 48, mo. with Co. 21 Jul 48.

DIEHL, WILLIAM S.: (Deal, Deihl): Pvt., enl. 16 Dec 46 at Reading, age 29, occ. carpenter, left sick at Puebla 7 Aug 47, died at Puebla 29 Aug 47 from diarrhea.

DIEHL, WILLIAM W.: (Deihl): 4th Sgt., enl. 16 Dec 46 at Reading, age 26, occ. carpenter, left sick at Puebla 7 Aug 47, wounded in the arm during the siege of Puebla, disc. at Puebla 17 Jan 48 on SCD for wound. Capt. Co. E, 50th P.V.I. 13 Sep 61 to 3 Feb 63. Died in 1873.

DONNELLY, JOHN: (Donnelley): Pvt., enl. 16 Dec 46 at Reading, age 22, occ. laborer, left sick at Perote 22 Jun 47, died at Perote 1 Sep 47 from diarrhea.

DUNBAR, CHARLES (Dunabar): Pvt., enl. 16 Dec 46 at Reading, age 22, occ. nail cutter, sent to Jalapa Hospital 28 Apr 47, died at Jalapa 29 Apr 47 from inflamation of the stomach and medical neglect.

EASON, JAMES: Pvt., enl. 16 Dec 46 at Reading, age 25, occ. laborer, left sick at Perote 22 Jun 47, died at Perote 19 Aug 47 from diarrhea.

EBBERT, JOSIAH (Joshua): Pvt., enl. 23 Dec 46 at Reading, age 32, occ. bricklayer, deserted at New Orleans 25 Jan 47.

FILBERT, HENRY A. M.: 2nd Lt., enl. 16 Dec 46 at Reading, age 25, occ. machinist, listed as sick on Sep-Oct 47 MR, on three months furlough from 1 Nov 47, continued on furlough in Mar & Apr 48 doing recruiting, tendered his resignation which was accepted 12 Apr 48. Capt. Co. K, 48th P.V.I. 1 Oct 61 until KIA 29 Aug 62 at Second Bull Run.

FISHER, AUGUSTUS: Pvt., enl. 16 Dec 46 at Reading, age 20, occ. laborer, mo. with Co. 21 Jul 48.

FISHER, JOHN: Pvt., enl. 16 Dec 46 at Reading, age 28, occ. laborer, left sick at Puebla 7 Aug 47, died at Puebla 25 Aug 47 from diarrhea.

FLICKINGER, CHARLES: (Fluckinger): Pvt., enl. 16 Dec 46 at Reading, age 35, occ. laborer, listed as sick on Sep-Oct 47 MR, reported disc. at Mexico City 1 Nov 47 on SCD, rejoined Co. 15 Apr 48, mo. with Co. 21 Jul 48.

FLICKINGER, WILLIAM: Pvt., enl. 16 Dec 46 at Reading, age 23, occ. miller, left sick at Puebla 7 Aug 47, died at Puebla 3 Nov 47 from diarrhea.

FORNEY, DANIEL L.: (Fawney, Forny): Pvt., enl. 16 Dec 46 at Reading, age 22, occ. carpenter, left sick at Puebla 7 Aug 47, died at Puebla 5 Sep 47 from diarrhea.

FREY, WILLIAM: (Fry): Pvt., enl. 16 Dec 46 at Reading, age 22, occ. shoemaker, hospitalized at Vera Cruz 8 Apr 47, disc. at Vera Cruz 17 May 47 on SCD.

FREYMORE, JOHN: (Freymer, Freymire, Frymier): Pvt., enl. 16 Dec 46 at Reading, age 22, occ. carpenter, slightly WIA in charge at Chapultepec 13 Sep 47, detailed to Commissary Dept. in Dec 47 & Jan 48, promoted to Cpl. 13 Apr 48, mo. with Co. 21 Jul 48.

FRITZ, EDWIN (Edward): (Fritey): Pvt., enl. 16 Dec 46 at Reading, age 19, occ. brass molder, hospitalized at Vera Cruz 8 Apr 47, disc. at Vera Cruz 17 May 47 on SCD, arrived in Reading 17 Jun 47.

GARDNER, HENRY: (Gardiner): Pvt., enl. 16 Dec 46 at Reading, age 30, occ. laborer, died in quarters at Puebla 20 Jul 47.

GAST, FREDERICK: Pvt., enl. 16 Dec 46 at Reading, age 22, occ. comb maker, left sick at Perote 22 Jun 47, rejoined Co. by 31 Dec 47, mo. with Co. 21 Jul 48.

GIBBS, GEORGE H.: Pvt., enl. 16 Dec 46 at Reading, age 21, occ. tailor, serving as attendant in regimental hospital at Mexico City from 16 Sep 47, hospitalized in Mexico City 19 Dec 47, rejoined Co. by 31 Jan 48, mo. with Co. 21 Jul 48.

GRAEFF, DANIEL: Pvt., enl. 16 Dec 46 at Reading, age 21, occ. tinsmith, on extra duty in hospital according to Sep-Oct 47 MR, died in quarters at San Angel 16 Feb 48.

GRAEFF, WILLIAM: (Greaeff): 1st Cpl., enl. 16 Dec 46 at Reading, age 23, occ. butcher, hospitalized at Jalapa 28 Apr 47, promoted to 1st Sgt. 1 Nov 47, promoted to 2nd Lt. 13 Apr 48, mo. with Co. 21 Jul 48.

HAMBRIGHT, JOHN G. (George I.): Pvt., enl. 16 Dec 46 at Reading, age 28, detailed as an assistant in hospital during Mar 47, promoted to 1st Sgt. 1 Apr 47, listed as sick on Sep-Oct 47 MR, died in Mexico City Hospital 8 Nov 47.

HARDEE, JOHN: Pvt., enl. 16 Dec 46 at Reading, age 21, occ. bricklayer, hospitalized at Jalapa 28 Apr 47, rejoined Co. by 31 Aug 47, mo. with Co. 21 Jul 48.

HEIL, JOHN A.: (Hiel): Pvt., enl. 16 Dec 46 at Reading, age 23, occ. jeweller, listed as on detached duty on Sep-Oct 47 MR, promoted to Cpl. 13 Apr 48, mo. with Co. 21 Jul 48.

HENRY, GEORGE: Pvt., enl. 16 Dec 46 at Reading, age 30, occ. wheelwright, severely WIA at Garita de Belen 13 Sep 47, hospitalized in Mexico City 14 Sep 47, died in Mexico City 29 Nov 47 from wounds.

HERBERT, WILLIAM: 4th Cpl., enl. 16 Dec 46 at Reading, age 24, occ. laborer, slightly WIA in charge at Chapultepec 13 Sep 47, promoted to 3rd Cpl. 1 Nov 47, promoted to Sgt. 13 Apr 48, mo. with Co. 21 Jul 48.

HERBST, WILLIAM: Pvt., enl. 16 Dec 46 at Reading, age 25, mo. with Co. 21 Jul 48.

HOGAN, PETER: Pvt., enl. 16 Dec 46 at Reading, age 21, occ. machinist, slightly WIA in charge at Chapultepec 13 Sep 47, promoted to Cpl. 1 Nov 47, promoted to Sgt. 13 Apr 48, mo. with Co. 21 Jul 48.

HORELL, CHARLES W.: (Horrell, Howell): Pvt., enl. 16 Dec 46 at Reading, age 23, occ. carpenter, left sick at Perote 22 Jun 47, disc. at Perote 29 Oct 47 on SCD.

HOTTENSTEIN, ISAAC: (Hottenstien, Hottenstine): Pvt., enl. 16 Dec 46 at Reading, age 33, deserted from Camp Jackson near New Orleans 25 Jan 47.

JONES, JESSE C.: Pvt., enl. 16 Dec 46 at Reading, age 21, occ. miller, left sick at Puebla 7 Aug 47, rejoined Co. by 31 Dec 47, mo. with Co. 21 Jul 48.

JONES, JOHN H.: Pvt., enl. 16 Dec 46 at Reading, age 24, occ. blacksmith, left sick at Puebla 7 Aug 47, rejoined Co. 31 Dec 47, mo. with Co. 21 Jul 48.

JORDAN, JOHN: (Jordon): Pvt., enl. 16 Dec 46 at Reading, age 22, deserted from Camp Jackson near New Orleans 25 Jan 47.

KARCHER, HENRY: (Kaercher, Karacher): Pvt., enl. 16 Dec 46 at Reading, age 27, occ. carpenter, left sick at Perote 22 Jun 47, died at Perote 30 Jul 47 from diarrhea.

KARCHER, ISRAEL: (Kaercher, Karacker, Karaker): Pvt., enl. 16 Dec 46 at Reading, age 22, occ. laborer, left sick at Perote 22 Jun 47, died at Perote 14 Jul 47 from rheumatism.

KLOTZ, VALENTINE: Pvt., enl. 16 Dec 46 at Reading, age 27, deserted from Camp Jackson near New Orleans 25 Jan 47.

KNERR, LEVI P.: 2nd Lt., enl. 16 Dec 46 at Reading, age 26, occ. machinist, on one months leave of absence for his health from 13 May 47, to consider himself disc. for disability on 13 Jun 47, arrived in Reading 17 Jun 47.

KOHLBERG, JOHN (Jacob, Joseph): (Kobburg, Kohlbergh, Kolebergh): Pvt., enl. 16 Dec 46 at Reading, age 22, occ. laborer, deserted from Camp Jackson near New Orleans 25 Jan 47.

KRAMER, GEORGE R. (P.): Pvt., enl. 16 Dec 46 at Reading, age 23, deserted from Camp Jackson near New Orleans 25 Jan 47, died in New Orleans.

KUTZ, JOHN: Pvt., enl. 16 Dec 46 at Reading, age 18, occ. laborer, wounded at Vera Cruz in right finger of right hand above the second joint & first finger of right hand was shot off, hospitalized at Vera Cruz 8 Apr 47, died at Vera Cruz 16 May 47 from Yellow Fever.

LANG, WILLIAM: (Laing): Pvt., enl. 16 Dec 46 at Reading, age 19, deserted at Jalapa 20 May 47, returned to Co. 15 Sep 47, deserted from San Angel 1 Mar 48.

LAY, EDWARD: Pvt., enl. 9 Oct 47 at York, age 23, joined Co. 30 Dec 47, mi. at San Angel 31 Dec 47, mo. with Co. 21 Jul 48.

LEADER, CHARLES: 3rd Cpl., enl. 16 Dec 46 at Reading, age 26, occ. carpenter, promoted to 2nd Cpl. 1 Nov 47, promoted to 3rd Sgt. date unknown, promoted to 2nd Sgt. 13 Apr 48, mo. with Co. 21 Jul 48.

LEOPOLD, HESS: (Hess, Leopold): Pvt., enl. 31 Oct 47 at York, age 25, mi. at Ft. Mifflin 10 Jan 48, reported at Ft. McHenry, Md. 20 Jan 48, joined Co. 29 Apr 48, mo. with Co. 21 Jul 48.

LEOSER, THOMAS S.: (Loeser): Capt., enl. 16 Dec 46 at Reading, age 27, fined two months pay by Court Martial 20 Apr 48 for not suppressing his men from throwing rotten eggs at a Massachusetts officer who attempted to buck & gag a guard for a trifling offense, mo. with Co. 21 Jul 48. Died in Phila. 12 Sep 49.

LINDERMAN, CHRISTIAN: (Lindeman): Pvt., enl. 16 Dec 46 at Reading, age 24, left sick at Perote 22 Jun 47, died at Perote 3 Aug 47 from diarrhea.

LONG, GEORGE: Pvt., enl. 16 Dec 46 at Reading, age 18, occ. machinist, listed as on extra duty on Sep-Oct 47 MR, mo. with Co. 21 Jul 48.

MARKS, WILLIAM: (Marx): Pvt., enl. 16 Dec 46 at Reading, age 18, occ. baker, listed as on detached duty on Sep-Oct 47 MR, detached as Baker in Nov & Dec 47, hospitalized in Mexico City 31 Dec 47, detached as Baker at San Angel according to Mar-Apr 48 MR, mo. with Co. 21 Jul 48. Supposedly served in the Civil War with Co. E, 15th Maryland Vol. Inf. (unconfirmed).

MATTHIAS, ADAM: (Mathias): Pvt., enl. 16 Dec 46 at Reading, age 27, deserted from Camp Jackson near New Orleans 25 Jan 47.

McDONALD, RANDALL W. (A.): (McDonal): Pvt., enl. 16 Dec 46 at Reading, age 26, occ. laborer, hospitalized at Jalapa 28 Apr 47, rejoined Co. by 31 Aug 47, listed as sick on Sep-Oct 47 MR, hospitalized in Mexico City from 19 Dec 47 through Apr 48, mo. with Co. 21 Jul 48.

McGEE, THOMAS: Fifer, enl. 16 Dec 46 at Reading, age 21, occ. moulder, slightly WIA in charge at Chapultepec 13 Sep 47, mo. with Co. 21 Jul 48.

McKARRACHER, SYLVESTER: (McCaragan, McCarraher, McKaracher, McKaraher): Pvt., enl. 16 Dec 46 at Reading, age 24, occ. railroad engineer, left sick at Puebla 7 Aug 47, died at Puebla 27 Sep 47 from diarrhea.

McMICHAEL, RICHARD: (McMichaels): Pvt., enl. 16 Dec 46 at Reading, age 30, occ. pattern maker, appointed Sgt. Maj. 7 Jan 47, promoted to 2nd Lt. 9 Sep 47, mo. with Co. 21 Jul 48. Lt. Col. 14th P.V.I. (3 mos.) 30 Apr 61 to 1 Aug 61. Lt. Col. 53rd P.V.I. 7 Nov 61 to 19 May 64. Lt. Col. 194th P.V.I. 24 Jul 64 to 6 Nov 64.

MEDARIER, PETER P. (B.): (Madarer, Madarie): Pvt., enl. 16 Dec 46 at Reading, age 21, occ. shoemaker, mo. with Co. 21 Jul 48. Died in 1922 at age 97.

MERCERON, NAPOLEON A.: (Maceron, Mirceron): Pvt., enl. 16 Dec 46 at Reading, age 24, occ. railroad conductor, left sick at Perote 22 Jun 47, died at Perote 27 Aug 47.

METZ, NATHAN: Pvt., enl. 16 Dec 46 at Reading, age 24, WIA at Garita de Belen 13 Sep 47, died in Mexico City Hospital 17 Oct 47 from wounds.

MILLER, JOHN: Pvt., enl. 16 Dec 46 at Reading, age 41, occ. laborer, slightly WIA before Mexico City 13 Sep 47, mo. with Co. 21 Jul 48.

MONCHERT, LEWIS: (Moncert, Monzert): Pvt., enl. 16 Dec 46 at Reading, age 21, occ. tailor, hospitalized at Jalapa 28 Apr 47, left sick at Puebla 7 Aug 47, disc. at Puebla 12 Dec 47 on SCD. Lived many years in Norristown, Pa.

MOSS, GEORGE L. (S.): Pvt., enl. 16 Dec 46 at Reading, age 26, occ. laborer, left sick at Perote 22 Jun 47, died at Perote 30 Aug 47.

MOYER, ISAAC: Pvt., enl. 16 Dec 46 at Reading, age 21, occ. blacksmith, left sick at Perote 22 Jun 47, rejoined Co. before 31 Aug 47, mo. with Co. 21 Jul 48.

MOYER, PETER: (Moyur): Pvt., enl. 16 Dec 46 at Reading, age 23, WIA at Chapultepec 13 Sep 47, died at Tacubuya Hospital 14 Sep 47 from wounds.

MYERS, ALBERT: Pvt., enl. 16 Dec 46 at Reading, age 20, occ. carpenter, left sick at Vera Cruz 9 Apr 47, disc. at Vera Cruz 17 May 47 on SCD, arrived in Reading 17 Jun 47.

MYERS, AUGUSTUS: Pvt., enl. 17 Nov 47 at Hollidaysburg, age 21, mi. at Ft. Mifflin 10 Jan 48, reported at Ft. McHenry, Md. 20 Jan 48, joined Co. 29 Apr 48, hospitalized at San Angel according to Mar-Apr 48 MR, mo. with Co. 21 Jul 48.

PATTERSON, WILLIAM: Pvt., enl. 16 Dec 46 at Reading, age 35, occ. mason, died at Perote Hospital 17 Jun 47 from diarrhea.

RAPP, JACOB: Pvt., enl. 16 Dec 46 at Reading, age 22, occ. teamster, detailed to U.S. Artillery 16 Apr 47, rejoined Co. by 31 Aug 47, slightly WIA in charge at Chapultepec 13 Sep 47, hospitalized at San Angel according to Mar-Apr 48 MR, mo. with Co. 21 Jul 48.

RISSLER, THOMAS C.: (Risler, Rister): Pvt., enl. 16 Dec 46 at Reading, age 32, occ. laborer, hospitalized at San Angel according to Mar-Apr 48 MR, mo. with Co. 21 Jul 48.

RITCHEY, CHARLES: (Richey): Pvt., enl. 16 Dec 46 at Reading, age 21, occ. laborer, left sick at Perote 22 Jun 47, rejoined Co. on the march home, mo. with Co. 21 Jul 48.

ROLAND, ABRAHAM: Pvt., enl. 16 Dec 46 at Reading, age 21, WIA at Cerro Gordo in his head at the right ear with the ball lodging under his tongue 18 Apr 47, died in Jalapa Hospital 27 Apr 47 from wound.

SAENER, FREDERICK: (Saena): Pvt., enl. 16 Dec 46 at Reading, age 30, deserted from Camp Jackson near New Orleans 25 Jan 47.

SAUL, DANIEL S. (C., G.): Pvt., enl. 16 Dec 46 at Reading, age 21, occ. teacher, severely WIA in charge at Chapultepec 13 Sep 47, hospitalized in Mexico City from 15 Sep 47, sent to Jalapa Hospital 19 Apr 48, mo. with Co. 21 Jul 48.

SCHERMERHORN, GARRETT (Ganet): (Schoemerhorn, Shermerhorn): Pvt., enl. 16 Dec 46 at Reading, age 26, occ. machinist, detailed as cook in Dec 47, mo. with Co. 21 Jul 48.

SHEETS, JOHN: (Sheetz): Pvt., enl. 16 Dec 46 at Reading, age 24, WIA in the calf of his left leg by a grape shot at Cerro Gordo 18 Apr 47, hospitalized at Jalapa, died at Jalapa 29 Apr 47 from lockjaw.

SMITH, WILLIAM M.: Pvt., enl. 16 Dec 46 at Reading, age 28, occ. jeweller, disc. at Vera Cruz 5 Apr 47 on SCD.

TRAYER, WILLIAM: Pvt., enl. 16 Dec 46 at Reading, age 20, left sick at Vera Cruz 9 Apr 47, disc. at Vera Cruz 17 May 47 on SCD, arrived in Reading 17 Jun 47.

UMPLEBY, WILLIAM: (Umplebey, Umpleblez): Pvt., enl. 16 Dec 46 at Reading, age 21, occ. blacksmith, left sick at Puebla 7 Aug 47, rejoined Co. by 31 Dec 47, mo. with Co. 21 Jul 48.

VAN DOREN, CORNELIUS: (Van Doane, Vandoren): Pvt., enl. 16 Dec 46 at Reading, age 40, deserted from Camp Jackson near New Orleans 25 Jan 47.

VAN THEIL, WILLIAM: (Van Thiel, Vanthield): Pvt., enl. 16 Dec 46 at Reading, age 28, died at Perote 11 Jun 47 from diarrhea.

VAUX, BERNHARD (Barnhart): Pvt., enl. 16 Dec 46 at Reading, age 22, listed as sick on Sep-Oct 47 MR, died in Mexico City Hospital 26 Nov 47.

WELCH, DAVID: (Welsh): Pvt., enl. 4 Oct 47 at Phila., age 32, occ. laborer, joined Co. 30 Dec 47, mi. at San Angel 31 Dec 47, mo. with Co. 21 Jul 48.

WUNDER, LEVI (Lewis) H.: (Wander, Wonder): 1st Sgt., enl. 16 Dec 46 at Reading, age 23, occ. tailor, disc. at Vera Cruz 5 Apr 47 on SCD for chronic nephritis.

WUNDER, WILLIAM: (Wander): 1st Lt., enl. 16 Dec 46 at Reading, age 36, occ. tailor, became sick at Jalapa, died in San Jose Hospital 14 Sep 47, buried in English burial plot in Mexico City, his body was removed and reburied in Reading on 13 May 48.

Company B, 2nd Regiment
American Highlanders

The American Highlanders were from Summit and the surrounding area of Cambria County. The company was probably in existence by 1846, and Captain John White Geary had, for a number of years, been involved in the militia activity of the county.

The Highlanders volunteered for war service as soon as they heard about the declaration of hostilities. Captain Geary received word in December that his company should report for duty with the 2nd Regiment of Pennsylvania Volunteers. The Highlanders marched to Pittsburgh, where First Lieutenant Horace B. Field, 3rd U.S. Artillery, mustered them into Federal service on 3 January 1847.

During their tour of duty they participated in the battles of La Hoya, Chapultepec and Garita de Belen. They returned to Pittsburgh where, on 14 July 1848, they were mustered out of the Army by Major George Wright, 4th U.S. Infantry. They then went directly to Summitt for a joyous reunion and the customary rounds of banquets and speeches.

A total of 96 men served in the company during the war, six of them recruits who joined it in Mexico. Seven men chose to desert. Fourteen men suffered battle related injuries, two of which proved fatal. In all, twenty-seven Highlanders died in service, and an additional sixteen received discharges before muster out.

ADAMS, IGNATIUS (Iqualius): Pvt., enl. 21 Dec 46 at Summitt, age 23, occ. saddler, deserted from Camp Jackson near New Orleans 24 Jan 47.

BARBOUR, SAMUEL S. G.: Pvt., enl. 21 Dec 46 at Hollidaysburgh, age 25, occ. baker, hospitalized at Puebla 8 Aug 47, disc. at Puebla 5 Nov 47 on SCD.

BEER, JOHN: (Beers): Pvt., enl. 21 Dec 46 at Summitt, age 25, occ. carpenter, listed as sick on Mar-Apr 47 MR, left sick at Puebla 8 Aug 47, wounded at Puebla, disc. at Puebla 5 Nov 47 on SCD for wounds.

BLACK, SAMUEL: 1st Lt., enl. 21 Dec 46 at Summitt, age 26, under arrest from 28 Feb 47 to 26 May 47 for disobedience of orders, on furlough from 8 Dec 47, resigned 31 Jan 48.

BROOKBANK, JOHN B.: 4th Sgt., enl. 21 Dec 46 at Summitt, age 23, occ. tinman, promoted to 3rd Sgt. 8 Jan 47, WIA at the storming of Chapultepec 13 Sep 47, promoted to 1st Sgt. 1 May 48, mo. with Co. 14 Jul 48.

CALDWELL, DAVID: Pvt., enl. 21 Dec 46 at Armagh, age 19, occ. farmer, mo. with Co. 14 Jul 48.

CAMPBELL, JOHN: Pvt., enl. 21 Dec 46 at Newry, age 20, occ. carpenter, hospitalized at Vera Cruz according to Mar-Apr 47 MR, WIA at the storming of Chapultepec 13 Sep 47, rejoined Co. in Oct 47, mo. with Co. 14 Jul 48.

CARLIN, WILLIAM: (Carland): Pvt., enl. 21 Dec 46 at Summitt, age 20, occ. pedlar, KIA at Garita de Belen 13 Sep 47.

CARR, JOSHUA: Pvt., enl. 21 Dec 46 at Summitt, age 23, occ. carpenter, listed as sick on Jan-Feb 47 & May-Jun 47 MRs, died at Puebla 29 Jul 47.

CASSIDY, JOHN: (Cassiday): Pvt., enl. 21 Dec 46 at Summitt, age 19, occ. boatman, deserted from Camp Jackson near New Orleans 24 Jan 47.

COLBURN, JOHN D.: (Colborn, Colbourn): Pvt., enl. 21 Dec 46 at Somersett, age 21, occ. lawyer, left sick at Perote 28 Jun 47, disc. at Perote 28 Oct 47.

CONFER, JACOB M.: (Carfer, Cenfer, Cowfer): Pvt., enl. 21 Dec 46 at Hollidaysburgh, age 21, occ. medical student, promoted to 4th Sgt. 8 Jan 47, detached to regimental hospital as Ward Master 5 Aug 47, reduced to Pvt. & appointed Hospital Steward 16 Nov 47, mo. with Co. 14 Jul 48. Surgeon 29th Indiana Vol. Inf. 10 Feb 63 to 8 Dec 63.

DANE, FREDERICK: (Dean, Deane): Pvt., enl. 21 Dec 46 at Summitt, age 25, occ. miner, died in hospital at Jalapa 7 May 47.

DAVIS, NATHANIEL: Pvt., enl. 3 Jan 47 at Pittsburgh, age 23, occ. cabinet maker, hospitalized at Perote according to May-Jun 47 MR, died in Mexico City Hospital 8 Oct 47.

DOPP, JOHN H.: Pvt., enl. 4 Jan 47 at Pittsburgh, age 37, occ. inn keeper, left sick at Vera Cruz 9 Apr 47, disc. at Vera Cruz 11 May 47 on SCD.

DRIPPS, ANDREW W.: (Drips): Pvt., enl. 3 Jan 47 at Pittsburgh, age 21, occ. printer, WIA at Chapultepec 13 Sep 47, hospitalized in Mexico City 14 Sep 47, returned to duty as orderly to Col. Geary Mar to May 48, mo. with Co. 14 Jul 48.

DUFF, DAVID: Pvt., enl. 26 Dec 46 at Huntingdon, age 25, occ. lawyer, on duty as clerk for Col. Geary from Nov 47 through May 48, promoted to Sgt. Maj. 10 Jun 48 to rank from 12 Feb 48, mo. with F & S 21 Jul 48.

DUNLAP, JOHN W.: Pvt., enl. 21 Dec 46 at Summitt, age 20, mo. with Co. 14 Jul 48.

DUNLAP, RICHARD F.: Pvt., enl. 21 Dec 46 at Summitt, age 22, listed as sick on Jan-Feb 47 MR, detailed to regimental hospital as Attendant 23 Feb 48, rejoined Co. by 30 May 48, mo. with Co. 14 Jul 48.

ESTEP, WILLIAM (Eslep): Pvt., enl. 21 Dec 46 at Summitt, age 21, occ. miner, hospitalized at Vera Cruz according to Mar-Apr 47 MR, hospitalized at Perote according to Jul-Aug 47 MR, died at Perote 21 Aug 47.

FARREN, THOMAS: (Farran): Pvt., enl. 21 Dec 46 at Summitt, age 27, occ. farmer, fell out of ranks 8 Sep 47 during march from San Augustin, not seen thereafter, listed as AWOL & supposing him to have been killed.

FISHER, JOHN: Pvt., enl. & mi. 11 Aug 47 at York, age 35, reported at Carlisle Barracks, Pa. 31 Aug 47, joined Co. 30 Dec 47, mo. with Co. 14 Jul 48.

FLESHOUR, JOHN: Pvt., enl. 21 Dec 46 at Reading, age 24, occ. teamster, left sick at Puebla 8 Aug 47, died at Puebla 22 Nov 47.

FRIEND, JACOB: Pvt., enl. 3 Jan 47 at Pittsburgh, age 43, occ. carpenter, left sick at Puebla 8 Aug 47, died at Puebla 17 Sep 47.

FRY, ISAAC: Pvt., enl. 21 Dec 46 at Summitt, age 23, occ. carpenter, listed as sick on Jan-Feb 47 MR, left sick at Perote 22 Jun 47, disc. at Perote 5 Oct 47 on SCD.

GARDNER, JOHN: (Gardiner): Pvt., enl. 21 Dec 46 at Summitt, age 19, occ. manufacturer, hospitalized at San Angel according to Mar-Apr 48 MR, promoted to 4th Cpl. 1 May 48, mo. with Co. 14 Jul 48.

GEARY, JOHN WHITE: Capt., enl. 21 Dec 46 at Summitt, age 28, elected Lt. Col. 6 Jan 47, assumed command of Regt. 1 Sep 47, slightly WIA in charge on Chapultepec 13 Sep 47, promoted to Col. 3 Nov 47, mo. with F & S 21 Jul 48. Col. 28th P.V.I. 28 Jun 61, Brig. Gen. of Vols. 25 Apr 62, Maj. Gen. of Vols. 12 Jan 65 to Jul 65. Died 8 Feb 73.

HARRISON, HENRY: (Henry, Harrison): 2nd Cpl., enl. 21 Dec 46 at Summitt, age 23, occ. blacksmith, promoted to 1st Cpl. 8 Jan 47, listed as sick on Jan-Feb 47 MR, died in Mexico City Hospital 22 Oct 47.

HASSETT, JOHN: Pvt., enl. 21 Dec 46 at Newry, age 21, left sick at Perote in Jun 47, died at Perote 20 Aug 47.

HEARD, JAMES HENRY: (Herd): Pvt., enl. 21 Dec 46 at Hollidaysburgh, age 23, occ. tailor, listed as sick on May-Jun 47 MR, died at Puebla Hospital 25 Jul 47.

HESHOUR, JOHN: Pvt., enl. 3 Jan 47 at Pittsburgh, age 24, died at Puebla Hospital 22 Nov 47.

HOLLAND, THOMAS: Pvt., enl. 21 Dec 46 at Summitt, age 25, occ. railroad hitcher, listed as sick on May-Jun 47 MR, WIA at Garita de Belen 13 Sep 47, promoted to 4th Sgt. 10 Jun 48 to rank from 1 May 48, mo. with Co. 14 Jul 48.

HUMPHREYS, JOHN: 1st Sgt., enl. 21 Dec 46 at Summitt, age 23, promoted to Capt. 7 Jan 47, mo. with Co. 14 Jul 48.

HUMPHREYS, THOMAS: (Humphrey): Pvt., enl. 21 Dec 46 at Summitt, age 19, WIA at Chapultepec 13 Sep 47, detailed as Attendant in regimental hospital 16 Sep 47 through Nov 47 & again in Feb 48, mo. with Co. 14 Jul 48.

HUMPHREYS, WILLIAM: Pvt., enl. 21 Dec 46 at Summitt, age 21, listed as sick on May-Jun 47 MR, severely WIA at Chapultepec 13 Sep 47, hospitalized in Mexico City 14 Sep 47, died in Mexico City Hospital 27 Sep 47 from wounds.

HUTCHINSON, GEORGE: (Huchison, Hutchenson, Hutchison): Pvt., enl. 3 Jan 47 at Pittsburgh, age 20, occ. teamster, mo. with Co. 14 Jul 48.

IREMAN, MICHAEL (McChall): (Ironman, Jremun): Pvt., enl. & mi. 11 Aug 47 at Pittsburgh, age 26, occ. farmer, reported at Carlisle Barracks, Pa. 31 Aug 47, joined Co. 30 Dec 47, hospitalized at San Angel according to Mar-Apr 48 MR, mo. with Co. 14 Jul 48.

IVORY, WILLIAM W. (H.): 3rd Sgt., enl. 21 Dec 46 at Summitt, age 20, occ. tinman, promoted to 2nd Sgt. 8 Jan 47, listed as sick on Jan-Feb 47 MR, hospitalized at Vera Cruz according to Mar-Apr 47 MR, promoted to 2nd Lt. 10 Jun 48 to rank from 1 Feb 48, mo. with Co. 14 Jul 48.

JOHNSTON, JAMES: Pvt., enl. 21 Dec 46 at Summitt, age 19, deserted from Pittsburgh 8 Jan 47.

KERR, WASHINGTON L.: Pvt., enl. 3 Jan 47 at Pittsburgh, age 21, occ. pedlar, left sick at Perote 22 Jun 47, died at Perote before 31 Aug 47.

KEYS, ELISHA (Elijah) I.: (Keyes): Pvt., enl. 21 Dec 46 at Summitt, age 24, occ. cabinet maker, promoted to 3rd Cpl. 8 Jan 47, listed as sick on May-Jun 47 MR, left sick at Puebla 8 Aug 47, died at Puebla 18 Sep 47.

KILLEN, SAMUEL D.: Pvt., enl. 21 Dec 46 at Summitt, age 21, promoted to 2nd Cpl. 10 Jun 48 to rank from 1 May 48, mo. with Co. 14 Jul 48. Pvt. Co. D, 70th Ohio Vol. Inf. 10 Sep 61 to 14 Jan 63.

LADOUCEUR, LEWIS: Pvt., age 33, listed only on Co. muster-in roll.

LANDIS, SAMUEL: (Landas, Landes): Pvt., enl. 21 Dec 46 at New Alexandria, Pa., age 25, occ. physician, left sick at Perote 28 Jun 47, disc. at Perote 29 Oct 47 on SCD.

LEWIS, THOMAS: Pvt., enl. 21 Dec 46 at Summitt, age 25, occ. carman, left sick at Puebla about 8 Aug 47, died at Puebla date unknown.

LUCKET, DEMETRIUS (Demetrous): Pvt., enl. 21 Dec 46 at Summitt, age 21, occ. farmer, deserted from Camp Jackson near New Orleans 24 Jan 47.

LUCKETT, ELISHA M.: (Lucket): 2nd Lt., enl. 21 Dec 46 at Summitt, age 24, was present but sick in May 47, resigned for health reasons 29 Jun 47.

MATTHEWS, WILLIAM: (Mathews): Pvt., enl. 21 Dec 46 at Armagh, age 24, occ. manufacturer, listed as sick on Jan-Feb 47 MR, died in Mexico City Hospital 12 Oct 47.

McCHESNEY, JAMES: (Machesney, Machezney): Pvt., enl. 21 Dec 46 at Hollidaysburgh, age 41, occ. teamster, on duty as clerk in Nov 47, on duty as hostler for Col. Geary Dec 47 through May 48, mo. with Co. 14 Jul 48.

McCLOSKEY, CORNELIUS K.: (McClosky): Pvt., enl. 21 Dec 46 at Summitt, age 28, occ. farmer, hospitalized at Perote according to May-Jun 47 MR, listed as sick in quarters on Sep-Oct 47 MR, disc. at Mexico City 8 Dec 47 on SCD for rupture.

McDADE, CHARLES: Pvt., enl. 30 Dec 46 at Summitt, age 21, occ. miner, serving as Attendant at Perote Hospital according to May-Jun 47 MR, mo. with Co. 14 Jul 48.

McILHATTON, FRANKLIN: (McElhatan, McElhattan, McIlhatan, McIlhatten, McIllhatan, McIllhaten): Pvt., enl. 21 Dec 46 at Hollidaysburgh, age 20, occ. painter, hospitalized at San Angel according to Jan-Feb 48 MR, disc. at San Angel 28 Feb 48 on SCD for heart disease.

McKEE, ANDREW: Pvt., enl. 21 Dec 46 at Summitt, age 22, occ. carman, listed as sick on Jan-Feb 47 MR, left sick at Vera Cruz 9 Apr 47, disc. at Vera Cruz 21 May 47 on SCD.

McKEE, FRANCIS: 2nd Sgt., enl. 21 Dec 46 at Summitt, age 26, occ. tinman, promoted to 1st Sgt. 8 Jan 47, listed as sick on Jan-Feb 47 MR & on May-Jun 47 MR, WIA at Garita de Belen 13 Sep 47, promoted to 2nd Lt. 10 Jun 48 to rank from 1 Aug 47, mo. with Co. 14 Jul 48.

McKENNA, MARK: (Makena): Pvt., enl. 21 Dec 46 at Summitt, age 31, occ. school teacher, died on board steamer *Cambria* at Cincinnati 13 Jan 47.

McLAUGHLIN, JAMES: 3rd Cpl., enl. 21 Dec 46 at Summitt, age 25, occ. cabinet maker, promoted to 2nd Cpl. 8 Jan 47, listed as sick in camp on Mar-Apr 47 MR, promoted to 2nd Sgt. 10 Jun 48 to date from 1 May 48, mo. with Co. 14 Jul 48.

McLAUGHLIN, JOHN J. (S.): Pvt., enl. 8 Dec 46 at Hollidaysburgh, age 25, occ. blacksmith, transferred from Co. F, 1st Pa. Regt. 27 Jun 47, WIA at Chapultepec 13 Sep 47, hospitalized at San Angel according to Jan-Feb 48 MR, disc. at San Angel 28 Feb 48 on SCD for wounds.

McLAUGHLIN, WILLIAM: Pvt., enl. 21 Dec 46 at Summitt, age 20, occ. blacksmith, mo. with Co. 14 Jul 48.

McNAMARA, JOHN: 4th Cpl., enl. 21 Dec 46 at Summitt, age 26, occ. merchant, reduced to Pvt. 8 Jan 47, listed as sick on May-Jun 47 MR, was orderly to Col. Geary Nov 47 through Feb 48, died at San Angel 25 Apr 48.

MEALEY, JAMES: (Mealy): Pvt., enl. 21 Dec 46 at Hollidaysburgh, age 24, occ. shoemaker, listed as sick in camp on Mar-Apr 47 MR, mo. with Co. 14 Jul 48.

MOORE, JOSEPH: Pvt., enl. & mi. 13 Oct 47 at Phila., age 23, joined Co. 30 Dec 47, mo. with Co. 14 Jul 48.

O'HARA, WILLIAM: (Oharo, O'Harra, Oharro): Pvt., enl. 21 Dec 46 at Summitt, age 20, occ. farmer, mo. with Co. 14 Jul 48. Died in his home in Munster Twp., Cambria County 22 Sep 05.

O'ROURKE, MICHAEL: Pvt., enl. 11 Nov 47 at Hollidaysburgh, age 19, mi. at Ft. Mifflin 10 Jan 48, reported at Ft. McHenry, Md. 20 Jan 48, joined Co. 18 Apr 48, mo. with Co. 14 Jul 48.

OTT, WILLIAM M.: Pvt., enl. 21 Dec 46 at Summitt, age 19, occ. boatman, listed as sick on Jan-Feb 47 MR, hospitalized at Perote according to May-Jun 47 MR, promoted to 3rd Cpl. 10 Jun 48 to rank from 1 May 48, mo. with Co. 14 Jul 48.

OWENS, THOMAS: (Owen): Pvt., enl. 21 Dec 46 at Summitt, age 20, occ. carman, left sick at Perote in Jun 47, died at Perote in Jul or Aug 47.

PALMER, MATTHIAS: Pvt., enl. 21 Dec 46 at Armagh, age 20, occ. farmer, died in Mexico City Hospital 27 Sep 47.

PALMER, ROBERT: Pvt., enl. 21 Dec 46 at Blairsville, age 19, occ. boatman, hospitalized at San Angel according to Mar-Apr 48 MR, mo. with Co. 14 Jul 48.

RAPP, JOHN: Pvt., enl. 21 Dec 46 at Summitt, age 26, occ. miner, listed as sick on May-Jun 47 MR, left sick at Puebla 8 Aug 47, died at Puebla 12 Sep 47.

REILLY, JOHN T.: (Reiley, Riley): Fifer, enl. 21 Dec 46 at Hollidaysburgh, age 17, occ. painter, deserted from Camp Jackson near New Orleans 24 Jan 47.

REVALON, DONALD (Daniel) F.: (Revelon): Pvt., enl. 21 Dec 46 at Blairsville, age 33, occ. manufacturer, promoted to Drummer 7 Jan 47, convicted of horse stealing & received 39 lashes on the bare back, fined four months pay by Court Martial 18 May 47, released from confinement & detailed as Attendant in Perote Hospital according to May-Jun 47 MR, rejoined Co. by 31 Dec 47, mo. with Co. 14 Jul 48.

RHOADS, ABRAHAM I.: (Rhoades, Rhodes): Pvt., enl. 21 Dec 46 at Summitt, age 22, occ. blacksmith, WIA in the storming of Chapultepec 13 Sep 47, mo. with Co. 14 Jul 48.

RIFFLE, JOHN: (Riffel, Riffell): Pvt., enl. 21 Dec 46 at Summitt, age 18, occ. boatman, detailed as cook in Nov 47 & from Mar to May 48, mo. with Co. 14 Jul 48.

RODERICK, JACOB: (Roderique, Rodrick, Rodrique): Pvt., enl. 21 Dec 46 at Summitt, age 19, occ. wood chopper, left sick at Puebla 8 Aug 47, disc. at Puebla about 5 Nov 47.

RUSSELL, JAMES: Pvt., enl. 21 Dec 46 at Summitt, age 25, occ. teamster, left sick at Perote 28 Jun 47, rejoined Co. in Mar or Apr 48, mo. with Co. 14 Jul 48.

SHARP, JOHN: (1st): Pvt., enl. 21 Dec 46 at Newry, age 31, occ. engraver, deserted from Camp Jackson near New Orleans 28 Jan 47.

SHARP, JOHN: (2nd): Pvt., enl. 21 Dec 46 at Summitt, age 30, occ. farmer, died at Jalapa Hospital 16 May 47.

SHARP, RICHARD: Pvt., enl. 21 Dec 46 at Summitt, age 22, occ. farmer, mo. with Co. 14 Jul 48.

SHEINTZBERG, HENRY: (Schnitberg, Schnitzberger, Snitberg, Snitburg): Pvt., enl. 21 Dec 46 at Summitt, age 40, occ. miner, promoted to 1st Cpl. 10 Jun 48 to rank from 1 May 48, mo. with Co. 14 Jul 48.

SHELCROSS, JAMES P.: (Schellcross, Shallcross, Shalleroys): Pvt., enl. 3 Jan 47 at Pittsburgh, age 39, appointed Q.M. Sgt. 8 May 47, mo. with F & S 21 Jul 48.

SHRIVER, FREDERICK: (Schriver): Pvt., enl. 21 Dec 46 at Hollidaysburgh, age 26, occ. carpenter, listed as sick in camp on Mar-Apr 47 MR, left sick at Puebla 8 Aug 47, rejoined Co. by 31 Dec 47, mo. with Co. 14 Jul 48.

SHULTZ, JACOB: (Schiltz, Shulz): Pvt., enl. & mi. 2 Aug 47 at Phila., age 32, occ. baker, joined Co. 30 Dec 47, listed as in confinement on Jan-Feb 48 MR, mo. with Co. 14 Jul 48.

STONE, WASHINGTON I.: Pvt., enl. 21 Dec 46 at Hollidaysburgh, age 20, occ. moulder, WIA in the leg at Chapultepec 13 Sep 47, disc. at Mexico City 7 Dec 47 on SCD for wound.

STORM, HUGH F.: Pvt., enl. 21 Dec 46 at Summitt, age 22, occ. carpenter, WIA at Chapultepec 13 Sep 47, mo. with Co. 14 Jul 48.

STORM, JOHN: Pvt., enl. 21 Dec 46 at Summitt, age 40, occ. carpenter, detailed as Asst. Hospital Steward at Jalapa from 7 May 47 to 27 Jun 47, died in Mexico City Hospital 27 Sep 47.

TINKCOM, JOHN L.: (Tinckcum, Tincom, Tinkem, Tinkom, Tinkum, Truckain): Drummer, enl. 21 Dec 46 at Armagh, age 23, occ. carpenter, appointed Drum Maj. 7 Jan 47, reduced to Pvt. 1 Mar 47, left sick at Perote 28 Jun 47, disc. at Perote 29 Oct 47 on SCD.

TODD, ANDREW: Pvt., enl. 21 Dec 46 at Summitt, age 26, occ. merchant, detailed as Hospital Steward 14 Jun 47, rejoined Co. by 31 Aug 47, served as Co. Commissary Mar to May 48, promoted to Fifer 1 May 48, mo. with Co. 14 Jul 48.

TODD, DAVID: Pvt., enl. 21 Dec 46 at Armagh, age 36, occ. shoemaker, deserted from Camp Jackson near New Orleans 23 Jan 47.

TOPPER, ANDREW: Pvt., enl. 21 Dec 46 at Summitt, age 40, occ. teamster, hospitalized at Vera Cruz according to Mar-Apr 47 MR, hospitalized at San Angel according to Mar-Apr 48 MR, mo. with Co. 14 Jul 48.

TROTTER, WILLIAM: Pvt., enl. 21 Dec 46 at Summitt, age 21, disc. at Vera Cruz 11 May 47 on SCD.

TROXELL, SAMUEL: (Troxel): Cpl., enl. 21 Dec 46 at Summitt, age 28, occ. inn keeper, reduced to Pvt. 8 Jan 47, hospitalized at San Angel according to Mar-Apr 48 MR, mo. with Co. 14 Jul 48.

WILLIAMS, WILLIAM: 2nd Lt., enl. 21 Dec 46 at Hollidaysburgh, age 20, left for recruiting duty 8 Jun 47 & never rejoined Co., promoted to 1st Lt. 10 Jun 48 to rank from 1 Feb 48, disc. effective 14 Jul 48.

WILLS, ALEXIS: (Willis): Pvt., enl. 21 Dec 46 at Summitt, age 24, occ. wood chopper, left sick at Perote in Jun 47, died at Perote 8 Aug 47.

WILSON, JOHN S.: Pvt., enl. 18 Dec 47 at Hollidaysburgh, mi. at Ft. Mifflin 10 Jan 48, reported at Ft. McHenry 20 Jan 48, joined Co. 18 Apr 48, mo. with Co. 14 Jul 48. Age 18 years.

WORTHINGTON, JOHN I.: Pvt., enl. 21 Dec 46 at Johnstown, age 23, occ. boot maker, promoted to 4th Cpl. 8 Jan 47, WIA at Chapultepec 13 Sep 47, promoted to 3rd Sgt. 10 Jun 48 to rank from 1 May 48, mo. with Co. 14 Jul 48. Sgt. Co. H, 6th Kansas Cav. 7 Jan 62 to 31 Mar 62. Sgt. Co. K, 6th Kansas Cav. 31 Mar 62 to 8 Apr 62. Capt. Co. H & Maj., 1st Arkansas Cav. 7 Aug 62 until KIA 11 Mar 65.

WRAPP, JOHN: Pvt., enl. 21 Dec 46 at Summitt, age 26, died at Puebla Hospital 12 Sep 47.

ZENTZ, GEORGE W.: (Zenty): Pvt., enl. 21 Dec 46 at Hollidaysburgh, age 21, occ. boatman, hospitalized at Vera Cruz according to Mar-Apr 47 MR, listed as sick on May-Jun 47 MR, left sick at Puebla 8 Aug 47, died at Puebla 17 Aug 47.

Company C, 2nd Regiment
Columbia Guards

The Columbia Guards was organized about 1817 at Danville, then the county seat of Columbia County. By the 1820s the company was one of the best known in that part of the state.

The Guards were the second Pennsylvania company to tender service to the government upon the declaration of war, but for political reasons they were not selected for the first regiment. When a second regiment was called for, the Guards were assured a position in it. They left Danville on the morning of 28 December and arrived in Pittsburgh on the afternoon of 3 January and were immediately mustered into Federal service by First Lieutenant Horace B. Field, 3rd U.S. Artillery.

In Mexico, the Columbia Guards was the first Pennsylvania company to exchange fire with enemy soldiers on the sand hills near Vera Cruz. In addition to taking part in the siege of that city they participated in the battles of Cerro Gordo, Chapultepec and Garita de Belen.

The company returned to Pittsburgh on 18 July 1848, and were mustered out by Major George Wright of the 4th U.S. Infantry on the 20th. They arrived home in Danville on 27 July to huge crowds and beautiful decorations and to participate in a parade, ceremonies and banquets.

The organization of the company was maintained, and in the three month's service of 1861 they became Company C of the 14th Regiment of Pennsylvania Volunteers. Although an attempt was made to recruit for a three year enlistment, too many of the men had already joined other units. Therefore, by the end of 1861 the Columbia Guards had ceased to exist.

A total of 109 men served in the company during the war, twelve of them recruits who joined it in Mexico. Eight men deserted. Three men suffered battle related injuries, and died of their wounds. In all, forty-one Guards died in service, and an additional fourteen received discharges before muster out.

ADAMS, CHARLES W.: Pvt., enl. 26 Dec 46 at Danville, age 18, left sick at Perote 28 Jun 47, disc. at Perote 29 Oct 47 on SCD.

ADAMS, JOHN: 1st Cpl., enl. 26 Dec 46 at Danville, age 34, occ. shoemaker, listed as sick on Jan-Feb 47 MR, disc. at Vera Cruz 8 Apr 47 on SCD.

ALLEN, ALVIN M.: Pvt., enl. 26 Dec 46 at Danville, age 26, occ. carpenter, hospitalized at Perote according to Jul-Aug 47 MR, left sick at Puebla 7 Aug 47, died at Puebla 17 Sep 47.

APP, JACOB: Pvt., enl. 26 Dec 46 at Danville, age 22, occ. farmer, mo. with Co. 20 Jul 48. Died in San Francisco, Calif. in Oct 49.

ARMSTRONG, GEORGE W.: Pvt., enl. 26 Dec 46 at Danville, age 22, disc. at New Orleans 28 Jan 47 on SCD.

BAKER, SAMUEL D.: Pvt., enl. 26 Dec 46 at Danville, age 21, occ. farmer, hospitalized at Perote 18 Jun 47, died at Perote date unknown.

BALL, RANDOLPH: Pvt., enl. 26 Dec 46 at Danville, age 21, left sick at Perote 28 Jun 47, died at Perote 23 Jul 47.

BANGHEART, WILLIAM: (Banghart, Barnheart, Baughart): Pvt., enl. 26 Dec 46 at Danville, age 37, occ. laborer, left sick at Vera Cruz 9 Apr 47, rejoined Co. before 30 Apr 47, left sick at Perote 28 Jun 47, died at Perote 11 Jul 47.

BEST, FRANCIS R.: Pvt., enl. 28 Dec 46 at Mifflinburg, age 21, occ. tailor, left sick at Perote 28 Jun 47, died at Perote 29 Jun 47.

BIRCHFIELD, WILLIAM H.: Pvt., enl. 26 Dec 46 at Danville, age 26, occ. saddler, detailed as teamster according to May-Jun 47 MR, left sick at Puebla 7 Aug 47, rejoined Co. 17 Jan 48, disc. at San Angel 4 Mar 48 on SCD.

BIRKENBINE, JOHN: Pvt., enl. 26 Dec 46 at Danville, age 18, occ. boatman, left sick at Perote 28 Jun 47, died at Perote 23 Aug 47.

BOBST, PETER: (Bopst, Brobst, Bropst): Pvt., enl. 26 Dec 46 at Danville, age 20, occ. tailor, left sick at Puebla 8 Aug 47, rejoined Co. 8 Dec 47, mo. with Co. 20 Jul 48. Supposed to have served in the Civil War (unconfirmed).

BONHAM, ELAM (Elatin) B.: Pvt., enl. 26 Dec 46 at Danville, age 22, occ. miller, listed as sick on Jan-Feb 47 MR, hospitalized at Perote 18 Jun 47, died at Perote date unknown.

BOOKS, SAMUEL: Pvt., enl. 28 Aug 47 at Pittsburgh, age 19, joined Co. 29 Dec 47, mi. at San Angel 31 Dec 47, died at San Angel 6 Apr 48.

BOWER, FRANCIS: Pvt., enl. 26 Dec 46 at Danville, age 25, occ. stone cutter, hospitalized at Jalapa according to Mar-Apr 47 MR, serving as Ward Master in regimental hospital from 2 Sep 47 through at least 30 Apr 48, mo. with Co. 20 Jul 48.

BRANDT, FREDERICK: Pvt., enl. 26 Dec 46 at Danville, age 34, occ. tanner, listed as sick on Jan-Feb MR, left sick at Vera Cruz 8 Apr 47, died at Vera Cruz 12 May 47.

BRINDLE, WILLIAM: 2nd Lt. enl. 26 Dec 46 at Danville, age 28, residence Muncy, elected Maj. 5 Jan 47, promoted to Lt. Col. 4 Nov 47, mo. with F & S 21 Jul 48. Died in Dec 1902, buried in Pottsville.

BRUNER, WILLIAM: (Brunner): Pvt., enl. 26 Dec 46 at Danville, age 21, occ. miller, mo. with Co. 20 Jul 48.

BURNS, SAMUEL: (Burms, Burnes): Pvt., enl. 26 Dec 46 at Danville, age 39, occ. laborer, transferred to Co. A, 2nd Pa. Regt. 1 May 47.

CARLEY, ABRAHAM (Abram) B.: Pvt., enl. 26 Dec 46 at Danville, age 22, occ. school teacher, left sick at Perote 18 Jun 47, disc. at Perote 29 Oct 47 on SCD.

CLARK, JESSE G.: Fifer, enl. 26 Dec 46 at Danville, age 22, occ. printer, appointed Fife Maj. 5 Jan 47, reduced to Co. Fifer 1 May 47, mo. with Co. 20 Jul 48.

CLARK, ROBERT C.: 3rd Sgt., enl. 26 Dec 46 at Danville, age 19, occ. puddler, sent to New Orleans 1 Nov 47 for health reasons, from there he went home to Danville, ordered on 5 Feb 48 to rejoin his Co. ASAP, promoted to 2nd Sgt. 8 Apr 48, mo. with Co. 20 Jul 48.

CLARK, THOMAS: Pvt., enl. 6 Dec 47 at Hollidaysburgh, age 21, occ. laborer, mi. at Ft. Mifflin 10 Jan 48, reported at Ft. McHenry, Md. 20 Jan 48, joined Co. 17 Apr 48, mo. with Co. 20 Jul 48.

CLARK, THOMAS: Drummer, enl. 26 Dec 46 at Danville, age 17, mo. with Co. 20 Jul 48. Pvt. Co. D, 2nd Ohio Vol. Inf. 9 Sep 61 to 10 Oct 64.

CORRIGAN, MICHAEL: (Carrigan): Pvt., enl. 26 Dec 46 at Danville, age 35, occ. laborer, left sick at Vera Cruz 8 Apr 47, nothing more given.

CROCKS, FREDERICK: Pvt., enl. 17 Sep 47 at Phila., age 36, joined Co. 29 Dec 47, mi. at San Angel 31 Dec 47, mo. with Co. 20 Jul 48.

DEWICK, WILLIAM E.: Pvt., enl. 16 Sep 47 at Phila., age 27, joined Co. 29 Dec 47, mi. at San Angel 31 Dec 47, mo. with Co. 20 Jul 48.

DIETRICK, WILLIAM H.: (Deiterich, Dieterich, Dietrich): Pvt., enl. 26 Dec 46 at Danville, age 23, occ. miller, WIA in the storming of Chapultepec 13 Sep 47, died in Mexico City Hospital 2 Oct 47 from wounds.

DORAN, PATRICK: Pvt., enl. 17 Sep 47 at Pottsville, age 38, occ. laborer, transferred from Co. I, 2nd Pa. Regt. 17 Apr 48, left behind when starting from San Angel for home 30 May 48, no record of disc.

ERB, WILLIAM: Pvt., enl. 26 Dec 46 at Danville, age 22, on duty as Co. cook in Jan 48, promoted to Cpl. 1 May 48, mo. with Co. 20 Jul 48.

EVANS, CHARLES: 4th Sgt., enl. 26 Dec 46 at Danville, age 22, occ. shoemaker, promoted to 3rd Sgt. 8 Apr 47, mo. with Co. 20 Jul 48. Commissary Sgt. 76th P.V.I. 6 Nov 61 to 7 Sep 64. 1st Lt. & Capt. Co. K, 76th P.V.I. 7 Sep 64 to 18 Jul 65.

FOLLMER, DANIEL S.: (Folimer, Folmer): Pvt., enl. 26 Dec 46 at Danville, age 26, occ. farmer, promoted to 2nd Cpl. 8 Apr 47, promoted to 1st Cpl. 28 May 47, promoted to 2nd Lt. 10 Jun 48 to rank from 13 Nov 47, mo. with Co. 20 Jul 48.

FORSTER, ROBERT H.: (Forter, Foster): Pvt., enl. 28 Dec 46 at Hartleton, age 19, occ. printer, listed as AWOL on May-Jun 47 MR, on extra duty at printing office in Mexico City in Sep & Nov 47, on duty as orderly for Court of Commissioners in Apr 48, mo. with Co. 20 Jul 48. Capt. Co. K & Maj. 148th P.V.I. 1 Sep 62 to 22 Dec 64, WIA at Chancellorsville, Gettysburg & Petersburg. Died at Harrisburg 2 May 01 & buried in Mifflinburg.

FORTNER, CHARLES W.: Pvt., enl. 26 Dec 46 at Danville, age 37, occ. school teacher, hospitalized at Jalapa according to Mar-Apr 47 MR, left sick at Perote 28 Jun 47, died at Perote 27 Aug 47.

FRICK, CLARENCE HENRY: 1st Lt., enl. 26 Dec 46 at Danville, age 28, occ. physician, promoted to Capt. 12 Nov 47, mo. with Co. 20 Jul 48. Died in Danville 21 Jan 61.

GARNER, GEORGE: Pvt., enl. 26 Dec 46 at Danville, age 19, died in Perote Hospital 23 Jun 47.

GEARHART, ARTHUR J.: (Gearheart): 3rd Cpl., enl. 26 Dec 46 at Danville, age 20, occ. moulder, promoted to 2nd Cpl. 28 May 47, promoted to 4th Sgt. 15 Dec 47 to rank from 1 Dec 47, reduced to 2nd Cpl. 1 May 48, mo. with Co. 20 Jul 48. Pvt. Co. B, 20th P.V.I. (3 mos.) 30 Apr 61 to 7 Jul 61. Pvt. Co. C, 210th P.V.I. 20 Sep 64 to 30 May 65. Died in Danville 9 Mar 77.

GIBBS, SEWELL: Pvt., enl. 26 Dec 46 at Danville, age 39, occ. distiller, died at Jalapa 16 Jun 47.

GIRTON, SHEPHERD W.: Pvt., enl. 26 Dec 46 at Danville, age 19, occ. chair maker, left sick at Perote 28 Jun 47, died at Perote 8 Aug 47.

GRAHAM, THOMAS: Pvt., enl. 26 Dec 46 at Danville, age 23, occ. cutler, mo. with Co. 20 Jul 48.

GROVE, EDWARD: Pvt., enl. 26 Dec 46 at Danville, age 19, occ. shoemaker, left sick at Perote 28 Jun 47, died at Perote 29 Jun 47 from consumption.

HAMILTON, SAMUEL: Pvt., enl. 1 Sep 47 at Pittsburgh, age 30, occ. tanner, joined Co. 29 Dec 47, mi. at San Angel 31 Dec 47, died in San Angel Hospital 10 Apr 48.

HEISLER, ADAM: Pvt., enl. 26 Dec 46 at Danville, age 29, occ. laborer, left sick at Puebla 8 Aug 47, rejoined Co. 8 Dec 47, on duty as Co. cook in Dec 47, mo. with Co. 20 Jul 48.

HELME, OLIVER: Pvt., enl. 26 Dec 46 at Danville, age 19, died at Puebla 18 Jul 47.

HORNCASTLE, HENRY: Pvt., enl. 26 Dec 46 at Danville, age 25, occ. machinist, on duty as cook in regimental hospital from 23 Feb 48, mo. with Co. 20 Jul 48.

HUNTINGDON, SAMUEL: (Huntington): Pvt., enl. 26 Dec 46 at Danville, age 30, occ. laborer, left sick at Perote 28 Jun 47, died at Perote 18 Dec 47.

KERTZ, WILLIAM S. (I.): (Kutz): Pvt., enl. 26 Dec 46 at Danville, age 19, occ. printer, deserted from Camp Jackson near New Orleans 26 Jan 47.

KING, WILLIAM: Pvt., enl. 26 Dec 46 at Danville, age 33, occ. laborer, detailed as cook to Mexico City Hospital 16 Dec 47, rejoined Co. by 30 Apr 48, mo. with Co. 20 Jul 48.

KLINE, GEORGE S.: 1st Sgt., enl. 26 Dec 46 at Danville, age 21, occ. blacksmith, mo. with Co. 20 Jul 48.

KONKLE, JEROME: (Kunkle): Pvt., enl. 26 Dec 46 at Danville, age 21, occ. laborer, hospitalized at Jalapa according to Mar-Apr 47 MR, serving as Co. Commissary in Apr & May 48, mo. with Co. 20 Jul 48.

LAFORM, BENJAMIN: (Laferm): Pvt., enl. 26 Dec 46 at Danville, age 21, occ. farmer, on duty as hospital attendant in Jan 48, mo. with Co. 20 Jul 48.

LANDSBERGER, GODFRIED (Godfrey): Pvt., enl. 16 Aug 47 at Pittsburgh, age 30, occ. laborer, reported at Carlisle Barracks 31 Aug 47, joined Co. 29 Dec 47, mi. at San Angel 31 Dec 47, mo. with Co. 20 Jul 48.

LeCLERC, EDWARD E.: 2nd Lt., enl. 26 Dec 46 at Danville, age 27, occ. lawyer, residence Wilkes-Barre, listed as sick on Sep-Oct 47 MR, appointed Q.M. 8 Nov 47, promoted to 1st Lt. 12 Nov 47, mo. with Co. 20 Jul 48. Died at Phila. 12 Aug 49.

LEWIS, DAVID D.: Pvt., enl. & mi. 9 Aug 47 at Pittsburgh, age 43, occ. laborer, reported at Carlisle Barracks 31 Aug 47, joined Co. 5 Jan 48, died in quarters at San Angel 24 Jan 48.

LOWERY, JOHN A.: (Lowrey, Lowry): Pvt., enl. 26 Dec 46 at Danville, age 36, occ. laborer, left sick at Perote 28 Jun 47, died at Perote 23 Aug 47.

LOWNSBERRY, IRA (Hiry): (Lonsberry, Lonsbury): Pvt., enl. 26 Dec 46 at Danville, age 24, occ. laborer, serving as Co. cook in Nov 47, hospitalized in Mexico City 19 Dec 47, rejoined Co. by 29 Feb 48, mo. with Co. 20 Jul 48.

LYON, ROBERT: (Lynn): Pvt., enl. 26 Dec 46 at Danville, age 20, occ. boatman, left sick at Perote 28 Jun 47, died at Perote 1 Aug 47.

LYTTLE, CHARLES: (Litle, Lytle, Lytte): Pvt., enl. 26 Dec 46 at Danville, age 35, occ. laborer, died at Jalapa Hospital 26 May 47.

MACK, NORMAN: Pvt., enl. 26 Dec 46 at Danville, age 21, occ. printer, promoted to 3rd Cpl. 28 May 47, mo. with Co. 20 Jul 48.

MALLON, JOHN G.: (Mellon): Pvt., enl. 26 Dec 46 at Danville, age 33, occ. laborer, left sick at Puebla 8 Aug 47, disc. at Jalapa 21 Dec 47 on SCD.

MANLEY, MAHLON K. (R.): (Manely, Manly): Pvt., enl. 26 Dec 46 at Danville, age 23, occ. shoemaker, left sick at Perote 28 Jun 47, disc. at Perote 29 Oct 47 on SCD. Capt. Co. E, 6th Pa. Reserves 14 May 61 to 22 Mar 63. 1st Lt. Co. D, 53rd Pa. Emergency Militia 28 Jun 63 to 19 Aug 63.

MARTIAL, DANIEL: (Marshall, Marstrad): Pvt., enl. 26 Dec 46 at Danville, age 23, occ. laborer, promoted to Cpl. 1 May 48, mo. with Co. 20 Jul 48.

MARTIN, BENJAMIN I. (A.): Pvt., enl. 26 Dec 46 at Danville, age 25, occ. confectioner, hospitalized at Jalapa according to Mar-Apr 47 MR, detached as clerk to "Commissary Brigade" in Dec 47, mo. with Co. 20 Jul 48.

McALMONT, ROBERT: (McAlmon): Pvt., enl. 26 Dec 46 at Danville, age 22, detached to Capt. Steptoe's Battery of U.S. Artillery 16 Apr 47, rejoined Co. 8 Jun 47, left sick at Puebla 8 Aug 47, died at Puebla date unknown.

McCLELLAND, JAMES: (McCelland): Pvt., enl. 2 Jan 47 at Blairsville, age 26, deserted from Camp Jackson near New Orleans 25 Jan 47.

McDONALD, ALEXANDER: Pvt., enl. 26 Dec 46 at Danville, age 22, occ. machinist, deserted from Camp Jackson near New Orleans 28 Jan 47.

McDONALD, WILLIAM: (McDonnal): Pvt., enl. 26 Dec 46 at Danville, age 19, occ. boat builder, listed as sick on Jan-Feb 47 MR, mo. with Co. 20 Jul 48.

McFADDEN, HUGH: (McFaddin): Pvt., enl. 26 Dec 46 at Danville, age 20, occ. saddler, residence Lewisburg, listed as sick on Jan-Feb 47 MR, left sick at Perote 28 Jun 47, died at Perote 15 Sep 47.

McGONNEL, EDWARD: Pvt., enl. 26 Dec 46 at Danville, age 34, occ. laborer, mo. with Co. 20 Jul 48.

McKEAN, RICHARD H.: Pvt., enl. 26 Dec 46 at Danville, age 40, occ. carpenter, left sick at Puebla 8 Aug 47, disc. at Jalapa 13 Dec 47 on SCD.

MILLER, GEORGE: Pvt., enl. 26 Dec 46 at Danville, age 19, occ. laborer, deserted from Camp Jackson near New Orleans 27 Jan 47.

MOONEY, ARCHIBALD: Pvt., enl. 26 Dec 46 at Danville, age 25, hospitalized at Jalapa in Apr 47, mo. with Co. 20 Jul 48. Cpl. Co. K, 8th Minnesota Vol. Inf. 21 Aug 62 to 11 Jul 65.

MOSER, WILLIAM: Pvt., enl. 26 Dec 46 at Danville, age 21, occ. laborer, hospitalized at Jalapa in Apr 47, mo. with Co. 20 Jul 48.

MOYNTHAN, CHARLES: (Moyntham): Pvt., enl. 26 Dec 46 at Danville, age 24, occ. laborer, hospitalized in Mexico City 19 Dec 47, disc. at Mexico City 5 Mar 48 on SCD.

MUSSLEMAN, JASPER: (Musselman): Pvt., enl. 26 Dec 46 at Danville, age 21, occ. moulder, left sick at Puebla 8 Aug 47, disc. at Puebla 5 Nov 47 on SCD, died at Plan del Rio on his way home.

NEFF, WILLIAM: Pvt., enl. 14 Sep 47 at Phila., age 20, joined Co. 29 Dec 47, mi. at San Angel 31 Dec 47, mo. with Co. 20 Jul 48.

OLIVER, JAMES: (Olliver): 2nd Cpl., enl. 26 Dec 46 at Danville, age 21, occ. carpenter, promoted to 1st Cpl. 8 Apr 47, promoted to 4th Sgt. 28 May 47, left sick at Perote 28 Jun 47, died at Perote 1 Nov 47.

OTENWELDER, CASPER: (Otenweller, Ottenwelder, Ottenwellder): Pvt., enl. 26 Dec 46 at Danville, age 20, occ. laborer, left sick at Puebla 8 Aug 47, rejoined Co. 8 Dec 47, mo. with Co. 20 Jul 48.

POORMAN, DANIEL: Pvt., enl. 26 Dec 46 at Danville, age 23, occ. blacksmith, left sick at Puebla 8 Aug 47, disc. at Puebla on SCD date unknown, died in New Orleans Hospital 31 Jan 48 on his way home.

RAKE, PHILIP: Pvt., enl. 26 Dec 46 at Danville, age 23, occ. laborer, left sick at Perote 28 Jun 47, died at Perote 19 Jul 47.

REED, PETER S.: Pvt., enl. 26 Dec 46 at Danville, age 23, occ. tanner, promoted to 2nd Lt. 6 Jan 47, left sick at Puebla 8 Aug 47, rejoined Co. 8 Dec 47, mo. with Co. 20 Jul 48. Capt. Co. A, 2nd Nebraska Vol. Cav. 23 Oct 62 to 21 Sep 63. Died at Golden City, Colorado 11 Jun 82 & buried there.

SANDERS, JONATHAN R.: Pvt., enl. 26 Dec 46 at Danville, age 23, occ. shoemaker, detailed to Capt. Steptoe's Battery of U.S. Artillery 16 Apr 47, rejoined Co. 8 Jun 47, left sick at Perote 28 Jun 47, died at Perote 4 Aug 47.

SARBA, JOHN: (Sarby): Pvt., enl. 26 Dec 46 at Danville, age 21, occ. laborer, started with Co. on march from Vera Cruz 9 Apr 47 but could not keep up, left behind & listed as a deserter, not heard from again. Pvt. Co. F, 56th P.V.I. 17 Dec 61 to ? Pvt. Co. D, 150th P.V.I. 29 Aug 62 until deserting 8 Jul 63. Pvt. Co. D, 51st P.V.I. 12 Oct 64 to 27 May 65.

SCHOFIELD, JOHN N.: (Scofield): Pvt., enl. 26 Dec 46 at Danville, age 21, occ. farmer, promoted to 2nd Sgt. 8 Apr 47, reduced to Pvt. by Court Martial 14 May 47, mo. with Co. 20 Jul 48.

SEIGFRIED, PETER: (Seigfrieds, Seyfield): Pvt., enl. 26 Dec 46 at Danville, age 35, occ. mason, detailed as cook to regimental hospital in Sep & Oct 47, detailed as cook for regimental band in Mar & Apr 48, mo. with Co. 20 Jul 48. Died in Espy, Pa. 22 Jan 54.

SEILER, EDWARD: (Siler): Pvt., enl. 26 Dec 46 at Danville, age 33, occ. mason, left sick at Puebla 8 Aug 47, died at Puebla 15 Sep 47.

SLATER, JAMES D.: 2nd Sgt., enl. 26 Dec 46 at Danville, age 25, occ. blacksmith, disc. at Vera Cruz 7 Apr 47 on SCD. Sgt., 2nd Lt., 1st Lt. & Capt. Co. B, 5th Pa. Reserves 21 Jun 61 to 1 Sep 63. Veteran Reserve Corps from 1 Sep 63 (unconfirmed).

SMITH, JOHN: 3rd Cpl., enl. 26 Dec 46 at Danville, age 20, occ. saddler, severely WIA in the face at Cerro Gordo by a canister shot 18 Apr 47, died at Jalapa Hospital 1 May 47 from wound.

SMITH, JOSEPH: Pvt., enl. 26 Dec 46 at Danville, age 24, occ. baker, left sick at Boalsburg during the march to Pittsburgh 29 Dec 46.

SNYDER, DAVID (Daniel): Pvt., enl. 26 Dec 46 at Danville, age 20, occ. laborer, deserted from Camp Jackson near New Orleans 27 Jan 47.

SNYDER, JOHN C.: Pvt., enl. 26 Dec 46 at Danville, age 23, occ. boat builder, hospitalized at Jalapa in Apr 47, severely WIA in the storming of Chapultepec 13 Sep 47, died at Tacubaya 17 Sep 47 from wound.

SPACE, PETER M.: Pvt., enl. 26 Dec 46 at Danville, age 30, occ. laborer, hospitalized at Jalapa in Apr 47, died at Perote 25 Jun 47.

STEPHENS, OLIVER C.: (Stevens): Pvt., enl. 26 Dec 46 at Danville, age 28, occ. plasterer, left sick at Perote 28 Jun 47, died at Perote date unknown.

STEWART, JAMES A.: Pvt., enl. 26 Dec 46 at Danville, age 27, occ. carpenter, left as nurse in Perote Hospital in Jun 47, rejoined Co. by 31 Aug 47, on duty as cook in Feb 48, mo. with Co. 20 Jul 48.

STRATTON, JOSEPH H.: (Stratten): Pvt., enl. 26 Dec 46 at Danville, age 22, occ. chair maker, left sick at Puebla 8 Aug 47, rejoined Co. 8 Dec 47, died in Mexico City Hospital 26 Dec 47.

SWANEY, WILLIAM W. (H.): (Sweney): Pvt., enl. 26 Dec 46 at Danville, age 39, occ. hatter, detailed as cook to regimental hospital in Sep & Oct 47, disc. at Mexico City 27 Nov 47 on SCD.

SWARTZ, WILLIAM: (Swarts, Swarty): Pvt., enl. 26 Dec 46 at Danville, age 26, occ. shoemaker, hospitalized at Jalapa in Apr 47, promoted to 4th Cpl. 28 May 47, left sick at Perote 28 Jun 47, died at Perote 12 Jul 47.

TOMLINSON, BENJAMIN W.: Pvt., enl. 12 Jan 48 at Harrisburg, age 21, occ. tailor, mi. at Ft. McHenry, Md. 19 Jan 48, joined Co. 17 Apr 48, mo. with Co. 20 Jul 48.

TROXEL, DANIEL (David): (Troxall): Pvt., enl. 18 Aug 47 at Pittsburgh, age 34, occ. laborer, joined Co. 29 Dec 47, mi. at San Angel 31 Dec 47, mo. with Co. 20 Jul 48.

TYLER, JACOB W.: (Tayler): Pvt., enl. 8 Oct 47 at York, age 20, joined Co. 29 Dec 47, mi. at San Angel 31 Dec 47, mo. with Co. 20 Jul 48.

WAGNER, GEORGE: (Wagoner, Warner): Pvt., enl. 26 Dec 46 at Danville, age 29, occ. laborer, left sick at Perote 28 Jun 47, died at Perote 1 Aug 47.

WALKER, JEROME: Pvt., enl. 26 Dec 46 at Danville, age 19, died in Perote Hospital 18 Jun 47.

WHITE, WILLIAM: Pvt., enl. 26 Dec 46 at Danville, age 30, occ. laborer, deserted from Camp Jackson near New Orleans 26 Jan 47.

WILLET, JACOB (George): (Willett, Willit): Pvt., enl. 26 Dec 46 at Danville, age 22, occ. farmer, left sick at Puebla 8 Aug 47, disc. at Jalapa 26 Dec 47 on SCD.

WILLET, LEFFERT: Pvt., enl. 26 Dec 46 at Danville, age 30, occ. laborer, rejected by Surgeon in Pittsburgh 3 Jan 47 due to poor eyesight.

WILSON, JOHN S.: Capt., enl. 26 Dec 46 at Danville, age 33, occ. machinist, granted leave of absence on 7 Apr 47, died on board ship off Vera Cruz 12 Apr 47, his remains were brought home to Danville by the Co. where they were buried 28 Jul 48.

WINGARD, GEORGE: (Wengard, Wingan, Wingar, Winger): Pvt., enl. 26 Dec 46 at Danville, age 21, occ. carpenter, listed as sick on Jan-Feb 47 MR, died at Jalapa Hospital 13 May 47.

WRAY, ADAM M.: Pvt., enl. 26 Dec 46 at Danville, age 23, occ. boatman, promoted to 3rd Cpl. 1 Nov 47, mo. with Co. 20 Jul 48. Pvt. Co. F, 7th Pa. Reserves 13 Jun 61 until disc. 31 Dec 62 for wounds received while bearing the Colors at Charles City Cross Roads 20 Jun 62, died in Danville 7 Nov 63 from wounds.

YARNALL, PETER M.: Pvt., enl. 28 Dec 46 at Mifflinburg, deserted at Pittsburgh 4 Jan 47.

Company D, 2nd Regiment
Cambria Guards

The Cambria Guards were a uniformed militia company, believed to have been formed and active before 1846. Their home territory was the Ebensburgh area of Cambria County. Captain James Murray, their commander, was also the County Sheriff.

The Guards sought to be one of Pennsylvania's companies from the very beginning of the war, and in December Captain Murray received word to have his company in Pittsburgh by 5 January to become part of the 2nd Regiment. They left Ebensburgh on 2 January and First Lieutenant Horace B. Field, 3rd U.S. Artillery, on 4 January, mustered them into Federal service.

While on active duty, some of the Cambria Guards caught smallpox, which kept them from being with the regiment at Vera Cruz and Cerro Gordo. They did, however, participate in the battles of La Hoya, Chapultepec and Garita de Belen. In July 1848 they returned to Pittsburgh, where they were mustered out on the 14th by Major George Wright of the 4th U.S. Infantry. The welcome they received in Ebensburgh was remembered by the participants with great joy for the rest of their lives.

A total of 94 men served in the company during the war, five of them recruits who joined it in Mexico. Five members became deserters. Five men suffered battle related injuries, two of them fatal. In all, twenty-two Guards died in service, and an additional seventeen received discharges before muster out.

ARMOR, HENRY L.: (Armour): Pvt., enl. 4 Jan 47 at Pittsburgh, age 27, occ. tailor, left sick at Perote Hospital 8 Jun 47, died at Perote 13 Jul 47 from diarrhea.

ASHCRAFT, JAMES: Pvt., enl. 31 Dec 46 at Ebensburgh, age 27, occ. farmer, died at San Augustin 4 Sep 47 from diarrhea.

BLAIR, JOHN A.: Pvt., enl. 4 Dec 46 at Ebensburgh, age 21, occ. carpenter, promoted to Cpl. 29 Oct 47, mo. with Co. 14 Jul 48. Was living in Ebensburgh in 1907.

BRADLEY, THOMAS: (Bradly): Pvt., enl. 4 Dec 46 at Ebensburgh, age 19, occ. chair maker, mo. with Co. 14 Jul 48.

BRUCE, WILLIAM: Pvt., enl. 4 Dec 46 at Ebensburgh, age 24, occ. farmer, serving as hospital attendant & chief cook from 16 Sep 47, rejoined Co. by 30 Apr 48, mo. with Co. 14 Jul 48.

BUCHANAN, DAVID: Pvt., enl. 2 Jan 47 at Armagh, age 39, occ. gunsmith, listed as sick on Jan-Feb 47 MR, left sick at Vera Cruz 14 Apr 47, disc. at Vera Cruz 11 May 47.

BUCK, JAMES P.: Pvt., enl. 4 Jan 47 at Pittsburgh, age 23, occ. saddler, left sick at Jalapa 30 Apr 47, disc. at Jalapa 20 May 47 on SCD for diarrhea.

BURKHART, ABRAM (Abraham, Alexander) H.: (Berkhart): Pvt., enl. 2 Jan 47 at Armagh, age 21, died at Mexico City 23 Sep 47 from diarrhea.

BYRNE, FRANCIS: (Byrnes): Pvt., enl. 11 Dec 46 at Ebensburgh, age 24, occ. blacksmith, mo. with Co. 14 Jul 48. Died near Carrolltown, Pa. in 1897.

CAMERON, JOHN W. (H.): Pvt., enl. 11 Dec 46 at Ebensburgh, age 30, occ. carpenter, appointed Lance Cpl. 18 Sep 47, promoted to 1st Cpl. 1 Nov 47, mo. with Co. 14 Jul 48. Died in Cambria County.

CAMPBELL, JOSHUA E.: Pvt., enl. 11 Dec 46 at Ebensburgh, age 35, occ. farmer, mo. with Co. 14 Jul 48. Moved to New Jersey.

COLE, LAYMAN (Lyman): Pvt., enl. 29 Dec 46 at Danville or 1 Jan 47 at Ebensburgh, age 26, occ. farmer or boatman, left sick at Perote 21 Jun 47, died at Perote 7 Aug 47 from diarrhea.

COLLINS, JAMES: Pvt., enl. 11 Dec 46 at Ebensburgh, age 20, occ. glass blower, mo. with Co. 14 Jul 48.

CRAIN, WILLIAM: (Crum): Pvt., enl. 11 Dec 46 at Ebensburgh, age 21, deserted at New Orleans 26 Jan 47.

CRAMER, DANIEL: Pvt., enl. 26 Dec 46 at Danville, age 21, occ. coach maker, mo. with Co. 14 Jul 48.

CROZIER, RICHARD J.: Pvt., enl. 4 Jan 47 at Pittsburgh, age 21, occ. carpenter, mo. with Co. 14 Jul 48. Capt. Co. M. 62nd P.V.I. 9 Aug 61 to 7 Mar 63. Capt. Co. B & Maj. McKeage's Independent Battalion 3 Jul 63 to 8 Aug 63. Died 15 May 00.

CUMMINGS, ALEXANDER B.: 1st Cpl., enl. 4 Dec 46 at Ebensburgh, age 28, occ. cabinet maker, left sick at Perote 25 Jun 47, died at Perote 18 Aug 47 from diarrhea.

CUMMINGS, WILLIAM: Pvt., enl. 1 Oct 47 at Phila., age 30, mi. at Phila. 28 Oct 47, joined Co. 29 Dec 47, mo. with Co. 14 Jul 48.

DAVIS, BENJAMIN F.: Pvt., enl. 4 Dec 46 at Ebensburgh, age 22, occ. carpenter, WIA in charge at Chapultepec 13 Sep 47, promoted to 4th Sgt. 7 Oct 47, hospitalized in Mexico City 23 Dec 47, rejoined Co. by 29 Feb 48, mo. with Co. 14 Jul 48. Died in Salem, Oregon.

DAVIS, THOMAS J.: Pvt., enl. 4 Jan 47 at Pittsburgh, age 22, occ. carder, disc. at Mexico City 27 Oct 47 on SCD.

DEAL, SAMUEL: Pvt., enl. 4 Jan 47 at Pittsburgh, age 24, occ. carder, hospitalized in Mexico City 18 Dec 47, disc. at San Angel 11 Apr 48 on SCD.

DONNEY, EDWARD A.: (Downey): Cpl., enl. 14 Dec 46 at Ebensburgh, age 27, occ. carpenter, WIA in the leg at Garita de Belen 13 Sep 47, hospitalized in Mexico City 14 Sep 47, his leg was amputated, died at Mexico City 7 Oct 47 from wound.

DONOGHUE, CORNELIUS: (Donohoe, Donoughe, Donoughu, Donoughue): Pvt., enl. 29 Dec 46 at Ebensburgh, age 30, occ. saddler, detailed as attendant in regimental hospital 16 Sep 47, rejoined Co. by 31 Dec 47, hospitalized at Jalapa 11 Apr 48, disc. at Jalapa 12 May 48 on SCD. Died in Cambria County.

DOUGHERTY, EDWARD: Pvt., enl. 29 Dec 46 at Ebensburgh, age 21, deserted at New Orleans 26 Jan 47. Died in Ebensburgh.

EVANS, DANIEL O.: Pvt., enl. 29 Dec 46 at Ebensburgh, age 30, occ. shoemaker, mo. with Co. 14 Jul 48. Died in Ebensburgh.

EVANS, EVAN D.: Pvt., enl. 29 Dec 46 at Ebensburgh, age 25, occ. carpenter, mo. with Co. 14 Jul 48. Died in Ebensburgh.

EVANS, JOHN E.: Pvt., enl. 29 Dec 46 at Ebensburgh, age 23, occ. blacksmith, mo. with Co. 14 Jul 48.

EVANS, THOMAS O.: Pvt., enl. 29 Dec 46 at Ebensburgh, age 41, occ. tailor, left sick at Vera Cruz 14 Apr 47, disc. at Vera Cruz 2 May 47 on SCD. Died in Ebensburgh.

EVY, HENRY: Pvt., enl. 26 Dec 46 at Danville, age 20, occ. farmer, mo. with Co. 14 Jul 48. Sgt., 2nd Lt. & 1st Lt. Co. H, 56th P.V.I. 1 Dec 61 until KIA at the Wilderness 6 May 64.

FRANCIS, JOHN: Pvt., enl. 29 Dec 46 at Ebensburgh, age 43, occ. teacher, left sick at Vera Cruz 17 Apr 47, disc. at Vera Cruz 21 May 47 on SCD, died at New Orleans.

FREDERICKS, JOHN W.: (Fredricks): Pvt., enl. 4 Jan 47 at Pittsburgh, age 21, occ. clerk, appointed Acting Commissary Sgt. 1 Oct 47, in which capacity he served through at least 30 Apr 48, mo. with Co. 14 Jul 48.

FULTON, SAMUEL: Pvt., enl. 4 Jan 47 at Pittsburgh, age 22, occ. gentleman, promoted to Sgt. 18 Mar 47, hospitalized at Mexico City according to Sep-Oct 47 MR, sent to New Orleans for his health on orders of 28 Oct 47, reduced to Pvt. 1 Nov 47, rejoined Co. at Pittsburgh from sick leave 11 Jul 48, mo. with Co. 14 Jul 48.

FULTZ, FRANCIS: Pvt., enl. 4 Jan 47 at Pittsburgh, age 28, occ. stage driver, hospitalized at Jalapa 11 Apr 48, disc. at Jalapa 13 May 48 on SCD, reported to have died in Mexico.

GARRISON, WILLIAM D.: (Garrettson): Pvt., enl. 21 Jan 47 at New Orleans, age 22, occ. clerk, mi. 27 Jan 47 at New Orleans, left sick at Jalapa 4 May 47, died at Perote 11 Jul 47 from diarrhea.

GIVEN, JOHN G. (J.): 2nd Lt., enl. 16 Dec 46 at Ebensburgh, age 26, occ. printer, appointed Acting Asst. Commissary of Subsistence 25 May 47, mo. with Co. 14 Jul 48. Supposed to have been living in Mexico, Indiana in 1907.

GOLDMAN, NOAH: (Golden): Pvt., enl. 25 Dec 46 at Ebensburgh, age 20, occ. clerk, promoted to Cpl. 10 Mar 47, left sick at Perote 27 Jun 47, died at Perote 28 Jul 47 from diarrhea.

GREGG, JOHN IRWIN: (Greg): Pvt., enl. 29 Dec 46 at Milesburgh, age 21, occ. gentleman, appointed 1st Lt. of Inf. in the Regular Army 18 Feb 47, assigned to 11th U.S. Inf. to rank from 9 Apr 47, furloughed from Co. D, 2nd Pa. Regt. at Jalapa 18 May 47 to accept his Regular commission, promoted to Capt. 5 Sep 47, mo. 14 Aug 48. Capt. Co. E, 5th Pa. Reserves 21 Jun 61 to 12 Jul 61. Concurrently appointed Capt. 3rd U.S. Cav. to rank from 14 May 61, transferred to 6th U.S. Cav. 3 Aug 61. Col. 16th Pa. Cav. 14 Nov 62 to 11 Aug 65. Bvt. Brig. Gen. 13 Mar 65. Col. 8th U.S. Cav. 28 Jul 66 until his retirement 2 Apr 79. Died 6 Jan 92.

HELZEL, ADAM: (Helsel): Pvt., enl. 29 Dec 46 at Ebensburgh, age 23, occ. blacksmith, detailed as attendant to regimental hospital 23 Feb 48, mo. with Co. 14 Jul 48. Pvt. Co. C, 91st Ohio Vol Inf. 25 Jul 62 to 24 Jun 65.

HENDRICKS, ABRAHAM: Pvt., enl. 29 Dec 46 at Ebensburgh, age 42, occ. carpenter, died in Jalapa Hospital 14 May 47 from diarrhea.

HEYER, CHARLES H.: 1st Lt., enl. 16 Dec 46 at Ebensburgh, age 25, occ. lawyer, assumed command of Co. 28 Oct 47, promoted to Capt. 10 Jun 48 to rank from 12 Feb 48, mo. with Co. 14 Jul 48.

HEYER, THEOPHILUS L.: Pvt., enl. 29 Dec 46 at Ebensburgh, age 19, occ. student, hospitalized in Mexico City 10 Dec 47, rejoined Co. by 29 Feb 48, mo. with Co. 14 Jul 48. Died in Baltimore, Md.

**John I. Gregg as a Captain in the
early days of the Civil War**
USAMHI

**Andrew Lewis as a Captain in the 11th
Pennsylvania Reserves**
USAMHI

Robert Litzinger pictured as a
Captain in the Civil War
Ronn Palm Collection

George W. Todd as Major of the 91st
Pennsylvania in the Civil War
Charles B. Oellig Collection

HOLLIDAY, SAMUEL M.: Pvt., enl. 4 Jan 47 at Pittsburgh, age 33, occ. tailor, hospitalized in Mexico City 23 Dec 47, disc. at San Angel 11 Apr 48 on SCD.

HOOD, WILLIAM: Pvt., enl. 2 Jan 47 at Blairsville, age 23, occ. clerk, mo. with Co. 14 Jul 48.

HOOVER, JOHN B.: Pvt., enl. 11 Dec 46 at Ebensburgh, age 22, occ. printer, appointed Fife Major 1 May 47, listed as sick in quarters on Sep-Oct 47 MR, hospitalized in Mexico City according to Nov-Dec 47 & Jan-Feb 48 MRs, mo. with F & S 21 Jul 48.

HOUSER, JACOB: (Honser, Howser): Pvt., enl. 26 Dec 46 at Danville, age 20, occ. farmer, left sick at Perote 21 Jun 47, died at Perote 27 Oct 47 from diarrhea.

HUGHES, JOHN D.: Pvt., enl. 29 Dec 46 at Ebensburgh, age 28, occ. tailor, hospitalized in Mexico City according to Sep-Oct 47 MR, hospitalized at San Angel according to Mar-Apr 48 MR, mo. with Co. 14 Jul 48. Died in Johnstown.

JACKSON, JAMES: Pvt., enl. 11 Dec 46 at Ebensburgh, age 19, occ. chair maker, detailed as attendant & cook to Mexico City Hospital 18 Dec 47, rejoined Co. by 30 Apr 48, mo. with Co. 14 Jul 48. Pvt. Co. F, 136th P.V.I. 22 Aug 62 to 29 May 63. Pvt. Battery A, 5th Pa. Heavy Art. 24 Aug 64 to 30 Jun 65.

JAMES, ENOCH G.: Pvt., enl. 4 Jan 47 at Pittsburgh, age 21, occ. chair maker, promoted to Cpl. 1 Nov 47, mo. with Co. 14 Jul 48.

JOHNSTON, WILLIAM: (Johnson): Pvt., enl. 23 Aug 47 at Phila., age 24, mi. 28 Oct 47 at Phila., joined Co. 29 Dec 47, mo. with Co. 14 Jul 48.

JONES, JOHN: Pvt., enl. 4 Jan 47 at Pittsburgh, age 21, deserted at Pittsburgh 9 Jan 47.

KAYLOR, MICHAEL G.: Pvt., enl. 25 Dec 46 at Ebensburgh, age 22, occ. blacksmith, left sick at Perote 22 Jun 47, rejoined Co. at Puebla 1 Aug 47, promoted to Cpl. 1 Nov 47, mo. with Co. 14 Jul 48. Died near Carrolltown, Pa.

KAYLOR, PETER: (Kayler): Pvt., enl. 1 Jan 47 at Ebensburgh, age 20, occ. blacksmith, mo. with Co. 14 Jul 48.

KELLY, MICHAEL: Pvt., enl. 2 Oct 47 at Phila., age 35, mi. 28 Oct 47 at Phila., joined Co. 29 Dec 47, mo. with Co. 14 Jul 48.

KELSO, JAMES W.: Pvt., enl. 4 Jan 47 at Pittsburgh, age 39, occ. blacksmith, mo. with Co. 14 Jul 48.

LAMBAUGH, JOHN S.: (Lambough): Pvt., enl. 11 Dec 46 at Ebensburgh, age 24, occ. tanner, listed as sick on Jan-Feb 47 MR, disc. at Jalapa 17 May 47 on SCD. Died in Ebensburgh.

LAUFMAN, WILLIAM: (Lauffman): Pvt., enl. 4 Jan 47 at Pittsburgh, age 24, deserted at Pittsburgh 5 Jan 47.

LEWIS, ANDREW: Pvt., enl. 4 Dec 46 at Ebensburgh, age 35, occ. plasterer, appointed Lance Cpl. 27 Jun 47, hospitalized in Mexico City according to Sep-Oct 47 MR, sent to New Orleans for his health 28 Oct 47, disc. at New Orleans 27 Feb 48 on SCD for diarrhea. 1st Lt. & Capt. Co. A, 11th Pa. Reserves 25 Jun 61 until KIA at Gaines Mill 27 Jun 62.

LITZINGER, DENNIS A.: Pvt., enl. 4 Dec 46 at Ebensburgh, age 23, occ. cabinet maker, mo. with Co. 14 Jul 48.

LITZINGER, JOHN R.: Fifer, enl. 4 Dec 46 at Ebensburgh, age 19, occ. printer, listed as Drummer on all MRs but the muster-in roll, died at San Angel 19 Apr 48 from typhoid fever.

LITZINGER, ROBERT: Drummer, enl. 4 Dec 46 at Ebensburgh, age 18, listed as Fifer on all MRs but the muster-in roll, mo. with Co. 14 Jul 48. Capt. Co. A & Maj. 11th Pa. Reserves 25 Jun 61 to 1 Apr 62. Col. 4th Pa. Emergency Militia 11 Sep 62 to 25 Sep 62. Capt. Co. A & Lt. Col. of Litzinger's Independent Battalion 23 Jun 63 to 8 Aug 63. Capt. Co. C, 209th P.V.I. 15 Sep 64 to 4 Jun 65.

MARDIS, JOSEPH: Pvt., enl. 29 Dec 46 at Ebensburgh, age 24, occ. laborer, mo. with Co. 14 Jul 48.

MARTIN, THOMAS J. (D.): Pvt., enl. 26 Dec 46 at Danville, age 33 or 34, occ. moulder or pudler, left sick at Perote 22 Jun 47, fined $2.00 by regimental Court Martial according to Jul-Aug 47 MR, disc. at Perote 29 Oct 47 on SCD, was reported to have died in Mexico.

McCUNE, ARCHIBALD S.: Pvt., enl. 4 Dec 46 at Ebensburgh, age 30, occ. saddler, listed as sick on Jan-Feb 47 MR, left sick at Vera Cruz 14 Apr 47, disc. at Vera Cruz 11 May 47 on SCD. Died at Summitt, Pa. 15 Apr 49.

McDERMITT, BARNABAS: (McDermit): Sgt., enl. 4 Dec 46 at Ebensburgh, age 25, occ. cabinet maker, promoted to 1st Sgt. 10 Sep 47, mo. with Co. 14 Jul 48. Lt. Col. 54th P.V.I. 30 Nov 61 to 29 Jan 63. Died at Altoona in 1890.

McDERMITT, CHARLES: (McDermit): 2nd Lt., enl. 16 Dec 46 at Ebensburgh, age 26, occ. mechanic, promoted to 1st Lt. 10 Jun 48 to rank from 12 Feb 48, mo. with Co. 14 Jul 48. Maj. & Lt. Col. 2nd California Vol. Cav. 7 May 65 until KIA by Indians at Queen's River, Nevada 7 Aug 65.

McDERMITT, FRANCIS C. (S.): (McDermit): Pvt., enl. 4 Dec 46 at Ebensburgh, age 18, occ. school teacher, WIA in charge at Chapultepec 13 Sep 47, listed as sick in quarters on Sep-Oct 47 MR, mo. with Co. 14 Jul 48.

McLAUGHLIN, WILLIAM (F. C.) R.: (McGlaughlin): Pvt., enl. 24 Dec 46 at Ebensburgh, age 35, occ. stage driver, listed as hospitalized in Mexico City on Sep-Oct 47 MR, sent to New Orleans for his health 28 Oct 47, died at New Orleans Hospital 3 Jan 48 from diarrhea.

MILLS, DAVID: Sgt., enl. 4 Dec 46 at Ebensburgh, age 28, occ. saddler, mo. with Co. 14 Jul 48.

MILLS, WILLIAM: Sgt., enl. 4 Dec 46 at Ebensburgh, age 27, occ. carpenter, reduced to Pvt. 18 Mar 47, left sick at Vera Cruz 14 Apr 47, disc. at Vera Cruz 21 May on SCD.

MOSES, GEORGE: Pvt., enl. 11 Dec 46 at Ebensburgh, age 19, occ. laborer, hospitalized in Mexico City 23 Dec 47 through Feb 48, hospitalized at San Angel according to Mar-Apr 48 MR, mo. with Co. 14 Jul 48.

MUMMY, EDWARD: (Mummey): Pvt., enl. 4 Jan 47 at Pittsburgh, age 23, occ. painter, left sick at Puebla 7 Aug 47, died at Puebla date unknown.

MURRAY, JAMES: Capt., enl. 16 Dec 46 at Ebensburgh, age 42, occ. sheriff, left on three months furlough 1 Nov 47, his resignation was accepted 11 Feb 48. Capt. Co. D, 115th P.V.I. 30 Oct 62 to 23 Apr 63.

MURRAY, PATRICK A.: Pvt., enl. 11 Dec 46 at Ebensburgh, age 22, occ. cabinet maker, died on march from Jalapa 18 Jun 47 from diarrhea.

NEFF, GEORGE W.: Pvt., enl. 26 Dec 46 at Danville, age 23, occ. moulder, WIA at Chapultepec 13 Sep 47, hospitalized in Mexico City, hospitalized again in Mexico City 18 Dec 47, rejoined Co. by 30 Apr 48, mo. with Co. 14 Jul 48.

PARRISH, JOSHUA D.: Pvt., enl. 11 Dec 46 at Ebensburgh, age 21, occ. carpenter, mo. with Co. 14 Jul 48. Living in Ebensburgh in 1907.

PARTUSH, JOHN H.: (Partuch, Partusch): Pvt., enl. 20 Aug 47 at Harrisburg, age 38, reported at Carlisle Barracks 31 Aug 47, mi. 28 Oct 47 at Phila., served as Drummer for the detachment according to Oct-Dec 47 MR, joined Co. 29 Dec 47, mo. with Co. 14 Jul 48.

PATTERSON, ARCHIBALD: Pvt., enl. 2 Jan 47 at Armagh, age 26, occ. carpenter, appointed Lance Cpl. 27 Jun 47, severely WIA in the arm at Chapultepec 13 Sep 47, his arm was amputated, died in Mexico City Hospital 10 Jan 48 from wound.

PLUMMER, DANIEL: Pvt., enl. 18 Dec 46 at Ebensburgh, age 21, occ. farmer, left sick at Puebla 7 Aug 47, died at Puebla 12 Oct 47 from diarrhea.

PLUMMER, JOHN: Pvt., enl. 18 Dec 46 at Ebensburgh, age 25, occ. farmer, left sick at Puebla 7 Aug 47, died at Puebla 30 Aug 47 from diarrhea.

PLUMMER, SILAS: Pvt., enl. 18 Dec 46 at Ebensburgh, age 21, occ. farmer, hospitalized in Mexico City according to Sep-Oct 47 MR, sent to New Orleans for his health 28 Oct 47, died at New Orleans 3 Jan 48 from diarrhea.

RHEY, JAMES W.: Pvt., enl. 11 Dec 46 at Ebensburgh, age 21, occ. clerk, disc. at Mexico City 29 Oct 47 having procured George Willis as his substitute. Died in Lancaster.

ROBBINS, JOHN J.: Pvt., enl. 2 Jan 47 at Milesburgh, age 21, occ. physician, detailed as nurse to Jalapa Hospital 8 May 47, moved with the hospital to Perote, disc. at New Orleans 11 Jul 48 on SCD.

ROBERTS, MILTON: 3rd Cpl., enl. 1 Jan 47 at Ebensburgh, age 23, occ. clerk, reduced to Pvt. 10 Mar 47, disc. at San Angel 28 Feb 48 on SCD. Died in Ebensburgh.

SKELLY, JAMES: (Kelly, Skelley): 2nd Cpl., enl. 11 Dec 46 at Ebensburgh, age 25, promoted to 3rd Sgt. 29 Oct 47, mo. with Co. 14 Jul 48.

SPENCER, JOHN: Pvt., enl. 29 Dec 46 at Milesburgh, age 19, occ. laborer, mo. with Co. 14 Jul 48.

SWORD, GEORGE: Pvt., enl. 2 Jan 47 at Armagh, age 20, occ. shoemaker, left sick at Puebla 7 Aug 47, died at Puebla 27 Oct 47 from diarrhea.

THOMPSON, JAMES: Pvt., enl. 4 Jan 47 at Pittsburgh, age 23, occ. clerk, mo. with Co. 14 Jul 48.

TODD, GEORGE W.: Pvt., enl. 4 Dec 46 at Ebensburgh, age 22, occ. clerk, promoted to 1st Sgt. 26 Jan 47, appointed Sgt. Maj. 10 Sep 47, promoted to 2nd Lt. 10 Jun 48 to rank from 11 Feb 48, mo. with Co. 14 Jul 48. Major 91st P.V.I. 4 Dec 61 until 19 Dec 62 when he died of wounds received at Fredericksburg 13 Dec 62, Bvt. Lt. Col. 13 Dec 62.

TODD, WILLIAM A.: 1st Sgt., enl. 16 Dec 46 at Ebensburgh, age 22, occ. lawyer, reduced to Pvt. 26 Jan 47, disc. at San Angel 28 Feb 48 on SCD. Had been appointed 2nd Lt. 11th U.S. Inf. 30 Dec 47, resigned 30 Jun 48. 1st Lt. Co. C, 71st P.V.I. 21 May 61 to 17 Oct 62. Died at Indiana, Pa.

VANRONK, DANIEL: Pvt., enl. 4 Jan 47 at Pittsburgh, age 21, occ. plasterer, originally enl. in Co. G, 1st Pa. Regt. 20 Nov 46 but was left sick in Pittsburgh 22 Dec 46, he therefore joined Co. D, 2nd Pa. Regt., deserted from New Orleans 17 Jan 47, returned to Co. by 30 Apr 47, left sick at Perote 8 Jun 47, disc. at Perote 29 Oct 47 on SCD. Moved to Danville. Sgt. Co. A, 132nd P.V.I. 14 Aug 62 until KIA at Antietam 17 Sep 62.

WEAKLAND, JAMES: (Weekland): Pvt., enl. 29 Dec 46 at Ebensburgh, age 20, occ. carpenter, mo. with Co. 14 Jul 48. Moved to California.

WEAKLAND, WILLIAM: (Weekland): Pvt., enl. 29 Dec 46 at Ebensburgh, age 23, occ. farmer, deserted in Mexico City 14 Dec 47.

WILLIS, GEORGE: Pvt., enl. & mi. 29 Oct 47 at Mexico City as a substitute for Pvt. James W. Rhey, mo. with Co. 14 Jul 48.

WISE, WILLIAM W.: Pvt., enl. 4 Jan 47 at Pittsburgh, age 23, occ. printer, on detached duty from 25 Dec 47, rejoined Co. by 30 Apr 48, mo. with Co. 14 Jul 48. Supposed to have been killed in the Civil War (unconfirmed).

Company E, 2nd Regiment
Westmoreland Guards

The Westmoreland Guards hailed from Greensburg, Westmoreland County, and it is supposed that they were already existing as an organized uniformed militia company before the war. Although disappointed at not being part of the first regiment, they were grateful to be selected to help fill the second.

The Guards left Greensburg on 30 December and arrived in Pittsburgh at near dark of the same day. First Lieutenant Horace B. Field, 3rd U.S. Artillery, mustered them into U.S. service on New Years Day, 1847. With numerous doctors, lawyers and students this was unquestionably one of the most highly educated companies in the entire Army.

The Westmoreland soldiers upheld the honor of their homes with unwavering dedication; participating in the investment of Vera Cruz and the battles of Cerro Gordo, Chapultepec and Garita de Belen.

The Guards reached Pittsburgh on 11 July 1848 and on the 14th were mustered out by Major George Wright of the 4th U.S. Infantry. The next day they returned to Greensburg to a warm welcome and rounds of entertainment.

A total of 95 men served in the company during the war. There were no deserters and no later recruits in this company. Seven of its members suffered battle related injuries, none fatal. In all, twenty-five Guards died in service, and an additional eighteen received discharges before muster out.

238

AIKENS, JOHN: (Aikins, Aitkens): Pvt., enl. 24 Dec 46 at Greensburgh, age 21, occ. tobacconist, left sick at Puebla 7 Aug 47, remained at Puebla until the march for home, mo. with Co. 14 Jul 48.

ALLSHOUSE, LEBBENS: (Allhouse, Alshouse): Pvt., enl. 24 Dec 46 at Greensburgh, age 21, occ. blacksmith, mo. with Co. 14 Jul 48.

ARMSTRONG, JAMES: 1st Lt., enl. 24 Dec 46 at Greensburgh, age 26, occ. lawyer, appointed in Jul 47 to temporarily command Co. H, arrested 10 Nov 47 by order of Col. Geary, sick in Mexico City in Feb 48, was sick but on duty in Mar 48, was sick in quarters in Apr 48, mo. with Co. 14 Jul 48.

BARCLAY, THOMAS I. (J.): 2nd Sgt., enl. 24 Dec 46 at Greensburgh, age 22, occ. lawyer, promoted to 1st Sgt. 21 Apr 47, appointed 2nd Lt. in 11th U.S. Inf. 19 Jan 48 to rank from 30 Dec 47, he accepted the commission & was transferred to the 11th Inf. 26 Feb 48, resigned 6 May 48. Died 24 Aug 81.

BATES, ANDREW J. (I.): Pvt., enl. 24 Dec 46 at Greensburgh, age 21, occ. coach maker, severely WIA in both thighs by musket balls while storming Chapultepec 13 Sep 47, hospitalized in Mexico City 19 Dec 47, rejoined Co. by 29 Feb 48, mo. with Co. 14 Jul 48.

BIGELOW, WILLIAM G.: 3rd Cpl., enl. 24 Dec 46 at Greensburgh, age 23, occ. store keeper, promoted to 2nd Sgt. 1 Mar 48, mo. with Co. 14 Jul 48.

BILLS, McCLURE: Pvt., enl. 24 Dec 46 at Greensburgh, age 20, occ. boatman, mo. with Co. 14 Jul 48.

BLOON, HENRY: Pvt., enl. 24 Dec 46 at Greensburgh, age 19, listed only on muster-in roll with a line drawn through entire entry.

BONNEN, GEORGE W.: (Bonnin): Pvt., enl. 24 Dec 46 at Greensburgh, age 27, occ. lawyer, promoted to 4th Cpl. 14 Jan 47, listed as sick on Sep-Oct 47 MR, promoted to 1st Sgt. 1 Mar 48, mo. with Co. 14 Jul 48.

BRADY, HUGH J. (I.): Pvt., enl. 24 Dec 46 at Greensburgh, age 21, occ. clerk, left sick at Vera Cruz 9 Apr 47, rejoined Co. by 30 Jun 47, was hospital attendant from 16 Sep 47, rejoined Co. by 31 Dec 47, mo. with Co. 14 Jul 48. Major 23rd Pa. Emergency Militia 21 Sep 62 to 30 Sep 62. Lt. Col. 177th Pa. Drafted Militia 28 Nov 62 to 7 Aug 63. Col. 206th P.V.I. 9 Sep 64 to 26 Jun 65. Died 7 Jan 03.

BYERLY, SAMUEL A.: Pvt., enl. 24 Dec 46 at Greensburgh, age 26, occ. wagon maker, promoted to 4th Sgt. 21 Apr 47, promoted to 3rd Sgt. 1 May 48, mo. with Co. 14 Jul 48.

CAMPBELL, WILLIAM A.: Pvt., enl. 24 Dec 46 at Greensburgh, age 21, occ. lawyer, disc. at Jalapa 8 Jun 47 on SCD for phthisis pulmonalis, died the second day after arriving at his parents' home in Blairsville 12 Jul 47.

CARNEY, HAGAN: Pvt., enl. 24 Dec 46 at Greensburgh, age 21, occ. carpenter, promoted to Cpl. 4 Oct 47, mo. with Co. 14 Jul 48.

Richard Coulter as Colonel of the 11th Pennsylvania in the Civil War
MOLLUS-Mass & USAMHI

CARPENTER, JAMES M.: 1st Cpl., enl. 24 Dec 46 at Greensburgh, age 25, occ. lawyer, hospitalized at Jalapa 28 Apr 47, disc. at Jalapa 23 May 47 on SCD.

CARSON, HUMPHREY: Pvt., enl. 24 Dec 46 at Greensburgh, age 19, occ. tailor, mo. with Co. 14 Jul 48.

CLOUD, MILTON: Pvt., enl. 24 Dec 46 at Greensburgh, age 29, occ. shoemaker, serving as attendant in regimental hospital from 16 Sep 47, serving as nurse in general hospital in Mexico City from 16 Dec 47, rejoined Co. by 30 Apr 48, mo. with Co. 14 Jul 48.

COULTER, JAMES: 2nd Lt., enl. 24 Dec 46 at Greensburgh, age 26, occ. lawyer, detached as courier to Vera Cruz 1 Nov 47 to 11 Dec 47, sick in quarters in Apr 48, mo. with Co. 14 Jul 48.

COULTER, RICHARD: Pvt., enl. 24 Dec 46 at Greensburgh, age 19, occ. law student, mo. with Co. 14 Jul 48. Lt. Col. 11th P.V.I. (3 mos.) 26 Apr 61 to 25 Jul 61. Col. 11th P.V.I. 27 Nov 61 to 1 Jul 65, WIA at Fredericksburg, Gettysburg & Spottsylvania. Bvt. Brig. Gen. 1 Aug 64 & Bvt. Maj. Gen. 1 Apr 65. Born 1 Oct 27 & died 14 Oct 08 at Greensburgh.

DECKAR, GEORGE: Pvt., enl. 1 Jan 47 at Pittsburgh, age 26, occ. saddler, WIA before Mexico City 13 Sep 47, mo. with Co. 14 Jul 48.

DOUGHERTY, ARCHIBALD: Pvt., enl. 24 Dec 46 at Greensburgh, age 30, occ. laborer, left sick at Jalapa 28 Apr 47, left sick at Perote 22 Jun 47, disc. at Puebla 5 Nov 47 on SCD.

ELLIOTT, JAMES L.: Pvt., enl. 24 Dec 46 at Greensburgh, age 26, occ. tailor, left sick at Vera Cruz 9 Apr 47, employed as Attendant in Vera Cruz Hospital according to Jul-Aug 47 & Sep-Oct 47 MRs, employed there as Hospital Steward according to Nov-Dec 47, Jan-Feb 48 & Mar-Apr 48 MRs, no record of his discharge is shown.

FISHEL, HENRY: (Fiskel): Pvt., enl. 24 Dec 46 at Greensburgh, age 25, occ. joiner, WIA before Mexico City 13 Sep 47, disc. at Mexico City 27 Oct 47 on SCD.

FORNEY, ANDREW JACKSON: Drummer, enl. 24 Dec 46 at Greensburgh, age 19, occ. cooper, left sick at Vera Cruz 9 Apr 47, disc. at Vera Cruz 18 May 47, died at Louisville, Kentucky on his way home.

GEESYN, HENRY: (Geesen): Pvt., enl. 24 Dec 46 at Greensburgh, age 24, occ. laborer, mo. with Co. 14 Jul 48. Cpl. Co. A, 14th Illinois Vol. Cav. 11 Sep 62 until transferred to the Veteran Reserve Corps.

GORDON, ANDREW D. (J.): Pvt., enl. 24 Dec 46 at Greensburgh, age 27, occ. scale builder, listed as sick on Sep-Oct 47 MR, promoted to 3rd Cpl. 1 Mar 48, mo. with Co. 14 Jul 48.

GORGAS, SAMUEL: Pvt., enl. 24 Dec 46 at Greensburgh, age 21, occ. laborer, died at Puebla 30 Jul 47 from typhus fever.

GROW, JOHN R. (L.): Pvt., enl. 24 Dec 46 at Greensburgh, age 21, occ. furnace keeper, left sick at Vera Cruz 9 Apr 47, disc. at Vera Cruz 22 May 47 on SCD.

HAGERTY, GEORGE: (Haggerty): Pvt., enl. 24 Dec 46 at Greensburgh, age 32, occ. mason, left sick at Puebla 7 Aug 47, died at Puebla 10 Sep 47.

HAINES, FREDERICK: (Hains): Pvt., enl. 24 Dec 46 at Greensburgh, age 18, occ. farmer, hospitalized at Mexico City according to Sep-Oct 47 MR, hospitalized at San Angel according to Jan-Feb 48 MR, mo. with Co. 14 Jul 48. Pvt. Co. H, 8th Kansas Vol. Inf. 20 Jan 62 to 24 Jan 65.

HANSBERRY, EDWARD: (Hansbery): Pvt., enl. 24 Dec 46 at Greensburgh, age 26, occ. weaver, hospitalized at Jalapa 28 Apr 47, rejoined Co. by 30 Jun 47, severely injured while on duty as advance guard before Mexico City 11 Sep 47 by a mortar carriage passing over both feet, hospitalized in Mexico City 19 Dec 47, disc. at Mexico City 5 Mar 48 on SCD for injuries.

HARTFORD, JAMES M.: Pvt., enl. 24 Dec 46 at Greensburgh, age 20, occ. school teacher, left sick at Vera Cruz 9 Apr 47, died in Vera Cruz Hospital 16 Apr 47 from consumption.

HARTMAN, GEORGE W.: Pvt., enl. 24 Dec 46 at Greensburgh, age 19, occ. tailor, mo. with Co. 14 Jul 48.

HAYS, JAMES: Pvt., enl. 24 Dec 46 at Greensburgh, age 24, occ. tailor, listed as sick on Sep-Oct 47 MR, mo. with Co. 14 Jul 48.

HEASLEY, MICHAEL: (Heasely): Pvt., enl. 24 Dec 46 at Greensburgh, age 25, occ. carpenter, left sick at Puebla 7 Aug 47, disc. at Puebla 5 Nov 47 on SCD, died upon his return home.

HOFFER, JACOB: Pvt., enl. 24 Dec 46 at Greensburgh, age 21, occ. tailor, hospitalized in Mexico City 19 Dec 47, sent to Jalapa Hospital 2 Apr 48, mo. with Co. 14 Jul 48.

HUSTON, ANDREW R.: Pvt., enl. 24 Dec 46 at Greensburgh, age 34, occ. painter, detailed as nurse to Vera Cruz Hospital 8 Mar 47 to date from 18 Feb 47, died in Vera Cruz Hospital 18 Jun 47.

JOHNSTON, JAMES: (Johnson, Johnstone): Pvt., enl. 24 Dec 46 at Greensburgh, age 27, occ. law student, appointed Q.M. Sgt. 7 Jan 47, disc. at Jalapa 22 May 47 on SCD.

JOHNSTON, JOHN W.: (Johnstone): Capt., enl. 24 Dec 46 at Greensburgh, age 26, left sick at Puebla 8 Aug 47, rejoined Co. 8 Dec 47, absent with leave during Mar 48, listed as sick in quarters during Apr 48, mo. with Co. 14 Jul 48. Col. 14th P.V.I. (3 mos.) 30 Apr 61 to 1 Aug 61. Lt. Col. 93rd P.V.I. 28 Oct 61 to 10 Jul 62. Died at Youngstown, Pa. 17 Dec 02. Was born 22 May 20.

JOHNSTON, RICHARD H. L.: Pvt., enl. 24 Dec 46 at Greensburgh, age 21, occ. laborer, appointed 2nd Lt. of Inf. in the Regular Army 5 Mar 47, assigned to 11th U.S. Inf. to date from 9 Apr 47, accepted the commission 25 Apr 47, KIA at Molino del Rey 8 Sep 47.

KEGARIZE, JACOB: (Kaganze, Kegarise): Pvt., enl. 24 Dec 46 at Greensburgh, age 22, occ. laborer, disc. at San Angel 28 Feb 48 on SCD for hernia.

KELLY, WILLIAM: (Kelley): Pvt., enl. 24 Dec 46 at Greensburgh, age 27, occ. blacksmith, left sick at Vera Cruz 9 Apr 47, disc. at Vera Cruz 19 May 47 on SCD.

KERR, JOHN: Pvt., enl. 24 Dec 46 at Greensburgh, age 26, occ. lawyer, died on ship *J. N. Cooper* 11 Mar 47 off Anton Lizardo.

KESLAR, HENRY: (Kestlar): Pvt., enl. 24 Dec 46 at Greensburgh, age 34, occ. turner, detailed as Co. commissary in Apr & May 48, mo. with Co. 14 Jul 48.

KETTERING, MICHAEL I.: Fifer, enl. 24 Dec 46 at Greensburgh, age 19, occ. tanner, mo. with Co. 14 Jul 48.

KUHN, JACOB: Pvt., enl. 24 Dec 46 at Greensburgh, age 23, occ. blacksmith, mo. with Co. 14 Jul 48.

KUHNS, DANIEL S.: Pvt., enl. 24 Dec 46 at Greensburgh, age 27, occ. printer, severely wounded in the left breast with a sword while walking in the streets of Mexico City 14 Sep 47, died in Mexico City Hospital 9 Dec 47 as a result of wound.

KUHNS, HENRY BYORS: 3rd Sgt., enl. 24 Dec 46 at Greensburgh, age 19, occ. law student, disc. at Vera Cruz 31 Mar 47 on SCD for chronic inflamation of the brain. Pvt. Co. K, 11th P.V.I. 1 Oct 61 to 15 Jun 65.

KUHNS, PHILIP: Pvt., enl. 24 Dec 46 at Greensburgh, age 23, occ. weaver, left sick at Puebla 7 Aug 47, disc. at Puebla 5 Nov 47 on SCD.

LANDON, EDMUND B.: (Laudon): Pvt., enl. 24 Dec 46 at Greensburgh, age 37, occ. teamster, left sick at Puebla 7 Aug 47, disc. at Puebla 5 Nov 47 on SCD.

LINSEBIGLER, JACOB: Pvt., enl. 24 Dec 46 at Greensburgh, age 19, occ. farmer, died at Mexico City Hospital 26 Sep 47 from general debility.

MARCHAND, HENRY C.: 1st Sgt., enl. 24 Dec 46 at Greensburgh, age 26, occ. lawyer, disc. at Vera Cruz 23 Apr 47 on SCD for fever and general debility.

John W. Johnston as Lieutenant Colonel, 93rd Pennsylvania in the Civil War
MOLLUS-Mass & USAMHI

MARCHAND, JACOB: Pvt., enl. 24 Dec 46 at Greensburgh, age 18, occ. tanner, mo. with Co. 14 Jul 48.

MARTZ, BENJAMIN: (Marts): Pvt., enl. 24 Dec 46 at Greensburgh, age 24, occ. painter, left sick at Vera Cruz 9 Apr 47, rejoined Co. 25 Jan 48, promoted to Drummer 1 May 48, mo. with Co. 14 Jul 48.

MAY, GEORGE: Pvt., enl. 24 Dec 46 at Greensburgh, age 27, occ. farmer, left sick at Vera Cruz 9 Apr 47, disc. at Vera Cruz 18 May 47 on SCD, died at Vera Cruz 19 May 47 from diarrhea.

McCABE, PETER: Pvt., enl. 24 Dec 46 at Greensburgh, age 21, occ. shoemaker, mo. with Co. 14 Jul 48.

McCLANEN, SAMUEL: (McClarren, McLarren): Pvt., enl. 24 Dec 46 at Greensburgh, age 27, occ. farmer, left sick at Puebla 7 Aug 47, rejoined Co. 8 Dec 47, mo. with Co. 14 Jul 48.

McCLELLAN, RICHARD: (McClelland, McLelland): Pvt., enl. 24 Dec 46 at Greensburgh, age 19, occ. laborer, WIA severely in the foot by a musket ball at Garita de Belen 13 Sep 47, hospitalized in Mexico City 19 Dec 47, disc. at Mexico City 5 Mar 48 on SCD for wounds.

McCOLLUM, JOHN: Pvt., enl. 24 Dec 46 at Greensburgh, age 22, occ. teamster, left sick at Perote 22 Jun 47, died at Perote 10 Aug 47.

McCREDIN, EDWARD: (McCreden, McCroden): Pvt., enl. 24 Dec 46 at Greensburgh, age 38, occ. plasterer, left sick at Vera Cruz 9 Apr 47, disc. at Vera Cruz 19 May 47 on SCD, died upon reaching home.

McCUTCHEON, DAVID R.: (McCulchen, McCutchen): Pvt., enl. 24 Dec 46 at Greensburgh, age 19, occ. saddler, left sick at Vera Cruz 9 Apr 47, rejoined Co. 9 Dec 47, mo. with Co. 14 Jul 48.

McDERMOTT, JAMES H.: (McDermot): Pvt., enl. 24 Dec 46 at Greensburgh, age 21, occ. blacksmith, deserted at New Orleans 27 Jan 47, died at New Orleans.

McGARVEY, CHARLES: Pvt., enl. 24 Dec 46 at Greensburgh, age 24, occ. furnace keeper, left sick at Vera Cruz 9 Apr 47, rejoined Co. 9 Dec 47, mo. with Co. 14 Jul 48.

McGINLEY, ROBERT C.: Pvt., enl. 24 Dec 46 at Greensburgh, age 24, occ. lawyer, promoted to 1st Cpl. 25 May 47, died in Mexico City Hospital 3 Oct 47.

McINTIRE, WILLIAM: Pvt., enl. 24 Dec 46 at Greensburgh, age 28, occ. saddler, disc. at Camp Washington near Vera Cruz 31 Mar 47 on SCD for hepatization of the lungs and general debility.

McLANE, AMON: (McClain): Pvt., enl. 24 Dec 46 at Greensburgh, age 23, occ. cooper, mo. with Co. 14 Jul 48.

McLAUGHLIN, JAMES M.: 4th Sgt., enl. 24 Dec 46 at Greensburgh, age 20, occ. law student, listed as sick on Jan-Feb 47 MR, promoted to 2nd Sgt. 21 Apr 47, on detached duty as forage master for U.S. Quartermaster Montgomery 27 Oct 47 through Nov 47, on furlough from Dec 47, arrived home 25 Dec 47, disc. at Greensburgh, Pa. 14 Jan 48 on SCD, died at his father's home in Greensburgh 30 Mar 48.

McWILLIAMS, JAMES: Pvt., enl. 24 Dec 46 at Greensburgh, age 22, occ. farmer, listed as sick on Mar-Apr 47 MR, mo. with Co. 14 Jul 48.

McWILLIAMS, WILLIAM: Pvt., enl. 24 Dec 46 at Greensburgh, age 30, occ. carpenter, mo. with Co. 14 Jul 48.

MECHLING, DAVID: (Mechlin): Pvt., enl. 24 Dec 46 at Greensburgh, age 27, occ. farmer, promoted to 3rd Sgt. 31 Mar 47, WIA before Mexico City 13 Sep 47, promoted to 2nd Lt. 1 May 48 to rank from 15 Jun 47, mo. with Co. 14 Jul 48.

MELLVILLE, WILLIAM H.: (Melville): Pvt., enl. 24 Dec 46 at Greensburgh, age 36, occ. painter, died at San Augustin Hospital 3 Sep 47 from dysentery.

MILLER, JACOB P.: Pvt., enl. 24 Dec 46 at Greensburgh, age 27, occ. farmer, seriously WIA in the thigh by a musket ball at Cerro Gordo 18 Apr 47, hospitalized at Jalapa 18 Apr 47, disc. at Jalapa 7 Jun 47 on SCD for wound.

MILNER, SAMUEL: (Milnor): Pvt., enl. 24 Dec 46 at Greensburgh, age 28, occ. blacksmith, missing in Mexico City from 1 Dec 47 and presumed to have been killed.

MONTGOMERY, SAMUEL HAYS: Pvt., enl. 24 Dec 46 at Greensburgh, age 36, occ. clerk, commissioned Asst. Q.M. U.S. Army with the rank of Capt. 5 Jan 47 to rank from 4 Jan 47, accepted the commission 9 Jan 47, dismissed 25 Feb 48, reinstated as Capt. A.Q.M. of Vols. 27 Jun 48, disc. 15 Oct 48. Appointed Military Store Keeper Q.M.D. 14 Mar 57. Died 15 Jun 64.

MOREHEAD, SAMUEL C.: (Moorehead, Moorhead): Pvt., enl. 24 Dec 46 at Greensburgh, age 26, occ. farmer, mo. with Co. 14 Jul 48. Pvt. Co. G, 2nd California Vol. Inf. 11 Nov 61 to 11 Nov 64.

MURRY, WASHINGTON: (Murray, Murrey): 2nd Lt., enl. 24 Dec 46 at Greensburgh, age 29, occ. lawyer, appointed Acting Commissary of Subsistence 15 Apr 47, on leave of absence from 24 May 47, disc. on SCD to be effective 15 Jun 47, died on his way home. His remains were buried in Westmoreland County.

MYERS, LEWIS: Pvt., enl. 24 Dec 46 at Greensburgh, age 21, occ. bricklayer, died at Vera Cruz Hospital 10 Apr 47.

PEASE, JONATHAN: Pvt., enl. 24 Dec 46 at Greensburgh, age 19, occ. coach maker, left sick at New Orleans 29 Jan 47, disc. at New Orleans date unknown.

RAGER, JAMES: (Roger): Pvt., enl. 24 Dec 46 at Greensburgh, age 23, occ. farmer, hospitalized at Jalapa 28 Apr 47, rejoined Co. by 30 Jun 47, left sick at Puebla 7 Aug 47, disc. at Puebla 5 Nov 47 on SCD.

REXROAD, FREDERICK: (Rexrode): Pvt., enl. 24 Dec 46 at Greensburgh, age 19, occ. boatman, hospitalized at Jalapa 28 Apr 47, disc. at Jalapa 19 May 47 on SCD for diarrhea and cough.

ROSS, ANDREW: 2nd Cpl., enl. 24 Dec 46 at Greensburgh, age 29, occ. lawyer, appointed 2nd Lt. of Infantry in the Regular Army 5 Mar 47, assigned to 11th U.S. Inf. to rank from 9 Apr 47, left Vera Cruz for furlough and died on his way home while crossing the Gulf of Mexico in May 47, buried at sea.

SARGEANT, CHAUNCEY F.: (Sargant, Sargent, Sergeant): Pvt., enl. 24 Dec 46 at Greensburgh, age 18, occ. printer, severely WIA through the wrist and in the thigh by musket balls at Chapultepec 13 Sep 47, rejoined Co. by 29 Feb 48, mo. with Co. 14 Jul 48.

SHAW, JOSEPH: Pvt., enl. 24 Dec 46 at Greensburgh, age 19, occ. laborer, listed as sick on Sep-Oct 47 MR, hospitalized in Mexico City from 19 Dec 47, died in Mexico City Hospital 17 Jan 48.

SHIELDS, WILLIAM R.: Pvt., enl. 24 Dec 46 at Greensburgh, age 29, occ. school teacher, promoted to 2nd Cpl. 21 Apr 47, left sick at Puebla 7 Aug 47, rejoined Co. 8 Dec 47, promoted to 4th Sgt. 1 May 48, mo. with Co. 14 Jul 48.

SIMMS, THOMAS: 4th Cpl., enl. 1 Jan 47 at Pittsburgh, age 23, occ. wagoner, left sick at Puebla 7 Aug 47, died at Puebla 9 Sep 47.

SMITH, JOSEPH: Pvt., enl. 24 Dec 46 at Greensburgh, age 21, occ. blacksmith, left sick at Puebla 7 Aug 47, rejoined Co. 7 Dec 47, mo. with Co. 14 Jul 48.

SPEARS, THOMAS: (Speers): Pvt., enl. 24 Dec 46 at Greensburgh, age 19, occ. carpenter, died on board ship *J. N. Cooper* 16 Mar 47 off Anton Lizardo.

STECK, FREDERICK D.: (Steek): Pvt., enl. 24 Dec 46 at Greensburgh, age 19, occ. butcher, promoted to 4th Cpl. 1 Mar 48, mo. with Co. 14 Jul 48.

STICHLE, HENRY: (Stickel, Stickle): Pvt., enl. 24 Dec 46 at Greensburgh, age 22, occ. laborer, left sick at Puebla 7 Aug 47, rejoined Co. 7 Dec 47, on duty as Co. cook in Apr & May 48, mo. with Co. 14 Jul 48.

TAYLOR, JOHN: Pvt., enl. 24 Dec 46 at Greensburgh, age 27, occ. tailor, left sick at New Orleans 29 Jan 47, disc. at New Orleans date unknown.

THOMAS, NATHANIEL: Pvt., enl. 24 Dec 46 at Greensburgh, age 19, occ. farmer, left sick at Puebla 7 Aug 47, died at Puebla 7 Sep 47.

UNCAPHER, ISRAEL: Pvt., enl. 24 Dec 46 at Greensburgh, age 23, occ. tanner & currier & lawyer, appointed Acting Ordnance Sgt. 28 Oct 47, appointed Acting Commissary Sgt. 1 Nov 47, served as clerk for Col. Geary in Mar 48, was Acting Ordnance Sgt. in Apr 48, promoted to Cpl. 1 May 48, mo. with Co. 14 Jul 48. 1st Lt. Co. F & Adjutant 11th P.V.I. 25 Oct 61 to 28 Nov 62. Born 10 Jan 24 & died 17 Feb 75.

This portrait is believed to be of Israel Uncapher while a First Lieutenant in the
11th Pennsylvania during the Civil War
*Division of Archives and Manuscripts,
Pennsylvania Historical and Museum Commission*

UNDERWOOD, JAMES: Pvt., enl. 24 Dec 46 at Greensburgh, age 22, occ. plasterer, left sick at Puebla 7 Aug 47, rejoined Co. 7 Dec 47, mo. with Co. 14 Jul 48.

WATERS, SAMUEL: (Watters): Pvt., enl. 24 Dec 46 at Greensburgh, age 20, occ. butcher, left sick at Puebla 7 Aug 47, rejoined Co. probably 7 Dec 47, mo. with Co. 14 Jul 48.

WENTZ, WILLIAM R.: (Wartz): Pvt., enl. 24 Dec 46 at Greensburgh, age 25, occ. farmer, died in quarters at Jalapa 15 May 47 from diarrhea.

WISE, JACOB T. (I.): Pvt., enl. 24 Dec 46 at Greensburgh, age 18, occ. laborer, left sick at Vera Cruz 9 Apr 47, rejoined Co. on the march home, mo. with Co. 14 Jul 48. Served in Co. C, 1st U.S. Sharp Shooters in the Civil War, when he enlisted from Michigan.

Company F, 2nd Regiment
Philadelphia Rangers

The Philadelphia Rangers are believed to have been active prior to the Mexican War. They were quick to respond to the government's first call for troops, and Captain Charles Naylor was given reason to believe his company would be in the state's first regiment. The Rangers were ready, but circumstances found them to be the eleventh company in a ten company regiment.

The Rangers were the first company accepted for service in the 2nd Regiment, and left Philadelphia on 14 December 1846. They were mustered into Federal service at Pittsburgh on 22 December by First Lieutenant Horace B. Field of the 3rd U.S. Artillery.

Captain Naylor's Rangers participated in the investment of Vera Cruz and the battles of Cerro Gordo, Chapultepec and Garita de Belen. The company spent the last eight months of their time in Mexico garrisoning the Mexico City area.

The Rangers returned to Pittsburgh where they were mustered out on 15 July 1848 by Major George Wright, 4th U.S. Infantry. They did not return home to Philadelphia until the other companies from that city had enjoyed the great festivities arranged for the returning veterans, thus their celebration paled in comparison to that of their predecessors.

A total of 101 men served in the company during the war, including one recruit who joined it in Mexico. Fourteen men deserted the colors. Fifteen men suffered battle related injuries, three of them dying as a result. In all, twenty-one Rangers died in service, and an additional thirteen received discharges before muster out.

ARESON, JOHN: (Aareson, Arison, Arrison): Pvt., enl. 1 Dec 46 at Phila., age 25, WIA at Chapultepec 13 Sep 47, promoted to 4th Cpl. 1 Feb 48, mo. with Co. 15 Jul 48. 1st Lt. Co. H, 20th P.V.I. (3 mos.) 30 Apr 61 to 6 Aug 61. Pvt. Co. B, Q.M. Sgt. & 2nd Lt. Co. B, 99th P.V.I. 28 Feb 62 to 1 Jul 65.

BARNES, WILLIAM H. T.: Pvt., enl. 1 Dec 46 at Phila., age 28, occ. preacher, transferred to the New York Regt. at Lobos Island 9 Mar 47 in exchange for Pvt. John Wheeler by order of Maj. Gen. Patterson.

BEATTY, SAMUEL H.: (Beaty): Pvt., enl. 1 Dec 46 at Phila., age 26, left sick at Vera Cruz 8 Apr 47, rejoined Co. 25 Jan 48, mo. with Co. 15 Jul 48.

BECHTEL, JOHN: (Bechtol): Pvt., enl. 1 Dec 46 at Phila., age 43, WIA at Gareta de Belen 13 Sep 47, listed as present sick through 30 Apr 48, mo. with Co. 15 Jul 48.

BECKETT, FRANCIS M.: Pvt., enl. 1 Dec 46 at Phila., age 21, left sick at Puebla 8 Aug 47, died at Puebla before 31 Dec 47 (date unknown), owing the sutler I. Dewney $4.08.

BELSTERLING, JOHN I. (J.): Pvt., enl. 1 Dec 46 at Phila., age 22, listed as present sick on Sep-Oct 47 MR, mo. with Co. 15 Jul 48. Capt. Co. C, 88th P.V.I. 13 Sep 61 until KIA at Second Bull Run 30 Aug 62.

BINGHAM, GEORGE: Pvt., enl. 1 Dec 46 at Phila., age 24, mo. with Co. 15 Jul 48. Pvt. Co. L, 2nd California Cav. 21 Jan 62 until transferred 1 Jul 62.

BLACK, DAVID: Pvt., enl. 1 Dec 46 at Phila., age 22, listed as sick on Sep-Oct 47 MR, mo. with Co. 15 Jul 48.

BOYD, EDWARD L.: Pvt., enl. 1 Dec 46 at Phila., age 19, disc. at Vera Cruz 7 Apr 47 on SCD.

BRIEST, LEWIS S.: Pvt., enl. 1 Dec 46 at Phila., age 30, hospitalized at Jalapa 29 Apr 47, left sick at Perote 27 Jun 47, disc. at Perote 29 Oct 47 on SCD.

BRUTCHE, GEORGE: Pvt., enl. 1 Dec 46 at Phila., age 21, left sick at Puebla 8 Aug 47, KIA at the siege of Puebla.

CAMPBELL, JOHN M.: Pvt., enl. 22 Dec 46 at Pittsburgh, age 23, deserted at New Orleans 27 Jan 47.

CAPEHART, DANIEL K.: (Cupehart): Pvt., enl. 1 Dec 46 at Phila., age 24, WIA in the leg at Garita de Belen 13 Sep 47 & hospitalized in Mexico City, listed as sick on Mar-Apr 48 MR, mo. with Co. 15 Jul 48.

CAREY, JOHN P.: (Carie): Pvt., enl. 1 Dec 46 at Phila., age 25, mo. with Co. 15 Jul 48. Capt. Co. I, 91st P.V.I. 10 Sep 61 to 10 Feb 63.

CHAMBERLIN, DANIEL (Donald): (Chamberlain): Pvt., enl. 1 Dec 46 at Phila., age 35, left sick at Puebla 8 Aug 47, died at Puebla in 1847.

CHAMBERS, JOHN: Pvt., enl. 1 Dec 46 at Phila., age 24, severely WIA in the back by a musket ball at Cerro Gordo 18 Apr 47 & hospitalized at Jalapa, rejoined Co. by 31 Aug 47, listed as under arrest on Sep-Oct 47 MR, mo. with Co. 15 Jul 48.

CHIPPEY, SAMUEL: (Chippy): Pvt., enl. 1 Dec 46 at Phila., age 35, mo. with Co. 15 Jul 48.

CHURCH, JOHN C.: Pvt., enl. 1 Dec 46 at Phila., age 23, was sick in Dec 46, listed as sick on Sep-Oct 47 MR, mo. with Co. 15 Jul 48.

CRUSE, EDWARD: (Cruze, Kruse): Pvt., enl. 1 Dec 46 at Phila., age 21, severely WIA in the back by a musket ball at Cerro Gordo 18 Apr 47 & hospitalized at Jalapa, as of 30 Apr 47 the ball was still in the wound, left sick at Perote 28 Jun 47, listed as AWOL on Jul-Aug 47 MR, listed as sick on Sep-Oct 47 MR, hospitalized at Mexico City according to Nov-Dec 47 & Jan-Feb 48 MRs, was AWOL from the hospital in Feb 48, rejoined Co. from the hospital 12 Apr 48, mo. with Co. 15 Jul 48.

CURRY, GEORGE W. (Washington): Pvt., enl. 1 Dec 46 at Phila., age 31, deserted at New Orleans 27 Jan 47.

DECKER, SIDNEY H.: Pvt., enl. 1 Dec 46 at Phila., age 23, deserted at New Orleans 27 Jan 47.

DUBACEE, JOHN M.: (Dubesee, Dubisee): Pvt., enl. 1 Dec 46 at Phila., age 28, deserted at New Orleans 27 Jan 47, apprehended 25 Apr 48, disc. at Ft. Mifflin 10 Jun 48 by order of the Adjutant General.

DUBACEE, JOSEPH: (Dubasee, Dubsey): Pvt., enl. 1 Dec 46 at Phila., age 26, listed as sick on Sep-Oct 47 MR, mo. with Co. 15 Jul 48.

DUTTON, BENJAMIN F.: 1st Lt., enl. 1 Dec 46 at Phila., age 30, appointed Adjutant 7 Jan 47, left Jalapa for recruiting duty 8 Jun 47, was recruiting in the State Fencibles' armory in Phila. by 27 Jul 47, rejoined Regt. 28 Dec 47, he was involved in a bank robbery and murder in Mexico City 4 Apr 48, removed from the post of Adjutant by Col. Geary 6 Apr 48, was in confinement according to Mar-Apr 48 MR, his sentence (hanging) was read to the troops 19 May 48, was reprieved, mo. with F & S 21 Jul 48.

EVANS, CHARLES: Pvt., enl. 1 Dec 46 at Phila., age 26, died at Perote 30 Jun 47 from diarrhea.

EVANS, EDWARD S.: Cpl., enl. 1 Dec 46 at Phila., listed as sick on Sep-Oct 47 MR, mo. with Co. 15 Jul 48. Died suddenly in his home 27 Jul 48.

FIELDS, JOHN: Pvt., enl. 1 Dec 46 at Phila., age 35, detailed as Attendant in regimental hospital from 16 Sep 47, rejoined Co. by 31 Dec 47, mo. with Co. 15 Jul 48.

FORCE, HENRY: Pvt., enl. 1 Dec 46 at Phila., age 29, left sick at Puebla 8 Aug 47, died at Puebla date unknown.

FORTINER, JOSEPH B.: Cpl., enl. 1 Dec 46 at Phila., age 22, promoted to 2nd Sgt. 18 May 47, promoted to 1st Sgt. 14 Aug 47, commanding Co. from Jan to Mar 48, mo. with Co. 15 Jul 48.

FOSTER, PETER: (Forster): Pvt., enl. 1 Dec 46 at Phila., age 27, promoted to Cpl. 1 Nov 47, mo. with Co. 15 Jul 48.

FOX, JOHN C.: Fifer, enl. 1 Dec 46 at Phila., age 21, listed as sick on Nov-Dec 47 MR, hospitalized according to Mar-Apr 48 MR, mo. with Co. 15 Jul 48.

GEDDES, EDWARD D.: Pvt., enl. 1 Dec 46 at Phila., age 26, deserted at Pittsburgh 8 Jan 47.

GILMORE, DAVID R.: (Gilmer): Pvt., enl. 1 Dec 46 at Phila., age 20, left sick at Puebla 8 Aug 47, disc. at Puebla date unknown.

HAMMITT, JOHN: Pvt., enl. 1 Dec 46 at Phila., age 40, died at U.S. Barracks below New Orleans 19 Jan 47.

HANN, THOMAS (Jacob): (Hand): Pvt., enl. 1 Dec 46 at Phila., age 35, severely WIA in the left shoulder by a musket ball or cannister shot at Cerro Gordo 18 Apr 47 & hospitalized at Jalapa, left sick at Perote 27 Jun 47, disc. at Perote 30 Oct 47 on SCD for wound.

HARE, ISAAC P.: 2nd Lt., enl. 1 Dec 46 at Phila., age 24, was sick in Mexico City in Mar 48, wounded in the arm and arrested during a bank robbery & murder in which he participated 4 Apr 48, confined in Mexico City, his sentence to hang was read to the troops 19 May 48, was reprieved, no record of disc.

HARTLEY, JOHN: (Heartley): Pvt., enl. 1 Dec 46 at Phila., age 21, left sick at Puebla 8 Aug 47, rejoined Co. by 31 Dec 47, mo. with Co. 15 Jul 48.

HIGH, ABRAHAM G.: Pvt., enl. 1 Dec 46 at Phila., age 29, promoted to Cpl. 8 Jul 47, disc. at Mexico City 27 Oct 47 on SCD, died and was buried in Phila. 1 Mar 48.

HOLMES, OLIVER: Pvt., enl. 1 Dec 46 at Phila., age 40, listed as doing hospital attendant duty on Mar-Apr 47 MR, serving as Hospital Steward from 1 Jun 47, on detached duty as Asst. Surgeon from 1 Oct 47, rejoined Co. by 31 Dec 47, mo. with Co. 15 Jul 48.

HUGHES, JAMES R.: Pvt., enl. 1 Dec 46 at Phila., age 21, promoted to Cpl. 18 May 47, reduced to Pvt. 8 Jul 47, on detached duty for Gen. Quitman according to Jul-Aug & Sep-Oct 47 MRs, on three months furlough from 1 Nov 47, disc. at Phila. before 29 Feb 48 on SCD.

ILLINGSWORTH, CALDER: Pvt., enl. 1 Dec 46 at Phila., age 22, left sick at Jalapa 28 Apr 47, died at Jalapa 20 May 47.

JACKSON, JOSEPH L.: Cpl., enl. 1 Dec 46 at Phila., age 23, disc. at Perote 23 Jun 47 on SCD.

JEFFREYS, ROBERT: (Jefreys): Pvt., enl. 1 Dec 46 at Phila., age 24, left Co. at Camp Washington near Vera Cruz 28 Mar 47 with a scouting party and he is believed killed by the enemy.

KAUFFMAN, ABRAHAM B. (G.): (Kaufman): Pvt., enl. 1 Dec 46 at Phila., age 24, mo. with Co. 15 Jul 48.

KEESEY, JOSEPH: Pvt., enl. 1 Dec 46 at Phila., age 22, left sick at Puebla 8 Aug 47, rejoined Co. by 31 Dec 47, mo. with Co. 15 Jul 48.

KELLY, JAMES: Pvt., enl. 1 Dec 46 at Phila., age 21, deserted at New Orleans 27 Jan 47.

KNOX, THOMAS I.: Pvt., enl. 1 Dec 46 at Phila., age 22, deserted at Pittsburgh 8 Jan 47.

KOPLIN, JUSTICE: Pvt., enl. 1 Dec 46 at Phila., age 26, left sick at Puebla 8 Aug 47, died at Puebla date unknown.

KUHN, JAMES G.: Pvt., enl. 1 Dec 46 at Phila., age 26, listed as sick on Jan-Feb 47 MR, serving as Col. Roberts' hostler according to Jul-Aug 47 MR, hospitalized at San Angel according to Mar-Apr 48 MR, mo. with Co. 15 Jul 48.

LANCASTER, WILLIAM: Pvt., enl. 1 Dec 46 at Phila., age 22, left sick at Puebla 8 Aug 47, rejoined Co. by 31 Dec 47, mo. with Co. 15 Jul 48.

LOGUE, WILLIAM HENRY: Pvt., enl. 1 Dec 46 at Phila., age 21, promoted to Cpl. 8 Jul 47, WIA at Chapultepec 13 Sep 47, hospitalized in Mexico City according to Jan-Feb 48 MR, mo. with Co. 15 Jul 48.

LUTZ, HENRY: Pvt., enl. 1 Dec 46 at Phila., age 23, mo. with Co. 15 Jul 48.

MAJOR, SAMUEL E.: Pvt., enl. 1 Dec 46 at Phila., age 24, WIA before Mexico City 13 Sep 47, detached to regimental band according to Jan-Feb 48 MR, mo. with Co. 15 Jul 48.

McCRACKEN, JAMES: Pvt., enl. 1 Dec 46 at Phila., age 43, promoted to Cpl. 18 May 47, died in Mexico City 8 Oct 47.

MERCER, ARCHIBALD: Pvt., enl. 1 Dec 46 at Phila., age 34, listed as hospital attendant on Mar-Apr 47 MR, left sick at Perote 27 Jun 47, disc. at Perote date unknown.

MILLER, GEORGE W.: Pvt., enl. 1 Dec 46 at Phila, age 22, KIA at Vera Cruz 28 Mar 47 when the Mexicans ambushed a scouting party he was with.

MOORE, HENRY S. (L.): (More): Drummer, age 28, transferred from 1st Massachusetts Regt. 1 Mar 48 in place of Drummer George M. Newell, no record of mo.

MORRIS, ELIAS: Pvt., enl. 1 Dec 46 at Phila., age 22, disc. at Jalapa 7 Jun 47 on SCD.

NAYLOR, CHARLES: Capt., enl. 1 Dec 46 at Phila., age 38, was sick in Jun & Jul 47, detached as Superintendent of the National Palace in Mexico City from Nov 47 through Apr 48, disc. 3 Aug 48. Died 24 Dec 72 & is buried in Laurel Hill Cemetery in Phila.

NEWELL, GEORGE M. (W.): (Neuell, Newal): Sgt., enl. 1 Dec 46 at Phila., age 26, appointed Drummer 8 Jan 47, appointed Drum Major 1 Mar 47, reduced to Co. Drummer 10 Jul 47, transferred to 1st Massachusetts Regt. 1 Mar 48 in trade for Drummer Henry S. Moore.

NICOLETTE, FRANCIS: (Nicoletti): Pvt., enl. 1 Dec 46 at Phila., age 32, detached to Well's Battery of the 3rd U.S. Artillery 25 Apr 47, rejoined Co. in May 47, missing at Mexico City since 18 Sep 47 & presumed murdered.

PETERS, HENRY: Pvt., enl. 1 Dec 46 at Phila., age 22, left sick at Perote 28 Jun 47, died at Perote 1 Jul 47 from diarrhea.

POTTS, THOMAS W.: Pvt., enl. & mi. 28 Jan 47 at New Orleans, deserted at New Orleans 28 Jan 47.

POWER, JOSEPH: (Powers): Pvt., enl. 1 Dec 46 at Phila., age 31, promoted to Sgt. 1 Nov 47, mo. with Co. 15 Jul 48.

PRINCE, LYSANDER (Lycinder): Pvt., enl. 1 Dec 46 at Phila., age 31, occ. mechanist, left as nurse in the hospital at Perote 27 Jun 47, disc. at Vera Cruz 28 Jan 48 on SCD for injury to his Achilles Tendon.

RANDOLPH, EDWARD F.: Pvt., enl. & mi. 28 Jan 47 at New Orleans, deserted at New Orleans 28 Jan 47.

REHR, WILLIAM F.: (Reeher): Pvt., enl. 1 Dec 46 at Phila., age 28, was sick from mi., died at Pittsburgh 11 Jan 47.

RICE, WILLIAM: Pvt., enl. 1 Dec 46 at Phila., age 43, WIA at Chapultepec 13 Sep 47, disc. at Mexico City 30 Oct 47 on SCD for wounds, died from disease on his way home, buried in Phila.

RODGERS, WILLIAM R.: Pvt., enl. 1 Dec 46 at Phila., age 43, left sick at Dr. Lusonberg's Hospital in New Orleans in Jan 47, rejoined Co. by 30 Apr 47, left sick at Puebla 8 Aug 47, died at Puebla date unknown.

SAMPLE, JAMES T.: Pvt., enl. 22 Dec 46 at Pittsburgh, age 25, listed as sick on Jan-Feb 47 MR, WIA in the right leg at Chapultepec 13 Sep 47, the leg was amputated, disc. at Mexico City 28 Feb 48 on SCD for wounds.

SCOTT, JOHN: Pvt., enl. 1 Dec 46 at Phila., age 24, mo. with Co. 15 Jul 48.

SHARP, JOSEPH: Pvt., enl. 1 Dec 46 at Phila., age 39, left sick at Dr. Lusonberg's Hospital in New Orleans in Jan 47, rejoined Co. by 30 Apr 47, died at Perote 22 Jun 47 from fever.

SHERIDAN, JAMES: Pvt., enl. 1 Dec 46 at Phila., age 35, was AWOL according to Jul-Aug 47 MR, listed as sick on Sep-Oct 47 MR, mo. with Co. 15 Jul 48.

SILCOX, MARK: Pvt., enl. 1 Dec 46 at Phila., age 22, left sick at Vera Cruz 8 Apr 47, listed as under arrest on Jul-Aug 47 MR, listed as sick on Sep-Oct 47 MR, mo. with Co. 15 Jul 48.

SIMONS, JACOB B.: Pvt., enl. 1 Dec 46 at Phila., age 22, severely WIA in the left breast by a musket or canister ball at Cerro Gordo 18 Apr 47, left sick at Perote 27 Jun 47, disc. at Perote 29 Oct 47 on SCD for wounds.

SIMONS, JAMES: Pvt., enl. 1 Dec 46 at Phila., age 19, hospitalized at Mexico City according to Nov-Dec 47 MR, mo. with Co. 15 Jul 48.

SLOAN, BENJAMIN: Pvt., enl. 1 Dec 46 at Phila., age 36, deserted at New Orleans 27 Jan 47.

SMITH, DANIEL R.: Pvt., enl. 1 Dec 46 at Phila., age 25, promoted to Cpl. 1 Nov 47, detached to regimental band according to Jan-Feb 48 MR, mo. with Co. 15 Jul 48.

SMITH, JOSEPH: Pvt., enl. 1 Dec 46 at Phila., age 21, died at Jalapa 16 Jun 47.

SMITH, SAMUEL B.: Pvt., enl. 1 Dec 46 at Phila., age 29, deserted at Pittsburgh 3 or 8 Jan 47 or at New Orleans 27 Jan 47.

SPEAR, MATTHIAS: Sgt., enl. 1 Dec 46 at Phila., age 33, mo. with Co. 15 Jul 48.

SPERRY, JACOB F.: 2nd Lt., enl. 1 Dec 46 at Phila., age 23, submitted his resignation at Puebla 5 Aug 47, it was accepted by Gen. Scott 7 Aug 47 & he was disc. that day, KIA at Puebla by guerrillas 26 Aug 47.

SPRINGER, ANDREW M.: Cpl., enl. 1 Dec 46 at Phila., age 36, deserted at New Orleans 27 Jan 47.

STROUD, ROBERT P.: Pvt., enl. 1 Dec 46 at Phila., age 22, listed as sick on Sep-Oct 47 MR, fined 6 months pay and confined at Chapultepec by Court Martial 18 Jan 48, mo. with Co. 15 Jul 48.

TAPPER, CHARLES M.: Sgt., enl. 1 Dec 46 at Phila., age 28, listed as sick on Nov-Dec 47 MR, hospitalized at Mexico City according to Jan-Feb 48 MR, mo. with Co. 15 Jul 48.

THAWLEY, THOMAS: (Thawly, Thorley): Pvt., enl. 1 Dec 46 at Phila., age 26, listed as sick on Sep-Oct 47 MR, hospitalized in Mexico City according to Jan-Feb 48 MR, rejoined Co. 26 Apr 48, mo. with Co. 15 Jul 48.

THOMPSON, RICHARD: Pvt., enl. 1 Dec 46 at Phila., age 21, deserted at New Orleans 27 Jan 47.

TOURISON, ASHTON S.: Drummer, enl. 1 Dec 46 at Phila., age 34, promoted to 2nd Sgt. 8 Jan 47, promoted to 1st Sgt. 18 May 47, promoted to 2nd Lt. 14 Aug 47, WIA in the leg at Garita de Belen 13 Sep 47, on four months furlough from 12 Jan 48 and assigned to do recruiting while at home, not mo. with Co. but disc. as of 20 Jul 48. Capt. Co. P, 28th P.V.I. 26 Sep 61 to 28 Oct 62. Capt. Co. E, 147th P.V.I. 28 Oct 62 to 5 Aug 63. Capt. Veteran Reserve Corps 5 Aug 63 to 28 Aug 63.

UNGER, DAVID J. (I.): 2nd Lt., enl. 6 Dec 46 at Harrisburg, age 24, occ. merchant, assigned to command Co. F from Co. G 7 Apr 48, mo. with Co. G 20 Jul 48.

WALLACE, EDMUND: Pvt., enl. 1 Dec 46 at Phila., age 21, mo. with Co. 15 Jul 48.

WALLACE, THOMAS: Pvt., enl. & mi. 7 Apr 47 at Vera Cruz, age 27, under arrest according to Sep-Oct 47 MR, mo. with Co. 15 Jul 48.

WARNER, JOHN: Pvt., enl. 1 Dec 46 at Phila., age 22, listed as sick on Jan-Feb 47 MR, died at Perote 28 Jun 47.

WEAVER, GEORGE W.: Pvt., enl. 1 Dec 46 at Phila., age 30, under arrest according to Mar-Apr 47 MR, left sick at Perote 27 Jun 47, later served as Hospital Steward at Perote, rejoined Co. for the march home, died aboard ship on the Gulf of Mexico 23 Jun 48.

WEAVER, MICHAEL: Pvt., enl. 1 Dec 46 at Phila., age 27, listed as sick on Sep-Oct 47 MR, detached to regimental band according to Jan-Feb 48 MR, mo. with Co. 15 Jul 48.

WHEELER, JOHN: Pvt., transferred from the 1st New York Regt. 9 Mar 47 in exchange for Pvt. William H. T. Barnes to date from 1 Mar 47, died at Jalapa Hospital 27 Jun 47.

WHITE, GEORGE W.: (Wite): Pvt., enl. 1 Dec 46 at Phila., age 21, occ. coach maker, promoted to Cpl. 16 Feb 47, reduced to Pvt. 8 Jul 47, transferred to Co. K, 2nd Pa. Regt. 1 Sep 47 at San Augustin in exchange for Pvt. John B. Wier.

WIER, JOHN B. (U.): (Weir): Pvt., enl. 20 Dec 46 at Mauch Chunk, age 26, occ. printer, transferred from Co. K, 2nd Pa. Regt. at San Augustin 31 Aug 47 in exchange for Pvt. George W. White, detached to printing office in Mexico City according to Sep-Oct 47 & Nov-Dec 47 MRs, was AWOL for 10 days according to Jan-Feb 48 MR, mo. with Co. 15 Jul 48.

WILLETTS, PETER H.: (Willets, Willits, Willitts): 1st Sgt., enl. 1 Dec 46 at Phila., age 30, wounded in the right hand losing his forefinger and having his hand shattered when his musket accidently discharged while drawing his load at Camp Washington near Vera Cruz 15 Mar 47, disc. at Jalapa 18 May 47 on SCD for wounds. Capt. Co. C, 72nd P.V.I. 10 Aug 61 until KIA at Antietam 17 Sep 62.

WOODMANCY, WASHINGTON: (Woodmansee, Woodmansie): Pvt., enl. 1 Dec 46 at Phila., age 22, listed as sick on Sep-Oct 47 MR, mo. with Co. 15 Jul 48.

WYKOFF, WILLIAM: Pvt., enl. 1 Dec 46 at Phila., age 22, was AWOL in Mexico City according to Nov-Dec 47 MR, mo. with Co. 15 Jul 48.

YOUNG, THOMAS: Pvt., enl. 1 Dec 46 at Phila., age 21, listed as sick on Sep-Oct 47 MR, in confinement according to Jan-Feb 48 MR, deserted from San Angel 9 Mar 48.

Company G, 2nd Regiment
Cameron Guards

The Cameron Guards were recruited and organized by Captain Edward C. Williams in Harrisburg specifically for service in the war with Mexico. They were named for Senator Simon Cameron. Through close contacts with political and military leaders in the state, Captain Williams was able to have the Guards accepted to serve with the 2nd Regiment.

The company left Harrisburg on 26 December and was mustered into federal service at Pittsburgh on 2 January by First Lieutenant Horace B. Field, 3rd U.S. Artillery.

Because they were quarantined for smallpox, with Companies B and D, the Guards didn't join the regiment until 23 April 1847. They then participated in the battles of La Hoya, Chapultepec and Garita de Belen. The company was mustered out at Pittsburgh by Major George Wright, 4th U.S. Infantry, on 20 July 1848. They reached Harrisburg about 26 July, and it is believed that upon their arrival and dismissal from the ranks the company ceased to exist.

A total of 97 men served in the company during the war, two of them recruits who joined it in Mexico. Nine men chose to desert their comrades. Ten of its members suffered battle related injuries, two of them dying of their wounds. In all, twenty-one Guards died in service, and an additional sixteen received discharges before muster out.

ALBERT, JOHN: Pvt., enl. 6 Dec 46 at Harrisburg, age 20, occ. tailor, deserted from Camp Jackson near New Orleans 24 Jan 47.

ALEXANDER, WILLIAM: Pvt., enl. 6 Dec 46 at Harrisburg, age 22, occ. tailor, deserted from Camp Jackson near New Orleans 24 Jan 47.

AUCHMUDY, SAMUEL S.: Pvt., enl. 6 Dec 46 at Harrisburg, age 22, occ. carpenter, mo. with Co. 20 Jul 48. 1st Lt. Co. D, 47th P.V.I. 31 Aug 61 to 18 Sep 64.

AUCHMUDY, SHIPMAN: Pvt., enl. 6 Dec 46 at Harrisburg, age 24, occ. tailor, detached to Capt. Steptoe's Battery of U.S. Artillery according to Jul-Aug 47 MR, promoted to Sgt. 29 Feb 48, mo. with Co. 20 Jul 48.

BODEN, HUGH: Pvt., enl. 6 Dec 46 at Harrisburg, age 26, occ. carpenter, wounded in Mexico City by an assassin 7 Oct 47, died 12 Oct 47 from these wounds.

BOLMER, JACOB: (Balmer): Pvt., enl. 6 Dec 46 at Harrisburg, age 19, occ. blacksmith, hospitalized in Mexico City according to Sep-Oct 47 MR, mo. with Co. 20 Jul 48. Supposed to have served in the Civil War (unconfirmed).

BOLTON, WILLIAM: (Bolten): Pvt., enl. 6 Dec 46 at Harrisburg, age 29, occ. blacksmith, KIA at Garita de Belen 13 Sep 47.

BOWMAN, GEORGE: Pvt., enl. 6 Dec 46 at Harrisburg, age 27, occ. carpenter, deserted from Camp Jackson near New Orleans 24 Jan 47.

BRESSLER, GEORGE: Cpl., enl. 6 Dec 46 at Harrisburg, age 22, occ. millwright, left sick at Puebla 8 Aug 47, rejoined Co. by 29 Feb 48, mo. with Co. 20 Jul 48.

BROBST, GEORGE: Pvt., enl. 6 Dec 46 at Harrisburg, age 22, occ. laborer, deserted from Camp Jackson near New Orleans 24 Jan 47.

BROWN, ALEXANDER: Pvt., enl. 6 Dec 46 at Harrisburg, age 21, occ. puddler, hospitalized at Puebla according to Sep-Oct 47 MR, mo. with Co. 20 Jul 48.

BRUA, JACOB: Pvt., enl. 6 Dec 46 at Harrisburg, age 38, occ. printer, left sick at Perote 25 Jun 47, died at Perote 3 Jul 47. He had been appointed 2nd Lt. in the 11th U.S. Infantry 25 May 47 but never served in that capacity.

CLENDENNIN, THOMAS: (Clendenen, Clendenin): Pvt., enl. 6 Dec 46 at Harrisburg, age 21, occ. carpenter, listed as sick on May-Jun 47 MR, left sick at Puebla 8 Aug 47, rejoined Co. by 30 Apr 48, mo. with Co. 20 Jul 48.

COLTON, ROBERT: Pvt., enl. 8 Dec 46 at Harrisburg, age 20, occ. shoemaker, deserted from Camp Jackson near New Orleans 24 Jan 47.

COSGROVE, JAMES S.: Pvt., enl. 6 Dec 46 at Harrisburg, age 23, occ. laborer, severely WIA in the calf of the right leg at storming of Chapultepec 13 Sep 47, disc. at Mexico City 7 Dec 47 on SCD for wounds.

COWHOECK, DANIEL: (Cowhick, Cowhock): Pvt., enl. 6 Dec 46 at Harrisburg, age 30, occ. farmer, died in Mexico City Hospital 15 Dec 47.

CRAFT, LEVI: Pvt., enl. 6 Dec 46 at Harrisburg, age 34, occ. coppersmith, promoted to Cpl. 1 Nov 47, mo. with Co. 20 Jul 48.

CROMLEIGH, DAVID (Daniel): Pvt., enl. 8 Dec 46 at Harrisburg, age 29, occ. merchant, deserted from Camp Jackson near New Orleans 24 Jan 47.

CROOKS, CLARK B.: (Cook): Pvt., enl. 6 Dec 46 at Harrisburg, age 20, occ. printer, promoted to Cpl. 16 Apr 47, reduced to Pvt. 1 Apr 48, mo. with Co. 20 Jul 48.

DALEY, JOSEPH: (Daily): Pvt., enl. 8 Dec 46 at Harrisburg, age 28, occ. stone mason, sent to a hospital in New Orleans 28 Oct 47, died at New Orleans Barracks 29 Nov 47.

DAVIS, HENRY: Pvt., enl. 8 Dec 46 at Harrisburg, age 20, occ. butcher, promoted to Cpl. 16 Apr 47, promoted to Sgt. 12 Aug 47, promoted to 1st Sgt. 1 Jan 48, mo. with Co. 20 Jul 48.

DEITRICH, GEORGE: (Deitrick, Deutrich): Pvt., enl. 8 Dec 46 at Harrisburg, age 38, occ. farmer, left sick at Vera Cruz 9 Apr 47, died at Vera Cruz 28 Apr 47.

DENNISON, BARTLETT: Pvt., enl. 8 Dec 46 at Harrisburg, age 28, occ. clerk, promoted to Cpl. 12 Aug 47, died in Mexico City Hospital 23 Oct 47.

DERRY, WILLIAM H. P.: Cpl., enl. 6 Dec 46 at Harrisburg, age 27, occ. boat builder, promoted to 2nd Sgt. 1 Jan 48, mo. with Co. 20 Jul 48.

ELDER, JAMES: Sgt., enl. 6 Dec 46 at Harrisburg, age 21, occ. gentleman, disc. at Jalapa 22 May 47 on SCD. Appointed 2nd Lt. 11th U.S. Infantry 24 Jul 47, mo. 17 Aug 48. Capt. Cameron Guards, District of Columbia Vols. 20 Apr 61 to 20 Jul 61. Capt. 11th U.S. Inf. 14 May 61 until dismissed 6 Jan 64.

EVANS, LEWIS (Levi): Pvt., enl. 8 Dec 46 at Harrisburg, age 24, occ. blacksmith, listed as sick on May-Jun 47 MR, hospitalized at Puebla 8 Aug 47, died at Puebla 9 Sep 47.

FLECK, JOHN J.: Sgt., enl. 6 Dec 46 at Harrisburg, age 29, occ. plasterer, hospitalized at Vera Cruz according to Mar-Apr 47 MR, disc. at Vera Cruz 21 May 47 on SCD.

FORSTER, WEIDMAN: (Foster): Pvt., enl. 8 Dec 46 at Harrisburg, age 21, occ. carpenter, promoted to Cpl. 1 Feb 47, appointed 2nd Lt. of Inf. in the Regular Army 16 Feb 47, he accepted the commission 13 Apr 47, was assigned to the 11th U.S. Inf. to rank from 9 Apr 47, promoted to 1st Lt. 4 Dec 47, mo. 15 Aug 48.

FURLEY, JAMES A.: Pvt., enl. 8 Dec 46 at Harrisburg, age 23, occ. blacksmith, hospitalized in Mexico City according to Sep-Oct 47 MR, hospitalized again in Mexico City 19 Dec 47, disc. at San Angel 28 Feb 48 on SCD.

GLASBY, LEWIS: (Glasbey, Glasbuy, Glassby): Pvt., enl. 8 Dec 46 at Harrisburg, age 29, occ. blacksmith, listed as sick on May-Jun 47 MR, left at Perote as Hospital Steward 26 Jun 47, disc. at San Angel 10 Apr 48 on SCD.

GOULD, JAMES S.: Pvt., enl. 8 Dec 46 at Harrisburg, age 30, occ. shoemaker, promoted to Sgt. 21 Apr 47, sent to a hospital at New Orleans for his health 28 Oct 47, went AWOL from New Orleans Hospital, disc. at Pittsburgh 17 Jan 48.

GRIFFITH, ROBERT: Pvt., enl. 8 Dec 46 at Harrisburg, age 21, occ. farmer, hospitalized at Vera Cruz according to Mar-Apr 47 MR, listed as sick on May-Jun 47 MR, left sick at Puebla 8 Aug 47, sent to U.S. for his health 28 Oct 47, rejoined Co. by 31 Dec 47, mo. with Co. 20 Jul 48.

GRIMSHAW, JAMES: Pvt., enl. 8 Dec 46 at Harrisburg, age 33, occ. physician, left sick at Perote 25 Jun 47, listed as Hospital Steward at Perote on Jan-Feb & Mar-Apr 48 MRs, appointed Asst. Surgeon 11th U.S. Inf. 29 Mar 48, disc. at Encero 16 May 48 to accept his commission, mo. 14 Aug 48.

HAGAN, JAMES P.: Pvt., enl. 1 Jan 47 at Fort Hamilton, N.Y., age 29, occ. stone cutter, mi. at Ft. Hamilton 1 Jan 47, transferred from the New York Regt. 31 Oct 47, mo. with Co. 20 Jul 48.

HAMBRIGHT, HENRY A.: 1st Sgt., enl. 6 Dec 46 at Harrisburg, age 26, occ. contractor, listed as sick on May-Jun 47 MR, promoted to 1st Lt. of Co. H 10 Aug 47, for Civil War & subsequent service see Co. H.

HESTER, FREDERICK: Pvt., enl. 8 Dec 46 at Harrisburg, age 24, occ. farmer, mo. with Co. 20 Jul 48.

HOVIS, JOHN D. (C.): Pvt., enl. 8 Dec 46 at Harrisburg, age 23, occ. printer, promoted to Cpl. 1 Apr 48, mo. with Co. 20 Jul 48.

IRVINE, MATHEW T. (C.): (Irvin, Irwin): Pvt., enl. 8 Dec 46 at Harrisburg, age 29, occ. shoemaker, mo. with Co. 20 Jul 48.

IRWIN, SAMUEL C.: (Irvin, Irvine): Pvt., enl. 8 Dec 46 at Harrisburg, age 29, occ. farmer, left sick at Puebla 8 Aug 47, disc. at Puebla 4 Nov 47 on SCD for dysentery, died after returning home.

JORDAN, THOMAS R.: (Jorden, Jordon): Cpl., enl. 6 Dec 46 at Harrisburg, age 23, occ. carpenter, promoted to 1st Cpl. 1 Feb 47, promoted to Sgt. 16 Apr 47, listed as sick on May-Jun 47 MR. Left sick at Puebla 8 Aug 47, disc. at Puebla 5 Nov 47 on SCD.

KAUFFMAN, FRANKLIN: Pvt., enl. 10 Dec 46 at Harrisburg, age 28, occ. carpenter, deserted from Camp Jackson near New Orleans 24 Jan 47.

KERR, JOHN: Pvt., enl. 8 Dec 46 at Harrisburg, age 29, occ. distiller, died in Mexico City Hospital 10 Oct 47.

KILLINGER, JOHN: Pvt., enl. 8 Dec 46 at Harrisburg, age 19, occ. butcher, mo. with Co. 20 Jul 48.

KLOTZ, WILLIAM: (Ilatz, Klatz): Pvt., enl. 8 Dec 46 at Harrisburg, age 33, occ. laborer, listed as sick on May-Jun 47 MR, died at Puebla 21 Jul 47.

KURTZ, LEWIS: Pvt., enl. 8 Dec 46 at Harrisburg, age 21, occ. hatter, listed as sick on Jan-Feb 47 MR, mo. with Co. 20 Jul 48.

LEIB, CHRISTIAN W.: (Lieb): Pvt., enl. 6 Dec 46 at Harrisburg, age 31, occ. butcher, appointed Ensign 22 Apr 47, slightly WIA at Chapultepec 13 Sep 47, promoted to 2nd Lt. and transferred to Co. H 12 Nov 47.

LOOKER, CHARLES: Pvt., enl. 6 Dec 46 at Harrisburg, age 29, occ. shoemaker, hospitalized at Vera Cruz according to Mar-Apr 47 MR, mo. with Co. 20 Jul 48.

LUKENS, WILLIAM: (Lookins, Lukins): Pvt., enl. 6 Dec 46 at Harrisburg, age 18, occ. laborer, mo. with Co. 20 Jul 48.

MAY, JACOB: Pvt., enl. 6 Dec 46 at Harrisburg, age 26, occ. laborer, died at San Angel 7 Sep 47 while on a march.

McWILLIAMS, PETER H.: (Williams): 1st Lt., enl. 6 Dec 46 at Harrisburg, age 25, occ. printer, left for recruiting duty 8 Jun 47, reported for duty at Ft. Mifflin 24 Feb 48, rejoined Co. at Pittsburgh 17 Jul 48, mo. with Co. 20 Jul 48.

MILLER, HENRY: Pvt., enl. & mi. 20 Jul 47 at Harrisburg, age 20, occ. printer, serving as Lance Sgt. in the recruiting party in Oct 47, reported at Ft. McHenry, Md. 20 Jan 48, joined Co. 17 Apr 48, mo. with Co. 20 Jul 48.

MILLS, GEORGE R.: (Mitts): Pvt., enl. 6 Dec 46 at Harrisburg, age 21, occ. stone cutter, promoted to 4th Cpl. 1 Jan 48, mo. with Co. 20 Jul 48.

MOSLEY, CHARLES: (Moseley, Mosely): Pvt., enl. 6 Dec 46 at Harrisburg, age 20, occ. puddler, mo. with Co. 20 Jul 48.

MOYER, JACOB: Pvt., enl. 6 Dec 46 at Harrisburg, age 22, occ. tinner, promoted to Cpl. 1 May 47, WIA at Chapultepec 13 Sep 47, died in Mexico City Hospital 28 Oct 47 from wounds.

MOYERS, EMANUEL: (Moyer): Pvt., enl. 6 Dec 46 at Harrisburg, age 21, occ. laborer, severely WIA at Garita de Belen 13 Sep 47, disc. at Mexico City 7 Dec 47 on SCD for wounds.

MULLEN, CHAMBERS C. (S.): Pvt., enl. 6 Dec 46 at Harrisburg, age 22, occ. brewer, listed as sick on May-Jun 47 MR, hospitalized in Mexico City 19 Dec 47, rejoined Co. 12 Mar 48, mo. with Co. 20 Jul 48.

MURRAY, WILLIAM GRAY: Sgt., enl. 6 Dec 46 at Harrisburg, age 22, occ. merchant, appointed 2nd Lt. of Inf. in the Regular Army 5 Mar 47, assigned to 11th U.S. Inf. to rank from 9 Apr 47, left Co. G, 2nd Pa. Regt. to accept his commission 16 Apr 47, mo. 14 Aug 48. Col. 84th P.V.I. 23 Dec 61 until KIA at Winchester, Va. 23 Mar 62.

MYERS, JACOB: (Meyers): Pvt., enl. 6 Dec 46 at Harrisburg, age 27, occ. cooper, mo. with Co. 20 Jul 48.

NOVINGER, GEORGE: (Noreinger): Pvt., enl. 6 Dec 46 at Harrisburg, age 27, occ. farmer, detailed as attendant in regimental hospital 16 Sep 47, rejoined Co. by 31 Dec 47, promoted to 1st Cpl. 1 Jan 48, mo. with Co. 20 Jul 48.

NOVINGER, HIRAM: Pvt., enl. 6 Dec 46 at Harrisburg, age 20, occ. farmer, listed as sick on May-Jun 47 MR, died while on a march at Beraugas 3 Jul 47.

PALMER, JOSEPH C.: Pvt., enl. 6 Dec 46 at Harrisburg, age 19, occ. boatman, slightly WIA at Mexico City 13 Sep 47 while on detached service with a battery of the 4th U.S. Artillery, left at New Orleans 3 Jul 48, disc. to date from 3 Jul 48. Pvt. & Artificer Co. E, 50th New York Engineers 22 Aug 62 to 13 Jun 65 under the name of Joseph Pound.

PATRICK, JOHN: Pvt., enl. 6 Dec 46 at Harrisburg, age 21, occ. shoemaker, listed as sick on Jan-Feb 47 MR, promoted to Cpl. 1 Nov 47, promoted to 4th Sgt. 1 Jan 48, reduced to Pvt. 29 Feb 48, mo. with Co. 20 Jul 48.

POWERS, JOHN: Pvt., enl. 6 Dec 46 at Harrisburg, age 36, occ. shoemaker, mo. with Co. 20 Jul 48.

PUCHALSKI, EUGENE: Pvt., enl. & mi. 29 Apr 48 at San Angel, age 32, mo. with Co. 20 Jul 48.

REES, DAVID: (Reese): Pvt., enl. 6 Dec 46 at Harrisburg, age 19, occ. moulder, left sick at Vera Cruz 12 Apr 47, rejoined Co. by 31 Aug 47, mo. with Co. 20 Jul 48.

REES, JAMES J.: (Reese): Pvt., enl. 6 Dec 46 at Harrisburg, age 18, occ. printer, left sick at Vera Cruz 12 Apr 47, died at Vera Cruz date unknown.

REES, WILLIAM: (Reese): Pvt., enl. 6 Dec 46 at Harrisburg, age 19, occ. moulder, deserted from Camp Jackson near New Orleans 24 Jan 47.

REIGHTER, HENRY: (Reichter, Richter): Pvt., enl. 6 Dec 46 at Harrisburg, age 21, occ. brick maker, listed as AWOL on Jan-Feb 48 MR, mo. with Co. 20 Jul 48.

REXFORD, ENSIGN: Pvt., enl. 6 Dec 46 at Harrisburg, age 22, occ. barber, deserted from Camp Jackson near New Orleans 24 Jan 47.

RIGGLE, SIMON: (Reggle, Reigle, Riegle): Pvt., enl. 6 Dec 46 at Harrisburg, age 23, occ. laborer, mo. with Co. 20 Jul 48. Pvt. New Co. K, 16th Wisconsin Vol. Inf. 12 Dec 63 to 12 Jul 65.

ROCK, DAVID B.: Pvt., enl. 6 Dec 46 at Harrisburg, age 19, occ. printer, left sick at Vera Cruz 12 Apr 47, disc. at Vera Cruz 21 May 47 on SCD.

RODGERS, ROBERT A.: (Rogers): Pvt., enl. 6 Dec 46 at Harrisburg, age 24, occ. carpenter, severely WIA at Garita de Belen 13 Sep 47, disc. at Mexico City 10 Apr 48 on SCD for wounds.

ROLLER, SAMUEL: (Roler): Pvt., enl. 6 Dec 46 at Harrisburg, age 21, occ. blacksmith, mo. with Co. 20 Jul 48.

SHAUM, FREDERICK: Pvt., enl. 6 Dec 46 at Harrisburg, age 25, occ. butcher, mo. with Co. 20 Jul 48.

SHAW, JAMES: Pvt., enl. 6 Dec 46 at Harrisburg, age 21, occ. printer, hospitalized at Vera Cruz according to Mar-Apr 47 MR, listed as sick on May-Jun 47 MR, died at Puebla 21 Jul 47.

SHOEMAKER, JOHN: Pvt., enl. 6 Dec 46 at Harrisburg, age 19, occ. shoemaker, listed as sick in quarters on Nov-Dec 47 MR, mo. with Co. 20 Jul 48.

SIMONS, GEORGE: Fifer, enl. 6 Dec 46 at Harrisburg, age 22, occ. blacksmith, mo. with Co. 20 Jul 48. Pvt. & Blacksmith Co. C, 9th Pa. Vol. Cav. 11 Oct 61 to 18 Jul 65.

SIMONS, JOHN: Cpl., enl. 6 Dec 46 at Harrisburg, age 31, occ. teamster, reduced to Pvt. 1 Feb 47, transferred to New York Regt. 31 Oct 47.

SIMONS, SAMUEL: Drummer, enl. 6 Dec 46 at Harrisburg, age 28, occ. blacksmith, appointed Drum Major 8 Nov 47, mo. with F & S 21 Jul 48. Musician Co. K, 2nd P.V.I. (3 mos.) 20 Apr 61 to 26 Jul 61.

SNYDER, JACOB: Pvt., enl. 6 Dec 46 at Harrisburg, age 23, occ. farmer, left sick at Puebla 8 Aug 47, died at Puebla 19 Aug 47.

SNYDER, JEREMIAH: Pvt., enl. 6 Dec 46 at Harrisburg, age 25, occ. boatman, hospitalized in Mexico City 19 Dec 47, rejoined Co. 12 Mar 48, mo. with Co. 20 Jul 48.

SPAYD, CHRISTIAN C. (K.) (C. King): (Spayel): Pvt., enl. 6 Dec 46 at Harrisburg, age 30, occ. printer, promoted to Sgt. 22 May 47, promoted to 1st Sgt. 12 Aug 47, listed as sick in quarters on Sep-Oct & Nov-Dec 47 MRs, was AWOL from 3 Jan 48, died in main guardhouse in Mexico City 7 Apr 48.

SPONG, GEORGE (John): Pvt., enl. 6 Dec 46 at Harrisburg, age 22, occ. miller, mo. with Co. 20 Jul 48.

STENTZ, HENRY: Pvt., enl. 6 Dec 46 at Harrisburg, age 36, occ. contractor, left sick at New Orleans 12 Apr 47, disc. at New Orleans 13 May 47 on SCD.

TREXLER, MICHAEL P.: (Traxler, Traxter): Pvt., enl. 12 Dec 46 at Harrisburg, age 21, occ. cabinet maker, slightly WIA at Chapultepec 13 Sep 47, mo. with Co. 20 Jul 48.

UNDERWOOD, EDMUND (Edward): Pvt., enl. 6 Dec 46 at Harrisburg, age 19, occ. school teacher, disc. at Jalapa 19 May 47 on SCD. Appointed 2nd Lt. in the 4th U.S. Inf. 3 Mar 48, promoted to 1st Lt. 24 Mar 53, promoted to Capt. 11 Mar 56, Maj. 18th U.S. Inf. 14 May 61 until retirement 27 Feb 62. Born 22 Feb 28 & died 5 Sep 63.

Edmund Underwood as a Second
Lieutenant in the 4th U.S. Infantry in the
late 1840s or early 1850s
Dickinson College Library

Edward C. Williams pictured during
the Civil War
*History of Susquehanna and
Juniata Valleys*

UNGER, DAVID J. (I.):   2nd Lt., enl. 6 Dec 46 at Harrisburg, age 24, occ. merchant, assigned to command Co. F, 2nd Pa. Regt. 7 Apr 48, mo. with Co.
20 Jul 48.

UNGER, FRANKLIN (Frederick):   Pvt., enl. 6 Dec 46 at Harrisburg, age 22,
occ. shoemaker, hospitalized at Vera Cruz according to Mar-Apr 47 MR,
listed as sick in quarters on Sep-Oct 47 MR, mo. with Co. 20 Jul 48.

WALTERS, JOHN: Pvt., enl. 6 Dec 46 at Harrisburg, age 33, occ. cordwainer,
listed as sick on May-Jun 47 MR, left sick at Puebla 8 Aug 47, died at Puebla
9 Nov 47 from chronic dysentery.

WARD, PATRICK: Pvt., enl. 6 Dec 46 at Harrisburg, age 19, occ. laborer,
severely WIA at the storming of Chapultepec 13 Sep 47, hospitalized in
Mexico City 19 Dec 47, disc. 5 Mar 48 on SCD for wounds.

WASHABAUGH, LEWIS: (Washbough):   Pvt., enl. 6 Dec 46 at Harrisburg, age
23, occ. carpenter, died in Mexico City Hospital 12 Oct 47 from chronic
dysentery.

WATERBURY, ISAAC S.: 2nd Lt., enl. 6 Dec 46 at Harrisburg, age 27, occ. tailor, appointed Acting Adjutant 8 Jun 47, rejoined Co. 28 Dec 47, listed as sick in quarters on Nov-Dec 47 MR, mo. with Co. 20 Jul 48. Adjutant 2nd P.V.I. (3 mos.) 20 Apr 61 to 26 Jul 61. Capt. Co. G, 55th P.V.I. 28 Aug 61 until dying at Bermuda Hundred 8 May 64.

WILLIAMS, EDWARD C.: Capt., enl. 6 Dec 46 at Harrisburg, age 27, occ. book binder, slightly WIA in storming of Chapultepec 13 Sep 47, listed as sick in quarters on Sep-Oct 47 MR, mo. with Co. 20 Jul 48. Brig. Gen. Pa. Vols. in three months service under Gen. Robert Patterson in 1861. Col. 9th Pa. Cav. 21 Nov 61 to 9 Oct 62. Died at Chapman, Pa. 18 Feb 00.

WILLIS, WILLIAM: Pvt., enl. 6 Dec 46 at Harrisburg, age 22, occ. stone mason, mo. with Co. 20 Jul 48.

WINOWER, GEORGE: (Weimower, Winour): Pvt., enl. 6 Dec 46 at Harrisburg, age 39, occ. bricklayer, listed as sick on May-Jun 47 MR, died at Puebla Hospital 8 Aug 47 from chronic dysentery.

WOLF, SAMUEL C.: Pvt., enl. 6 Dec 46 at Harrisburg, age 20, occ. blacksmith, left sick at Puebla 8 Aug 47, disc. at Puebla 26 Feb 48 on SCD.

WOOD, HENRY B.: Pvt., enl. 6 Dec 46 at Harrisburg, age 21, occ. law student, disc. at Jalapa 1 Jun 47 on SCD.

Company H, 2nd Regiment
Fayette County Volunteers

Four uniformed militia companies had volunteered before 15 July 1846 to represent their county in Mexico. When it became clear that only a limited number could be selected, the Fayette County Volunteers was organized so as to include many members of the older companies. The Volunteers were chosen to be part of the 2nd Regiment, and William B. Roberts, a field grade officer of the county militia brigade, was elected captain.

The Volunteers left Uniontown on 3 January and were mustered in at Pittsburgh the next day by First Lieutenant Horace B. Field, 3rd U.S. Artillery. They performed their duty admirably, taking part in the siege of Vera Cruz and the engagements of Cerro Gordo, Chapultepec and Garita de Belen. They returned to Pittsburgh, where on 12 July 1848, Major George Wright, 4th U.S. Infantry, mustered the men out of the Federal service.

The company reached Uniontown on 14 July to the cheers and tears of families and friends. When the men broke ranks in Uniontown, the Fayette County Volunteers passed out of existence.

A total of 113 men served in the company during the war, twelve of whom joined it in Mexico. Thirteen deserters left the ranks. Eight of its members suffered battle related injuries, and two of them proved to be fatal. In all, thirty-nine Volunteers died in service, and an additional seventeen received discharges before muster out.

ABERCROMBIE, EPHRAIM: Pvt., enl. 16 Dec 46 at Uniontown, age 22, listed as sick on Jan-Feb 47 MR, listed as sick at Vera Cruz on Mar-Apr 47 MR, disc. at Vera Cruz 19 May 47 on SCD.

ALLEN, MATHEW (Nathan): Pvt., enl. 16 Dec 46 at Uniontown, age 25, listed as sick on Jan-Feb 47 MR, listed as sick at camp on Mar-Apr 47 MR, sick at Perote from 28 Jun 47, died at Perote date unknown.

BAINE, ALEXANDER: (Bain, Bane): Pvt., enl. 16 Dec 46 at Fayette, age 33, occ. miner, hospitalized in Mexico City 19 Dec 47, rejoined Co. 14 Jan 48, mo. with Co. 12 Jul 48. Moved to Missouri.

BAKER, WILLIAM: Pvt., enl. & mi. 28 Oct 47 at Mexico City as a substitute for Pvt. John W. Skiles, age 27, occ. bricklayer, mo. with Co. 12 Jul 48.

BARNES, ZEPHANIAH ELLIS (G.) (L.): Pvt., enl. 16 Dec 46 at Connelsville, age 19, occ. laborer, listed as sick on Sep-Oct 47 MR, hospitalized in Mexico City 19 Dec 47, rejoined Co. in Mar 48, hospitalized at Jalapa 13 Apr 48, disc. at Jalapa 11 May 48 on SCD. Died in Connelsville.

BAYES, WILLIAM C.: (Baize, Barge, Bays, Bayse): Pvt., enl. 16 Dec 46 at Connelsville, age 22, listed as sick on Jan-Feb 47 MR, left sick at Vera Cruz 9 Apr 47, transferred to New Orleans Hospital, disc. at New Orleans 31 Dec 47 on SCD. Pvt. Co. I, 20th Ohio Vol. Inf. 9 Dec 61 to 2 Mar 64.

BEDKAR, DAVID: (Bedker): Pvt., enl. 16 Dec 46 at Connelsville, age 26, deserted at New Orleans 23 Jan 47.

BEESON, EDMUND: (Beesin): Pvt., enl. 16 Dec 46 at Uniontown, age 26, mo. with Co. 12 Jul 48.

BIRD, NOAH: Pvt., enl. 16 Dec 46 at Petersburgh, age 23, occ. shoemaker, listed as sick in camp on Mar-Apr 47 MR, mo. with Co. 12 Jul 48. Pvt. & Cpl. Batt. L, 3rd Pa. Heavy Artillery 29 Feb 64 to 9 Nov 65. Died at Harnedsville, Pa. 13 May 13.

BISHOP, JOHN: Pvt., enl. 16 Dec 46 at Connelsville, age 21, occ. shoemaker, mo. with Co. 12 Jul 48. Died in Connelsville.

BRADFORD, HENRY: (Braford): Pvt., enl. 16 Dec 46 at Fayette, age 33, occ. laborer, apprehended as a deserter in Puebla according to Jul-Aug 47 MR, returned to duty by order of Lt. Col. Geary 12 Oct 47, left San Angel for Tacubaya 26 May 48 & supposed to have been murdered or a deserter.

BRYAN, HENRY: Pvt., enl. 16 Dec 46 at Fayette, age 22, died at Mexico City 11 Nov 47.

CAINWORTHY, SAMUEL: (Canworthy): Pvt., enl. 16 Dec 46 at Petersburgh, age 25, left sick at Perote 28 Jun 47, died at Perote 27 Jul 47.

CHIPPS, HARVEY (Harry): (Chips): Pvt., enl. 16 Dec 46 at Fayette, age 24, died at Mexico City 21 Oct 47 from diarrhea.

CONNER, CYRUS LUSION: Pvt., enl. 16 Dec 46 at Fayette, age 22, occ. clerk, promoted to Sgt. 1 May 48, mo. with Co. 12 Jul 48. Capt. Co. D, 8th Pa. Reserves 21 Jun 61 to 25 Dec 62, being a POW from 27 Jun 62 to 19 Aug 62. Pvt., Sgt., 2nd Lt. & Capt. Co. I, 7th Pa. Cav. 25 Feb 64 into 1865. Major 137th U.S.C.T. 8 Apr 65 to 15 Jan 66. Died at Masontown, Pa.

COUCH, GEORGE: Pvt., enl. 4 Jan 47 at Pittsburgh, age 20, deserted at Pittsburgh 8 Jan 47.

CRAWFORD, JOHN R.: Cpl., enl. 16 Dec 46 at Uniontown, age 22, occ. laborer, promoted to Sgt. 1 May 48, mo. with Co. 12 Jul 48. Died from the kick of a horse in Uniontown.

CROSSLAND, CALEB: Fifer, enl. 16 Dec 46 at Uniontown, age 29, left sick at Vera Cruz 9 Apr 47, deserted from U.S. Hospital at New Orleans 15 Dec 47, rejoined Co. at Pittsburgh 10 Jul 48, mo. with Co. 12 Jul 48.

CUMMINGS, JOHN (James) A.: Pvt., enl. 8 Dec 46 at Pittsburgh, age 24, occ. laborer, transferred from Co. K, 1st Pa. Regt. 30 Mar 47, promoted to 1st Sgt. 1 May 47, WIA at Garita de Belen 13 Sep 47, reduced to Pvt. by Court Martial 20 Apr 48, mo. with Co. 12 Jul 48. He had served in the War for Texas Independence.

DAVENPORT, LEWIS (Louis): Pvt., enl. 17 Aug 47 at Phila., age 29, occ. sailor, joined Co. & mi. at San Angel 31 Dec 47, mo. with Co. 12 Jul 48.

DAVIS, JOHN (1st) (long): Pvt., enl. 16 Dec 46 at Uniontown, age 21, transferred to Co. C, 2nd U.S. Dragoons at Vera Cruz 8 Apr 47 in exchange for Pvt. William Thompson.

DAVIS, JOHN (2nd) (short): Pvt., enl. 16 Dec 46 at Waynesburgh, age 18, deserted at New Orleans 24 Jan 47.

DOWNER, HIRAM: Pvt., enl. 16 Dec 46 at Fayette, age 40, was sick at Vera Cruz & disc. there 7 Apr 47 on SCD, died on his way home 6 May 47 at Mills Point, was eventually buried in Uniontown.

DOWNER, JAMES P.: Cpl., enl. 16 Dec 46 at Uniontown, age 27, occ. saddler, promoted to Sgt. 12 Nov 47, promoted to 2nd Sgt. 1 May 48, mo. with Co. 12 Jul 48. Pvt. Co. C, 2nd Kansas Cav. 3 Dec 61 to 10 Jan 65. Died at Sagauche, Colorado.

DUCKET, GEORGE: (Duchet): Pvt., enl. 16 Dec 46 at Fayette, age 32, was sick at Vera Cruz & disc. there 7 Apr 47 on SCD, died on his way home.

FEE, WILSON: (Fen, Fer): Pvt., enl. 16 Dec 46 at Fayette, age 23, left sick at Perote 28 Jun 47, died at Perote 19 Jul 47.

FERGUSON, ANDREW: (Fergurson, Furgerson, Furguson): Pvt., enl. 16 Dec 46 at Waynesburgh, age 40, occ. carpenter, mo. with Co. 12 Jul 48.

FETTER, JOHN W. S.: Pvt., enl. 16 Dec 46 at Petersburgh, age 22, occ. physician, died at Vera Cruz 24 Mar 47.

FORREY, DANIEL: (Forney, Forry): 1st Sgt., enl. 16 Dec 46 at Connelsville, age 26, listed as present sick on Jan-Feb 47 MR, died at Vera Cruz 13 Apr 47.

FOWG, HENRY: (Fogg, Forey, Foug): Pvt., enl. 4 Jan 47 at Pittsburgh, age 25, left sick at Vera Cruz 9 Apr 47, disc. at Vera Cruz 22 May 47.

FREEMAN, WILLIAM: Pvt., enl. 16 Dec 46 at Uniontown, age 22, occ. laborer, listed as sick on Jan-Feb 47 MR, mo. with Co. 12 Jul 48. Pvt. Co. A, 97th P.V.I. 30 Sep 64 to 28 Jun 65. Died at Middle Run, Pa. 31 Aug 11.

FREY, BENJAMIN F.: (Fry): Pvt., enl. 16 Dec 46 at Uniontown, age 22, accidently shot in the breast with a musket by Pvt. Edmund Beeson while on a foraging party without leave at Vera Cruz 11 Mar 47, disc. at Vera Cruz 4 Apr 47 on SCD for wounds. Pvt. Co. B, 61st P.V.I. 16 Jul 63 to 16 Jun 65. Died at Dunbar, Pa. sometime after the Civil War.

GADD, ELISHA (Elijah): Pvt., enl. 20 Dec 46 at Uniontown, age 19, left sick at Vera Cruz 9 Apr 47, disc. at Vera Cruz 19 May 47. Died at Bowling Green, Ky.

GARDNER, JESSE BEESON: Pvt., enl. 20 Dec 46 at Fayette, age 22, occ. pedlar, promoted to Ensign 1 May 48, mo. with Co. 12 Jul 48. 1st Lt. & Capt. Co. G, & Major 8th Pa. Reserves 24 Apr 61 to 23 May 62. Died at Uniontown 7 Jan 98. Born 10 Jun 24.

GIBSON, JOHN H. (W.): Pvt., enl. 4 Jan 47 at Pittsburgh, age 21, left sick at Vera Cruz 9 Apr 47, disc. at New Orleans 6 Dec 47. Entered Soldiers' Home at Dayton, Ohio in 1906.

GILLIS, JOHN: Pvt., enl. 20 Dec 46 at Connelsville, age 18, deserted at New Orleans 27 Jan 47.

GORDON, JAMES: Pvt., enl. 20 Dec 46 at Uniontown, age 38, left sick at Puebla 8 Aug 47, disc. at Puebla date unknown, died at New Orleans in Nov 47.

GREGG, ELI M.: Pvt., enl. 20 Dec 46 at Uniontown, age 47, listed only on Co. muster-in roll.

GUILER, ABSOLOM: 2nd Sgt., enl. 16 Dec 46 at Uniontown, age 28, occ. tailor, promoted to 1st Sgt. 1 May 48, mo. with Co. 12 Jul 48. Major 85th P.V.I. 4 Nov 61 to 31 May 62. Died at Uniontown 28 Apr 73.

HAMBRIGHT, HENRY A. (Augustus): 1st Sgt., enl. 6 Dec 46 at Harrisburg, age 26, occ. contractor, transferred from Co. G & promoted to 1st Lt. 10 Aug 47, mo. with Co. 12 Jul 48. Capt. Co. K, 1st P.V.I. (3 mos.) 20 Apr 61 to 26 Jul 61. Col. 79th P.V.I. 18 Oct 61 to 12 Jul 65, had brevets to Maj., Lt. Col., Col. & Brig. Gen. Held concurrent commission as Capt. 11th U.S. Inf. 14 May 61 to 21 Sep 66. Capt. 29th U.S. Inf. 21 Sep 66 to 27 Jan 69. Maj. 32nd U.S. Inf. 27 Jan 69 to 15 Mar 69. Maj. 19th U.S. Inf. 15 Mar 69 to retirement 6 May 79. Born 24 Mar 19 & died at Lancaster, Pa. 19 Feb 93.

Henry A. Hambright in the Uniform of a Colonel and wearing the insignia of a
Brigadier General during the Civil War

MOLLUS-Mass & USAMHI

HARDESTY, DANIEL: Pvt., enl. 4 Jan 47 at Pittsburgh, age 20, occ. laborer, mo. with Co. 12 Jul 48.

HARVEY, HENDERSON: Pvt., enl. 16 Dec 46 at Brownfield, Va., age 25, deserted at New Orleans 24 Jan 47.

HAZARD, DANIEL: Pvt., enl. 16 Dec 46 at Uniontown, age 36, listed as sick on Jan-Feb 47 MR, left sick at Vera Cruz 9 Apr 47, disc. at Vera Cruz date unknown.

HEADMAN, ANDREW: (Hedman): Pvt., enl. & mi. 10 Aug 47 at Phila., age 27, joined Co. at San Angel 31 Dec 47, died at San Angel Hospital 3 Mar 48.

HENRY, JOHN: Pvt., enl. 17 Nov 47 at Hollidaysburg, age 20, mi. at Ft. Mifflin 10 Jan 48, reported at Ft. McHenry, Md. 20 Jan 48, joined Co. 20 Apr 48, mo. with Co. 12 Jul 48.

HESSER, EDWIN: Pvt., enl. 21 Oct 47 at Phila., age 23, occ. laborer, mi. & joined Co. at San Angel 31 Dec 47, mo. with Co. 12 Jul 48.

HICKS, GEORGE: Pvt., enl. 7 Apr 47 at Vera Cruz, age 35, mi. at Vera Cruz 8 Apr 47, died at Jalapa 10 Jun 47.

HOOD, ALEXANDER H.: Pvt., enl. 16 Dec 46 at Connelsville, age 20, occ. tailor, died in Mexico City Hospital 2 Oct 47 from diarrhea.

HUTCHINSON, JAMES: Pvt., enl. 4 Jan 47 at Pittsburgh, age 21, deserted at New Orleans 27 Jan 47, died at Madison on his way home.

HUTCHINSON, JOHN: (Hutcheson): Pvt., enl. 4 Jan 47 at Pittsburgh, age 37, listed as sick at Vera Cruz on Mar-Apr 47 MR, disc. at Vera Cruz 19 May 47 on SCD.

HYDE, SAMUEL: Pvt., enl. 16 Dec 46 at Uniontown, age 25, promoted to Cpl. 6 Jan 47, left sick at Puebla 8 Aug 47, died at Puebla 11 Sep 47.

INKS, HEZEKIAH: (Juks): Pvt., enl. 4 Jan 47 at Pittsburgh, age 30, listed as sick at Jalapa on Mar-Apr 47 MR, died at Perote 24 Jun 47.

IRWIN, RICHARD: (Erwin): 4th Sgt., enl. 16 Dec 46 at Uniontown, age 19, promoted to 2nd Lt. 12 Nov 47, on detached duty in Puebla in Mar 48, mo. with Co. 12 Jul 48.

JACKMAN, WILLIAM: Pvt., enl. 18 Aug 47 at Pittsburgh, age 24, occ. laborer, reported at Carlisle Barracks, Pa. 31 Aug 47, mi. & joined Co. at San Angel 31 Dec 47, mo. with Co. 12 Jul 48.

JARRETT, DANIEL: (Janett, Jarred): Drummer, enl. 16 Dec 46 at Morgantown, Va., age 29, occ. currier, detailed as attendant to regimental hospital 16 Sep 47, hospitalized in Mexico City 19 Dec 47, rejoined Co. in Mar 48, promoted to Cpl. 1 May 48, mo. with Co. 12 Jul 48.

JOHNS, PETER A.: Cpl., enl. 16 Dec 46 at Connelsville, age 29, occ. cooper, promoted to Sgt. in May or Jun 47, remained in Puebla without leave 8 Aug 47, was clerk in Jalapa Hospital in Apr 48, disc. at New Orleans 16 Jun 48 on SCD. 1st Lt. Co. F, Adjutant & Major 11th Pa. Reserves 23 May 61 to 30 Mar 63. Died in Fayette County 20 Sep 76.

JONES, OLIVER E.: Pvt., enl. 16 Dec 46 at Uniontown, age 23, deserted at New Orleans 24 Jan 47. Moved to Kentucky.

KILPATRICK, JACKSON: Pvt., enl. 16 Dec 46 at Connelsville, age 22, listed as sick at camp on Mar-Apr 47 MR, disc. at Jalapa 19 May 47 on SCD. Pvt. in Cos. B, G & D, 28th P.V.I. 28 Jun 61 to 18 Jul 65.

KILPATRICK, JOHN P.: Pvt., enl. 16 Dec 46 at Connelsville, age 24, occ. wagon maker, listed as sick on Jan-Feb 47 MR, mo. with Co. 12 Jul 48. Died at Connelsville 14 Mar 98.

KING, JOHN: Pvt., enl. 4 Jan 47 at Pittsburgh, age 25, deserted at Pittsburgh 8 Jan 47.

LEIB, CHRISTIAN W.: (Lieb): Pvt., enl. 6 Dec 46 at Harrisburg, age 31, occ. butcher, transferred from Co. G & promoted to 2nd Lt. 12 Nov 47, was sick on duty from Mar to May 48, mo. with Co. 12 Jul 48.

LOWER, JOHN: (Lawer): Pvt., enl. 10 Aug 47 at Pittsburgh, age 26, occ. blacksmith, reported at Carlisle Barracks, Pa. 31 Aug 47, mi. & joined Co. at San Angel 31 Dec 47, mo. with Co. 12 Jul 48.

McBRIDE, THOMAS: Pvt., enl. 16 Dec 46 at Connelsville, age 32, KIA in a skirmish at Buena Vista 14 Aug 47.

McCONNELL, JOHN: Pvt., enl. 23 Aug 47 at Pittsburgh, age 37, occ. stone cutter, mi. & joined Co. at San Angel 31 Dec 47, mo. with Co. 12 Jul 48.

McMICHAEL, CORNELIUS: (McMickle, McMicle): Pvt., enl. 16 Dec 46 at Uniontown, age 38, left sick at Vera Cruz 9 Apr 47, disc. at Vera Cruz date unknown, died at New Orleans 17 Jul 47 on his way home.

McNAMEE, JOHN: (McNamen): Pvt., enl. 4 Jan 47 at Pittsburgh, age 23, deserted at Pittsburgh 8 Jan 47.

MENDENHALL, WILLIAM: (Mendenhull): Pvt., enl. 16 Dec 46 at Fayette, age 23, WIA in the heel at Garita de Belen 13 Sep 47, disc. at Mexico City 6 Dec 47 on SCD for wounds.

MITTS, JOHN: (Mits, Mittz): Pvt., enl. 16 Dec 46 at Connelsville, age 35, listed as sick on Jan-Feb 47 MR, left sick at Vera Cruz 9 Apr 47, disc. at New Orleans Hospital 31 Dec 47 on SCD. Died in Connelsville.

MOORE, WILLIAM: (More): Pvt., enl. 16 Dec 46 at Uniontown, age 32, died at Puebla 21 Jul 47.

MORGAN, SAMUEL: Pvt., enl. 16 Dec 46 at Fayette, age 23, occ. laborer, WIA in the breast at Chapultepec 13 Sep 47, hospitalized in Mexico City 19 Dec 47, rejoined Co. in Mar 48, hospitalized at Jalapa 13 Apr 48, disc. at Jalapa 11 May 48 on SCD for wounds, died at home.

MOTES, THOMAS: Pvt., enl. 16 Dec 46 at Fayette, age 28, listed only on Co. muster-in roll.

MURPHY, HUGH: Pvt., enl. 13 Aug 47 at Pittsburgh, age 18, occ. laborer, reported at Carlisle Barracks, Pa. 31 Aug 47, mi. & joined Co. at San Angel 31 Dec 47, mo. with Co. 12 Jul 48.

MURPHY, JOHN: Pvt., enl. 16 Dec 46 at Fayette, deserted at Pittsburgh 8 Jan 47.

MUSTARD, JOHN: Pvt., enl. 16 Dec 46 at Uniontown, age 41, left sick at Perote 28 Jun 47, died at Perote 1 Jul 47.

NICHOLSON, ALBERT G.: Pvt., enl. 4 Jan 47 at Pittsburgh, age 32, occ. laborer, mo. with Co. 12 Jul 48. Died near New Geneva, Pa. about 1853.

NICHOLSON, WILLIAM F.: Pvt., enl. 16 Dec 46 at Fayette, age 30, was sick at Jalapa in Apr 47, disc. at Mexico City 27 Oct 47 on SCD, died on the Mississippi River near Vicksburg while on his way home, buried at New Geneva, Pa.

ORWIN, JACOB: Pvt., enl. 4 Jan 47 at Pittsburgh, age 33, deserted at New Orleans 24 Jan 47.

PAGE, SAMUEL: Pvt., enl. 16 Dec 46 at Connelsville, age 18, occ. shoemaker, mo. with Co. 12 Jul 48. Died at Connelsville.

PALMER, MICHAEL J.: (Parmer): Pvt., enl. 30 Aug 47 at Pittsburgh, age 22, occ. huckster, mi. & joined Co. at San Angel 31 Dec 47, mo. with Co. 12 Jul 48.

POLLOCK, JOHN: Pvt., enl. 16 Dec 46 at Fayette, age 27, occ. miner, mo. with Co. 12 Jul 48. Served in the Civil War, unit unknown. Died at Soldiers' Home in Dayton, Ohio.

PRITCHARD, ANDREW: (Prichard): Pvt., enl. 16 Dec 46 at Connelsville, age 26, listed as sick on Jan-Feb 47 MR, left sick at Perote 28 Jun 47, died at Perote 28 Sep 47.

QUAIL, WILLIAM: 1st Lt., enl. 16 Dec 46 at Connelsville, age 26, elected Capt. 7 Jan 47, listed as sick on Jan-Feb 47 MR, left sick at Puebla 8 Aug 47, left for recruiting duty 30 Dec 47, rejoined Co. at Pittsburgh 10 Jul 48, mo. with Co. 12 Jul 48. Buried in Uniontown.

RINE, EDMUND: (Rian): 3rd Sgt., enl. 16 Dec 46 at Uniontown, age 38, elected 2nd Lt. 7 Jan 47, disc. at Jalapa 16 May 47 on SCD. Buried at Soldiers' Home in Dayton, Ohio.

RIST, HENRY: Pvt., enl. 16 Dec 46 at Connelsville, age 18, occ. laborer, was sick at Jalapa in Apr 47, WIA at Chapultepec 13 Sep 47, listed as sick on Sep-Oct 47 MR, mo. with Co. 12 Jul 48.

ROBERTS, WILLIAM B.: Capt., enl. 16 Dec 46 at Uniontown, age 38, occ. furniture maker, elected Col. 6 Jan 47, was sick from Sep 47, died in Mexico City 3 Oct 47, his remains were returned to Uniontown for burial.

RUDY, JOSEPH: (Roody): Pvt., enl. 16 Dec 46 at Connelsville, age 20, left sick at Perote 28 Jun 47, died at Perote 25 Jul 47.

SEALS, VINCENT: Pvt., enl. 16 Dec 46 at Waynesburgh, age 18, died at Vera Cruz 3 Apr 47.

SHAW, DAVID K. (R.): Pvt., enl. 16 Dec 46 at Connelsville, age 19, died at Puebla 4 Aug 47.

SHAW, JAMES: Pvt., enl. 16 Dec 46 at Connelsville, age 28, occ. shoemaker, WIA at Cerro Gordo 18 Apr 47 causing the amputation of the 3rd finger of his left hand, mo. with Co. 12 Jul 48. Sgt. Co. E, 140th P.V.I. 22 Aug 62 to 22 Feb 63. Died at Connelsville.

SHAW, SOLOMON: Pvt., enl. 16 Dec 46 at Connelsville, age 21, occ. laborer, promoted to Cpl. 1 May 48, mo. with Co. 12 Jul 48. Died at Connelsville.

SHAW, WILLIAM B.: Pvt., enl. 4 Jan 47 at Pittsburgh, age 24, occ. printer, listed as sick on Sep-Oct 47 MR, promoted to Cpl. 12 Nov 47, mo. with Co. 12 Jul 48. Died at Connelsville.

SHRIVER, EVANS: Pvt., enl. 16 Dec 46 at Uniontown, age 22, occ. tailor, listed as sick at Vera Cruz on Mar-Apr 47 MR, promoted to Cpl. 12 Nov 47, mo. with Co. 12 Jul 48.

SILVEY, DAVID: (Silrey): Pvt., enl. 16 Dec 46 at Uniontown, age 26, occ. stage driver, left sick at Puebla 8 Aug 47, died at Puebla date unknown.

SKILES, JOHN W.: Pvt., enl. 16 Dec 46 at Uniontown, age 21, detached to Commissary Dept. according to Mar-Apr, May-Jun & Jul-Aug 47 MRs, disc. at Mexico City 28 Oct 47 due to his providing a substitute in the person of Pvt. William Baker. Major 88th Ohio Vol. Inf. 29 Jul 63 to 26 Jul 65, Bvt. Col. 7 Jun 65. Died at Denver, Colorado 6 Apr 94.

SMITH, JESSE: Pvt., enl. 16 Dec 46 at Fayette, age 18, died at Mexico City 1 Oct 47.

SNYDER, JOHN: Pvt., enl. 17 Aug 47 at Harrisburg, age 27, occ. laborer, reported at Carlisle Barracks, Pa. 31 Aug 47, joined Co. 31 Dec 47, died at San Angel 21 May 48.

SPEERS, STEWART: 2nd Lt., enl. 16 Dec 46 at Uniontown, age 33, was wounded in the left hand when the pistol which he was loading accidentally discharged 21 Mar 47, disc. at Vera Cruz 3 Apr 47 on SCD for wounds.

STANLEY, MARTIN S.: (Stanly, Stenly): Pvt., enl. 16 Dec 46 at Uniontown, age 36, died at Puebla 18 Jul 47.

STEPHENS, BENJAMIN: (Stevens): Pvt., enl. 16 Dec 46 at Uniontown, age 20, died at Mexico City Hospital 1 Oct 47 from diarrhea.

STILWAGON, HENRY L. (N.): (Stillwager, Stillwagon): Cpl., enl. 16 Dec 46 at Connelsville, age 31, promoted to Sgt. 7 Jan 47, left sick at Vera Cruz 9 Apr 47, disc. at Vera Cruz 19 May 47 on SCD.

STILWELL, JOHN: (Stillwell): Pvt., enl. 16 Dec 46 at Fayette, age 28, deserted at New Orleans 24 Jan 47. Eventually moved west.

STURGEON, JOHN: (Sturgen): 2nd Lt., enl. 16 Dec 46 at Uniontown, age 24, elected 1st Lt. 7 Jan 47, died at Puebla 22 Jul 47, his body was stolen by Mexicans before it could be sent home for burial.

SUTTON, JOHN: Pvt., enl. 16 Dec 46 at Uniontown, age 23, died at Tacubaya Hospital 13 Sep 47.

THOMPSON, WILLIAM: Pvt., age 20, occ. sailor, transferred from Co. C, 2nd U.S. Dragoons at Vera Cruz 8 Apr 47, mo. with Co. 12 Jul 48.

TURNER, JAMES: Pvt., enl. 16 Dec 46 at Petersburgh, age 21, died on board the ship *James N. Cooper* off Lobos Island 1 Feb 47.

TURNER, WILLIAM: Pvt., enl. 16 Dec 46 at Connelsville, age 25, occ. laborer, hospitalized in Mexico City 19 Dec 47, rejoined Co. 2 Jan 48, mo. with Co. 12 Jul 48. Died at Connelsville.

WALKER, HUGH: Pvt., enl. 16 Dec 46 at Connelsville, age 26, occ. laborer, listed as sick on Jan-Feb 47 MR, mo. with Co. 12 Jul 48, died at home the day after his return.

WARD, JAMES F. (P.): Pvt., enl. 16 Dec 46 at Fayette, age 19, occ. laborer, promoted to Cpl. 1 May 48, mo. with Co. 12 Jul 48.

WEST, WILLIAM: Pvt., enl. 16 Dec 46 at Uniontown, age 24, deserted at New Orleans 21 Jan 47.

WIDDOWS, JOSEPH: (Widdens, Widows): Pvt., enl. 16 Dec 46 at Morgantown, Va., age 31, occ. shoemaker, mo. with Co. 12 Jul 48.

WINDERS, JOSIAH (Jonah) M. (I.): (Winden, Window): Pvt., enl. 16 Dec 46 at Uniontown, age 19, severely WIA at Garita de Belen 13 Sep 47 being disemboweled by a ball, died 14 Sep 47 from wounds, his remains were later buried in Fayette County.

WOLVERTON, ISAAC: (Woolverton): Pvt., enl. 16 Dec 46 at Waynesburgh, age 25, left sick at Puebla 8 Aug 47, died at Puebla 11 Oct 47.

YEAMAN, CHARLES C.: (Yeamans): Pvt., enl. 16 Dec 46 at Petersburgh, age 20, left sick at Puebla 8 Aug 47, died at Puebla 12 Nov 47.

Company I, 2nd Regiment
Independent Irish Greens

The Independent Irish Greens existed at least as early as 1845 and were part of the Pittsburgh Volunteer Regiment. They offered their services to the government soon after hearing of the war with Mexico. In December they were accepted to be part of the second regiment from Pennsylvania. First Lieutenant Horace B. Field, 3rd U.S. Artillery, mustered them in on 4 January 1847.

During their active service, the Greens took part in the siege of Vera Cruz and the battles of Cerro Gordo, Chapultepec and Garita de Belen. The company returned to Pittsburgh in mid-July 1848 and was mustered out of Federal service by Major George Wright, 4th U.S. Infantry, on 20 July.

It is possible that the Greens continued their organization and activity for several years after their return. However, it is more likely that by the end of 1849 they had ceased to exist as an active company.

A total of 117 men served in the company during the war, nine of which were recruits who joined it in Mexico. Sixteen deserters fled from the life of order and discipline. Five of its members suffered battle related injuries, one of them being killed in action. In all, twenty-six Greens died in service, and an additional fourteen received discharges before muster out.

BERGER, JOHN: (Barger, Beyer, Burger): Pvt., enl. 20 Dec 46 at Pittsburgh, age 36, listed as sick on Jan-Feb 47 MR, left sick at Perote 28 Jun 47, died at Perote 28 Jun 47.

BLACK, WILSON S.: Pvt., enl. 20 Dec 46 at Pittsburgh, age 28, hospitalized at Jalapa according to Mar-Apr 47 MR, disc. at Jalapa 22 May 47 on SCD.

BRERGE, JOHN: Pvt., enl. 20 Dec 46 at Pittsburgh, age 40, shown only on Co. muster-in roll.

BROWN, JOHN D.: Pvt., enl. 20 Dec 46 at Pittsburgh, age 25, left sick at Puebla 8 Aug 47, died at Puebla 5 Oct 47 from fever.

BUGLEY, FRANCIS: (Bueglie, Bugelea, Bugely): Pvt., enl. 20 Dec 46 at Pittsburgh, age 35, died in Mexico City 19 Oct 47 from diarrhea.

BURKE, JOSEPH: (Burk): Pvt., enl. 20 Dec 46 at Pittsburgh, age 22, promoted to 4th Cpl. 1 Nov 47, detailed to special duty about 22 May 48 of securing the bodies of fallen Pittsburgh comrades to take them home, he became missing during this duty and it was supposed that he had been killed.

BURNETT, NATHAN S.: Pvt., enl. 31 Dec. 46 at Storstown, age 43, left sick at Vera Cruz 8 Apr 47, disc. at Vera Cruz 18 May 47 on SCD.

CANNON, MICHAEL: Pvt., enl. 20 Dec 46 at Pittsburgh, age 22, shown only on Co. muster-in roll.

CARR, LEMUEL: (Kerr): Pvt., enl. 20 Dec 46 at Pittsburgh, age 35, deserted from Camp Jackson near New Orleans 25 Jan 47.

CARR, THOMAS: (Kerr): Pvt., enl. 20 Dec 46 at Pittsburgh, age 16, disc. at New Orleans 26 Jan 47 on SCD.

CASSIDY, HENRY: (Cassiday): 4th Sgt., enl. 20 Dec 46 at Pittsburgh, age 36, disc. at New Orleans 29 Jan 47 on SCD for rheumatism.

CHRISTIAN, JOHN: Pvt., age 33, shown only on Co. muster-in roll.

COLLINS, PATRICK: Pvt., enl. 20 Dec 46 at Pittsburgh, age 26, in confinement in main guardhouse at San Angel with charges preferred according to Jan-Feb & Mar-Apr 48 MRs, deserted from guardhouse 30 Apr 48, mo. with Co. 20 Jul 48.

CRAWFORD, WILLIAM: Pvt., enl. 20 Dec 46 at Pittsburgh, age 28. mo. with Co. 20 Jul 48.

DAVIDSON, DAVID M.: Pvt., enl. 4 Jan 47 at Pittsburgh, age 34, WIA in the leg by a bayonet at Cerro Gordo 18 Apr 47, AWOL from 23 Feb 48, returned to Co. by 30 Apr 48, mo. with Co. 20 Jul 48.

DENNY, HUGH: Pvt., enl. 20 Dec 46 at Pittsburgh, age 26, shown only on Co. muster-in roll.

DEVLIN, FRANCIS G. (J.): (Develin, Develine, Develon): 1st Cpl., enl. 20 Dec 46 at Pittsburgh, age 20, left sick at Puebla 8 Aug 47, died at Puebla 11 Oct 47 from chronic bronchitis.

DININGER, FREDERICK: (Deedenger, Denninger, Dieneiger, Dillingham): Pvt., enl. 20 Dec 46 at Pittsburgh, age 34, left sick at Vera Cruz 8 Apr 47, disc. at Vera Cruz 19 May 47 on SCD.

DITCH, JOSEPH: Drummer, enl. 20 Dec 46 at Pittsburgh, age 19, shown only on Co. muster-in roll.

DORAN, PATRICK: Pvt., enl. 17 Sep 47 at Pottsville, age 38, joined Co. 30 Dec 47, mi. at San Angel 31 Dec 47, transferred to Co. C, 2nd Pa. Regt. 1 Apr 48.

DOUGHERTY, DIONYSIUS: Pvt., enl. 20 Dec 46 at Pittsburgh, age 27, shown only on Co. muster-in roll.

DOUGHERTY, GEORGE: 3rd Sgt., enl. 20 Dec 46 at Pittsburgh, age 35, under arrest in quarters according to Jan-Feb 48 MR, mo. with Co. 20 July 48.

DURNYAN, JAMES: Pvt., enl. 30 Dec 46 at Pittsburgh, deserted at Pittsburgh 9 Jan 47.

ENGLES, JOHN (Fisher G.) F. (P.): (Englis): Pvt., enl. 20 Dec 46 at Pittsburgh, age 33, left sick at Puebla 8 Aug 47, disc. at Puebla 17 Jan 48 on SCD.

FISHER, MICHAEL: Pvt., enl. 11 Aug 47 at Pittsburgh, joined Co. 30 Dec 47, mi. at San Angel 31 Dec 47, died at San Angel Hospital 6 Apr 48 from typhus fever.

FRABER, JOHN: Pvt., enl. & mi. 28 Jan 47 at New Orleans, disc. at Jalapa 25 May 47 on SCD. See Unassigned 2nd Regt.

FRIEDLIN, JACOB: Pvt., enl. & mi. 28 Jan 47 at New Orleans, deserted from Camp Jackson near New Orleans 29 Jan 47.

GALLAGHAN, JOHN: (Gallagan, Gallegen, Galleghan, Gallogher): Pvt., enl. 20 Dec. 46 at Pittsburgh, age 35, left sick at Perote 28 Jun 47, died at Perote 14 Aug 47.

GALLAGHAN, THOMAS: Pvt., enl. & mi. 28 Jan 47 at New Orleans, deserted from Camp Jackson near New Orleans 29 Jan 47.

GALVIN, ANTHONY: Pvt., enl. & mi. 28 Jan 47 at New Orleans, mo. with Co. 20 Jul 48.

GARRET, EDWARD: Pvt., enl. 20 Dec 46 at Pittsburgh, age 24, shown only on Co. muster-in roll.

GARRETT, WILLIAM: (Garnett): Pvt., enl. 20 Dec 46 at Pittsburgh, deserted from Camp Jackson near New Orleans 25 Jan 47.

GILSTIN, JOHN: (Gelson, Gelston): Pvt., enl. 20 Dec 46 at Pittsburgh, age 22, deserted at Pittsburgh 9 Jan 47.

GRAFF, FREDERICK: (Kraft): Pvt., enl. & mi. 28 Jan 47 at New Orleans, left sick at Vera Cruz 9 Apr 47, disc. at Vera Cruz 19 May 47 on SCD.

GRAHAM, ARCHIBALD: (Grahem): Pvt., enl. 20 Dec 46 at Pittsburgh, age 22, WIA at Chapultepec 13 Sep 47, mo. with Co. 20 Jul 48.

GRANZ, ADAM: (Grans, Grantz): Pvt., enl. 20 Dec 46 at Pittsburgh, age 19, left sick at Vera Cruz 9 Apr 47, died at Vera Cruz 20 May 47 from chronic rheumatism.

GUTHRIE, JAMES: Pvt., enl. 20 Dec 46 at Pittsburgh, age 30, left sick at Puebla 8 Aug 47, rejoined Co. 28 Jan 48, mo. with Co. 20 Jul 48.

HAGUE, JOHN: Pvt., enl. 20 Dec 46 at Pittsburgh, age 21, died in Mexico City Hospital 27 Sep 47.

HARPER, JAMES: Pvt., enl. 20 Dec 46 at Pittsburgh, age 34, left sick at Puebla 8 Aug 47, rejoined Co. between 31 Dec 47 and 29 Feb 48, in confinement in main guardhouse at San Angel according to Jan-Feb & Mar-Apr 48 MRs, deserted from guardhouse 30 Apr 48, mo. with Co. 20 Jul 48.

HART, BERNARD: Pvt., enl. 20 Dec 46 at Pittsburgh, age 31, deserted at Pittsburgh 9 Jan 47.

HART, GEORGE: (Hard): Pvt., enl. 20 Dec 46 at Pittsburgh, age 26, mo. with Co. 20 Jul 48.

HENRYHAN, TIMOTHY: (Henryhen): Pvt., enl. 30 Dec 47 at Phila., age 29, mi. at Ft. Mifflin 10 Jan 48, reported at Ft. McHenry, Md. 20 Jan 48, joined Co. 18 Apr 48, mo. with Co. 20 Jul 48.

HOLMES, JOHN (James): Pvt., enl. 20 Dec 46 at Pittsburgh, age 29, left sick at Puebla 8 Aug 47, died at Puebla 31 Mar 48 from phthisis pulmonalis.

HOOPS, ISAAC N.: (Hoopes): Pvt., enl. & mi. 28 Jan 47 at New Orleans, WIA and had his musket destroyed at Chapultepec 13 Sep 47, disc. in Mexico City 27 Nov 47 on SCD for deafness.

HOPPER ROBERT: (Hooper): Pvt., enl. 20 Dec 46 at Pittsburgh, age 27, hospitalized at Jalapa according to Mar-Apr 47 MR, died at Jalapa 9 May 47 from diarrhea.

HOYT, ISAAC: Pvt., enl. 20 Dec 46 at Pittsburgh, age 26, shown only on Co. muster-in roll.

HUNT, JOHN: Pvt., enl. 11 Aug 47 at Pittsburgh, reported at Carlisle Barracks, Pa. 31 Aug 47, joined Co. 30 Dec 47, mi. at San Angel 31 Dec 47, mo. with Co. 20 Jul 48.

HUTTON, AUGUSTUS C.: Pvt., enl. 20 Dec 46 at Pittsburgh, age 33, left sick at Vera Cruz 8 Apr 47, disc. at Vera Cruz 22 May 47 on SCD.

JOHNS, CHRISTOPHER (Kristopher): (Jahns, John): Pvt., enl. 20 Dec 46 at Pittsburgh, age 33, died at San Angel 12 or 15 Sep 47.

JONES, EDWARD: Pvt., enl. 20 Dec 46 at Pittsburgh, age 27, shown only on Co. muster-in roll.

KANE, HENRY: Pvt., enl. 20 Dec 46 at Pittsburgh, age 27, shown only on Co. muster-in roll.

KANE, JAMES: (Kean): 2nd Lt., enl. 20 Dec 46 at Pittsburgh, age 20, given furlough from 29 Oct 47, on recruiting duty from Dec 47 through May 48, mo. with Co. 20 Jul 48.

KAUFFMAN, ADAM: Pvt., enl. 20 Dec 46 at Pittsburgh, age 30, shown only on Co. muster-in roll.

KELLY, MICHAEL: Pvt., enl. 20 Dec 46 at Pittsburgh, age 27, had his musket destroyed at Garita de Belen 13 Sep 47, mo. with Co. 20 Jul 48.

KELLY, ROBERT H.: (Kelley): Pvt., enl. 20 Dec 46 at Pittsburgh, age 26, listed as Musician or Bugler on all MRs after muster-in roll, listed as AWOL on Jan-Feb 48 MR, mo. with Co. 20 Jul 48.

KENNEDY, ROBERT: (Kenneday): Pvt., enl. 20 Dec 46 at Pittsburgh, age 29, left sick at Vera Cruz 8 Apr 47, hospitalized 9 Apr 47, died at Vera Cruz 20 Apr 47 from hernia.

KERR, ROBERT: (Carr): listed only on Co. MR of Jul-Aug 47 stating he was paid to place of enrollment.

KESSLER, MICHAEL: (Kesler, Kessloe, Kisslow): Pvt., enl. 20 Dec 46 at Pittsburgh, age 23, mo. with Co. 20 Jul 48. Moved to Danville. Pvt. Co. C, 14th P.V.I. (3 mos.) 26 Apr 61 to 8 Aug 61. Pvt. & Sgt. Co. A, 132nd P.V.I. 14 Aug 62 to 24 May 63, WIA at Fredericksburg 13 Dec 62. Pvt. Co. A, 87th P.V.I. 12 Jul 64 until WIA at Cedar Creek 19 Oct 64, still hospitalized for wounds at mo. 29 Jun 65. Died at Danville before 1880.

KIMMELL, HENRY R.: (Kemell, Kemmell): Pvt., enl. 20 Dec 46 at Pittsburgh, age 43, in guardhouse from 28 Dec 47, died in Mexico City Hospital 8 Jan 48.

KINNEY, ROBERT (Samuel): (Kenny): Pvt., enl. 20 Dec 46 at Pittsburgh, age 25, deserted from Camp Jackson near New Orleans 25 Jan 47.

KLINE, HENRY: Pvt., enl. 11 Oct 47 at York, joined Co. 30 Dec 47, mi. at San Angel 31 Dec 47, mo. with Co. 20 Jul 48.

KOUP, JOHN: (Kaoop): Pvt., enl. 23 Aug 47 at Pittsburgh, joined Co. 30 Dec 47, mi. at San Angel 31 Dec 47, mo. with Co. 20 Jul 48.

LANE, SHADRICK (Shadrach, Shadrack): Pvt., enl. 20 Dec 46 at Pittsburgh, age 27, listed as sick on Jan-Feb 47 MR, left sick at Vera Cruz 8 Apr 47, disc. at Vera Cruz 19 May 47 on SCD.

LARKINS, JOHN: (Larkin): Pvt., enl. 20 Dec 46 at Pittsburgh, age 25, promoted to Cpl. before 28 Feb 47, listed as sick in quarters on Nov-Dec 47 MR., mo. with Co. 20 Jul 48.

LAVERTY, EDWARD: (Lafferty): Pvt., enl. 20 Dec 46 at Pittsburgh, age 24, mo. with Co. 20 Jul 48.

LUSK, DAVID: Pvt., enl. 20 Dec 46 at Pittsburgh, age 23, mo. with Co. 20 Jul 48.

MAGEE, JOHN: (Mage, McGee): Pvt., enl. 4 Jan 47 at Pittsburgh, deserted 16 Aug 47, rejoined Co. 4 Mar 48, not listed as mo.

MAHON, JOHN D.: Pvt., enl. 20 Dec 46 at Pittsburgh, disc. at Mexico City 30 Oct 47, for youth and inability to perform the duties of a soldier.

MASONHEIMER, FREDERICK: (Masonhimer, Massinghamer, Massinghemer, Mensonheimer): Pvt., enl. 20 Dec 46 at Pittsburgh, age 35, died at Perote 20 Jun 47.

McCANN, HUGH: 2nd Sgt., enl. 20 Dec 46 at Pittsburgh, age 27, mo. with Co. 20 Jul 48.

McDONALD, FELIX: Pvt., enl. & mi. 28 Jan 47 at New Orleans, mo. with Co. 20 Jul 48.

McDONALD, JOHN: Pvt., enl. 20 Dec 46 at Pittsburgh, age 29, mo. with Co. 20 Jul 48.

McDONOUGH, HUGH: Pvt., enl. 20 Dec 46 at Pittsburgh, age 24, shown only on Co. muster-in roll.

McKINNEY, EDWARD: (McKenney): Pvt., enl. 20 Dec 46 at Pittsburgh, age 27, deserted at Pittsburgh 9 Jan 47.

MEARS, PATRICK: (Means): Pvt., enl. 20 Dec 46 at Pittsburgh, age 27, deserted from Camp Jackson near New Orleans 25 Jan 47.

MEYER, FREDERICK: (Meyor, Myer): Pvt., enl. 20 Dec 46 at Pittsburgh, age 31, lost a musket at Cerro Gordo and another at Chapultepec, WIA at Chapultepec 13 Sep 47, mo. with Co. 20 Jul 48.

MILLER, GEORGE H.: (Millar): Pvt., enl. 1 Sep 47 at Pittsburgh, joined Co. 30 Dec 47, mo. with Co. 20 Jul 48.

MINK, MICHAEL: (Menk): Pvt., enl. 20 Dec 46 at Pittsburgh, age 29, left sick at Puebla 8 Aug 47, died at Puebla 17 Oct 47 from diarrhea.

MONTGOMERY, FLEMING (Henry): Pvt., enl. 20 Dec 46 at Pittsburgh, age 25, killed in his tent at Camp Jackson near New Orleans 20 Jan 47 by unknown party or parties, being stabbed in the shoulder.

MULLIN, TIMOTHY: Pvt., enl. 20 Dec 46 at Pittsburgh, age 22, shown only on Co. muster-in roll.

MURPHY, JOHN: (Murphey): Pvt., enl. 20 Dec 46 at Pittsburgh, age 25, mo. with Co. 20 Jul 48.

MURPHY, PETER: (Murphey): 4th Cpl., enl. 20 Dec 46 at Pittsburgh, age 22, promoted to 4th Sgt. 18 Jan 47, mo. with Co. 20 Jul 48.

MURRAY, HENRY: Pvt., enl. 20 Dec 46 at Pittsburgh, age 28, deserted from Camp Jackson near New Orleans 25 Jan 47.

NEMEYER, FREDERICK: (Newmeyer, Newmyer, Neymmeyr, Neymyer): Pvt., enl. 20 Dec 46 at Pittsburgh, age 28, left sick at Perote 28 Jun 47, disc. at Perote 29 Oct 47 on SCD.

NICHOLSON, ROBERT D.: Pvt., enl. 20 Dec 46 at Pittsburgh, age 22, detailed to special duty about 22 May 48 of securing the bodies of fallen Pittsburgh comrades to take home, he became missing during this duty and it was supposed that he had been killed.

NOLAN, THOMAS: (Noland, Nolen, Nooland): Pvt., enl. at Harrisburg, age 19, left sick at Vera Cruz 8 Apr 47, disc. at Vera Cruz 19 May 47 on SCD.

NOLAND, CHARLES: Pvt., enl. 20 Dec 46 at Pittsburgh, age 22, shown only on Co. muster-in roll.

O'BRIEN, EDWARD: (O'Brian, O'Brion): Pvt., enl. 20 Dec 46 at Pittsburgh, age 27, promoted to 4th Cpl. 23 Feb 47, hospitalized in Mexico City 19 Dec 47, rejoined Co. by 29 Feb 48, mo. with Co. 20 Jul 48. Capt. Co. F, 12th P.V.I. (3 mos.) 25 Apr 61 to 5 Aug 61. Capt. Co. D, Lt. Col. & Col. 134th P.V.I. 14 Aug 62 to 26 May 63. Died 9 Jul 77.

O'BRIEN, PATRICK: (O'Brian): Pvt., enl. 20 Dec 46 at Pittsburgh, age 27, deserted at Jalapa 19 Jun 47.

OPLIGER, JOHN: (Oblinger, Oplegar, Opligar): Pvt., enl. 20 Dec 46 at Pittsburgh, age 29, left sick at Perote 28 Jun 47, died at Perote 28 Jun 47.

PORTER, ROBERT: Capt., enl. 20 Dec 46 at Pittsburgh, age 30, left for recruiting duty 1 Nov 47, rejoined Co. in Pittsburgh, mo. with Co. 20 Jul 48.

POWELL, CHARLES: Pvt., enl. 20 Dec 46 at Pittsburgh, age 21, mo. with Co. 20 Jul 48.

RANKIN, WILLIAM: 1st Lt., enl. 20 Dec 46 at Pittsburgh, age 26, hospitalized in Mexico City 19 Dec 47, assumed command of Co. 21 Feb 48, mo. with Co. 20 Jul 48.

REED, JOHN W.: Cpl., enl. 20 Dec 46 at Pittsburgh, age 30, shown only on Co. muster-in roll.

RICHIE, PETER: (Richey): Pvt., enl. & mi. 28 Jan 47 at New Orleans, mo. with Co. 20 Jul 48.

ROBINSON, JAMES: Pvt., enl. 30 Dec 46 at Pittsburgh, deserted from Camp Jackson near New Orleans 25 Jan 47.

RONNER, JACOB: (Renner, Roener, Roenor, Rouner): Pvt., enl. 20 Dec 46 at Pittsburgh, age 33, mo. with Co. 20 Jul 48.

SALLY, JOHN J.: (Sallea): Pvt., enl. 20 Dec 46 at Pittsburgh, age 21, left sick at Puebla 8 Aug 47, died at Puebla 17 Oct 47 from pleuritis.

SCHREIDER, ADAM: (Schneider, Shrader, Shreader, Shreider): Pvt., enl. 20 Dec 46 at Pittsburgh, age 26, died in regimental hospital in Mexico City 14 Oct 47 from acute dysentery.

SCHULTZ, JOHN: (Sculter, Shultz): Pvt., enl. 20 Dec 46 at Pittsburgh, age 25, deserted at Jalapa 20 May 47.

SHEARING, CALEB: (Schearing, Shearer): Pvt., enl. 20 Dec 46 at Pittsburgh, age 29, listed as sick having lost the power of his legs on Jan-Feb 47 MR, mo. with Co. 20 Jul 48.

SKELLY, WILLIAM P. (S.): (Kelly, Skelley): 2nd Lt., enl. 20 Dec 46 at Pittsburgh, age 22, commanding Co. from 19 Dec 47 to 21 Feb 48, was sick in Mar 48, mo. with Co. 20 Jul 48.

SMITH, DANIEL: Pvt., enl. 20 Dec 46 at Pittsburgh, age 24, mo. with Co. 20 Jul 48.

SMITH, EDWARD: Fifer, enl. 20 Dec 46 at Pittsburgh, age 19, reduced to Pvt. before 28 Feb 47, mo. with Co. 20 Jul 48.

SMITH, JAMES: Pvt., enl. 20 Dec 46 at Pittsburgh, age 24, died in regimental hospital in Mexico City 25 Nov 47 from chronic bronchitis.

SMITH, PETER M.: Pvt., enl. 20 Dec 46 at Pittsburgh, age 29, died in regimental hospital in Mexico City 11 Dec 47 from diarrhea.

SOLOMON, CHARLES E.: Cpl., enl. 20 Dec 46 at Pittsburgh, age 21, listed as sick on Jan-Feb 47 MR, hospitalized in Mexico City from 19 Dec 47 to 26 Jan 48, mo. with Co. 20 Jul 48.

STAUGH, PETER M.: Pvt., enl. 12 Oct 47 at York, joined Co. 30 Dec 47, mi. at San Angel 31 Dec 47, died at San Angel 20 May 48.

STEWART, CHARLES: (Stuart): Pvt., enl. 20 Dec 46 at Pittsburgh, age 31, KIA at Garita de Belen 13 Sep 47 OR AWOL from 30 Apr 48, listed as AWOL on muster-out roll, conflicting information appears on the rolls.

STRICKER, CHARLES: (Striker): Drummer, enl. & mi. 7 Apr 47 at Vera Cruz, mo. with Co. 20 Jul 48.

THOMAS, JOHN: Pvt., enl. 20 Dec 46 at Pittsburgh, age 26, shown only on Co. muster-in roll.

VANSWARTMAN, FRANCIS: (VanSwarttouw, Vanswarttow): 1st Sgt., enl. 20 Dec 46 at Pittsburgh, age 34, mo. with Co. 20 Jul 48.

VULSE, FRANCIS: (Feels, Fuls, Veels, Voultz, Vuls): Pvt., enl. 20 Dec 46 at Pittsburgh, age 29, left sick at Perote 28 Jun 47, died at Perote 28 Jun 47.

WEIDY, NICHOLAS: (Werdy): Pvt., enl. 20 Dec 46 at Pittsburgh, age 26, shown only on Co. muster-in roll.

WISE, FREDERICK: Pvt., enl. 20 Dec 46 at Pittsburgh, age 34, deserted from Camp Jackson near New Orleans 25 Jan 47.

WISEMAN, ROBERT: Pvt., enl. 20 Dec 46 at Pittsburgh, age 22, shown only on Co. muster-in roll.

YOST, HENRY: (Yoste):   Pvt., enl. 20 Dec 46 at Pittsburgh, age 35, left sick at Perote 28 Jun 47, died at Perote 12 Jul 47.

Company K, 2nd Regiment
Stockton Artillerists

The Stockton Artillerists, named for Navy Commodore Robert F. Stockton, had already existed for several years when the Mexican War broke out, and by 15 July they had offered their services to the government. They left their homes in the Mauch Chunk area of Carbon County on 24 December and proceeded to Pittsburgh by way of Pottsville, Philadelphia, Baltimore and Cumberland, Maryland. They arrived on New Years Day and were that day mustered in by First Lieutenant Horace B. Field, 3rd U.S. Artillery.

During their active war service, the Artillerists took part in the siege of Vera Cruz and the battles of Cerro Gordo, Chapultepec and Garita de Belen.

The company returned to Pittsburgh, where on 12 July 1848 they were mustered out by Major George Wright, 4th U.S. Infantry. On 20 July the Artillerists arrived at Mauch Chunk where they were treated to rounds of banquets and receptions. It is believed that the company's history ended with its return from the Mexican War.

A total of 95 men served in the company during the war, three of them recruits who joined it in Mexico. The company was plagued by five desertions. Sixteen of its members suffered battle related injuries, with only one being killed. In all, twenty of the Artillerists died in service, and an additional nine received discharges before muster out.

BACHMAN, JOHN F.: (Bauchman): Pvt., enl. 20 Dec 46 at Mauch Chunk, age 19, occ. printer, on extra duty as printer in Mexico City from 26 Oct 47, rejoined Co. by 30 Apr 48, mo. with Co. 12 Jul 48.

BELFORD, JAMES: (Bedford): Pvt., enl. 20 Dec 46 at Mauch Chunk, age 28, occ. blacksmith, mo. with Co. 12 Jul 48.

BERG, CHARLES M.: Sgt., enl. 24 Dec 46 at Phila., age 26, occ. clerk, resigned his appointment as Sgt. to become Pvt. 18 Jan 47, on extra duty with the Commissary Dept. aboard the ship *Ocean* in Feb 47, employed by the Gen. as clerk according to Mar-Apr 47 MR, transferred to 2nd U.S. Dragoons 30 Jun 47 in exchange for Pvt. Henry Levi.

BLAIN, EDWARD: Pvt., enl. 20 Dec 46 at Mauch Chunk, age 20, occ. carpenter, slightly WIA in the cheek in the charge at Chapultepec 13 Sep 47, mo. with Co. 12 Jul 48.

BLAIN, JESSE: Pvt., enl. 20 Dec 46 at Mauch Chunk, age 22, occ. laborer, promoted to 2nd Cpl. 1 Sep 47, mo. with Co. 12 Jul 48.

BROWN, STEPHEN: Pvt., enl. 20 Dec 46 at Mauch Chunk, age 22, occ. carpenter, died at Perote 23 Jun 47.

BUSTARD, JAMES: (Busthard): Pvt., enl. 20 Dec 46 at Mauch Chunk, age 21, occ. shoemaker, severely WIA in the right leg at Garita de Belen 13 Sep 47, hospitalized in Mexico City from 14 Sep 47, disc. at Mexico City 5 Mar 48 on SCD for wounds.

CAMPBELL, BROOKS: (Campble): Pvt., enl. 20 Dec 46 at Mauch Chunk, age 20, occ. founder, confined to guardhouse according to Sep-Oct 47 MR, mo. with Co. 12 Jul 48.

CLARK, GEORGE E. A.: (Clarck): Pvt., enl. 20 Dec 46 at Mauch Chunk, age 21, occ. printer, mo. with Co. 12 Jul 48.

CLEMMENS, WILLIAM: (Clemence, Clemens, Clements): Pvt., enl. 20 Dec 46 at Mauch Chunk, age 22, occ. laborer, fined $3.50 by Court Martial according to May-Jun 47 MR, WIA in right shoulder at Chapultepec 13 Sep 47, attached to regimental hospital as attendant 16 Sep 47, rejoined Co. by 31 Dec 47, mo. with Co. 12 Jul 48.

COLLINS, JONATHAN N.: Pvt., enl. 20 Dec 46 at Mauch Chunk, age 19, occ. collier, died in regimental hospital at San Angel 14 Feb 48 from typhus fever.

COLLINS, PETER: Pvt., enl. 20 Dec 46 at Mauch Chunk, age 23, occ. collier, mo. with Co. 12 Jul 48.

CONNELLY, JOHN (Joseph): Pvt., enl. 20 Dec 46 at Mauch Chunk, age 23, occ. laborer, deserted at New Orleans 20 Jan 47.

CRELLEN, THOMAS R.: (Crellin): 1st Sgt., enl. 20 Dec 46 at Mauch Chunk, age 23, occ. carpenter, listed as sick in Mexico City on Sep-Oct 47 MR, disc. at Mexico City 27 Nov 47 on SCD. Living in Mauch Chunk in 1884.

CUTLER, CHARLES: (Cuttler): Pvt., enl. 20 Dec 46 at Mauch Chunk, age 23, occ. shoemaker, mo. with Co. 12 Jul 48.

DARFLING, CONRAD: (Derfling, Dorfling): Pvt., enl. 20 Dec 46 at Mauch Chunk, age 31, occ. miner, listed as sick in camp on Mar-Apr 47 MR, on extra duty at the Palace with Capt. Naylor according to Sep-Oct 47 MR, hospitalized at San Angel according to Mar-Apr 48 MR, mo. with Co. 12 Jul 48.

DAVIS, EMOR M.: Pvt., enl. 20 Dec 46 at Mauch Chunk, age 20, occ. shoemaker, severely WIA in the foot at Garita de Belen 13 Sep 47, hospitalized in Mexico City from 14 Sep 47, disc. at Mexico City 5 Mar 48 on SCD for wounds.

DETWILER, JOHN P.: (Detweiler, Detwilder): Pvt., enl. 20 Dec 46 at Mauch Chunk, age 23, occ. butcher, on extra duty from 20 Mar to 30 Mar 47, left sick at Perote 28 Jun 47, disc. at Perote 29 Oct 47 on SCD.

DILLY, LYMAN: (Dilley): Pvt., enl. 20 Dec 46 at Mauch Chunk, age 21, occ. carpenter, died at Jalapa 29 Apr 47 from congestion of the brain.

EMORY, ABRAHAM H. (D.): (Emery): Pvt., enl. 20 Dec 46 at Mauch Chunk, age 26, occ. carpenter, died at Puebla Hospital 27 Jul 47.

FENNER, GEORGE W.: Pvt., enl. 20 Dec 46 at Mauch Chunk, age 22, occ. carpenter, accidently shot and killed a teenager named Lewis Malisee in Pittsburgh 6 Jan 47, listed as sick in camp on Mar-Apr 47 MR, hospitalized at Perote according to May-Jun 47 MR, mo. with Co. 12 Jul 48.

FERRIS, WILLIAM A.: (Fennis, Ferres): Pvt., enl. 20 Dec 46 at Mauch Chunk, age 30, occ. laborer, hospitalized at Jalapa according to Mar-Apr 47 MR, left sick at Puebla 8 Aug 47, disc. at Puebla 4 Nov 47 on SCD.

FIELD, MICHAEL: (Fields): Pvt., enl. 24 Dec 46 at Phila., age 28, occ. baker, employed by the artillery in Apr 47, listed as sick in quarters on Sep-Oct 47 MR, mo. with Co. 12 Jul 48. Pvt. Co. I, 15th Kansas Vol. Cav., enl. 16 Sep 63.

FIELDS, GEORGE W.: Pvt., enl. 24 Dec 46 at Phila., age 19, occ. baker, on detached duty as baker according to Jul-Aug & Sep-Oct 47 MRs, on extra duty as baker from 19 Dec 47, rejoined Co. by 29 Feb 48, mo. with Co. 12 Jul 48.

FOESIG, JACOB: (Faesich, Faesig, Feasig, Folsig): Pvt., enl. 25 Dec. 46 at Reading, age 26, occ. butcher, left sick at Puebla 8 Aug 47, died at Puebla 20 Aug 47.

FRITZINGER, JOHN: Pvt., enl. 20 Dec 46 at Mauch Chunk, age 28, occ. laborer, left sick at Vera Cruz 9 Apr 47, died at Vera Cruz 2 May 47 from debility.

GALLOGHER, DAVID E.: (Galagher, Galeher, Gallacher, Gallagher): Pvt., enl. 24 Dec 46 at Phila., age 23, occ. laborer, listed as sick at Jalapa on Mar-Apr 47 MR, died at Perote 21 Jun 47.

GRAY, ISAAC: Pvt., enl. 20 Dec 46 at Mauch Chunk, age 28, occ. laborer, confined in guardhouse according to Sep-Oct 47 MR, mo. with Co. 12 Jul 48.

GUTH, HORACE: Pvt., enl. 20 Dec 46 at Mauch Chunk, age 23, occ. cobbler, left sick at Puebla 8 Aug 47, rejoined Co. by 31 Dec 47, mo. with Co. 12 Jul 48.

HANDMANDEL, JOHN: (Handmandle): Pvt., enl. 20 Dec 46 at Mauch Chunk, age 29, occ. laborer, left sick at Puebla 8 Aug 47, rejoined Co. by 31 Dec 47, mo. with Co. 12 Jul 48.

HARRIOTT, WILLIAM: Pvt., enl. 20 Dec 46 at Mauch Chunk, age 30, occ. carpenter, left sick at Perote in Jun 47, died at Perote 2 Aug 47.

HASSEN, MICHAEL: (Hasson): Pvt., enl. & mi. 18 May 47 at Jalapa, age 40, occ. miner, slightly WIA in the hip in the charge at Chapultepec 13 Sep 47, listed as confined on Sep-Oct 47 MR, mo. with Co. 12 Jul 48.

HEATH, CLARK: Pvt., enl. 20 Dec 46 at Mauch Chunk, age 21, occ. collier, mo. with Co. 12 Jul 48.

HEISTAND, JOHN W.: (Hestand, Hiestand): Pvt., enl. 26 Dec 46 at Phila., age 21, occ. clerk, left sick at Puebla 8 Aug 47, detached to Jalapa Hospital as cook 1 Jan 48, mo. with Co. 12 Jul 48.

HENRY, ALEXANDER: Pvt., enl. 20 Dec 46 at Mauch Chunk, age 32, occ. miner, confined in guardhouse according to Sep-Oct 47 MR., mo. with Co. 12 Jul 48.

HERTER, SAMUEL: (Horter): Pvt., enl. 20 Dec 46 at Mauch Chunk, age 33, occ. miner, fined $7.00 by Court Martial according to May-Jun 47 MR, confined in guardhouse according to Sep-Oct 47 MR, mo. with Co. 12 Jul 48.

HILEMAN, JOSEPH: 3rd Cpl., enl. 20 Dec 46 at Mauch Chunk, age 23, occ. carpenter, reduced to Pvt. in Sep or Oct 47, promoted to Cpl. 1 Feb 48, mo. with Co. 12 Jul 48.

HORN, JOHN: Pvt., enl. 20 Dec 46 at Mauch Chunk, age 20, occ. laborer, listed as sick in camp on Mar-Apr 47 MR, severely WIA in the neck at Chapultepec 13 Sep 47, hospitalized at San Angel according to Jan-Feb 48 MR, mo. with Co. 12 Jul 48.

HORN, JOSIAH: Pvt., enl. 20 Dec 46 at Mauch Chunk, age 21, occ. machinist, WIA in the thigh at Cerro Gordo 18 Apr 47, left sick at Puebla 8 Aug 47, rejoined Co. by 31 Dec 47, attached to regimental band 1 Jan 48 until mo. with Co. 12 Jul 48.

HORN, SAMUEL: (Horne, Horner): Drummer, enl. 20 Dec 46 at Mauch Chunk, age 44, occ. hatter, appointed Drum Major 10 Jul 47, listed as absent on Sep-Oct 47 F & S MR, reduced to Co. Drummer in Nov or Dec 47, listed as sick in quarters on Nov-Dec 47 MR, mo. with Co. 12 Jul 48.

HORN, WILLIAM: Pvt., enl. 20 Dec 46 at Mauch Chunk, age 22, occ. miner, hospitalized at San Angel according to Jan-Feb & Mar-Apr 48 MRs, mo. with Co. 12 Jul 48.

HOWELL, WILLIAM: Pvt., enl. 20 Dec 46 at Mauch Chunk, age 27, occ. shoemaker, left sick at Puebla 8 Aug 47, disc. at Puebla 4 Nov 47 on SCD.

KAVENY, PHILIP: (Caveny): Pvt., enl. 20 Dec 46 at Mauch Chunk, age 20, occ. moulder, listed as sick in camp on Mar-Apr 47 MR, hospitalized in Mexico City 25 Nov 47, hospitalized in San Angel according to Mar-Apr 48 MR, mo. with Co. 12 Jul 48.

KITLER, JOHN B. (D.): (Ketler, Kettler): Pvt., enl. 20 Dec 46 at Mauch Chunk, age 25, occ. laborer, mo. with Co. 12 Jul 48.

KLINE, FREDERICK C.: (Cline): Bugler, enl. 20 Dec 46 at Mauch Chunk, age 25, occ. shoemaker, listed as sick in camp on Mar-Apr 47 MR, attached to regimental band according to Jan-Feb 48 MR, mo. with Co. 12 Jul 48.

KLOTZ, ROBERT: 2nd Lt., enl. 20 Dec 46 at Mauch Chunk, age 27, occ. merchant, on furlough from 4 May 47, while marching from Vera Cruz to rejoin his Co. he was detailed to Co. K, 11th U.S. Inf. & participated in the skirmish of Puente Nationale, rejoined Co. 7 Dec 47, on furlough in Mar 48, appointed Adjutant 7 Apr 48, absent on leave at mo. Col. 19th Pa. Emergency Militia 15 Sept 62 to 27 Sep 62. Died 1 May 95.

KOENIG, HENRY: Pvt., enl. 20 Dec 46 at Mauch Chunk, age 22, occ. laborer, deserted at Pittsburgh 9 Jan 47.

KRAMER, JOSEPH: Pvt., enl. 20 Dec 46 at Mauch Chunk, age 27, occ. miner, deserted at New Orleans 20 Jan 47.

LEVI, HENRY: (Levy): Pvt., enl. 1 Jul 47 at Perote, age 20, occ. pedlar, transferred from 2nd U.S. Dragoons 1 Jul 47 in exchange for Pvt. Charles M. Berg, procured a Substitute (David McFadden) and was accordingly disc. 1 Apr 48.

LINK, ORLANDO: Pvt., enl. 20 Dec 46 at Mauch Chunk, age 19, occ. blacksmith, left sick at Perote 22 Jun 47, rejoined Co. by 31 Dec 47, mo. with Co. 12 Jul 48.

LIPPINCOTT, SAMUEL: Pvt., enl. 20 Dec 46 at Mauch Chunk, age 30, occ. laborer, confined in guardhouse according to Nov-Dec 47 MR, died in San Angel 8 Feb 48 from diarrhea.

McALLISTER, ROBERT: (McCallister): Pvt., enl. 20 Dec 46 at Mauch Chunk, age 25, occ. shoemaker, promoted to Cpl. 1 Sep 47, mo. with Co. 12 Jul 48.

McFADDEN, DAVID: Pvt., enl. & mi. 1 Apr 48 at San Angel, age 19, occ. laborer, procured as a substitute for Pvt. Henry Levi, mo. with Co. 12 Jul 48.

McFALL, HENRY: Pvt., enl. 20 Dec 46 at Mauch Chunk, age 18, occ. boatman, killed near San Augustin 28 Aug 47.

McKEEN, JAMES, JR.: (McKean): 2nd Lt., enl. 20 Dec 46 at Mauch Chunk, age 24, occ. lawyer, serving as Q.M. according to Mar-Apr 47 MR, was Acting Asst. Q.M. in Jun 47, left sick at Puebla 8 Aug 47, WIA at Puebla, died at Puebla 25 Sep 47.

MILLER, JAMES: Capt., enl. 20 Dec 46 at Mauch Chunk, age 23, occ. watchmaker, severely WIA in the right arm at Chapultepec 13 Sep 47, left 1 Nov 47 for recuperation and recruiting duty in Pa., arrived in Phila. 15 Dec 47, left home for return to Mexico by 18 Mar 48, rejoined Co. 11 Apr 48, was sick in Apr 48, mo. with Co. 12 Jul 48. Col. 81st P.V.I. 8 Aug 61 until KIA at Fair Oaks 31 May 62.

MOORE, WILLIAM O.: Pvt., enl. 24 Dec 46 at Phila., age 19, occ. miner, promoted to Cpl. 7 Aug 47, killed near San Augustin 28 Aug 47.

NOLAN, JOHN: (Noland, Nolen, Nolin): Pvt., enl. 24 Dec 46 at Phila., age 19, occ. moulder, served as nurse in Mexico City Hospital from 19 Dec 47, rejoined Co. by 29 Feb 48, mo. with Co. 12 Jul 48.

PAUL, JOHN YATES: Pvt., enl. 20 Dec 46 at Mauch Chunk, age 20, shown only on Co. muster-in roll.

PRIOR, JOHN W.: (Pryor): Cpl., enl. 20 Dec 46 at Mauch Chunk, age 21, occ. moulder, promoted to Sgt. 15 Feb 47, mo. with Co. 12 Jul 48. 1st Lt. Co. G & Capt. Co. D, 81st P.V.I. 16 Sep 61 to 4 Feb 64, WIA at Charles City Crossroads, Fredericksburg & Gettysburg.

REARICH, MICHAEL: Pvt., enl. 20 Dec 46 at Mauch Chunk, age 19, shown only on Co. muster-in roll.

REMMELL, EDWARD: Pvt., enl. 20 Dec 46 at Mauch Chunk, age 21, occ. shoemaker, mo. with Co. 12 Jul 48. Living in Mauch Chunk in 1913.

REMMELL, JACOB: (Remmit): Pvt., enl. 20 Dec 46 at Mauch Chunk, age 27, occ. wheelwright, mo. with Co. 12 Jul 48.

RENINGER, WILLIAM: (Ryninger): Pvt., enl. 24 Dec 46 at Phila., age 27, occ. cap maker, serving as orderly to Capt. Naylor in the Palace according to Sep-Oct 47 MR, listed as sick in quarters on Nov-Dec 47 MR, attached to regimental band as of 1 Apr 48, mo. with Co. 12 Jul 48.

REX, HENRY: (Red): Pvt., enl. 20 Dec 46 at Mauch Chunk, age 27, occ. tanner, listed as sick in quarters on Nov-Dec 47 MR, mo. with Co. 12 Jul 48.

RHUE, EDWARD: (Rhu): Pvt., enl. 24 Dec 46 at Phila., age 20, occ. clerk, left sick at Puebla 7 Aug 47, died at Puebla 22 or 25 Oct 47 from diarrhea.

RICHARDS, JOSEPH: Pvt., enl. 24 Dec 46 at Phila., age 19, occ. laborer, listed as sick in Vera Cruz on Mar-Apr 47 MR, died in Mexico City 19 Oct 47 from diarrhea.

ROSS, CHARLES K. (R.): Pvt., enl. 24 Dec 46 at Phila., age 24, occ. cabinet maker, promoted to Sgt. 18 Jan 47, listed as sick in quarters on Nov-Dec 47 MR, mo. with Co. 12 Jul 48.

SAPP, ISAAC: Pvt., enl. 24 Dec 46 at Phila., age 27, occ. laborer, left sick at Puebla 7 Aug 47, died at Puebla 17 Oct 47 from harmoptysis.

SHERLOCK, SAMUEL: (Shurlock): Pvt., enl. 20 Dec 46 at Mauch Chunk, age 24, occ. sailor, detailed to Capt. Steptoe's Battery of U.S. Artillery in Apr & May 47, appointed Color Sgt. 1 Oct 47, promoted to 4th Sgt. 1 Feb 48, mo. with Co. 12 Jul 48. Sgt. Co. I & Capt. Co. D, 81st P.V.I. 15 Oct 61 until KIA at Fair Oaks 15 Jun 62.

SMITH, BENJAMIN: Pvt., enl. 20 Dec 46 at Mauch Chunk, age 19, occ. laborer, mo. with Co. 12 Jul 48.

SMITH, WILLIAM W.: 3rd Sgt., enl. 20 Dec 46 at Mauch Chunk, age 23, occ. blacksmith, reduced to Pvt. 15 Feb 47, WIA in the right leg at Chapultepec 13 Sep 47, listed as sick in quarters on Nov-Dec 47 MR., mo. with Co. 12 Jul 48.

SNYDER, WILLIAM: Pvt., enl. 20 Dec 46 at Mauch Chunk, age 21, occ. carpenter, listed as sick in camp on Mar-Apr 47 MR, WIA in the leg at Chapultepec 13 Sep 47, mo. with Co. 12 Jul 48.

SOLINSKI, WILLIAM (C.H.W.) (C.W.H.): (Solensky, Solinsky): 1st Cpl., enl. 20 Dec 46 at Mauch Chunk, age 29, occ. artist, promoted to 2nd Lt. 27 Oct 47, mo. with Co. 12 Jul 48.

SOLOMON, JOHN: (Sollomon): Pvt., enl. 20 Dec 46 at Mauch Chunk, age 22, occ. moulder, severely WIA in the right foot at Chapultepec 13 Sep 47, re-joined Co. by 29 Feb 48, mo. with Co. 12 Jul 48.

SOMMERS, FREDERICK: (Somers): Pvt., enl. 20 Dec 46 at Mauch Chunk, age 23, occ. butcher, WIA in the left arm at Cerro Gordo 18 Apr 47, left sick at Perote in Jun 47, rejoined Co. by 31 Dec 47, mo. with Co. 12 Jul 48.

STADON, SAMUEL G.: (Stadden, Staddon, Straddon): 2nd Cpl., enl. 20 Dec 46 at Mauch Chunk, age 28, occ. clerk, died at Puebla 3 Aug 47.

STAPLES, THOMAS (Joseph R.): Pvt., enl. 20 Dec 46 at Mauch Chunk, age 25, occ. shoemaker, was sick in Jalapa in Apr 47, left sick at Perote in Jun 47, died at Perote 24 Jul 47.

STARK, CHARLES: Pvt., enl. 20 Dec 46 at Mauch Chunk, age 23, occ. laborer, listed as sick in quarters on Sep-Oct & Nov-Dec 47 MRs, mo. with Co. 12 Jul 48.

STEPHENS, JOHN: Pvt., enl. 20 Dec 46 at Mauch Chunk, age 28, occ. laborer, deserted at New Orleans 20 Jan 47.

STRAUS, WILLIAM: (Strous): Sgt., enl. 20 Dec 46 at Mauch Chunk, age 34, occ. butcher, left sick at Puebla 8 Aug 47, rejoined Co. by 31 Dec 47, listed as sick in quarters on Nov-Dec 47 MR, promoted to 1st Sgt. 1 Feb 48, mo. with Co. 12 Jul 48.

STREET, JOHN: Pvt., enl. 25 Dec 46 at Reading, age 20, occ. fireman, left sick at Vera Cruz 9 Apr 47, rejoined Co. by 31 Aug 47, KIA at Chapultepec 13 Sep 47.

SWAIN, JOHN: (Swayne): Pvt., enl. 24 Dec 46 at Phila, age 21, occ. tailor, on extra duty at hospital according to Sep-Oct 47 MR, mo. with Co. 12 Jul 48.

THOMAN, FREDERICK A.: Pvt., enl. 20 Dec 46 at Mauch Chunk, age 25, occ. clerk, left sick at Perote 28 Jun 47, disc. at Perote 4 Oct 47 on SCD for chronic rheumatism.

THOMAS, HEZEKIAH: Pvt., enl. 20 Dec 46 at Mauch Chunk, age 21, occ. machinist, was sick at Jalapa in Apr 47, severely WIA in the right shoulder at Chapultepec 13 Sep 47, mo. with Co. 12 Jul 48.

WALLACE, ROBERT: Pvt., enl. 20 Dec 46 at Mauch Chunk, age 23, occ. laborer, promoted to Cpl. 15 Feb 47, mo. with Co. 12 Jul 48.

WALTERS, WILLIAM: Pvt., enl. 25 Dec 46 at Reading, age 23, occ. sailor, detailed as Attendant in hospital according to Mar-Apr 47 MR, left sick at Perote 28 Jun 47, died at Perote 19 Jul 47.

WARREN, WILLIAM: Pvt., enl. 20 Dec 46 at Mauch Chunk, age 29, occ. machinist, was sick at Jalapa in Apr 47, died at Jalapa 16 May 47 from febris intermittent.

WHITE, GEORGE W.: (Wite): Pvt., enl. 1 Dec 46 at Phila., age 21, occ. coach maker, transferred from Co. F, 2nd Pa. Regt. at San Augustin 1 Sep 47 in exchange for Pvt. John B. Wier, disc. at Mexico City 1 Dec 47 on SCD to date from 27 Nov 47.

WIER, JOHN B. (U.): (Weir): Pvt., enl. 20 Dec 46 at Mauch Chunk, age 26, occ. printer, on furlough according to Mar-Apr 47 MR, transferred to Co. F, 2nd Pa. Regt. 31 Aug 47 at San Augustin in exchange for Pvt. George W. White.

WILHELM, WILLIAM: (Willhelm): Pvt., enl. 20 Dec 46 at Mauch Chunk, age 19, occ. laborer, WIA in the left leg at Cerro Gordo 18 Apr 47, left sick at Perote 28 Jun 47, rejoined Co. by 31 Aug 47, attached to regimental band from 1 Jan 48 through 30 Apr 48, fined $7.00 by Court Martial according to Mar-Apr 48 MR, mo. with Co. 12 Jul 48.

WITHINGTON, WILLIAM: Pvt., enl. 20 Dec 46 at Mauch Chunk, age 21, occ. laborer, deserted at New Orleans 20 Jan 47.

WOLF, HIRAM: 1st Lt., enl. 20 Dec 46 at Mauch Chunk, age 23, occ. clerk, on furlough in Jun 47, under arrest in Dec 47, under arrest from 13 Feb 48 through Apr 48, fined by Court Martial 1 Apr 48, mo. with Co. 12 Jul 48. Died at Danville 5 Mar 66 and is buried there.

YOUNG, JOHN W.: Pvt., enl. 20 Dec 46 at Mauch Chunk, age 26, occ. laborer, left sick at Puebla 8 Aug 47, died at Puebla 20 Sep 47.

YOUNG, SAMUEL: Pvt., enl. 20 Dec 46 at Mauch Chunk, age 24, occ. laborer, was sick at Jalapa in Apr 47, left sick at Puebla 8 Aug 47, rejoined Co. 19 Apr 48, mo. with Co. 12 Jul 48.

Company L, 2nd Regiment
Independent Grays

The Independent Grays of Bedford, by 1846, had already attained a high reputation in their area for discipline and military efficiency. They had been among the ninety companies to volunteer at the outbreak of the Mexican War. However, it was not until about 15 March 1847 that they were accepted for service under the third call for Pennsylvania troops.

The Grays left Bedford on 22 May and arrived in Pittsburgh on the 26th. That same day they were mustered into Federal service by First Lieutenant Horace B. Field, 3rd U.S. Artillery. It was decided that they should become part of the 2nd Regiment, and so they joined it at Puebla on 7 August. They participated in the storming of Chapultepec and Garita de Belen, where their full ranks proved to be an asset.

The Independent Grays arrived at Pittsburgh on 10 July and were mustered out there on the 14th by Major George Wright, 4th U.S. Infantry. A few days later they returned to Bedford to be the center of attention and to enjoy a hero's welcome.

A total of 87 men served in the company during the war. No recruits joined the ranks despite the desertion of eighteen members. Nine Grays suffered battle related injuries, and three of them proved fatal. In all, fourteen Grays died in service, and an additional nine received discharges prior to muster out.

ADAMS, CHARLES: Pvt., enl. 6 May 47 at Bedford, age 21, deserted at Pittsburgh 27 May 47.

AKE, CHAUNCEY (Chauncy): Pvt., enl. 6 May 47 at Buckstown, age 20, occ. farmer, deserted at Pittsburgh 27 May 47.

AKE, SAMUEL: Pvt., enl. 6 May 47 at Buckstown, age 20, occ. farmer, deserted at Pittsburgh 27 May 47.

BAKER, JACOB: Pvt., enl. 16 Jun 47 at New Orleans, age 21, occ. shoemaker, mi. at Vera Cruz 8 Jul 47, mo. with Co. 14 Jul 48.

BELLVILLE, ARCHIBALD: (Belleville): Pvt., enl. 30 May 47 at Wheeling, Va., age 25, occ. farmer, mi. at New Orleans 15 Jun 47, mo. with Co. 14 Jul 48.

BISHOP, WILLIAM: Pvt., enl. 6 May 47 at Bethel Township, age 19, occ. farmer, slightly WIA in the leg by a musket ball at Chapultepec 13 Sep 47, promoted to 4th Sgt. after 30 Apr 48, mo. with Co. 14 Jul 48.

BOWMAN, DANIEL: (Bowhan): Pvt., enl. 26 May 47 at Pittsburgh, age 39, occ. blacksmith, deserted at New Orleans 21 Jun 47.

CAMPBELL, THOMAS: Pvt., enl. 6 May 47 at Dublin Township, age 22, occ. farmer, left sick at Perote 1 Aug 47, disc. at Perote 29 Oct 47 on SCD.

CARNEY, ANDREW J.: Pvt., enl. 6 May 47 at Dublin Township, age 19, occ. farmer, left sick at Puebla 8 Aug 47, rejoined Co. 20 Dec 47, mo. with Co. 14 Jul 48.

CHESTNUT, JOHN: Pvt., enl. 6 May 47 at Dublin Township, age 21, occ. farmer, deserted at Cincinnati 2 Jun 47.

COWAN, JAMES: (Cowen): Pvt., enl. 6 May 47 at Dublin Township, age 21, occ. farmer, hospitalized in Mexico City 19 Dec 47, rejoined Co. by 29 Feb 48, mo. with Co. 14 Jul 48.

DANIELS, CHARLES: Pvt., enl. 6 May 47 at Belfast Township, age 22, occ. tinner, listed as sick on Sep-Oct 47 MR, mo. with Co. 14 Jul 48.

DAVIS, BIVEN R.: Sgt., enl. 6 May 47 at Bedford, age 20, promoted to 2nd Lt. 7 Dec 47, under arrest according to Jan-Feb 48 MR, suspended from command for two months and to lose pay by General Court Martial 22 Mar 48, mo. with Co. 14 Jul 48.

DAVIS, THOMAS: Pvt., enl. 6 May 47 at Shellsburg, age 23, occ. chair maker, severely WIA in the head by a musket ball at Chapultepec 13 Sep 47, mo. with Co. 14 Jul 48.

DAVIS, WILLIAM: Pvt., enl. 6 May 47 at Adamsburg, age 20, occ. cooper, deserted at New Orleans 21 Jun 47.

DUNAHOE, GEORGE: (Donahue, Dunehoe): Pvt., enl. 23 Jun 47 at New Orleans, age 27, occ. farmer, mi. at Vera Cruz 15 Jul 47, died in Mexico City 5 Oct 47 from chronic bronchitis.

ECKERT, JESSE: (Eckart): Pvt., enl. 6 May 47 at Shellsburg, age 21, occ. tailor, on duty as tailor in Co. fixing clothes during Dec 47, mo. with Co. 14 Jul 48.

ERNST, GEORGE (John) P.: (Earnest, Earnst): Pvt., enl. 6 May 47 at Adamsburg, age 35, deserted at New Orleans 19 Jun 47.

FABLE, CHRISTOPHER: Pvt., enl. 6 May 47 at Bedford, age 29, occ. shoemaker, mo. with Co. 14 Jul 48.

FADICK, WILLIAM: (Faddick): Pvt., enl. 6 May 47 at Shellsburg, age 41, occ. shoemaker, mo. with Co. 14 Jul 48.

FEATHER, JOHN: Pvt., enl. 6 May 47 at Shellsburg, age 20, occ. tanner, promoted to Cpl. after 30 Apr 48, mo. with Co. 14 Jul 48.

FINLEY, RUSSELL H.: (Findley): Pvt., enl. 26 May 47 at Pittsburgh, age 25, occ. farmer, mo. with Co. 14 Jul 48.

FORE, DAVID: (Stove): Cpl., enl. 6 May 47 at Ayr Township,, age 25, occ. farmer, mo. with Co. 14 Jul 48.

FRIEND, ELI: Pvt., enl. 6 May 47 at West Providence, age 23, occ. blacksmith, died in San Augustin Hospital 30 Aug 47.

GABE, FREDERICK: (Gabl): Pvt., enl. 6 May 47 at Shellsburg, age 24, occ. tobacconist, hospitalized at Vera Cruz 15 Jul 47, died at Vera Cruz 25 Jul 47 from "Quot. Int. Fever."

GARDNER, GEORGE: (Gardener): Pvt., enl. 6 May 47 at Bedford, age 18, occ. farmer, mo. with Co. 14 Jul 48.

GATES, WILLIAM: Pvt., enl. 6 May 47 at Shellsburg, age 20, occ. tobacconist, listed as sick on Sep-Oct 47 MR, mo. with Co. 14 Jul 48.

GILMORE, JOHN M. (W.): 1st Sgt., enl. 6 May 47 at Bedford, age 21, occ. book seller, left sick at New Orleans 21 Jun 47, disc. at New Orleans 26 Jan 48 on SCD.

GRIMES, WILLIAM: Pvt., enl. 6 May 47 at Bedford, age 22, deserted at Cincinnati 2 Jun 47.

GRUBB, WILLIAM: Pvt., enl. 28 May 47 at Pittsburgh, age 19, occ. shoemaker, mi. at New Orleans 15 Jun 47, KIA at Garita de Belen 13 Sep 47.

HARMAN, NICHOLAS: (Harmon, Harmun): Sgt., enl. 7 Jun 47 at Memphis, Tenn., age 23, occ. blacksmith, mi. at New Orleans 15 Jun 47, promoted to 1st Sgt. 7 Dec 47, promoted to 2nd Lt. 11 Feb 48, mo. with Co. 14 Jul 48.

HARTMAN, LEVI: Pvt., enl. 6 May 47 at Bedford, age 18, occ. laborer, mo. with Co. 14 Jul 48.

HEESLEY, MOSES: (Husly, Kesley): Pvt., enl. 6 May 47 at Shellsburg, age 20, deserted at Pittsburgh 27 May 47.

HELSEL, HENRY T.: (Heltzell, Helzell): Pvt., enl. 6 May 47 at Buckstown, age 19, occ. distiller, detailed as Attendant to regimental hospital 16 Sep 47, rejoined Co. by 31 Dec 47, detailed as Attendant to regimental hospital 23 Feb 48, mo. with Co. 14 Jul 48.

HOFINS, DAVID H.: (Hofius): 2nd Lt., enl. 6 May 47 at Bedford, age 27, listed as sick on Sep-Oct 47 MR, resigned 1 Nov 47.

HOUCK, SOLOMON: (Houk): Pvt., enl. 6 May 47 at Shellsburg, age 28, deserted on the Ohio River 6 Jun 47.

JONES, ALEXANDER I.: Cpl., enl. 6 May 47 at Shellsburg, age 25, occ. tinner, mortally WIA at Chapultepec 13 Sep 47 having his right leg shot off at the body by a cannon ball, died 16 Oct 47.

KEEFE, JOHN, JR.: (Keeffe, Keeffer): 2nd Lt., enl. 6 May 47 at Bedford, age 24, WIA in the shoulder at Chapultepec 13 Sep 47, on three months furlough from 1 Nov 47, rejoined Co. in Jan 48, his resignation was accepted 11 Feb 48.

KEGG, WILLIAM: Pvt., enl. 6 May 47 at Bedford, age 24, occ. farmer, left sick at Puebla 8 Aug 47, died at Puebla about 1 Sep 47.

KITTLE, FRANCIS: Pvt., enl. 6 May 47 at Licking Creek, age 21, occ. shoemaker, left sick at Vera Cruz 15 Jul 47, sent on to Regt. 14 Sep 47, died at Perote before 29 Feb 48.

KUHLE, JACOB: Pvt., enl. 6 May 47 at Shellsburg, age 40, occ. laborer, left sick at Perote 1 Aug 47, died at Perote date unknown.

LAMBERT, CASPER: (Lumbert): Pvt., enl. 6 May 47 at Adamsburg, age 19, occ. farmer, listed as sick on Sep-Oct 47 MR, died in Mexico City Hospital 5 Nov 47.

LEADER, GEORGE: Pvt., enl. 6 May 47 at Bedford, age 18, occ. stone mason, promoted to Sgt. after 30 Apr 48, mo. with Co. 14 Jul 48.

LINN, GEORGE: Pvt., enl. 6 May 47 at Bethel Township, age 21, occ. miller, on duty as Acting Co. Commissary in Dec 47, mo. with Co. 14 Jul 48.

LUTZ, JOSEPH: Pvt., enl. 6 May 47 at Adamsburg, age 20, occ. laborer, slightly WIA in the shoulder by a musket ball at Chapultepec 13 Sep 47, mo. with Co. 14 Jul 48.

MALONE, CHRISTOPHER (Christian): Pvt., enl. 6 May 47 at Martinsburg, age 33, occ. saddler, slightly WIA in the wrist by a musket ball at Chapultepec 13 Sep 47, mo. with Co. 14 Jul 48.

MARTIN, WILLIAM: Pvt., enl. 11 Jun 47 at New Orleans, age 30, occ. laborer, mi. at Vera Cruz 8 Jul 47, mo. with Co. 14 Jul 48.

McKELLIP, GEORGE W.: (McCalleb, McCelleb, McKellips, McKillip): Cpl., enl. 6 May 47 at Licking Creek, age 21, occ. cabinet maker, listed as sick on Sep-Oct 47 MR, sent to New Orleans for his health 1 Nov 47, disc. at New Orleans 6 Mar 48 on SCD.

McMULLIN, JOHN: Pvt., enl. 6 May 47 at Bedford, age 19, occ. chair maker, disc. at Pittsburgh 29 May 47 at SCD.

McMULLIN, NATHAN: Fifer, enl. 6 May 47 at Bedford, age 18, occ. laborer, mo. with Co. 14 Jul 48.

MILLER, DANIEL: Pvt., enl. 6 May 47 at Bedford, age 21, occ. farmer, mo. with Co. 14 Jul 48.

MILLER, JOHN: Pvt., enl. 6 May 47 at Licking Creek, age 21, occ. carpenter, mo. with Co. 14 Jul 48.

MILLER, LEVI: Pvt., enl. 6 May 47 at Bedford, age 27, occ. blacksmith, detailed as Attendant to Mexico City Hospital from 19 Dec 47, rejoined Co. by 30 Apr 48, mo. with Co. 14 Jul 48.

MILLER, SOLOMON: Pvt., enl. 6 May 47 at Bedford, age 28, occ. blacksmith, mo. with Co. 14 Jul 48.

MINICK, SAMUEL: (Minich): Pvt., enl. 6 May 47 at Bedford, age 22, occ. cabinet maker, mo. with Co. 14 Jul 48. Pvt. Co. E, 15th Iowa Vol. Inf. from 30 Aug 62.

MOCK, PAUL: Pvt., enl. 6 May 47 at Buckstown, age 19, occ. laborer, mo. with Co. 14 Jul 48.

MORELAND, JOHN: (Mooreland, Morland): Pvt., enl. 26 May 47 at Pittsburgh, age 22, deserted at Cincinnati 2 Jun 47.

MORTZ, PETER: Pvt., enl. 6 May 47 at Licking Creek, age 33, occ. laborer, listed as sick on Sep-Oct 47 MR, mo. with Co. 14 Jul 48.

MOWER, A. WAYNE: Drummer, enl. 6 May 47 at Bedford, age 23, occ. stage driver, disc. at Pittsburgh 29 May 47 on SCD.

NULTON, WILLIAM: (Nalton): Pvt., enl. 6 May 47 at Bedford, age 19, occ. saddler, promoted to Drummer before 31 Aug 47, mo. with Co. 14 Jul 48.

OILER, HIRAM: Pvt., enl. 6 May 47 at Shellsburg, age 19, occ. blacksmith, deserted at New Orleans 18 Jun 47.

OVER, DAVID: Pvt., enl. 6 May 47 at Bedford, age 22, occ. printer, listed as sick on Sep-Oct 47 MR, mo. with Co. 14 Jul 48.

PICKING, JACOB: Pvt., enl. 6 May 47 at Shellsburg, age 36, occ. blacksmith, listed as sick on Sep-Oct 47 MR, mo. with Co. 14 Jul 48.

REED, GEORGE W.: Pvt., enl. 6 May 47 at Buckstown, age 18, occ. blacksmith, died in quarters at San Augustin 5 Sep 47.

REED, JOSEPH P.: Sgt., enl. 6 May 47 at Shellsburg, age 23, occ. cabinet maker, listed as sick on Sep-Oct 47 MR, sent to New Orleans for his health 1 Nov 47, disc. at New Orleans 10 Mar 48 on SCD.

REMBY, GEORGE: (Rimbez, Rimby): Pvt., enl. 6 May 47 at Bedford, age 26, occ. bricklayer, deserted at Pittsburgh 27 May 47.

ROBB, JOHN: (Rebb): Pvt., enl. 6 May 47 at Shellsburg, age 39, occ. blacksmith, deserted at New Orleans 21 Jun 47.

SCHELL, ABRAHAM E.: Sgt., enl. 6 May 47 at Shellsburg, age 22, occ. farmer, promoted to 2nd Lt. after 30 Apr 48 to rank from 7 Dec 47, mo. with Co. 14 Jul 48.

SIGLE, STEPHEN (Christian): (Seigle): Pvt., enl. 6 May 47 at West Providence, age 21, occ. farmer, mo. with Co. 14 Jul 48.

SIPES, JAMES A.: (Sipe): Cpl., enl. 6 May 47 at Licking Creek, age 25, occ. carpenter, listed as sick on Sep-Oct 47 MR, promoted to 1st Sgt. after 30 Apr 48, mo. with Co. 14 Jul 48.

SLEEK, ALLEN: (Slick): Pvt., enl. 6 May 47 at Shellsburg, age 32, occ. farmer, promoted to Cpl. after 30 Apr 48, mo. with Co. 14 Jul 48. Pvt. Co. H, 55th P.V.I. 2 Mar 64 until KIA at Cold Harbor 3 Jun 64.

SLEEK, NICHOLAS: Pvt., enl. 6 May 47 at Shellsburg, age 21, occ. shoemaker, mo. with Co. 14 Jul 48.

SMITH, JACOB: Pvt., enl. 6 May 47 at West Providence, age 36, occ. farmer, mo. with Co. 14 Jul 48.

SMITH, JOHN: Pvt., enl. 6 May 47 at Bedford, age 18, occ. shoemaker, deserted at New Orleans 18 Jun 47.

SMITH, LEWIS W.: 1st Lt., enl. 6 May 47 at Bedford, age 34, promoted to Capt. 7 Dec 47, mo. with Co. 14 Jul 48.

SMITH, WILLIAM: Pvt., enl. 26 May 47 at Pittsburgh, age 29, occ. stone cutter, had his right leg shot off by a cannon ball at Chapultepec 13 Sep 47, died in Mexico City Hospital 10 Oct 47 from wounds.

SNARE, SOLOMON D.: Pvt., enl. 6 May 47 at Shellsburg, age 21, occ. clerk, mo. with Co. 14 Jul 48.

STEWART, JAMES: (Stuart): Pvt., enl. 6 May 47 at Bedford, age 18, occ. tobacconist, slightly WIA in the foot by a musket ball at Chapultepec 13 Sep 47, mo. with Co. 14 Jul 48.

STIFFLER, HENRY: Pvt., enl. 6 May 47 at Bedford, age 18, occ. farmer, mo. with Co. 14 Jul 48.

TARN, JOHN: (Tane, Yarn): Pvt., enl. 26 May 47 at Pittsburgh, age 31, occ. stone mason, missing from 20 Sep 47, died in Mexico City Hospital 25 Dec 47.

TAYLOR, ROBERT: Pvt., enl. 6 May 47 at Shellsburg, age 18, occ. farmer, promoted to Cpl. after 30 Apr 48, mo. with Co. 14 Jul 48.

TAYLOR, SAMUEL M.: Capt., enl. 6 May 47 at Bedford, age 31, died in quarters in Mexico City 6 Dec 47.

WAGONER, GEORGE: (Wagner): Pvt., enl. 6 May 47 at Shellsburg, age 26, deserted at New Orleans 21 Jun 47.

WASKELLER, JOHN: Pvt., enl. 6 May 47 at Shellsburg, age 32, occ. laborer, died in Mexico City Hospital 19 Oct 47.

WILLIAMS, THOMAS: Pvt., enl. 6 May 47 at Bedford, age 32, deserted at New Orleans 18 Jun 47.

WILSON, ABRAHAM: Pvt., enl. 6 May 47 at Shellsburg, age 18, deserted on the Ohio River 6 Jun 47.

WINDERS, WILLIAM: (Wenders, Wonders): Pvt., enl. 8 Jun 47 at Memphis, Tenn., age 32, occ. blacksmith, mi. at New Orleans 15 Jun 47, listed as sick on Sep-Oct 47 MR, hospitalized in Mexico City 19 Dec 47, disc. at San Angel 11 Apr 48 on SCD.

Company M, 2nd Regiment
Wayne Guards

The Wayne Guards came from the area centering around Newton Hamilton in Mifflin County, with some twenty-five or so joining from Williamsburg in Blair County. The Guards volunteered their services to the government and were selected as one of the two companies in the President's third call. The Wayne Guards reported to Pittsburgh, where they were mustered into the U.S. Army on 18 May 1847 by First Lieutenant Horace B. Field, 3rd U.S. Artillery.

The Guards reached Verz Cruz and marched for the interior, catching up with General Scott's Army at Puebla. There on 7 August they were attached to the 2nd Regiment. The men bore their share of the charge upon Chapultepec and the fighting at Garita de Belen. Their Captain, James E. Caldwell, was mortally wounded in the latter action.

Returning to Pittsburgh, the Guards were mustered out on 21 July 1848 by Major George Wright, 4th U.S. Infantry. The men then went to Newton Hamilton where grand festivities awaited them. It is believed that the Wayne Guards ceased to exist as a unit when they were dismissed in Newton Hamilton.

A total of 100 men served in the company during the war, with one man joining as a recruit. The rolls were marred by the desertion of sixteen men. Nine of the Guards suffered battle related injuries, which resulted in the deaths of three men. In all, fifteen Guards died in service, and an additional seven received discharges before muster out.

Jacob C. Higgins pictured as Lieutenant Colonel of the 1st Pennsylvania Cavalry in the Civil War
MOLLUS-Mass & USAMHI

Charles Bower as Surgeon of the 6th Pennsylvania Reserves
USAMHI

AKE, JOHN: Pvt., enl. 5 May 47 at Williamsburgh, age 23, occ. farmer, deserted at Pittsburgh 29 May 47.

ASH, DAVID: Pvt., enl. 5 May 47 at Trough Creek, age 18, occ. farmer, hospitalized at San Angel according to Jan-Feb 48 MR, hospitalized at Jalapa from 13 Apr 48, disc. at Jalapa 13 May 48 on SCD.

BARGER, WILLIAM: Pvt., enl. 5 May 47 at Stone Valley, age 28, occ. farmer, deserted at Louisville, Ky. 3 Jun 47.

BARNARD, LEWIS (Louis): (Barnitz): Pvt., enl. 5 May 47 at Newton Hamilton, age 27, occ. millwright, WIA in the arm in the charge at Chapultepec 13 Sep 47, mo. with Co. 21 Jul 48.

BARRETT, ROBERT: Pvt., enl. 18 May 47 at Pittsburgh, age 22, occ. laborer, left sick at Perote 1 Aug 47, died at Perote 15 Aug 47 or 14 Sep 47.

BIGHAM, SAMUEL A.: (Bingham): Pvt., enl. 18 May 47 at Pittsburgh, age 26, occ. hatter, deserted at Pittsburgh 29 May 47.

BOND, JOHN B.: (Bend): Pvt., enl. 5 May 47 at Newton Hamilton, age 29, occ. farmer, left sick at Perote 1 Aug 47, rejoined Co. 9 Dec 47, mo. with Co. 21 Jul 48.

BOWER, CHARLES: (Brown): 2nd Lt., enl. 5 May 47 at Newton Hamilton, age 30, occ. physician, appointed Acting Asst. Surg. 26 May 47 upon departure from Pittsburgh, acted in that capacity through 31 Oct 47, on 3 months furlough from 1 Nov 47 because of diarrhea, tendered his resignation 29 May 48, it was accepted 5 Jun 48. Surgeon 6th Pa. Reserves 22 Jun 61 to 11 Jun 64. Surgeon 193rd P.V.I. 19 Jul 64 to 9 Nov 64. Bvt. Lt. Col. & Col. 13 Mar 65. died in 1867.

CALDWELL, ALEXANDER: Pvt., enl. 5 May 47 at Newton Hamilton, age 18, occ. clerk, detached to assist regimental commissary at Vera Cruz 1 Jul 47, detached duty continued in Mexico City & Toluca, still on detached duty at mo., considered mo. when his Co. mo. 21 Jul 48.

CALDWELL, JAMES: Capt., enl. 5 May 47 at Newton Hamilton, age 37, occ. iron master, WIA at Garita de Belen 13 Sep 47, died 19 Sep 47 from wounds, buried in Methodist Church Cemetery, Newton Hamilton, Pa.

CAMPBELL, SYLVESTER H.: (Cambell, Campell): Pvt., enl. 5 May 47 at Stone Valley, age 21, occ. tailor, left sick at Vera Cruz 15 Jul 47, rejoined Co. in Jan 48, mo. with Co. 21 Jul 48.

CLARKSON, ADAM W.: (Clarkeson, Clarksen): Cpl., enl. 5 May 47 at Casville, age 25, listed as sick on Sep-Oct 47 MR, mo. with Co. 21 Jul 48.

COLABINE, ANTHONY: (Colebine, Colobine): Pvt., enl. 5 May 47 at Stone Valley, age 21, occ. laborer, mo. with Co. 21 Jul 48.

COPELAND, DAVID: (Copland, Coplin): Pvt., enl. 5 May 47 at Stone Valley, age 21, occ. farmer, mo. with Co. 21 Jul 48.

CORNELIUS, JACKSON: Pvt., enl. 5 May 47 at Newton Hamilton, age 20, occ. farmer, mo. with Co. 21 Jul 48.

DANIEL, JOHN: Pvt., enl. 18 May 47 at Pittsburgh, age 22, deserted at Pittsburgh 29 May 47.

DITCH, DAVID: (Deitch, Dutch): Pvt., enl. 5 May 47 at Stone Valley, age 21, occ. miller, mo. with Co. 21 Jul 48.

DIVEN, CHARLES: (Divin): Pvt., enl. 5 May 47 at Shirleysburgh, age 18, occ. laborer, mo. with Co. 21 Jul 48.

DIXON, CORNELIUS: Pvt., enl. 5 May 47 at Newton Hamilton, age 21, occ. laborer, deserted at Pittsburgh 29 May 47.

DIXON, THEODORE: (Dixion): Pvt., enl. 5 May 47 at Newton Hamilton, age 18, occ. laborer, mo. with Co. 21 Jul 48.

DOYLE, JOHN A.: 2nd Lt., enl. 5 May 47 at Newton Hamilton, age 23, occ. physician, promoted to 1st Lt. 12 Nov 47, listed as sick on Jan-Feb 48 MR, mo. with Co. 21 Jul 48.

DRAKE, THOMAS: Pvt., enl. 5 May 47 at Newton Hamilton, age 20, occ. farmer, disc. at Mexico City 1 Nov 47 on SCD.

DUNCAN, DANIEL D.: (Duncon): Pvt., enl. 18 May 47 at Pittsburgh, age 30, occ. hatter, listed as sick on Sep-Oct 47 MR, hospitalized in Mexico City 29 Dec 47, disc. in Mexico City 9 Apr 48 on SCD.

DUNLAP, MATTHEW: Pvt., enl. 5 May 47 at Williamsburgh, age 18, occ. shoemaker, mo. with Co. 21 Jul 48.

EDWARDS, JONATHAN: Pvt., enl. 5 May 47 at Williamsburgh, age 25, occ. tailor, detailed as Attendant in regimental hospital starting 23 Feb 48, mo. with Co. 21 Jul 48.

EPLER, CHARLES: (Eplar, Eppler): Pvt., enl. 1 Jun 47 at Wheeling, Va., age 19, mi. at New Orleans 15 Jun 47, WIA in the abdomen in the charge at Chapultepec 13 Sep 47, mo. with Co. 21 Jul 48.

FARREN, WILLIAM: (Farran): Pvt., enl. 18 May 47 at Pittsburgh, age 26, occ. laborer, hospitalized at San Angel according to Mar-Apr 48 MR., mo. with Co. 21 Jul 48.

FILEY, GEORGE W.: (Hiley): 1st Sgt., enl. 5 May 47 at Williamsburgh, age 30, occ. millwright, died 3 Jun 47 on the steamer *Col. Yell* at Louisville, Ky. & buried there 3 Jun 47.

FOCKLER, ELI: Pvt., enl. 5 May 47 at Stone Valley, age 23, occ. miller, detailed as Attendant in Mexico City Hospital according to Mar-Apr 48 MR., mo. with Co. 21 Jul 48.

GARDNER, JOSEPH W. (H.): Pvt., enl. 5 May 47 at Stone Valley, age 23, occ. carpenter, mo. with Co. 21 Jul 48. 1st Lt. Co. B., 3rd P.V.I. (3 mos.) 20 Apr 61 to 30 Jul 61. Capt. Co. K, 125th P.V.I. 16 Aug 62 to 18 May 63.

GARRETT, SAMUEL F.: Pvt., enl. 5 May 47 at Trough Creek, age 18, occ. distiller, mo. with Co. 21 Jul 48.

GUIN, HUGH: (Gwinn): Pvt., enl. 5 May 47 at Stone Valley, age 41, occ. machinist, mo. with Co. 21 Jul 48.

HAMILTON, JOSEPH (Thomas): (Hamelton): Pvt., enl. 18 May 47 at Pittsburgh, age 26, occ. laborer, severely WIA at Garita de Belen 13 Sep 47, died at Chapultepec 15 Sep 47.

HANNAH, DAVID W.: (Hanna): Drummer, enl. 5 May 47 at Williamsburgh, age 26, occ. cabinet maker, mo. with Co. 21 Jul 48.

HARRIS, RUSSEL: Pvt., enl. 5 May 47, age 28, occ. shoemaker, left sick at Perote 1 Aug 47, nothing further given on MRs.

HENNEY, JOHN: (Haney, Hanney, Henry): Pvt., enl. 18 May 47 at Pittsburgh, age 34, deserted at Pittsburgh 29 May 47.

HENNING, JOHN: Pvt., enl. 5 May 47 at Burnt Cabins, age 33, occ. laborer, missing aboard steamer *Col. Yell* near Cincinnati 1 Jun 47 & believed to be drowned.

HESHLEY, SAXFEAR: (Hashley, Heshly): Pvt., enl. 5 May 47 at Newton Hamilton, age 21, occ. bricklayer, WIA in the head at Garita de Belen 13 Sep 47, mo. with Co. 21 Jul 48.

HIGGINS, JACOB C.: Pvt., enl. 5 May 47 at Williamsburgh, age 21, occ. carpenter, hospitalized at San Angel according to Jan-Feb 48 MR, mo. with Co. 21 Jul 48. Capt. & Q.M. of Vols. 2nd Brig. of Patterson's Army 20 Apr 61 to Jul 61. Capt. Co. G & Lt. Col. 1st Pa. Cav. 18 Aug 61 to 8 Oct 61. Col. 125th P.V.I. 16 Aug 62 to 18 May 63. Col. 22nd Pa. Cav. 5 Mar 64 to 21 Jul 65. Died in Johnstown 1 Jun 93.

HILLS, FRANCIS M.: Pvt., enl. 5 May 47 at Williamsburgh, age 18, occ. book seller, hospitalized at San Angel according to Jan-Feb 48 MR, left sick at Jalapa 13 Apr 48, disc. at Jalapa 13 May 48 on SCD. Capt. Co. I & Lt. Col. 45th P.V.I. 18 Oct 61 to Aug 64. Born 15 Jun 29 & died 16 Apr 1915.

HOFFMEYER, GUSTAVUS: Pvt., enl. 18 May 47 at Pittsburgh, age 22, shown only on Co. muster-in roll.

HOGENBERRY, HENRY: (Haughenberg, Haughenberry, Hogenbury, Houghenberry): Pvt., enl. 5 May 47 at Burnt Cabins, age 22, occ. farmer, listed as sick on Sep-Oct 47 MR, died in quarters at San Angel 19 Jan 48 from hemorrhage.

HOLDER, JOHN: Pvt., enl. 5 May 47 at Newton Hamilton, age 24, occ. laborer, detailed as wagoner from 15 Jul 47 to 7 Aug 47, mo. with Co. 21 Jul 48. Pvt. Co. M, 62nd P.V.I. 2 Sep 61 to 16 Jun 63.

HOOVER, JEFFENIAH: Pvt., enl. 5 May 47 at Williamsburgh, age 22, occ. laborer, deserted at Pittsburgh, 29 May 47.

HOOVER, JOEL L.: Pvt., enl. 5 May 47 at Trough Creek, age 19, occ. laborer, hospitalized at Mexico City 29 Dec 47, mo. with Co. 21 Jul 48. Pvt. Co. G, 5th Pa. Reserves 21 Jun 61 to 13 Sep 62.

HOUCK, DORSEY B.: Pvt., enl. 5 May 47 at Williamsburgh, age 22, left sick at Puebla 8 Aug 47, rejoined Co. 9 Dec 47, mo. with Co. 21 Jul 48.

HOUCK, JAMES: Pvt., enl. 5 May 47 at Trough Creek, age 18, occ. saddler, detailed as wagoner from 15 Jul 47 to 7 Aug 47, listed as sick on Sep-Oct 47 MR, hospitalized in Mexico City 29 Dec 47, died in Mexico City Hospital 17 Jan 48 from diarrhea.

HURST, JOHN: (Horst): Pvt., enl. 5 May 47 at Stone Valley, age 31, occ. baker, detailed as baker at Tacubuya in Dec 47 & Jan 48, disc. at Mexico City 9 Apr 48 on SCD.

JENKINS, IRA: Pvt., enl. 5 May 47 at Stone Valley, age 26, occ. laborer, hospitalized at San Angel according to Mar-Apr 48 MR, mo. with Co. 21 Jul 48.

JOHNSON, GEORGE W. (N.): (Johnston): Pvt., enl. 18 May 47 at Pittsburgh, age 25, occ. printer, left sick at Perote 1 Aug 47, rejoined Co. in May 48, mo. with Co. 21 Jul 48.

KEEVER, JOHN: (Keefer): Pvt., enl. 5 May 47 at Newton Hamilton, age 21, occ. laborer, WIA in the neck at Garita de Belen 13 Sep 47, promoted to Cpl. in Nov or Dec 47, mo. with Co. 21 Jul 48.

KENSINGER, GEORGE: Pvt., enl. 5 May 47 at Williamsburgh, age 39, occ. laborer, listed as sick on Nov-Dec 47 MR, mo. with Co. 21 Jul 48.

KESSNER, JAMES M. C.: (Kepner, Kesner): Pvt., enl. 5 May 47 at Mifflin, age 23, occ. laborer, deserted at Cincinnati 1 Jun 47.

KIDD, JOSEPH L.: Cpl., enl. 5 May 47 at Williamsburgh, age 23, occ. coach maker, AWOL on Jan-Feb 48 MR, mo. with Co. 21 Jul 48.

LAWREMORE, JAMES: (Laramore, Larimer, Larrimer, Laurimore, Lorimer): Pvt., enl. 5 May 47 at Johnstown, age 21, occ. physician, promoted to Sgt. before 31 Aug 47, promoted to 1st Sgt. before 31 Dec 47, detached as Hospital Steward to Mexico City Hospital from 1 Mar 48 through Apr 48, mo. with Co. 21 Jul 48.

LONG, JAMES: Pvt., enl. 5 May 47 at Newton Hamilton, age 19, occ. shoemaker, left sick at Mexico City 29 Dec 47, rejoined Co. by 29 Feb 48, mo. with Co. 21 Jul 48.

MADSON, JOSEPH L.: Sgt., enl. 5 May 47 at Newton Hamilton, age 28, occ. clerk, listed as sick on Sep-Oct 47 MR, promoted to 1st Sgt. 1 Nov 47, promoted to 2nd Lt. 12 Nov 47, AWOL according to Jan-Feb 48 MR, listed as under arrest on Mar-Apr 48 MR, mo. with Co. 21 Jul 48.

McCARDLE, ROBERT: Pvt., enl. 5 May 47 at Stone Valley, age 24, occ. farmer, detailed as wagoner from 15 Jul 47 to 7 Aug 47, listed as sick on Sep-Oct & Nov-Dec MRs, mo. with Co. 21 Jul 48.

McCLANAHAN, JACOB M. (James C.): (McClonahan, McLanahan): Pvt., enl. 5 May 47 at Williamsburgh, age 21, occ. drover, KIA at Garita de Belen 13 Sep 47.

McDONALD, EDWARD: (McDowell): Pvt., enl. 19 May 47 at Pittsburgh, age 18, deserted at Pittsburgh 29 May 47.

McDOWELL, WILLIAM: Pvt., enl. 5 May 47 at Newton Hamilton, age 18, occ. farmer, mo. with Co. 21 Jul 48.

McKAMEY, ALEXANDER: (McKamy): 1st Lt., enl. 5 May 47 at Williamsburgh, age 31, occ. physician, promoted to Capt. effective 12 Nov 47, mo. with Co. 21 Jul 48.

McKIMAN, JOHN S.: (McKernan, McKiernan, McKurnan): Pvt., enl. 5 May 47 at Williamsburgh, age 19, occ. laborer, left sick at Perote 1 Aug 47, disc. at Perote date unknown.

McMONAGLE, WILLIAM A.: (McManagle, McManigal, McMonigal): Sgt., enl. 5 May 47 at Newton Hamilton, age 28, served as wagon master from 17 Jul to 7 Aug 47, died in Mexico City 20 Oct 47 from disease.

MENSHEMEYER, ANDREW: (Menshemoyer, Menshenroyer, Menthemeyer): Pvt., enl. 5 May 47 at Newton Hamilton, age 22, occ. laborer, deserted at New Orleans 22 Jun 47.

MONTGOMERY, JOHN: Pvt., enl. 5 May 47 at Williamsburgh, age 20, occ. tailor, left sick at Puebla 8 Aug 47, rejoined Co. 9 Dec 47, mo. with Co. 21 Jul 48. 1st Lt. Co. G, 172nd Pa. Drafted Militia 1 Nov 62 to 31 Jul 63.

MORGAN, ADAM: Pvt., enl. 5 May 47 at Burnt Cabins, age 18, occ. farmer, hospitalized in Mexico City 29 Oct 47, died in Mexico City Hospital 21 Jan 48 from diarrhea.

NEICE, REUBEN (Ruben): (Neece, Neese, Nice): Pvt., enl. 5 May 47 at McVeytown, age 18, occ. farmer, detailed as Attendant in U.S. Hospital in Mexico City from 19 Dec 47, rejoined Co. by 29 Feb 48, mo. with Co. 21 Jul 48.

NORTON, GEORGE: Pvt., enl. 5 May 47 at Newton Hamilton, age 21, occ. wagon maker, died in Mexico City Hospital 22 Nov 47.

NUGEN, JAMES: (Nugent): Pvt., enl. 5 May 47 at Newton Hamilton, age 19, occ. farmer, hospitalized at New Orleans 11 Jun 47, died there 19 Jun 47.

O'BRIEN, EDWARD: Pvt., enl. 18 May 47 at Pittsburgh, age 27, shown only on Co. muster-in roll.

O'BRYAN, ARTHUR: (O'Brien, Obryon): Pvt., enl. 5 May 47 at Newton Hamilton, age 35, occ. stone cutter, listed as sick on Sep-Oct 47 MR, mo. with Co. 21 Jul 48.

PEFFER, HENRY: (Pepper): Pvt., enl. 13 Dec 47 at Hollidaysburg, age 22, mi. at Fort Mifflin 10 Jan 48, reported at Ft. McHenry, Md. 20 Jan 48, joined Co. 17 Apr 48, mo. with Co. 21 Jul 48.

RAMSEY, SAMUEL: Pvt., enl. 5 May 47 at Stone Valley, age 42, occ. distiller, hospitalized at San Angel according to Jan-Feb 48 MR, sent from San Angel Hospital to Jalapa Hospital 13 Apr 48, did not return home with Co., further information not shown.

REED, SAMUEL: Pvt., enl. 18 May 47 at Pittsburgh, age 20, deserted at Pittsburgh 29 May 47.

RICHARDSON, THOMAS: Pvt., enl. 5 May 47 at Newton Hamilton, age 25, occ. carpenter, detailed as wagoner from 15 Jul 47 to 7 Aug 47, hospitalized at San Angel according to Jan-Feb 48 MR, mo. with Co. 21 Jul 48.

ROACH, THOMAS: (Roch, Roche): Pvt., enl. 5 May 47 at Newton Hamilton, age 30, occ. laborer, in confinement according to Jan-Feb 48 MR, mo. with Co. 21 Jul 48.

ROBLEY, JOHN: (Robbly): Pvt., enl. 5 May 47 at Newton Hamilton, age 18, occ. brick maker, deserted at Pittsburgh 29 May 47.

SCHNEE, JACOB F.: (Schree, Shnee): Pvt., enl. 5 May 47 at Freeport, age 22, occ. farmer, mo. with Co. 21 Jul 48. Pvt. Co. C, 45th P.V.I. 26 Feb 64 to 17 Jul 65, POW 30 Sep 64 to 30 Mar 65.

SHADE, JACOB: Cpl., enl. 5 May 47 at Newton Hamilton, age 23, occ. farmer, reduced to Pvt. before 31 Aug 47, hospitalized at San Angel according to Jan-Feb 48 MR, mo. with Co. 21 Jul 48.

SHIN, BENJAMIN: (Shim): Pvt., enl. 5 May 47 at Burnt Cabins, age 19, occ. laborer, WIA in the leg at Chapultepec 13 Sep 47, hospitalized at San Angel according to Jan-Feb & Mar-Apr 48 MRs, died at San Angel 9 May 48.

SHIVE, DAVID: Pvt., enl. 5 May 47 at Newton Hamilton, age 40, occ. carpenter, WIA in the groin in the charge at Chapultepec 13 Sep 47, mo. with Co. 21 Jul 48.

SMITH, GEORGE: Pvt., enl. 5 May 47 at Trough Creek, age 33, occ. tailor, mo. with Co. 21 Jul 48.

SMITH, JAMES R.: Pvt., enl. 5 May 47 at McVeytown, age 25, occ. carpenter, deserted at Cincinnati 1 Jun 47.

SNYDER, AUSTIN B.: Pvt., enl. 5 May 47 at Johnstown, age 23, occ. tailor, mo. with Co. 21 Jul 48. Capt. Co. G, 51st P.V.I. 17 Oct 61 to 12 Feb 62. Born 1824 & died 6 Feb 92.

SPECK, DANIEL: Pvt., enl. 5 May 47 at Franklin, age 24, occ. farmer, deserted at Cincinnati 1 Jun 47.

TAYLOR, JAMES R.: Pvt., enl. 5 May 47 at Newton Hamilton, age 18, occ. laborer, mo. with Co. 21 Jul 48.

TEMPLE, OLIVER: Pvt., enl. 5 May 47 at Newton Hamilton, age 19, occ. farmer, left sick at New Orleans 11 Jun 47, no further information given.

THOMPSON, WILLIAM L.: Pvt., enl. 5 May 47 at Morrison Cove, age 20, occ. tailor, died in quarters at San Angel 24 Jan 48 from erysipelas.

TOBEY, EDWIN: (Toby): Pvt., enl. 5 May 47, age 24, occ. shoemaker, absent with leave in Nov 47, sick in Mexico City in Jan 48, died in Mexico City in Feb 48.

WEEKS, JACOB F.: Pvt., enl. 5 May 47 at Shirley, age 28, occ. farmer, deserted at Pittsburgh 29 May 47.

WESTHOVEN, WILLIAM: (Westhooven, Westhover): Sgt., enl. 5 May 47 at Newton Hamilton, age 37, occ. clerk, mo. with Co. 21 Jul 48.

WHITE, LORENZO E.: Fifer, enl. 5 May 47 at Williamsburgh, age 26, occ. cabinet maker, listed on all subsequent MRs as Cpl., mo. with Co. 21 Jul 48.

WILSON, CYRUS B.: Cpl., enl. 5 May 47 at Newton Hamilton, age 24, occ. printer, on leave in Mexico City from 19 Dec 47, working as a printer in Mexico City from Nov 47 through Feb 48, AWOL on 29 Feb 48, mo. with Co. 21 Jul 48.

WILSON, JOHN S.: Pvt., enl. 11 Jun 47 at New Orleans, age 32, occ. coppersmith, mi. at Vera Cruz 8 Jul 47, died in Mexico City Hospital 30 Oct 47.

WILSON, WILLIAM H.: Pvt., enl. 5 May 47 at Stone Valley, age 19, occ. shoemaker, mo. with Co. 21 Jul 48.

WINGLER, JOHN: Pvt., enl. 5 May 47 at Stone Valley, age 19, occ. laborer, hospitalized at San Angel according to Jan-Feb 48 MR, mo. with Co. 21 Jul 48.

WINGLER, MOSES: Pvt., enl. 5 May 47 at Stone Valley, age 21, occ. laborer, hospitalized in Mexico City 29 Dec 47, rejoined Co. by 29 Feb 48, mo. with Co. 21 Jul 48.

ZIEDERS, GEORGE W.: (Zeiders, Ziders, Zillers): Pvt., enl. 5 May 47 at Trough Creek, age 18, mo. with Co. 21 Jul 48.

ZIMMERMAN, ISAAC: (Zimmermon): Pvt., enl. 5 May 47 at Burnt Cabins, age 26, deserted at Pittsburgh 29 May 47.

Unassigned Recruits, 2nd Regiment

ADAMS, JACOB: Pvt., enl. 4 Jun 48 at Johnstown, age 19, mi. at Ft. Mifflin 7 Jun 48, mo. at Ft. Mifflin 13 Jul 48.

AIKINS, WILLIAM: Pvt., enl. 13 Mar 48 at Phila., age 32, mi. at Ft. Mifflin 30 Apr 48, mo. at Ft. Mifflin 13 Jul 48.

ALEXANDER, AMOS W. (His real name was Alexander McNutt): Pvt., enl. 26 Mar 48 at Phila., age 26, mi. at Ft. Mifflin 30 Apr 48, mo. at Ft. Mifflin 13 Jul 48.

BAILEY, WILLIAM: Pvt., enl. 1 Oct 47 at Phila., age 34, deserted 18 Oct 47.

BICKING, GEORGE: Pvt., enl. 23 Jan 48 at Phila., age 21, mi. at Ft. Mifflin 29 Feb 48, disc. at Ft. Mifflin 22 Mar 48 on Habeas Corpus because he was a minor.

BOUND, JOSEPH: Pvt., enl. 22 Apr 48 at Phila., mi. at Ft. Mifflin 30 Apr 48, mo. at Ft. Mifflin 13 Jul 48, age 23.

BRINDLE, GEORGE: Pvt., enl. 14 Mar 48 at Phila., age 22, rejected by surgeon, disc. 17 Mar 48.

CALDWELL, ALEXANDER: Pvt., enl. 22 Jan 48 at Phila., age 21, mi. at Ft. Mifflin 29 Feb 48, employed by Lt. Deaney as Recruiting Sgt. in Phila., mo. at Ft. Mifflin 13 Jul 48.

CAMPBELL, JAMES: Pvt., enl. 14 Aug 47 at Pittsburgh, age 37, reported at Carlisle Barracks 31 Aug 47, disc. at Phila. 1 Oct 47 on SCD.

CARLTON, CHARLES: Pvt., enl. 23 Dec 47 at Phila., age 23, mi. at Ft. Mifflin 10 Jan 48, reported at Ft. McHenry, Md. 20 Jan 48, no further information given.

CARMICHAEL, JAMES: Pvt., enl. 14 Aug 47 at Pittsburgh, age 39, reported at Carlisle Barracks 31 Aug 47, serving as recruiting Sgt. for Lt. Williams in Phila. on 30 Apr 48 MR, mo. at Ft. Mifflin 13 Jul 48.

CARROLL, HUGH: Pvt., enl. 18 Dec 47 at Hollidaysburg, age 39, mi. at Ft. Mifflin 10 Jan 48, reported at Ft. McHenry, Md. 20 Jan 48, no further information given.

CODE, WILLIAM F.: Pvt., enl. 4 Jun 48 at Johnstown, age 21, mi. at Ft. Mifflin 30 Jun 48, mo. at Ft. Mifflin 13 Jul 48.

DAVIS, JOHN D.: Pvt., enl. 6 Jan 48 at Phila., age 24, mi. at Ft. Mifflin 10 Jan 48, appointed Lance Sgt. 15 Jan 48, mo. at Ft. Mifflin 13 Jul 48.

DIMINGER, FREDERICK: Pvt., enl. 20 Nov 47 at York, age 33, rejected before 10 Jan 48 because of varicose veins.

DINWOODIE, THOMAS: Pvt., enl. 10 Jan 48 at Phila., age 31, mi. at Ft. Mifflin 29 Feb 48, mo. at Ft. Mifflin 13 Jul 48.

DOTHARD, ALBERT B.: Pvt., enl. 21 Apr 48 at Phila., age 21, mi. at Ft. Mifflin 30 Apr 48, mo. at Ft. Mifflin 13 Jul 48.

FOLEY, WILLIAM: (Foly): Pvt., enl. 15 Sep 47 at Hollidaysburg, age 41, mi. at Ft. Mifflin 31 Mar 48, served as recruiting Sgt. at Lt. Williams' rendezvous in Phila. in Apr 48, mo. at Ft. Mifflin 13 Jul 48.

FORD, GEORGE: Pvt., enl. 28 Apr 48 at Phila., age 34, rejected by surgeon, disc. at Ft. Mifflin 29 Apr 48.

FRABER, JOHN: Pvt., enl. 1 Feb 48 at Pittsburgh, age 26, mi. at Ft. Mifflin 7 Jun 48, mo. at Ft. Mifflin 13 Jul 48. See Co. I, 2nd Pa. Regt.

GARY, DAVID: Pvt., enl. 10 Feb 48 at Johnstown, age 23, mi. at Ft. Mifflin 7 Jun 48, mo. at Ft. Mifflin 13 Jul 48.

GLATHOUSE, LAWRENCE: (Glatchier): Pvt., enl. 11 Aug 47 at Harrisburg, reported at Carlisle Barracks 31 Aug 47, nothing further given.

GLENN, HENRY: Pvt., deserted, caught and returned to the rendezvous in York by a William Martin according to the MR dated 16 Oct 47, nothing further given.

GOULDING, JOHN: Pvt., enl. 19 Nov 47 at Hollidaysburg, reported at Ft. McHenry, Md. 20 Jan 48, nothing further given.

HERZOG, CHARLES: Pvt., enl. 25 Jan 48 at Reading, age 28, mi. at Ft. Mifflin 30 Apr 48, mo. at Ft. Mifflin 13 Jul 48.

HITE, HEZEKIAH: Pvt., enl. 4 Jun 48 at Johnstown, age 21, mi. at Ft. Mifflin 7 Jun 48, mo. at Ft. Mifflin 13 Jul 48.

HOLDER, JOSEPH W.: Pvt., enl. 20 Apr. 48 at Pittsburgh, age 22, mi. at Ft. Mifflin 7 Jun 48, mo. at Ft. Mifflin 13 Jul 48.

HOUK, SOLOMON: Pvt., enl. 25 Apr 48 at Johnstown, age 2?, mi. at Ft. Mifflin 7 Jun 48, mo. at Ft. Mifflin 13 Jul 48.

HOWARD, LAWSON: Pvt., enl. 28 May 48 at Pittsburgh, age 21, mi. at Ft. Mifflin 7 Jun 48, mo. at Ft. Mifflin 13 Jul 48.

HUBBARD, CHRISTOPHER: Pvt., enl. 14 Oct 47 at Phila., listed only on detachment rolls of 31 Oct 47 & 28 Feb 48.

HUTCHINSON, ALEXANDER: Pvt., enl. 19 May 48 at Johnstown, age 18, mi. at Ft. Mifflin 7 Jun 48, mo. at Ft. Mifflin 13 Jul 48.

KIERNAN, GEORGE S.: Pvt., enl. 6 Jun 48 at Phila., age 2?, mi. at Ft. Mifflin 7 Jun 48, mo. at Ft. Mifflin 13 Jul 48.

KIPP, HENRY: Pvt., enl. 27 Jan 48 at Phila., age 2?, mi. at Ft. Mifflin 29 Feb 48, mo. at Ft. Mifflin 13 Jul 48.

KRINKS, JOHNSON: Pvt., enl. 18 Jan 48 at Phila., age 2?, mi. at Ft. Mifflin 29 Feb 48, mo. at Ft. Mifflin 13 Jul 48.

McBRIDE, THEOPHILUS: Pvt., enl. 8 Mar 48 at Phila., age 23, mi. at Ft. Mifflin 30 Apr 48, mo. at Ft. Mifflin 13 Jul 48.

McCLOSKEY, THOMAS M.: Pvt., enl. 17 Aug 47 at Harrisburg, age 33, deserted at Harrisburg 18 Aug 47.

McDONALD, JOHN: Pvt., enl. 8 Oct 47 at Phila., deserted at Phila.

McDONALD, JOHN: Pvt., enl. 19 Dec 47 at Hollidaysburg, age 27, deserted from Ft. McHenry, Md. 17 Jan 48.

McWILLIAMS, MICHAEL: Pvt., enl. 15 Nov 47 at Hollidaysburg, age 35, rejected by surgeon, disc. 20 Apr 48.

METZEL, WILLIAM J.: Pvt., enl. 4 Mar 48 at Reading, age 21, mi. at Ft. Mifflin 30 Apr 48, mo. at Ft. Mifflin 13 Jul 48.

MILLS, LEWIS: Pvt., enl. 12 Apr 48 at Phila., age 34, mi. at Ft. Mifflin 30 Apr 48, mo. at Ft. Mifflin 13 Jul 48.

MOMIN, GUSTAVE: Pvt., enl. 6 Aug 47 at Pittsburgh, age 38, listed only on Carlisle Barracks detachment roll of 31 Aug 47.

MORAN, DANIEL: Pvt., enl. 21 Aug 47 at Harrisburg, deserted at Harrisburg 25 Aug 47.

MURLEY, GEORGE: Pvt., enl. 23 Jan 48 at Phila., age 22, mi. at Ft. Mifflin 29 Feb 48, mo. at Ft. Mifflin 13 Jul 48.

MYER, WELDE: Pvt., enl. 19 Nov 47 at Hollidaysburg, age 35, rejected due to hernia on right side.

NIXON, ROBINSON: Pvt., enl. 21 May 48 at Johnstown, age 32, deserted at Johnstown 30 May 48.

NOBLE, ARTHUR: Pvt., enl. 18 Apr 48 at Pittsburgh, age 26, mi. at Ft. Mifflin 7 Jun 48, mo. at Ft. Mifflin 13 Jul 48.

PINCH, JOHN: Pvt., enl. 7 Feb 48 at Reading, age 33, mi. at Ft. Mifflin 31 Mar 48, mo. at Ft. Mifflin 13 Jul 48.

RICHARDS, JOHN F.: Pvt., enl. 29 Jan 48 at Reading, age 25, rejected by surgeon, disc. 29 Apr 48.

RICKERSON, JOHN: Pvt., enl. 30 Apr 48 at Phila., age 21, mi. at Ft. Mifflin 30 Apr 48, mo. at Ft. Mifflin 13 Jul 48.

ROBERSON, HENRY: (Robinson): Pvt., enl. 28 Aug 47 at Harrisburg, reported at Carlisle Barracks 31 Aug 47, deserted at Phila. 4 Sep 47.

SCOTT, WILLIAM: Pvt., enl. 23 Nov 47 at York, age 36, deserted from York 30 Nov 47.

SCOTT, WILLIAM F.: Pvt., enl. 21 Jan 48 at Phila., age 22, mi. at Ft. Mifflin 29 Feb 48, mo. at Ft. Mifflin 13 Jul 48.

SLEVIN, PATRICK W.: Pvt., enl. 18 Apr 48 at Pittsburgh, age 34, mi. at Ft. Mifflin 7 Jun 48, mo. at Ft. Mifflin 13 Jul 48.

SMITH, EDWARD: Pvt., enl. 27 May 48 at Phila., age 33, deserted at Phila. 3 Jun 48.

STERLING, PASCHAL: Pvt., enl. 27 Apr 48 at Phila., age 33, rejected by surgeon, disc. 29 Apr 48.

STRICKLER, JOHN: (Stricklin): Pvt., enl. 27 Apr 48 at Phila., age 27, rejected by surgeon, disc. 29 Apr 48.

SWEETHELM, HENRY: Pvt., enl. 10 Apr 48 at Reading, age 30, rejected by surgeon, disc. 29 Jun 48.

SWEITZER, CHARLES G.: (Sweitzler): Pvt., enl. 28 Apr 48 at Phila., age 24, rejected by surgeon, disc. 29 Apr 48.

WAGGONER, SAMUEL: Pvt., enl. 19 Jan 48 at Phila., age 21, mi. at Ft. Mifflin 29 Feb 48, deserted from Ft. Mifflin 9 Apr 48.

WALKER, JAMES: Pvt., enl. 13 Aug 47 at Pittsburgh, age 35, reported at Carlisle Barracks 31 Aug 47, disc. 1 Oct 47 on SCD.

WALKER, THOMAS: Pvt., enl. 10 May 48 at Pittsburgh, age 44, mi. at Ft. Mifflin 7 Jun 48, mo. at Ft. Mifflin 13 Jul 48.

WENDER, LEWIS C.: Pvt., enl. 11 Aug 47 at Harrisburg, age 35, deserted from Harrisburg 18 Aug 47.

WILLIAMSON, MONTREVILLE A.: Pvt., enl. 26 Jan 48 at Phila., age 22, mi. at Ft. Mifflin 29 Feb 48, mo. at Ft. Mifflin 13 Jul 48.

WINEGARDNER, JOSEPH: Pvt., enl. 3 Aug 47 at Harrisburg, age 21, served as Lance Sgt. in Harrisburg recruiting party in Nov 47, stationed at Ft. Mifflin from before 29 Feb 48, mo. at Ft. Mifflin 13 Jul 48.

WISE, DANIEL P.: Pvt., enl. 12 Apr 48 at Phila., age 31, mi. at Ft. Mifflin 30 Apr 48, mo. at Ft. Mifflin 13 Jul 48.

WOLF, ABRAM: Pvt., enl. 16 Aug 47 at Pittsburgh, age 41, deserted near Carlisle 30 Aug 47.

ZELWICK, EBENHARDT: Pvt., enl. 8 Sep 47 at Phila., deserted from Phila. 23 Oct 47.

APPENDIX I

Proclamation of War

In the name and by the Authority of the Commonwealth of Pennsylvania. By FRANCIS R. SHUNK, Governor of the said Commonwealth.

A Proclamation

Whereas, the President of the United States, in his Proclamation of the 13th instant, has announced that by the acts of the Republic of Mexico, a state of war exists between that Government and the United States.

And whereas, It is our first to acknowledge our dependence upon the Great Ruler of the Universe:—I do therefore, invoke the good people of the Commonwealth, by their religion and their patriotism, to submit as freemen should, to this dispensation of Providence, and humbly ask of Him, who alone can give counsel and strength, to sustain us in the last resort of injured Nations.

And whereas, The President has been authorized by Congress, to call for and accept the services of fifty thousand volunteer soldiers, to protect and maintain the honor and security of the Union. And whereas, All the force that may be required promptly and efficiently to conduct the War, and bring it to a speedy and successful termination, should be in readiness to meet every contingency that may occur in its progress.

And whereas, The Union of the States binds together the separate Sovereignties, and secures one common feeling and interest, in which the people of Pennsylvania largely participate.

The Officers and Soldiers of this Commonwealth will, therefore, with that alacrity and zeal which animate Freemen, and for which they are distinguished, hold themselves in readiness promptly to meet and repel the enemies of the Republic, and to preserve the rights and honor, and secure the perpetuity of the Union.

All Persons who have charge of public arms, and other munitions of war, are reminded by our existing relations, that it is their imperative duty immediately to prepare them for the Public Service.

313

And Whereas, The power of the Union is made effective for protection and defence, in all emergencies, by the harmony and energy of the people of each state: Therefore, All the citizens of the Commonwealth are exhorted to be united, firm and decided "in preserving order, and promoting concord, in maintaining the efficiency of the laws, and in supporting and invigorating all the measures which may be adopted by the constituted authorities for obtaining a speedy, just and honorable peace."

Given under my hand and the Great Seal of the Commonwealth, at Harrisburg, this sixteenth day of May, in the year of our Lord one thousand eight hundred and forty-six, and of the Commonwealth the seventieth.

By the Governor.

J. Miller,

Secretary of the Commonwealth.

APPENDIX II

Governor's Response to the President

Head-Quarters, Harrisburg, Pa., July 15, 1846.

Sir:

Immediately upon the receipt of the letter of the Secretary of War, of the 19th to muster in the service of the United States, six regiments of Volunteer Infantry, I gave directions to the Adjutant General to adopt effective measures to secure a prompt compliance. I have now the honor to inform you that I have received the report of that officer, which is herewith transmitted, and from which it appears that ninety companies, each containing the full complement of officers and men, and most of them an excess, regularly organized agreeably to the regulations adopted, and making an aggregate of seven thousand four hundred and seventy-five freemen of Pennsylvania, have voluntarily enrolled their names and tendered their services to fight the battles of the country. In addition, the 1st and 2d battalions, commanded by Col. James Beatty, of Fayette county, and attached to the 2d brigade 13th division, numbering one thousand officers and men, have tendered their services, but their muster rolls have not been received.* It is also proper to refer to the offer of Col. Wynkoop's regiment of volunteers, of Schuylkill county, made to you at a very early period, and to numerous other offers of regiments, battalions and companies which could not be received, because the companies did not contain the full number of men required by the regulations, or because of other informalities, which I regret prevent me from reporting them as being ready to be mustered into the service. The officers and men of these corps have manifested the strongest disposition to enter the service, and should they be required by any emergency, I have no doubt they will promptly comply with the regulations.

Having thus reported to you the organization of the companies, and their readiness to be mustered into the services of the U.S., I shall await your further orders in regard to them.

The Adjutant General limited the time for receiving offers to the 11th July instant. As the formation of the companies depend upon the voluntary action of the citizens, in every part of the Commonwealth, it was impossible to make any order, by which the exact number required, and no more, should be tendered. This accounts for the fact that more companies have been organized and volunteered their services, than your request contemplated.

Should the services of all those who have enrolled themselves, and who are ready to be mustered into the service, not be required, it will be an unpleasant duty to make a selection as all are desirous of the distinction and honor of participating in the patriotic service of the country. Your direction in the premises will govern my action in relation thereto.

It is earnestly hoped that in case these troops are required to be mustered into the service, a reasonable time will be allowed for the organization of the regiments, and for their discipline, before they shall be ordered to march. In concluding this report, I cannot refrain from expressing the gratification I derive from the patriotism, and ardor of the citizen soldiers of my native State, who, remote from the scene of action, have responded to the country's call with so much promptitude.

The superiority of our republican system over all others, is thus strikingly illustrated. Here we require no large standing armies to maintain a balance of power, and keep the people in subjection. Every man is part of the government, and realizes the interest he has in it. He is therefore ready whenever the country or her institutions are invaded or treated with injustice, to stand out in their defence. This not only protects us from the dangers incident to the maintenance of large bodies of regular troops, but saves us from the payment of an enormous and onerous expense. In my judgment, some substantial recognition of their patriotic action is due by the general government to the citizens who have enrolled themselves in the present emergency, and who are now spending their time and money in discipline and preparation for the public service. That suitable provision should be made to remunerate those who have complied with the request of your Excellency, whether they are called into service or not, appears to me to be not only the duty of the government as an act of justice, but is also dictated by the soundest principles of public policy.

With the highest respect, I am yours, &c.,

FRS. R. SHUNK.

To his Excellency James K. Polk, President of the U.S.

1. Patterson Guards, Capt. Wm. A. Stokes, 1st Lt. R. H. Woolworth, 77 men, Philadelphia.

2. Steuben Fusillers, Capt. Arnold Seyberg, 1st Lt. Chas. Angroth, 2nd Lt. J. Schoenleber, 78 men, Philadelphia.

3. Independent Guards, Capt. Edwin Chander, 1st Lt. _____ Tyler, 2nd Lt. Robt. Michaels, 77 men, Philadelphia.

4. National Guards, Capt. S. B. Kingston, 1st Lt. S. Wilson, 2nd Lt. G. M'Gee, 77 men, Philadelphia.

5. State Fencibles, Capt. James Page, 1st Lt. John Middleton, 2nd Lt. R. J. Parke, 78 men, Philadelphia.

6. State Fencibles, 2nd Company, Capt. Joseph Murray, 2nd Lt. W. Robertson, 77 men, Philadelphia.

7. Washington Blues, Capt. Wm. Patterson, 1st Lt. F. E. Patterson, 2nd Lt. J. A. Shutt, 77 men, Philadelphia.

8. City Guards, Capt. Joseph Hill, 1st Lt. Anthony Tully, 2nd Lt. D. Vincent, 77 men, Philadelphia.

9. Lafayette Light Guards, Capt. Wm. G. Smith, 1st Lt. T. M. Pierce, 2nd Lt. Casper M. Berry, 88 men, Philadelphia.

10. National Artillery, Capt. John K. Murphy, 1st Lt. Edwin Ward, 2nd Lt. Joseph Sinex, 82 men, Philadelphia.

11. Philadelphia Repeal Volunteers, Capt. Wm. Dixon, 1st Lt. Nathaniel Holland, 2nd Lt. M. Sweeney, 79 men, Philadelphia.

12. Monroe Guards, Capt. Wm. F. Small, 77 men, Philadelphia.

13. Frankford Artillery, Capt. John F. Pechell, 1st Lt. Isacher Pugh, 2nd Lt. E. F. Duffield, 81 men, Philadelphia.

14. National Grays, Capt. Peter Fritz, 1st Lt. Wm. A. Thorpe, 2nd Lt. Jacob Glause, 85 men, Philadelphia.

15. Cadwallader Grays, Capt. R. K. Scott, 1st Lt. S. T. Bruce, 2nd Lt. S. W. Palmer, 84 men, Philadelphia.

16. Union Fencibles, Capt. R. M. Lee, 1st Lt. Jos. K. Miller, 2nd Lt. S. C. Winslow, 85 men, Philadelphia.

17. Philadelphia Light Guards, Capt. John Bennett, 1st Lt. Malon Higs, 2nd Lt. R. G. Tomlinson, 84 men, Philadelphia.

18. Philadelphia Grays, Capt. N. H. Graham, 1st Lt. S. B. H. Vance, 2nd Lt. James Hanna, 82 men, Philadelphia.

19. Harrison Blues, Capt. Geo. Cadwallader, 1st Lt. Geo. McCulloh, 2nd Lt. James York, 83 men, Philadelphia.

20. Washington Light Infantry, Capt. F. W. Bender, 2nd Lt. J. C. Kritchmarr, 80 men, Philadelphia.

21. Irish Volunteers, Capt. Amable J. Brazler, 1st Lt. M. J. Williams, 2nd Lt. P. W. Pomroy, 78 men, Philadelphia.

22. Montgomery Guards, Capt. Rush Van Dyke, 1st Lt. John Marlow, 2nd Lt. Terrence Riley, 82 men, Philadelphia.

23. Washington National Guards, Capt. John Reiss, 1st Lt. Anthony Vagner, 90 men, Philadelphia.

24. Jefferson Guards, Capt. T. G. Morehead, 1st Lt. Mont. P. Young, 2nd Lt. Wm. Bryan, 79 men, Philadelphia.

25. Tyler Guards, Capt. Robert Tyler, 1st Lt. M. Kennedy, 2nd Lt. P. Caragan, 84 men, Philadelphia.

26. Junior Artilleries, Capt. Frederick Fritz, 1st Lt. Jacob Lawson, 2nd Lt. R. Beckenback, 78 men, Philadelphia.

27. Germantown Blues, Capt. John D. Miles, 1st Lt. H. L. Hagner, 2nd Lt. Wm. H. Cox, 78 men, Philadelphia.

28. Jackson Artillery, Capt. Jacob Hubeli, 1st Lt. A. Larentree, 2nd Lt. David Hanley, 79 men, Philadelphia.

29. Mechanic Rifle, 1st Lt. Jacob H. Battis, 2nd Lt. Wm. McCoy, 77 men, Philadelphia.

30. Montgomery Guards, Capt. Michael McCoy, 1st Lt. Wm. Dougherty, 2nd Lt. Jeremiah Hanly, 86 men, Philadelphia.

31. Union Guards, Capt. Joseph Morrison, 1st Lt. John G. Hills, 2nd Lt. J. J. Morrison, 77 men, Bucks county.

32. Doylestown Grays, Capt. Chas. H. Mann, 1st Lt. John S. Bryan, 2nd Lt. John Pidcock, 80 men, Bucks county.

33. National Guards, Capt. J. K. Zeilin, 1st Lt. C. H. Clayton, 2nd Lt. J. G. Denister, 77 men, Delaware county.

34. National Grays, Capt. Thomas Sloan, 1st Lt. John G. Mills, 2nd Lt. C. R. McDonnell, 77 men, Chester county.

35. Jackson Riflemen, Capt. Fred'k. Hambright, 1st Lt. Michael Tressler, 2nd Lt. S. E. Gundaker, 82 men, Lancaster county.

36. Lancaster Fencibles, Capt. J. H. Duckman, 1st Lt. George Ford, 2nd Lt. D. W. Patterson, 77 men, Lancaster county.

37. Gettysburg Guards, Capt. D. M. Smyser, 1st Lt. Aaron De Goff, 77 men, Adams county.

38. York Penna. Rifles, Capt. George Hay, 1st Lt. D. A. Stillinger, 2nd Lt. Isaac Elliott, 80 men, York county.

39. Washington Artillerists, Capt. R. Bruce, 1st Lt. J. C. Cochran, 78 men, York county.

40. Reading Artillery, Capt. Thomas S. Leoser, 1st Lt. Wm. Wunder, 2nd Lt. Herman Baird, 77 men, Berks county.

41. Washington Grays, Capt. H. A. Muhlenberg, 1st Lt. Levi Heister, 2nd Lt. H. L. Miller, 87 men, Berks county.

42. Harrisburg Rifle, Capt. C. Seiler, 1st Lt. G. W. Kinzer, 2nd Lt. E. A. Lesley, 100 men, Harrisburg.

43. Washington Rifle, Capt. John Weidman, 1st Lt. James W. Eber, 2nd Lt. C. Zimmerman, 78 men, Lebanon.

44. Dauphin Guard, Capt. Wm. Watson, 1st Lt. David Pool, 2nd Lt. D. A. Kepner, 97 men, Harrisburg.

45. National Grays, Capt. Joel Ritter, 1st Lt. H. A. M. Filbert, 2nd Lt. C. H. Richards, 77 men, Reading.

46. Hibernia Jackson Guards, Capt. C. F. Jackson, 1st Lt. I. S. McMichen, 2nd Lt. B. Reily, 86 men, Schuylkill county.

47. Washington Artillery, Capt. James Nagle, 1st Lt. Simon S. Nagle, 2nd Lt. J. K. Fernsler, 98 men, Schuylkill county.

48. Swatara Light Infantry, Capt. Wm. Rewalt, 2nd Lt. D. H. Fackler, 78 men, Dauphin county.

49. National Light Infantry, Capt. J. H. Campbell, 1st Lt. Wm. Pollock, 2nd Lt. James Rossell, 112 men, Schuylkill county.

50. Stockton Artillerists, Capt. J. H. Siewers, 77 men, Carbon county.

51. Columbia Guards, Capt. John S. Wilson, 1st Lt. Clarence H. Frick, 2nd Lt. W. D. Moore, 91 men, Columbia county.

52. Wyoming Artillerists, Capt. Edward L. Dana, 1st Lt. Martin Lawn, 2nd Lt. E. B. Collings, 78 men, Luzerne county.

53. Wyoming Yagers, Capt. John Richard, 1st Lt. Christian Goeltz, 2nd Lt. Jacob Walder, 78 men, Luzerne county.

54. Northumberland Infantry, Capt. David Taggart, 77 men, Northumberland county.

55. Jackson Infantry, Capt. John Cummings, 77 men, Union county.

56. Washington Guards, Capt. Michael Creswell, 1st Lt. W. Machlin, 2nd Lt. A. Holliday, 77 men, Mifflin county.

57. Warrior's Mark Fencibles, Capt. James Bell, 1st Lt. James Thompson, 2nd Lt. James A. Gano, 85 men, Huntingdon county.

58. Lewistown Artillerists, Capt. John Hamilton, 1st Lt. German Jacobs, 2nd Lt. Daniel Wise, 77 men, Mifflin county.

59. Centre Guards, Capt. Andrew Gregg, 1st Lt. J. I. Gregg, 2nd Lt. D. H. Smith, 83 men, Centre county.

60. Williamsburg Blues, Capt. Thomas R. Fluke, 1st Lt. James Kincaid, 2nd Lt. Alex. McKaney, 79 men, Blair county.

61. Lewistown Guards, Capt. J. A. Cunningham, 1st Lt. G. W. Gibson, 2nd Lt. Joseph Sourbeck, 78 men, Mifflin county.

62. St. Thomas Artillery, Capt. T. McAlister, 1st Lt. John Bricker, 2nd Lt. W. C. McDowell, 88 men, Franklin county.

63. Carlisle Light Infantry, Capt. Samuel Crop, 1st Lt. Wm. Parks, 2nd Lt. H. J. Keller, 82 men, Cumberland county.

64. Landisburg Guards, Capt. H. K. Wilson, 1st Lt. Wm. Power, 2nd Lt. Sol De Walt, 90 men, Perry county.

65. Bloomfield Light Infantry, Capt. T. A. Smith, 1st Lt. T. M. Graham, 2nd Lt. Wm. H. Oles, 83 men, Perry county.

66. Mercersburg Artillerists, Capt. Jas. McDonnel, 1st Lt. J. J. Chambers, 2nd Lt. John McCane, 77 men, Franklin county.

67. Cambria Guards, Capt. James Murray, 1st Lt. Robert Davis, 2nd Lt. C. M'Dermett, 78 men, Cambria county.

68. American Highlanders, Capt. J. W. Geary, 1st Lt. Samuel Black, 2nd Lt. E. M. Luckett, 96 men, Cambria county.

69. Independent Grays, Capt. S. M. Taylor, 1st Lt. L. W. Smith, 2nd Lt. Samuel Shupp, 82 men, Bedford county.

70. Conemaugh Guards, Capt. John Linton, 1st Lt. R. B. Gagley, 2nd Lt. R. Bingham, 87 men, Cambria county.

71. Schellsburg Artillerists, Capt. Robert Fry, 1st Lt. J. C. Statler, 2nd Lt. Jos. S. Reed, 77 men, Bedford county.

72. Franklin Blues, Capt. Hugh Irvin, 1st Lt. G. R. Haymaker, 2nd Lt. J. M. Rugh, 86 men, Westmoreland county.

73. Union Volunteers, Capt. S. S. Austin, 1st Lt. Stewart Speers, 2nd Lt. John Knight, 107 men, Fayette county.

74. Youghiogheny Blues, Capt. Wm. Quail, 1st Lt. Daniel Forrey, 2nd Lt. J. Kilpatrick, 91 men, Fayette county.

75. Westmoreland Guards, Capt. J. W. Johnson, 1st Lt. J. C. Gilchrist, 2nd Lt. W. Murray, 82 men, Westmoreland county.

76. Washington Patriots, Capt. Isaac P. Kendall, 1st Lt. James Dawson, 2nd Lt. James Hudson, 77 men, Fayette county.

77. Sewickley Artillery, Capt. M. N. Dick, 1st Lt. M. D. Campbell, 2nd Lt. J. L. Markle, 114 men, Westmoreland county.

78. Fayette Riflemen, Capt. Geo. W. Hertzog, 1st Lt. J. M. Pixler, 2nd Lt. Levi Zerry, 85 men, Fayette county.

79. Washington County Guards, Capt. John McAlister, 1st Lt. Samuel Morton, 2nd Lt. Jas. Murray, 115 men, Washington county.

80. Jefferson Grays, Capt. Wm. S. Callahan, 1st Lt. Michael Wolf, 2nd Lt. R. Sutton, 77 men, Washington county.

81. Waynesburg Blues, Capt. Bradley Mahanna, 1st Lt. John T. Hook, 2nd Lt. J. C. Fleniken, 77 men, Green county.

82. Centre Guards, Capt. John Vanatta, 1st Lt. Wm. Churchhill, 77 men, Green county.

83. Franklin Rangers, Capt. Neely Mahanna, 1st Lt. James Garnier, 2nd Lt. Hiram Hook, 77 men, Green county.

84. Pittsburg City Blues, 1st Lt. Robert Cornell, 77 men, Pittsburg.

85. Irish Greens, Capt. Joseph O'Brien, 1st Lt. James Dignan, 2nd Lt. M. Connelly, 77 men, Pittsburg.

86. Duquesne Grays, Capt. John Herron, 1st Lt. C. H. Poulson, 2nd Lt. Geo. Beal, 94 men, Pittsburg.

87. Independent Blues, Capt. Alexander Hays, 1st Lt. G. L. Drane, 2nd Lt. J. O. H. Denny, 119 men, Pittsburg.

88. Birmingham Guards, Capt. Samuel McKee, 1st Lt. Robert Duncan, 2nd Lt. D. Cunningham, 77, Pittsburg.

89. Pennsylvania Blues, Capt. Geo. S. Hays, 1st Lt. J. S. Bonnett, 2nd Lt. W. S. Cuddy, 77 men, Pittsburg.

90. Mercer Volunteers, Capt. James Galloway, 1st Lt. J. H. Williamson, 2nd Lt. D. Wadsworth, 78 men, Mercer.

*After the foregoing report was made to the President, the rolls of the following Companies, belonging to the 1st and 2d Battalions as above were received:

1st Com., officers' names not designated, numbering 172 men.

2d Com., Capt. Joseph Andrews; 1st Lt. Martin Becht; 2d Lt. James Hoke, numbering 133.

4th Com., Capt. Samuel Strickler; 1st Lt. John Vanosdal; 2d Lt. David Hutchison, numbering 111.

5th Com., Capt. Michael Culler, numbering 89.

7th Com., officers not designated, numbering 78.

8th Com., Capt. Zachariah Ball, numbering 94.

9th Com., Capt. Wm. Ball, numbering 117.

11th Com., Capt. Geo. Bower, numbering 105 men; making an aggregate 899 men.

APPENDIX III

Pillow's Report of 18 April

Head-Quarters 1st Brigade, Volunteer Division,

Plan del Rio, April 18, 1847.

Sir: I have the honor to report, for the information of the general commanding the division, that, in compliance with general orders No. 111, I took up a position with my brigade in front of the works occupied by the enemy's right wing, but I had not time to gain this position before the attack on his left commenced.

My command was composed of the 1st and 2d Tennessee and the 1st and 2d Pennsylvania foot, and a small detachment of Tennessee horse, commanded by Captain Caswell, and Captain William's company of Kentucky volunteers. It was divided into two storming parties, each supported by a strong reserve. It was my intention to assail with these parties, simultaneously, the adjacent angles of batteries Nos. 1 and 2-those points having been indicated by the engineer officer on duty with the brigade, as those proper for the assault-and thus, if possible, turn the whole line of works; but before the proper dispositions for the assault could be made, our movements were discovered by the enemy, who immediately opened upon our ranks with a most galling fire of musketry, grape, and canister. In this critical position of affairs, I found myself compelled either to retire beyond the range of the enemy's guns to complete my dispositions for the assault, or commence it at once with such force as I had already in position; but apprehending the moral effect which a retreat might produce upon troops, many of whom were comparatively inexperienced and unaccustomed to fire, I resolved to adopt the latter alternative.

I therefore directed Colonel Haskell, who commanded the assaulting force intended for the attack of battery No. 2, to assail that work with vigor, and carry it at the point of the bayonet; his party moved onward to the assault with great energy and enthusiasm, but owing to the many serious obstacles, such as dense chaparal thickets and brush entanglements, the unexpected weight

323

of artillery fire concentrated upon it from seven guns, and to the strong supporting force of infantry, it was compelled to retire with a great loss of both officers and men.

In the meantime Colonel Wynkoop, who commanded the storming party designed to attack battery No. 1, succeeded in gaining the position where the assault was to have been made; but finding that the fire of the main attack on the enemy's left had ceased, I deemed it prudent to suspend further operations until it should recommence, or until further instructions should be received from the general-in-chief. My whole force being drawn up for the attack of battery No. 1, I remained in this position until the news of the enemy's surrender arrived, when I withdrew my command to the national road. It is proper to state here, that Lieutenant Ripley, of the artillery, assisted by Lieutenant Laidley, of the ordnance, although separated from the rest of my command by their position, were actively engaged in the service of an eight-inch howitzer, which, with extraordinary exertions, they succeeded in having dragged over the heights upon the right bank of the river, and which they established so as to obtain an enfilading fire upon the enemy's lines.

Colonel Haskell's assaulting force, composed of his own regiment, (2d Tennessee foot,) Captain William's Kentucky company, and Captain Naylor's company of the 2d Pennsylvania regiment, being, from the nature of its duties, most exposed to the terrible fire of the enemy, sustained the shock-both officers and men-with a firmness and constancy worthy of high commendation.

In the action, Colonel Campbell, finding that I was too severely wounded for the moment to give orders, assumed temporary command, and began, with his accustomed energy and promptitude, dispositions for another attack, which was only deferred by myself for reasons before stated.

Lieutenants Tower and McClellan, of the corps of engineers, displayed great zeal and activity in the discharge of their duties in connexion with my command.

My staff-composed of Captain Winship, A. A. G., Lieutenant Rains, my aid-de-camp, and Lieutenant Anderson, 2d Tennessee foot, acting aid-de-camp, were of essential service to me; for, on account of my wound in the early part of the action, I was compelled to rely more than ordinarily upon their assistance.

I should do violence to my own feelings, as well as injustice to my command, were I to omit a notice of their coolness and good conduct generally upon this occasion. Although, at the time of the assault, the enemy was found to have a much larger amount of artillery bearing upon the approach of our troops than had been supposed, and which had been, until the moment, concealed by the nature of the ground, as well as by artificial arrangements, still none seemed to doubt its final accomplishment, or to shrink from its performance.

Respectfully submitted.

G. J. Pillow,

Brigadier General U. S. A.

APPENDIX IV

Wynkoop's Account of 18 April

Letter from F. M. Wynkoop, Hacienda Garcia, 4 May 1847.

.... Privious to the attack, I spoke to the men and instructed them not to cock a gun or pull a trigger, until the order was given by me, or the commanding officer, in case I was down. At the same time I ordered the music to "let out" with a strong Yankee Doodle, as Soon as they heard the Pennsylvania yell. We moved on to the position which we were ordered to take previous to the attack — that position, as we afterwards ascertained, was within 150 yards of the muzzles of 17 pieces of artillery, and under the fire of 2,000 muskets. My column of attack numbered but 450 men. (This was in consequence of my regiment having been divided to fill up the Tennessee regiments, which were very weak.) About 200 yards from the position, an ambuscade of more than 1,000 muskets opened on us from the chapparal, and grape and canister was poured upon us from the batteries. We had been discovered through the bushes whilst crossing a ravine and the ambuscade had been thrown out to stop us. A number of men were struck down with the first volley, but the line did not quiver. I called out to keep steady and to push on, but it was all unnecessary. The lads never looked behind at the wounded, but moved up rapidly behind me. The fire all this time was pouring upon us from both batteries and ambuscade. With the first call to "Forward," the men broke out into a regular fireman's yell, and the music struck up as though they were blowing their last. The Mexicans couldn't stand it, but "vamosed," as the saying is, straight for their breastwork. We never cocked a gun. Not a shot was fired. We formed our line of attack parallel with the breastworks, and awaited with great impatience the promised order to charge. General Pillow had directed me to form my line of attack, and hold it ready until he sent an officer ordering the charge . . . .

Printed in the *Bedford Gazette*, 4 June 1847.

APPENDIX V

Childs' Report of 12 July

Head-Quarters, 1st Artillery, Puebla, July 12, 1847.

Sir: Agreeably to your request of this date, I have the honor to report the operations of the brigade under my command, on the march from Jalapa to Perote.

The second brigade was composed of four companies of the 2d dragoons, the 1st regiment of artillery, (including Captain Magruder's battery of two 12-pounders and one mountain howitzer,) and the 2d Pennsylvania volunteers; commanded respectively, by Captain Blake, Major Dimick, and Colonel Roberts.

The command left Jalapa on the 18th of June, in the afternoon, and encamped at Barderilla. At daylight, on the morning of the 19th, the troops were in motion; the advance, a portion being interspersed between the divisions of the train, composed of the 2d brigade, with flankers thrown out to the right and left, occupying such positions and heights as might be advantageous for the enemy, and then remained until relieved by the successive columns as they came up; and in this way the march was continued to La Hoya, where we encamped for the night, without anything very special having occurred during the day. On the morning of the 20th, four companies under Captain Winder were sent, in advance, to occupy the successive heights in the pass of La Hoya, where the enemy were supposed to have posted themselves in considerable force. They were at last discovered, as we emerged from the pass, on the last and most difficult height to ascend, and on the left of the road.

Capt. Winder, with two companies, was directed to dislodge the enemy, and on gaining a mountain next to the one alluded to above, he reported the enemy in force on the height that he had already gained, when Major Dimick, with two companies, was sent to reinforce him. The cautious approach of Captain Winder enabled him to fire with effect upon the enemy, killing four and taking three prisoners. Three prisoners were likewise taken by Major Dimick. The Mexicans, finding that the troops were approaching in a different direction from what they anticipated, precipitately left the mountain, passed over

326

to the right of the road, when falling in with a portion of the command of Colonel Wynkoop, a brisk fire was opened from both parties. The advance of the 2d brigade coming up, drove the enemy in confusion from hill to hill for two and a half miles, they leaving seven or eight dead upon the field. The enemy was computed at from six to seven hundred.

The command encamped that night four miles beyond La Hoya at Rio Frio, and at 12, m., on the 21st, arrived at Perote without any further incident.

I have the honor to be, very respectfully, your obedient servant,

Thomas Childs,

Colonel Commanding 2d Brigade.

Wynkoop's Report of 23 June

Head-Quarters, Department of Perote, June 23, 1847.

I have the honor to report the following to the commander-in-chief:

On the 15th of June, a courier reported with letters from head-quarters, stating that Alvarez was on the road between this place and Puebla.

At the same time, hearing of a force of about five hundred in our immediate vicinity, I sent Captain Walker to seize and bring down to the castle 30 fine mustang horses which were secured at San Antonio, and which I thought might be seized and used against us.

The next day, I learnt from a Mexican courier that a force of fifteen hundred men were stationed at La Hoya with the determination of attacking General Cadwalader and train.

Ascertaining afterwards that this information was correct, and also learning the period at which General C. would arrive at La Hoya, I sent to Jalapa a courier, telling General Cadwalader I would meet him at the pass in the rear of the enemy on Sunday morning early.

At 10 o'clock on Saturday evening I left the castle and moved down the national road with Walker's rifles and five companies of my own regiment, (B, C, F, H, and K,) in all about 250 men. We reached the enemy's pickets about a mile beyond Las Vegas and drove them in before daybreak, killing one of them.

In this charge, Captain Walker, who was in advance, encountered a fence which threw his men, injuring some of them severely; and in the melee he lost his own horse and the horses of eight of his men. The accident I consider unavoidable, and think that no blame can accrue to the captain for the consequences.

At about seven o'clock, finding a party of the enemy's horsemen occupying the hills around us, I sent out skirmishers, who succeeded in driving them off, killing five of them. We then halted to rest, the men having walked a distance of 25 miles. Captain Walker requested permission to ride on, in order to get

328

some feed for his horses, a short distance in advance, and had been absent but ten minutes when he was hotly engaged with the enemy. I hurried up with my command, and found him fighting about 500 in a deep valley beyond Las Vegas. Upon the approach of the infantry, the Mexicans broke, and I turned the battalion rapidly so as to cut off their retreat. I followed them for several miles, fighting them upon every favorable piece of ground upon which they rallied, and killing a number. All this time, General Cadwalader with Colonel Childs were engaged in pursuing them; a most complete rout was the consequence. As near as I can estimate, the loss on the part of the enemy was at least 50 men killed; among the killed was an officer who was shot through the body by my orderly.

It is but just to state to the commander-in-chief, that the officers and men behaved themselves bravely and well. They went into the fight cheerfully, ignorant that General Cadwalader's force was at hand, and were desperately determined to drive the enemy off the ground alone. Major Bowman, who was in charge of my infantry, distinguished himself by his coolness and courage, and was among the last to quit the pursuit. Captain Walker and his company deserve the greatest share in the honor of the fight. Before the arrival of the infantry he held his position with 30 rifles against 500 of the enemy, and had killed a number of them.

I am further happy to state that none of my command were wounded.

All of which I have the honor, most respectfully, to submit to the general-in-chief.

F. M. Wynkoop,

Colonel commanding
head-quarters at Perote.

APPENDIX VII

Quitman's Report of 29 September

Head-Quarters of the Volunteer Division,

National Palace, Mexico, September 29, 1847.

Sir: I have the honor to transmit, for the information of the general-in-chief, a report of the movements and operations of that portion of the army under my command, from the afternoon of the 11th instant to the 14th, when our flag was raised on the national palace of Mexico.

The general-in-chief having concluded to carry the strong fortress of Chapultepec, and through it advance upon the city, ordered me, on the 11th, to move my division, after dark, from its position at Coyoacan to Tacubaya. Steptoe's battery and Gaither's troop of horse having been directed to report to General Twiggs, the remainder of the division, consisting of the battalion of marines, New York and South Carolina regiments, under Brigadier General Shields, and the 2d Pennsylvania regiment, under command of Lieutenant Colonel Geary, moved during daylight to the village of Piedad, and at night proceeded thence to their position at Tacubaya, where the troops lay upon their arms until daylight.

Two batteries, Nos. 1 and 2 on the map—the former put up by Lieutenants Tower and Smith, of engineers, under direction of Captain Lee, of the same corps, on the road from Tacubaya to Chapultepec, about eight hundred yards from the fortress; the latter under the direction of Captain Huger, of ordnance, at some distance to the left of the former—had been erected during the night. My division being intended to support these batteries, and to advance to the attack by the direct road from Tacubaya to the fortress, was placed in position near battery No. 1, early on the morning of the 12th, —detachments from its left extended to the support of battery No. 2. At 7 o'clock the guns—two sixteen pounders and an eight-inch howitzer—were placed in battery No. 1, in position so as to rake the road, sweep the adjoining grounds, and have a direct fire upon the enemy's batteries and the fortress of Chapultepec.

Our fire was then opened and maintained with good effect throughout the day, under the direction of that excellent and lamented officer, Captain Drum, of the 4th artillery, zealously aided by Lieutenant Benjamin and Porter, of his company. The fire was briskly returned from the castle with round shot, shells and grape. During the day, I succeeded, under cover of our batteries, in making an important reconnoisance of the grounds and works immediately at the base of the castle, a rough sketch of which was made by my aid, Lieutenant Lovell, on the ground. This disclosed to us two batteries of the enemy—one on the road in front of us, mounting four guns, and the other a flanking work of one gun, capable of sweeping the low grounds on the left of the road, and between it and the base of the hill.

The supporting party on this reconnoisance was commanded by the late Major Twiggs, of the marines, and sustained during the observation a brisk fire from the batteries and small arms of the enemy, who, when the party were retiring, came out of the work in large numbers; and, although repeatedly checked by the fire of our troops, continued to advance as the supporting party retired until they were dispersed, with considerable loss, by several discharges of canister from the guns of Captain Drum's battery, and a well-directed fire from the right of the 2d Pennsylvania regiment posted on the flank of the battery for its support. Our loss in this affair was seven men wounded; but the information gained was of incalculable advantage to the operations of the succeeding day. In the evening, Captain Drum's company was relieved by Lieutenant Andrew's company, 3d artillery, by whom a steady and well-directed fire was kept up from the battery, until the fortress could no longer be seen in the darkness. During the day, my command was reinforced by a select battalion from General Twigg's division, intended as a storming party, consisting of thirteen officers and two hundred and fifty men and non-commissioned officers and privates, chosen for this service out of the rifles, 1st and 4th regiments of artillery, and 2d, 3d, and 7th regiments of infantry—all under the command of Captain Silas Casey, 2d infantry.

Having received instructions from the general-in-chief to prevent, if possible, reinforcements from being thrown into Chapultepec during the night, Captain Paul, of the 7th infantry, with a detachment of fifty men, was directed to establish an advanced picket on the road to Chapultepec. During the night a brisk skirmish occurred between this detachment and the advanced posts of the enemy, which resulted in driving back the enemy; but, apprehensive that this demonstration was intended to cover the passage of reinforcements into Chapultepec, I ordered Lieutenant Andrews to advance a piece of artillery and rake the road with several discharges of canister. This was promptly executed; and, during the remainder of the night, there were no appearances of movements in the enemy's lines. During the night, the platforms of battery No. 1 were repaired, under the direction of Lieutenant Tower, of engineers, who had reported to me for duty, and a new battery for the gun established in advance of No. 1, a short distance, by Lieutenant Hammond of General Shields's staff.

The protection of battery No. 2, which was completed on the morning of the 12th, under the direction of Captain Huger, was intrusted to Brigadier General Shields. This battery, after the guns had been placed, opened and maintained a steady fire upon the castle, under the skilful direction of that experienced officer, Lieutenant Hagner, of ordnance.

At dawn, on the morning of the 13th, the batteries again opened an active and effective fire upon the castle, which was returned by the enemy with spirit and some execution, disabling, for a time, the eighteen pounder in battery No. 1, and killing one of the men at the guns.

During this cannonade, active preparations were made for the assault upon the castle. Ladders, pickaxes, and crows were placed in the hands of a pioneer storming party of select men from the volunteer division, under command of Captain Reynolds, of the marine corps, to accompany the storming party of one hundred and twenty men which had been selected from all corps of the same division, and placed under the command of Major Twiggs, of the marines. Captain Drum had again relieved Lieutenant Andrews at the guns, retaining from the command of the latter Sergeant Davidsin and eight men to man an eight-pounder, which it was intended to carry forward to operate upon the enemy's batteries in front of us; and, to relieve the command from all danger of attack on our right flank from reinforcements which might come from the city, that well-tried and accomplished officer, Brevet Brigadier General Smith, with his well-disciplined brigade, had reported to me for orders. He was instructed to move in reserve on the right flank of the assaulting column, protect it from skirmishers, or more serious attack in that quarter, and, if possible, on the assault, cross the aqueduct leading to the city, turn the enemy, and cut off his retreat. Those dispositions being made, the whole command, at the signal preconcerted by the general-in-chief, with enthusiasm and full of confidence, advanced to the attack. At the base of the hill constituting part of the works of the fortress of Chapultepec, and directly across our line of advance, were the strong batteries before described, flanked on the right by some strong buildings, and by a heavy stone wall about fifteen feet high, which extended around the base of the hill towards the west. Within two hundred yards of these batteries were some dilapidated buildings, which afforded a partial cover to our advance. Between these and the wall extended a low meadow, the long grass of which concealed a number of wet ditches by which it was intersected. To this point the command, partially screened, advanced by a flank, the storming parties in front, under a heavy fire from the fortress, the batteries, and breastworks of the enemy. The advance was here halted under the partial cover of the ruins, and upon the arrival of the heads of the South Carolina and New York Regiments, respectively, General Shields was directed to move them obliquely to the left, across the low ground, to the wall at the base of the hill. Encouraged by the gallant general who had led them to victory at Churubusco, and in spite of the obstacles which they had to encounter in wading through several deep ditches, exposed to a severe and galling fire from the enemy, these tried regiments promptly executed the movement, and effected a lodgment at the wall. The same order was given to Lieutenant Colonel Geary, and executed by his regiment with equal alacrity and success. These dispositions, so necessary to the final assault upon the works, were not made without some loss. In directing the advance, Brigadier General Shields was severely wounded in the arm. No persuasions, however, could induce that officer to leave his command, or quit the field. The brave Captain Van O'Linda, of the New York regiment, was killed at the head of his company. Lieutenant Colonel Baxter, of the same regiment, a valuable and esteemed officer, while gallantly leading his command, fell mortally wounded near the wall. And Lieutenant Colonel Geary, 2d Pennsylvania regiment, was for a time, disabled from command by a severe contusion from a spent ball.

In the meantime, Brigadier General Smith on our right was driving back skirmishing parties of the enemy; Lieutenant Benjamin, from battery No. 1, was pouring shot after shot into the fortress and woods on the slope of the hill; and Lieutenant H. J. Hunt, 2d artillery, who had on the advance reported to me with a section of Duncan's battery, had obtained a favorable position in our rear, from which he threw shells and shrapnel shot into the Mexican lines with good effect. Perceiving that all the preliminary dispositions were made, Major Gladden, with his regiment, having passed the wall by breaching it, the New York and Pennsylvania regiments having entered over an abandoned battery on their left, and the battalion of marines being posted to support the storming parties, I ordered the assault at all points.

The storming parties led by the gallant officers who had volunteered for this desperate service, rushed forward like a resistless tide. The Mexicans behind their batteries and breastworks stood with more than usual firmness. For a short time the contest was hand-to-hand; swords and bayonets were crossed, and rifles clubbed. Resistance, however, was vain against the desperate valor of our brave troops. The batteries and strong works were carried, and the ascent of Chapultepec on that side laid open to an easy conquest. In these works were taken seven pieces of artillery, one thousand muskets, and five hundred and fifty prisoners—of whom one hundred were officers—among them, one general and ten colonels.

The gallant Capt. Casey having been disabled by a severe wound directly before the batteries, the command of the storming party of regulars in the assault devolved on Captain Paul, 7th infantry, who distinguished himself for his bravery. In like manner, the command of the storming party from the volunteer division devolved on Capt. James Miller, of the 2d Pennsylvania regiment, by the death of its chief, the brave and lamented Major Twiggs, of the marine corps, who fell on the first advance at the head of his command.

Simultaneously with these movements on our right, the volunteer regiments, with equal alacrity and intrepidity, animated by a generous emulation, commenced the ascent of the hill on the south side. Surmounting every obstacle, and fighting their way, they fell in and mingled with their brave brethren in arms who formed the advance of Major General Pillow's column.

Side by side, amid the storm of battle, the rival colors of the two commands struggled up the steep ascent, entered the fortress, and reached the buildings used as a military college, which crowned its summit. Here was a short pause; but soon the flag of Mexico was lowered, and the stars and stripes of our country floated from the heights of Chapultepec high above the heads of the brave men who had planted them there. The gallant New York regiment claims for their standard the honor of being first waved from the battlements of Chapultepec. The veteran Mexican General, Bravo, with a number of officers and men, were taken prisoners in the castle. They fell into the hands of Lieutenant Charles Brower, of the New York regiment, who reported them to me. The loss of the enemy was severe, especially on the eastern side adjoining the batteries taken. It should also be mentioned, that, at the assault upon the works, Lieutenant Frederick Steele, 2d infantry, with a portion of the storming party, advanced in front of the batteries towards the left, there scaled the outer wall through a breach near the top, made by a cannon shot, ascended the hill directly in his front, and was among the first upon the battlements. The young and promising Lieutenant, Levi Gantt, 7th infantry, was of this party. He had actively participated in almost every battle since the opening of the war, but was destined here to find a soldier's grave.

After giving the necessary directions for the safe-keeping of the prisoners taken by my command, and ordering the several corps to form near the aqueduct, I hastily ascended the hill for the purpose of reconnoitring the positions of the enemy in advance towards the city. I there had the pleasure of meeting Major General Pillow, who, although seriously wounded, had been carried to the heights to enjoy the triumph in which he and his brave troops had so largely shared.

Perceiving large bodies of the enemy at the several batteries in the direct road leading from Chapultepec to the city, by the garita or gate of Belen, my whole command, after being supplied with ammunition, was ordered to be put in readiness to march by that route. When the batteries were taken the gallant rifle regiment, which had been deployed by General Smith on the right of his brigade, formed under the arches of the aqueduct in position to advance by the Chapultepec or Tacubaya road. As the remainder of General Smith's brigade came up from their position in reserve, that officer, with his usual foresight, caused them to level the parapets and fill the ditches which obstructed the road where the enemy's batteries had been constructed, so as to permit the passage of the heavy artillery, which was ordered up by the general-in-chief immediately upon his arrival at the batteries. In the meantime, while General Shields, with the assistance of his and my staff officers, was causing the deficient ammunition to be supplied, and the troops to be formed for the advance, Captain Drum, supported by the rifle regiment, had taken charge of one of the enemy's pieces, and was advancing towards the first battery occupied by the enemy on the road towards the city in our front.

The Chapultepec road is a broad avenue, flanked with deep ditches and marshy grounds on either side. Along the middle of this avenue runs the aqueduct, supported by arches of heavy masonry, through the garita or gate of Belen into the city. The rifles, supported by the South Carolina regiment, and folowed by the remainder of Smith's brigade, were now advanced, from arch to arch, towards another strong battery which had been thrown across the road, about a mile from Chapultepec, having four embrasures with a redan work on the right.

At this point, the enemy in considerable force made an obstinate resistance; but, with the aid of the effective fire of an 8-inch howitzer directed by the indefatigable Captain Drum, and the daring bravery of the gallant rifle regiment, it was carried by assault. The column was here reorganized for an attack upon the batteries at the garita of the city. The regiment of riflemen, intermingled with the bayonets of the South Carolina regiment, were placed in advance— three rifles and three bayonets under each arch. They were supported by the residue of Shields's brigade, the 2d Pennsylvania regiment, and the remainder of Smith's brigade, together with a part of the 6th infantry under Major Bonneville, who had fallen into this road. In this order the column resolutely advanced from arch to arch of the aqueduct, under a tremendous fire of artillery and small arms from the batteries at the garita, the Paseo, and a large body of the enemy on the Piedad road to the right, extending from the left of the garita.

Lieutenant Benjamin having brought up a 16-pounder, Captain Drum and his efficient subalterns were pouring a constant and destructive fire into the garita. As the enfilading fire of the enemy from the Piedad road became very annoying to the advance of the column, a few rounds of canister were thrown by our artillery in that direction, which effectually dispersed them. The whole column was now under a galling fire, but it continued to move forward steadily and firmly. The rifles, well sustained by the South Carolinians, gallantly pushed on to the attack; and at twenty minutes past one the garita was carried, and the city of Mexico entered at that point. In a few moments nearly the whole command was compactly up—a large part of it within the garita.

The obstinacy of the defence at the garita may be accounted for by our being opposed at that point by General Santa Anna in person, who is said to have retreated by the Paseo to the San Cosme road, there to try his fortune against General Worth.

On our approach to the garita, a body of the enemy, who were seen on a cross road threatening our left, were dispersed by a brisk fire of artillery from the direction of the San Cosme road. I take pleasure in acknowledging that this seasonable aid came from Lieut. Colonel Duncan's battery, which had been kindly advanced from the San Cosme road in that direction by General Worth's orders.

Upon the taking of the garita, the riflemen and South Carolina regiment rushed forward and occupied the arches of the aqueduct, within a hundred yards of the citadel. The ammunition of our heavy guns having been expended, a captured 8-pounder was turned upon the enemy and served with good effect until the ammunition taken with it was also expended. The piece, supported by our advance, had been run forward in front of the garita. Twice had Major Gladden, of the South Carolina regiment, furnished additional men to work the gun, when the noble and brave Captain Drum, who, with indomitable energy and iron nerve, had directed the artillery throughout this trying day, fell mortally wounded by the side of his gun. A few moments afterwards Lieutenant Benjamin, who had displayed the same cool, decided courage, met a similar fate.

The enemy, now perceiving that our heavy ammunition had been expended, redoubled their exertions to drive us out of the lodgment we had effected. A terrible fire of artillery and small arms was opened from the citadel, 300 yards distant, from the batteries on the Paseo, and the buildings on our right in front. Amid this iron shower, which swept the road on both sides of the aqueduct, it was impossible to bring forward ammunition for our large guns. While awaiting the darkness, to bring up our great guns, and place them in battery, the enemy, under cover of their guns, attempted several sallies from the citadel and buildings on the right, but were readily repulsed by the skirmishing parties of rifles and infantry. To prevent our flank from being enfiladed by musketry from the Paseo, Captains Naylor and Loeser, 2d Pennsylvania regiment, were ordered with their companies to a low sand-bag defence about a hundred yards in that direction. They gallantly took this position, and held it in the face of a severe fire, until the object was attained.

At night the fire of the enemy ceased. Lieutenant Tower, of engineers, who before and at the attack upon the batteries at Chapultepec had given important aid, had been seriously wounded. It was, therefore, fortunate that, in the commencement of the route to the city, Lieutenant Beauregard, of engineers, joined me. I was enabled, during the day, to avail myself of his valuable services; and although disabled, for a time, by a wound received during the day, he superintended, during the whole night, the erection of two batteries, within the garita for our heavy guns, and a breastwork on our right for infantry, which, with his advice, I had determined to construct. By the indefatigable energy of my acting assistant adjutant general, Lieutenant Lovell, my volunteer aid, Captain G. T. M. Davis, and Lieutenant H. Brown, 3d artillery, the sand-bags and ammunition were procured; Lieutenant Beauregard, assisted by Lieutenant Coupe, directing the construction of one battery in person, and Lieutenant W. H. Wood, 3d infantry, the other. Before the dawn of day, by the persevering exertions of Captains Fairchild and Taylor, of the New York regiment, who directed the working parties, the parapets were completed, and a 24-pounder, an 18-pounder, and 8-inch howitzer placed in battery by Captain Steptoe, 3d artillery; who, to my great satisfaction, had rejoined my command in the evening. The heavy labor required to construct these formidable batteries, under the very guns of the citadel, was performed with the utmost cheerfulness by the gallant men whose strong arms and stout hearts had already been tested in two days of peril and toil.

During the night, while at the trenches, Brigadier General Pierce—one of whose regiments (the 9th infantry) had joined my column during the day—reported to me in person. He was instructed to place that regiment in reserve at the battery in rear, for the protection of Steptoe's light battery and the ammunition at that point. The general has my thanks for his prompt attention to these orders.

At dawn of day on the 14th, when Captain Steptoe was preparing his heavy missiles, a white flag came from the citadel, the bearers of which invited me to take possession of this fortress, and gave me the intelligence that the city had been abandoned, by Santa Anna and his army. My whole command was immediately ordered under arms. By their own request, Lieutenants Lovell and Beauregard were authorized to go to the citadel, in advance, to ascertain the truth of the information. At a signal from the ramparts, the column, General Smith's brigade in front, and the South Carolina regiment left in garrison at the garita, marched into the citadel. Having taken possession of this work, in which we found 15 pieces of cannon mounted, and as many not up, with the extensive military armaments which it contained, the 2d Pennsylvania regiment was left to garrison it. Understanding that great depredations were going on in the palace and public buildings, I moved the column in that direction in the same order, followed by Captain Steptoe's light battery, through the principal streets into the great plaza, where it was formed in front of the national palace. Captain Roberts, of the rifle regiment, who had led the advance company of the storming party at Chapultepec, and had greatly distinguished himself during the preceding day, was detailed by me to plant the star-spangled banner of our country upon the national palace. The flag, the first strange banner which had ever waved over that palace since the conquest of Cortez, was displayed and saluted with enthusiasm by the whole command. The palace, already crowded with Mexican thieves and robbers, was placed in charge of Lieutenant Colonel Watson, with his battalion of marines. By his active exertions, it was soon cleared and guarded from further spoliation.

On our first arrival in the plaza, Lieutenant Beauregard was despatched to report the facts to the general-in-chief, who was expected to enter the city by the Alameda, with the column under General Worth. About 8 o'clock, the general-in-chief arrived in the plaza, and was received and greeted with enthusiasm by the troops. The populace, who had begun to be turbulent immediately after our arrival in the plaza, appeared for a time to be checked; but, in one hour afterwards, as our troops began to disperse for quarters, they were fired upon from the tops of houses and windows. This continued that day and the succeeding, until, by the timely and vigorous measures adopted by the general-in-chief, the disturbances were quelled.

Two detachments from my command, not heretofore mentioned in this report, should be noticed. Captain Gallagher and Lieutenant Reid, who, with their companies of New York volunteers, had been detailed on the morning of the 12th by General Shields to the support of our battery No. 2, well performed this service. The former, by the orders of Captain Huger, was detained at that battery during the storming of Chapultepec. The latter, a brave and energetic young officer, being relieved from the battery on the advance to the castle, hastened to the assault, and was among the first to ascend the crest of the hill where he was severely wounded.

In all the operations of the several corps under my command, to which this report refers, it gives me great pleasure to testify to the devoted courage with which they faced every danger, and the cheerfulness and alacrity with which they met every toil and exposure. A simple narrative of those military events, crowned as they were with complete success, is a higher compliment than any expressions of my opinion can bestow upon the general good conduct of the whole command.

I have already alluded to the gallant conduct of the storming parties. They deserve the highest commendation. The losses sustained by Captain Drum's heroic little band of artillerists from the 4th artillery, evince their exposure during the day. I do them, officers and men, but justice when I add that no encomium upon their conduct and skill would be misplaced.

This report has already shown the prominent part taken by the regiment of riflemen under the command of the brave and intrepid Major Loring, who fell severely wounded by my side, while receiving orders for the final charge upon the garita. After the taking of the batteries of Chapultepec, in which portions of this corps took an active part, this efficient and splendid regiment were employed as sharp-shooters in the advance, through the arches of the aqueduct, where their services were invaluable. My only concern was to restrain their daring impetuosity.

The gallant and unassuming Palmetto regiment, which had charged up the ascent of Chapultepec without firing a gun, was also employed to support and aid the rifles. In this service their loss was severe. Among others, their brave and efficient commander, Major Gladden, was severely wounded, and Lieutenants J. B. Moraigne and William Canty killed. But they well sustained the reputation they had acquired at Vera Cruz, Contreras, and Churubusco.

For the admirable conduct of the other corps of my command, I refer to the reports of Brigadier Generals Shields and Smith, and of Lieutenant Colonel Geary. The brilliant successes of the day were not acquired without considerable loss. The reports herewith transmitted show that, in my whole command, eight officers and sixty-nine non-commissioned officers and privates were killed, and four hundred and fifty-four officers and men were wounded, and nine men missing—making total of casualties five hundred and forty, besides those in the 9th regiment of infantry, while under my command, not reported to me.

Brigadier General Shields had solicited from me the command of the storming parties in the morning of the 13th. Not feeling justified in permitting so great an exposure of an officer of his rank with an inadequate command, and requiring his invaluable services with his brigade, the application was declined. Until carried from the field on the night of the 13th, in consequence of the severe wound received in the morning, he was conspicuous for his gallantry, energy, and skill. In brevet Brigadier General Smith, who was ever cool, unembarrassed, and ready, under the trying exposures of the day, I found an able and most efficient supporter. Lieutenant Colonel Geary, who, in the illness of Colonel Roberts, commanded the 2d Pennsylvania regiment, constituting the 2d brigade of my division, was wounded before the walls of Chapultepec at the head of his corps, but soon resumed command and rendered good service.

To Majors Loring and Dimick, and Captains Simonson and Alexander, commanders of regiments in Smith's brigade; Lieutenant Colonel Watson, Majors Gladden and Burnham, and Captain Donovan, commanders in Shields's brigade, and to Major Brindle, who for a time commanded his regiment, I am indebted for the active and fearless discharge of their duties in the direction of the operations of their respective corps while under their orders.

Of the storming parties, in addition to those already named in this report, Captain Dobbins, 3d infantry; Lieutenant Hill, 4th artillery; Lieutenant Westcott, 2d infantry; Lieutenant Stewart, of the rifles; Lieutenant Haskins, 1st artillery; Captain Reynolds, of marines; Captain Miller, 2d Pennsylvania regiment; Lieutenant Ball, South Carolina battalion; and Lieutenant Wolf, 2d Pennsylvania regiment, were highly distinguished for their gallantry. Captains Backenstos, Porter, and Tucker; Lieutenants Morris, Hatch, and Granger, of the rifles; Captains Blanding, Desaussure, Marshall, and Lieutenants Selleck, Lilly, and May, of the South Carolina regiment; Captain Taylor, New York regiment; Adjutant Baker, of the marines; Lieutenant F. J. Porter, 4th artillery; and Lieutenant Hare, 2d Pennsylvania regiment, whose conduct happened to fall under my own eye, were conspicuous for their bravery and efficiency. In the reports of the several commanders of brigades, the following officers are named with high credit: Captains Barclay and Pierson, New York regiment; Lieutenants McLean, Russel, and Gibbs, of the rifles; and Lieutenant Sheppard, 3d infantry; Surgeons Edwards, of Marines, and McMillan, 2d Pennsylvania regiment; and Assistant Surgeons McSherry and Bower, engaged in division hospital, deserve all praise for their attention to the wounded.

I take great pleasure by extending my cordial concurrence in the high commendation bestowed in the official reports of their respective chiefs upon the good conduct of Captain F. N. Page and Lieutenant R. P. Hammond, aids, both of General Shields's staff; and Lieutenant Earl Van Dorn, aid to General Smith.

I have before noticed the valuable services of Lieutenants Beauregard and Tower, of the engineers. A draught of the field of operations, planned by the later gentleman, accompanies this report.

Under the late orders, a list of the non-commissioned officers and privates of the command under my orders, who have been conspicuous for their services in the late actions, is transmitted.

I close this report with presenting to the notice of the general-in-chief the important services and excellent conduct of my personal staff. From the commencement of our movements, my aid and acting assistant adjutant general,

Lieutenant Mansfield Lovell, 4th artillery, was intrusted with the most responsible and arduous duties, and exposed frequently to imminent danger and severe fatigue. These duties were all fearlessly, cheerfully, and promptly performed, with a judgment and skill that promises the highest distinction in his profession. Although his arm was disabled by a wound received at the garita, he remained to the last in the active performance of his duties. The distribution of my command also imposed upon my aid, Lieutenant C. M. Wilcox, 7th infantry, dangerous duties. These were performed by him promptly and efficiently, facing danger fearlessly wherever his duty called him. Captain G. T. M. Davis, late of the 1st Illinois regiment, and Captain Danley, late of the Arkansas cavalry, acted as volunteer aids. The former was actively and constantly engaged in every part of the field, conveying my orders, and bringing up ammunition and supplies. The latter, after having conveyed my orders to the volunteer regiments through a galling fire, was severely wounded while resuming his position near me in front of the first battery on the Chapultepec road. Both of these gentlemen acted with distinguished gallantry.

Transmitting herewith a report of my division on the morning of the 18th, and lists of the killed and wounded.

I have the honor to remain, very respectfully, your obedient servant,

J. A. Quitman,

Major General U.S. Army, commanding Vol. Div.

APPENDIX VIII

Geary's Report of 15 September

City of Mexico, September 15, 1847.

Sir: — In compliance with the instructions of your note of yesterday, I have the honor to report the operations of the Second Pennsylvania Regiment, on the 12th and 13th inst.: the command devolving upon me in consequence of the extreme illness of Col. Wm. B. Roberts.

My command, on the morning of the 12th, was composed of eleven companies, (company K having been detailed on the 11th in the light infantry battalion,) in all about four hundred and fifty rank and file.

Early on the morning of the 12th, by order of Brig. Gen. Shields, I detailed four companies (E, I, L and M) of my regiment, under command of Major Brindle, to report to Capt. Huger, Chief of Ordnance, for special duty. For the service of this detachment, I refer you to the reports of Major Brindle and Capt. Huger.

The remaining seven companies, under my immediate command, were actively employed during the morning of the 12th, in constructing and supporting the batteries on the road fronting the fortress of Chapultepec. During the afternoon of the same day, I supported the light infantry battalion under Major Twiggs, of the Marine corps, and remained in position some time after their return, exposed to a constant fire of grape, canister and musketry from the works on Chapultepec, and a large force of infantry scattered through the adjoining fields and ditches.— During the afternoon, nine of my men were wounded.

The conduct of my command, while at work on the batteries and in support of the skirmishers, was highly commendable. The officers and men obeyed all orders cheerfully and promptly, and behaved with the greatest coolness, though exposed to a hot fire from the enemy without an opportunity of retaliating.

On the morning of the 12th [13th], having been joined by the detachment under Maj. Brindle, the regiment took its proper place in the division, and under your own immediate command, moved forward to the charge of Chapultepec.

341

While crossing the swamp between the road and the fortress, where greatly exposed to the fire of the enemy, I was struck in the groin by a grape shot, which prevented me from proceeding with the regiment, and, for a short time, the command devolved upon Maj. Brindle, who I have directed to submit a detailed statement of the occurrences during my absence.

Although my wound prevented me from moving forward for some time, I had an opportunity of witnessing the conduct of the regiment upon the fortress, and am proud to say, that it was such as to reflect credit on themselves as soldiers, and did honor to the state they represent. From my own observation, as well as from the reports of my subalterns, I am well convinced they were among the first to enter the enemy's works. Having sufficiently recovered from the shock which I had received, I joined my regiment as soon as they reached the summit of the hill, and resumed the command.

My regiment again took its proper position in the division and advanced on the city. In the support of the batteries at the Garita, the men and officers of my command cheerfully performed such duties as you assigned them, and fully sustained the character they had gained in the morning. As the subsequent operations were carried on under your immediate observation, and all orders were communicated by you, in person, it would be an act of supererogation on my part to particularize. Nor will it be necessary to mention the movements in taking the citadel, as your position was such as to render you fully cognizant of all the facts.

It is a matter of peculiar difficulty for the commander of a regiment to do justice to all under his command, in a brief report, such as this is expected to be. All of my command, officers and men, deserve and have my unqualified commendation.

Maj. Brindle deserves particular notice, not only for his coolness, courage and gallantry generally, during the day, but also for the promptness with which he resumed the command when I was compelled to stop. In fact, his conduct in the charge upon Chapultepec was such as to elicit the commendation of all who witnessed his actions.

Surgeon M'Millen has my thanks for the promptness and efficiency with which he performed the duties of his station during the day.

Adjutant Waterbury was prompt, active, and energetic in the discharge of his duties, and I take great pleasure in bringing him particularly to your notice.

My non-commissioned staff, Sergt. Maj. Todd and Quartermaster Sergeant Shellcross, rendered me valuable assistance.

Capt. Miller, with company K, was detailed on the 11th, into the light infantry battalion, and although their conduct did not come under my own observation, I learn that they acquitted themselves with great credit. Capt. Miller, although severely wounded early in the day, did not relinquish the command of his company.— Lieut. Wolf, of this company, is also highly spoken of for his gallantry and strict attention to his duties.

Company A, commanded by Capt. T. S. Loeser, allowed no one to surpass them in the performance of their duty; in crossing the swamp; ascending the hill, and in fact, during the whole day, they maintained their position well. I would here beg leave to call to your recollection the gallant conduct of Capt. Loeser and Lt. M'Michal, of this company, as well as Captains Humphreys and Naylor, of companies B and F, in crossing from the Garita to the breastwork near the citadel, during the afternoon. The great coolness with which they acted, in an unusually exposed position, will, I hope, receive your particular notice.

Company B, Capt. Humphreys, were on constant duty during both the 12th and 13th; on the former I sent him with a command of twelve men, to drive in what I supposed to be a few of the enemy's riflemen, who, by a continual firing from a corn field, annoyed us much. To our mutual surprise, he found the enemy in considerable force. After a smart contest, in which five of his party were wounded, he rejoined the regiment with his command in good order. For this conduct, and that of himself and company, on the 13th, I recommend him to your notice.

Company C, on this occasion, was under the command of Lieut. Frick, who, with his company acted very gallantly. I will also bring to your notice Lieut. LeClerc, of this company, who, not only in the discharge of his appropriate duties, but also by his intelligence and courage in reconnoitering and reporting the force and position of the enemy, afforded me valuable assistance.

Company D, under command of Lieut. Heyer, in consequence of the severe illness of Capt. Murray, distinguished themselves on both days as excellent marksmen, and fully sustained the character of the Mountaneers [sic.] of Pennsylvania.

Company E, commanded by Lieuts. Armstrong and Coulter, fully sustained their reputation during the whole fight, and were unsurpassed in the charge upon the Castle.

Capt. Naylor, of company F, a part of whose conduct has already been brought to your notice, joined his company from a sick bed, and continued in the command until he reached the citadel and the enemy had surrendered. I would respectfully ask for him the notice which his conduct so eminently deserves. Lieut. Fourison supported Capt. Naylor, and although wounded, I am happy to say not dangerously.

Company G, with its officers, Capt. Williams and Lieut. Unger, were always where duty called them, and although wounded, Capt. Williams continued in command till the close of the action.

Company H was commanded by Lt. Hambright. This officer entered the service a private, and gained his present position by his uniform good conduct. As a drill officer and tactician, he has no superior in the regiment, and in the action he and his company fully sustained their reputation. Sergeants Cummings and Irvin, of this company, also distinguished themselves.

Company I, commanded by Lieut. Rankin, distinguished themselves for gallantry, and cool, indomitable courage. This corps is composed principally by the sons of the Emerald Isle; their conduct reflects the highest honor upon them and the noble city they represent. It is much to be regretted that they were deprived of the services of their gallant Captain, (Porter,) who was confined to his bed dangerously ill.

Companies L and M, Captains Taylor and Caldwell, belong to the late levies, and but recently been attached to my command, their conduct would have done honor to veterans.

I refer you to the list herewith submitted for the casualties of my regiment.

I cannot close this report without referring you to the conduct of the men under my command on the 11th inst., when I was called upon to detail a small number to act as a storming party. I regret that it is not in my power to notice them more particularly. Lieuts. Hare, LeClerc and Heyer all came forward promptly and contended for the honor of leading them, and Lieut. Hare, the successful applicant, acted as I would have wished. Ten out of the fifteen, you will observe, are either killed or wounded.

At the request of the officers and men of M company, I appointed Mr. D. M. Dull, a citizen of Pennsylvania, to act as a Lieutenant during the engagement. Capt. Caldwell reports highly favorable of his conduct, and as his services on the occasion were entirely gratuitous, I ask for him your particular notice.

I was joined in the engagement by Major M'Micken, a gentleman from my own State, accompanying the army, who, by his appeals to the State and National pride of the men, contributed much to the enthusiasm of the regiment, and has my sincere thanks.

Mr. Dull and Maj. M'Micken being purely amateur soldiers, I mention them thus particularly as their conduct might not otherwise receive the notice it deserves.

You will observe from the appended list, that the number of our killed is 8, wounded 89. I am, sir, very respectfully, your obedient servant,

John W. Geary

Lt. Col. Com'g.
2d Reg't. Pa. Volunteers.

Printed in *The Pennsylvanian* (Philadelphia), Dec. 17, 1847.

APPENDIX IX

Brindle's Report of 15 September

Head-Quarters, Second Brigade, Vol. Division,

Citadel, City of Mexico, September 15, 1847.

Shortly before daybreak on the 13th instant Lieut. Richard Hammond, an aid of General Shields, conveyed an order to me for the General of the Division to join the Second Pennsylvania Regiment at Battery No. 1, near Tacubaya, with my command, to participate in an assault upon the Fortress of Chapultepec .... On the meadows, and under my eye, Captain E. C. Williams, of Company G "Cameron Guards" of Harrisburg, Pa., was struck by a ball, near the top of the shoulder, high enough up to turn the shoulder. It threw him forward on his hands and knees, severely wounded. He was quickly on his feet again, and continued on duty with his company until the fighting was concluded in the City of Mexico. Had the ball struck his shoulder slightly lower it would have been a mortal wound. ... As soon as the Second Pennsylvania Regiment had passed the wall of the Fortress, it encountered its garrison, about 800 strong, composed of artillery and infantry, which we drove back to the arch on the front of the Fortress, and under it where it surrendered.

I placed a guard over the prisoners, and then hastened to the eastern end of the Fortress, where I met the aged General Bravo, its commander, who stood with his arms folded over his chest, in the attitude of surrender. He was an ex-President of Mexico, and had fought gallantly to make it independent of Spain. I did not deem it necessary to humiliate him by taking his sword. At this moment General Quitman came up the roadway leading into the Fortress on the southeast. I met him and turned over to him the Fortress and the prisoners the Second Pennsylvania Regiment had taken in it. He directed me to have the Second Pennsylvania Regiment replenish its ammunition and proceed to the attack on the Garita-de-Belen, about two miles from the Fortress. At the moment when I met General Bravo, Lieutenant Charles B. Bowers, of Captain Gallagher's company of (F) the New York Regiment, then serving with

345

Battery No. 2, approached. Apparently he had been separated from his company and regiment; and attempted to assault General Bravo with his sword. I ordered him to halt, and called his attention to the fact that General Bravo, with his arms folded over his chest had surrendered, and ordered Bowers to put up his sword. . . . Captain E. C. Williams, of Company G, Second Pennsylvania Regiment soon after we entered the Fortress, ascended to the top of it, with the first American Flag made by Betsy Ross, of Philadelphia, which was presented to General Washington just before the battle of Trenton, during the Revolution of 1776, which Captain Williams had obtained from the State Library at Harrisburg, Pa., and carried with him to Mexico, with the purpose of raising it over the enemy's works at every opportunity, and which he raised over the Fortress of Chapultepec about the same time that a sergeant of one of the old infantry regiments raised a blue regimental flag over it. To Captain Williams belongs the honor of having raised the first American Flag over the Fortress. . . . Shortly before daylight on the 14th instant an Englishman who owned and operated a cotton factory, near the Citadel, whose property would have been destroyed if the batteries had opened fire, came running with a white flag to the General of the Division, who was about to open fire with the batteries, and informed him that General Santa Anna had marched out of the city by the Northeast Gate with his army. The General put the bearer of the white flag in my charge, to hold him with us until we ascertained whether his information was true or false. The General immediately ordered his command "forward". We found the battery at the Southeast of the Citadel abandoned, and also the Citadel, when I released the bearer of the white flag, with thanks. The Second Pennsylvania Regiment was placed as a garrison in the Citadel, when Captain E. C. Williams ran up over it that American Flag which he had so proudly raised over the Fortress. To Captain Williams also belongs the honor of having raised the First American Flag over any public building in the city of Mexico. . . . I cannot conclude my report without expressing my admiration of the good conduct and gallantry of every officer and man of the Second Pennsylvania Volunteer Regiment. I also express my thanks to them for the splendid and regular order in which they charged up the hill and into the Fortress which elicited the applause of all who witnessed their charge. The Second Pennsylvania Regiment lost eight killed, and eighty-nine wounded. A detailed list of the killed and wounded will accompany the report of Lieutenant Colonel Geary.

I am, very respectfully, Your obedient servant,

William Brindle, Major Commanding

Second Brigade, Volunteer Division.

Printed as shown here, in partial form, in: Dewey S. Herrold, "Brigadier-General Edward Charles Williams," *The Snyder County Historical Society Bulletin*, II (Bulletin No. 4), pp. 504-505.

APPENDIX X

Casualties Before Mexico City

Casualties of the 2nd Pennsylvania Regiment, 12 and 13 September

Chapultepec
    Field & Staff
        Lt. Col. John W. Geary, WIA

    Co. A
        Pvt. Jacob Armbriester, WIA
        Pvt. John E. Arthur, WIA
        Pvt. Henry Boyer, WIA
        Pvt. John Freymore, WIA
        Cpl. William Herbert, WIA
        Pvt. Peter Hogan, WIA
        Fifer Thomas McGee, WIA
        Pvt. Peter Moyer, WIA, DoW 14 Sep
        Pvt. Jacob Rapp, WIA
        Pvt. Daniel S. Saul, WIA

    Co. B
        Sgt. John B. Brookbank, WIA
        Pvt. John Campbell, WIA
        Pvt. Andrew W. Dripps, WIA
        Pvt. Thomas Humphreys, WIA
        Pvt. William Humphreys, WIA, DoW 27 Sep
        Pvt. John McLaughlin, WIA
        Pvt. Abraham I. Rhoads, WIA
        Pvt. Washington I. Stone, WIA
        Pvt. Hugh F. Storm, WIA
        Cpl. John I. Worthington, WIA

Co. C
>   Pvt. William H. Dietrick, WIA, DoW 2 Oct
>   Pvt. John Snyder, WIA, DoW 17 Sep

Co. D
>   Pvt. Benjamin F. Davis, WIA
>   Pvt. Francis C. McDermitt, WIA
>   Pvt. George W. Neff, WIA
>   Pvt. Archibald Patterson, WIA, DoW 10 Jan 48

Co. E
>   Pvt. Andrew J. Bates, WIA
>   Pvt. Chauncey F. Sargeant, WIA

Co. F
>   Pvt. John Areson, WIA
>   Pvt. William H. Logue, WIA
>   Pvt. William Rice, WIA
>   Pvt. James T. Sample, WIA

Co. G
>   Pvt. James S. Cosgrove, WIA
>   Ensign Christian W. Leib, WIA
>   Cpl. Jacob Moyer, WIA, DoW 28 Oct
>   Pvt. Michael P. Trexler, WIA
>   Pvt. Patrick Ward, WIA
>   Capt. Edward C. Williams, WIA

Co. H.
>   Pvt. Samuel Morgan, WIA
>   Pvt. Henry Rist, WIA

Co. I
>   Pvt. Archibald Graham, WIA
>   Pvt. Isaac N. Hoops, WIA
>   Pvt. Frederick Meyer, WIA

Co. K.
>   Pvt. Edward Blain, WIA
>   Pvt. William Clemmens, WIA
>   Pvt. Michael Hassen, WIA
>   Pvt. John Horn, WIA
>   Capt. James Miller, WIA
>   Pvt. William W. Smith, WIA
>   Pvt. William Snyder, WIA
>   Pvt. John Solomon, WIA
>   Pvt. John Street, KIA
>   Pvt. Hezekiah Thomas, WIA

Co. L
    Pvt. William Bishop, WIA
    Pvt. Thomas Davis, WIA
    Cpl. Alexander I. Jones, WIA, DoW 16 Oct
    2nd Lt. John Keefe, Jr., WIA
    Pvt. Joseph Lutz, WIA
    Pvt. Christopher Malone, WIA
    Pvt. William Smith, WIA, DoW 10 Oct
    Pvt. James Stewart, WIA

Co. M
    Pvt. Lewis Barnard, WIA
    Pvt. Charles Epler, WIA
    Pvt. Joseph Hamilton, WIA, DoW 15 Sep
    Pvt. Benjamin Shin, WIA
    Pvt. David Shive, WIA

Garita de Belen
    Co. A
        Pvt. George Henry, WIA, DoW 29 Nov
        Pvt. Nathan Metz, WIA, DoW 17 Oct

    Co. B
        Pvt. William Carlin, KIA
        Pvt. Thomas Holland, WIA
        1st Sgt. Francis McKee, WIA

    Co. D
        Cpl. Edward A. Donney, WIA, DoW 7 Oct

    Co. E
        Pvt. Richard McClellan, WIA

    Co. F
        Pvt. John Bechtel, WIA
        Pvt. Daniel K. Capehart, WIA
        2nd Lt. Ashton S. Tourison, WIA

    Co. G
        Pvt. William Bolton, KIA
        Pvt. Emanuel Moyers, WIA
        Pvt. Robert A. Rodgers, WIA

    Co. H
        Sgt. John A. Cummings, WIA
        Pvt. William Mendenhall, WIA
        Pvt. Josiah M. Winders, WIA, DoW 14 Sep

Co. I
    Pvt. Charles Stewart, KIA

Co. K
    Pvt. James Bustard, WIA
    Pvt. Emor M. Davis, WIA

Co. L
    Pvt. William Grubb, KIA

Co. M
    Capt. James Caldwell, WIA, DoW 19 Sep
    Pvt. Saxfear Heshley, WIA
    Pvt. John Keever, WIA
    Pvt. Jacob M. McClanahan, KIA

Location not specified
    Co. A
        Pvt. John Miller, WIA

    Co. E
        Pvt. George Deckar, WIA
        Pvt. Henry Fishel, WIA
        Sgt. David Mechling, WIA

    Co. F
        Pvt. Samuel E. Major, WIA

    Co. G
        Pvt. Joseph C. Palmer, WIA

Childs' Report of 13 October

Head-Quarters, Military Department of Puebla,

Puebla, October 13, 1847.

Sir: I have the honor to report that, after twenty-eight days close invest-ment, the enemy yesterday raised the siege and left for Atlixco.

I will avail myself of this opportunity to submit to the general-in-chief a brief account of the operations of the troops at this point, from the period of my assuming command to the termination of the siege, and the arrival of Brigadier General Lane with reinforcements.

On entering upon duties as civil and military governor, I found myself in command of Captain Ford's company of cavalry, 46 strong; Captains Kendrick's and Miller's companies of artillery, numbering 100; together with six companies of the 1st Pennsylvania volunteers, commanded by Lieutenant Colonel Black-his total effective strength being 247-and hospitals filled with 1,800 sick.

With this command, San Jose, the grand depot in the city, Loreto, and Guadalupe, were to be garrisoned, and held against the combined efforts of the military and populace.

The isolated positions selected for the hospitals compelled me to remove them within the protection of San Jose, on the first demonstration of hostility. This was not long in exhibiting itself, when I put myself, with such means as I had at my disposal, in the best possible state for defence, confining my efforts to the squares immediately around San Jose; and from these points the enemy, during the entire siege, were not able to force in (but for a single moment) a sentinel.

No open acts of hostility, other than the murdering of straggling soldiers, occurred until the night of the 13th of September, when a fire was opened from some of the streets. On the night of the 14th it recommenced, and from every street, with a violence that knew of no cessation for twenty-eight days and nights.

The enemy, with their numerous cavalry, succeeded in cutting off, at once, every kind of supply, and vainly attempted to change the current of the stream of water, that we might become a more easy prey. The night, however, before the cattle and sheep disappeared from the vicinity, two well-directed parties obtained 30 of the former and 400 of the latter.

The various points to be defended for the preservation of San Jose, on which the safety of the other posts depended, demanded the untiring vigilance of every officer and man.

The enemy augmented in numbers daily, and daily the firing was increased; and finally, on the 22d of September, General Santa Anna arrived with large reinforcements from Mexico, much to the delight of the besiegers, on which occasion a general ringing of bells took place, and was only stopped-as it had been several times before-by a discharge of shells and round-shot from Loreto into the heart of the city.

On the 25th of September General Santa Anna demanded my surrender. A copy of his demand, together, with the reply, are herewith enclosed, marked A.

I here beg to pay a passing tribute to my gallant troops. So soon as I had despatched my answer, I supposed not a moment would be lost by the general, who was to attack me at all points with his 8,000 troops. I rode to the different posts, and announced to the troops the demand, the force with which it was backed, and my reply. Their response convinced me that all was safe; that a hard and bloody battle must be fought ere the great captain of Mexico could overcome my little band.

The point of attack was San Jose, commanded by Lieutenant Colonel Black, with Captain Ford's company of cavalry, and Captain Miller's company of 4th artillery, and four companies of his own regiment, and one hospital, the guard of which was in command of Captain Rowe, of the 9th regiment of infantry.

The duty required of this command, as I have before observed, in consequence of the various points to be defended, demanded an untiring effort on the part of every officer and soldier. A shower of bullets was constantly poured from the streets, the balconies, the house-tops, and churches, upon their devoted heads.

Never did troops endure more fatigue by watching night after night, for more than thirty successive nights, nor exhibit more patience, spirit, and gallantry. Not a post of danger could present itself, but the gallant fellows were ready to fill it. Not a sentinel could be shot, but another was anxious and ready to take his place. Officers and soldiers vied with each other to be honored martyrs in their country's cause. This is the general character of the troops I had the honor to command, and I was confident the crown of victory would perch upon their standard when the last great effort should be made. Their bold and determined front deprived them of what they anxiously desired.

On the 30th ult. General Santa Anna had established his battery bearing upon San Jose, and opened with much spirit. Having anticipated this movement, I had thrown up a traverse on the plaza, and withdrawn a 12-pounder from Loreto, by which means I was enabled to answer his shot. Towards night his battery ceased, and on the next morning was withdrawn, together with from 3,000 to 4,000 of the besieging force, to meet the reinforcements then daily expected at Pinal.

On the 2d instant I availed myself of some reduction of the enemy's numbers to make a sortie against certain barricades and buildings, whose fire had become very annoying. One of the expeditions was confined to Captain Small of the 1st Pennsylvania volunteers. Passing through the walls of an entire square with fifty men, he gained a position opposite the barricade, and drove the enemy with great loss, they leaving seventeen dead on the ground. The barricade, consisting of 150 bales of cotton, was consumed. In this affair, Captain Small and his command behaved with great gallantry, and for twenty-four hours were unceasing in their labors in accomplishing the object; when I sent Lieutenant, of the ordnance corps, to blow up a prominent building, which was done by that excellent officer in good style; when the entire party was withdrawn, with few wounded.

At the same time Lieutenant Morgan, of the 14th regiment, with a detachment of marines, and Lieutenant Merryfield, of the 15th regiment, with a detachment of rifles, attempted to gain possession of certain buildings from which we were receiving a most galling fire. Lieutenant Merryfield entered the building. Lieutenant Morgan was not so fortunate. The enemy being in great force, I directed him to fall back, with the loss of one man killed. On the 5th instant Captain Herron was detached with his company to take possession of a building, from which the enemy had been enfilading the plaza. This he did in a very handsome manner, and to my entire satisfaction, with only a few men wounded.

Other minor acts of gallantry and good conduct were exhibited by officers and men at San Jose; and from Guadalupe one or two successful sorties were made upon the enemy, when engaged in their daily attacks on San Jose.

From Lieutenant Colonel Black, the immediate commander of San Jose, and his officers, I have received the most cordial support. Colonel Black for more than thirty days was untiring in his efforts and zeal for the safety of that point. Officers and men were at their posts night and day, without regarding the pelting storm; and I cannot say too much in praise of the gallant colonel, and his officers and men, before and during the siege.

Lieutenant Laidley, of the ordnance corps, commanded the 12-pounder, the mountain howitzer, and four rocket batteries at the barricade, and there stationed himself night after night; and, as often as these batteries were opened, it was with effect. Captain Ford, commanding the cavalry, although no opportunity occurred, in consequence of the limited number of his troops, to engage the enemy, was at all times ready. Captain Miller of the 4th artillery was particularly successful in managing the 12-pounder in one of the general attacks, and showed himself a good officer, and skilful artillerist.

Major Gwynn, commanding Loreto, although not attacked, was vigilant, and his command was of great assistance to me. Several detachments from his post occupied exposed points, and received heavy fires from the enemy-especially detachments under Lieutenants Carroll and Moore, who for forty-eight hours stood their guard, and were of essential service to me.

I cannot speak too highly of Captain Kendrick and his management of his batteries. His shells and shots fell beautifully upon houses and churches where the enemy were in great numbers. Whenever his shot took effect the firing soon ceased. The limited number of these missiles compelled us to use them with great caution. I am much, very much, indebted to Captain Kendrick for his vigilance and exertion before and during the siege. I will take this occasion to mention Sergeant Owell, of company B, 2d artillery, as a most skilful artillerist. I never saw shot thrown with more accuracy than from his gun.

I take great pleasure in speaking of Captain Morehead, commanding Guadalupe. The place and defences were in a most dilapidated condition. Captain Morehead, with his command, succeeded in placing himself in a perfect state of defence, by great and constant labor. The enemy several times felt him, but, finding him always on the alert, made no serious attack. By sorties upon the enemy, when attacking San Jose, he was of essential service to us, and killed many of them. I consider him an excellent and gallant officer. Lieutenant Edwards, 2d artillery, in charge of the mountain howitzer, threw his shells with great accuracy, and commanded a successful sortie.

To Captain Rowe, of the 9th infantry, who commanded the guard of one of the hospitals, (a constant point of attack, both day and night,) I am greatly indebted for his able defence of that position, and his gallant bearing before the enemy.

To Surgeon Mills, chief of the medical department, and to his assistants great praise is due for their unwearied and laborious services. Left with 1,800 sick, and limited supplies, with but six assistants, their utmost exertions were necessary to administer timely remedies to so many patients. Their attention to the wounded deserves my notice and thanks. These gentlemen were not only occupied in their professional duties, but the want of officers and men compelled me to make large requisitions for the defence of the hospitals, on surgeons and invalids, and they were nightly on guard, marshalling their men upon the roofs and other points. To them I am greatly endebted.

Captain Webster, A. Q. M., and Lieutenant Rhett, A. C. S., rendered valuable services in defending their premises with men in their employ; and with men in the quartermaster's department I was enabled to occupy a position that was all-important, and to which I had neither officers nor soldiers to send. Messrs. Spencer and Brown were particularly active and of great service.

I should be unjust to myself, and to the spy company under Captain Pedro Arria, if I did not call the attention of the general-in-chief to their invaluable services. From them I received the most accurate information of the movements of the enemy, and the designs of the citizens; through them I was enabled to apprehend several officers and citizens in their nightly meetings to consummate their plans for raising the populace. The spy company fought gallantly, and are now so compromised that they must leave the country when our army retires.

I have now only to speak of my A. A. A. General, Mr. Waelder, of the 1st Pennsylvania volunteers, and my secretary, Mr. Wengierski. The gallant charge of Lieutenant Waelder upon the enemy, although rash, exhibits him as an officer not to be intimidated by numbers. His duties have been arduous and dangerous, having daily to carry orders through the thickest of the fire. I take great pleasure in recommending him to the favorable notice of the general-in-chief.

To Mr. Wengierski, secretary and translator, I am much indebted for invaluable services. Mr., in addition to his appropriate duties, conducted the operations of the spy company, and through his suggestions and active exertions, I received much valuable information, and many successful expeditions of spies into the city were made. Mr. W. commanded the detachment on the roof of my quarters, and was the first man wounded. From his after efforts, his wound proved severe and painful; still he performed his various duties night and day, and is worthy of my approbation.

I regret that the health of Captain DeHart, lieutenant governor, prevented him from taking an active part in the stirring scenes I have related, and in which he was so anxious to participate. Until confined to his quarters by sickness, he was of great assistance to me in directing the defences of Guadalupe, and heading a command into the city to disperse the populace.

I herewith enclose a return of the killed and wounded, together with the sub-reports.

Respectfully submitted.

Thomas Childs,

Colonel U. S. A., Civil and Military Governor.

APPENDIX XII

Black's Report of 13 October

Head-Quarters, De San Jose, Puebla, Mexico, October 13, 1847.

Sir: I have the honor to report the operations of the troops under my command during the siege begun on the 13th of September and ended on the 12th instant. A minute detail of all that was done I have not the courage to undertake. I will, therefore, in this report be both brief and general. On the 13th the enemy, numbering about four thousand, surrounded this post. Towards midnight they commenced firing from the main street leading to the Plaza, the Tivoli, and the tops of houses on every side. I remained with my command on the roof of San Jose during the night, and the firing was brisk on both sides. Their assaults were repeated much in the same way up to the 22d, except that on the 18th they made a more decided attack, approaching nearer the Quartel than they had done before. A howitzer, placed by your order at the end of the main street, and a few volleys from the roofs of the Quartel and the houses adjacent, dispersed them in utter confusion. From the 22d to the 25th we were allowed reasonable rest. On the 25th I received your notice that General Santa Anna, having arrived with a large additional force, had sent in a formal demand for the evacuation of the points occupied by the American troops. The demand, and your prompt answer, I communicated at once to the officers and men under my command; their shouts of exultation and defiance reached the ears and hearts of our enemies. Contrary to all expectations, there was no attack that night nor the next day. On the 27th, their assaults were vigorously resumed and kept up until the 1st of October, although in every instance they were repulsed with considerable loss. During the night of the 29th, they got two 6-pounders into position above the Tivoli, and with them they opened on the morning of the 30th. Throughout the day the firing was heavy on both sides. On the 1st, General Santa Anna left the city with four thousand men, and the siege was conducted by sundry other generals with continuous and severe firing. A large additional force arrived on the 8th, and in the afternoon a close

356

demonstration was made; as usual, they were driven back. On the 10th, hostilities were suspended and our annoyance was confined to scattered shots until the night of the 11th. On the morning of the 12th, the enemy began to retire from their positions, and on your orders I moved down the main street towards the plaza, with two companies, for the purpose of silencing a fire maintained at the fourth corner from our breastworks. At our approach a body of lancers fled from the corner. I ordered Captain Herron to move round the square with his company, and if possible cut off their retreat, while I attacked, in front. They did not wait for the attack, and I halted at the point you directed me to occupy. Captain Herron did not join me as I expected, and in a short time sharp firing was heard a few streets above. I immediately hastened with the other company (Captain Hill's, 1st Pennsylvania volunteers) to the spot, and found Captain Herron enveloped by the enemy, and not less than five hundred lancers had charged from different streets and completely surrounded the company, whom we found fighting with the utmost desperation. Our arrival was fortunate, and I think saved the gallant company from being entirely cut to pieces. The enemy suffered severely, and in a short time were scattered. I regret to say our loss was great, both in numbers and value. Thirteen men of company K fell in the unequal contest, besides four severely wounded, whom we were able to save. I may be allowed to say that braver or better men never died a soldier's death.

I respectfully transmit to you Captain Small's report of his operations on the nights of the 2d and 3d instant. It is manifest that he conducted everything in the most skilful manner. The enemy's breast-works on our west side were entirely demolished, which stopped their firing from that quarter. For his admirable services on this occasion, and many others, I desire to express my warmest acknowledgements. I also enclose Captain Herron's report of his labors in removing the large wall and brick shed at the Tivoli, from which, for many days, the enemy had been pouring a constant and annoying fire.

That gallant officer speaks with characteristic modesty of the important and dangerous services himself and his company so well performed. On the 28th of September, Adjutant Waelder, with 13 men, in supporting our sentinels under a heavy fire from the breastwork, received and resisted the fire of more than 200 of the enemy. Our loss was one man (private William Einich, Pennsylvania volunteers) killed. The enemy in this affair suffered severely in both killed and wounded. I would do violence to my own feelings and to justice if I refrained from making particular mention of the gallant and fine behavior of our sentinels in every attack, and throughout the entire siege. To all the non-commissioned officers and soldiers I regret that I have not words to show forth the excellence of their good conduct. When patient and cheerful submission to broken rest, and every several sorrow of a long siege, shall meet their due reware, [sic.] these cannot nor will not be unremembered. And when, in bright letters, the manly encounter of all dangers is published, the names of the living and the memory of the dead will not be covered.

To the brave and accomplished officers of the Quartel my thanks are due for most faithful and uniform support.

The difficulty with me is not who to name, but who to leave unnamed. I must, however, say that Captain J. H. Miller, of company A, 4th artillery, Captain Ford, 3d dragoons, Captain Denny, 1st Pennsylvania volunteers, and his lieutenants, Captain Small and his lieutenants, Captain Dana and his lieutenants, Captain Herron and his lieutenants, and Lieutenant Blakey, of the voltigeurs, commanding a small detachment of his regiment, I feel indebted for most faithful and valuable services. Everything their country could expect or hope for, these gallant officers performed; and most worthily did they command the brave men to whom I have already referred. Lieutenant Laidley, of the ordnance, who had charge of the howitzers, managed his pieces with the utmost coolness and skill. In the hour of danger I had never to ask a second time if Mr. Laidley was at his post. Lieutenant Ehreinger, to whom was confided the management of two pieces, employed them with good effect against the enemy.

To Dr. Bunting, surgeon of the Pennsylvania battalion, I feel deeply indebted for his kindness and attention to the sick and wounded; wherever his services were needed they were promptly given, in the midst of every danger.

To Captain Hill, his officers and men, who were engaged during part of the siege near the Quartel, many thanks are due for most efficient and gallant services.

Lieutenant Woods, of company A, and Lieutenant Carroll, of company D, 1st Pennsylvania volunteers, are entitled to especial notice for gallantry in maintaining, with a small force, an important out-post at the Tivoli.

Captain Denny, of company A, and Captain Dana, of company I, were sent out, on the morning of the 12th, on important and dangerous expeditions; each was in command of his own company and was entirely successful. Mr. Waelder, my adjutant, with the arduous duties of his office doubled, rendered constant and essential service. I beg to give him my admiration and gratitude.

The behavior of the troops has been so manly, I think it is not wrong to say the good name of our country has not suffered in the long and difficult defence of San Jose.

> Very respectfully, & c.,
>
> Sam. W. Black,
>
> Lt. Col. 1st Penn. Vols., com'd San Jose.

APPENDIX XIII

Gwynn's Report of 15 October

Fort Loretto, Puebla, October 15, 1847.

Sir: In obedience to your instructions of the 12th instant, communicated by the acting assistant adjutant general, I have the honor to report that Fort Loretto, under my command, was, during the late siege, garrisoned by about 350 men, the greater part of whom were convalescent, and belonging to different regiments now in the city of Mexico.

About the 13th of September, the enemy commenced firing upon our principal depot of San Jose, in which were stored the supplies for the subsistence and service of the troops.

The battery of two 12-pounder field-guns, and our 10-inch mortar, commanded by Captain Kendrick, 2d regiment artillery, was skilfully managed, with reasonable success, during the seige. We opened our fire upon the city where the enemy had assaulted at different points and fired from, or wherever there was a chance of annoying him. The fire was continued, at intervals, from about the 15th until the 20th ultimo, the day on which Santa Anna demanded a surrender of the American garrison; and on the 25th, 26th, 27th, 28th, 29th, and 30th, it was brisk and continuous. Also, at periods between the 30th and the 8th instant, the firing was warm on all sides; and I am of opinion that the enemy must have suffered considerably.

The infantry were only engaged with the enemy when sent out to act as pickets towards San Jose, our principal station in the city. The detail of infantry pickets commenced on the 27th September, and one 12-pounder gun, with its complement of gunners, was ordered to San Jose on the 28th. The gunners and details were thus continued for that point until the 12th instant.

The following officers were stationed in this fort:

> Captain H. L. Kendrick, 2d artillery.
> Captain J. Hill, 1st Pennsylvania volunteers.
> First Lieutenant R. P. Maclay, 8th infantry.
> Second Lieutenant H. R. Selden, 5th infantry.

359

Second Lieutenant J. J. Booker, 8th infantry.
Second Lieutenant J. Swift Totten, 2d artillery.
Second Lieutenant G. Moore, 1st Pennsylvania volunteers.
Second Lieutenant E. Carroll, 1st Pennsylvania volunteers.

The officers and men under my command were attentive to every duty, and anxious to engage the enemy. Captain Kendrick was active and zealous in the discharge of his duties.

I take pleasure on the present occasion to speak of the skill and good conduct of first Sergeant Orvell, of B company, 2d artillery, in the management of the 12-pounder guns.

Very respectfully, I have the honor to be, sir, your most obedient servant,

Th. P. Gwynn,

Maj. 6th Inf'y, com'ding Fort Loretto, Puebla, Mexico.

Morehead's Report of 16 October

Guadaloupe Heights, Puebla, Mexico, October 16, 1847.

Sir: I have the honor to transmit to your excellency a detailed report of the proceedings of the garrison at Guadaloupe heights during the siege, commencing September 13th and ending October 12, 1847. As you are aware, a large guerrilla force arrived in this city on the 13th ultimo, under General Rea. All at this place was in readiness, and the garrison kept under arms all night. During the day we witnessed a dropping fire from the enemy from the house tops, and other available places, on San Jose; but no attack was made on this place until the 23d ultimo, when part of the enemy's forces was sent against this post, but were repulsed with severe loss by the men under my command, and retired in great haste and disorder. None of our men were injured, and no further attempt was made on us that day, although parties coming within the range of the howitzers were fired on, and some execution done on the enemy, which deterred them from venturing in the vicinity of the post for some time. On the afternoon of the 24th a party, numbering about 500, and under command of a general officer, approached to within 150 yards of the breastwork and discharged their pieces, but a brisk fire dispersed them with the loss of ten men and two horses killed and apparently a much greater number wounded. On the 25th, I had the honor to receive from your excellency a copy of a communication from Santa Anna, with your reply, which, being read to the troops being garrisoned at this place, was received with shouts of exultation, and the confidence of officers and men, in the skill and courage of the commander-in-chief of the forces at Puebla was redoubled, and a universal pledge given to perish sooner than surrender. On the 29th, a party was sent out under Lieutenant Lewis to attack a body of men who were keeping up a hot fire on San Jose. After a hot fire of three hours, killing eight and wounding a greater number, a heavy rain commenced and rendered the guns useless, and, the enemy having ceased firing, orders were sent to recall the party, which returned to quarters with one man severely and two slightly wounded.

361

The same afternoon a party under Lieutenant Bryan made an attack on the enemy, and killed and wounded many. No further attempt was made on us by the enemy. On the 6th of October, a party under Lieutenant Edwards, accompanied by Lieutenant Lewis, made an attack on a body of infantry near the Tivoli, of whom they killed five and wounded many more. After an hour's severe fighting they were able to make a breach in the wall of a church commanding the Tivoli; unable to spare a necessary force from Guadaloupe to garrison it, the place was abandoned after driving the enemy from the vicinity. They retired with one private severely, and Lieutenant Edwards and Lewis slightly, wounded. On the 8th instant, Captain Johnson was sent with a force to drive a party of the enemy from their position, in which he succeeded with no loss to himself, but considerable to the enemy. The subsequent operations of the garrison were confined to annoying the enemy when within musket range; and of the fifty men detailed on the 13th and engaged in the streets of Puebla, none were wounded or missing; and, as they fought under your own eye, it would be superfluous for me to mention their conduct on that occasion. It is difficult, when all have behaved so gallantly, to designate individuals who have distinguised themselves above the rest; but let me call to your attention the gallant conduct of corporal Salkeld, of company F, 2d artillery, corporal Meron, 4th artillery, artificer Jenkins, privates Barnes, company I, 2d artillery, Williams, company C, 2d infantry, James Wilkner, company G, 1st Pennsylvania volunteers, Daniel Ryan, a fifer, a boy of 15 years, company G, 1st Pennsylvania volunteers. To Lieutenants Morgan and Merrifield, previous to their being attached, I owe thanks for their gallant conduct. To Captain Johnson, Lieutenants Edwards, Bryan, and Lewis, I must also return thanks for their efficiency and gallantry in executing all orders. And let me particularly recommend for favorable notice Lieutenant Mont. P. Young, of company G, 1st Pennsylvania volunteers, now deceased, who, up to the time of fatal illness, rendered the most gallant and effectual services. He died of fever contracted by constant exposure on duty. The hour of death alone was able to draw him from his post. For the memory of this accomplished officer and gentleman I beg to bespeak your affection and respect.

I am with sentiments of deep respect, your excellency's obedient servant,

T. G. Morehead,

Capt. 1st Penn. volunteers, commanding Guadaloupe.

Casualties at Puebla

First Regiment
  Co. A
        Pvt. James Bowden, WIA
        Pvt. John Dolan, WIA
        Pvt. Emanuel Edwards, WIA
        Pvt. John B. Garman, WIA, DoW 14 Oct
        Pvt. John H. Hoover, WIA
        Pvt. David Lindsey, WIA
        Pvt. Henry Lynch, WIA
        Pvt. Mansfield B. Mason, WIA
        Pvt. James McKutcheon, WIA
        Pvt. George Richerberger, WIA
        Pvt. Robert Wilson, WIA

  Co. B
        Pvt. John Doyle, KIA 12 Oct

  Co. C
        Pvt. Charles Collison, WIA
        Cpl. William Eurich, KIA 28 Sep
        Pvt. John B. Herron, WIA, DoW 9 Nov

  Co. D
        Cpl. Charles Andrews, WIA
        Pvt. Sylvester Beesley, WIA
        Pvt. James W. Lambert, WIA, DoW 29 Oct

  Co. G
        Pvt. Samuel Houpt, WIA
        Fifer Daniel Ryan, WIA
        Pvt. William N. Shultz, WIA
        Pvt. James Wilkner, WIA
        Pvt. Joseph P. Willis, WIA

Co. I

    Sgt. Dominick Devanny, WIA
    Pvt. James Ellis, WIA
    Pvt. Luke Floyd, WIA
    Pvt. John Preece, KIA 26 Aug
    Pvt. David W. Yarlott, WIA

Co. K

    Pvt. Charles W. Blakeman, WIA
    Pvt. Johnson Elliott, WIA
    Pvt. Thomas B. Furman, WIA
    Pvt. John C. Gilchrist, KIA 12 Oct
    Pvt. John H. Herod, KIA 12 Oct
    Capt. John Herron, WIA
    Pvt. Francis B. Johns, KIA 12 Oct
    Pvt. Edward H. Jones, KIA 12 Oct
    Pvt. Henry Krutzleman, KIA 12 Oct
    Pvt. Andrew E. Marshall, WIA
    Pvt. James S. Negley, WIA
    Pvt. James Phillips, KIA 12 Oct
    Pvt. William A. Phillips, KIA 12 Oct
    Pvt. Robert Reid, WIA
    Pvt. William Schmitdz, KIA 12 Oct
    Pvt. Samuel D. Sewell, KIA 12 Oct
    Pvt. Samuel Sloop, WIA
    Pvt. Thomas Thornburgh, WIA
    Pvt. Samuel Troyer, KIA 12 Oct
    Pvt. Francis Van Dyke, KIA 12 Oct
    Pvt. David S. Vernovy, KIA 12 Oct
    Pvt. Joseph Wilson, KIA 12 Oct
    Pvt. William C. Winibiddle, WIA

Second Regiment

    Co. A

        Sgt. William W. Diehl, WIA

    Co. B

        Pvt. John Beer, WIA

    Co. F

        Pvt. George Brutche, KIA 8 Aug
        2nd Lt. Jacob F. Sperry, KIA 26 Aug

    Co. K

        2nd Lt. James McKeen, Jr., WIA

Ahl, Peter, Jr. Letter to Edward Danner, Feb. 12, 1848. Harry A. Diehl Collection.

Albright, Raymond W. *Two Centuries of Reading, Pa., 1748-1948, A History of the County Seat of Berks County.* Reading, Pa.: The Historical Society of Berks County, 1948.

Altoona Tribune. June 22, 1882.

Anonymous. "Famous Pennsylvania Regiments, 176th F. A. Pittsburgh," *National Guard And Community,* Vol. IV, No. 6, Dec. 1933-Jan. 1934.

Anonymous. "Flags Given To The State Museum," *Pennsylvania Heritage,* Vol. XI, No. 1, Winter 1985.

Anonymous. "Mexican War Battle-Flags Presented To The Historical Society Of Pennsylvania," *Pennsylvania Magazine Of History and Biography,* Vol. XVII, 1893.

Anonymous. "Official History of the Militia and National Guard of the State of Pennsylvania," *Our State Army And Navy Journal,* Vol. XXVII, Mar. 1924 & Apr. 1924.

Anonymous. *The Philadelphia Grays' Collection Of Official Reports Of Brigadier-General George Cadwalader's Services during the Campaign of 1847, In Mexico.* Philadelphia: T. K. and P. G. Collins, Printers, 1848.

Anson, Bert. "Colonel William Barton Roberts In The Mexico City Campaign - 1847," *Western Pennsylvania Historical Magazine,* Vol. XXXIX, No. 4, Winter 1956.

Bates, Samuel P. *History Of Pennsylvania Volunteers.* 5 Vols. Harrisburg, Pa.: B. Singerly, State Printer, 1869-1871.

Bates, Samuel P. *Martial Deeds of Pennsylvania.* Philadelphia: T. H. Davis & Co., 1876.

Battle, J. H. *History Of Columbia And Montour Counties, Pennsylvania.* Chicago: A. Warner & Co., 1887.

Bauer, K. Jack. *The Mexican War 1846-1848.* New York: Macmillan Publishing Co., Inc., 1974.

Bazelon, Bruce S. *Defending The Commonwealth.* Providence, R.I.: Mowbray Company - Publishers, 1980.

Bedford Gazette. May, 1846 through Aug. 13, 1847.

Beers, Paul. "A Profile: John W. Geary," *Civil War Times Illustrated,* June 1970.

Blackburn, E. Howard and Welfley, William H. *History of Bedford And Somerset Counties, Pennsylvania.* 3 Vols. New York: The Lewis Publishing Company, 1906.

Blackwood, Emma Jerome, (ed.). *To Mexico With Scott, Letters Of Captain E. Kirby Smith To His Wife.* Cambridge: Harvard University Press, 1917.

Bodson, Robert L. "A Description Of The United States Occupation Of Mexico As Reported By American Newspapers Published In Vera Cruz, Puebla, And Mexico City September 14, 1847 to July 31, 1848," D.Ed. Disertation, Ball State University, 1970.

Bonner, John. "Scott's Battles In Mexico," *Harper's New Monthly Magazine,* Vol. XI, No. 63, Aug. 1855.

Boucher, John N. *A Century And A Half Of Pittsburg And Her People.* New York: The Lewis Publishing Company, 1908.

Boucher, John N. *Old and New Westmoreland.* 2 Vols. New York: The American Historical Society, Inc., 1918.

Brenckman, Fred. *History of Carbon County, Pennsylvania.* Harrisburg, Pa.: James J. Nungesser, Publisher, 1913.

Brooks, N. C. *A Complete History Of The Mexican War.* Philadelphia: Grigg, Elliot & Co., 1849.

Brower, D. H. B. *Danville, Montour County, Pennsylvania.* Harrisburg, Pa.: Lanes S. Hart, Printer, 1881.

Burgess, Milton V. *Minute Men Of Pennsylvania.* Martinsburg, Pa.: Morrisons Cove Herald, 1962.

Cambria County Historical Society. John A. Blair Diary.

Cambria County Historical Society. Mexican War Documents.

Cambria Herald. Mar. 13, 1895.

Claiborne, John Francis Hamtramck. *Life And Correspondence Of John A. Quitman, Major-General, U.S.A., And Governor Of The State Of Mississippi.* 2 Vols. New York: Harper & Brothers, 1860.

Clark, William P. *Official History of the Militia and National Guard of the State Of Pennsylvania From the Earliest Period Of Record To The Present Time.* 2 Vols. Capt. Charles J. Hendler, Publisher, 1912.

Collins, Herman LeRoy and Jordan, Wilfred. *Philadelphia, A Story Of Progress.* 3 Vols. New York: Lewis Historical Publishing Co., 1941.

Coulter, Richard. "The Westmoreland Guards In The War With Mexico, 1846-1848," *Western Pennsylvania Historical Magazine*, Vol. XXIV, No. 2, June 1941.

Daily Morning Post (Pittsburgh). May, 1846 through Aug., 1848.

Danville Intelligencer. May, 1846 through Aug., 1848.

Democratic Press (Reading). Feb. 23, 1847 through Feb. 15, 1848.

Democratic Union (Harrisburg). May, 1846 through Aug., 1848.

Dillon, Lester R., Jr. *American Artillery in the Mexican War, 1846-1847.* Austin, Texas: Presidial Press, 1975.

Duncan, Louis C. "Medical History Of General Scott's Campaign To The City Of Mexico In 1847," *The Military Surgeon*, Vol. XLVII, Nos. 4 & 5, Oct. & Nov. 1920.

Dunkelberger, George Franklin. *The Story Of Snyder County.* Selinsgrove, Pa.: Snyder County Historical Society, 1948.

Egle, William H. *An Illustrated History of the Commonwealth of Pennsylvania, Civil, Political, And Military.* Harrisburg, Pa.: DeWitt C. Goodrich & Co., 1876.

Elliott, Ella Zerbey. *Blue Book of Schuylkill County.* Pottsville, Pa.: "Republican," 1916.

Ellis, Franklin, (ed.). *History Of Fayette County, Pennsylvania.* Philadelphia: L. H. Everts & Co., 1882.

Evans, John R. "The Reading Artillerists In The Mexican War," *The Historical Review of Berks County*, Vol. XV, No. 1, Oct. 1949.

Freeze, John G. *A History Of Columbia County, Pennsylvania*. Bloomsburg, Pa.: Elwell & Bittenbender, Publishers, 1883.

G.A.R. Memorial Hall, Philadelphia. Norton McGiffin Diary.

Geary, Mary deForest. *A Giant In Those Days, A Story About The Life Of John White Geary*. Brunswick, Ga.: Coastal Books, 1980.

Godcharles, Frederick A. *Chronicles of Central Pennsylvania*. 4 Vols. New York: Lewis Historical Publishing Company, Inc., 1944.

Godcharles, Frederick A. *Pennsylvania Political, Governmental, Military And Civil. Military* Vol. New York: The American Historical Society, Inc., 1933.

Greer, James K., (ed.). "Diary of a Pennsylvania Volunteer in the Mexican War," *Western Pennsylvania Historical Magazine*, Vol. XII, No. 3, 1929.

Hackenburg, Randy W. "Pennsylvania Volunteers In The War With Mexico," *Pennsylvania Heritage*, Vol. IV, No. 2, Mar. 1978.

Hackenburg, Randy W. "The Columbia Guards, Danville's Volunteer Infantry, 1817-1861." Master's Thesis, Bloomsburg State College, 1975.

Hadden, James. *A History of Uniontown, The County Seat Of Fayette County, Pennsylvania*. Evansville, Ind.: Unigraphic, Inc., 1978, (Reprint of the 1913 book).

Hartman, George W. *A Private's Own Journal Giving an Account of the Battles in Mexico. . . .* Greencastle, Pa.: E. Robinson, 1849.

Harvey, Oscar J. and Smith, Ernest G. *A History Of Wilkes-Barre, Luzerne County, Pennsylvania*. 4 Vols. Wilkes-Barre, Pa.: 1929.

Heitman, Francis B. *Historical Register And Dictionary Of The United States Army, From Its Organization, September 29, 1789, To March 2, 1903*. 2 Vols. Washington: Government Printing Office, 1903.

Herrold, Dewey S. "Brigadier-General Edward Charles Williams," *The Snyder County Historical Society Bulletin*, Vol. II, No. 4.

Heyer, Charles H. "A Mexican War Letter," *The Magazine Of History With Notes And Queries*, Vol. XVII, Jul.-Dec. 1913.

Hill, Daniel H. "Battle of Cerro Gordo," *The Southern Quarterly Review*, Vol. XXI, No. 41, 1852.

Historical and Biographical Annals Of Columbia and Montour Counties Pennsylvania. 2 Vols. Chicago: J. H. Beers & Co., 1915.

Historical Society of Pennsylvania. John Kritser Journal.

History Of Luzerne, Lackawanna And Wyoming Counties, Pa. New York: W. W. Munsell & Co., 1880.

History Of That Part Of The Susquehanna And Juniata Valleys Embraced In The Counties Of Mifflin, Juniata, Perry, Union And Snyder, In The Commonwealth Of Pennsylvania. 2 Vols. Philadelphia: Everts, Peck & Richards, 1886.

Hunsicker, Clifton S. *Montgomery County, Pennsylvania — A History*. New York: Lewis Historical Publishing Company, Inc., 1923.

Jenkins, John S. *History Of The War Between The United States And Mexico, From The Commencement Of Hostilities To The Ratification Of The Treaty Of Peace.* Philadelphia: John E. Potter And Company.

Kitchen, D. C. *Record of the Wyoming Artillerists.* Tunkhannock, Pa.: Alvin Day, Printer, 1874.

Lanard, Thomas S. *One Hundred Years With The State Fencibles,* 1813-1913. Philadelphia: Nields Company, 1913.

Larner, John William, Jr. "A Westmoreland Guard In Mexico, 1847-1848: The Journal Of William Joseph McWilliams," *Western Pennsylvania Historical Magazine,* Vol. LII, No. 3, Jul. 1969 & No. 4, Oct. 1969.

Linn, John Blair. *Annals Of Buffalo Valley, Pennsylvania, 1755-1855.* Harrisburg, Pa.: Lane S. Hart, Printer, 1877.

Mansfield, Edward D. *The Mexican War. . .* New York: A. S. Barnes & Co., 1848.

Mathews, Alfred, and Hungerford, Austin N. *History of the Counties of Lehigh And Carbon In The Commonwealth Of Pennsylvania.* Philadelphia: Everts & Richards, 1884.

May, Robert E. *John A. Quitman, Old South Crusader.* Baton Rouge, La.: Louisiana State University Press, 1985.

McClenathan, J. C.; Edie, William A.; Burgess, Ellis B.; Coll, J. Aloysius; and Norton, Eugene T. *Centennial History of the Borough of Connellsville, Pennsylvania, 1806-1906.* Columbus, Ohio: The Champlin Press, 1906.

Millikan, Paul. *The Manual Of Arms.* Mattawan, Mich,: Paul Millikan, Catalog No. 7, 1986.

Miners' Journal (Pottsville). May, 1846 through Aug., 1848.

Montgomery, Morton L. *History of Berks County In Pennsylvania.* Philadelphia: Everts, Peck & Richards, 1886.

Montgomery, Thomas Lynch (ed.). *Pennsylvania Archives,* Sixth Series, Vol. X. Harrisburg, Pa.: Harrisburg Publishing Co., 1907.

Morgan, George H. *Annals, Comprising Memoirs, Incidents and Statics Of Harrisburg From The Period Of Its First Settlement.* Harrisburg: George A. Brooks, 1858.

Mountain Sentinel (Ebensburg). Apr. 19, 1849.

Myers, William S. (ed.). *The Mexican War Diary Of George B. McClellan.* Princeton: Princeton University Press, 1917.

National Archives. Microfilm Publication M-1028, *Compiled Service Records of Volunteer Soldiers Who Served During the Mexican War in Organizations From the State of Pennsylvania.* 13 Rolls.

National Archives. Record Group 94, Records of the Adjutant General's Office, 1780's-1917, Papers of the 1st & 2nd Pennsylvania Infantry Regiments, 1846-1848.

Newell, W. H. "Schuylkill County in the Mexican War," *Publications of the Historical Society of Schuylkill County,* Vol. I, 1907.

Niebaum, John H. *History Of The Pittsburgh Washington Infantry, 102nd (Old 13th) Regiment Pennsylvania Veteran Volunteers And Its Forebears.* Pittsburgh, Pa.: Burgum Printing Co., 1931.

Now And Then. Muncy, Pa.: Muncy Historical Society, Vol. VII, No. 2, Apr. 1942 and Vol. XI, No. 12, Apr. 1957.

Oswandel, J. Jacob. *Notes Of The Mexican War 1846=47=48.* Philadelphia: 1885.

Pearce, Stewart. *Annals of Luzerne County.* Philadelphia: J. B. Lippincott & Co., 1866.

Pennsylvania Argus (Greensburg). May, 1846 through Aug., 1848.

Pennsylvania Historical And Museum Commission, Division Of Archives And Manuscripts. Columbia Guards Diary.

Pennsylvania Historical And Museum Commission, Division Of Archives And Manuscripts. Records of the Department of Military Affairs, Letter from Henry Petrikin to John S. Wilson, Nov. 30, 1846.

Pennsylvania Telegraph (Harrisburg). May, 1846 through May 30, 1848.

Pennsylvanian (Philadelphia). May, 1846 through Aug., 1848.

Pittsburgh Daily Gazette. May, 1846 through Aug., 1848.

Reading Gazette. May, 1846 through Jan. 1, 1848.

Reed, George Edward, (ed.). *Pennsylvania Archives.* Fourth Series, Vol. VII. Harrisburg, Pa.: The State of Pennsylvania, 1902.

Ripley, R. S. *The War With Mexico.* 2 Vols. New York: Burt Franklin, Reprint of 1970.

Scharf, J. Thomas and Westcott, Thompson. *History of Philadelphia, 1609-1884.* 3 Vols. Philadelphia: L. H. Everts & Co., 1884.

Simmons, Edward H. "Who Was First At Chapultepec?" *Fortitudine,* Vol. XI, No. 4 and Vol. XII, No. 1, Spring-Summer, 1982.

Sioussat, St. George L. (ed.). "Mexican War Letters of Col. William Bowen Campbell, of Tennessee," *Tennessee Historical Magazine,* Vol. I, 1915.

Smith, Justin H. *The War With Mexico.* 2 Vols. New York: The Macmillan Company, 1919.

Stearns, Morton E. "Pittsburgh In The Mexican War," *Western Pennsylvania Historical Magazine,* Vol. VII, No. 4, 1924.

Storey, Henry W. *History of Cambria County, Pennsylvania.* 2 Vols. New York: The Lewis Publishing Company, 1907.

Tinkcom, Harry M. *John White Geary, Soldier-Statesman, 1819-1873.* Philadelphia, Pa.: University Of Pennsylvania Press, 1940.

U.S. Army Military History Institute. Manuscript Archives, Descriptive Book of the Columbia Guards. Columbia County Historical Society Collection.

U.S. Army Military History Institute. Manuscript Archives, Letter from John B. Brookbank to Sarah Brookbank, Jul. 12, 1847. Mexican War Miscellaneous Collection.

U.S. Army Military History Institute. Manuscript Archives, Letter from Clarence H. Frick to Arthur W. Frick, Mar. 28, 1847. Mexican War Miscellaneous Collection.

U.S., Congress, Senate. *After Action Reports of Commanders in the Army in Mexico.* Senate Document 1, 30th Congress, 1st Session, 1847.

U.S., Congress, Senate. *Proceedings of the Two Courts of Inquiry in the Case of Major General Pillow.* Senate Document 65, 30th Congress, 1st Session, 1848.

Washington And Jefferson College Library Archives. Norton McGiffin Family Papers.

Wilcox, Cadmus M. *History Of The Mexican War.* Washington, D.C.: The Church News Publishing Co., 1892.

Williams, T. Harry (ed.). *With Beauregard In Mexico: The Mexican War Reminiscences of P. G. T. Beauregard.* Louisiana State University Press.

Wilson, Erasmus (ed.). *Standard History of Pittsburgh, Pennsylvania.* Chicago: H. R. Cornell & Company, 1898.

Wilson, John S. Letter to Martha Wilson, Feb. 21, 1847. In a private collection.

Wynkoop, J. M. (ed.). *Anecdotes And Incidents: Comprising Daring Exploits, Personal And Amusing Adventures Of The Officers And Privates of The Army, And Thrilling Incidents Of The Mexican War.* Pittsburgh: 1848.

Zerbey, Joseph Henry. *History of Pottsville and Schuylkill County Pennsylvania.* Vols. IV and V. Pottsville: "Republican" - "Morning Paper" Print, 1934-1935.

Zierdt, William Henry. *Narrative History Of The 109th Field Artillery Pennsylvania National Guard, 1775-1930.* Wilkes-Barre, Pa.: Wyoming Historical And Geological Society, 1932.